ISBN 978-1-331-08470-9
PIBN 10142797

1 MONTH OF
FREE
READING

at

www.ForgottenBooks.com

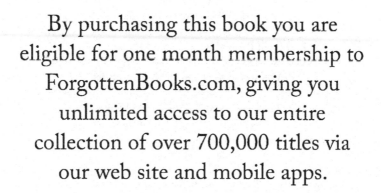

By purchasing this book you are
eligible for one month membership to
ForgottenBooks.com, giving you
unlimited access to our entire
collection of over 700,000 titles via
our web site and mobile apps.

To claim your free month visit:

www.forgottenbooks.com/free142797

Similar Books Are Available from
www.forgottenbooks.com

A HISTORY

OF THE

NATIONAL TUBERCULOSIS ASSOCIATION

THE ANTI-TUBERCULOSIS MOVEMENT IN THE UNITED STATES

By

S. ADOLPHUS KNOPF, M.D.

NATIONAL TUBERCULOSIS ASSOCIATION
370 SEVENTH AVENUE
NEW YORK CITY
1922

PREFACE

THE completion of fifteen years of the active work of the National Tuberculosis Association in January, 1920, seemed to me an opportune time for recording in some more or less permanent form a history of the beginning of the great anti-tuberculosis movement in the United States and a record of the progress made. This is the reason for this volume.

My own personal interest in tuberculosis work, extending over a quarter of a century, and my intimate acquaintance with the National Tuberculosis Association from its inception to its present development, led me to suggest to the Association that such a history should be written. The committee appointed to undertake the matter asked me to write the history and submit it to them for criticism, modification, and approval. The committee was composed of Dr. Hermann M. Biggs, Chairman, Dr. Henry Barton Jacobs, Dr. George M. Kober, Dr. Charles J. Hatfield, and the author. Each member of the committee has read and approved the manuscript and offered helpful suggestions which have been incorporated in the text.

Their suggestion that my own biography should be added was very flattering, but I have not complied with it for the following reasons: First, not having been an officer of the Association I was not entitled to appear among those who have held such positions; and secondly, there is nothing of sufficient importance in my own life to be worth recording. I have been a humble soldier in the war against tuberculosis which has been led by great generals. In the early days I had my trials and tribulations like all those who endeavor to do pioneer work. I have been amply rewarded for my work by the good will and friendship of my teachers and colleagues and that of the officers and directors of the Association who have granted me the privilege of writing the history and have been helpful in making its publication possible. I have acceded to the request of my colleagues of the Historical Committee to add to the tuberculosis bibliographies of the presidents, vice-presidents, secretaries, and treasurers a list of my own publications on tuberculosis. I hope the readers will bear with the length of it, as an excuse for which I may say that I have scarcely written on any other subject than tuberculosis. Thus my bibliography represents in a measure my life's work.

I am particularly indebted to Dr. Philip P. Jacobs, the Publicity Director, for his helpful co-operation in writing the chapter on the Sixth International Congress, the biographies of Dr. Flick and Dr. Fulton, and several other chapters in Part I. He has also been most helpful in the preparation and editing of the entire work and in facilitating its printing and publication. The arrangement of the material and the rereading of the page proof were done by Dr. Philip P. Jacobs and his able assistant, Miss Eleanor B. Conklin. To both I desire to express my grateful appreciation.

It would be ungracious on my part if I did not also express my grateful appreciation of the valuable information furnished by the relatives, friends, and pupils of our departed presidents and vice-presidents. I wish to extend my thanks to Professor John H. Finley, who helped me in writing the biographical sketch of Grover Cleveland, ex-president of the United States and honorary vice-president of the Association; to Mrs. Douglas Robinson, who sent me valuable data concerning her brother, Theodore Roosevelt, ex-president of the United States and honorary vice-president of the Association; to Lady Osler, Mrs. William C. Gorgas, Mrs. John H. Lowman, Mrs. Theodore B. Sachs, Mrs. George M. Sternberg for biographical notes and photographs of their late husbands; to Mrs. Mathilda Janeway Wisner for an excellent photograph, data, and notices of her father, the late Dr. Edward G. Janeway. To Dr. Edward R. Baldwin I am indebted for the bibliography of Dr. Edward Livingston Trudeau; and to Dr. David R. Lyman for a photograph of and a touching tribute to his teacher and friend, the late Dr. John P. Foster. Lastly I wish to express my grateful appreciation to Mr. George B. Christian, secretary to the president, and to Mr. Judson C. Welliver, the president's private secretary, for their helpfulness in obtaining interesting data for the biographical sketch of Warren

G. Harding, president of the United States and honorary vice-president of the National Tuberculosis Association.

In preparing the history, I wrote first an introductory part, outlining in a general way the beginning and development of the tuberculosis movement in general and the National Tuberculosis Association in particular, and including a section on the Sixth International Congress and a chapter on the work of the various state associations. The remaining parts of the book deal with the proceedings of the various annual meetings of the Association, the biographies of the officers, lists of their contributions to tuberculosis literature, a description of the war work in tuberculosis of the Surgeon Generals of the U. S. Army, the U. S. Navy, and the U. S. Public Health Service, a list of books, pamphlets, and leaflets issued by the Association, and lastly, the tuberculosis bibliography of the author. In this way the history has become not a mere chronicle of events alone, but a record of the men who brought these events to pass.

S. ADOLPHUS KNOPF, M.D.

NEW YORK, April 1, 1922.

TABLE OF CONTENTS

PART III

Biographies of the Officers of the Association

TABLE OF CONTENTS

LIST OF ILLUSTRATIONS

xi

PART I
EARLY HISTORY *and* DEVELOPMENT

CHAPTER I
BEGINNINGS

THE history of the National Tuberculosis Association and, in fact, the history of the anti-tuberculosis movement in America, may well be recorded in terms of the work done. A mere chronological summary of efforts would be of little general interest did it not show the spirit of the men and women who have contributed to the development of the campaign against tuberculosis in the United States. It is this spirit that makes the history worth recording. Tuberculosis had been known chiefly because of its pestilential character and because of the apparent hopelessness of its prevention or cure. This was a condition not peculiar to the United States; indeed, not more than two generations ago it was the prevailing conception of the disease throughout the world.

In this introductory part the history of the campaign against tuberculosis will be sketched under two phases of its development—first, those early pioneer efforts in treatment, prevention, and organization that led up to the formation of the National Tuberculosis Association; and second, the kaleidoscopic changes in the health map of the country which have been made during the last fifteen years under the able leadership of the National Association.

Among the earliest American physicians who made pulmonary tuberculosis a special study must be mentioned Dr. Benjamin Rush, who published his "Thoughts Upon the Causes and Cure of Pulmonary Tuberculosis" as early as 1783. Regarding Rush's ideas on the treatment of tuberculosis, Dr. Henry Barton Jacobs speaks as follows:[1]

"His treatment of consumption, as of most diseases, depended upon the state of the patient's system; if in the plethoric state, *i. e.*, with high bounding

[1] "Some Distinguished American Students of Tuberculosis," *Johns Hopkins Hosp. Bull.*, vol. xiii, Nos. 137, 138, 1902.

pulse and fever, then depletion was demanded by frequent bleeding, low diet, and purges; if in the debilitated state, *i. e.*, with weak, small pulse, with or without night-sweats and hemoptysis, then a sustaining treatment was indicated—full diet, alcohol, tonics. In either condition the radical treatment consisted of exercise in the open air, graduated so as to induce fatigue—active exercise if possible, passive, if necessary. In the question of food and air and exercise, it is remarkable how exactly his ideas coincide with ours to-day a full hundred years after."

The next distinguished student of tuberculosis, one whom we may justly call a pupil of Laennec, was Samuel George Morton, who published his book on pulmonary consumption in 1834.[1] Other names which should not be forgotten as American pioneers of the study and treatment of tuberculosis are Leonard Hopkins (1750–1801), James Jackson, Jr. (1810–1834), William W. Gerhardt (1809–1872), Austin Flint (1812–1886). The latter was the first to propose the term "cavernous respiration" for the character of the breathing heard over pulmonary cavities, a form of breathing distinctly different from so-called tabular breathing. He also introduced the term "bronchovesicular respiration" to indicate the breath-sounds over areas more or less infiltrated with disease, yet not so consolidated as to produce the tabular quality.

The first systematic movement toward the study of the causes and prevention of tuberculosis in the United States in relation to topography, geography, and climatology was made by Dr. Henry Ingersoll Bowditch between the years 1850 and 1860. He was then busily engaged in correspondence with medical men throughout New England to determine, if possible, the factors which favored the production of pulmonary diseases. Dr. Bowditch was particularly anxious to determine the relation of soil moisture to the prevalence of tuberculosis.

The first authentic record of the use of the open-air treatment for tuberculosis in the United States dates back to about 1808, when Nathaniel Bowditch, the celebrated mathematician, father of Dr. Henry Ingersoll Bowditch, mentioned above, and grandfather of Dr. Vincent Y. Bowditch, of Boston, treated himself by that then unique method. Professor Nathaniel Bowditch, having

---

[1] Morton, Samuel George: "Illustration of Pulmonary Consumption; Its Anatomical Characteristic Causes, Symptoms and Treatment," Key and Biddle, Philadelphia, 1834, p. 183.

had a hemorrhage with evident signs of tuberculosis at the age of thirty-five, succeeded in arresting the disease by a prolonged journey with horse and buggy, living and sleeping in the open air. Another remarkable case in that early period was one treated by Dr. Henry Ingersoll Bowditch after the example given him by his father. An old man at the age of ninety-two wrote in 1917 to Dr. Vincent Y. Bowditch that sixty years before, being declared tuberculous, he had followed the advice of Dr. H. I. Bowditch, who had sent him to the wilds of Minnesota with the following injunction: "Have pluck and patience and don't be afraid of the cold open air, it is the coming treatment."

Among the early pioneers in the rational treatment of pulmonary tuberculosis we must not forget to mention Dr. William A. McDowell, the distinguished nephew of his distinguished uncle, Dr. Ephraim McDowell, who, without the aid of an anesthetic, performed the first ovariotomy in Danville, Ky., in 1809. In the year 1843 Dr. William A. McDowell published a book entitled, "The Curability of Pulmonary Consumption in All its Stages," based on the results of his own experiments and investigations. When we consider that blood-letting, purging, an invalid diet of weak broth, and protection from cold air constituted the treatment for tuberculosis in those days, we cannot help admiring young McDowell for his courage in opposing the ideas then endorsed by high medical authorities. He disapproved strongly of blood-letting and purging, and approved of four meals a day, outdoor air, and graduated exercises. He opposed violent exercise, which some of his colleagues recommended. "A Heretic of the Last Century," a name bestowed upon him by his daughter, Mrs. Madeline McDowell Breckenridge, in an admirable article which appeared in the *Journal of the Outdoor Life* of November, 1916, seems to be appropriate.

The communicability of pulmonary tuberculosis had been recognized by American physicians even before the discovery of the tubercle bacillus by Koch. Dr. Edward G. Janeway published an article on this subject as early as 1882.[1] It is of historic interest to note that the idea of making tuberculosis a reportable

[1] Janeway, Dr. Edward G.: "Possible Contagion of Phthisis," *Archives of Medicine*, 1882, vol. viii, p. 219.

disease dates back even further than Dr. Janeway's paper.   Dr. Stephen Smith, that venerable Nestor of the medical profession of the United States, now in his ninety-ninth year, wrote the author, in an autograph letter dated July 2, 1920, as follows: "When a Commissioner of Health from 1868 to 1875, I endeavored to have tuberculosis reported as contagious, but failed."

It was not until 1889 that the communicability of tuberculosis was officially recognized by the New York City Health Department.   Thus the year 1889 marks the most important epoch in the control of tuberculosis in New York city, as well as in the United States, if not in the entire civilized world.   In that year Dr. Hermann M. Biggs, Dr. T. Mitchell Prudden, and Dr. H. P. Loomis presented to the Health Department of New York city a communication calling attention to the communicability of tuberculosis and recommending that measures be taken to prevent the spread of this disease and outlining these measures.   The Department of Health submitted this communication to 12 prominent physicians and asked for their suggestions and recommendations.   The only ones of this group who favored the recommendations of Drs. Biggs, Prudden, and Loomis were Dr. Edward G. Janeway and Dr. Frank P. Foster, at that time editor of the *New York Medical Journal*.   The Department of Health, however, considered the matter with more or less favor, and in that same year, 1889, published a leaflet giving the essential facts with regard to the nature, causation, and prevention of tuberculosis, and distributed the leaflet in large quantities, particularly in the tenement houses of the city.   The leaflet was also placed in the hands of every family where a death from tuberculosis had occurred.   So far as we are able to ascertain, this is the first leaflet ever published for distribution among the general public.   It is certainly the first one published and distributed by a health department, and as such marks an epoch in tuberculosis education.

On account of its historic interest a copy of this leaflet is reproduced herewith:

Contagious Consumption

The following report on consumption as a contagious disease was yesterday approved by the Health Department:

Health Department
Division of Contagious Diseases
309 Mulberry Street, July 9, 1889

Rules to be Observed for the Prevention of the Spread of Consumption

Pulmonary tuberculosis (consumption) is directly communicated from one person to another. The germ of the disease exists in the expectoration of persons afflicted with it. The following extract from the report of the pathologists of the Health Department explains the means by which the disease may be transmitted:

"Tuberculosis is commonly produced in the lungs (which are the organs most frequently affected) by breathing air in which living germs are suspended as dust. The material which is coughed up, sometimes in large quantities, by persons suffering from consumption contains these germs often in enormous numbers. This material when expectorated frequently lodges in places where it dries, as on the street, floors, carpets, handkerchiefs, etc. After drying in one way or another, it is very apt to become pulverized and float in the air as dust."

By observing the following rules the danger of catching the disease will be reduced to a minimum:

1. Do not permit persons suspected to have consumption to spit on the floor or on cloths unless the latter be immediately burned. The spittle of persons suspected to have consumption should be caught in earthen or glass dishes containing the following solution: Corrosive sublimate 1 part, water 1,000 parts.

2. Do not sleep in a room occupied by a person suspected of having consumption. The living rooms of a consumptive patient should have as little furniture as practicable. Hangings should be especially avoided. The use of carpets, rugs, etc., ought always to be avoided.

3. Do not fail to wash thoroughly the eating utensils of a person suspected of having consumption as soon after eating as possible, using boiling water for the purpose.

4. Do not mingle the unwashed clothing of consumptive patients with similar clothing of other persons.

5. Do not fail to catch the bowel discharges of consumptive patients with diarrhœa in a vessel containing corrosive sublimate 1 part, water 1,000 parts.

6. Do not fail to consult the family physician regarding the social relations of persons suffering from suspected consumption.

7. Do not permit mothers suspected of having consumption to nurse their offspring.

8. Household pets (animals or birds) are quite susceptible to tuberculosis; therefore do not expose them to persons afflicted with consumption; also do not keep, but destroy at once, all household pets suspected of having consumption, otherwise they may give it to human beings.

9. Do not fail to thoroughly cleanse the floors, walls, and ceilings of the living and sleeping rooms of persons suffering from consumption at least once in two weeks.

By order of the Board,

(*Signed*)   EMMONS CLARK, *Secretary.*

No further action was taken by the Department of Health of New York city with reference to pulmonary tuberculosis until 1893, after Dr. Biggs became pathologist and director of the laboratories of the Department.   He then, with Dr. Prudden, submitted another communication urging that action be taken with reference to the reporting of pulmonary tuberculosis as a communicable disease.   This letter was followed by a resolution of the Health Department requiring notification of pulmonary tuberculosis from all public institutions and establishing voluntary notification for private cases.   It also provided for the free examination of sputum for diagnostic purposes, for the visitation of cases in the homes by Health Department inspectors, and for the renovation of premises vacated.   This resolution went into effect in 1894.   In 1897 compulsory notification of cases of pulmonary tuberculosis for physicians in private practice as well as for public institutions was established by resolution of the Board of Health, largely at the instigation of Dr. Biggs.

The opposition to the action of the Department of Health in establishing compulsory notification of pulmonary tuberculosis in 1897 presents an interesting chapter in medical history and in tuberculosis control, especially by way of contrast with present-day conditions.   In 1897 the New York County Medical Society and the Kings County Medical Society were so bitterly opposed to the action of the Health Department that they secured the introduction of bills in the State Legislature at Albany rescinding the provision of the charter of New York city which gave authority to the Health Department of New York city to deal with tuberculosis as an infectious disease. During the legislative session of 1898 and 1899 Dr. Biggs spent much of the winter in Albany fighting these bills and blocking their passage. The opposition, however, continued to be intense, and the feeling aroused in medical circles was extremely bitter. At Dr. Biggs' request the New York Academy of Medicine appointed a committee to consider the entire question. Dr. Edward G. Janeway was president of the Academy at that time, and he and Dr. T. Mitchell Prudden served with others on the committee. Numerous meetings of the committee were held. The discussions were bitter and heated. After several weeks the committee reported back to the Academy that they considered the action of the Health Department "inexpedient and inadvisable." The influence of Dr. Janeway and Dr. Prudden prevented the committee from making more drastic recommendations which some of the members favored.

On February 13, 1904, the New York City Board of Health finally passed a resolution favoring compulsory reporting of tuberculous disease in all forms, but it was not until January 18, 1907, that tuberculosis was declared a communicable and infectious disease, and as such reportable in all instances (Sect. 153, Code of 1907). New York's example of reporting tuberculous cases to the Health Department has since been followed by most of the principal cities of the Union.

To the city of Boston, the home of Dr. Bowditch, belongs the honor of having established the first free hospitals for the treatment of consumption. The Channing Home, named after the celebrated Unitarian divine, was founded in Boston in 1857, for the treatment of white women in all stages of pulmonary tuberculosis. In 1861, in Boston, Miss Anne Smith Robbins founded the House of the Good Samaritan for women with advanced consumption who were without means of support. For fifty-nine years this House has been a beautiful home to many a poor dying woman. In 1918, 69 cases were treated. In 1864, in the same city, the Cullis Consumptives' Home, named after Dr. Charles Cullis, was established. This is a hospital for the treatment of men and women in the last stages of pulmonary tuberculosis who are without means of support. The fourth oldest institution of this kind is the one established in 1876 by the Philadelphia Protestant Episcopal City Mission. It is known as the Home for Consumptives at Chestnut Hill.

The first private sanatorium in the United States was established in 1875 in Asheville, N. C., by Dr. Joseph W. Gleitzmann. The first sanatorium for the poor and those of moderate means was founded by Dr. E. L. Trudeau at Saranac Lake in 1884, under the name "Adirondack Cottage Sanitarium." The first sanatorium established near a large city without regard to climatic advantages was the Sharon Sanatorium, near Boston. It was opened in 1890 and owes its existence to the enthusiasm and personal work of Dr. Vincent Y. Bowditch.

In 1896 there was established the second private sanatorium situated at Liberty, but a few hours by rail from New York city. The institution was named in honor of the late Professor Alfred Loomis, who had been so active in helping in the creation of the Adirondack Cottage Sanitarium, now the Trudeau Sanatorium. The late Dr. Herbert Maxon King became physician-in-chief of the Loomis institution, and thanks to his devotion, scientific attainment, and charming personality the institution has grown to be one of the most important private sanatoria in the United States.

In the same year was established a semi-philanthropic institution known as the Eudowood Sanatorium. The name has since been changed to The Hospital for Consumptives of Maryland. It receives the white citizens of Maryland and has a capacity of 105 patients. The first officers of the hospital were Daniel W. Hopper, president, and W. B. Canfield, M.D., secretary; the present officers are Henry Barton Jacobs, M.D., president, and W. Graham Bowdoin, secretary.

Thanks to the enthusiasm and energy of Miss Louisa F. Loring, of Massachusetts, Dr. Charles F. McMahan, Dr. Ernest S. Cross, and other prominent citizens of Aiken, S. C., an admirable little institution was established in that community in 1897, known as the Aiken Cottage Sanatorium. It has since grown to considerable proportions and is doing excellent work for tuberculous invalids whose finances do not permit their being

"THE LITTLE RED COTTAGE" WHERE TRUDEAU BEGAN HIS SANA-
TORIUM

received and cared for in private institutions. Miss Loring, the founder, is still, after 25 years, the president of the institution.

The first state sanatorium for the tuberculous was established by an act of the Legislature of the State of Massachusetts in 1895, and was opened for the reception of patients in October, 1898. It was called the Massachusetts State Sanatorium and is located at Rutland.

The first municipal hospital for the consumptive poor in the United States was established in Cincinnati, Ohio, in July, 1897. The second one was established in New York city at Blackwell's Island in 1902, by the Department of Charities, under the direction of Mr. Homer Folks. It is known as the Metropolitan Hospital.

The United States Government in 1899 established a United States Army General Hospital at Fort Bayard, N. M., for discharged tuberculous soldiers of the United States Army, who are beneficiaries of the Soldiers' Home, Washington, D. C., for officers of the Army on the active or retired list who have tuberculosis, for wives of officers, and for Army nurses who are tuberculous. It has a capacity at present of 1,500. A second hospital was established by the United States Public Health Service about the same time at Fort Stanton, N. M. It was designed for the treatment of tuberculous civilian government employees. Both institutions are now under the United States Public Health Service and at the present time are almost entirely occupied by tuberculous ex-soldiers of the world war.

In 1903 and 1904 there were established two institutions for the treatment of tuberculosis, each unique in its own way. The first was the Stony Wold Sanatorium, built in the Adirondacks at Lake Kushaqua, N. Y., for the treatment of consumptive working women and children. The sanatorium is maintained by philanthropic women of wealth. The other institution was Sea Breeze, a seaside sanatorium for tuberculous and scrofulous children, established in 1904 by the New York Association for Improving the Condition of the Poor, at Coney Island. It is now operated by the city of New York at Neponsit Beach, Long Island.

Interest in the treatment of tuberculosis had developed to

such an extent that in 1905 the American Sanatorium Association was organized, and held its first meeting at the American Museum of Natural History, New York city, on December 1st of that year, with seventeen members present. The object of the Association is "to promote the professional and social rela tions of the members and to advance the knowledge of sanatorium treatment of pulmonary tuberculosis."

It was decided that the Association should consist of active and honorary members. All physicians engaged in active sanatorium work, who are also members of the National Tuberculosis Association, are eligible for active membership. Honorary members are nominated by the executive committee, consisting of the president, vice-president, and secretary-treasurer. Later on the privilege of membership was extended also to non-resident, visiting, and consulting physicians of sanatoria or tuberculosis hospitals, so that the membership which started with nineteen in 1906, is now over 225.

At the first meeting, Doctors Vincent Y. Bowditch, of Boston, Lawrence F.˙ Flick, of Philadelphia, and Lawrason Brown, of Saranac Lake, were elected president, vice-president, and secre tary-treasurer, respectively. Doctors Bowditch, Flick, and E. L. Trudeau were made life members in recognition of their work in establishing and propagating sanatorium treatment in the United States.

In 1906 the first municipal sanatorium for early cases was established at Otisville, N. Y., by the New York City Health Department, under the direction of Dr. Hermann M. Biggs. In 1904, when our Association was organized, there were in operation in the United States 96 sanatoria and special hospitals for tuberculosis.

The first dispensary class in the United States devoted exclusively to the treatment of tuberculosis was inaugurated in 1894 by Dr. Edward J. Bermingham, of New York city, at the New York Throat and Nose Hospital. Nine years later, on October 30, 1903, Dr. John H. Huddleston established a class for tuberculous patients in connection with the general dispensary of the Gouverneur Hospital, thus creating the first tuberculosis dispensary under the auspices of the City Department of Bellevue and Allied Hospitals. A dispensary exclusively for the treatment of the consumptive poor, and having its own building, was established by the city of New York under the auspices of the Health Department and opened in March, 1904. This was located at the corner of Fifty-fifth Street and Sixth Avenue, and was known as the Clinic for Pulmonary Diseases of the Health Department. It was started mainly through the initiative of Dr. Hermann M. Biggs, then General Medical Officer of the city. Dr. Biggs acted as director and Drs. John S. Billings and S. Adolphus Knopf as associate directors, with a staff of 10 attending physicians.

Following is an enumeration of the dispensaries in operation prior to the founding of The National Association for the Study and Prevention of Tuberculosis: In Connecticut 1, District of Columbia 1, Illinois 1, Maryland 1, Massachusetts 2, Minnesota 2, New Jersey 1, New York 8, Ohio 2, Pennsylvania 4, Rhode Island 1—a total of 24.

The idea of forming a society to create auxiliaries to tuberculosis clinics originated in New York in 1905 with Mrs. Willard Straight, Mrs. J. Borden Harriman, Dr. Andrew J. McCush and Dr. Hermann M. Biggs. In 1907 the first auxiliary to a tuberculosis dispensary was established in connection with the tuberculosis clinic of the Presbyterian Hospital of New York city. It owes its existence to the enthusiasm and devotion of Mrs. J. Borden Harriman, Mrs. Willard Straight, and Mrs. Rumsey.

The Chelsea Clinic auxiliary and other auxiliaries were later developed. An active association under the name of "Society for Prevention and Relief of Tuberculosis" was incorporated in 1915. Mrs. J. Borden Harriman was elected honorary president, Mrs. Willard Straight an honorary member, Miss Beatrice Bend, president, and Mrs. Hermann M. Biggs, vice-president. In 1916 Mrs. Biggs succeeded to the presidency and remained in this position until 1920, when she was made honorary president and was succeeded by Miss Ruth Twombly. The activities of the Society are varied. Besides providing for medical attention, it gives relief in food, clothing, transportation to sanatoria, and employment, and has installed in the various clinics day nurseries, physical culture classes, dental clinics, and workshops.

The first exhibit on tuberculosis in this country was held in Baltimore in January, 1904, under the joint auspices of the Tuberculosis Commission of the Maryland State Board of Health and the Maryland Public Health Association. The exhibit was an objective presentation of the history, distribution, varieties, causes, cost, prevention, and cure of tuberculosis, and was undertaken at the suggestion of Dr. John S. Fulton, Secretary of the Maryland State Board of Health.

In 1908 the first open-air school in the United States was established in Providence, R. I., by Dr. Ellen R. Stone, of the school board of that city. In 1909 the first tuberculosis preventorium was established at Farmingdale, N. J. It owes its inception to the munificence of the New York philanthropist, Mr. Nathan Straus. The first day camp was established in Boston in 1905, under the direction of the Boston Association for Relief and Control of Tuberculosis.

The first municipal preventorium was inaugurated on September 24, 1920. It has a capacity of 200 beds, and is located at West New Brighton, Staten Island, N. Y., forming a part of Sea View Hospital. This preventorium owes its inception to the Hon. Bird S. Coler, Commissioner of the Department of Public Welfare of the city of New York.

In 1908, after a meeting at the tuberculosis exhibition in New York, the Metropolitan Life Insurance Company decided to establish a sanatorium for its consumptive employees. After some litigation concerning the right of such a company to do this, permission was granted by the courts and a magnificent institution was erected at Mount McGregor, N. Y. It was inaugurated on June 20, 1914.

The need for special undergraduate instruction in tuberculosis was first recognized in 1901, when a chair of tuberculosis was established in Tufts College Medical School in Boston. Dr. Edward O. Otis was placed in charge, with the title of Professor of Tuberculous Diseases and Climatology. In 1908 the New York Post-Graduate Medical School created the first chair of phthisiotherapy, which was occupied by the author until the adequate development of the work had to be given up during the war for lack of funds.

In 1917 the Trudeau School of Tuberculosis, named in honor of Edward Livingston Trudeau, was founded at Saranac Lake, N. Y., and three years later the Colorado School of Tuberculosis was established at Colorado Springs, with Dr. Gerald B. Webb as Dean.

In 1913 Dr. John H. Pryor, of Buffalo, returned from Europe, after having studied the Rollier system of heliotherapy for the treatment of local and general tuberculosis. He was fortunate enough to secure funds sufficient to erect proper buildings for this treatment, as part of the J. N. Adam Memorial Hospital for incipient tuberculosis at Perrysburg, N. Y. This was the first institution where this beneficial treatment for bone, joint, and glandular tuberculosis was put in practice in this country on a large scale.

The first periodical in America to be devoted entirely to tuberculosis was the *Journal of Tuberculosis*, which made its initial appearance in June, 1899, under the editorship of Cárl von Ruck, B.S., M.D., of Asheville, N. C. In 1903 the *Journal of the Outdoor Life* saw the light of day at Saranac Lake, N. Y., under the able editorship of Dr. Lawrason Brown. This journal has been productive of a great deal of good, and has now no less than 6,500 subscribers. It is published monthly by the National Tuberculosis Association, 370 Seventh Avenue, New York city. The editorial staff is composed of the following: James Alexander Miller, M.D., editor-in-chief; H. R. M. Landis, M.D., Lawrason Brown, M.D., Fred H. Heise, M.D., Allen K. Krause, M.D., Charles L. Minor, M.D., Philip King Brown, M.D., A. W. Jones, Jr., Homer Folks, George Thomas Palmer, M.D., John Tombs, Charles J. Hatfield, M.D., associate editors; and Philip P. Jacobs, Ph.D., managing editor. The aim of this journal is to be helpful to persons seeking health by an outdoor life, and to disseminate reliable information looking to the prevention and cure of tuberculosis.

In the year 1916 American tuberculosis workers felt the need of a scientific publication similar to the German *Zeitschrift*, which then arrived very irregularly in this country owing to war conditions, and the National Tuberculosis Association laid plans for a monthly publication to be called *The American Review of Tuber-*

culosis.   Today it is universally conceded that the *Review* is in every way equal, if not superior, to the veteran German journal. The first number of *The American Review of Tuberculosis* appeared in March, 1917, with Edward R. Baldwin, of Saranac Lake, as editor-in-chief, and Allen K. Krause, of Johns Hopkins Hospital, Baltimore, as managing editor.   Lawrason Brown, H. R. M. Landis, Paul A. Lewis, M. J. Rosenau, Henry Sewall, and Borden S. Veeder complete the editorial staff; George Mannheimer is abstract editor.   The *Review* is now in its fifth year, and it is constantly growing in excellence.   Each number contains from four to six original articles, often beautifully illustrated by original drawings or radiographic pictures.   Besides the original articles, the *Review* contains abstracts on tuberculosis and allied subjects from all the leading medical journals of the world.

The first endowed institute for the study, treatment, and prevention of tuberculosis was founded in Philadelphia, Pa., in 1903. It owes its existence to the well-known philanthropist, Mr. Henry Phipps, of New York.   This Institute is now a part of the University of Pennsylvania.   The story of its foundation is an interesting one, and shows how enthusiasm for a great cause seldom remains unrewarded.   The Institute was conceived by Dr. Lawrence F. Flick, who was about to start a tuberculosis clinic with a total backing of $1,000, when he met Mr. Henry Phipps and discussed the venture with him.   Mr. Phipps at once offered to underwrite a much more extensive enterprise to be aimed at the extermination of tuberculosis.   On February 1, 1903, the Institute began work in an old remodeled building equipped with 52 beds, a small laboratory, and facilities for operating a large dispensary.   During the ten years that followed its work was so successful that Mr. Phipps not only agreed to continue his support, but also supplied funds for the purchase of land and the erection of the splendid building in which the Institute is now housed.   Dr. Flick, the moving spirit in the founding of the Institute, resigned as director in 1909.   In order that the standing of the Institute might be assured and the integrity of the enterprise guaranteed, it was placed in charge of the trustees of the University of Pennsylvania on July 1, 1910, with the understanding that Mr. Phipps would be responsible for its support over a stipulated period of time. The new building erected at Mr. Phipps' expense provided adequate facilities for every branch of medical and sociological research bearing upon the problem of tuberculosis.

Most thorough and interesting indeed is the work which this institution is doing. By its pre-natal clinic it gives a baby a chance to enter life unhandicapped by physical deformity, and safeguards the prospective mother from the attacks of tuberculosis. Its baby clinic corrects tuberculous tendencies in infants. A children's clinic is held each Saturday morning, so that it will not interfere with school hours. This clinic is similar in purpose to the baby clinic, and examines an average of 50 children each week. The nutrition clinic makes growing "fat and strong" an interesting game for children predisposed to be tuberculous. Gold stars awarded weekly to children gaining most weight make the fight for health a joyous contest which even the youngsters can appreciate.

The Negro clinic, supervised by Negro physicians, nurses, and social service workers, is meeting a special problem. Clinics for adults dispose of 200 cases weekly. The syphilis clinic provides for the diagnosis and treatment of the many obscure cases in which tuberculosis is complicated by syphilis. All clinics supply cases necessary for observation and research work, and through them an effort to discover a more reliable clinical diagnosis, especially a diagnosis applicable to children, is being made. Social service workers see that treatment is observed in the homes as directed by physicians in charge of the clinics.

The personal attitude of the staff and the methods by which they work make it possible to state that no medical institution has so far succeeded in entering into the lives of its patients more sympathetically or more helpfully than has the Henry Phipps Institute. The research work of the Institute in the fields of clinical medicine, bacteriology, and chemistry are a pattern for similar work wherever tuberculosis is being fought.

The personnel of the Institute consists of an advisory council, the members of which are Drs. William H. Welch, Theobald Smith, Simon Flexner, Hermann M. Biggs, Lawrason Brown, Gideon Wells, Livingston Farrand, James Alexander Miller,

2

Joseph H. Pratt, David R. Lyman, William Charles White, Mr. William H. Baldwin, Prof. Samuel McC. Lindsay, and ex officio the Commissioner of Health of Pennsylvania and the Director of Public Health and Charities of Philadelphia. The Provost and a committee of trustees represent the University of Pennsylvania. The executive director is Dr. Charles J. Hatfield. The director of the clinical and sociological department is Dr. H. R. M. Landis; the director of the laboratory is Dr. Paul A. Lewis. Associate directors of the clinical and sociological departments are Drs. A. J. Cohen, Frank A. Craig, and I. Kauffman.

The first association for the prevention of tuberculosis in the United States was the Pennsylvania Society for the Prevention of Tuberculosis formed by Dr. Lawrence F. Flick, of Philadelphia, in 1892. From its very beginning this society commenced to agitate for the reporting and registration of living cases of tuberculosis and to disburse information regarding the nature and communicability of the disease. At the present time the Pennsylvania Tuberculosis Society is one of the most influential organizations in the State. It has affiliated with it 97 local associations. For many years it was the only state tuberculosis association in the United States.

In January, 1902, 11 physicians, Drs. Hermann M. Biggs, Joseph D. Bryant, John H. Huddleston, A. Jacobi, Walter B. James, Edward G. Janeway, Alexander Lambert, Henry P. Loomis, T. Mitchell Prudden, Andrew H. Smith, Stephen Smith, and the author decided to call a tuberculosis committee or association into life in New York city. Professor Edward T. Devine, Ph.D., at that time general secretary of the Charity Organization Society, offered his services as secretary, and another distinguished layman, the Hon. Charles P. Cox, was chosen as chairman. As the objects of the committee, the following program was decided upon:

1. Research into the social, as distinct from the medical, aspects of tuberculosis. For example, into the relations between the disease and overcrowding, infected tenements, and unhealthy occupations, and also into the influence upon recovery of improved diet and hygienic living.
2. Education. The publication of leaflets and pamphlets, the giving of lectures, and the promulgation in every possible way of the fact that tuberculosis

is a communicable and preventable disease; the widest distribution of the results of scientific research in this field, and of the results of modern treatment, both in sanatoria and at home.

3. The encouragement of movements for suitable public and private sanatoria, both for advanced and for incipient cases; for adults and for children; for free care and also for the care of those who can pay moderate fees.

4. The relief of indigent consumptives by the provision of suitable food and medicine, by the payment of rent when this is necessary to secure adequate light and air, and by transportation and maintenance at a distance, when, in the judgment of the committee, this is essential.

The public interest taken in New York in this then entirely new movement may be shown by the response to an appeal for subscriptions to carry on the work of the committee. Within two weeks many relatively small gifts had amounted to a total of $5,000. This Committee, working under the auspices of the powerful Charity Organization Society of the city of New York, in time has become one of the leading anti-tuberculosis organizations in the United States.

Among the earliest western tuberculosis associations mention should be made of the Chicago Tuberculosis Institute, founded· in 1906. Its influence has been felt in Chicago, Illinois, the Mississippi Valley, and the entire country. The calling of this organization into life was largely due to the devotion and enthusiasm of a group of pioneers in the anti-tuberculosis field, among whom we must mention the late Henry B. Favill; a president of the National Tuberculosis Association, Theodore B. Sachs; the great blind physician, Robert H. Babcock; and the skilled clinician, one of the founders of the American Medical Association, Nathan S. Davis. Of those early workers in the Chicago Tuberculosis Institute who are still with us we must mention Drs. Frank Billings, William A. Evans, Ethan A. Gray, Arnold C. Klebs, Edwin W. Ryerson, and George W. Webster. Among the distinguished lay persons who gave their help and support in those early days there should be mentioned Miss Jane Addams, Mrs. James L. Houghteling, and the Hon. Julian W. Mack. Mr. Charles L. Allen served the Institute as its first honorary counsel, Mr. David R. Forgan as its first treasurer, Mr. Alexander M. Wilson, and Mr. Sherman C. Kingsley as its first and second secretaries.

The work of the Institute is divided into a department of education, a department of dispensaries, a department of immunity research, and a department of sanatoria, camps, and hospitals. Two of the outstanding achievements of the Chicago Tuberculosis Institute have been, first, the establishment of the Edward Sanatorium at Naperville, Ill., which opened its doors on June 15, 1907; and, second, its work with the county board in the establishment of the great Municipal Tuberculosis Sanitarium of the city of Chicago, at 5601 North Crawford Avenue. This institution, with a capacity for 1,000 cases of ambulant tuberculous patients and 300 bed cases, was opened on March 1, 1915. The central office of the dispensary department is at 105 West Monroe Street, and there are eight branches throughout the city.

About the time the New York Committee was formed, local associations were being organized in Washington, D. C.; New Haven County, Conn.; Chicago; Boston, Cambridge, and Worcester, Mass.; St. Louis; Minneapolis; Orange, N. J.; Binghamton, Rochester, and Buffalo, N. Y.; Scranton, Pa.; and Newport, R. I. By 1904 only 24 associations had been formed, including one in Cuba. These organizations were distributed over 16 different States, Pennsylvania and Massachusetts each having four. Only a few of these original associations have survived to this date.

In 1913 there was established in New York city the first workshop for arrested tuberculous patients whose condition was such that they could work for a few hours a day without fear of relapse. This institution took the name of Altro Manufacturing Company. Patients with or without previous experience in garment-making find remunerative employment there for as many hours a day as their condition will safely permit. This workshop from its beginning has been under the able direction of Mr. Edward Hochhauser. In 1920 another type of workshop was established for arrested tuberculous cases, known as the Reco Manufacturing Company. It owes its existence to the enthusiasm of the officers of the New York Tuberculosis Association and a subsidy from the National Tuberculosis Association. Patients are taught watchmaking, jewelry manufacturing and cabinet making, trades which enable them to earn a good living after they have acquired the necessary skill.

As an item of historical interest in the combat of tuberculosis in animals, we must not fail to remember the pioneer work of Dr. Leonard Pearson. In the *Journal of the American Veterinary Medical Association* of January, 1921, Dr. L. A. Klein has this to say about Pearson's work:

"The first tuberculin test made on this continent was applied in 1892 near Villa Nova, 20 miles west of Philadelphia, to a herd of pure-bred Jersey cattle by L. Pearson. There were 76 cattle in the herd, some of them imported and all pure-bred; and 51 reacted to the test. On March 16, 1892, six of them were brought to the veterinary school and killed for postmortem examination. Pearson was a student in Germany in 1890 when Koch discovered tuberculin. During the following three years Pearson used the tuberculin test in his private practice. Its efficiency and reliability were recognized by veterinarians, physicians, sanitary officials and the more progressive livestock owners when they became more familiar with it. But the opposition of some of the livestock owners and journals continued for a long time. In 1895, when the Pennsylvania State Livestock Sanitary Board was organized and Pearson became its secretary, he introduced the principle of testing herds on the voluntary application of the owner. This principle was the keystone of what became known as the Pennsylvania plan for controlling tuberculosis, and it is also one of the features of the accredited herd plan. Viewed from a purely economic standpoint, and laying aside the question of public health, the control and eradication of tuberculosis in cattle is a matter of great importance not only to the cattle owner, but also to all consumers of meat and milk."

CHAPTER II

ORGANIZATION OF THE NATIONAL TUBER CULOSIS ASSOCIATION

THE need of a National Tuberculosis Association in the United States was apparent as early as 1898, when Dr. Lawrence F. Flick suggested the formation of such an organization. From the foregoing chapter it will be seen that anti-tuberculosis work was going forward here and there all over the country, and the need of some central association to co-ordinate the varied activities and to extend the work was beginning to make itself felt. By 1903 such an organization had become an imperative necessity.

In that year there had sprung up suddenly two tuberculosis congresses, one calling itself the American Congress on Tuberculosis and planning for an international tuberculosis congress the following year, the other styled the American Congress for the Prevention of Consumption. Furthermore, two tuberculosis exhibitions were planned for the year 1904, one to be held in Baltimore and another one in St. Louis. Besides these American congresses and tuberculosis exhibitions, an international tuberculosis congress with an exhibition was planned to be held in Paris during September, 1904.

In an effort to clear up this bewildering situation, Dr. S. A. Knopf, of New York, made the suggestion in a letter, published in the *Journal of the American Medical Association* of December 5, 1913, that all of those interested in the question of congresses or associations should meet for a conference at Baltimore during the Tuberculosis Exposition to be held there in January, 1904. This letter is given in full as follows:

"NEW YORK, November 27, 1903.

"*To the Editor:* During the past few months I have received many inquiries concerning the various tuberculosis congresses (American and international)

22

which have been projected for the years 1904–5. The multiplicity of these various congresses and the similarity of their names lead naturally to great confusion.

"It is announced that a congress on tuberculosis is to be held in St. Louis in October, 1904, under the name of 'International Congress on Tuberculosis.' On careful inquiry I learned the following facts about this congress: Mr. Francis, the president of the St. Louis Exhibition, has been approached by the officers of the 'American Congress on Tuberculosis,' which was founded some years ago by Clark Bell, a lawyer of the city of New York, to sanction the holding of an international congress on tuberculosis in connection with the Louisiana Purchase Exposition. From a letter received from Dr. E. J. Barrick of Toronto, Canada, the president of this congress, I learn that Mr. Francis has appointed the above mentioned Mr. Clark Bell chairman of the committee on organization. Mr. Clark Bell is also the treasurer and chairman of the executive committee of the 'American Congress on Tuberculosis,' season 1903–1904; a Mr. Samuel Bell Thomas, of 290 Broadway, New York, is the secretary of the latter. The officers of the international congress are not yet elected. I was desirous to learn the names of other medical men interested in this congress, and Dr. Barrick very kindly wrote me November 16th that he had asked Mr. Bell to furnish me the desired additional information, but nothing has thus far been received.

"The other international tuberculosis congress announced is the one to meet in Washington, D. C., April, 1905. It is to be held under the auspices of 'The American Congress on Tuberculosis for the Prevention of Consumption,' of which Dr. Daniel Lewis, New York, is president, and Dr. George Brown, Atlanta, Ga., is secretary.

"I want to call attention to the difference in name of the two American congresses, one is 'American Congress on Tuberculosis,' the other 'The American Congress on Tuberculosis for the Prevention of Consumption.'

"The congress which was to meet under the name of 'Congress International de la Tuberculose' at Paris from September 26 to October 1, 1904, has been recently postponed to the year 1905. The president of this congress is Professor Brouardel, honorary dean of the Faculty of Medicine of Paris. The general secretary is Dr. M. Letulle, professor agrégé of the Faculty of Medicine, residing at 7 rue Magdebourg, Paris.

"There will be held during the coming year independently of the above-mentioned congresses two tuberculosis exhibitions, one in Baltimore and the other in St. Louis. The Baltimore Tuberculosis Exhibition will be held in January, 1904, under the combined auspices of the tuberculosis commission of the Maryland Board of Health and the Maryland Public Health Association.

"The other tuberculosis exhibition will be held in St. Louis, in connection with the Exhibition of Social Economy and under the sub-section of hygiene, of which Dr. J. N. Hurty, of Indianapolis, is superintendent. All indications point toward success of both exhibits, and it is to be hoped that they will fulfil their high purpose and at the same time be a credit to American physicians and hygienists.

"Considering the various congresses, I do not hesitate to express a feeling of deep anxiety. The first one mentioned, which for reason of brevity I will call 'The Bell Congress,' because it owes its inception to Mr. Clark Bell, has not, to my knowledge, the support of our best men. The second congress in point of time, which again, for the sake of brevity and clearness, I may call 'The Lewis-Brown Congress' (names of the president and secretary), while it has many distinguished men of various State and provincial boards of health among the members, has, like the Bell Congress, thus far not among them the men we are wont to look up to as leaders in movements of this kind.

"What are our confréres across the water to think if they hear of two American congresses on tuberculosis and each having an international one under its auspices? The European authorities found it best, instead of having a triennial congress, to have one more year intervene. This will make the congress in Washington and the one in Paris convene in the same year (1905).

"If President Francis, of the St. Louis Exposition, desires that a tuberculosis congress shall be held in St. Louis, let him call to his aid some of the men who are recognized as leaders in our profession. They will counsel with him on the advisability of such a congress, and if it is decided that one should be held, Mr. Francis can be assured that the best element of Europe and America will come to St. Louis to contribute to its success.

"The officers and members of the Lewis-Brown Congress must realize that they cannot expect their international meeting in Washington to be successful, when, six months later, there will be held an international congress in Paris. I hope that there will be enough patriotism and national pride for all interested to realize that to have two American congresses on tuberculosis is an anomaly, and that, if the St. Louis Congress is to be a success, it must be in the hands of medical men well and favorably known in this country and abroad.

"As a solution of the problem I beg leave to suggest the following: During the Tuberculosis Exposition in Baltimore next January all interested should meet on a certain date on this neutral ground for the purpose of coming to an agreement about a single representative national or international tuberculosis congress which will convene in Paris."

Prior to its publication the letter had been submitted to a few prominent men who were particularly interested in the situation, as the author did not wish to assume the entire responsibility in so important a matter. Following are some of the encouraging replies which made the publication of such a letter seem most timely. Sir William Osler, then Professor of Medicine of Johns Hopkins Medical School, wrote:

"BALTIMORE, MD., Nov. 25, 1903.
"Excellent in every way! There is not a word to alter, and I have nothing to suggest. It hits the nail fairly and squarely on the head. I feel that we should organize a national committee which should be in touch with the Con-

gress in Paris, and it should be composed of good men from each state. That we could do during the Baltimore meeting. The *Maryland Medical Journal* is the one in which the letter should also be published."

Dr. Edward G. Janeway, Professor of Medicine of Bellevue Medical College, wrote:

"NEW YORK, December 25, 1903.

"I think that the ground which you have taken as regards the American International Congress on Tuberculosis is correct. Any such body to be successful must originate in a desire to accomplish good results for the victims of tuberculosis, and must be so constituted as to have the confidence of the medical profession. Moreover the true status of these organizations may be tested by the attitude of their officers towards a movement such as you indicate, which will endeavor to unite under such leadership as will have medical and lay support, those who earnestly desire to conduct a combat against this dread disease. The judgment of Solomon may thus have an analogy in this warfare of interests."

Dr. Arnold C. Klebs, of the Committee on the Prevention of Tuberculosis of the Visiting Nurse Association in Chicago, wrote as follows:

"CHICAGO, December 12, 1903.

"Your letter of recent date makes unnecessary a step which I contemplated and which coincides with yours entirely. I hope you will be successful to get the chief men together in Baltimore. I shall, of course, come. If I may suggest something in regard to this meeting, I believe it would be wise to call only a few men, not more than 15 or 20. I think it would expedite matters and facilitate a national understanding. Our attitude toward these tuberculosis congresses is really of secondary importance. The formation of a Central Committee seems to me more important than anything else. At any rate, I am with you in anything of that kind."

Dr. Edward O. Otis, of Boston, wrote:

"I read your letter on Tuberculosis Congresses and Exhibits and thank you most heartily for enlightening us all upon this mixed matter. I approve heartily of your suggestion of the meeting in Baltimore, and, as far as I know now, I think I can be present on the evening of January 28th."

Because of the good standing of some of the men connected with the "American Congresses," and in order to be just and fair, the editor of the *Journal of the American Medical Association* sent the manuscript of the letter and of his editorial approving of it to a number of men well known for their high medical and ethical standing, asking for an unbiased opinion. As a result of this precaution the following communications were received from three gentlemen to whom the author had also written directly for advice and counsel in this delicate matter.

Dr. Vincent Y. Bowditch, of Boston, wrote:

"Dr. Simmons, the editor of the *Journal of the American Medical Association*, sent me your letter with the proof sheet of his editorial upon it, asking me to give him my frank opinion of his editorial. I replied saying that I thought both were admirable and that I thought the subject ought to be thoroughly aired. It certainly would seem as though some definite committee should be formed to represent the respectable profession on this matter, and, if Dr. Osler or Welch would head it, it would be the best means of ensuring its success."

Dr. J. H. Musser, of Philadelphia, wrote:

"Concerning the Tuberculosis Congresses, I am heartily in sympathy with you. I saw your letter and the editorial which were published in the *Journal of the American Medical Association*. I was asked by the editor to *visé* them before they were published in order that he might have the thoughts of two or three others. These editorials are therefore an expression of my views, and I think uphold you."

Dr. Frank Billings, of Chicago, wrote:

"I have read your letter and the editorial. In addition I had several interviews with Dr. Simmons and with Dr. Osler on the subject under discussion. I most emphatically agree with all that has been written by you and by the editors of the medical journals, who have discussed the subject. It is a very serious business. If we cannot head off both of these so-called 'Congresses on Tuberculosis,' it will be a disgrace to American medicine. A properly conducted International Congress on Tuberculosis, in America, at the proper time, after the Paris Congress, will, I think, be a very desirable and proper procedure on your part."

How very serious the situation had become may be gathered from an editorial which appeared in the *Journal of the American Medical Association* the week following the publication of Dr. Knopf's letter, under the heading "Tuberculosis Congresses." After quoting an official communication which had been sent by the Assistant Secretary of State to the American ambassadors in England, France, Denmark, and The Netherlands, inviting those governments to send delegates to the Clark Bell Congress, the editor continued as follows:

"This letter of instruction to our ambassadors to England, France, Denmark, and The Netherlands, without referring to others, is sufficient to show

how seriously and earnestly the United States Government has endorsed the movement. The fact that these people have succeeded in obtaining the support of the government is unfortunate, for as a natural result physicians of foreign countries interested in the subject will be led to come to this congress. If, having come so far, they find that the 'congress' is not supported by the better element of the profession—by those prominent in tuberculosis work in the United States; if, to use a familiar expression, they find the play of Hamlet with Hamlet left out, they will feel that they have been imposed on. The result will not be complimentary to us, but will in a measure reflect on the medical profession of the United States, irresponsible as it is for the conditions.

"We are neither ready, nor is the time opportune, for an international congress on tuberculosis. But when we have one, let it be one that shall have its inception in some reputable and recognized body; one that shall have the indorsement and support of the profession, and especially of those who are recognized as authorities on the subject; one whose utterances shall be authoritative and command respect, and one that shall redound to the credit of America and of which Americans can be proud.

"We believe that those who are working in behalf of the organization known as the Lewis-Brown congress are animated by pure motives, and by the belief that its contemplated meeting will be beneficial. Nevertheless, we cannot but think that under the circumstances it will be a mistake for them to go on. They have inherited with their 'congress' all its former stigma, and the only way to get rid of the stigma is to quickly let the 'congress' die and start anew. The title of the Lewis-Brown congress—the American Congress on Tuberculosis for the Prevention of Consumption—is too much like that of the Bell congress—the American Congress on Tuberculosis—and it will be impossible for them to free themselves from the odium the name carries with it.

"As far as the other congress is concerned, the so-called 'Bell Congress,' it seems to us that the time has come to do something more than simply ignore it. If it is to become a reality under conditions in which it cannot receive the support and coöperation of those best qualified to represent the American medical profession in the discussion of the subject, and we believe such to be the case, it is well that the world should know the fact."

As a result of Dr. Knopf's suggestion, a conference was held in McCoy Hall, Baltimore, on January 28, 1904, at which the following men, representing various agencies, activities, and interests were present:

Drs. Daniel Lewis, New York city; John B. Huber, New York city; Thomas Darlington, New York city; W. Freudenthal, New York city; S. A. Knopf, New York city; Lawrason Brown, Saranac Lake, N. Y.; Herbert D. Pease, Albany, N. Y.; Walter J. Marcley, Rutland, Mass.; Edward O. Otis, Boston, Mass.; Vincent Y. Bowditch, Rutland, Mass.; M. G. Overlock, Worcester, Mass.; J. A. Egan, Springfield, Ill.; Charles L. Minor, Asheville, N. C.; J. N. Hurty, Indianapolis, Ind.; H. M. Bracken, Minneapolis, Minn.; William M. Angney, Philadelphia, Pa.; Joseph J. Kinyoun, Glen Olden, Pa.; David R. Lyman, New Haven, Conn.; Theodore Eugene Oertel, Atlanta, Ga.; Robert H. Babcock, Chicago, Ill.; Arnold C. Klebs, Chicago, Ill.; William W. Ford, White Water, Mo.; P. H. Bryce, Montreal, Canada; J. G. Adami, Montreal, Canada; A. J. Richer, Montreal, Canada; J. H. Elliott, Ontario, Canada; W. A. Young, Toronto, Canada; William H. Welch, Baltimore, Md.; John S. Fulton, Baltimore, Md.; William Osler, Baltimore, Md.; William S. Thayer, Baltimore, Md.; Marshall L. Price, Baltimore, Md.; J. H. Mason Knox, Baltimore, Md.; John Ruhrah, Baltimore, Md.; Joseph E. Gichner, Baltimore, Md.; Harry Taylor Marshall, Baltimore, Md.; Henry Barton Jacobs, Towson, Md., and Mr. Paul Kennaday, New York city.

The following resolution, which paved the way for the foundation of the National Tuberculosis Association, was unanimously adopted:

"Moved, that the Chair be authorized to appoint a committee with power to act to consider the conditions existing with regard to the proposed Tuberculosis Congress and other National Anti-Tuberculosis Associations in the United States, also to consider the formation of a National Committee to represent this country at the International Congress at Paris, and that the members of this Conference will abide by the action of the committee—also that this Committee have power to add to its membership."

In accordance with this motion Professor William H. Welch, the Chairman of the conference, appointed the following committee: Drs. William Osler, Baltimore, Md.; Edward L. Trudeau, Saranac Lake, N. Y.; Theobald Smith, Boston, Mass.; J. G. Adami, Montreal, Canada; Vincent Y. Bowditch, Boston, Mass.; S. A. Knopf, New York city; Mazÿck P. Ravenel, Philadelphia, Pa.; Arnold C. Klebs, Chicago, Ill.; Edward G. Janeway, New York city; Henry Barton Jacobs, Baltimore, Md.; H. M. Bracken, St. Paul, Minn.; Lawrence F. Flick, Philadelphia, Pa., and Hermann M. Biggs, New York city. To this committee were added the names of Drs. William H. Welch, Baltimore, Md., and A. Jacobi, New York city.

The committee appointed by Dr. Welch arranged for a meeting

in Philadelphia on March 28, 1904, under the auspices of the Henry Phipps Institute, the immediate occasion being a lecture by Professor Maragliano, of Italy, which was read in his absence. Dr. William Osler presided at this meeting and Dr. Henry Barton Jacobs of Baltimore, served as secretary. After a full discussion by the entire group of about 100 physicians and laymen, the following resolution, presented by Dr. Flick, of Philadelphia, and seconded by Dr. Forchheimer, of Cincinnati, was unanimously adopted

"*Resolved*, That we here assembled do now organize ourselves into a United States Society for the Study and Prevention of Tuberculosis."

Besides providing for a constitutional committee, the group also voted that

"It is the sense of this meeting that the committee call us together for organization at Atlantic City during the week of the meeting of the American Medical Association" (June, 1904).

The committee appointed by the chair consisted of Drs. Edward L. Trudeau, Hermann M. Biggs, Lawrence F. Flick, William H. Welch, and General George M. Sternberg, together with the chairman, Dr. William Osler, and secretary, Dr. Henry Barton Jacobs, as ex-officio members of the committee. This committee met at the home of Dr. Hermann M. Biggs, of New York, some weeks later, when an organization under the name of "National Association for the Study and Prevention of Tuberculosis" was suggested. This name was chosen so as to make it distinctive from the other organizations in the field. Only recently, after the death of Mr. Clark Bell, and with him all that was left of his former organization, was the much more simple name of "National Tuberculosis Association" adopted. The committee at its meeting at Dr. Biggs' home formulated a constitution and by-laws which, on Monday, June 6, 1904, at the meeting in Atlantic City, were adopted by a large group of physicians and laymen interested in tuberculosis. The objects of the new society were stated to be: (1) The study of tuberculosis in all its forms and relations. (2) The dissemination of knowledge about the causes, treatment, and prevention of tuberculosis. (3) The encouragement of the prevention and scientific treatment of tuberculosis.

The officers elected at the meeting in Atlantic City were: Dr. Edward L. Trudeau, of Saranac Lake, N. Y., president; Dr. William Osler, of Baltimore, and Dr. Hermann M. Biggs, of New York, vice-presidents; General George M. Sternberg, of Washington, D. C., treasurer; Dr. Henry Barton Jacobs, of Baltimore, secretary. The first board of directors consisted of Drs. Norman Bridge, of California; S. B. Solly, of Colorado; John P. C. Foster, of Connecticut; George M. Sternberg, of Washington, D. C.; Arnold C. Klebs and Robert H. Babcock, of Illinois; J. N. Hurty, of Indiana; William H. Welch, William Osler, Henry Barton Jacobs, and John S. Fulton, of Maryland; Henry M. Bracken, of Minnesota; William Porter, of Missouri; Edward O. Otis and Vincent Y. Bowditch, of Massachusetts; Mr. Frederick L. Hoffman, of New Jersey; Drs. Hermann M. Biggs, S. A. Knopf, Edward L. Trudeau and Mr. Edward T. Devine, of New York; Drs. Charles L. Minor, of North Carolina; Charles O. Probst, of Ohio; Lawrence F. Flick, Mazÿck P. Ravenel, H. S. Anders and Leonard Pearson, of Pennsylvania; M. M. Smith, of Texas; Col. George E. Bushnell, of the United States Army Hospital, and Surgeon General Walter Wyman, of the United States Marine Hospital Service.

It was decided that the membership of the Association should consist of three classes: (1) Members—those who are elected by the Board of Directors and who pay annual membership dues of $5.00; (2) Life Members—those who pay $200 and are already members of the Association; (3) Honorary Members—persons distinguished for original researches relating to tuberculosis, eminent as sanitarians or as philanthropists, who have given material aid in the study and prevention of tuberculosis.

The government of the Association, the planning of work, the arrangement for meetings and congresses, and everything appertaining to legislation and direction, was to be left in the hands of the board of directors, and committees were to have the power to execute only what was directed by the board.

The board of directors was empowered, however, to appoint an executive committee of seven members, to which was to be entrusted the executive work of the Association. This committee was chosen at the meeting in Atlantic City and consisted of Drs. Edward L. Trudeau, Henry Barton Jacobs, Edward O.

Otis, Mazÿck P. Ravenel, Arnold C. Klebs, John N. Hurty, and Mr. Edward T. Devine.

The board of directors was empowered to appoint representatives to the International Committee on Tuberculosis. It was decided at the first meeting of the board that this representation was to be headed by Dr. William Osler, his associates to be selected later. The board was authorized also to appoint such committees as might be necessary for scientific and educational work, and for the holding of meetings and congresses.

This meeting at Atlantic City was one that will be long remembered by all those who were privileged to be present. Drs. Osler, Trudeau, Biggs, Barrier, Flick, Huber, Knopf, Mr. Devine, and others spoke on the scope of the work which was before the Association. The various addresses were received with enthusiastic applause, but the ovation given when Dr. Trudeau appeared on the platform surpassed anything the writer has ever been privileged to witness. It was spontaneous, genuine, and lasted for many minutes. It was a grand tribute from the vast assembly, not only to the pioneer of the sanatorium treatment in America, but to the great qualities of Dr. Trudeau as a physician, scientist, and humanitarian. In response Dr. Trudeau spoke as follows:

"I cannot find words suitable to express my appreciation of the great honor you have done me in electing me as President of this Association. While struggling for so many years alone and in a remote region with the tuberculosis problem about me, my wildest fancy never pictured the possibility of such a wide-spread and earnest movement as this, and much less that I would ever be accorded the inestimable privilege of standing before such a gathering as I see here to-day as its leader. That I have been permitted to do so will be to me a satisfaction which will last as long as life does."

Concerning the character of the new organization, Edward T. Devine, the editor of *Charities*, then the organ of the New York Charity Organization Society, wrote in this magazine the week after the meeting as follows:

"There are two conspicuous and equally gratifying features in this national movement. It is thoroughly representative of the leaders of the medical profession; and at the same time there are ample evidences of their determination to make the Association of direct practical value in legislation, in the education of the public, and in bringing about a coördination of philanthropic, medical, and educational agencies for the conquest of the great scourge.

"While the scope of the Association has not been officially outlined, it is evident from the stirring addresses made on the evening of the first meeting, that it will work directly for the better education of the public as to the means by which tuberculosis is communicated; for the erection of hospitals and sanatoriums; for the adoption by local Boards of Health of such measures as have been so effective in reducing the death rate from the disease in New York city; for the formation of local committees and associations in various communities, and for the intelligent coöperation of State and municipal authorities, private voluntary agencies, and the medical profession.

"The question as to whether a special journal shall be established, was left over for later consideration; but either through a special periodical or through the use of the medical or the lay press, the Association will aim to bring about a practical and beneficial interchange of experiences, and a more intimate knowledge on the part of those who are at work in any community of the measures which have been found effective elsewhere. The executive committee was empowered to select an executive secretary, who will probably be a layman, and as soon as the condition of the Association's treasury warrants it, a determined and aggressive campaign will be opened.

"It will be a source of pride and gratification, not only to physicians but to all who have taken a sympathetic interest in the warfare against tuberculosis, that there now is a national body to which local associations and committees, hospitals and sanatoriums, legislatures and local municipal administrations may turn with confidence for the last word on any disputed subjects, and for encouragement and sympathy for all good work on lines which experience has approved as promising of good results."

An immediate effort was made to secure funds for the infant organization, with the result that by January, 1905, sufficient money was on hand to warrant the opening of an office. The Association was fortunate in securing the services of Dr. Livingston Farrand, at that time assistant professor of anthropology at Columbia University, and connected with the American Museum of Natural History. On January 14, 1905, Dr. Farrand opened the office of the National Tuberculosis Association in room 515 of the United Charities Building, at 105 East 22d Street, New York.

Dr. Farrand continued as executive secretary of the Association until January, 1914, when he resigned to become president of the University of Colorado. Dr. Charles J. Hatfield succeeded Dr. Farrand in charge of the executive office. Philip P. Jacobs, Ph.D., who became connected with the work on March 1, 1908, as assistant to Dr. Farrand, is at present publicity director of the Association.

CHAPTER III

EARLY PROBLEMS

THE problem that confronted the National Tuberculosis Association at the outset was a two-fold one. There was, first of all, the necessity of an extensive campaign of education, and secondly, the necessity for organization that would intensify the message concerning tuberculosis and make facilities for the control of the disease available to every individual in every community in the United States. It would be too much to claim that the Association has always moved forward consciously with this two-fold problem in mind. Sometimes it has gone forward urged by the stress of immediate needs; sometimes halting because of lack of funds; sometimes diverted from its aim by certain pressing and urgent situations; but always in the long run developing toward the goal that every community in America should have facilities for the control of tuberculosis. Even in its earliest days the Association started out with the realization that tuberculosis, if it is to be controlled, must be controlled by local machinery, and that the object of the National Association is to provide the local machinery.

With this idea in mind, the first educational work of the Association was the development of a large traveling exhibit which, under the leadership of Mr. E. G. Routzahn, toured the States east of the Mississippi from Toronto to the city of Mexico for over seven years, from the winter of 1905 until the spring of 1912. Similarly in 1909 a second exhibit started out to tour the States west of the Mississippi, and under the direction of Mr. W. L. Cosper covered practically all of the States to the Pacific Coast. These exhibits, coupled with the publicity bureau of the National Association started in 1908, and with the annual meetings and other sources of spreading information that the Association had at its disposal in those early days, soon began to arouse such

3

interest in the tuberculosis campaign far and wide that there developed a demand for organization. As one might have expected, there were at that time many well-meaning people who thought that the formation of an association to combat tuberculosis would solve the problem automatically. This line of thinking led to the formation of hundreds of paper organizations during the period from 1906 to 1912.

In 1905, at the International Tuberculosis Congress in Paris, an invitation was extended by the official American delegation to hold the next session in the United States in 1908. Dr. Jacobs cabled from Paris to Dr. Welch in Baltimore requesting him to see President Roosevelt and to ask him to present an invitation through the American Embassy in Paris. This was necessary because no invitation could be accepted by the Congress unless it came from the head of the Government. The principal addresses expressing this invitation were made by Drs. Henry Barton Jacobs, of Baltimore, Lawrence F. Flick, of Philadelphia, and Henry G. Beyer, Medical Inspector of the United States Navy. The invitation extended by America was accepted by the representatives of the various governments assembled in Paris and it was agreed that the Sixth International Congress should be held in Washington, D. C., in 1908. This program was carried out and the meeting in Washington was considered to be one of the most successful of all the various congresses. (See Chapter VIII.)

Entirely aside from the contributions to the knowledge of tuberculosis made at the International Congress of 1908, that gathering will live forever in the minds of those who are interested in the campaign against tuberculosis in the United States because of the stimulus it gave to the organization of associations, dispensaries, and institutions in every section of the country. In conjunction with the International Congress there was held the largest tuberculosis exhibit ever gathered together.

Under the skilful leadership of Dr. Farrand, the Association early in its career adopted a policy with reference to local associations that has made it in no small degree what it is to-day. Instead of a policy of centralized control with a strong National Association and local branches tied completely to the central organization, or even one of federated local organizations, the plan of having a strong National Association, but with independent and autonomous state and local organizations, was conceived. This independence and autonomy has been the secret of the development of the campaign against tuberculosis in the United States.

With the development of organization, however, the National Association was at once confronted with a number of serious questions. First of all, the problem of financing the local organizations had to be solved; secondly, the question of providing programs and of stimulating new organizations to a true conception of their task was continually in the foreground; thirdly, the problem of proper organization to prevent ambitious or selfish-minded individuals from gaining control of associations had to be met in a very definite way; and fourthly, the problem of providing in the home office a clearing-house for information and education that would answer the ever-growing needs.

To meet the first problem, that of finance, the alliance of the National Association with the Red Cross in the Red Cross Seal Campaign was an extremely fortuitous and happy one. The Red Cross Seal started more or less as a fad, and even those in the Red Cross and the National Association who were most interested in it expected it to live only a few years. It has become, however, the most important, and in many instances the only, means for financing the non-official tuberculosis work in the United States. By means of the Red Cross Seal (now the Tuberculosis Christmas Seal) associations in every State have been financed. It would have been almost impossible to establish such organizations otherwise. Probably the most difficult type of organization to finance is a State association—much more difficult, in fact, than a local or national one. The early policy adopted in the Red Cross Seal Sale of leaving the major portion of the funds from the Seal Sale in the communities where the seals were sold proved to be the biggest stimulus imaginable in creating sound organization. It is not too much to say that without the Red Cross Seal the development of the National Association would undoubtedly have been very much retarded.

From 1910 up to and including the Christmas season of 1919

the National Tuberculosis Association and the American Red Cross continued their plan of coöperation in the sale of the Red Cross Christmas Seals.   There was only one break in the succession of Christmas Seal Sales, this being in 1918.   In the summer of 1918, before the armistice was signed, when the Red Cross was planning for the continuation of its work with the army abroad and at home, it entered into negotiations with the National Tuberculosis Association whereby the Tuberculosis Association agreed to discontinue its plans for a Red Cross Christmas Seal Sale in December.   In lieu of this sale, and in order to perpetuate the work carried on under the National Tuberculosis Association and its affiliated agencies, the Red Cross made a direct appropriation of $2,500,000 to the National Association for distribution to its allied agencies.   In the spring of 1919 the Red Cross, having entered upon its peace-time program, notified the National Tuberculosis Association that in order to avoid confusion and in order to concentrate its own work more fully, it would be compelled to withdraw its name and emblem from the Red Cross Christmas Seal after the sale of 1919.   This was done.   Consequently, in the fall of 1919 and the spring of 1920 the National Tuberculosis Association began plans for the conduct of a seal sale in December, 1920, featuring the double-barred cross and omitting, for the first time since the inauguration of the seal in 1908, the Red Cross emblem.   The success of this sale, which reached nearly $4,000,000, clearly proved the wisdom and possibilities of the new plan.   (See Chapter VI.)

The second problem, that of providing programs and stimulating local effort, was a somewhat more difficult one.   This was particularly true in the early days of the movement, when funds for the National Association were hard to secure.   Thanks, however, to the generous coöperation of the Russell Sage Foundation in standing by the Association during this crucial developmental period, field and other educational service was provided, and gradually the National Association began to standardize programs and methods of work.   This standardization has steadily progressed until at the present time the machinery for this purpose is the most extensive part of the Association's equipment.

The third problem, that of organization, was one which went

NATIONAL ASSOCIATION OFFICES

hand in hand to some degree with the problem of stimulation and the developing of programs. In its organization effort, the National Association gradually moved westward, developing first the Atlantic Coast States, then the Middle Western and Southern States, and finally pushing on to the Southwestern and Northwestern States, confining itself for the most part to state associations. It has always acted upon the theory that dealings with local groups should come through the state association, and this practice has become more and more rigid as the years have passed. In organizing state work, the Association always considered the question of whether the new association had funds available or in sight for carrying out a program. The insistence upon fulltime paid executives as contrasted with volunteer service has produced a machine in each of the states that is working more and more effectively toward the desired goal. At the present time each of the 48 states has an organization and a fulltime secretary. A somewhat similar service has also been secured for Porto Rico, the Philippine Islands, and Hawaii.

The fourth problem of the Association, to provide a clearinghouse for information and education, has been solved by the gradual accumulation of knowledge and experience. As State and local organizations developed and as institutions sprang up apace, the National Association became more and more the central clearing-house for providing literature, furnishing data, gathering together groups in conference, etc. At the present time the Association maintains elaborate machinery for the dispensing of information through its executive office, through correspondence, through its field service, through its three monthly publications, through conferences and meetings and in other ways.

It will not be necessary in this part of the history to deal with individual state problems nor even to record the development of work in different parts of the country. These facts are recorded in a separate chapter. It will be necessary here simply to call attention to this significant fact, that wherever State and local tuberculosis associations have been formed there have sprung into existence almost automatically, it would seem, hospitals and sanatoria, open-air schools and preventoria, dispensaries and clinics, nurses and other machinery for home care and relief, and all the other agencies that go to make up a well-rounded campaign for the control of tuberculosis. It is not too much to say, furthermore, that the increased efficiency in public health work on the part of state and local departments of health has been due in no small degree, and in many instances entirely, to local and state tuberculosis associations. The coördination of health activities, which is now progressing with agreeable rapidity, is also being stimulated by the organizations brought into existence through the National Tuberculosis Association.

CHAPTER IV

DEVELOPMENT OF THE ASSOCIATION'S PROGRAM

THE trend of development has been steady and consistent. It may be remarked, from a study of the records of the Association, that the number of associations has apparently decreased. This is not an indication, however, of a decline in the movement. In the earlier stages of development it was considered desirable to form as many associations as possible. Later experience has shown that a smaller number of associations, more adequately manned and better financed, is the better method of organization. For this reason in New York and other states the number of associations and committees recorded in the earlier years of the Association's history has been greatly cut down and there has been a consistent effort toward concentration and increased efficiency, which has resulted in a better covering of the ground than was indicated by the larger number of associations in previous years.

In the case of dispensaries and clinics, the rapid development in the earlier years of work was due to the inauguration of large state systems of clinics and dispensaries in Pennsylvania, Delaware, and other states. Within recent years there has been an effort toward increasing efficiency in this work and the number of dispensaries has shown a slower rate of increase. Omitting these local considerations, the development of work in all lines shows a steady expansion.

That the National Association has made itself felt in the public health field and in the lives of millions of people is evident from the wide-spread interest exhibited in the subject of tuberculosis to-day as contrasted with that of ten or fifteen years ago. In addition to conducting the Sixth International Congress on Tuberculosis and organizing the traveling tuberculosis exhibits, which have been spoken of above, some of the most significant achievements of the Association during the last fifteen years may be briefly summarized as follows:

1. On the side of research and publication the Association has, either through its executive office or through its membership, accomplished much. Most of the results of this research are published in the annual volumes of Transactions. In addition to the Transactions, the Association has put out a number of special volumes and monographs, including its "Tuberculosis Directory," issued in four editions, 1908, 1911, 1916, and 1919; "Fresh Air and How to Use It"; and "Tuberculosis Hospital and Sanatorium Construction." Pamphlets on the "Influence of Tuberculosis Sanatoria on Surrounding Property"; "Tuberculosis Legislation in the United States"; "Tuberculosis Dispensary Method and Procedure"; "Sleeping and Sitting in the Open Air"; "What You Should Know About Tuberculosis"; "Workingmen's Organization in the Anti-Tuberculosis Campaign"; "What Tuberculosis Workers Should Know About Discharged and Rejected Soldiers," and "An Outline of Lectures on Tuberculosis," have also been published from time to time. The results of studies of a less extensive character have been published in the three periodicals issued by the Association, viz., the monthly *Bulletin*, the *Journal of the Outdoor Life*, and the *American Review of Tuberculosis*.

2. One of the most significant achievements of the Association has been its promotion of the Red Cross Christmas Seal. The Seal Sale, starting with a little over $100,000 in 1908, reached a total in 1920 of nearly $4,000,000. The educational and financial assistance rendered through the Red Cross Seal Sale, now the Tuberculosis Christmas Seal Sale, has proved of incalculable benefit.

3. The National Association recognized before the entrance of America into the World War that tuberculosis constituted a serious war problem. The insistence of the National Association that the government recognize this problem brought tuberculosis, for the first time in the history of warfare, to a prominence that it had never before occupied. The war program carried out by the National Association may be briefly summarized as follows:

(a) Coöperation with various governmental and semi-governmental agencies interested in the health of the soldier was inevitable. To such agencies as the American Red Cross, Federal Board for Vocational Education, Y.M.C.A., Bureau of War Risk Insurance, United States Public Health Service, and many others generous coöperation was extended, but among the agencies with which the Tuberculosis Association coöperated, and perhaps the most important of all in the way of sympathy and results, was the office of the Surgeon General of the Army, both under the late Major General Gorgas and his successor, Major General Ireland.

(b) The Association assumed an active responsibility in educating the soldiers, both in camps at home and abroad, regarding the necessity of preserving their health. The distribution of great quantities of literature and exhibit material helped materially in this connection.

(c) The Association served as an adviser to a number of agencies, governmental and extra-governmental, interested in the health of the soldier and in this capacity greatly stimulated activity on the part of these agencies.

(d) Through the office of the Surgeon General of the United States Army, the names of men rejected on account of tuberculosis were transmitted to the National Association's office and thence to state and local tuberculosis agencies and other groups who were interested in following up and securing for these men the best care and supervision.

(e) The war program of the National Association has extended and is still (even in 1921) extending over the country. The Association is exercising its responsibility to the men discharged from the army and those still in government tuberculosis hospitals, and is maintaining an active and varied interest in the agencies dealing with these men.

4. The Association has been called upon to deal with a large number of questionable agencies which have traded upon the tuberculosis campaign for various reasons, including such associations as the National White Cross League, the Children's National Tuberculosis Society, the McKinley Memorial League, etc. Similarly the Association has been called upon to investi-

gate and publish data regarding so-called cures for tuberculosis. Through the newspaper press and the *Journal of the Outdoor Life*, with the coöperation of the American Medical Association, a large amount of helpful information has been disseminated on this subject.

5. In legislation, federal, state, and local, the Association has always maintained and still maintains active interest. Through its Committee on Federal Legislation and in other ways the Association has secured the passage of bills that have been helpful in the tuberculosis campaign and has disseminated information regarding standard laws on tuberculosis.

6. Among some of the general educational features initiated or promoted by the National Association, the following may be mentioned:

(*a*) Tuberculosis Week, growing out of Tuberculosis Sunday established in 1910, is now a part of the Christmas Seal Sale and reaches many people annually.

(*b*) The Association's standard pamphlets, such as "What You Should Know About Tuberculosis," "Sleeping and Sitting in the Open Air," "Periodical Medical Examination," "Don't Card," etc., have been distributed in English and foreign languages to the extent of 5,000,000 copies.

(*c*) The use of motion pictures has led to the inauguration of a special service of this character for selling and renting films. The service now has over a dozen subjects in constant circulation, reaching hundreds of thousands of people yearly.

(*d*) In the use of plays for health work, the National Association has been a pioneer. A series of over 15 plays is sold to those who wish them. Marionettes have been developed as a health educational feature, and are used with a standard puppet theater and also by means of a cardboard theater called "Tiny Tim's House." The Association in May, 1921, added to its staff a "health clown."

(*e*) In the education of special groups, such as tuberculosis secretaries, nurses, physicians, and others, the Association has made valuable contributions through its institutes, conferences, and course outlines.

7. The demonstration of new ideas in tuberculosis work has

NAT ONAL ASSOCIAT ON OFFICES

always been a prominent feature of the Association. The principal activity of the Association in this connection has been the Framingham Community Health and Tuberculosis Demonstration established in the fall of 1916, at Framingham, Massachusetts. The Demonstration closed its initial period of three years in December, 1919, and as a result of a report of an independent committee of appraisal was continued for another period of years from a grant of the Metropolitan Life Insurance Company, which had originally advanced $100,000 for this purpose. A more complete discussion of the Framingham Demonstration will be found in Chapter VII.

In connection with its work for the United States Public Health Service, the Bureau of War Risk Insurance, and the Federal Board for Vocational Education, the Association has also exercised its function of demonstration.

8. In 1917 the National Association inaugurated a movement for the creation of correct habits for health among school children, known as the Modern Health Crusade. The Crusade grew out of the Christmas Seal Sale and at the start numbered a handful of crusaders. Its conception and development have been due largely to Charles M. DeForest, of the Association staff. At the present time over 7,000,000 children are enrolled in this movement in the United States alone. If to this number were added the crusaders in France, Italy, Czechoslovakia, China, and elsewhere, the total would run into many millions more.

The Modern Health Crusade is not an organization. It is a system of health education. It is based upon the following 11 standard chores:

1. I washed my hands before each meal to-day.
2. I washed not only my face, but my ears and neck, and I cleaned my finger-nails to-day.
3. I kept fingers, pencils, and everything likely to be unclean or injurious out of my mouth and nose to-day.
4. I brushed my teeth thoroughly after breakfast and after the evening meal to-day.
5. I took ten or more slow, deep breaths of fresh air to-day. I was careful to protect others if I spit, coughed, or sneezed.
6. I played outdoors or with open windows more than thirty minutes to-day.
7. I was in bed ten hours or more last night and kept my windows open.

8. I drank four glasses of water, including a drink before each meal, and drank no tea, coffee, nor other injurious drinks to-day.

9. I tried to eat only wholesome food and to eat slowly. I went to toilet at my regular time.

10. I tried hard to-day to sit up and stand up straight; to keep neat, cheerful, and clean-minded; and to be helpful to others.

11. I took a full bath on each of the days of the week that are checked.

By doing these chores daily, by scoring them on a sheet prepared for that purpose, and (see page 45) by reporting the score to teacher or Crusade leader, the child progresses steadily through the ranks of squire, knight, knight banneret, and even to a seat at the "round table" in this new health chivalry. The Crusade makes the routine and burdensome daily health duties of the average child interesting by giving to them the elements of romance and competition.

The testimony of hundreds of parents and teachers, as well as the observation of thousands of children, shows that the Crusade contributes largely to these results:

(a) Correction of nutritional defects and habits.

(b) Improved cleanliness of body and mind.

(c) Correct posture, and proper exercise and rest.

(d) General physique and health and the steady building of weight and resistance.

Recognition of the Modern Health Crusade as an integral part of the school curriculum has been accorded in several States and in a large number of cities in the United States, as well as in Czechoslovakia, the Philippine Islands, and Porto Rico. It is hoped that eventually the Crusade will become as much a part of a child's required schooling as the "Three R's."

9. The organization work of the National Association has been for years one of its principal activities. Thirty-six of the 48 States have been organized or reorganized directly by the National Association. This has meant an increased amount of field service and intensive educational propaganda.

10. The Association has endeavored to standardize methods and programs in a variety of different ways. The Institutes for the Training of Tuberculosis Workers, established in 1916, have

DAILY CHORES
See notes on other side

1 I ashed my ahds before eah real today.

2 I washed my fa, ears and neck, and I aned my fingernails.

3 I kept fingers, pencils and everything likely to be unclean or injurious out of my outh and os.

4 I brushed my teth oily after rst ard after the evening meal.

5 I took ten or ae slow, deep breaths of fresh air. I proted others if I spit, coughed or z...

6 I played hrs or with windows open ae than thirty ... I tried hard to sit and stand straight.

7 I was in bed ten ohrs or more last h, and kept my windows open.

8 I drk fr glasses of at, hng. soe before eah eal, and drank no tea, coffee or agus. ds.

9 I tried to eat bg, and only holesome food including milk, vegetables, fruit. I at to toilet at agar ta.

10 I tried hard to keep neat; to be at, straightforward and clean-minded; and to be pdul to others.

11 I took a full bath on each day of the week that is od (x).

Total ar of chores done each e. . . . .

THE STANDARD "CHORE RECORD" OF THE MODERN HEALTH CRUSADE

materially contributed toward the standardization of methods and programs.   The standardization of hospital planning and administration has for years been given careful attention and consideration by the Association and through the influence of the executive office much has been accomplished along this line.   In more recent years the standardization of nursing and medical service has been attempted with gratifying results.   In this connection the publication of standards of diagnosis might be mentioned.

CHAPTER V

ORGANIZATION AND METHODS

O N APRIL 1, 1921,[1] the staff of the National Association consisted of 19 members of the administrative force and 33 members of the clerical force. The present executive force is organized into six services as follows:

1. *Administrative Service.*—The head of the Administrative Service is Dr. Charles J. Hatfield, Managing Director, and immediately under him is Mr. Frederick D. Hopkins, the Administrative Secretary. All of the problems of administration of the Association, including the business management of the office, the handling of supplies, and the general supervision of all other services fall under the administrative service. In addition to Dr. Hatfield and Mr. Hopkins, the administrative service has the following members: Mr. S. M. Sharpe, Business Manager; Mr. L. B. Whitcomb, Purchasing Agent; Miss Grace Douglass, Office Secretary, and Miss Amelia T. Dutcher, Administrative Assistant.

2. *Field Service.*—The field service is the outgrowth of the original exhibit started by the National Association in the winter of 1905. Following the extensive educational campaign and the demand for organization the Association was called upon to an increasing degree not only to organize, but also to help promote programs of work in different parts of the country. In 1918, at the specific request of certain states, the Association extended its field service by establishing five branch or regional offices in different parts of the country. In the summer of 1920 it was found necessary to discontinue these offices because of lack of funds. The service, therefore, at present consists simply of Mr. Arthur J. Strawson, Supervisor of Field Service, stationed at the home office. The field service fulfils the valuable function of not only keeping the executive office in closer touch with the various state and local activities, but also in bringing to bear upon state and local activities the very facilities of the executive office.

[1] For staff on January 1, 1922, see Chapter XXVII.

3. *Modern Health Crusade Service.*—The Modern Health Crusade Service conducts the Crusade.   The service prepares literature and works out the plans for national supervision and conduct of the movement.   As at present organized the service consists of Mr. Charles M. De Forest, Crusader Executive; Miss M. Grace Osborne, Assistant Crusader Executive; and Miss Mildred Terry, Assistant Crusader Executive.

4. *Medical Service.*—The medical service is one of the newest developments of the Association. It is an outgrowth of the demand on the part of state and local associations that more atten tion be given to the medical problems involved in tuberculosis control.   The service is headed by Dr. H. A. Pattison.   Mr. T. B. Kidner, Institutional Secretary, serves the field as adviser to sanatoria in matters of construction and maintenance, and also occupational therapy and vocational training.   Miss Mary E. Marshall, Secretary for Nursing, is specifically entrusted with the responsibility for standardizing and stimulating tuberculosis nursing service.   Dr. Benjamin K. Hays, a fourth member of the service, is in charge immediately of the educational work in certain of the Army and U. S. Public Health Service Hospitals.

5. *Research Service.*—The research service is designed to answer the numerous questions that pour into the executive office from individuals and organizations in every part of the world. The personnel of the service at the present time consists of Miss Jessamine S. Whitney, Research Secretary, who works particularly on statistical research; Miss Eleanor B. Conklin, Research Secretary, whose particular responsibility is editing and reviewing; and Miss Isabel L. Towner, Librarian, who is responsible for cataloguing, indexing, and handling all of the library files and records.

6. *Publicity and Publications Service.*—The publicity and publications service is charged directly with the distribution of educational and publicity material, the conduct of the Christmas Seal Campaign, the conduct of membership and financial appeals, the handling of the free publications of the National Association, and the editing and management of all periodicals.   Philip P. Jacobs, Ph.D., Publicity Director, is head of this service.   In addition to Mr. Jacobs, the service consists of Mr. B. G. Eaves as Campaign

Secretary, Miss Helena V. Williams and Miss Elizabeth Cole as Assistant Publicity Secretaries. The service has a varied responsibility: It not only puts out the newspaper publicity, but it organizes campaigns and furnishes educational material, such as motion pictures, slides, scrap-books on methods of anti-tuberculosis work, etc., and in addition edits the monthly *Bulletin*, the *Journal of the Outdoor Life* and the Transactions, and handles the business details of these publications and the *American Review of Tuberculosis*. The managing editor of the *Review*, Dr. Allen K. Krause, with offices in Baltimore, and the abstract editor, Dr. George Mannheimer, are on the staff of this service.

In addition to the six services, the National Association is responsible for the Framingham Community Health and Tuberculosis Demonstration. Dr. Donald B. Armstrong, Associate Secretary of the Association, is the Executive Officer, and Dr. P. Challis Bartlett, the Medical Director, with offices in Framingham.

The methods of work of the Association may be briefly summarized as follows:

1. *Correspondence and Personal Conference.*—By this means direct questions concerning problems of work as between states and local committees are taken care of.

2. *Conferences and Meetings.*—Besides its annual meeting, the Association holds six sectional conferences in each of the six districts into which the country has been divided and in addition several special conferences and institutes where groups of workers may receive intensive training and discuss specific problems.

3. *Distribution of Newspaper Publicity, Literature, Motion Pictures, etc.*—By this means the Association endeavors to interest the public concerning the treatment and prevention of tuberculosis.

4. *Field Visits and Conferences Through the Regional Secretaries and Members of the Home Office Staff.*—This work is designed to take up the specific problems of interest in each state and to help a local group in settling its difficulties and solving its problems.

5. *Publications.*—The Association has three monthly publications: the monthly *Bulletin*, published primarily for workers in the field; the *Journal of the Outdoor Life*, a popular journal for

4

laymen and anti-tuberculosis workers; and the *American Review of Tuberculosis*, a medical journal for physicians and those interested in the scientific phases of tuberculosis. In addition, the Association publishes an annual volume of Transactions and frequent monographs on certain specific topics of vital interest to people engaged in the tuberculosis field.

6. *Research.*—The Association is constantly engaged in medical and social research, both through its home office and through its members and workers in the field at large. The results of this research are published in monographs, in the Transactions, in the various journals of the Association, and elsewhere.

7. *Clearing-house.*—The Association acts as a general clearing-house for information on several phases of the tuberculosis movement. Its staff consists of specialists in various kinds of work who help in the solution of problems dealing with institutions, education, organization, medicine and other phases of the campaign.

8. *Modern Health Crusade.*—The Association has organized and is the national director of the Modern Health Crusade, a movement for the training of children in proper health habits.

9. *Publicity.*—By means of newspaper publicity, and through the promotion of the use of exhibits, motion pictures, lantern slides, etc., the Association stimulates educational work in various parts of the field.

10. *Experimental and Demonstration Work.*—The Association has for three years been conducting a demonstration on the control of tuberculosis at Framingham, Mass., with the idea of trying to show how a normal American town may best control tuberculosis within its own limits.

Program and Policies

The National Association has always conceived its function in relationship to the other agencies in the field to be that of a servant rather than that of a master or autocrat. While most of the tuberculosis agencies throughout the country owe their existence directly or indirectly to the National Association, the Association has no branch organizations. In 1921 the by-laws of the Association were amended to provide for definite representation of State associations on its directorate, thereby giving to these organizations a more controlling interest in the national program and policies. The thousand or more State and local associations are affiliated with it, but are entirely autonomous. The National Association has endeavored through the Christmas Seal Sale and in other ways to secure funds for the support of State and local work and because of this has sought to secure the wisest possible expenditure of such funds, but it has always deemed it the function of the State and local organization to determine the general way in which its funds should be spent.

The program of the National Association in general includes the organization of a local unit for the control of tuberculosis to cover every section of the United States. Such local communities will not be uniform either as to their administrative control or as to their size. Some of them will cover large areas, some of them relatively small areas. On the other hand, the National Association realizes that tuberculosis is essentially a local problem, and that the people must be reached through local channels. The National Association may furnish the ideas for organization, the standards of work, suggestions regarding program and methods, but the ultimate achievement of the work must be local.

Recognizing that tuberculosis in its various social ramifications reaches almost every avenue of industrial and community life, the National Tuberculosis Association has adopted as a general policy the broadest possible coöperation with public health and social agencies that are seeking to relieve human suffering and promote community betterment. With this idea in mind, formal policies of coöperation have been worked out between such groups as the American Red Cross, the Conference of State and Territorial Health Authorities, the National Organization for Public Health Nursing, and others.

In line with this policy, the Association has become a member of the National Health Council and the National Child Health Council. In April 1921, it moved into new quarters and became associated in certain common services with the American Social Hygiene Association, the National Committee on Mental Hygiene, and the National Organization for Public Health Nursing, all these organizations occupying adjoining offices on the same floor. These joint services are being developed under the direction of a Common Service Committee consisting of representatives of the four organizations and the National Health Council.

FINANCIAL SUPPORT

The financial support of the National Tuberculosis Association is derived from three sources: (*a*) A percentage of the sale of Tuberculosis Christmas Seals, usually amounting to 5 per cent. of the gross sale; (*b*) membership dues and donations; and (*c*) sale of supplies. The Association receives no government subsidy or appropriation, except where it does a special piece of work and is compensated therefor.

Any reputable physician in good medical standing and any layman who is interested in the control of tuberculosis and is not engaged in an enterprise foreign to the ideals of the Association is welcomed to membership in the National Association. The membership dues are $5.00 per year. Members of the Association are entitled to receive a number of valuable publications, including the *Journal of the Outdoor Life*, a monthly magazine and the official organ of the Association and the monthly *Bulletin* of the Association, as well as various publications which are issued from time to time, such as the Transactions, Tuberculosis Directory, and various special volumes and studies. Members are also entitled to receive the *American Review of Tuberculosis*, another monthly publication of the Association, at the reduced price of $3.00 per year (price to non-members, $6.00 per year). Checks should be drawn to the order of Henry B. Platt, Treasurer, and should be sent to 370 Seventh Avenue, New York City.

An active organization doing such extensive humanitarian work as ours cannot and should not depend for a considerable portion of its entire financial support on the small annual dues of its members. We must look to our well-to-do fellow-citizens for substantial help to carry on our work effectively. We should have a larger number of life members to assure a permanent income to the Association, but bequests of larger and smaller amounts are also needed.

It would be ungracious to close this historical review without paying our tribute and expressing our gratitude to the men and women who have made the Association what it is to-day. In 1904 the Association started with a membership of 26; to-day we have 25 life members and over 3,500 regular members. Among the life members, many of whom have contributed $5,000 or more, we have such names as Finley Barrel, Chicago; George Blumenthal, New York; F. A. Clark, New York; Harvey Edward Fisk, New York; Henry C. Frick,* New York; Edward S. Harkness,* New York; Emma Gale Harris, Chicago; Henry L. Higginson,* Boston; Mrs. H. Knickerbacker, New York; Ejnar Larsen, Wayne, Neb.; Henry C. Lea, Philadelphia; Adolph Lewisohn, New York; Cyrus H. McCormick, Chicago; V. Everit Macy, New York; Martin Maloney, Philadelphia; Louis Marshall, New York; Samuel Mather, Cleveland; Francis E. May, Chicago; Henry Phipps, New York; John D. Rockefeller, New York; Jacob H. Schiff,* New York; L. F. Swift, Chicago; Rodman Wanamaker, Philadelphia; Felix M. Warburg, New York.

Prior to June, 1904, there were in the United States 23 tuberculosis associations and committees, to-day there are over 1,100 associations. Before our Association was organized, there were in the United States 96 sanatoria and special hospitals, 24 tuberculosis dispensaries, no open-air schools, no preventoria. There are now nearly 700 sanatoria, special hospitals and camps; over 550 tuberculosis dispensaries; at least 3,000 open-air schools and fresh-air classes, and more than 15 preventoria. In 1904 there existed no tuberculosis nurses, to-day we have about 3,500 specially trained tuberculosis nurses.

From the humblest citizen to our greatest philanthropist, from the lowliest medical or social worker to the highest authority on tuberculosis, all, who by their affiliation with us, their financial help or personal service, have shown their interest in our work, deserve our most heartfelt thanks.

What has been said in the preceding pages of our various achievements and what the statistics just given show of the growth of the anti-tuberculosis movement in the United States since the formation of our society, indicate that much has been done. There is, however, more to do. Let every one who is able

* Deceased.

to help bear in mind that tuberculosis is a disease of all people, rich and poor, the educated and uneducated; that it is not confined to climates or races, but that it is universal; and that every one should be interested in combating it. Even those with no means can help by acquainting themselves with the simple precautions to prevent the disease and by imparting what they know to others who do not know. Personal service is as essential as financial aid in fighting the great white plague.

Pasteur, to whom the world owes so much as the father of modern preventive and curative medicine, has pointed out our duties in the following words: *"En 'fait de bien à répandre, le devoir ne cesse que là où le pouvoir manque."* (In doing good the duty ceases only when the power fails.)

CHAPTER VI

THE TUBERCULOSIS CHRISTMAS SEAL

THE compelling force of an idea is nowhere better illustrated than in the history of the tuberculosis Christmas seal. The seal grew out of one woman's interest in a small tuberculosis hospital in Wilmington, Del. From that original idea and interest have developed the funds which have made the tuberculosis campaign in the United States what it is to-day. Starting with an initial sale of $3,000, the Christmas seal idea has produced over $20,000,000, largely for the benefit of the non-official local, state and national tuberculosis associations.

It was in 1907 that Jacob A. Riis received from a friend in Copenhagen a letter bearing on its back a peculiar seal. He wrote to his friend for further information and then published an article in the *Outlook* on the Norwegian tuberculosis Christmas seal. In Wilmington, Del., Miss Emily P. Bissell with Dr. John Black was struggling to maintain a tuberculosis shack of eight beds on the banks of the Brandywine. As she read the article in the *Outlook*, an inspiration came to her that here was a good way to secure money for the tuberculosis camp. She interested Howard Pyle, the famous artist, who produced an attractive design. She then approached the Philadelphia *North American*, which has a wide circulation in Wilmington and surrounding territory, and secured its support of the idea. With Miss Bissell's enthusiasm and the Philadelphia *North American's* backing, this initial Christmas seal sale produced the sum of $3,000.

The success of this first seal sale gave to Miss Bissell the idea of a wider extension of the Christmas seal plan. She had always been an enthusiastic supporter of the American Red Cross and at that time was secretary of the Delaware Chapter. She took the matter up with Washington headquarters and found the officials at first inclined to be unresponsive and fearful of venturing into a nation-wide Christmas seal project. Miss Bissell, however, urged upon them the necessity for a peace-time program and pointed out that interest was being aroused in tuberculosis by the recently formed National Association for the Study and Prevention of Tuberculosis and by the organization for the International Congress on Tuberculosis. She even offered to finance the initial production of a national Christmas seal. As a result, in 1908 the first nation-wide seal sale was held. The sale was conducted very largely under the direction of women's clubs and Red Cross chapters. About $135,000 was realized from this sale. The Red Cross was at once convinced of the immediate possibilities of the seal. In 1909 the second seal sale was held and over $200,000 was realized.

Up to this time the American Red Cross had considered the seal as peculiarly its own. The National Tuberculosis Association at that time was struggling for existence. It was not as widely known as the Red Cross. Its program was still far from being fixed and its organization was faulty. For the most part it was passing through that necessary early stage of extensive education and had not yet arrived at the second stage of intensive organization.

In 1910, however, Dr. Livingston Farrand, then executive secretary of the National Tuberculosis Association, approached the American Red Cross and suggested a liaison arrangement between that organization and the National Tuberculosis Association. As a result of these negotiations the two organizations entered into what was virtually a partnership arrangement which, because of the far-seeing vision of its framers, has proved to be the most effectual policy in the development of the tuberculosis movement in the United States that could possibly have been devised.

Because of their historical significance, copies of letters under date of June 25 and August 6, 1910, creating this initial agreement and signed by Ernest P. Bicknell, then National Director of the American Red Cross, are quoted in full:

June 25, 1910.

Dr. Livingston Farrand,
    Executive Secretary, National Association for the Study and Prevention
        of Tuberculosis, 105 East 22nd Street, New York, N. Y.
Dear Dr. Farrand:
    Pursuant to my promise to you when in New York the other day I am writing to elaborate somewhat the idea which I had as to a co-operative ar-

rangement between your Association and the Red Cross in the conduct of the Christmas stamp campaign.

In deciding upon retaining 12½ per cent. as the Red Cross proportion of the gross sale of Christmas stamps this year, we went into the matter of expenses and the probabilities of the sale with a good deal of care. Last year we sold, in round numbers, twenty-five million stamps. This year, if we sell ten million stamps, the 12½ per cent. will just cover our outlay. It may not cover the time of our regular force devoted to the work of the campaign but will cover our actual expenditures for printing, postage, express charges and extra services. Should we sell as many stamps this year as we sold last, our 12½ per cent. would bring us a profit of probably $18,000 after all expenses have been deducted.

Our study of the outlook does not lead us to expect a sale so large as that of last year. It will probably be considerably smaller and may be very much smaller. Several factors enter into our conclusion that the sale this year will show a falling off. One factor is the probability that there will be a large number of rival stamps in the market. We are told that in a number of States the State Federation of Women's Clubs are considering the issuing of stamps of their own, the proceeds to be used in promoting such interests as the Women's Clubs may be pursuing at the time. As the Women's Clubs in the past have been a strong help in the sale of our Red Cross stamps, their defection would very seriously hurt our sale in any State in which they issued a stamp of their own. In the State of Kentucky, for instance, the State Tuberculosis Society wrote us that the Federation of Women's Clubs was likely to issue its own stamp in which case the Tuberculosis Society would feel that it must cast in its lot with the Federation and discontinue the sale of Red Cross stamps. This is but an illustration of what may possibly occur in several states.

Another factor is the passing of the vogue of the Christmas stamp. We cannot positively assert that the tide has reached its height and begun to ebb, but there are some indications that it has. The most important indication is to be found in the fact that in 1909 some of our more important agencies sold fewer stamps than in 1908 and are expressing doubt as to the success of the campaign this year. The increase last year in total sales over the year before was due in part to a sustained interest and in part to the awakening of new interest in territory which was not reached in 1908. Last year, however, we entered most of the territory of the country from which large returns could be expected and I feel that we cannot reasonably expect any great growth this year through entering new fields. The issuance of a multiplicity of rival stamps, many of them purely local in character, will not only interfere directly with our sale but will tend to surfeit the public with the whole stamp business. A third factor to be considered is the recent ruling of the Post Office Department which is that non-postage stamps must not be affixed to the face of any envelope or mailed package. This fact must be emphasized in our advertising and is an item which adds somewhat to the complexity of the situation. Many people will overlook this prohibition and their letters will be returned to them or forwarded to the dead letter office. The result will be discontent, newspaper complaint and something of a lessening of enthusiasm on the part of those in charge of the sale of stamps in the various localities. Other factors may occur to you, but I need not weary you further on this point. I speak of it somewhat fully in order that you may understand quite fully why we are not expecting so large a sale of stamps this year as last. Whether these diverse influences will slightly or greatly affect the sale is a matter largely of conjecture.

I should hope that the active participation of your organization in the campaign through its direct and indirect influence might serve in some measure to stem the receding tide. If we enter into a co-operative arrangement, such as I have mentioned, we shall, of course, hope for your very active and enthusiastic support in every practicable way. I should be glad if you will write me something of the methods and machinery by which you feel that you could help in the campaign. The publicity work which we have heretofore maintained has consisted broadly of two forms. One is made up of the various posters, placards and envelope slips which are distributed to the agents in such quantities as may be ordered.. The other consists of newspaper articles, publicity circulars, containing miscellaneous collections of stories and items which the agents in turn may give out to their local press as they see fit, lantern slides for use in motion picture shows, etc. The printing of the posters, placards, envelope slips, etc., can probably better be carried out and the distribution made by the Red Cross as heretofore. In the miscellaneous publicity matter for the press, it seems to me that you can be of very great assistance. Through your publicity channels, which are extensive, you can give wide circulation to such matter as we prepare, as well as that which you prepare yourself. On this side of the work we should hope for especial benefit from our relations with you. Last year our publicity circulars were put up in the form which the word "circular" suggests. This year we have thought it wiser to issue publicity stuff in the form of galley proofs. Upon this point, however, we shall be glad to have your judgment and to put our matter into uniform shape with yours or into such shape as your experience indicates to be the best.

I probably have failed to cover some points which may arise in your mind but no doubt have given you in general a fair idea of what we are thinking of. At your convenience I shall be glad to hear from you as fully as may be.

Yours very truly,

(Signed) ERNEST P. BICKNELL,

National Director.

* * * * * * * * * * * * * * * * * * *

August 6, 1910.

Dr. Livingston Farrand,

Executive Secretary, National Association for the Study and Prevention of Tuberculosis, 105 East 22nd Street, New York.

Dear Dr. Farrand:

I am now prepared to propose to your association that the Red Cross will divide equally with you the net profits of the Christmas seal sale in the season of 1910. The Red Cross will first pay all its expenses in connection with the conduct of the work and then divide equally with you the remainder.

From you we will expect the heartiest of co-operation, to be made as practical and effective as possible. We shall hope that you will not only use your active influence in getting the tuberculosis agencies throughout the country enthusiastically lined up for the Red Cross Christmas seals, but shall hope to have a great deal of valuable help from your publicity department.

I may add that we are hearing from a good many important tuberculosis organizations which are applying for the agency for the seals this year and that the prospects for a good year seem to be promising.

I should be glad if you will have all the tuberculosis societies in the country notified of this arrangement for the division of net proceeds if the plan meets with your acceptance. In sending out a notice, it would perhaps be well for you to call attention to the fact also that the Red Cross percentage is only 12½ per cent. this year as against 20 per cent. last. If you care to mention the fact, you might state that there will probably be greater profit to the tuberculosis societies this year in handling the Red Cross seals than in getting out seals of their own and that in addition to this inducement there is also the advantage that the National Tuberculosis Association is to share in the profits.

I am taking the liberty of sending a copy of this letter to Kingsbury for his information.

Yours very truly,
(Signed) ERNEST P. BICKNELL,
National Director.

* * * * * * * * * * * * * * * * * *

A copy of a letter from Dr. Farrand to Mr. Bicknell under date of April 26, 1911, following the sale of 1910, is also of vital interest in showing the further development of Christmas seal relations and policy:

April 26, 1911.

Mr. Ernest P. Bicknell,
   715 Union Trust Building,
      Washington, D. C.
Dear Mr. Bicknell:

Referring to our conversation the other day I wish to say that I have conferred with the Executive Committee of the National Association and we are ready to take over, as you suggested, the responsibility for the appointment of agents for the sale of Red Cross Christmas seals for the coming year.

As soon as may be, I think it would be advisable for us to have a conference upon details and methods of conducting the campaign for this season. A number of suggestions of value have naturally come in from various agents during the year which call for attention.

There is one matter of chief importance which I think we ought to consider with care. There was, as you know, last year a very considerable amount of dissatisfaction, well or ill grounded as the case may be, on the part of some of the important agents in different parts of the country. As nearly as I can analyze the reasons for this dissatisfaction they were based upon a feeling that the business administration of the campaign was not as satisfactory as it might have been.   I do not sympathize with this attitude to any great extent, although I am bound to say that in certain instances the point was well taken. I feel nevertheless that in order to retain and increase the interest of all concerned something must be done to meet and allay these sentiments.

In view of this situation I should like to offer for the consideration of the National Red Cross the following propositions:

It is obvious that the ultimate responsibility for and control of the Christmas seals should rest in the National Red Cross.   It seems equally obvious that the co-operation of The National Association for the Study and Prevention of Tuberculosis is essential to results in any way approaching the possibilities of the situation.   The co-operation last year showed the good results which can be obtained and we all feel sure that this success can be heightened in the future.   It is also clear, I think, that negotiations with the state and local tuberculosis associations who become the agents for the sale of the Red Cross seals can best be carried on by the National Association on account of our more or less constant and intimate relations.

Would it not be better therefore if the entire administration of the Christmas seal campaign were placed in the hands of the National Association acting as National agent for the Red Cross?

Without going into the matter in its details it would seem to me a desirable and workable proposition.   My idea would be that the National Red Cross having decided upon a seal should delegate the entire administration of the campaign to the National Association, reserving the right to approve or disapprove all matters of general policy and expenditure and to be the body of ultimate authority throughout.   On the other hand the details of administration, dealings with individual agents, ordering, printing and shipping seals and advertising material, when once approved by the Red Cross, to be carried out by the National Association.   The financial responsibility and distribution would remain, presumably, as at present.

Should such a proposition be favorably considered by the National Red Cross it would seem to me probably the part of wisdom to open a special office for the period of the campaign in Washington for handling the work.

The preliminary negotiations with agents and publicity campaign could probably best be administered from the New York office of the National Association.   I think this would be the most satisfactory and most workable plan that could be devised.   Will you not take it up with your Board and give it careful consideration?

May I add that I think the sooner we can plan our campaign for next season the better?   We are taking up now the question of agents in a preliminary way and hope to have the matter practically settled in the early summer. The sooner all such questions as the design of the seal, contracts for printing, the kind of advertising material to be prepared and the many details to be decided upon can be settled the more successful, I feel sure, the campaign will be.

I might add that at a meeting of the Board of Directors of the National

Association held last week I was empowered to act in this matter and can therefore say that we are ready to assume the added responsibility should the Red Cross view the proposition with favor.

Yours very truly,

(Signed) LIVINGSTON FARRAND,

Executive Secretary.

As will be noted from the correspondence under the agreement between the American Red Cross and the National Tuberculosis Association, the latter organization became the general agent of the Red Cross for the sale of Christmas seals with the privilege of appointing such other state or local agents as it might desire, and with full power and responsibility for controlling the expenditure of the funds derived from the Christmas seal sale. In other words, the policy of the American Red Cross in the Christmas seal sale from the beginning until the termination of this agreement was to act always in the capacity of general sponsor for the seal sale, leaving to the National Tuberculosis Association the widest possible latitude in the achievement of results from the funds derived through this method.

It is a matter of interesting record that the sponsors of the Christmas seal sale both in the American Red Cross and the National Tuberculosis Association considered it in its earlier days largely a fad which would soon die out and would have to be replaced by some other means of raising money. The reason why the Christmas seal outlived that dangerous fad period of development and has become a permanent institution in American communities is organization, spelled in large letters.

From 1910 until 1919 the American Red Cross and the National Tuberculosis Association maintained their virtual partnership in the Christmas seal sale. Each year an annual conference of state and other interested executives was held, usually at Washington, and plans for the Christmas seal sale of the ensuing year were perfected. The increasing development of the seal sale meant an increasing investment of funds for the printing of the seals and advertising matter. The Red Cross assumed this financial responsibility each year, reimbursing itself out of the returns of the seal sale.

In 1918 no national Christmas seal sale was conducted. In

July of that year the American Red Cross approached the National Tuberculosis Association with the suggestion that the seal sale be discontinued for the following Christmas. After a series of conferences, in September an agreement was reached whereby the Red Cross appropriated the sum of $2,500,000 to the tuberculosis movement in the United States to be distributed by the National Tuberculosis Association to the states and through the states to the local associations. This sum was in lieu of the seal sale which was not conducted that year. In 1919, the last Red Cross seal sale was held. It is significant to note that in that year the seal design bore both the emblem of the American Red Cross and the double-barred cross of the National Tuberculosis Association. The sale of 1919 aggregating $3,872,622 terminated the arrangement with the American Red Cross begun in 1910. The tuberculosis movement in the United States will never be able to repay the American Red Cross for the assistance it gave through the loan of its name, its funds, and the support of the Red Cross Seal during those critical years of development from 1910 to 1919.

In 1920 the first strictly tuberculosis Christmas seal, featuring the double-barred cross emblem alone, was issued. Although confronted by a radical change in policy and by unfavorable financial conditions, the power of the penny Christmas seal is shown in the fact that the total result in 1920 reached the sum of $3,662,312 for the United States. In 1921 the seal sale totaled over $3,500,000.

It is interesting to record here the ways in which the Christmas seal has helped to develop tuberculosis work. It would be difficult or almost impossible to record all of the many ways, but a few of the more significant will be of value.

First of all, the Christmas seal has always been and still is the greatest means for spreading the educational message of the tuberculosis campaign that has ever been devised. Because the penny Christmas seal reaches everyone, rich and poor, there is afforded an opportunity for bringing the message of tuberculosis to all kinds of groups. The Christmas seal furthermore furnishes the opportunity for widespread publicity. Every year at Christmas time the educational campaign of the tuberculosis movement

MRS. HARDING BUYS CHRISTMAS SEALS FROM A MODERN HEALTH
CRUSADER

is condensed into a few weeks of intensive effort to bring to the men, women and children of the country the message of their responsibility for the control of this preventable disease.

Secondly, the Christmas seal has provided the funds that have made organizations possible. The National Tuberculosis Association has always operated upon this axiom in organization, viz., that an association without funds or program is of no value. Some associations have had programs but no funds with which to execute them. Some have had funds but no program. In both instances the Christmas seal has been the means for providing proper organization. In the former instance where state and local associations have had a program and no funds, the Christmas seal has in hundreds of instances, both on a state-wide basis and in local communities, furnished the original funds with which to start a proper association and to employ the necessary full-time service. The businesslike organization of the tuberculosis campaign is due almost entirely to this policy of supplementing a local program with funds through the Christmas seal. Similarly there have been many instances where communities have had funds but no vision nor program. Here the state tuberculosis association through the Christmas seal sale has been able to furnish the necessary leadership and guidance with which to develop a practical program.

Thirdly, the Christmas seal has been the most potent means available to the tuberculosis movement for the development of correct standards of organization and work. With the development here and there throughout the country of local groups interested in education, nursing, hospitals, sanatoria, open air schools, and various other phases of tuberculosis work, the greatest danger that has confronted the tuberculosis movement has been the establishment of agencies without an appreciation of their functions and methods. This, to a certain degree, is still a problem. The Christmas seal has helped to standardize work of this sort in two ways—first, by giving to the state and national associations that authority through contractual relations that would more or less compel the organizations in question to adopt approved standards; and secondly, by providing the means for developing standards and bringing them to the agencies interested in tuberculosis.

Fourthly, the Christmas seal has been the means of attracting to the tuberculosis movement the most diversified interests of the community. Labor unions and industrial and religious organizations, school children, women's clubs and societies, bankers and bakers, in fact all the elements of American community life have contributed not only financially but in many other ways to making the Christmas seal sale a success. The Christmas seal, in other words, furnishes an opportunity for everyone, rich and poor, high and low, to participate in the community program for the prevention of tuberculosis.

In the conduct of the Christmas seal sale the policy of relations between the National Tuberculosis Association and the state and local groups has been the deciding factor in the success of the seal sale. As is implied in the correspondence passing between Mr. Bicknell and Dr. Farrand, the original policy of the Christmas seal sale was that the money derived from the sale of seals shall so far as possible remain in the community where the seals are sold. There have been varying degrees of modification of this policy. The National Tuberculosis Association at the present time makes a fixed contract with each of the state associations whereby a definite percentage from the gross sale of seals is paid into the treasury of the National Association. Arrangements between state and local associations vary in different states. In some the percentages are high and in some they are low. They range anywhere from 10 per cent. over and above the percentage to the National Association to as high as 40 per cent. or even 50 per cent. In unorganized territory where there is no association and no agency for expending the funds in approved ways, it is customary in most instances for the state association to take all of the proceeds and spend them for the benefit of the local community or hold them in trust for an organization to be developed. Thus, out of every dollar's worth of seals sold in city or town, a percentage goes to the support of both national and state work as well as local work. The returns from the Christmas seal by years, beginning with 1907, are as follows:

1907......... $3,000	1914....:.... $550,932
1908.........135,000	1915........ 760,000
1909.........250,000	1916........1,050,000
1910.........300,000	1917........1,780,000
1911.........320,000	1918........ no sale
1912.........402,256	1919........3,872,622
1913.........449,505	1920........3,662,312

It will be of interest to record typical seal sales, that of 1919 and 1920, by states, showing the gross amount received in each state and the per capita sale. The following table gives these facts:

A TABLE SHOWING COMPARATIVE RESULTS OF THE CHRISTMAS SEAL SALE, 1919 AND 1920

State	1920 Population	1920 Seal Sale		1919 Seal Sale	
		Total Sale in Dollars	Per Capita Sale in Cents	Total Sale in Dollars	Per Capita Sale in Cents
TOTAL.........	105,710,620	$3,662,312.57	3.4	$3,872,622.78	3.6
Alabama.........	2,348,174	68,730.15	2.9	40,717.85	1.7
Arizona..........	334,162	18,802.13	5.6	23,113.47	6.9
Arkansas.........	1,752,204	22,459.40	1.3	47,973.93	2.7
Brooklyn & Queens	2,487,398	90,539.86	3.6	78,347.14	
California. ...	3,426,861	199,343.18	5.8	156,261.07	4.5
Chicago (Cook Co.)	3,053,017	91,050.85	3.0	101,356.08	3.3
Colorado.........	939,629	43,021.25	4.6	71,470.67	7.6
Connecticut.......	1,380,631	78,518.72	5.7	82,324.94	5.9
Delaware.........	223,003	13,204.59	5.9	26,693.15	11.9
Dist. of Columbia..	437,571	19,907.39	4.5	19,836.34	4.6
Florida.	968,470	25,731.68	2.	21,995.07	2.2
Georgia	2,895,832	22,578.20	·6	2,030.06	..
Idaho..	431,866	19,374.16	4.5	20,024.90	4.6
Illinois (Excl. Cook Co.)...	3,432,263	141,295.98	4.1	135,767.74	3.9
Indiana	2,930,390	131,685.67	4.	115,705.68	3.9
Iowa.............	2,404,021	71,744.40	3.5	91,845.95	3.7
Kansas..........	1,769,257	43,190.58	2.4	57,825.39	3.2
Kentucky ..	2,416,630	25,488.88	1.0	36,779.63	1.
Louisiana	1,798,509	30,032.20	1.7	51,523.36	2.5
Maine...	768,014	22,748.99	3.0	32,290.51	4.2
Maryland ...	1,449,661	57,094.36	3.9	57,642.61	3.9
Massachusetts.....	3,852,356	122,918.79	3.2	141,604.77	3.6
Michigan.........	3,668,412	123,805.22	3.·	78,231.54	2.1
Minnesota........	2,387,125	104,175.39	4.4	143,659.56	6.0

A TABLE SHOWING COMPARATIVE RESULTS OF THE CHRISTMAS SEAL SALE, 1919 AND 1920
Continued

State	1920. Population	1920 Seal Sale		1919 Seal Sale	
		Total Sale in Dollars	Per Capita Sale in Cents	Total Sale in Dollars	Per Capita Sale in Cents
Mississippi........	1,790,618	$8,595.44	0.5	$32,184.03	1.7
Missouri..........	3,404,055	90,672.58	2.7	117,091.48	3.4
Montana..........	548,889	19,729.16	3.6	21,564.72	3.9
Nebraska.........	1,296,372	19,751.79	1.5	31,257.78	2.4
Nevada..........	77,407	4,217.16	5.4	4,551.23	5.8
New Hampshire...	443,083	24,023.31	5.4	52,908.85	11.9
New Jersey.......	3,155,900	136,796.37	4.3	126,323.06	4.1
New Mexico......	360,350	7,374.80	2.0	13,443.25	3.7
New York State (Excl. of N.Y.C.)..	4,765,179	392,864.50	8.2	374,867.49	7.8
New York City (Excl. of Brooklyn and Queens)	3,132,650	152,002.91	4.9	263,526.66	8.4
North Carolina....	2,559,123	36,728.38	1.4	42,407.18	1.6
North Dakota.....	646,872	15,659.14	2.4	17,263.04	2.6
Ohio.....	5,759,394	197,529.25	3.4	197,063.84	3.4
Oklahoma..	2,028,283	53,533.32	2.6	57,277.18	2.6
Oregon....	783,389	38,763.09	5.0	33,290.76	4.2
Pennsylvania (Excl. of Allegheny Co.)..	7,534,209	283,369.18	3.7	289,129.18	3.8
Pittsburgh (Allegheny Co.)......	1,185,808	84,989.45	7.2	46,126.86	3.8
Rhode Island......	604,397	32,508.79	5.4	39,895.63	6.6
South Carolina....	1,683,724	22,738.92	1.3	28,057.27	1.6
South Dakota.....	636,547	34,587.60	5.4	38,716.44	6.0
Tennessee........	2,337,885	26,857.32	1.1	69,202.00	2.9
Texas............	4,663,228	92,592.40	2.0	96,891.35	2.0
Utah.............	449,396	27,373.03	6.1	11,255.10	2.5
Vermont.........	352,428	8,288.89	2.3	6,790.77	1.9
Virginia..........	2,309,187	54,075.35	2.3	34,311.60	1.4
Washington.......	1,356,621	62,533.65	4.6	57,939.06	4.2
West Virginia.....	1,463,701	38,154.97	2.6	25,194.42	1.7
Wisconsin..	2,632,067	100,659.00	3.9	97,752.48	3.7
Wyoming.........	194,402	7,964.20	4.1	11,318.66	5.8

If one were to recite the various influences and factors that have contributed most to the success of the campaign against tuberculosis in the United States, he could not help but place at the head of any such list the Tuberculosis Christmas Seal.

CHAPTER VII

THE FRAMINGHAM DEMONSTRATION

NO HISTORY of the tuberculosis movement in the United States would be complete that did not chronicle the origin, development and results to date of the unique Framingham Community Health and Tuberculosis Demonstration at Framingham, Mass. For over four years, with the co-operation of its citizens, Framingham has been developing a program to show to the world the effectiveness of the methods of control of tuberculosis.

It may not be amiss as a matter of historical interest to state here how the Framingham Demonstration originated. To do this we must go back to the year 1908, when the interest of the officers of the Metropolitan Life Insurance Company in the tuberculosis problem was first aroused. The late Dr. John Henry Huddleston was mainly responsible for a meeting to which all the New York employees of the Metropolitan Life Insurance Company and its officers were invited. The occasion was the tuberculosis exhibition in the Museum of Natural History, New York City, which had been brought from Washington, D. C., largely through the efforts of Dr. Alfred Meyer of New York. Later it was also sent to Philadelphia through the efforts of Dr. Lawrence F. Flick. It had attracted great throngs of visitors during the Tuberculosis Congress in the capital city and in Philadelphia, but the crowds which visited the exhibit in New York were even greater. Various organizations, corporations and schools visited the museum in bodies, and each meeting was addressed by one or two physicians specially interested in tuberculosis. The Metropolitan Life Insurance Company's meeting at which Mr. Haley Fiske, now the president, then the vice-president of the Company, presided, was attended by no less than 1200 agents and clerks of the Company. Officers and employees listened attentively to the various addresses made by Mr. Fiske, Dr. John Henry Huddleston, Dr. Augustus S. Knight, one of the medical directors of the Company, and others. In the course of the address by the author of this history the suggestion was made that the time had come when life insurance companies should take a deeper interest in the tuberculosis problem, and very profitably might begin by taking care of their own tuberculous employees. The suggestion was taken up by Mr. Fiske and his fellow officers, and on June 20, 1914, a model sanatorium for the tuberculous employees of the company was dedicated at Mount McGregor, N. Y. This institution has been in operation ever since and has done a splendid life-saving service.

Thus as far back as 1908 the Metropolitan Life Insurance Company had evinced an active interest in the prevention of tuberculosis. In 1911 the Company began an intensive educational and nursing campaign among its policyholders which has resulted in the saving of millions of dollars and thousands of lives. Because of the fact that about one in every five people in the United States is insured in this Company, the Metropolitan has consistently extended its service and support to enterprises that did not reach its policyholders directly but that affected them through the general population.

In line with and as an outgrowth of this broad interest, Dr. Lee K. Frankel, third vice-president of the Company, proposed to his board an experiment to demonstrate if it was possible to control tuberculosis in a limited area. This proposal was accepted and on May 3, 1916, Dr. Frankel wrote Dr. E. R. Baldwin, then president of the National Tuberculosis Association, the following letter:

"The Metropolitan Life Insurance Company is much interested by reason of the fact that over 16 per cent. of the deaths in its Industrial Department are due to tuberculosis. In 1915 the Company paid claims of over $4,000,000 on the lives of 14,325 policyholders dying from this disease.

"The Company believes that an intensive experiment might well be made in the United States to determine whether it is possible to substantially reduce the mortality and morbidity of tuberculosis in the hope that the disease may eventually be eradicated.

"To this end, we are prepared to place at the disposal of The National Association for the Study and Prevention of Tuberculosis the sum of One Hundred

Thousand Dollars ($100,000) for the purpose of conducting a community experiment over a period of three years in the control of tuberculosis, on condition that the Association selects a community of approximately five thousand (5,000)* inhabitants, preferably in New York or Massachusetts, in which conditions would be favorable for such an experiment and that a special committee of the Association be appointed, on which the Company shall be represented, to whom full power shall be given to institute the necessary preliminary survey and to conduct the experiment along the lines finally determined upon by this committee.

"We would further suggest that in making the experiment, stress should be placed on

1. Periodic medical examination of all members of the community.
2. Medical and nursing care of all cases of tuberculosis.
3. Sanatorium or hospital care for such cases as may need it.
4. A tuberculosis clinic or dispensary.
5. Co-operation of local and state health officers, employers, labor unions, school authorities, etc.

"It is our hope that this experiment will be a practical contribution towards the study of the etiology of tuberculosis and that the results obtained may indicate a method for the prevention and elimination of the disease.

"I shall be glad to be advised by you of the acceptance of the Company's offer."

The Company's offer was enthusiastically accepted at the annual meeting of the National Tuberculosis Association in May, 1916, by the following resolution·

"The National Association for the Study and Prevention of Tuberculosis expresses its hearty appreciation of the generous proposition of the Metro_politan Life Insurance Company to contribute $100,000 for conducting a community experiment in the control of tuberculosis. In undertaking this trust the Association hopes that the results of the experiment may be commensurate with the desires which inspired the offer."

A National Committee consisting of the following was appointed: Dr. Edward R. Baldwin, chairman, Saranac Lake, N. Y.; Dr. Charles J. Hatfield, secretary, Philadelphia, Pa.; Dr. Lee K. Frankel, New York City, N. Y.; Dr. Charles, L. Minor, Asheville, N. C.; Mr. Homer Folks, New York City, N. Y.; Dr. Arthur K. Stone, Framingham, Mass.; Dr. Eugene R. Kelley, Boston, Mass.; Dr. Stephen J. Maher, New Haven, Conn.; Dr. William Charles White, Pittsburgh, Pa.; Dr. Victor Safford, Boston, Mass.; Dr. F. C. Smith, New York City, N. Y.;

* Subsequently this population limit was raised to fifteen or sixteen thousand.

Mr. Theodore F. Rice, Framingham, Mass.; Dr. Enos H. Bigelow, Framingham, Mass.; Mr. Henry S. Dennison, Framingham, Mass.

Dr. Donald B. Armstrong was selected as executive officer in July, 1916. For several months he worked with the committee in the selection of a town. Framingham was finally chosen because it was an average American town of about 16,000 population, with average conditions as to mortality and other factors. In December, 1916, Dr. Armstrong moved to Framingham and the Demonstration itself was launched.

The Demonstration started out to find, if possible, a solution to these four community problems: (a) to discover and place under adequate medical, nursing, and relief supervision all cases of tuberculosis, incipient and advanced, active and arrested; (b) to ascertain with some degree of definiteness the responsible social and economic factors in disease causation, particularly as regards tuberculosis; (c) to utilize in the most efficient way the existing means for discovery and treatment of tuberculosis and to find out what percentage of disease is preventable; (d) to find and organize the best community health machinery for preventing sickness and death from tuberculosis.

In order to evaluate the results and methods of the Demonstration after the initial three-year period of work, the Surgeon General of the United States Public Health Service, at the request of the National Tuberculosis Association, appointed the following group as a Committee on Appraisal: Dr. Allan J. McLaughlin, U. S. Public Health Service, chairman; Prof. C.-E. A. Winslow, Yale University, New Haven, Conn., secretary; Dr. Edgar T. Sydenstricker, U. S. Public Health Service; Dr. Charles V. Chapin, Health Commissioner, Providence, R. I.; Dr. Victor G. Heiser, Rockefeller Foundation, N. Y. City; Miss Helen R. Stewart, National Organization for Public Health Nursing; Mr. George J. Nelbach, State Charities Aid Association, New York; Dr. Emery R. Hayhurst, State Department of Health, Ohio; Dr. Thomas A. Storey, American School Hygiene Association; Dr. Samuel McClintock Hamill, University of Pennsylvania, Philadelphia, Pa.; Dr. Louis Hamman, Johns Hopkins Medical School, Baltimore, Md.; Dr. Lawrason Brown, Trudeau Sanatorium, Saranac Lake, N. Y.; Dr. H. R. M. Landis, Phipps Institute, Philadelphia, Pa.

The Appraisal Committee reported favorably on the results of the Demonstration and recommended its continuation for a limited period, a recommendation which has been adopted.

The report of the Committee summarizes the results of the Demonstration as follows:

"1. THE EXTENT OF TUBERCULOSIS

"The first step, a determination of the actual prevalence of tuberculosis infection, has been accomplished with a high degree of success, giving us for the first time a fairly complete picture of the amount of tuberculosis actually existing in a typical American community.

"2. THE CONSULTATION SERVICE

"The most important of all the practical contributions made by the Demonstration is the working out of a plan for medical consultation service, which is clearly the most promising means yet devised for securing a reasonably complete knowledge of the amount of tuberculosis existing in a given community. The consultation service plan has attracted wide attention throughout the country.

"3. TUBERCULOSIS TREATMENT

"The machinery adopted for the treatment of cases of tuberculosis after they have been discovered has been modeled along generally accepted lines. The work has been accomplished efficiently and successfully.

"4. STANDARDS OF DIAGNOSIS

"The officers of the Demonstration have prepared a scheme of diagnostic standards for tuberculosis which has attracted wide attention.

"5. DEATH CERTIFICATION ANALYSIS

"The careful analysis of death certificates, showing that the actual deaths from tuberculosis in Framingham were 22 per cent. in excess of the reported deaths from this disease, also constitutes a valuable contribution.

"6. SANITARY STUDIES

"From the standpoint of general environmental causes effecting the spread and development of tuberculosis, the staff of the Demonstration has conducted valuable studies of schools, factories, and municipal health conditions.

"7. GENERAL SICKNESS PREVALENCE

"The medical examination drives have yielded some of the most complete data in regard to the prevalence of disease of all sorts in a random section of the population that have ever been collected in this country.

"8. THE TUBERCULOSIS DEATH-RATE

"From the standpoint of mortality, the tuberculosis death-rate has fallen from 93 per 100,000 in 1917 to a rate corresponding to 76 for the first five months of 1919.   This is an encouraging showing, in view of the fact that the tuberculosis death-rate in similar Massachusetts communities has in general materially increased.

"9. THE TOWN'S RESPONSE

"The town of Framingham has responded with vision and effectiveness to the remarkable opportunities offered by the establishment of the Demonstration.   The Local Board of Health, the School Committee, the Civic League, and many of the employers of labor, have met the challenge to make Framingham the model "Health Town" with constructive responses of a high order.

"10. LOCAL HEALTH DEVELOPMENT

"Even more important from the practical standpoint has been the notable development of public health work in Framingham along a wide variety of lines.

"11. THE HEALTH AND SCHOOL DEPARTMENTS

"The local health department has grown to be a strong and effective one, and the system of medical inspection of school children, organized under the Department of Education, represents one of the best examples of such service to be found in the United States.

"12. THE COMMUNITY BENEFITED

"It seems clear that if the Framingham Demonstration should cease on January 1, 1920, the local community will have benefited materially and many important contributions will have been made to the practical control of tuberculosis.

"13. NEED FOR LOCAL CO-ORDINATION

"It seems to us if the Demonstration is to be continued that it might be of service to organize in Framingham a Health Council which would include the Health Officer, or a Board of Health representative as Chairman, with representatives of the School Committee, the Civic League, the Framingham Hospital, the Red Cross, the medical society, and the Demonstration,—this council to serve as a clearing-house for the co-ordination of health activities and the planning of the most effective public health machinery for the community as a whole.   We deem it to be of great importance to transfer the work to them (the local agencies) as rapidly as possible.

"14. THE FOUNDATION LAID

"The foundation has been well laid; a program for the control of tuberculosis by early diagnosis and hygienic care has been organized on ideal lines; local sentiment both in the medical and lay circles has been successfully developed in support of the campaign; and all conditions are favorable to its success.

"15. CONTINUATION VITAL

"These statistical calculations have led us to the conclusion that the Framingham Demonstration should be continued for a period of at least five years in order to render the attainment of definite results of reasonable certainty It would furnish for the first time a definitely established working program for the practical control of tuberculosis."

The Framingham Demonstration endeavors as one of its distinct aims to show to other communities how tuberculosis may be controlled. Framingham is, in other words, a community laboratory where methods that can be universally applied are tested. Dr. Armstrong in a recent article has emphasized this phase of the work under the pertinent title "Framingham Yardsticks." Since this article shows in brief some of the most significant achievements of the Demonstration from the point of view of methods, it is quoted in full as follows:

"I. HOW MUCH TUBERCULOSIS IS THERE?

"The examination of thousands of men, women and children in Framingham shows that approximately 1 per cent. were suffering from active tuberculosis.

"In a city of 100,000 people this would mean, therefore, about 1,000 active cases.

"II. HOW MANY CASES SHOULD BE UNDER CARE?

"In Framingham intensive medical work among infants, in schools, in factories and elsewhere, brought to light 9 or 10 active cases for every annual death.

"In a city of 100,000, therefore, with a death-rate, say, of 100 per hundred thousand, or 100 deaths a year, there should be 900 or 1,000 active cases under care. (Variations in the death-rate may, of course, affect this ratio.)

"III. WHAT PERCENTAGE OF CASES SHOULD BE REPORTED IN THE EARLY STAGE?

"Before the Demonstration started in Framingham, the physicians of Framingham reported only 45 per cent. of the cases in the early stage; now about 75 per cent. of the cases are being reported as early-stage tuberculosis.

"IV. WHAT ARE THE MINIMUM INSTITUTIONAL NEEDS?

"In Framingham the minimum bed requirement has been from one to two beds for every annual death in the community. This hypothetical city of 100,000, with 100 deaths a year, will need, therefore, at least 100 hospital or sanatorium beds to care for its adult and child tuberculosis cases needing institutional care.   In fact, 200 beds will more nearly meet the needs disclosed by intensive search for tuberculosis.

"V. WHAT PERCENTAGE OF CASES SHOULD BE GIVEN HOSPITAL OR SANATORIUM TREATMENT?

"In Framingham the cases during any one year needing and being benefited by institutional care constitute about 33 per cent. of the total number of active cases under observation or treatment.   This, of course, includes many early cases, given the educational and hygienic advantages of perhaps only a few months' stay in a sanatorium.

"VI. WHAT CONSTITUTES A COMPREHENSIVE EDUCATIONAL PROGRAM?

"An educational program should fight:

"a. Infection—by promoting respiratory hygiene, by improving milk supplies, by improving general sanitation, etc.

"b. Disease—by lessening stress or strain, mental or physical; by improving economic, social and nutritional conditions; by promoting constructive personal hygiene.

"c. Death—by popularizing and making adequate provision for institutional and home treatment.

"VII. WHAT COMMUNITY MACHINERY IS NECESSARY?

"a. Medical machinery to find tuberculosis cases—a school or factory physician for every 3,000 individuals, a clinic and consultation service, etc.

"b. An adequate nursing service—tuberculosis nurses (or general public health nurses—at least 1 to every 2 or 3,000 people), infant welfare, school, factory and home nursing, arrested case follow-up, etc.

"c. Adequate institutional equipment.

"d. An educational program.

"e. Proper community organization, adequate legislation, general sanitation, research, etc.

"VIII. WHAT WILL IT COST?

"It is impossible to separate the cost of tuberculosis work from the cost of general health work.   In Framingham for all kinds of health work, including tuberculosis, before the Demonstration there was being spent 40 cents per capita per year.   Now the community is spending over $2.00 per capita per year from both public and private sources.

"In our city of 100,000, therefore, an adequate health budget would be at least $200,000 a year.   Probably $100,000 of this should come from public sources through taxation, and another $100,000 from private sources, to carry on civic, social, industrial and other non-official activities.

"IX. WHAT RESULTS MAY BE HOPED FOR?

"In Framingham it is too early, of course, to announce final conclusions. It may be said, however, that the Demonstration is now finding fewer cases, and in particular it is finding fewer advanced cases—which would indicate a beginning reduction in tuberculosis morbidity.

"As to mortality, the death-rate has declined during the Demonstration from a pre-Demonstration rate of 121 per 100,000 to a current rate of 35 or 40 per 100,000 (corrected for residence and certification errors)—a reduction of over two-thirds in 5 years.

"In the city of 100,000, with 100 deaths a year, this would mean a saving of 65 or 70 lives a year, which represents, when measured in money terms alone, thousands and thousands of dollars. The same methods, if successfully applied throughout our country, will mean a saving of over 80,000 lives a year,—many more than were lost by this country in the great war.

"That is the Framingham story in a nutshell. Of course, it is not yet complete, and the future may alter these tentative conclusions. However, if they are suggestive to your community, if you think a similar procedure can be applied with advantage and want more detail as to method, write the Community Health Station, Framingham, Mass."

It is significant to note in closing this chapter that the idea and methods of the Framingham Demonstration have stimulated the National Child Health Council to establish a similar demonstration on child welfare with a fund of $200,000 granted by the American Red Cross. This most conspicuous illustration is one of a great many instances where agencies and communities, throughout the United States and the world, are being benefited by the application of the methods tested and verified by the Framingham Demonstration.

CHAPTER VIII

THE STATE TUBERCULOSIS ASSOCIATIONS

A HISTORY of the National Tuberculosis Association should logically include a brief survey of the work of the various state associations.

For many years the National Association's work was largely that of organizing state bodies. Within the last four or five years, however, it has been the stimulation and standardization of tuberculosis work throughout the state organizations.

At the present time there is a state association in every state and in the District of Columbia.

The local associations in New York City, Brooklyn, Pittsburgh, and Chicago are treated by the National Tuberculosis Association in the same relation as state associations, and are designated as "affiliated associations."

This section, therefore, will deal with the history of the work in each of the 48 state associations, the District of Columbia, and the four affiliated associations.

For purpose of convenience the state and affiliated associations are grouped alphabetically.

The information contained in this section has been compiled from reports received by the author and from records on file in the office of the National Tuberculosis Association.

The information concerning deaths and death-rates is taken entirely from the records of the United States Census Bureau for the Registration Area of the United States in order that the figures may be uniform and comparable. While figures are available from state registrars for most of the states, they are not as comparable, one with another, as those from the Registration Area. Where no death-rate figures are given, it may be assumed that none are available, the state not being included in the Registration Area.

76

ALABAMA TUBERCULOSIS ASSOCIATION

The active campaign against tuberculosis in Alabama is about seven years old.

As early as 1906 a standing committee on tuberculosis of the Medical Association of the State of Alabama, with Dr. Glenn Andrews as chairman, had been formed, and through the influence of this committee legislation was secured in 1907 declaring tuberculosis to be an infectious disease, and making it reportable. Up until 1914, however, comparatively little had been done, chiefly for the reason that funds were not available for a state-wide campaign.

A local association had been formed in Montgomery in 1908, and in Birmingham in 1910. The work of these organizations, however, was largely local and centered chiefly about the supervision of sanatorium and hospital care for a limited number of tuberculous patients.

With the inauguration of a state-wide Christmas seal sale in 1914, the real campaign against tuberculosis in Alabama began. Educational work was conducted on a state-wide basis, and local communities were stimulated to organization.

At the close of 1921 there were 4 sanatoria in the state, with a bed capacity of 115, 5 dispensaries, and 17 local associations. There are 15 county public health nurses and a state supervising nurse, with 2 other state nurses on part time.

The Modern Health Crusade has been introduced widely throughout the state. The state association has an executive secretary and a Crusader executive, and an additional staff.

In 1915 a State Tuberculosis Commission was created for the purpose of promoting county and district hospitals. The Commission has coöperated with the State Tuberculosis Association and has been instrumental in stimulating a wide interest in the institutional care of the tuberculous. The unfavorable financial conditions of recent years have hindered the development of work along this line.

The problem of tuberculosis control in Alabama is seriously complicated by the large Negro population. The State Tuberculosis Association has stimulated such an interest among the

Negroes, however, in their own health that early in the year 1922 a state-wide Negro tuberculosis association was organized, closely affiliated with the Alabama Tuberculosis Association.

The headquarters of the Alabama Tuberculosis Association are at 308 North Twenty-first Street, Birmingham, Alabama, and the acting secretary is Mrs. H. E. Pearce.

ALASKA

There is no organized tuberculosis work in Alaska.

As a disease, tuberculosis presents a most serious menace, particularly to the native population. Through a few of the mission centers and government agencies, particularly through the Bureau of Education, a certain amount of literature has been distributed and some talks on tuberculosis have been given.

Medical and nursing care is available for a very limited number of patients.

For the most part, however, the problem of tuberculosis is untouched in Alaska. The distance and inaccessibility of the territory for a large part of the year has made it extremely difficult for the National Tuberculosis Association to undertake work there.

ARIZONA ANTI-TUBERCULOSIS ASSOCIATION

As early as 1909 an Arizona Association for the Study and Prevention of Tuberculosis had been formed. The association, however, existed largely on paper, and did no active work of education or organization on a state-wide basis until it was completely reorganized in 1916. At that time, at the instance of the National Tuberculosis Association, a new association, now known as the Arizona Anti-Tuberculosis Association, was formed and a full-time executive secretary was employed. The immediate stimulus in reorganizing the association was the Christmas seal.

While Christmas seals had been sold in more or less desultory fashion in Arizona for several years, after the reorganization of the work and the employment of a full-time executive the seal sale was multiplied more than three times, and a sufficient fund was given to begin a real campaign of organization and education.

The tuberculosis problem in Arizona is peculiar in that the state is widely known throughout the world as a health resort for the tuberculous. A very considerable percentage of the population have tuberculosis or have come to the state because of some member of their family who has the disease.

The migratory indigent consumptive is everywhere present and presents a serious relief and health problem. The paucity of population also, combined with the fact that much of the wealth of the state is controlled by individuals who have their business headquarters outside of Arizona, has made it very difficult for a State Association to get a firm foothold.

In spite of these obstacles, however, local centers have been developed in Phoenix, Tucson, Prescott, and other cities, and at the present time there is an increasing amount of institutional, nursing, and dispensary provision for indigenous tuberculosis as contrasted with the institutions that are in existence purely for the care of private cases largely from outside of the local communities in which the sanatoria are located.

The state association has conducted a public health survey in coöperation with the State Board of Health and has stimulated the establishment of the Modern Health Crusade and the employment of full-time county health officers.

There are at present 35 public health nurses working at full time. Ten years ago there were no nurses of this character in the state.

The problem of tuberculosis in Arizona may best be visualized by a report of a survey in Phoenix of 481 tuberculosis cases. Fifty-seven of these cases were absolutely indigent, 82 were receiving some support from relatives, friends, fraternal organizations, or other groups, and many of the patients were working when they should have been resting. Fifteen were tuberculous husbands supported by their wives. Thirty-three were living upon savings which were rapidly being exhausted. Most of the patients had been sent to Arizona by eastern physicians and social agencies. The majority of them at the time of arrival were in an advanced stage of the disease, and without sufficient funds to provide for proper care.

The headquarters of the Arizona Anti-Tuberculosis Association are at 300 East Adams Street, Phoenix, Arizona, and the executive secretary is Mr. T. C. Cuvellier.

ARKANSAS TUBERCULOSIS ASSOCIATION

The first state association on record in Arkansas is the Arkansas Association for the Relief and Control of Tuberculosis, formed in 1908. The Association was developed largely out of the State Committee for the Sixth International Congress on Tuberculosis. As a state-wide body, however, it never functioned.

It was not until 1917 that the real state-wide campaign against tuberculosis in Arkansas began. At that time, as a result of a field survey by the National Tuberculosis Association and the stimulus of the Christmas seal, a full-time executive was employed. Since that date there has been a rapid development of interest and enthusiasm in the state of Arkansas in tuberculosis and public health. There are now seven local centers of work.

The state sanatorium was established in 1907, and now has 145 beds. In addition to this institution there are 2 sanatoria with 32 beds, 3 free clinics, and about 25 tuberculosis and public health nurses, including those employed by the Red Cross.

The state association carries on a vigorous campaign of education through the Modern Health Crusade, exhibits, motion pictures, and in other ways. The aroused interest in tuberculosis work has been the means for improving public health conditions throughout the entire state of Arkansas.

It is not too much to say that a great part of the revival of interest in public health in the state of Arkansas is due to the activities and energy of the Arkansas Tuberculosis Association.

Arkansas has a large Negro population, and in the northern part of the state there are many mountaineers. This population composition, together with the rural and scattered condition of the people, makes it difficult to carry on a progressive work in many of the counties. The state association, however, has penetrated practically every portion of the state and has local representatives and committees allied with it in some way in practically every community.

The headquarters of the Arkansas association are at 201

Donaghey Building, Little Rock, Arkansas, and the executive secretary is Miss Erle Chambers.

CALIFORNIA TUBERCULOSIS ASSOCIATION

Among the earliest efforts at organization of tuberculosis work in California were the Southern California Anti-Tuberculosis League, formed in 1903, with Dr. F. M. Pottenger as president, and the Tuberculosis Committee of the State Medical Society, formed in the same year. These organizations operated largely in southern California and San Francisco. Their principal work was the distribution of a limited amount of literature.

The California Association for the Study and Prevention of Tuberculosis, of which Dr. George H. Kress was the secretary for several years, was formed in 1907 largely out of the interest stimulated by the International Congress Committee.

This latter organization carried on a state-wide propaganda and stimulated considerable interest by the distribution of literature, holding of meetings, and the work that was accomplished in Los Angeles through its clinic.

It was in 1914, however, that the most progressive step in state tuberculosis work was taken, when the Association was reorganized and a full-time executive secretary was employed. The increase in the Christmas seal sale immediately justified the employment of the state executive, Mrs. E. L. M. Tate-Thompson, in 1915. As a result largely of Mrs. Thompson's perseverance and energy, the State Legislature enacted a law providing for a State Bureau of Tuberculosis in the Department of Health and for a state subsidy for counties which built tuberculosis hospitals along lines approved by the State Bureau.

Up to this time it had been almost impossible to secure local provision for tuberculosis cases, primarily because of the fear of communities that the establishment of county hospitals would bring in an influx of indigent migratory consumptives. The experience of the last six years demonstrates clearly that such fears were largely groundless.

Mrs. Thompson was appointed as the head of the State Bureau of Tuberculosis, and retained her position also as head of the State Tuberculosis Association, in which dual capacity she has

6

developed a work of unusual significance. At the present time there are 28 counties in the state operating subsidized tuberculosis hospitals, with a bed capacity of 1,900. All of these hospitals are supervised and inspected by the State Bureau and must maintain adequate standards in order to retain the state subsidy. Twelve cities are operating tuberculosis clinics. There are 9 summer camps, 4 preventoria, and open-air schools in 4 cities. There are nearly 60 tuberculosis nurses, besides a much larger number of nurses doing general public health work, including tuberculosis.

The educational work of the state association has covered a wide range, including lectures, distribution of printed matter, Modern Health Crusade, motion pictures, billboards, etc.

The state association has greatly stimulated occupational therapy by the employment of teachers to visit sanatoria under the supervision of the State Bureau.

The traveling motor clinic, organized in 1920, toured the rural districts of the state.

The State Tuberculosis Association has also greatly stimulated all the public health work of the state, particularly that relating to medical examination of school children.

When it is recalled that in 1915, outside of San Francisco and Los Angeles, there was not a single decent place in the entire state for consumptives without means to receive examination or treatment, the present status of the work in California exhibits a phenomenal progress. The State Tuberculosis Association may justly take the credit for most of this progress.

The tuberculosis death-rate in California has steadily declined in spite of the influx of migratory consumptives and the fact that southern California particularly is widely used as a resort for the tuberculous.

The death-rate from tuberculosis in 1907, when the first state association was formed, was 2,198. In 1914 it had declined to 195.0, and in 1920 to 159.6.

The headquarters of the California Tuberculosis Association are at 418 Griffith McKenzie Building, Fresno, California, and the executive secretary is Mrs. E. L. M. Tate-Thompson.

COLORADO TUBERCULOSIS ASSOCIATION

The Colorado State Committee of the International Congress was incorporated in April, 1908, and virtually became a State Tuberculosis Association.

As early as 1910 the Association employed a full-time secretary.

For several years the work was carried on with vigor. A state law requiring the reporting of tuberculosis was enacted notwithstanding a great deal of opposition. The educational campaign was extended throughout the state. The Christmas seal sale was gradually increased.

In 1918 the Association was reorganized with a new executive. Its work since that time has been state-wide; it has been instrumental in stimulating the organization of committees and interested groups in the larger centers throughout the state.

There are now ten well-organized branch associations. The Denver Tuberculosis Society, the first and largest of these, was formed in 1917. Its outstanding achievements are: obtaining the construction of a municipal tuberculosis sanatorium; inaugurating in the schools the Modern Health Crusade; weighing and measuring; follow-up work in the homes; school luncheons; establishing nutrition classes and an open-air school; and carrying on country-wide propaganda against the migration of the indigent tuberculous.

Colorado is another state in which the indigent migratory consumptive is a most serious problem. As in Arizona and California, this fact has retarded the development of local institutional provision. While there are a number of private sanatoria in Denver and Colorado Springs, there is very little local provision elsewhere. The Association, however, has stimulated the establishment of four dispensaries and is creating interest in public health nursing throughout the state.

The Modern Health Crusade has been extended into nearly every county in the state, enlisting half of the school children in its ranks.

Educational publicity has been carried on through the distribution of several hundred thousand circulars and folders, by newspaper articles, and by many health talks.

The Association has been instrumental in stimulating a demand for reorganization of the State Health Department.   While its efforts have not yet proved successful, the constantly increasing interest in public health will surely accomplish the desired result.

In 1918 less than $10,000 was available for tuberculosis educational work in the entire state.   In 1922 expenditures of the state and local associations will total over $43,000.   These figures epitomize the progress of the tuberculosis campaign in Colorado.

The death-rate from tuberculosis in Colorado in 1908 was 256.2, and in 1920 it was 225.4.

The headquarters of The Colorado Tuberculosis Association are at 409 Barth Building, Denver, Colorado, and the executive secretary is Miss G. I. Pelton.

CONNECTICUT STATE TUBERCULOSIS COMMISSION

In Connecticut, the anti-tuberculosis campaign is conducted by the State Tuberculosis Commission.   Connecticut has never had a state tuberculosis association in the sense in which this term is used in most other states.   Public tuberculosis work was started in 1902 by the New Haven County Anti-Tuberculosis Association, the establishment of the Gaylord Farm Sanatorium at Wallingford, and the Wildwood Sanatorium at Hartford.   Out of the interest generated by the establishment of these two sanatoria, and the report of a special investigation commission appointed by Governor Woodruff in 1907, the legislature in 1909 created the Connecticut State Tuberculosis Commission primarily for the establishment of a series of joint state and county tuberculosis hospitals.   Dr. J. P. C. Foster was the first chairman of this Commission.

With the development of interest in tuberculosis work throughout the state, the State Commission by legal enactment and common consent assumed such a place of leadership that it became the logical agency through which the National Tuberculosis Association worked.   For several years, therefore, the State Tuberculosis Commission has served as the agent for the sale of Christmas seals and has stood in the same relationship to the National Tuberculosis Association as a state association.

While the primary business of the Commission has been the construction and administration of the splendid series of five state sanatoria, as required by statute, it has also been the leader in conducting of campaigns of education on tuberculosis. Through the money derived from the Christmas seal sale it has been able to stimulate the organization of local tuberculosis work in about thirty or more different centers throughout the state. Clinics, nurses, open-air schools and educational agencies have developed in practically every city and town of the state. The coöperation of working men in the Employees' Tuberculosis Relief Associations has been particularly helpful in stimulating tuberculosis work in the large industries so prominent throughout the state.

In addition to the 5 state sanatoria, which include one sea-side hospital for crippled children, there are 6 special tuberculosis hospitals or wards of general hospitals, 23 clinics, 1 day camp, 5 preventoria, 9 open-air schools and classes, and 40 public health nurses giving either full- or part-time to tuberculosis nursing.

The death-rate from tuberculosis in 1909 was 152.5. In 1920 the death-rate had been reduced to 119.4.

The headquarters of the Connecticut State Tuberculosis Commission are at the State Capitol, Hartford, Connecticut, and the field secretary is Hubert M. Sedgwick. The chairman of the Commission is Dr. Stephen J. Maher, of New Haven.

DELAWARE ANTI-TUBERCULOSIS SOCIETY

Out of the Delaware Anti-Tuberculosis Society grew the Red Cross seal, and out of the Red Cross seal grew the tuberculosis Christmas seal.

The Delaware Anti-Tuberculosis Society was organized through the interest of Miss Emily P. Bissell and Dr. John Black, of Wilmington. Their first work was the erection of a little sanatorium of eight beds on the banks of the Brandywine, which to-day has developed into Hope Farm, a sanatorium of 60 beds. The needs of this sanatorium prompted Miss Bissell to undertake the first Christmas seal sale.

In 1909 the Delaware State Tuberculosis Commission came into existence. Since that time there has been a certain amount of division of responsibility, and a definite amount of coöperation between the Delaware Anti-Tuberculosis Society and the Commission. The joint work of the two bodies has resulted in the establishment of the first state sanatorium for Negroes, three tuberculosis dispensaries, and a number of public health nurses. The educational campaign has been extended into every corner of the state.

The death-rate from tuberculosis in 1920 was 146.0.

The headquarters of the Delaware Anti-Tuberculosis Society are at 911 Delaware Avenue, Wilmington, Delaware.

The headquarters of the Delaware State Tuberculosis Commission are at 213 West Seventh Street, Wilmington, Delaware, and the secretary is Dr. Albert Robin.

DISTRICT OF COLUMBIA TUBERCULOSIS ASSOCIATION

Among the earliest active local tuberculosis associations in the United States is the District of Columbia organization. It was established originally as the Committee on Prevention of Consumption of the Associated Charities of the District of Columbia. It changed its name later to the Association for the Prevention of Tuberculosis of the District of Columbia, now popularly known as the District of Columbia Tuberculosis Association.

Among the earliest efforts of the Association were the distribution of educational literature, the institution of public lectures, the successful advocacy of legislation for the compulsory registration of tuberculosis cases, and the free examination of sputum by the Health Department.

The Association has contributed to practically every stage of the development of tuberculosis and public health work in the District of Columbia, including the establishment of a tuberculosis hospital, the opening of various tuberculosis clinics, the open-air schools, nutrition classes, and similar activities.

The Modern Health Crusade has been made an integral part of the school curriculum and has attracted the attention of leaders in the capital from the president down.

The death-rate from tuberculosis in Washington has been reduced from 279.5 in 1902 to 151.6 in 1919.

The headquarters of the District of Columbia Tuberculosis

Association are at 923 H Street, N. W., Washington, D. C., and the executive secretary is Mr. Walter S. Ufford.

FLORIDA PUBLIC HEALTH ASSOCIATION

The State Public Health Association in Florida is among the youngest of the state organizations. It was organized in March, 1916. The Christmas seal is immediately responsible for the state association. An effort was made to employ a full-time executive secretary in 1917, but partly due to war conditions, this endeavor was abandoned after four months' trial. After the armistice a full-time executive was secured. It would be difficult to estimate the progress that has been made in Florida in knowledge of tuberculosis and public health within the last four years.

Through the State Board of Health and the State Federation of Women's Clubs there had been a certain amount of interest in tuberculosis prior to the formation of the Florida Public Health Association. It was the putting of the state-wide work on a business basis with a full-time executive that pushed the entire campaign forward by leaps and bounds.

At the present time there is one county tuberculosis hospital, and provision is being made for others. There are two permanent and one traveling clinic. There are more than a dozen public health nurses in different parts of the state.

The Modern Health Crusade and other methods of education are being extended rapidly.

The work in Florida is still in its beginnings, and it has been hampered by unfavorable financial conditions. The problem is further complicated by the large number of Negroes in the state.

The death-rate from tuberculosis in 1920 was 104.1.

The headquarters of the Florida Public Health Association are at 507 Dyal-Upchurch Building, Jacksonville, Florida, and the executive secretary is Mr. R. H. Hixson.

GEORGIA TUBERCULOSIS ASSOCIATION

Among the earliest tuberculosis activities in Georgia was the formation of a committee on tuberculosis in the Georgia Medical

Association, and the appointment of a State Commission to "investigate the extent of tuberculosis in Georgia and the means of stamping out the disease," both of which came into existence in 1904.

The Georgia Anti-Tuberculosis and Sanatoria Society grew out of the Medical Society's committee in 1909, but because of lack of funds it did very little in the way of state-wide work.

In 1913, on the death of one of Georgia's most philanthropic citizens, Captain W. G. Raoul, there was created the Raoul Foundation, with an endowment fund of $50,000, the income from which was to be expended annually for the prevention of tuberculosis in the state. The Raoul Foundation functioned as a state tuberculosis association until the fall of 1921, when a re-organization was effected and the Georgia Tuberculosis Association formed, the Raoul Foundation becoming one of its financial contributors and backers.

In Atlanta an active group of workers, led by Captain Raoul, as early as 1907, began a pioneer campaign in that city and demonstrated clearly the possibilities of organized tuberculosis work. The Raoul Foundation, extending the work begun in Atlanta, with the assistance of the National Association, made an extensive survey of the ravages of tuberculosis in this state, conducted state-wide educational campaigns, and developed a state organization. The Foundation was the chief factor in securing legislative provision for full-time county health officers and better health administration. Meanwhile, the tuberculosis campaign was pushed throughout the state with great vigor. The result of this extensive activity is shown not only in the institutional provision available, but in the wide-spread interest in public health to-day as contrasted with 1913. There is a state sanatorium with 100 beds, and a local sanatorium in Atlanta with 190 beds. There are 7 clinics, 2 open-air schools, and more than 103 public health nurses, all of them doing some kind of tuberculosis work.

The headquarters of the Georgia Tuberculosis Association are at 602 Chamber of Commerce Building, Atlanta, Georgia, and the executive secretary is Mr. James P. Faulkner.

HAWAII

The campaign against tuberculosis was inaugurated in Hawaii in 1909 as a result of the interest of James A. Rath and some of his associates connected with the Palama Settlement in Honolulu.

The interest, stimulated by the Anti-Tuberculosis League of Hawaii, grew steadily until in 1920 the territorial Government took over the entire activities of the League and expanded the work in the form of nursing, institutional and educational provision. The League has now gone out of existence, but the entire tuberculosis campaign is being carried on in a much broader and extensive form than ever before.

IDAHO ANTI-TUBERCULOSIS ASSOCIATION

Through the accidental interest of the energetic proprietor of a leading department store in Boise, Mr. Henry L. Falk, the Idaho Anti-Tuberculosis Association developed. During the Christmas season of 1914 a customer at Mr. Falk's store asked for Christmas seals. Not knowing what they were, he wrote to one of his buyers in New York and ascertained where they could be had. He then sold them to some of his customers.

The following year, in 1915, the National Tuberculosis Association, capitalizing the interest created, formed the Idaho Anti-Tuberculosis Association and conducted, with the coöperation of Mr. Falk, a mail sale campaign of the Christmas seal to provide the initial funds with which to start the organization. The next year an executive secretary was employed.

In spite of large territory, sparse population, and difficulties of communication, in the past three years the Idaho Association has secured legislation for two tuberculosis hospitals; secured the location at Boise of Public Health Service Hospital No. 52 for ex-service men; placed the Modern Health Crusade in the curriculum of the public school system, enrolling 80,000 children and thereby winning the National Crusade Cup in 1921; organized and financed 18 county associations; put on nursing demonstrations and school inspections in 22 of the 44 counties of the state.

While in 1916, when the work of the Association began there

was relatively little interest in community health, at the present time there are 12 county nurses, 9 school nurses and 3 other general public health nurses.   The interest in community health surveys, the Modern Health Crusade, poster contests and other methods of bringing tuberculosis to the attention of the public has been greatly stimulated.   There is hardly a community in the state where the message of the Idaho Anti-Tuberculosis Association has not been carried in some way or other.

The headquarters of the Idaho Anti-Tuberculosis Association are at 222 Boise City National Bank Building, Boise, Idaho, and the executive secretary is Mrs. Catherine R. Athey.

ILLINOIS TUBERCULOSIS ASSOCIATION

[*Note:*   The work of the Illinois Tuberculosis Association and the Chicago Tuberculosis Institute will be treated under separate sections.]

As early as 1905 an Illinois State Association for the Prevention of Tuberculosis, with Ernest P. Bicknell as secretary, was formed. Two years earlier the Committee on the Prevention of Tuberculosis of the Visiting Nurse Association of Chicago had been organized.

In 1904 a Committee on Tuberculosis of the Illinois State Medical Society was formed, primarily for the purpose of securing a state sanatorium through legislative enactment.

Out of these early beginnings, and particularly from the work of the Visiting Nurse Association and the enthusiasm of the late Dr. Theodore B. Sachs, the Chicago Tuberculosis Institute was formed on May 1, 1906.   For nearly five years this association served both in the capacity of a local and state organization.

In June, 1910, at the stimulus of the National Tuberculosis Association, the Illinois Association for the Prevention of Tuberculosis was completely reorganized and an executive office was established in Chicago with Frank E. Wing as executive secretary and Arthur J. Strawson as assistant secretary.   The president of the Association was Dr. W. A. Evans.

Since 1910 the Illinois Association has carried on a progressive campaign of education and organization throughout the state.

The office was later moved to Springfield where it now is.

Dr. George Thomas Palmer, who has served as president of the

Illinois Tuberculosis Association since October, 1913, has been largely instrumental in the development of the state program. The interest of the Association centered first of all on the passage of legislation making possible municipal and county tuberculosis hospitals in the "down state" sections outside of Chicago. As a result of the activities of the Association following the passage of this legislation there are now in existence, or already provided for in the State of Illinois, outside of Chicago and Cook County, 62 tuberculosis hospitals with a bed capacity of 3,814. In addition there are 38 tuberculosis clinics, open-air schools, and over 100 public health nurses working largely in the rural sections of the state.

Most of the hospital and other provision for the care of the tuberculous has been secured by referendum campaigns. With very few exceptions, whenever the question of taxation for the establishment of a tuberculosis hospital and provision of other agencies for this disease has been put up to voters it has been passed by a large majority. In 1916, 8 communities voted for tuberculosis sanatoria, in 1918 there were 33, and in 1920 there were 6, a total of 47 provided for at such general elections. In this respect Illinois leads the country.

The creation of health promotion week, an educational campaign focusing attention on health during the session of the legislature, and the Sanatorium Pilgrimage, a tour of interested executives and physicians from one institution to another throughout the state, have been unique contributions to tuberculosis methods.

In 1920 the death-rate from tuberculosis in Illinois was 100.6.

The headquarters of the Illinois Tuberculosis Association are at 516 East Monroe Street, Springfield, Illinois, and the managing director is Mr. Joseph W. Becker

CHICAGO TUBERCULOSIS INSTITUTE

[*Note:* The Chicago Tuberculosis Institute is recognized by the National Tuberculosis Association as an affiliated association, and as such is treated in the same category with state associations.]

The Chicago Tuberculosis Institute was organized in May, 1906, to carry on the work of the Committee on the Prevention of Tuberculosis of the Chicago Visiting Nurse Association.

Dr. Theodore B. Sachs had in 1903 begun to lecture on tuberculosis, and had made a survey of the prevalence of tuberculosis in some of the congested districts of Chicago, the results of which were widely published.

Following the organization of the Institute, one of its first activities was the establishment of a tuberculosis camp, known as Camp Norwood, in which 20 tuberculous women were successfully treated in the open air during the winter of 1906–7. Camp Norwood was under the immediate direction of Dr. Theodore B. Sachs and Dr. Ethan A. Gray.

Directly following this came the erection of Edward Sanatorium at Naperville, Illinois. This institution, made possible through the generosity of Mrs. E. L. Gaylord, was placed under the direction of Dr. Sachs, and was intended for the care of people of moderate means. Later Dr. Sachs placed the sanatorium under the general authority of the Chicago Tuberculosis Institute as its sanatorium department. He remained in full charge of the institution until his death in 1916.

The opening of the sanatorium marked an interesting epoch. It was more than an attempt to provide institutional care. It was a definite protest against the all too prevalent view of the day that climate, and especially the southwestern climate, was necessary in the treatment of tuberculosis. At the Edward Sanatorium, the Chicago Tuberculosis Institute, under the leadership of Dr. Sachs, definitely proved, as had already been proved by Bowditch, Trudeau, King, Flick, and others on the Atlantic seaboard, that tuberculosis could be cured anywhere if proper medical supervision and the other requisites of hygiene and diet could be provided.

The Institute next established a chain of seven tuberculosis dispensaries under the direction of Dr. E. A. Gray. They were transferred to the control of the Municipal Sanitarium Board in 1910.

In 1908 the Chicago Tuberculosis Institute secured the passage of the original Glackin law, under which the city of Chicago was given permission to vote on the question of the establishment of the Municipal Tuberculosis Sanitarium. Immediately following the passage of the law the Institute conducted a whirlwind campaign the slogan of which was "Vote 'Yes' for the tuberculosis hospital!"   The proposition was carried by a large vote and assured a sufficient fund from taxation to make possible the Municipal Sanitarium.   It took nearly seven years of self-sacrificing and diligent work, the burden of which fell chiefly upon Dr. Sachs and Mr. Frank E. Wing, before the Municipal Sanitarium was opened in 1915.   There are few institutions in the United States that owe their existence more distinctly to the personal interest and clear vision of a non-official agency than the Chicago Municipal Tuberculosis Sanitarium.

With the Municipal Sanitarium, and under its supervision, there has been provided a chain of ten municipal tuberculosis dispensaries, a staff of tuberculosis nurses, and other facilities.

Chicago has also led the way, under the Tuberculosis Institute and the Elizabeth McCormick Memorial Fund, in the open-air school campaign.

In recent years the work of the Institute has been extended to Cook County, outside of Chicago, where it now maintains a corps of 15 nurses and a clinical director.   Twenty-four towns are now organized and coöperate with the Institute in the various phases of its work.

The death-rate from tuberculosis in Chicago in 1906 was 191.9. As a partial indication of the activity of the Chicago Tuberculosis Institute and the agencies which it has brought into existence, the death-rate from tuberculosis has declined in 1920 to 97.4.

The headquarters of the Chicago Tuberculosis Institute are at 8 South Dearborn Street, Chicago, Illinois, and the superintendent is Mr. James Minnick.

INDIANA TUBERCULOSIS ASSOCIATION

The first attempt at the organization of tuberculosis work in Indiana was the establishment of the Anti-Tuberculosis Society of Indiana in October, 1904, which followed the enthusiasm generated by a lecture given by Dr. S. A. Knopf.   The organization, however, never functioned and soon passed out of existence.

In 1907 the Indiana Association for the Prevention of Tuberculosis was formed, and carried on for a time a more or less desultory campaign, chiefly in Indianapolis.   A number of county organizations, existing largely on paper, were formed throughout the state.

In 1914 the National Tuberculosis Associations assisted in the reorganization of the Indiana Association, establishing the work on a firm business basis. Since that date the Association has made phenomenal progress. At the present time there are 89 city and county tuberculosis associations in the state, covering practically every community. Besides the State Sanatorium there are 5 county and municipal tuberculosis hospitals with a bed capacity of 564. There are 28 permanent tuberculosis clinics and 8 infant welfare clinics. There are 18 open-air schools or open-window rooms, and one preventorium. Fully 250 tuberculosis and public health nurses are working in the state either under official or non-official auspices.

The Indiana Association, through its legislative program, has made a distinct contribution to tuberculosis work in the state. The Association has been responsible for practically all of the legislation relative to the control of tuberculosis in Indiana, and assisted materially in bringing about the creation of the Bureau of Tuberculosis in the State Board of Health.

The death-rate from tuberculosis has shown a distinctly favorable downward trend, from 171.3 in 1907 to 108.8 in 1920.

The headquarters of the Indiana Tuberculosis Association are at 1134 K. of P. Building, Indianapolis, Indiana, and the executive secretary is Mr. Murray A. Auerbach.

IOWA TUBERCULOSIS ASSOCIATION

The history of tuberculosis work in Iowa illustrates the value and significance of a non-official agency in the public health movement. As early as 1905, an Iowa Association for the Study and Prevention of Tuberculosis was formed, but its activities were very limited, and after a brief career it ceased to exist except on paper.

Meanwhile, in 1907, the legislature made provision for an annual appropriation of $5,000 for a lecturer on tuberculosis, under the State Board of Control, and primarily for the development of an educational campaign against the disease. While the work of this department was well done, the Board, largely because it was an official body, was limited in its power to criticize or commend.

It was not until 1915 that the present State Association was organized, and the work of the Association, starting with a shoe string, has developed into one of the most vigorous and effective organizations in the entire State of Iowa. At the present time there are 29 local associations, The State Association coöperates with more than 15 different state-wide civic and social organizations, and has especially helpful coöperative arrangements with such public agencies as the Board of Control of State Institutions, the Board of Health, Department of Public Instruction, Housing Commission, Bureau of Animal Husbandry, State University, State Agricultural College, State Teachers' College, Governor's Office and Legislature. Six sanatoria, including a well run state sanatorium, with a bed capacity of 417, 13 clinics and dispensaries, 2 open-air schools and nearly 200 tuberculosis nurses make up in part the present fighting equipment against tuberculosis.

Iowa has been a leader in the development of the Modern Health Crusade. The silver loving cup, awarded by the National Tuberculosis Association, was won in the year 1920. At the present time Iowa and Idaho are in close competition for the permanent retention of this cup.

According to the 1920 report of the Association, no less than 1,300,000 pieces of printed matter have been distributed. The propaganda of the Association has extended into many avenues of social, civic and political life in the state covering schools, rural and farm organizations, industries, women's clubs, churches and many other similar organizations.

The headquarters of the Iowa Tuberculosis Association are at 518 Century Building, Des Moines, Iowa, and the executive secretary is Mr. T. J. Edmonds.

KANSAS STATE TUBERCULOSIS ASSOCIATION

As was the case in a number of other states, in Kansas the State Tuberculosis Association grew out of the International Congress Committee.

In the fall of 1908, a group of people interested in tuberculosis formed the Kansas Association for the Study and Prevention of Tuberculosis.

The State Association has always worked in very close relationship with the State Board of Health, largely because the primary enthusiasm and interest in the organization came from the State Health Officer, Dr. S. J. Crumbine and his associate, Dr. Charles H. Lerrigo.   The advantages of this close relationship have been many.

Because of the rural nature of the state and the absence of large centers of population the emphasis has been laid primarily upon nursing and general community welfare.

There are only two local sanatoria in Kansas besides the State Sanatorium, which serves practically the entire population. There are 5 dispensaries and a traveling clinic covering rural districts.   There are 8 special tuberculosis nurses, and in addition there are a large number of general public health nurses.

The Modern Health Crusade and other educational methods approved by the National Association have been vigorously pushed.

The death-rate in Kansas has always been low due largely to the character and constitution of the population.   There has, however, been a significant decline from 58.7 in 1914 to 48.2 in 1920.

The headquarters of the Kansas State Tuberculosis Association are at 601 Mills Building, Topeka, Kansas, and the executive secretary is Dr. Charles H. Lerrigo.

KENTUCKY TUBERCULOSIS ASSOCIATION

Organized tuberculosis work in Kentucky dates back to 1905 when the so-called Kentucky Anti-Tuberculosis Association was formed.   While the name of the Association indicates that it was a state-wide organization it functioned almost exclusively in Louisville and Jefferson County.   About the same time a local association was formed at Lexington.

Out of the Louisville Association grew the Hazelwood Sanatorium, the first institutional provision for the care of the tuberculous in the state, and later the Louisville Municipal Sanatorium, provided for in 1908.

In 1909 the Kentucky Association for the Study and Prevention of Tuberculosis was organized and opened an office in Louisville. Thus began the first real state-wide campaign against tuberculosis. Out of the activities of this Association grew the Kentucky Board of Tuberculosis Commissioners, established by act of legislature in 1912. With the establishment of this Board, the State Association, assuming that its work was completed, passed out of existence and turned over its work and property to the Board. By 1919, however, it became apparent to the National Tuberculosis Association that the state movement against tuberculosis, outside of a few of the larger centers, was not progressing as it should. In March of that year, accordingly, the entire work was reorganized. The present Kentucky Tuberculosis Association is a development from that reorganization.

Probably the most distinct feature of the campaign against tuberculosis in Kentucky at the present time is the close relationship, amounting almost to amalgamation, of the State Association with the State Board of Health. The public health leaders in Kentucky consider this intimate relationship as extremely advantageous. From the perspective of National Association, and in view of the inhibitions that such a close relationship compels, there is doubt in the minds of other leaders as to whether the union of the non-official state tuberculosis association with the state board of health is a wise and desirable procedure.

At the present time there are 5 sanatoria in Kentucky with a bed capacity of 396. There are 4 clinics and dispensaries and 3 open-air schools and classes. More than 50 county and rural public health nurses outside of the city of Louisville are giving considerable attention to tuberculosis. Within the city of Louisville there are some 20 more nurses.

Although Kentucky has a large Negro population the death-rate from tuberculosis has shown a consistent decline from 229.5 in 1911 to 152.9 in 1920.

The headquarters of the Kentucky Tuberculosis Association are at 532 West Main Street, Louisville, Kentucky, and the executive secretary is Dr. J. S. Lock.

LOUISIANA ANTI-TUBERCULOSIS LEAGUE

The Louisiana Anti-Tuberculosis League was formed in December, 1906, and was one of the first state associations in the south. For many years its activities centered largely about the city of New Orleans, but a number of local associations were formed prior to 1911 in various parishes and in the city of Shreveport.

As was the case with several of the state organizations established before the International Congress, one of the first problems of the Louisiana Anti-Tuberculosis League was the provision of institutional care for cases needing treatment.

In March, 1908, the tuberculosis camp of the Louisiana Anti-Tuberculosis League was opened. In the same year a tuberculosis clinic was established. The value of these two pioneer agencies in Louisiana can hardly be fully estimated. They have served as stimuli both to communities in Louisiana and other communities in the south.

At the present time there are a number of local associations in the state, but only a few of them are actively functioning. Besides the sanatorium of the Anti-Tuberculosis League, now known as Camp Hygeia, there is an excellent and up-to-date sanatorium, recently opened at Shreveport, a camp for Negroes and a camp for whites, with a certain amount of provision for both whites and Negroes in the State Charity Hospital at New Orleans. There are twelve public health nurses serving tuberculous cases and two special tuberculosis nurses, besides a number of other nurses.

A State Commission was provided by act of legislature in 1912. This Commission has plans for the establishment of one or more state sanatoria. The League has recently purchased a property at Greenwell Springs with the intention of giving it over to the Commission for a tuberculosis hospital.

The death-rate from tuberculosis in Louisiana in 1918 was 185.8, and in 1920 it was 141.2.

The tuberculosis problem is seriously complicated by the large number of Negroes in Louisiana.

The headquarters of the Louisiana Anti-Tuberculosis League are at 730 Common Street, New Orleans, Louisiana.

MAINE PUBLIC HEALTH ASSOCIATION

The first attempt at organization of tuberculosis work in Maine, was in 1901, when the Maine State Sanatorium Association was formed, with Dr. Estes Nichols as medical director, and Dr. A. G. Young, of the State Board of Health as secretary. The association was formed primarily to establish a tuberculosis sanatorium which was opened in Hebron in 1904 and which the Sanatorium Association operated until 1915 when it was taken over by the State at a nominal sum.

Largely through the influence of the original sanatorium group, the Central Maine Association for the relief and control of Tuberculosis, in 1911, opened a second sanatorium at Fairfield, Maine. In 1915 this sanatorium was taken over by the State at a nominal sum. A third state sanatorium at Presque Isle, was opened in 1920.

In 1908 largely as a result of the interest generated by the International Congress, the Maine Society for the Study and Prevention of Tuberculosis was formed. This organization did very little active work. It did lead, however, to the organization of the Maine Anti-Tuberculosis Association, in Lewiston in 1911, with Bishop Robert Codman as president and Dr. A. D. Downes, as secretary. Although its funds were limited, an executive secretary was engaged and a state-wide campaign was started.

Local tuberculosis activity had been developed in the meantime at Bangor, Lewiston, Waterville, Portland and in sections of Aroostook and Washington Counties.

In 1918 the association was re-christened and reorganized as the Maine Public Health Association, the general feeling being that the sparseness of the population made it undesirable to encourage a number of specialized state associations and that the entire tuberculosis and public health work would be furthered by one organization.

At the present time the State Association has a number of di visions such as tuberculosis, child welfare, cancer, prevention of blindness, social hygiene, dental hygiene, mental hygiene, etc.

In addition to the three state tuberculosis sanatoria at Hebron, Fairfield, and Presque Isle, with a total bed capacity of 297, there are the three private sanatoria and a hospital for tuberculous ex-service men, three tuberculosis dispensaries, four fresh-air schools, and twelve local associations.

The death-rate from tuberculosis in Maine has shown a steady decline from 149.6 in 1910 to 103.8 in 1920.

The headquarters of the Maine Public Health Association are at 318 Water Street, Augusta, Maine. The executive secretary is Mr. Walter D. Thurber.

MARYLAND TUBERCULOSIS ASSOCIATION

As has been pointed out elsewhere in these pages (see pp. 10 and 14), the campaign against tuberculosis in Maryland was among the earliest and best conceived of any of the state movements.

In 1902 the legislature of the state of Maryland passed a law authorizing the appointment of a tuberculosis commission to investigate the means of preventing tuberculosis in the state and the feasibility of establishing a state sanatorium. The men appointed by this commission were among the leaders in civic, social, and public health work of the state; such men as the late Sir William Osler, Dr. William H. Welch, Dr. Henry Barton Jacobs, Dr. John S. Fulton, Dr. William S. Thayer, and others. As a result of a survey conducted by this commission, the first well-developed effort of its kind, the Maryland Association for the Prevention and Relief of Tuberculosis was formed at the suggestion of the commission in December, 1904. The Association selected an executive secretary and began its active work in 1905.

One of the earliest activities was the development of the tuberculosis exhibit, which had been created by the commission in 1904, and was the first of its kind. As has been noted in other pages of this history (see p. 22), the national meeting, out of which the National Tuberculosis Association grew, was held in connection with this exhibit.

Under the leadership of the Maryland Association some of the pioneer tuberculosis nursing work of the country was developed. By 1907 the Association was supporting three special tuberculosis nurses, and its traveling exhibit had been seen by over 100,000 persons. Local associations had been established in two counties, a special tuberculosis dispensary had been located in one of the congested districts in Baltimore, and a considerable amount of other progressive work had been carried on.

In connection with the development of the state program in Maryland, mention should be made of the pioneer work of the Hospital for Consumptives of Maryland, popularly known as the Eudowood Sanatorium, located at Towson. This institution had been established in 1896 for white patients in the early stages of tuberculosis who were unable to pay for their full cost of maintenance in private institutions. It has been a pioneer in the development of the farm colony idea, and has contributed much to the interest in tuberculosis work throughout the state of Maryland.

There are at the present time 15 local associations in Maryland, a state sanatorium and 6 local sanatoria and hospitals with a combined bed capacity of 501, a preventorium, 13 clinics and dispensaries, 5 open-air schools, and approximately 175 public health and tuberculosis nurses. Of the 23 counties in the state, 14 are undertaking active educational work.

The Maryland Association was one of the earliest to develop the railroad car exhibit, and later to work out the automobile clinic and exhibit.

In 1919 the Association established a preventorium for children, and in 1921 secured the site for a Negro open-air health school, the first institution of its type to be proposed in this country.

The death-rate from tuberculosis in Maryland, in spite of the large Negro population, has shown a constant decline from 208.1 in 1906 to 165.8 in 1919, and 146.7 in 1920.

The headquarters of the Maryland Tuberculosis Association are at 704 North Howard Street, Baltimore, Maryland, and the executive secretary is Mr. A. E. Sinks.

MASSACHUSETTS TUBERCULOSIS LEAGUE

Although the campaign against tuberculosis in Massachusetts dates in point of development back at least to 1898, the Massachusetts Anti-Tuberculosis League was not formed until 1914.

In 1898, as is pointed out in Chapter XXXVII, Dr. Vincent Y. Bowditch secured from the legislature of Massachusetts an appropriation for the first state sanatorium, located at Rutland. The state sanatorium grew out of Dr. Bowditch's experience at the Sharon Sanatorium, established seven years earlier in 1891.

The interest of men like Dr. Bowditch, Dr. Edward O. Otis, Dr. James J. Minot, and others brought about, in 1903, the organization of the Boston Association for the Relief and Control of Tuberculosis.

In the same year a group of workers in Cambridge formed the Tuberculosis Aid and Education Association of Cambridge, now known as the Cambridge Anti-Tuberculosis Association.

For more than ten years the Boston Association served as a state association much in the same way as the Chicago Tuberculosis Institute had done in Illinois.   Local associations sprang up in various parts of the state, particularly in the larger centers of population.

In 1914, however, it became apparent that there was necessity for closer coördination as well as need for covering the territory more adequately.   Out of this need grew the Massachusetts Anti-Tuberculosis League in February, 1914.

Meanwhile, in 1907, largely as a result of the activity of the Boston group, a State Commission had been appointed to erect three tuberculosis hospitals in different parts of the state.

In 1906 the State Medical Society created a group of its local organizations on the prevention of tuberculosis.   All of its activities were later merged either in the State Department of Health, or in the new State Anti-Tuberculosis League.

Credit for the present existing machinery for the control of tuberculosis in Massachusetts belongs, therefore, not entirely to the State League, but to various agencies.   Much of it owes its existence to the Boston Association and to the other associations at Cambridge, Lawrence, Salem, New Bedford, Holyoke, Springfield, Fall River, and Brookline, all of which had been active for several years previous to the organization of the State League. Credit also belongs to the State Department of Health, including its district health officers and nurses, to the visiting nurses' associations, and to such men as the late Dr. William J. Gallivan, who were active in securing progressive health legislation before the State League was organized.

The work of the Massachusetts Tuberculosis League during its early history was conducted through the coöperation of the Boston Association, the League having no independent paid staff or offices of its own. Since 1918 the League has assumed full responsibility for state-wide activities, and has organized a large portion of the state on the county and district unit plan, and has increased its local Seal Sale Committee from 91 to 350.

At the present time there are in Massachusetts 4 state sanatoria, 6 county hospitals, 40 municipal and private institutions with a combined bed capacity of 4,356, which will be increased to approximately 5,000 when the county hospital program is completed. The county hospital law is mandatory and must be complied with not later than 1925. There are 56 tuberculosis dispensaries, 1 preventorium, 35 open-air schools registering 3,120 pupils, and about 800 public health nurses.

The passage of legislation making it mandatory for communities with a population of 10,000 or over to establish tuberculosis dispensaries, the provision of 4 state hospitals, the establishment of the Framingham Demonstration, and the reorganization of the State Department of Health are among the high lights of achievement to which the campaign against tuberculosis in Massachusetts has contributed very largely.

The mortality from tuberculosis in Massachusetts has been declining in recent years. In 1905 the death-rate was 192.7; in 1910 it was 162.7; in 1915 it was 141.6, and in 1920 it was 113.8.

The headquarters of the Massachusetts Tuberculosis League are located at 80 Boylston Street, Boston, Massachusetts, and the executive secretary is Mr. R. V. Spencer.

MICHIGAN TUBERCULOSIS ASSOCIATION

In February, 1908, the Michigan Association for the Prevention and Relief of Tuberculosis was formed, a group of physicians headed by Dr. Victor C. Vaughan, Jr. and Dr. A. S. Wharton of the University of Michigan Medical School being the leaders in the formation of the new organization.

As early as 1905 the Grand Rapids Tuberculosis Society had

been formed, and by 1908 it had already secured a municipal tuberculosis sanatorium.

The Detroit Society for the Study and Prevention of Tuberculosis had been organized in 1905. Except for these two centers, relatively little work in tuberculosis prevention had been done throughout the state.

The state sanatorium was established in 1907. Since that time 19 county sanatoria and one private sanatorium have come into existence or are provided for. There are 24 permanent local clinics and about as many irregular local clinics. The State Board of Health in coöperation with the State Association maintains a traveling clinic. There are 4 preventoria, 35 open-air schools, 12 special tuberculosis nurses, and approximately 150 other public health nurses.

The State Association has brought into existence local organizations in about 60 different communities. Most of the state is now covered with associations and in some of these full-time executives are employed.

One of the most significant achievements of the Michigan Association was the famous Michigan survey conducted from 1915 to 1917 by the State Board of Health in coöperation with the State Association, under an appropriation of $50,000. This survey was the first state-wide effort of its kind, and brought to light, in the rural communities particularly, a large amount of tuberculosis that was previously unknown.

The State Association followed up the survey in 1918–1920 with a series of traveling clinics working in coöperation with the State Board of Health. In this way many of the rural communities of the state have been able to secure expert diagnostic facilities which otherwise would have been impossible to them.

The death-rate in Michigan, as in most of the states bordering on the Great Lakes, has always been low, but as a result of the extensive activity of the State Association and the State Board of Health it has shown a steady decline from 99.3 in 1908 to 83.6 in 1920.

The headquarters of the Michigan Tuberculosis Association are at 209 Shiawassee St., West, Lansing, Michigan, and the executive secretary is Mr. Theodore J. Werle.

MINNESOTA PUBLIC HEALTH ASSOCIATION

One of the first expressions of tuberculosis activity in Minnesota was in 1901, when at the instance of a group of physicians, headed by Dr. H. Longstreet Taylor, the legislature passed an act providing for the establishment of a State Commission on Tuberculosis, one of the earliest bodies of its kind. The Commission was created primarily for the purpose of studying the advisability of a state sanatorium, which was opened in 1905.

The Associated Charities of Minneapolis at about the same time began to take a considerable amount of interest in tuberculosis, largely because of its contact with families in which the disease was present. In 1903, the Anti-Tuberculosis Committee of the Associated Charities of Minneapolis was formed and began a work which has been of great significance not only to Minnesota but to the entire country.

The Minnesota Association for the Prevention and Relief of Tuberculosis was organized in 1906, but for two years it remained in a somewhat dormant condition. In 1908 it was reorganized and an executive secretary was secured.

In July, 1914, the association was again reorganized under the name of the Minnesota Public Health Association although its program was and has been very largely a tuberculosis one.

As a result of the activities of the original state association, in 1913 the legislature passed a law providing for state aid in the erection and maintenance of county tuberculosis hospitals. The stimulus of state subsidy, together with the supervising oversight accorded to the State Commission as a result of the subsidy, has greatly helped in the establishment of county and district hospitals. At the present time hospitalization is available for practically every section of the state. There are 14 such local institutions besides the state sanatorium, with an aggregate bed capacity of 1,164.

The Association has developed 87 local affiliated organizations. There are a very large number of public health nurses working in coöperation with the county hospitals and in other ways.

The death-rate from tuberculosis in Minnesota has declined from 109.1 in 1910 to 89.5 in 1920.

The headquarters of the Minnesota Public Health Association are at 300 Shubert Building, St. Paul, Minnesota, and the executive secretary is Dr. William F. Wild.

MISSISSIPPI TUBERCULOSIS ASSOCIATION

The first attempt at organization of tuberculosis work in Mississippi was in 1907, when the Mississippi State Anti-Tuberculosis League was formed.   The Association, however, while starting out with a laudable purpose and with a certain amount of educational activity, did not long survive.   It was not until 1913 that another effort at organization was made when the Mississippi Anti-Tuberculosis Committee was formed with headquarters at Jackson.   The present Mississippi Tuberculosis Association is a rechristening of this earlier organization.   Considering the sparsity of population, the large Negro element and the lack of great industrial centers, Mississippi has made a record of itself in the development of tuberculosis work since 1913 of which it may well be proud.   Much still remains to be done, but the progress indicates favorable development in the future.

The national campaign of education, developed out of Christmas seal funds by the State Association, gradually bore fruit until in 1918 the Mississippi State Tuberculosis Sanatorium came into existence with Dr. Henry Boswell as superintendent.   With the opening of the sanatorium, the need for such an institution became more and more apparent.   In connection with the State Association, therefore, Dr. Boswell began a campaign before the meeting of legislature in 1919, which resulted in the hitherto unprecedented appropriation by the Mississippi Legislature of $1,000,000, for the enlargement of the state sanatorium and the extension of its work throughout the state.   The completed plan of the institution provides for 1,000 beds.   Less than five years ago there was not a single bed for the care of the tuberculous patients in Mississippi.

The State Association has also aroused interest locally and now has 22 affiliated county tuberculosis committees.   Besides the state sanatorium there is a county hospital.   The state also maintains an excellent traveling clinic and the State Association maintains a state nurse.   There are about 20 public health nurses.

All told, the stimulus that the tuberculosis campaign has given to public health work in Mississippi is truly remarkable.

The death-rate from tuberculosis in Mississippi in 1920 was 127.8.

The headquarters of the Mississippi Tuberculosis Association are in the Merchants Bank Building, Jackson, Mississippi, and the executive secretary is Mrs. R. S. Phifer, Jr.

MISSOURI TUBERCULOSIS ASSOCIATION

The earliest attempt at community organization for tuberculosis prevention in Missouri was in St. Louis. The local Society for the Prevention of Tuberculosis was organized in that city in May, 1904. Three years later, in 1907, the Missouri Association for the Relief and Control of Tuberculosis was formed. A state sanatorium had been assured by an act of legislature of 1905, furthered largely by Dr. James Stewart.

In 1910, a State Commission, supported by private funds, was appointed by the Governor and conducted a vigorous state-wide campaign on tuberculosis, the first effort of its kind. Following this campaign the work of the State Association lapsed somewhat until in the fall of 1911 when a reorganization was effected.

In 1918 the association's offices were moved from Columbia to St. Louis. The Missouri Tuberculosis Association conducts a unique and vigorous campaign of education centering largely about the public schools and the school machinery of the state. The Modern Health Crusade has been used since 1918 as the basis for this educational campaign. Legislation has been secured providing for: the strengthening of the State Board of Health including the establishment of a Division of Child Hygiene; state aid to county hospitals; municipal and county public health nurses; improving sanitary conditions in the lead and zinc mining districts as a means of lessening tuberculosis; and instruction in physical education in the public schools of the state, including the preparation of teachers, nurses and medical health supervisors for such service.

In St. Louis, the local tuberculosis society has developed its campaign independently of the State Association. There are few cities in the country where greater interest in tuberculosis has been aroused than in St. Louis.   A splendid corps of municipal tuberculosis nurses, a municipal sanatorium, a series of municipal tuberculosis clinics, a system of open-air schools and a developing plan on municipal control of tuberculosis, speak volumes for the educational work accomplished by the St. Louis Society.

In Kansas City, St. Joseph, Columbia and Springfield the local societies have been active in establishing open-air schools and tuberculosis visiting nurse service;   in Jasper County, a county tuberculosis hospital has been established and nurse service maintained.

In the state as a whole, the present machinery for the control of tuberculosis consists of 1 state sanatorium, 1 county hospital, 2 municipal hospitals, 1 night and day camp and 1 preventorium. Tuberculosis clinics are found in Kansas City, St. Joseph, Springfield, and St. Louis, 11 in all.   There are 3 open-air schools and about 150 nurses outside of St. Louis giving whole or part time to tuberculosis work.   Besides the larger cities of the state, several small cities conduct the physical examination of school children and maintain baby clinics.

The death-rate from tuberculosis in Missouri has declined from 154.6 in 1911 to 106.9 in 1920.

The headquarters of the Missouri Tuberculosis Association are located at 706 Pontiac Building, St. Louis, Missouri, and the executive secretary is Dr. W. McN. Miller.

MONTANA TUBERCULOSIS ASSOCIATION

In 1908 a Montana Association for the Prevention and Study of Tuberculosis was formed, but its existence was largely on paper as it never functioned in a state-wide capacity.   When the National Tuberculosis Association, therefore, in 1915 conducted a Christmas seal sale by mail for the benefit of a Montana Association it secured a welcome response and enough funds to assure the organization.

In June, 1916, a new association was organized and a sufficient fund was provided, together with a program, to assure continuity of work.

Montana is a state of huge distances and of difficult travel. Many of its counties are isolated for months at a time.   It is largely agricultural with a certain amount of mining industry. In view of these circumstances, the development of tuberculosis work in Montana is doubly significant.

In 1913 the state sanatorium was begun by act of legislature. It has now increased its capacity to 138. It is the only sanatorium in the state except for a federal institution exclusively for Indians. Besides the sanatorium there are 4 clinics, 3 full time health officers and about 30 public health nurses. The State Association has 4 local organizations. These figures, however, do not indicate the enormous amount of interest aroused by the Modern Health Crusade, poster and essay contests, exhibits, etc. throughout the state.

The State Association works in close coöperation with the State Board of Health and has hundreds of representatives in the women's clubs, rotary clubs, parent-teachers associations and similar organizations centered throughout the state. The unfavorable financial situation during the past four years has had some effect upon the development of active work in Montana, but this has not been so serious as to retard the work altogether, as will be noted from the figures and facts quoted above.

The death-rate from tuberculosis in Montana has declined from 107.3 in 1916 to 75.1 in 1920.

The headquarters of the Montana Tuberculosis Association are at the State Capitol, Helena, Montana, and the executive secretary is Mrs. Sara E. Morse.

NEBRASKA TUBERCULOSIS ASSOCIATION

The Nebraska Association for the Study and Prevention of Tuberculosis, out of which the present association has grown, was formed in December, 1907. Its secretary, Mrs. K. R. J. Edholm, has served in that capacity since June, 1908.

The present equipment for the prevention of tuberculosis in Nebraska consists of a state sanatorium, established in 1912, one county pavilion, two clinics, two open-air classes, three special tuberculosis nurses, and a very considerable number of city and county school nurses and Red Cross nurses who devote a certain amount of attention to tuberculosis.

Under the direction of the Nebraska Association, and partially financed by the National Association, a thorough survey of the Winnebago Indians was made in 1919 and 1920.   The survey has been published by the Nebraska Historical Society.

The death-rate from tuberculosis in Nebraska was 43.0 in 1920.

The headquarters of the Nebraska Tuberculosis Association are located at 483 Brandeis Theatre Building, Omaha, Nebraska, and the executive secretary is Mrs. K. R. J. Edholm.

NEVADA PUBLIC HEALTH ASSOCIATION

The Nevada Public Health Association was organized in 1916, on much the same basis as the associations in Idaho, Montana and Wyoming.   All of these associations were formed out of funds secured through the Christmas seal sale by the National Association.

The entire population of the State of Nevada, according to the 1921 census, was only 77,000, less than the population of a city like Trenton, New Jersey, or Syracuse, New York.   The problem of developing a state-wide interest in public health and tuberculosis under such circumstances will readily be seen to present peculiar difficulties.   It is gratifying, however, to note that in the last five years the State Association has developed an unusual amount of interest in tuberculosis.   A very considerable number of patients have been taken care of, chiefly in California institutions.   The Modern Health Crusade has been extended throughout the schools.   The mining camps have spread information about health and disease.   At least six public health nurses have been secured for state or local work.   At present there is a determined effort to secure some definite state provision for tuberculosis patients and for the development of a better state public health system.   It is not too much to say that all this interest and activity can be traced to the Nevada Public Health Association.

The headquarters of the Nevada Public Health Association are at Reno, Nevada, and the secretary is Mrs. Martha O. Davis.

NEW HAMPSHIRE TUBERCULOSIS ASSOCIATION

The earliest history of tuberculosis activity in New Hampshire is that of a commission appointed by joint resolution of the legislature in 1901.   The report of this commission led to the establishment of the New Hampshire State Sanatorium in 1909. In many respects the New Hampshire Commission report of 1902 ranks with the now famous Maryland Commission report of about the same time.

In 1904 the New Hampshire Society for the Prevention of Consumption was formed. The membership was largely medical. As the society lacked funds it soon passed out of existence.

As early as 1901 a local sanatorium at Concord (the Pembroke Sanatorium) had been established, the first institution for the treatment of tuberculosis in the state.

After the New Hampshire Society for the Prevention of Consumption had ceased to be active, the New Hampshire Red Cross took an interest in the development of tuberculosis work, and for several years fostered interest both in the Pembroke Sanatorium and to a certain degree in educational effort.

In 1916, at the instance of the National Tuberculosis Association, the work of the state was reorganized and the present New Hampshire Tuberculosis Association was formed. The remarkable development of tuberculosis activity in New Hampshire since that time is due largely to the activity of the state association.

Besides the state sanatorium and the Pembroke Sanatorium there is only one other institution that makes provision for tuberculous patients in the state. The total bed capacity for tuberculous patients is 207. There are 20 tuberculosis clinics. At the present time there are 12 nurses whose entire time is devoted to case finding and educational work, both in the homes and the community, and about 170 public health nurses engaged in various forms of public health work throughout the state. Many of these give valuable assistance to the tuberculosis nurse and coöperate in every way.

The constructive educational campaign being carried on throughout the state utilizes every device for the promotion of its work. The Modern Health Crusade is particularly active. Through the state association, facilities are available for the advice, diagnosis and treatment of patients in any part of the state.

Since 1916 the death-rate from tuberculosis in New Hampshire has shown a drop from 114.5 to 97.0 in 1920.

The headquarters of the New Hampshire Tuberculosis Association are located in the Manchester City Mission Building, Merrimac and Beech Streets, Manchester, New Hampshire, and the executive secretary is Dr. Robert B. Kerr.

NEW JERSEY TUBERCULOSIS LEAGUE

The first organization for the prevention of tuberculosis in New Jersey was the Anti-Tuberculosis Committee of the Oranges, established in 1904.

The New Jersey Association for the Prevention and Relief of Tuberculosis was established in 1906, with headquarters in Newark.   For seven years the association conducted a more or less active campaign until, in 1913, it became necessary to reorganize the work.   By that time local associations had been formed in most of the larger cities in the state.   The state association became, as in the case of Massachusetts, a league of societies as its name implies.   It has, since reorganization, gone beyond the original limits set for the League, and developed a large amount of unorganized territory in the localities where it has not been possible up to this time to organize local associations.   There are 38 local associations definitely affiliated with the League, indicating that the state is fairly well served, especially in view of the fact that most of the local associations have full-time executives.

Under the county hospital laws of 1910 and 1912 the League has developed 9 county hospitals and 4 city sanatoria.   In addition there is the state sanatorium and one private sanatorium, with a total bed capacity of 1,688.   There are 18 clinics and dispensaries, 5 camps, 2 preventoria, and 40 open-air classes. Eighty-four towns and cities have public health nursing service, the number of nurses being considerably in excess of the number of towns.

The legislative activity of the State League, besides that already mentioned, has resulted in the prevention of public spitting, the abolition of the roller towel and public drinking cup, better housing laws, improved factory conditions, and the compulsory reporting of tuberculosis.

The educational campaign of the State League and its affiliated local groups has been broad and extensive and, furthermore, has been intensive enough to reach practically every group in the population.

The mortality from tuberculosis in 1906 was 196.0, and in 1920, 114.0.

The headquarters of the New Jersey Tuberculosis League are at 45 Clinton Street, Newark, New Jersey, and the secretary is Mr. Ernest D. Easton.

NEW MEXICO TUBERCULOSIS ASSOCIATION

The first state association in New Mexico was the New Mexico Society for the Study and Prevention of Tuberculosis, formed in 1909, a development of the International Congress Committee. This society, however, never functioned as a state-wide organization and, except for a small amount of activity centered largely in Albuquerque, its headquarters did very little work.

In 1917, at the instance of the National Association, the society was reorganized under the name of the New Mexico Public Health Association with an executive office in Albuquerque.

The tuberculosis problem in New Mexico is complicated by three outstanding factors; first, the indigent migratory consumptive; second, the large Mexican population, and third, the scattered character of the communities. Considering these three conditions, the development of tuberculosis work in New Mexico since 1917, under the leadership largely of the State Association, has been remarkable in many ways.

One of the first tasks of the Association was to secure, in co operation with the United States Public Health Service, legislation providing for a State Department of Health with a full-time health officer. The outgrowth of this legislation has been the se curing of full-time county health officers in several of the counties of the state.

A traveling clinic, in 1919, covered many of the Spanish-speaking districts of the state, and for the first time brought the message of tuberculosis and its prevention to these villages.

8

The Modern Health Crusade has, during the last year, been presented to over 20,000 children. There has also been a very considerable amount of education on tuberculosis in other ways.

New Mexico is a health resort state. It has no provision for the local care of tuberculous patients.

There are 18 sanatoria but they are all private institutions. Through the activity of the State Association and the State Department of Health, however, there are nearly 20 public health nurses now working in New Mexico. The public health interest centers largely about tuberculosis and child welfare.

The headquarters of the New Mexico Tuberculosis Association are at Albuquerque, New Mexico.

NEW YORK STATE TUBERCULOSIS ASSOCIATION

[*Note:* The work of the New York City and Brooklyn Tuberculosis organizations will be treated under separate sections.]

The campaign against tuberculosis in New York State, outside of Greater New York, has since 1907 been conducted by the Committee on Prevention of Tuberculosis of the State Charities Aid Association recently reorganized into the Committee on Tuberculosis and Public Health.

In July 1907 the Russell Sage Foundation, at that time recently established, made available a sum of money to the State Charities Aid Association for the development of a state-wide campaign against tuberculosis in New York with a view to demonstrating the possibility of organization on a state basis. Up to that time none of the state tuberculosis associations in the United States had had sufficient funds with which to organize a proper campaign. The first task of the new committee, under the immediate direction of John A. Kingsbury and the general supervision of Homer Folks, the general secretary of the State Charities Aid Association, was to reach, with an exhibit and an educational campaign, the larger cities of the state.

By 1908 it became apparent that the immediate need of the state was local hospital provision.

In 1909 a law was enacted providing for county tuberculosis hospitals. Then began a campaign which had for its slogan "No uncared-for tuberculosis in New York State." The following out

of that slogan has resulted, by January 1, 1922, in the establishment of county hospitals in 37 counties. In addition the City of
Buffalo has provided 2 municipal institutions. Municipal provision has also been secured in Albany, and the capacity of the
State Sanatorium at Raybrook has been doubled.

The total bed capacity of New York State, outside of New
York City in 1907 was 324. On January 1, 1922, the total bed
capacity in New York State was 3,360. Along with this progressive growth in institutional provision has gone a corresponding
development in dispensaries, nurses, open-air schools, preventoria
and similar agencies. By this time there are 68 sanatoria, 40 dispensaries, 232 nurses, 49 open-air schools, and 4 preventoria.

Furthermore the archaic public health law of New York, at the
instance of the State Tuberculosis Committee, was completely
revised and an up-to-date department of health was created,
placing New York State in a leading position for the entire country. The significance of this public health law with its district
supervisors and its entire machinery for relaying the state health
facilities to the local health departments can hardly be overestimated in the prevention of tuberculosis.

As might have been expected, the State Tuberculosis Committee has been obliged to organize its work extensively throughout
the state. During the formative period of this work it formed
a large number of county and local committees, over 300 all told.
More recently, however, the development has been along intensive
lines, particularly in the formation of strong county associations
with full-time paid executives. At the present time there are 52
such associations, and in addition there are other local committees.

The New York State Committee's campaign is probably the
most striking example of the way in which a non-official voluntary
association can by intensive effort secure institutions, nurses, dispensaries and other machinery for the control of tuberculosis.
The amount of money spent by the state committee and its affiliated agencies is relatively small when compared with the millions
of dollars invested from public funds and the hundreds of thousands of dollars being spent each year from the same sources.

The death-rate from tuberculosis in New York State, outside

of Greater New York, has steadily declined.*   In 1907 it was 152.7.   In 1915 it was 135.9.   In 1920 it was 112.4.

The headquarters of the Committee on Tuberculosis and Public Health of the State Charities Aid Association (New York State Association) are at 105 East 22d Street, New York City, and the executive secretary is Mr. George J. Nelbach.

NEW YORK TUBERCULOSIS ASSOCIATION

[*Note:* This section will treat of the work of the New York Tuberculosis Association covering the boroughs of Manhattan, Bronx and Richmond of Greater New York.   The next section will treat of the work of the boroughs of Brooklyn and Queens.]

Organized tuberculosis work in New York City dates back to the year 1902 when the Committee on Prevention of Tuberculosis of the Charity Organization Society of New York was formed (see page 18).   The work was carried on under this committee until 1919 when the New York Tuberculosis Association was formed, taking over the activities of the committee.

Among the first local tuberculosis associations to develop an active program for prevention of tuberculosis was the New York Committee.   Its first secretary was Paul Kennaday.   A handbook on the prevention of tuberculosis was published by the committee as its first annual report.   This document was one of the first attempts in this country to point out the social incidence of tuberculosis.

In 1904, a directory of institutions and societies dealing with tuberculosis in the United States and Canada was published, the first of a series since continued by the National Tuberculosis Association.

The New York Committee continued its activities, working with various groups such as the medical society, labor union, industrial organizations, department of health and similar groups.   Through its coöperation with the city administration, the institutional facilities of New York were greatly expanded, first in the provision of a sanatorium at Otisville, then in the establishment of a large

---

* These rates are not directly available from the mortality records of the U. S. Census Bureau.   They were obtained by using the deaths in N. Y. State outside of N. Y. City as given by the Census Bureau and the estimated midyear populations for the given years.

hospital for moderately advanced cases at Staten Island, and later in the development of an admirable system of tuberculosis clinics, public and private, under the Association of Tuberculosis Clinics. The Committee was also responsible for the introduction of open-air classes in the schools, and the New York Association still exercises a degree of supervision over this valuable adjunct for the building up of children.

The Committee coöperated with the department of health in the securing of more than 150 tuberculosis and public health nurses, and in other ways stimulated the increased budgets for the city departments dealing with tuberculosis.

The Committee also took an active part in state legislation, particularly the modification of tenement house laws and the development of New York's Health Department.

In 1919, following the first attempt at a Greater City Christmas seal sale, the New York Tuberculosis Association was organized with Dr. James Alexander Miller as its president.

One of the most significant activities of the Association since its development has been the establishment of a vocational workshop largely for ex-service men who have had sanatorium treatment. The shop follows the lines of activity successfully developed by the Altro Manufacturing Company, conducted by the Committee on the Care of Jewish Tuberculous.

The New York Association has also succeeded in developing strong work in the outlying boroughs of the Bronx and Richmond.

The traveling exhibit of former years has been expanded into a full and complete health exhibit with social workers, lecturers, and even a physician in attendance to answer requests for information with real knowledge as against the usual method of having only ordinary attendants at such exhibits.

The educational work being carried on among labor unions and industrial organizations is particularly worthy of mention as well as the work in the schools.

A notable movement in the anti-tuberculosis field in New York City is that of the auxiliaries or committees of women attached to many of the tuberculosis clinics which not only have undertaken to provide funds for emergency relief, but, especially in the cases of the New York Society for the Prevention and Relief of

Tuberculosis and the Woman's Auxiliary to the Bellevue Tuberculosis Clinic, have stepped into the breach and have organized day camps and nurseries, have supported educational classes, and strengthened the clinic work wherever it needed support. These auxiliaries under the leadership of the New York Tuberculosis Association, have been confederated into an organization known as the Associated Tuberculosis Auxiliaries.

In connection with the work of the New York Tuberculosis Association mention should be made also of the activities of the New York Association for Improving the Condition of the Poor, under the leadership of Bailey B. Burritt. This Association, while largely a relief agency, has been instrumental in developing a unique contribution to tuberculosis methodology, namely, the Home Hospital. Here the tuberculous patient and his family may receive treatment under home environment, with intensive medical and nursing care approximating that secured in a sanatorium.

The death rate from tuberculosis in Greater New York has declined from 240.6 in 1902 to 127.8 in 1920.

The headquarters of the New York Tuberculosis Association are at 10 East 39th Street, New York City, and the Director is Mr. J. Byron Deacon.

COMMITTEE ON THE PREVENTION OF TUBERCULOSIS OF THE BROOKLYN BUREAU OF CHARITIES

[*Note:* This section will treat of the work in the boroughs of Brooklyn and Queens of the city of Greater New York.]

Organized tuberculosis work in Brooklyn dates back to 1905, when the Committee on the Prevention of Tuberculosis of the Brooklyn Bureau of Charities was formed. It is interesting to note that in Brooklyn, as in Manhattan, the original tuberculosis committee was a branch of the leading relief organization of the city. This committee relationship in Brooklyn is still maintained. There is no independent tuberculosis association as in Manhattan.

The Brooklyn Committee has made a number of signal contributions to tuberculosis work in that borough, and in the country at large, notably the development of the Medford Sanatorium, through the active participation, financial and otherwise, of the Brooklyn Federation of Labor; the perfection of the ferry-boat day camp service in coöperation with the city department of health; organization of one of the first health centers in the city, and the early use of health places as a means of education on tuberculosis.

In 1919, following the Greater New York Christmas seal sale, to which reference has been made in the preceding section, a committee covering the Borough of Queens was organized under the supervision of the Brooklyn Committee.

In 1921 the Queens Committee became an independent association known as the Queens County Tuberculosis Association. This organization is now developing an extensive educational campaign throughout this large and diversified borough of Greater New York.

The death-rates from tuberculosis given in the preceding section for New York city apply to Greater New York and include Brooklyn and Queens. The same relative decline in this borough has been marked as in the whole city.

The headquarters of the Committee on the Prevention of Tuberculosis of the Brooklyn Bureau of Charities are at 69 Schermerhorn Street, Brooklyn, New York. Dr. Thomas J. Riley is the general secretary and Mr. Nels A. Nelson is the secretary.

NORTH CAROLINA TUBERCULOSIS ASSOCIATION

In 1906 a North Carolina Association for the Prevention of Tuberculosis was organized. With no money and without a very definite program, the Association soon passed out of existence.

In 1913, at the suggestion of the National Tuberculosis Association, a Red Cross Seal Commission for North Carolina was formed. Out of the energetic activity of that commission a new state association, known as the North Carolina Tuberculosis Association, was organized in 1920. The Red Cross Seal Commission, from its beginning in 1913, was closely related to the State Bureau of Tuberculosis and the State Sanatorium, of which Dr. L. B. McBrayer was the head, and has naturally developed its program in close coöperation with these official agencies.

The formation of the independent association in 1920 grew

out of the feeling that an independent association could be more effective and more representative of the state as a whole.

The tuberculosis program in North Carolina has shown distinct advance, particularly in the development of educational work for Negroes, public health nursing, the admirable state sanatorium, and medical education. The traveling clinic of the state association has also been a distinct feature of the work.

At the present time, beside the state sanatorium, with a capacity for 200 white patients and a state sanatorium for Negroes in process of erection, there are two county sanatoria with a bed capacity for 48 white and colored, and two other county sanatoria in process of erection, to cost $100,000 and $150,000 respectively, both maintained by tax, six private sanatoria, one general hospital with a tuberculosis pavilion, four tuberculosis clinics, and 45 public health nurses doing tuberculosis work.

The death-rate from tuberculosis in North Carolina in 1916 was 147.2. In 1920 it had declined to 116.5.

The headquarters of the North Carolina Tuberculosis Association are at Sanatorium, North Carolina, and the executive secretary is Dr. L. B. McBrayer.

NORTH DAKOTA TUBERCULOSIS ASSOCIATION

The original stimulus for organization of the North Dakota Anti-Tuberculosis Association came from a group of people who had been interested in tuberculosis work at the International Congress.

In 1909 the North Dakota Anti-Tuberculosis Association was formed. Its first activity was to urge the establishment of a state sanatorium, which was opened in 1911. The activity of the state association has resulted since then in the expansion of the state sanatorium to a bed capacity of 140, and in the establishment of two open-air schools and several open-window rooms, and about 35 public health nurses. The traveling clinic of the association is also a feature of its work.

The original group of workers in North Dakota, as in most states, was hardly a dozen people. Today the entire state is aroused and active in the fight against tuberculosis.

The headquarters of the North Dakota Tuberculosis Association are in the Tribune Building, Bismarck, North Dakota, and the executive secretary is Miss Carrie Haugen.

OHIO PUBLIC HEALTH ASSOCIATION

The Ohio Society for the Prevention of Tuberculosis, formed in the fall of 1901, is, next to the Pennsylvania Society for the Prevention of Tuberculosis, the earliest state association still in existence.

In 1902 a state commission was formed which presented a report to the legislature and was discharged from office in 1903.

The original Ohio Society existed for a number of years without a very active program. In the fall of 1908 it was reorganized on a firmer financial basis and has since that time been a leader in the development of the tuberculosis and public health program in the state of Ohio.

In 1911 the Society was incorporated.

In 1920 it was entirely reorganized under the name of Ohio Public Health Association.

In Ohio, largely as a result of the activity of the state associa tion, the tuberculosis campaign has developed intensively in most parts of the state. There are 12 district sanatoria serving practi cally all of the populous counties of the state. In addition there are 51 clinics, 20 camps, 650 public health nurses most of whom do tuberculosis work, and 69 local associations.

Among the principal achievements of the Ohio Association have been the establishment of the Ohio State Sanatorium, the passage of the county and district hospital law and the subsequent establishment of institutions, the establishment of a Division of Tuberculosis in the State Department of Health, the first in the United States, a very remarkable development in public health nursing, the establishment of a department of public health and sanitation in the state university, the reorganization of the state and local health departments of the state and the subsequent increase in the number of full-time local health officers, and the general development of the program along broad public health lines.

The death rate in Ohio has shown an interesting decline from 150.8 in 1910 to 102.8 in 1920.

The headquarters of the Ohio Public Health Association are at

83 South 4th Street, Columbus, Ohio, and the executive secretary is Dr. Robert G. Paterson.

OKLAHOMA PUBLIC HEALTH ASSOCIATION

The earliest recorded attempt at tuberculosis organization in Oklahoma was the formation of the Oklahoma City Anti-Tuberculosis League in 1908. No records are available regarding the later history of this association, which seems to have gone out of existence shortly after its formation.

In 1910 the Oklahoma State Anti-Tuberculosis Association was formed. This association existed for seven years, conducting a somewhat cursory campaign of education throughout the state.

· In 1917 it became necessary to reorganize the work. Through the field staff of the National Tuberculosis Association the present tuberculosis association was formed, with an entirely new board and a new executive secretary. Without any immediate capital, but with a Christmas seal sale ahead, the Association undertook a vigorous campaign of education and organization which resulted in the first year in securing nearly $40,000. Since that time the Association has steadily progressed. In 1919 the name of the Association was changed to the Oklahoma Public Health Association. Its educational work has been unique and has set an example for many other public health associations.

The development of the Modern Health Crusade, the use of posters, publication of bulletins, newspaper publicity, films and lantern slides, and the use of exhibits are only a few of the many educational methods employed.

Demonstration public health nurses engaged in welfare and school nursing surveys have been furnished to about 25 communities for periods of from two weeks to two months each. The public health surveys, conducted in eight of the largest cities in the state in 1918-1919, received national recognition for their remarkable thoroughness.

Almost entirely as a result of the activity of the Oklahoma Association there are now in the state 10 local associations, 65 county public health committees, 3 state sanatoria, 1 county sanatorium, 1 state sanatorium for tuberculous ex-service men, 2 county clinics, a summer camp, 2 open-air schools, and nearly 40 nurses working in whole or in part in the tuberculosis campaign.

The headquarters of the Oklahoma Public Health Association are at 315 Oklahoman Building, Oklahoma City, Oklahoma, and the acting secretary is Miss Helen M. Hastings.

OREGON TUBERCULOSIS ASSOCIATION

Out of the State Committee for the International Congress an Oregon State Association for the Study and Prevention of Tuberculosis was formed in December, 1908. Like several similar organizations its existence was soon terminated because of lack of funds.

Even before 1908, the Portland Open Air Sanatorium for the treatment of tuberculosis had been established in 1905. Dr. Woods Hutchinson, who was State Health Officer of Oregon from 1903 to 1905, interested Mr. A. L. Mills of Portland and some others in the establishment of a camp for tuberculosis patients. Out of this plan developed the Portland Open Air Sanatorium, the pioneer sanatorium in the entire Pacific Northwest. The influence of this institution has radiated far and wide in that part of the United States.

In 1909, the Visiting Nurses' Association of Portland established a tuberculosis division and for nearly six years it served as a pioneer, the only tuberculosis association in the entire state of Oregon.

For two or three years prior to 1915, the State Federation of Women's Clubs had conducted a seal sale, and had carried on a certain amount of tuberculosis relief work. In 1915 a state association was organized under the direction of the National Tuberculosis Association. The difficulties of finance delayed rapid progress, but the association has steadily gone forward until in 1922 there are 16 local associations besides the original Visiting Nurses' Association in Portland, a state tuberculosis hospital, 2 private tuberculosis hospitals, 1 clinic, 1 open-air school and 3 open-air classes, and 16 county public health nurses. The State Association has also secured a Bureau of Public Health Nursing in the State Board of Health. Too much cannot be said of the

pioneer work of the association in rural counties with sparse popu
lation aggregating as large an area as whole states like Connecti
cut.   Figures do not indicate the full achievement of the State
Association.   The organization has made itself felt in every part
of the state, and has brought public health to the front in a strik
ing way.

The death-rate from tuberculosis in Oregon in 1920 was 89.1.

The headquarters of the Oregon Tuberculosis Association are
at 1010 Selling Building, Portland, Oregon, and the executive
secretary is Mrs. Saidie Orr-Dunbar.

PENNSYLVANIA TUBERCULOSIS SOCIETY

[*Note:* This section discusses tuberculosis work in Pennsylvania outside
of Allegheny County and Pittsburgh which is treated separately in the following section.]

The Pennsylvania Society for the Prevention of Tuberculosis,
formed in 1892, is the first tuberculosis association on record
anywhere in the world.   It grew out of the interest and experience of Dr. Lawrence F. Flick, of Philadelphia (see Chapter LX).

The institutional care of the tuberculous had received earlier
consideration in Philadelphia and Boston than in any other
parts of the United States.   The hospital for diseases of the
lungs at Chestnut Hill, Philadelphia, dates back to 1876.

The formation of the Pennsylvania Society, however, was a
definite move on the part of Dr. Flick and his associates to
spread information about tuberculosis in the poorer districts
of Philadelphia.   For nearly twenty years the work of the
Pennsylvania Society was concentrated largely in Philadelphia.
Since 1908 its program has been increasingly state-wide.

At the present time there are about 100 local associations
outside of Allegheny County.   There are in Pennsylvania 24
sanatoria and special tuberculosis hospitals, with a capacity of
3,924.   Three of these are state sanatoria, with a combined
bed capacity of over 2,000.   The State Department of Health
conducts 90 tuberculosis clinics, with the coöperation of tuberculosis and other agencies.   Besides the nurses connected with
these clinics, there are about 1,000 other public nurses in the
state.   There are 20 open-air schools and classes.

In 1921 the Pennsylvania Society coöperated with the State Department of Health in securing the passage of a bill authorizing county tuberculosis hospitals, reversing the policy that had existed in the State Department of Health for nearly fifteen years. Referendum campaigns in the fall of 1921 resulted in the establishment of seven hospitals.

Henry Phipps Institute for the Study and Prevention of Tuberculosis, established in 1903, also through the interest of Dr. Flick, has exercised a marked influence upon the development of tuberculosis work throughout the state, as well as in the city of Philadelphia. Through its clinical and pathologic research its influence has been cast throughout the United States; in fact, throughout the country.

The result of organized tuberculosis work in Pennsylvania is exhibited in the decline in death-rate from 150.9 in 1906, 133.7 in 1910, and 105.0 in 1920.

The headquarters of the Pennsylvania Tuberculosis Society are at 10 South 18th Street, Philadelphia, Pa., and the executive secretary is Mr. Arthur M. Dewees.

TUBERCULOSIS LEAGUE OF PITTSBURGH

The Tuberculosis League of Pittsburgh was organized in February, 1907, first under the name of Pittsburgh Sanatorium and then under its present name, after consolidating with the Pittsburgh Association for the Prevention of Tuberculosis. For various reasons, the Pittsburgh League, covering Allegheny County, operates independently of the state association and in direct affiliation with the National Association.

The Tuberculosis League operates a hospital, a central dispensary and five division dispensaries, a research laboratory, an educational division in conjunction with the public school system; is the center of education for the undergraduate medical students of the University of Pittsburgh; provides special training and postgraduate training in coöperation with the hospitals and Public Health Nursing Association for this district, and operates an open-air school in conjunction with the board of education.

Under the auspices of the League the second open-air school in the United States was formed, and the first open-air school in an orphanage. One of the first attempts in training undergraduate nurses in tuberculosis was made at the hospital of the League.

The death-rate from tuberculosis in Pittsburgh in 1908 was 146.2 and in 1920 was 120.0.

The headquarters of the Tuberculosis League of Pittsburgh are at Bedford and Wandless Streets. The medical director is Dr. William Charles White, and the superintendent, Miss Alice E. Stewart.

PHILIPPINE ISLANDS ANTI-TUBERCULOSIS SOCIETY

At a meeting of the Philippine Islands Medical Association, in the spring of 1908, a committee consisting of Dr. Richard P. Strong, now with the League of Red Cross Societies, and Dr. Harry T. Marshall, now Dean of the University of Virginia, was appointed to confer with the National Tuberculosis Association relative to the possibilities of coöperation in an educational campaign in the Islands. Out of the work of this committee grew the Philippine Islands Anti-Tuberculosis Society formed in 1910. The Society was fortunate in securing close coöperation and patronage of the United States Public Health Service, and for several years was actively directed by Dr. Victor G. Heiser, now with the International Health Board. The unusually high caliber of medical men connected with the association in its initial stages has given it a firm foundation.

In recent years the general direction and supervision of the Society has been largely under native auspices. The tuberculosis work is subsidized from government sources, and is also supported in part from voluntary contributions. Christmas seals have been sold in the Philippine Islands for several years past.

The general plan of campaign now being employed covers practically all of the approved methods used in continental United States.

In 1920 the Society showed its progressive interest by sending Dr. Carmelo Peñaflor, one of the members of its staff, to this country for a period of study.

At the present time there are in the Philippine Islands four institutions for the care of the tuberculous, with a combined bed capacity of 285, and ten tuberculosis despensaries.

The headquarters of the Philippine Islands Anti-Tuberculosis Society are in the Fajard Building, Manila, Philippine Islands, and the secretary is Dr. Antonio Hernandez.

ANTI-TUBERCULOSIS LEAGUE OF PORTO RICO

As in the Philippine Islands, the activities of the United States Public Health Service furnished the indirect inspiration for the establishment of an association. In the spring of 1906 the Anti-Tuberculosis League of Porto Rico was formed. Its chief purpose was the establishment of a sanatorium which was opened in 1907 at San Juan. There are now two sanatoria, providing 75 beds.

The interest of the League, unlike that in the Philippine Islands, however, has been centered largely on institutional care.

During its early years, with a small government subsidy, a small amount of educational work was carried on throughout the island, but within recent years the League has had practically no territorial program. An effort is now being made to reorganize the League.

RHODE ISLAND TUBERCULOSIS ASSOCIATION

Before a state association was formed in Rhode Island, active anti-tuberculosis work had been started in Newport with the formation of the Newport Association for the Relief and Control of Tuberculosis. Dr. Henry Barton Jacobs, of Baltimore, who was one of the founders of the National Tuberculosis Association, was largely instrumental in the establishment of this local organization in Rhode Island. At the time of the formation of the National Association, in 1904, it was one of the few local associations in the entire country that had a paid executive secretary.

The Rhode Island Anti-Tuberculosis Association was formed in the fall of 1907, and since that date has had an enviable reputation as a state-wide organization. The activity of a group of physicians, largely in Providence, was responsible for the formation of the state association.

Definite legislation on tuberculosis in Rhode Island dates back to 1894, when an act was passed authorizing the State Board of Health to investigate the causes and prevention of tuberculosis, and appropriated $1,000 for the purpose.   In 1901 another thousand dollars was appropriated for a similar purpose.

In 1902 a commission was formed to consider the establishment of a state sanatorium, which was opened in 1905.   In the same year the St. Joseph's Hospital of Providence opened an annex for tuberculosis patients.

From these facts it will be seen that there was a considerable amount of early interest in tuberculosis in Rhode Island.

One of the most significant contributions of Rhode Island to the tuberculosis movement was the establishment of the first open-air school in 1908.

The state association has been influential also in promoting an extensive educational campaign extending into every section of the state and well organized through the various industries of the state.

At the present time there are 21 local tuberculosis associations in Rhode Island.   Besides the state sanatorium and the state hospital for advanced cases, located at Wallum Lake, there are five other institutions, providing a total bed capacity of 604. There is also a preventorium of 50 beds for children predisposed to tuberculosis.   The state has nine dispensaries and clinics. There are 112 public health nurses in Rhode Island, representing practically every community in the state.   Because of its small area, this state has been intensively organized.

The death-rate from tuberculosis in Rhode Island has declined from 198.5 in 1907 to 131.3 in 1920.

The headquarters of the Rhode Island Tuberculosis Association are at 109 Washington Street, Providence, Rhode Island, and the executive secretary is Mr. Willis E. Chandler.

SOUTH CAROLINA TUBERCULOSIS ASSOCIATION

Previous to the formation of the South Carolina Tuberculosis Association, in March, 1917, there had been in existence a number of local associations in various parts of the state. The Richland Association at Columbia built a camp for incipient cases in 1914, and carried on some educational work. The Greenville Association also had established a camp.

In 1913 a state-wide Christmas seal sale was held under the

direction of a Red Cross Seal Commission. For three years funds were accumulated in this way, and in 1917 a full-fledged state association took the place of the commission. In spite of unusual financial difficulties, inherent both in the sparsity and character of the population as well as in the cotton and tobacco situation of recent years, the South Carolina Association has been able to maintain its executive office and has stimulated an increasing amount of local interest in tuberculosis.

The presence of the state sanatorium and well-developed work in such centers as Columbia, Charleston, and Greenville, are evidences of its activity.

The present institutional facilities of the state represent practically 100 per cent gain over those in existence five years ago. Besides a state sanatorium for white and colored patients, there are three county hospitals and one private sanatorium, the Aiken Cottage Sanatorium, operated largely for northern patients, and opened in 1896 (see p. 10). There are three permanent clinics, two open-air schools, and over 90 public health nurses doing some form of tuberculosis work.

The death-rate from tuberculosis in South Carolina in 1916 was 146.1, and in 1920 it was 120.0.

The headquarters of the South Carolina Tuberculosis Association are at 209–210 Liberty Bank Building, Columbia, South Carolina, and the field secretary is Miss Chauncey Blackburn.

SOUTH DAKOTA PUBLIC HEALTH ASSOCIATION

The present South Dakota Public Health Association and, in fact, practically all of the present tuberculosis and public health movement in the state, with the possible exception of the state sanatorium, owes its existence directly or indirectly to the enthusiasm of one woman, a Mrs. E. P. Wanzer, of Armour. In 1913 Mrs. Wanzer was interested in the Christmas seal sale and was made chairman of a temporary Red Cross Seal Commission created by the National Association. At that time the State of South Dakota never had seen a public health nurse. No campaign for health education had ever been carried on in the state. The entire appropriation for the State Board of Health amounted to only $600. With relatively little instruction, but with a great

9

deal of enthusiasm and with the wide acquaintance and splendid coöperation of the women's organizations of the state, Mrs. Wanzer began a campaign which in its historical development is one of the most remarkable of any state campaigns in the United States. Considering that the entire population of South Dakota is only a little over 635,000, and considering the large area of the state, the difficulties of organization will be readily appreciated.

Probably the principal contribution of the South Dakota Association has been in the number of public health nurses. There are now 32 nurses doing community work throughout the state. There is a state sanatorium and two other sanatoria with a combined capacity of 285. The Modern Health Crusade has been organized in practically all of the schools.. The message of tuberculosis and public health has been carried largely by the women's clubs and allied organizations into almost every village, town, and hamlet, even in the remotest portions of the state. With this message has gone the Christmas seal. In 1920 the per capita sale of seals in South Dakota amounted to 5.4. The State Board of Health has now been completely reorganized and is gradually coming up to the standard of similar bodies in neighboring states.

Out of the Red Cross Seal Commission of South Dakota the South Dakota Public Health Association was formed in 1920. The work is now on a firm foundation, strongly entrenched and well supported.

The headquarters of the South Dakota Public Health Association are at Huron, South Dakota, and the managing director is Mr. H. M. Cass.

TENNESSEE ANTI-TUBERCULOSIS ASSOCIATION

Tuberculosis work in Tennessee dates back to 1906 when the Nashville Anti-Consumption League was formed following the American exhibit of the National Tuberculosis Association. The League, however, soon passed out of existence for lack of funds. Other local associations were formed from time to time, but none of them maintained an active program.

In 1912 the Tennessee Anti-Tuberculosis Association was established with headquarters at Nashville. In 1916 it became necessary to reorganize the association. Since this latter date state-wide work has developed rapidly.

There are now three county hospitals and three other tuberculosis sanatoria with a total number of 465 beds. There are five tuberculosis dispensaries and 15 others furnishing opportunity for diagnosis. There are three open-air schools and over 50 public health nurses.

The State Association works in close coöperation with the Peabody College for Teachers, and has been influential, through that institution, in developing public health instruction for nurses and others.

In 1920 the State Association formed the Tennessee Colored Anti-Tuberculosis Society which has, since that time, been doing valuable educational work among the Negroes throughout the state.

The new county hospital at Memphis (The Oakdale Memorial Sanatorium) and the Pine Breeze Sanatorium at Chattanooga, a semi-private institution for local patients, are two of the finest institutions of their type in the south.

The death rate from tuberculosis in Tennessee was 199.1 in 1917 and 164.6 in 1920.

The headquarters of the Tennessee Anti-Tuberculosis Association are at 309 Church Street, Nashville, Tennessee, and the executive secretary is Mr. James P. Kranz.

TEXAS PUBLIC HEALTH ASSOCIATION

Out of the state committee for the International Congress the Texas Anti-Tuberculosis Association was formed in the fall of 1908, with headquarters at Austin. For about four years the association did little or no active work. In 1912 an executive secretary was secured and the first attempt at a state-wide campaign against tuberculosis was begun. A county hospital law was passed at the instance of the organization in 1913.

In 1917 the work was reorganized under the name of the Texas Public Health Association. Since that date the association has conducted a broad educational campaign on tuberculosis and public health and has succeeded in organizing many of the larger local centers in this, the largest state of the union. The difficulties of organization in Texas may be visualized when one considers that it takes 36 hours to travel from El Paso to Austin.

The problem of the indigent migratory consumptive is an acute one in Texas.   In 1909 an attempt was made to arrive at a solution of the problem by securing an appropriation of $10,000, to return indigent migratory cases to their homes, but this did not produce the desired effect.

The State Association has been and is still coöperating with the American Legion in the building of a tuberculosis hospital for ex-service men.   The state operates a sanatorium with 360 beds. When the plans for the American Legion Sanatorium are completed the capacity of the state institution will be increased to 600 beds.   Besides the state sanatorium, there are now five county tuberculosis hospitals, six clinics, 13 local associations, and a very large number of public health nurses doing tuberculosis work. Because of the large Mexican and Negro population in Texas, special secretaries for each of these groups have been provided by the State Association.

The headquarters of the Texas Public Health Association are at 616 Littlefield Building, Austin, Texas, and the executive secretary is Mr. D. E. Breed.

UTAH PUBLIC HEALTH ASSOCIATION

The Utah Public Health Association grew out of a "nest-egg" secured by the National Tuberculosis Association in a Christmas seal sale in the fall of 1915.   One-thousand dollars was secured in this way and with this little fund the Utah Association was formed in the fall of 1916, and an executive secretary was secured.   The multiplication of the original $1,000 has made the present organization possible.

The progress of the work in Utah may be indicated by the seal sale in 1921 which amounted to $28,000.

While the State of Utah had had, for several years prior to the formation of a state association, an active health officer in the person of Dr. T. B. Beatty, the development of tuberculosis and public health work since 1916 has clearly shown the wisdom and need for a non-official agency.

The amount of interest aroused in Utah by newspaper publicity, posters, the Modern Health Crusade and other forms of educational propaganda is almost incredible when compared with that of 1916.   Besides the methods just mentioned, the Association has used health clowns, motion pictures, clean school contests, and its monthly journal to good advantage.   At the present time, the only bed contribution in the state of Utah is a tuberculosis ward in the Salt Lake County Hospital, accommodating 25 patients.   There is now on foot an extended agitation to secure a state sanatorium at the next session of the legislature.   There are 53 public health and school nurses.

In 1921 the State Association, in coöperation with the State Board of Health and the United States Public Health Service, organized a traveling clinic which is touring every part of the state examining for tuberculosis and children's diseases especially, and conducting an educational campaign along public health lines.

The death rate from tuberculosis in Utah has declined from 50.7 in 1916 to 39.1 in 1920.

The headquarters of the Utah Public Health Association are in the State Capitol Building, Salt Lake City, Utah, and the executive secretary is Mr. James H. Wallis.

VERMONT TUBERCULOSIS ASSOCIATION

That Vermont should have taken an early interest in tuberculosis might logically be presumed by those who know of the pioneer health activities of the State Board of Health under the leadership of the late Dr. Henry D. Holton.

In 1902 a commission of five was appointed by the Governor to investigate the extent of tuberculosis, and for several years this commission, with an annual appropriation from the legisla ture, carried on an extensive educational campaign throughout the state.   In this same year tuberculosis was made a reportable disease by act of the legislature, one of the earliest state laws of this character in the country.

The Vermont Society for the Study and Prevention of Tuberculosis was also formed in 1902, but no records are available to indicate that it ever functioned in any capacity.

Four years later, in 1906, the Vermont State Anti-Tuberculosis Society was organized, but, like its predecessor, it apparently has no history of activity.

In 1907 the Vermont Sanatorium at Pittsford was opened.

This sanatorium is a gift to the state of Vermont from the late Senator Redfield Proctor. The Proctor family, whose large marble quarry interests are centered in Vermont, have been very generous in furthering tuberculosis work in that state.

For several years prior to 1916, and after the establishment of the Vermont Sanatorium, the Vermont Red Cross Chapter was practically the only agency in the state attempting to do tuberculosis work on a state-wide basis. Because of lack of funds this organization accomplished very little.

In 1916, at the instance of the National Tuberculosis Association, the Vermont Tuberculosis Association was formed, and sufficient funds were secured at once to appoint an executive secretary. Since that date the Association has steadily advanced the tuberculosis work of Vermont. At the present time, besides the sanatorium mentioned with a bed capacity of 47, and a county sanatorium of 46 beds, there are 15 clinics, a preventorium, and 5 nurses doing tuberculosis work. The association employs a physician who has had special training in the diagnosis of tuberculosis, and has an arrangement of part time with two other physicians who are specially qualified for this work. The educational campaign is carried on by lectures, distribution of printed matter, the Modern Health Crusade, a monthly story paper for children, motion pictures, etc.

In 1920 the preliminary results of a preventorium established by the state association moved two citizens to offer 45 acres and $50,000 for a new preventorium, providing the people of the state contributed a like amount for the general work of the Vermont Association. As a result, nearly $55,000 was raised. This assured the new preventorium, which will be opened in 1922.

The State of Vermont appropriates $50,000 annually for the care of indigent tuberculous patients in hospitals.

The National Tuberculosis Association has for several years, ending with 1921, conducted a study of tuberculosis among the granite workers of Barre, which study has contributed greatly to a better knowledge of the prevention of tuberculosis in this dominant industry of the state.

The death-rate from tuberculosis in Vermont has steadily declined from 113.4 in 1910, to 110.8 in 1916, and 81.8 in 1920.

The headquarters of the Vermont Tuberculosis Association are at 139 Church Street, Burlington, Vermont, and the secretary is Mr. Harold W. Slocum.

VIRGINIA TUBERCULOSIS ASSOCIATION

The Virginia Anti-Tuberculosis Association was formed in October, 1909, largely as a result of the interest of Captain W. W. Baker and some of his associates, of the State Board of Health, in tuberculosis.

Previous to the formation of the State Association the Anti-Tuberculosis League of Norfolk had been organized in 1906, and was at that time conducting an active work. The State Association's program remained somewhat indefinite for a number of years until in 1915, under the leadership of Miss Agnes D. Randolph, it began to arouse general interest throughout the state in tuberculosis. Since that date the tuberculosis campaign in Virginia has shown steady progress.

A state sanatorium had been established in 1909, but after the formation of the State Association it was considerably expanded until its present bed capacity is 300. In addition to this Catawba State Sanatorium there are two other state sanatoria, one of which is exclusively for Negro patients, one of the pioneer institutions of its type in this country. With the private tuberculosis hospitals and other institutional facilities the bed capacity for tuberculosis in Virginia is 750. There are 17 open-air schools, 172 public health nurses, (exclusive of Metropolitan whole time nurses) 7 dispensaries and clinics, and 19 local associations affiliated with the State Association. At the present time there is a Division of Tuberculosis in the State Board of Health which has been coöperating with the State Association in the development of traveling clinics and diagnostic facilities for rural districts.

Virginia has also been successful in developing a very large amount of organization and active work among the Negroes of the State. The establishment of the Piedmont Negro State Sanatorium has been of great value in arousing interest. The Negro

Organization Society donated $5,000 as the initial gift in the establishment of this institution.

Mortality from tuberculosis work in Virginia has declined from a death-rate of 167.6 in 1913 to 142.9 in 1920.

The headquarters of the Virginia Tuberculosis Association are located at 611 Chamber of Commerce Building, Richmond, Virginia, and the executive secretary is Mr. Irving Lewis Spear.

WASHINGTON TUBERCULOSIS ASSOCIATION

The Washington Tuberculosis Association formed in September, 1907, as the Washington Association for the Prevention and Relief of Tuberculosis, represents the first organized activity against tuberculosis in the Pacific Northwest. The Association has set an example for the neighboring states of Oregon, Idaho, Utah, Nevada and Montana in the steady development of work against tuberculosis. The first few years of work were largely spent in laying foundations and in general education.

In 1910 a more intensive program was begun and three years later, in 1913, an act was passed as a result of the State Association's activity, authorizing counties to erect sanatoria for the care of the tuberculous and to employ public health nurses, whose first duty was to be the care and instruction of tuberculous cases. An appropriation of $50,000 was made with this act to provide state subsidies of $3.00 a week (in 1919 raised to $5.00) for local patients of such hospitals. This was one of the earliest state subsidy acts in the country.

The energetic leadership of the present executive secretary, Mrs. Bethesda Beals Buchanan, who has been with the Association since 1910, has contributed largely to its present development. The program has always been educational but has centered about the formation of county anti-tuberculosis leagues and assisting them to secure the establishment of institutions and the county nursing service. As a result of this program there are at the present time in Washington 30 such county leagues. There are 4 county sanatoria, 1 municipal sanatorium and 1 private sanatorium. There are 24 clinics and dispensaries operating in connection with the sanatoria or under the Association and leagues, and 117 nurses in the various phases of public health work.   Practically all of this work has been established since 1913.

As a further indication of the development of interest in tuberculosis work it is interesting to note that in 1910 only 618 cases of tuberculosis were reported although 1,197 deaths from the disease were recorded in that year.   In 1920, 6,888 cases were reported and 1,320 deaths.   The value of educational propaganda is indicated in these figures.   The mortality in the state of Washington has always been low, due largely to the racial and age composition of the population.   In 1913 it was 102.4 and in 1920 it was 98.4.

The headquarters of the Washington Tuberculosis Association are at 601–603 Thompson Building, Seattle, Washington, and the executive secretary is Mrs. B. B. Buchanan.

WEST VIRGINIA TUBERCULOSIS ASSOCIATION

The West Virginia Anti-Tuberculosis League was formed in the fall of 1908, and grew out of the interest of a group of women headed by Dr. Harriet B. Jones, of Wheeling, whose enthusiasm had been aroused at the International Congress.   Too much cannot be said of the self-sacrificing, enthusiastic service of Dr. Jones in the development of state tuberculosis work in West Virginia.

One of the first acts of the new state association was to secure a resolution at a special session of the state legislature, called for this purpose, appointing a committee of five to make a study of tuberculosis in the state and to report on a state sanatorium. It was not until January, 1913, however, that the state sanatorium was opened at Terra Alta.

Meanwhile the state association, under the leadership of Dr. Jones, kept steadily promoting interest in tuberculosis work. Active groups in Wheeling, Charleston, and New Martinsville were formed early in the movement, and contributed largely to the success of the state organization.

In 1913 an appropriation of $9,900 for a two-year campaign against tuberculosis was secured from the legislature. With this money Dr. Jones and her associates toured the most remote sections of the state, penetrating into districts where the message of tuberculosis and health education had never before reached.

Thousands of miles were covered on foot and in automobile, and a very considerable portion of the population was reached.

In 1920 it became necessary to reorganize the association. Since that time the work has developed on a broader basis, with more funds and greater interest.

At the present time there are 39 local committees, 2 state sanatoria, 1 of which is for Negroes, 2 local sanatoria, 8 tuberculosis clinics, 1 preventorium, 3 open-air schools and classes, and 36 nurses doing tuberculosis work.

The headquarters of the West Virginia Tuberculosis Association are at Room 412, Davidson Building, 910 Quarrier Street, Charleston, West Virginia, and the executive secretary is Mr. George C. Rowell.

WISCONSIN ANTI-TUBERCULOSIS ASSOCIATION

Active interest in tuberculosis in Wisconsin began about 1903 when a state tuberculosis commission was appointed by act of legislature, to investigate the prevalence of tuberculosis and to report on the desirability of establishing a state sanatorium.   The report of this commission was a noteworthy document and was widely circulated.

In 1905 the legislature made an appropriation for the establishment of a sanatorium which was opened in 1907.   In the same year, 1907, tuberculosis was included in the list of diseases to be reported by physicians.

In June, 1908, the Wisconsin Anti-Tuberculosis Association was organized from the state committee of the International Congress. Since that date Wisconsin has carried on one of the most active and unique campaigns against tuberculosis and for the promotion of public health of any state in the Union.   The leader in this campaign, since the beginning, has been Dr. Hoyt E. Dearholt.

Following a general campaign of education in which the Christmas seal played a prominent part (Wisconsin had its own Christmas seal before the Red Cross seal became generally known), in 1911 the State Association secured a law authorizing the establishment of county hospitals and providing for a state subsidy.

Unlike most of the state associations in the country, the Wisconsin Anti-Tuberculosis Association has always proceeded upon the policy that a strong centralized association is preferable to the ordinary procedure of strong local associations with a relatively strong state body. The State Association has, therefore, made itself much more felt in local communities throughout the state than has been the case in many other parts of the country. There are 62 affiliated organizations.

Out of the leadership of the Wisconsin State Association and as a result of the county sanatorium law of 1911 there have been opened in that state, besides the state sanatorium, a state convalescent forestry camp and 14 county sanatoria. In addition there is one semi-philanthropic sanatorium and one private sanatorium. The total bed capacity of Wisconsin is 1,400. The State Association operates a demonstration and traveling clinic and conducts public health courses for graduate nurses and social workers. Through demonstrating nurses sent from the office of the State Association, Wisconsin communities became familiar with the public health nurse.* The contributions of the Wisconsin Anti-Tuberculosis Association to educational methods have been many. It was one of the first states to utilize the motorcycle and automobile for campaigning in rural districts. Its early rural surveys opened the eyes of the country to the prevalence of tuberculosis in rural districts. Its children's work, through the Modern Health Crusade health stories and the Christmas seal sale, and in other ways, has been widely imitated.

The close coördination of the state association with the extension work of the University of Wisconsin has been a remarkable factor in contributing to the success of the state program.

The decline of the tuberculosis death-rate in Wisconsin has been steady. In 1908 the death rate was 109.3. In 1915 it was 95.8. In 1920 it was 85.6.

The headquarters of the Wisconsin Anti-Tuberculosis Association are at 558 Jefferson Street, Milwaukee, Wisconsin, and the executive secretary is Dr. Hoyt E. Dearholt.

* The employment of a nurse or health instructor in every county is now compulsory.

WYOMING PUBLIC HEALTH ASSOCIATION

The Wyoming Public Health Association is a direct outgrowth from the Christmas seal sale. The association was formed in 1916, following a Christmas seal sale conducted by the National Tuberculosis Association the preceding year.

With a population of no more than that of the city of Syracuse or Scranton, Wyoming, in both 1916 and 1917 won the National per capita banner for the sale of Christmas seals, selling over a million in 1917.

Wyoming was the last state in the Northwest Division (perhaps in the U. S.) to form and organize a public health association. It is the youngest in anti-tuberculosis work.

When the association was started there was practically no interest in tuberculosis work. The State Board of Health was largely apathetic, and in the state at large tuberculosis was not supposed to be a problem of sufficient moment to be given consideration.

The Wyoming Public Health Association has clearly demonstrated that tuberculosis is not only a serious problem, but the most serious disease problem of the state. Surveys have clearly established this fact. As a result of these surveys, the Christmas seal sale, the Modern Health Crusade and other methods of education, there are now five public health nurses doing tuberculosis work, and a number of other nurses will soon be actively engaged in different parts of the state. The State Board of Health has been completely reorganized, and a full-time health officer has been secured. Legislation is being considered to make provision for tuberculous patients. The largest financial interests in the state are taking an active part in the tuberculosis campaign. What it means to arouse interest in a state with so sparse a population as that of Wyoming and an area equal to all of the New England states is difficult for one who has not lived in Wyoming to appreciate. The steady development of interest in tuberculosis and public health in that state is highly gratifying to those who have been in close touch with it.

The headquarters of the Wyoming Public Health Association are located at Industrial Club, Box 637, Cheyenne, Wyoming, and the executive secretary is Miss Etta M. Dobbin.

CHAPTER IX

THE SIXTH INTERNATIONAL CONGRESS

By PHILIP P. JACOBS, Ph.D.

AS HAS been pointed out elsewhere in these pages, the National Tuberculosis Association really grew out of discussions centering around an International Congress on Tuberculosis. The confusion incident to the proposals of Clark Bell and Dr. Daniel Lewis and the discussions pro and con concerning the merits of their respective congresses crystallized a growing desire for a national association that might represent the United States properly in any such international gathering.

After The National Association for the Study and Prevention of Tuberculosis was formed in 1904, one of the first acts of the board of directors was to take up the question of an international meeting of some sort to be held in the United States.

In 1905 Dr. Hermann M. Biggs, Dr. Lawrence F. Flick, Dr. William Osler, Dr. Henry Barton Jacobs, and others represented The National Association for the Study and Prevention of Tuberculosis at the Fifth International Congress on Tuberculosis held in Paris; Medical Inspector Henry G. Beyer, of the U. S. Navy, representing the United States Government. Acting as spokesman for the United States organization, Dr. Flick presented its invitation to the International Congress to meet in this country in 1908. The invitation was seconded by Dr. Henry Barton Jacobs on behalf of the Association. But as a rule of the Congress prevented it from accepting any invitation which did not come from the government of the country extending the invitation, Dr. Jacobs cabled to Dr. William H. Welch to secure from Mr. Roosevelt, the President of the United States, such an invitation and transmit it through the American Embassy in Paris. Immediately on receipt of the cable Dr. Welch went to Washington and secured the invitation to meet in the United States in 1908, which was accepted unanimously.

To the board of directors of the infant national association, struggling hard to raise a budget of $10,000, the assumption of such responsibility as an International Congress indicated great faith in the giving public of the United States. It was estimated by various members of the board that to bring an International Congress here, to house it properly, and to conduct it in a manner compatible with the dignity of this country would cost at least $100,000, and probably considerably more. In December, 1905, Dr. Flick proposed to the board of directors a plan for raising the money and for organizing the Congress. Briefly stated, Dr. Flick's plan included, among other features:

1. That 20 men be secured to give $5,000 each, these men to act as patrons of the Congress and to become life members of the association.

2. That the interest on this $100,000 be allowed to accumulate and be set aside for prizes of various kinds to be awarded in connection with the Congress.

3. That the Congress be held in Washington and that it extend over a period of at least three weeks.

The board of directors approved of the general plan outlined by Dr. Flick and appointed him as a committee of one to take action at once to put the plan of raising money into effect. Dr. Flick associated with himself in this initial effort, as members of his committee, Dr. Vincent Y. Bowditch, of Boston, Dr. Alfred Meyer, of New York, Dr. Lawrence Litchfield, of Pittsburgh, and Dr. Joseph Walsh and Dr. Charles J. Hatfield, of Philadelphia. By the end of the year 1906 this committee had collected between $30,000 and $35,000, chiefly in large contributions.

The committee, which was enlarged from time to time by the addition of representative men and women, held meetings at monthly intervals beginning with December 18, 1906. During the fall of 1906 Dr. John S. Fulton, of Baltimore, secretary of the State Board of Health of Maryland, was engaged as secretary-general of the Congress. Most of the administrative work devolved upon Dr. Fulton. At the meetings of the committee the general policies were worked out and the outlines of the Congress were decided upon. Committees of various kinds were appointed. The executive committee of the Congress consisted of Dr. Flick, as chairman, Dr. Livingston Farrand, at that time the executive secretary of The National Association for the Study and Prevention of Tuberculosis, Dr. Joseph Walsh, of Philadelphia, and Dr. John S. Fulton, the secretary-general.

Volume V of the Transactions of the Sixth International Congress contains a complete list of all of the officers, committees, and sub-committees. It will not be necessary to give them in detail in this place.

In the spring of 1907 it became necessary to expand the scope and membership of the original committee, headed by Dr. Flick. It also became necessary to elect a president of the Congress. Dr. William H. Welch was elected president, but he found it impossible to serve. After a considerable amount of discussion it was decided by the board of directors of The National Association for the Study and Prevention of Tuberculosis, under whose auspices the entire Congress was conducted, to select the Honorable Theodore Roosevelt, then President of the United States, as President of the Congress. Dr. Edward Livingston Trudeau, of Saranac Lake, Dr. Robert Koch, of Berlin, Dr. Louis Landouzy, of Paris, and Dr. C. Theodore Williams, of London, were elected honorary vice-presidents. On May 12, 1908, President Roosevelt sent his acceptance of the presidency of the International Congress in the following letter:

THE WHITE HOUSE,
Washington, May 5, 1908.

Sir: It is with great pleasure that I accept the presidency of "The International Congress on Tuberculosis" which is to meet in this city on September 21, 1908, and extend its session to October 12, 1908. Official duties, however, may prevent my presiding at the initial meeting of the Congress, in which case I will deputize Secretary Cortelyou.

The importance of the crusade against tuberculosis, in the interest of which this Congress convenes, cannot be overestimated when it is realized that tuberculosis costs our country two hundred thousand lives a year, and the entire world over a million lives a year, besides constituting a most serious handicap to material progress, prosperity, and happiness, and being an enormous expense to society, most often in those walks of life where the burden is least bearable.

Science has demonstrated that this disease can be stamped out, but the rapidity and completeness with which this can be accomplished depend upon the promptness with which the new doctrine about tuberculosis can be inculcated into the minds of the people and engrafted upon our customs, habits, and laws. The presence in our midst of representatives of world-wide workers in this magnificent cause gives an unusual opportunity for accelerating the educational part of the process.

The modern crusade against tuberculosis brings hope and bright prospects of recovery to hundreds of thousands of victims of the disease, who under old teachings were abandoned to despair. The work of the Congress will bring the results of the latest studies and investigations before the profession at large and place in the hands of our physicians all the newest and most approved methods of treating the disease—a knowledge which will add many years of valuable life to our people and will thereby increase our public wealth and happiness.

The International Congress on Tuberculosis is in the interest of universal peace. By joining in such warfare against a common foe the peoples of the world are brought closer together and made to better realize the brotherhood of man; for a united interest against a common foe fosters universal friendship. Our country, which is honored this year as the host of other nations in this great gathering of leaders and experts, and as the custodian of the magnificent exhibit which will be set up by the entire world, should manifest its appreciation by giving the Congress a setting worthy of the cause, of our guests, and of ourselves. We should endeavor to make it the greatest and most fruitful Congress which has yet been held, and I assure you of my interest and services to that end.

With expressions of appreciation for the compliment conferred in extending the invitation to become president of the Congress.

Very respectfully,
(Signed) THEODORE ROOSEVELT.

The dates of the Congress were definitely fixed for September 28 to October 12, 1908. For some time there was doubt as to the actual housing arrangements for the meeting, but after considerable negotiation arrangements were made through a special appropriation of the Congress of the United States of $40,000 for the use of the National Museum Building, at that time just nearing completion. All of the sessions and the exhibit of the Congress were held in this building.

For about a year and a half prior to the Congress itself, under the leadership of Dr. Fulton and his staff, an extensive organization and educational campaign was carried out. In every state of the Union special committees were formed, for the most part under the patronage of the health departments and the governors of the states. A vigorous publicity campaign was conducted, with a favorable response from the newspapers of the country. A considerable amount of printed matter, consisting of posters, circulars, booklets, and similar material, was distributed. The aims of the Congress were presented by word of mouth to all of the leading medical and health organizations at that time in existence. In foreign countries similar committees were organized and similar propaganda was conducted.

In preparation for the Congress itself an elaborate exhibit representing tuberculosis work throughout the world was prepared. No similar exhibit has ever been gathered together either in this country or elsewhere. The greater part of the main floor of the large National Museum Building was given over to the purpose. Arrangements for the exhibit itself were perfected by the late Dr. Henry G. Beyer, U.S.N., who served as director of the exhibit. Much of the detail work in arranging and managing the exhibit was carried on by E. G. Routzahn, at that time director of the traveling exhibit of the National Association and at the present time associate director of the Department of Surveys and Exhibits of the Russell Sage Foundation. A complete description of all of the exhibits, with a list of winners of prizes, will be found in Volume V of the Transactions of the Sixth International Congress. As a matter of historical record, however, it will be significant to mention in this place that, after the close of the International Congress, most of the exhibit was shipped intact to New York and set up in the American Museum of Natural History, where for a month hundreds of thousands of people viewed it. Following the exhibit in New York, it was also shown in Philadelphia.

Regarding the Congress itself, the eight volumes of Transactions, authorized by the general committee and prepared jointly by the Committee on Printing and Publication, the Editorial and the Executive Committees, give such voluminous details that only a comparatively brief mention need be made in this place.

The Congress opened in the Assembly Hall of the new National Museum on the morning of September 28. The Secretary of the Treasury, the Honorable George Bruce Cortelyou, called the meeting to order and formally announced the names of the hon-

10

orary vice-presidents.   The opening ceremonies were of a most impressive character.   Following addresses of welcome by Secretary Cortelyou, and the Honorable Henry B. Macfarland, President of the Commissioners of the District of Columbia, representative delegates from the following 'participating countries responded, outlining in brief the organization of the campaign against tuberculosis in their respective countries: Dr. Fermin Rodriguez, Jr., of Argentina; Dr. Hermann von Schrötter and Dr. Laislaus Detre, of Austria-Hungary; Professor Josef Denys, of Belgium; Mr. Sylvino Gurgel do Amaral, of Brazil; Dr. Arthur Newsholme, of the British Government; Dr. Frederick Montizambert, of Canada; Dr. L. Sierra, of Chile; Dr. Shinfwe P. M. Jee, of China; Dr. Juan J. Ulloa, of Costa Rica; Dr. Joaquin L. Jacobsen, of Cuba; Dr. Bernard Bang, of Denmark; Dr. C. W. Richardson, of Ecuador; Dr. J. B. Piot (Bey), of Egypt; Professor Dr. Louis Landouzy, of France; Professor Robert Koch, of Germany; Mr. Lambros Coromilas, of Greece; Dr. Ramon Bengoechea, of Guatemala; Professor N. Ph. Tendeloo, of Holland; Dr. Antonio Stella, of Italy; Professor Dr. S. Kitasato, of Japan; Dr. Eduardo Liceaga, of Mexico; Dr. F. Harbitz, of Norway; Dr. M. J. Echeverria, of Panama; Mr. Sylvino Gurgel do Amaral, of Portugal; Dr. S. Irimescu, of Rumania; Dr. A. Wladimiroff, of Russia; Dr. Paul G. Woolley, of Siam; Dr. Camilo Calleja, of Spain; Hon. Conrad Cedercrantz, of Sweden; Professor Fritz Egger, of Switzerland, and Mr. Luis Melian Lafinur, of Uruguay.

The Congress itself was organized into seven sections, as follows·

Section 1.—Pathology and Bacteriology, with Dr. William H. Welch of Baltimore, as president.

Section 2.—Clinical Study and Therapy of Tuberculosis— Sanatoriums, Hospitals, and Dispensaries, with Dr. Vincent Y. Bowditch of Boston, as president.

Section 3.—Surgery and Orthopedics, with Dr. Charles H. Mayo, of Rochester, Minnesota, as president.

Section 4.—Tuberculosis in Children—Etiology, Prevention, and Treatment, with Dr. Abraham Jacobi, of New York, as president.

Section 5.—Hygienic, Social, Industrial, and Economic Aspects of Tuberculosis, with Mr. Edward T. Devine, of New York, as president.

Section 6.—State and Municipal Control of Tuberculosis, with Surgeon-General Walter Wyman, U.S.P.H.S., Washington, as president.

Section 7.—Tuberculosis in Animals and Its Relations to Man, with Dr. Leonard Pearson, of Ithaca, as president.

Simultaneous meetings of the various sections were carried on throughout the duration of the Congress. In addition there were a number of special lecturers and special addresses. Two general meetings, the opening and the closing ceremonies, were also held.

In conjunction with the Congress a series of public lectures was given in Washington, Philadelphia, Baltimore, New York, and Boston. It was originally planned by the committee to have these special lectures given by world-famous experts in all of the large cities of the country, but for reasons of economy this plan could not be carried out. The names of the special lecturers and the titles of their addresses follow: Dr. Shibasaburo Kitasato, "Tuberculosis and Its Prevention in Japan"; Dr. Andres Martinez Vargas, "Tuberculosis of the Heart, of the Blood, and of the Lymph-Vessels"; Professor Gotthold Pannwitz, "Social Life and Tuberculosis"; Professor A. Calmette, "On the Modern Procedures for the Early Diagnosis of Tuberculous Infection"; Dr. Arthur Newsholme, "The Causes of the Past Decline in Tuberculosis and the Light Thrown by History on Preventive Measures for the Immediate Future"; Dr. C. Theodore Williams, "The Evolution of the Treatment of Pulmonary Tuberculosis"; Dr. A. Wladimiroff, "The Biology of the Tubercle Bacillus"; Professeur L. Landouzy, "Cent Ans de Phtisiologie, 1808–1908"; Prof. N. Ph. Tendeloo, "Collateral Tuberculous Inflammation"; Prof. Bernard Bang, "Studies on Tuberculosis in Domestic Animals, and What We May Learn from Them Regarding Human Tuberculosis"; Dr. Maurice Letulle and M. Augustin Rey, "The Fight against Tuberculosis in Large Cities—The Sanitary Dwelling as a Factor in the Prevention of Tuberculosis—The City Antituberculous; Scientific Methods of Construction"; Dr.

R. W. Philip, "The Antituberculosis Program: Coördination of Preventive Measures."

At the Congress itself practically all of the leading nations of the world were represented, and in the case of such nations as Great Britain, Germany, France, Italy, and others, representatives from the various provinces were also in attendance. The total number of delegates and representatives attending the Congress was considerably over 5,000. The total attendance at the various meetings aggregated nearly 100,000 people.

The medal of the Congress presented to each member was reproduced in handsome bronze from a design prepared by Victor Brenner. It represents the figure of a beautiful woman, in one hand holding the hour-glass of time, standing on the conquered dragon representing disease. On the reverse is the American eagle, with the stars and stripes; and underneath appear the words, "International Congress on Tuberculosis, Washington, 1908," and the double-barred cross, the insignia of the tuberculosis campaign.

It was only through the generosity of the Congress of the United States and the influence of President Roosevelt and Secretary Cortelyou that a building large enough to house the Congress could be secured in the city of Washington. The incomplete condition of the New National Museum made it possible to use to good advantage the large floor area for exhibits.

In connection with the Congress The National Association for the Study and Prevention of Tuberculosis prepared a memorial volume entitled, "The Campaign Against Tuberculosis in the United States." The expense of publication was met from a special grant of the Russell Sage Foundation. The book was prepared for the Association by Philip P. Jacobs. It outlined, in the form of a directory, the facilities for fighting tuberculosis at that time in existence in this country, consisting of sanatoria, hospitals, day camps, dispensaries, clinics, associations, and committees, special provision for the care of the criminal and insane, legislation, both state and national, and other features of interest. The National Association also had an exhibit showing in graphic form the extent of the tuberculosis movement in this country at the time of the Congress.

The closing session of the Sixth International Congress was held on the morning of October 5, 1908. The Secretary of the Treasury, Hon. George B. Cortelyou, presided. The Committee on Resolutions, of which Dr. Livingston Farrand was the secretary had, during the sessions of the Congress, considered numerous resolutions. To summarize the work of the Congress in a few brief statements of purpose was found to be a difficult task; but the following resolutions, adopted unanimously by the Congress, accomplished the task in a commendable manner:

Resolved, That the attention of the state and central governments be called to the importance of proper laws for the obligatory notification, by medical attendants, to the proper health authorities, of all cases of tuberculosis coming to their notice, and for the registration of such cases, in order to enable the health authorities to put in operation adequate measures for the prevention of the disease.

Resolved: That the utmost efforts should be continued in the struggle against tuberculosis to prevent the conveyance of tuberculous infection from man to man as the most important source of the disease.

Resolved: That preventive measures be continued against bovine tuberculosis, and that the possibility of the propagation of this to man be recognized.

Resolved: That we urge upon the public and upon all governments (*a*) the establishment of hospitals for the treatment of advanced cases of tuberculosis, (*b*) the establishment of sanatoriums for curable cases of tuberculosis, (*c*) the establishment of dispensaries, day camps, and night camps for ambulant cases of tuberculosis which cannot enter hospitals or sanatoriums.

Resolved: That this Congress indorses such well-considered legislation for the regulation of factories and workshops, the abolition of premature and injurious labor of women and children, and the securing of sanitary dwellings, as will increase the resisting power of the community to tuberculosis and other disease.

Resolved: That this Congress indorses and recommends the establishment of playgrounds as an important means of preventing tuberculosis through their influence upon health and resistance to disease.

Resolved: That instruction in personal and school hygiene should be given in all schools for the professional training of teachers.

Resolved: That whenever possible such instruction in elementary hygiene should be intrusted to properly qualified medical instructors.

Resolved: That colleges and universities should be urged to establish courses in hygiene and sanitation, and also to include these subjects among their entrance requirements, in order to stimulate useful elementary instruction in the lower schools.

On recommendation of the Committee on Resolutions also, an invitation from the Italian Ambassador, Baron Des Planches, to hold the next International Congress in Rome in 1911, was accepted.   At the closing session brief addresses were given by representatives of practically all of the foreign countries, and in addition by His Excellency, Theodore Roosevelt, President of the Congress, and President of the United States; Dr. Lawrence F Flick, chairman of the General Committee; and the Honorable Henry B. MacFarland, president of the Commissioners of the District of Columbia.

The report of the treasurer of the Congress shows that the entire amount collected by the General Committee amounted to $102,841.35.   The total expenditures were approximately $150,000, as originally estimated by Dr. Flick.   The National Association for the Study and Prevention of Tuberculosis was relieved of the entire responsibility for raising and distributing this sum, and except for a few hundred dollars, was not obliged to expend any of its comparatively limited resources on the Congress itself.   This fact enabled the Association to reap the utmost benefit from the Congress without any direct financial burden.

Of the influence of the Sixth International Congress on Tuberculosis work much might be written.   It has proved unquestionably to be the most significant milestone in the progress of this great movement in the United States.

The educational and organization campaign centering around the preparation for the Congress paved the way for the development of state and local associations throughout the entire country.   The state committees in many instances became the nuclei around which permanent state associations were later formed. The individuals interested in the Congress from various local communities in turn received from the Congress itself such an inspiration that hundreds of them immediately began to develop community effort in their respective towns and cities.   The extensive education that the publicity preceding and during the Congress afforded laid the foundation for much of the later constructive development in the tuberculosis campaign.

The conclusions reached by the Congress, both as evidenced in the resolutions and as brought out in the various discussions, formed the basis for the programs of national, state, and local tuberculosis associations for nearly a decade. For example, the emphasis laid upon hospital care for advanced cases as a preventive agency at once changed the trend of thought from cure to prevention as the most desirable measure of procedure. For years after the Congress this emphasis proved of the greatest value in securing additional hospital provision. The discussions in regard to tuberculosis in children focused the attention of workers in almost every department of the tuberculosis campaign upon this phase of the work, and has had the greatest influence in shaping the tuberculosis movement.

While no significant new discovery was announced at the Congress, the accumulation of experience, pathological, clinical, and social, from every part of the world, unquestionably stimulated and inspired the workers in The National Association for the Study and Prevention of Tuberculosis and gave to them a new vision. The present campaign against tuberculosis is in itself a testimony to the vision created by the Sixth International Congress.

CHAPTER X

THE DOUBLE-BARRED CROSS

AT ITS second annual meeting in 1906 the National Tuberculosis Association adopted the double-barred cross as its official emblem. A historical statement regarding this emblem, quoted from an article by Philip P. Jacobs, Ph.D., in the *Journal of the Outdoor Life* for April, 1922, may not be amiss in these pages:

The double-barred cross was adopted as the emblem of the tuberculosis movement at the International Conference on Tuberculosis held in Berlin in 1902. The proposer of the emblem was Dr. G. Sersiron, of Paris. Some persons in connection with the Conference had been discussing the desirability of an emblem for several years. Dr. Sersiron made the definite proposal to adopt the Lorraine Cross. The emblem was adopted without any hesitation and with practically no opposition.

The Lorraine Cross itself, to which the tuberculosis emblem, as will be noted, is closely related, dates back to the Patriarchal or Jerusalem Cross carried by the patriarchs of Jerusalem and Constantinople. This form of cross was and still is used by the Greek Catholic Church as its emblem. The double-barred cross as a symbol of various movements, religious, political, fraternal and otherwise has been in use for centuries.

The medieval crusades of the eleventh, twelfth, thirteenth and fourteenth centuries familiarized Europe with the double-barred cross as it was seen upon the Greek Churches of Asia Minor and Turkey. Godfrey, Duke of Lorraine, who was a leader of the first Crusade, saw the cross in vogue in Jerusalem and adopted it as his standard when he was elected ruler of Jerusalem in 1099. Apparently on his return to France the double-barred cross became the emblem of the then rising house of Lorraine. It has remained in France as the Lorraine Cross to this day, but is distinguished from the Patriarchal Cross by having the lower bar nearer the base. Many people will recall that one of the divisions of the A. E. F. used the Lorraine Cross as its insignia, not adopting the tuberculosis emblem, but utilizing the Lorraine emblem which was very much in vogue in certain sections of France where this division happened to be quartered.

The Masonic Order has used the double-barred cross also as an emblem for many centuries. It seems likely that they in turn also adopted it from the Jerusalem Cross and not from the House of Lorraine.

When the tuberculosis movement adopted the cross, in 1902, no effort was made to standardize its form or its proportion.

In 1906 the National Tuberculosis Association, by a special

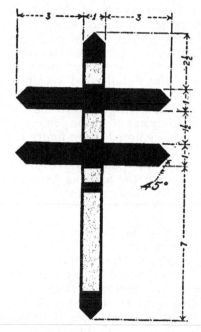

THE DOUBLE-BARRED CROSS, SHOWING THE TRUE PROPORTIONS
All the Angles in the Points are of 45 Degrees. The Width of the Cross is the Unit of Measurement.

resolution, adopted the double-barred cross as the emblem of the campaign against tuberculosis in the United States. For about six years no effort was made to standardize its form. Everywhere crosses were used of all sorts and shapes, some with long points and some with short points.

In 1912 a definite effort was made to standardize the double-barred cross and a committee was appointed for that purpose. In 1913 the committee made its report at the annual meeting of the National Tuberculosis Association. After a careful study of the history and the artistic merits of numerous designs the committee reported in favor of a double-barred cross with equal cross arms, the upper standard being shorter, and the lower standard longer than the cross arms, and the ends of both arms and standards to be pointed instead of square.   The committee was influenced in its decision by the following reasons.

1. Because the design selected is farthest removed from any design having a religious significance.

2. Because it is farthest removed from the well-known emblem used by the American National Red Cross.

3. Because its wide-spread use in this country by many anti-tuberculosis associations over a long period of years has associated it in the minds of the public with the tuberculosis movement.

In the first report the committee did not recommend any definite proportions, but it was given power to work these out and later to submit the details and specifications to all anti-tuberculosis agencies.   The committee's final choice of design is shown in the accompanying illustration.   The width of the standards and arms (they are all of the same width) is taken as the standard unit.   It will be noted, from figure 1, that the length of the lower standard below the cross arms is 7 units; the arms are 3 units on either side; the point above the arms is 2½ units; and the distance between the arms is 1½ units.   As the width of the cross remains the constant, standard unit, these measurements hold good for crosses of any size.

With the separation of the National Tuberculosis Association from the American Red Cross in relation to the Christmas seal sale, it became increasingly necessary for the tuberculosis movement to popularize the double-barred cross.   It also became necessary to conserve the emblem so that it would not be used by unscrupulous vendors of patent medicines and organizations that were not approved by the National Tuberculosis Association. Accordingly in February, 1920, the emblem was protected by registry in the United States Patent Office with the number 137345.

The National Tuberculosis Association has made liberal arrangements whereby permits for the use of the emblem may be secured from its representative directors in the states.   Such permit must specify the particular kinds of printed matter on which the cross is to be used, and must give samples and must pass muster with the representative director who files a copy of the permit with the state association and with the National Tuberculosis Association.   In this way any reputable tuberculosis agency, association, dispensary, sanatorium or other agency can use the double-barred cross.

PART II

THE ANNUAL MEETINGS OF THE NATIONAL TUBERCULOSIS ASSOCIATION

INTRODUCTORY NOTE

This part of the history records the principal happenings at each of the seventeen annual meetings. It includes the resolutions adopted, the officers and directors elected, and a brief financial summary for each meeting.

CHAPTER XI

FIRST ANNUAL MEETING

THE first annual meeting of The National Association for the Study and Prevention of Tuberculosis was held in Washington, D. C., May 18 and 19, 1905. The sessions were held at the New Willard Hotel, the headquarters of the Association, the local arrangements being in the hands of a committee consisting of Dr. George M. Kober, chairman, Dr. D. Perčy Hickling and Dr. William C. Woodward.

The following list of officers and directors held office at this meeting:

President, Dr. Edward L. Trudeau, Saranac Lake; vice-presidents, Dr. William Osler, Baltimore, Md., and Dr. Hermann M. Biggs, New York, N. Y.; treasurer, Dr. George M. Sternberg, Washington, D. C.; secretary, Dr. Henry Barton Jacobs, Baltimore, Md.; directors, Dr. Norman Bridge, Los Angeles, Cal.; Dr. S. E. Solly, Colorado Springs, Colo.; Dr. John P. C. Foster, New Haven, Conn.; Dr. George M. Sternberg, Washington, D. C.; Dr. Arnold C. Klebs, Chicago, Ill.; Dr. Robert H. Babcock, Chicago, Ill.; Dr. John N. Hurty, Indianapolis, Ind.; Dr. William H. Welch, Baltimore, Md.; Dr. William Osler, Baltimore, Md.; Dr. Henry Barton Jacobs, Baltimore, Md.; Dr. John S. Fulton, Baltimore, Md.; Dr. Henry M. Bracken, St. Paul, Minn.; Dr. William Porter, St. Louis, Mo.; Dr. Edward O. Otis, Boston, Mass.; Dr. Vincent Y. Bowditch, Boston, Mass.; Mr. Frederick L. Hoffman, Newark, N. J.; Dr. S. Adolphus Knopf, New York, N. Y.; Dr. Edward L. Trudeau, Saranac Lake, N. Y.; Mr. Edward T. Devine, New York, N. Y.; Dr. Charles L. Minor, Asheville, N. C.; Dr. Charles O. Probst, Columbus, Ohio; Dr. Lawrence F. Flick, Philadelphia, Pa.; Dr. Mazÿck P. Ravenel, Philadelphia, Pa.; Dr. Howard S. Anders, Philadelphia, Pa.; Dr. Leonard Pearson, Philadelphia, Pa.; Dr. M. M. Smith, Austin, Texas; Maj. George E. Bushnell, M.D., Fort Bayard, N. M.; Gen. Walter Wyman, M.D., Washington, D. C.

Executive secretary, Dr. Livingston Farrand.

In preparing the program the executive committee had provided for three sections; a sociological, a clinical and climatolog ical, and a pathological and bacteriological. Each of these sections held two sessions, and in addition there were two general meetings of the Association, one on the morning of May 18 and the other on the evening of the same day. The regular business of the Association was transacted on the morning of May 18, fol‑ lowing the presidential and vice-presidential addresses, and on the evening of May 18, following the public address of Mr. Talcott Williams. The president of the Association, Dr. Edward L. Trudeau, presided at both general meetings.

A summary of the transactions follows: On motion of Dr. Lawrence F. Flick, of Philadelphia, it was voted that the president appoint a committee on resolutions, to consist of five members, to which all resolutions should be referred before being brought before the Association for action. The president appointed as members of the committee on resolutions, Dr. William H. Welch, chairman, Dr. Edward G. Janeway, Dr. DeLancey Rochester, Mr. Edward T. Devine, and Dr. H. R. M. Landis.

The secretary announced that six directors retired by expiration of term of office and that one vacancy existed by resignation. The secretary presented the nominations of the board of directors for the vacant directorships as follows: Dr. William S. Carter, of Galveston, in place of Dr. William Osler, resigned. For directors to serve for a term of five years: E. P. Bicknell, of Chicago; Dr. Vincent Y. Bowditch, of Boston; Dr. John S. Fulton, of Baltimore; Dr. Arnold C. Klebs, of Chicago; Henry Phipps, of New York; Dr. C. O. Probst, of Columbus. There being no other nominations, on motion of Dr. DeLancey Rochester the secretary cast a ballot for the names presented, and the gentlemen were declared elected.

The committee on resolutions made its report through the chairman, Dr. William H. Welch, the following resolutions being recommended for adoption:

Resolved, That the sincere thanks of The National Association for the Study and Prevention of Tuberculosis be tendered to Mr. Henry Phipps for his noble benefaction in connection with the study, prevention and cure of tuberculosis.

WHEREAS, Dr. William Osler, one of our founders and a potent factor in the development of our organization, has been called to another field of labor, be it *Resolved*, That we express our appreciation of his valuable service.

Resolved, That we elect him an Honorary Vice-President as a mark of our appreciation and esteem.

The National Association for the Study and Prevention of Tuberculosis hails with gratification the establishment and successful operation of national sanatoria for the treatment of tuberculous patients belonging to the army, the navy, and the Marine Hospital and Public Health Service, and trusts that their usefulness may be enlarged in every possible manner in the study and prevention of tuberculosis.

Resolved, That in the interest of preventive medicine and the cause of industrial hygiene this Association respectfully recommends to the Chief Executive of the Nation the desirability of instituting an inquiry through the proper officers of the government as to the sanitary conditions existing in all government offices and workshops where a large number of persons are employed, especially with a view of recommending, if necessary, measures for the prevention of tuberculosis therein.

Resolved, That the attention of all municipal and State authorities be especially directed to the enormous economic importance to every community of the tuberculosis problem and the wisdom of and the necessity for the provision of adequate funds and the enactment of proper regulations for combating the prevalence of this disease.

Resolved, That the officers of the Association be directed to request the directors and officers of insurance associations to unite themselves with this Association and to consider the advisability of giving financial aid to sanatoria for the treatment and prolongation of life of those insured in their companies.

Resolved, That the directors and officers of insurance associations be invited to attend the next meeting of this Association.

Inasmuch as President Roosevelt in his last message to Congress has emphasized the importance and the possibility of making the national capital a model city in sanitary and social matters, and

Inasmuch as the President has suggested the formation of a "Special Commission on Housing and Health Conditions in the National Capital," to be composed of unpaid prominent citizens of Washington, provided with money for necessary expenses by congressional appropriation, served by a competent paid secretary for the twelve or sixteen months which would be requisite for the work, therefore be it

Resolved, That the National Association for the Study and Prevention of Tuberculosis earnestly recommends to the Congress of the United States the early passage of legislation providing for the appointment of such a commission either by the President of the United States or the Commissioners of the District.

This resolution met with opposition and was referred back to the board of directors.

At a meeting of the board of directors held on the evening of May 18 the following officers were elected for the ensuing year: president, Dr. Hermann M. Biggs; first vice-president, Dr. Lawrence F. Flick; second vice-president, Dr. Vincent Y. Bowditch; secretary, Dr. Henry Barton Jacobs; treasurer, Gen. George M. Sternberg. In addition to the president and secretary and the vice-presidents, Mr. E. T. Devine and Drs. Foster, Klebs, Ravenel, Trudeau, and Welch were elected members of the executive committee.

The meeting closed with a testimonial banquet to the president, Dr. Edward L. Trudeau, on the evening of May 19.

The summarized report of the treasurer, Gen. George M. Sternberg, is as follows:

Receipts to April 30, 1905	$10,367.15
Expenditures	3,364.96
Balance on hand April 30, 1905	$7,002.19

The following is a list of papers read before the respective sections at the meeting of May 18–19, 1905:

The winning fight—Talcott Williams.
Health as an investment—Homer Folks.
A working program—Edward T. Devine.
The progress of the sanatorium movement in America—William H. Baldwin.
Infection in transportation—H. M. Bracken, M.D.
The therapeutic value of Marmorek's anti-tubercular serum—Arthur J. Richer, M.D.
The natural and artificial protection of man against tuberculosis—F. Figari, M.D.
The serum diagnosis of tuberculosis—Hugh M. Kinghorn, M.D.
Studies in agglutination—Mazÿck P. Ravenel, M.D., and H. R. M. Landis, M.D.
The properties of the serum of immunized rabbits—E. R. Baldwin, M.D., H. M. Kinghorn, M.D., and A. H. Allen, M.D.
An histological study of the lesions of immunized rabbits—Joseph L. Nichols, M.D.
Two experiments in artificial immunity against tuberculosis—Edward L. Trudeau, M.D.
Examination of the blood in pulmonary tuberculosis, with special reference to prognosis—J. T. Ullom, M.D., and Frank A. Craig, M.D.
Tuberculosis of the thoracic duct and acute miliary tuberculosis—Warfield T. Longcope, M.D.

Vicarious action of the bowels for the kidneys in tuberculosis—Lawrence F. Flick, M.D., and Joseph Walsh, M.D.

Note on the stability of the cultural characters of tubercle bacilli; with special reference to the production of capsules—Theobald Smith, M.D.

The vitality of tubercle bacilli in sputum—David C. Twichell, M.D.

Studies in mixed infection in tuberculosis—Mazÿck P. Ravenel, M.D., and J. Willoughby Irwin, M.D.

The thyroid in tuberculosis—William B. Stanton, M.D.

Landry's paralysis complicating pulmonary tuberculosis—D. J. McCarthy, M.D.

Impalpable sputum, as a usually overlooked danger in tuberculosis—Norman Bridge, M.D.

Result of the open-air treatment of surgical tuberculosis—W. S. Halsted, M.D.

The influence of the event of the tuberculous upon native population—Charles F. Gardiner, M.D.

Sanatorium provision with industrial opportunities for indigent consumptives —Herbert M. King, M.D., and Henry B. Neagle, M.D.

Detention institutions for ignorant and vicious consumptives—John P. C. Foster, M.D.

What cases are suitable for admission to a state sanatorium for tuberculosis, especially in New England?—Herbert C. Clapp, M.D.

Six years' experience at the Massachusetts state sanatorium for tuberculosis at Rutland, Mass.—Vincent Y. Bowditch, M.D., and Henry B. Dunham, M.D.

Tent colonies in management of tuberculosis—J. W. Pettit, M.D.

Sanatorium treatment in an appropriate climate—Maj. G. E. Bushnell.

The treatment and care of advanced cases of pulmonary tuberculosis—S. Adolphus Knopf, M.D.

Home treatment of tuberculosis, either in favorable or unfavorable climates— Edward O. Otis, M.D.

The after treatment of pulmonary tuberculosis—J. A. Wilder, M.D.

Clinical suggestions from the study of 500 cases of pulmonary tuberculosis— Henry P. Loomis, M.D.

Clinical studies at Mount St. Rose—William Porter, M.D.

History and work of the Bedford sanitarium for consumptives—Alfred Meyer, M.D.

Report of the Committee on the Influence of Climate in Pulmonary Tuberculosis.

Report of the Committee on Clinical Nomenclature.

Report of the Committee on Early Diagnosis of Tuberculosis.

Report of the Committee on an Educational Leaflet for Distribution Among the People.

CHAPTER XII

SECOND ANNUAL MEETING

THE second annual meeting of The National Association for The Study and Prevention of Tuberculosis was held at the New Willard Hotel, Washington, D. C., Wednesday, Thursday, and Friday, May 16, 17, and 18, 1906.

In preparing the program the executive committee had provided for two new sections, a Surgical section and one on Tuberculosis in Children, in addition to the three previously existing. Each of the older sections held two sessions and the newly formed sections one each.

In the absence of Dr. Hermann M. Biggs, the president of the Association, Dr. Lawrence F. Flick, vice-president, occupied the chair. The opening meeting on the evening of May 16 was a joint session of the National Association with the Association of American Physicians, at which the president of the latter society, Dr. Frank Billings, presided, the address on that occasion being by Dr. Simon Flexner, of New York.

At the business meeting of the Association, held on the evening of May 17, following the vice-presidential address of Dr. Flick, the six directors whose terms of office expired by limitation were reëlected, namely, Drs. H. M. Bracken, Minnesota; W. S. Carter, Texas; Henry Barton Jacobs, Maryland; E. O. Otis, Massachusetts; Edward L. Trudeau, New York; and William H. Welch, Maryland.

By the amendment to the by-laws providing for the enlargement of the board of directors to 60, the following new directors were nominated by the board and elected by the Association: Mr. Redfield Proctor, Jr., Vermont; W. T. Sedgwick, Massachusetts; Rowland G. Hazard, Rhode Island; Homer Folks, New York; Dr. Walter B. James, New York; Dr. Edward G. Janeway, New York; Dr. Alfred Meyer, New York; John Seely Ward, Jr.,

New York; Charles M. Lea, Pennsylvania; Dr. Joseph Walsh, Pennsylvania; Otis H. Childs, Pennsylvania; Dr. John J. Black, Delaware; Robert Garrett, Maryland; William H. Baldwin, District of Columbia; Samuel Gompers, District of Columbia; Dr. George M. Kober, District of Columbia; Dr. C. F. McGahan, South Carolina; Dr. T. D. Coleman, Georgia; Dr. John H. Lowman, Ohio; Charles W. Fairbanks, Indiana; Dr. Frank Billings, Illinois; A. A. Sprague, 2d, Illinois; David R. Francis, Missouri; C. E. Perkins, Iowa; James J. Hill, Minnesota; Dr. Sherman G. Bonney, Colorado; Dr. Henry Sewall, Colorado; Dr. W. H. Flint, California; and Benjamin I. Wheeler, California.

The following resolutions, having been endorsed by the committee on resolutions, were unanimously adopted:

Resolved, That the National Association for the Study and Prevention of Tuberculosis adopt the double red cross as the official emblem of the Association.

Resolved, That in the interests of clearness and uniformity of nomenclature the Association employ in its official publications the term *tuberculous* to refer to lesions or conditions caused by the tubercle bacillus, and the term *tubercular* to describe conditions resembling tubercles, but not caused by the tubercle bacillus.

WHEREAS, Recent experience in Europe and in this country has shown that outdoor life in pure air has the same curative effect in surgical tuberculosis as in tuberculosis of the lungs, therefore, be it

Resolved, That, in the opinion of the members of this Association, hospitals and sanatoria should be established outside of cities, either in the country or on the seashore, for the treatment, from its incipiency, of tuberculosis of bones, joints, and glands in children.

At a meeting of the board of directors held on Friday, May 18, the following officers were elected for the ensuing year: Dr. Hermann M. Biggs, president; Dr. Lawrence F. Flick and Dr. Vincent Y. Bowditch, vice-presidents; Dr. Henry Barton Jacobs, secretary; General George M. Sternberg, treasurer. The following directors were elected to serve on the executive committee for the ensuing year: W. H. Baldwin, Homer Folks, Drs. Vincent Y. Bowditch, Lawrence F. Flick, J. P. C. Foster, E. C. Janeway,

Arnold C. Klebs.   Dr. Edward L. Trudeau was elected an Honorary Member of the Association.

There are no available records of the second annual report of the treasurer.

Prior to the first meeting of the National Association in Washington, there existed in the United States 23 tuberculosis associations, to which were added during the year 1905 no less than nine.   To the 24 dispensaries were added three during the same period, and 10 sanatoria and special hospitals to the already existing 96.

A list of officers and directors for 1905 to 1906 follows:

President, Dr. Hermann M. Biggs; honorary vice-presidents, Theodore Roosevelt, Grover Cleveland, and Dr. William Osler; vice-presidents, Dr. Lawrence F. Flick, and Dr. Vincent Y. Bowditch; treasurer, Gen. George M. Sternberg; secretary, Dr. Henry Barton Jacobs; directors, Dr. Howard S. Anders, Philadelphia; Ernest P. Bicknell, Chicago; Dr. Hermann M. Biggs, New York; Dr. Vincent Y. Bowditch, Boston; Dr. Henry M. Bracken, St. Paul; Dr. Norman Bridge, Los Angeles; Maj. George E. Bushnell, Fort Bayard, N. M.; Dr. William S. Carter, Galveston; Otis H. Childs, Pittsburgh; Edward T. Devine, New York; Dr. Lawrence F. Flick, Philadelphia; Homer Folks, New York; Dr. John P. C. Foster, New Haven; Dr. John S. Fulton, Baltimore; Frederick L. Hoffman, Newark, N. J.; Dr. John N. Hurty, Indianapolis; Dr. Henry Barton Jacobs, Baltimore; Dr. Edward G. Janeway, New York; Dr. Arnold C. Klebs, Chicago; Dr. S. A. Knopf, New York; Dr. Charles L. Minor, Asheville; Dr. Edward O. Otis, Boston; Dr. Leonard Pearson, Philadelphia; Henry Phipps, New York; Dr. William Porter, St. Louis; Dr. Charles O. Probst, Columbus, O.; Dr. Mazÿck P. Ravenel, Philadelphia; Dr. S. E. Solly, Colorado Springs; Gen. George M. Sternberg, Washington; Dr. Edward L. Trudeau, Saranac Lake; Dr. Victor C. Vaughan, Ann Arbor; Dr. Joseph Walsh, Philadelphia; Dr. William H. Welch, Baltimore; Gen. Walter Wyman, Washington.

Executive secretary, Dr. Livingston Farrand.

The following is a list of papers read before the respective sections at the meeting of May 16–18, 1906.

Immunity in tuberculosis—Simon Flexner, M.D.
The influence of a tuberculosis sanatorium on the value of surrounding property —William H. Baldwin.
Tuberculosis nostrums—Samuel Hopkins Adams.
Tuberculosis among the Oglala Sioux Indians—James R. Walker, M.D.
Tuberculosis among the Negroes—Thomas Jesse Jones, Ph.D.
Effective methods of educating the public—Paul Kennaday.

Insurance of industrial workingmen as an instrument of tuberculosis prevention—Arnold C. Klebs, M.D.

Localized tuberculous leptomeningitis—D. J. McCarthy, M.D.

The liver in tuberculosis—Josephus T. Ullom, M.D.

The kidneys in tuberculosis—Joseph Walsh, M.D.

The clinical and pathological comparison of cavities—H. R. M. Landis, M.D.

Tuberculosis of the placenta—Alfred Scott Warthin, M.D.

Notes on some common errors in the technique of sputum staining for tubercle bacilli—Charles L. Minor, M.D., and Paul Ringer, M.D.

Concerning Bacillus X—Stephen J. Maher, M.D.

Further notes on the serum diagnosis of tuberculosis—Hugh M. Kinghorn, M.D., and David C. Twichell, M.D.

The technique of tuberculo-opsonic test—Hugh M. Kinghorn, M.D., and David C. Twichell, M.D.

Studies on immunity in tuberculosis, III. Experiments with leucocytes. Lymph gland and bone marrow extracts of immunized animals—E. R. Baldwin, M.D., and J. Woods Price, M.D.

The scope and aim of state sanatoria for tuberculosis—Vincent Y. Bowditch, M.D.

The therapeutic use of tuberculin combined with sanatorium treatment of tuberculosis—E. L. Trudeau, M.D.

The treatment of tuberculous laryngitis with watery extract of tubercle bacilli, with observations upon the action of specific inoculations in the treatment of tuberculosis—F. M. Pottenger, M.D.

Review of the work upon the opsonic index (Wright and Douglas) in tuberculosis—Nathaniel Bowditch Potter, M.D.

Hæmatological studies in tuberculosis—Arnold C. Klebs, M.D., and Henry Klebs, M.D.

On the use and abuse of pulmonary gymnastics in the treatment of tuberculosis—Charles L. Minor, M.D.

Use and abuse of pulmonary gymnastics—Edward O. Otis, M.D.

Diet in tuberculosis—Herbert Maxon King, M.D.

Statistics of diet in sanatoria for consumptives—Irving Fisher, Ph.D.

Diet in pulmonary tuberculosis—Sherman G. Bonney, M.D.

Climate as a factor in the treatment of tuberculosis—Frederick I. Knight, M.D.

The relative value of home treatment of tuberculosis—Lawrence F. Flick, M.D.

A suggestion in the treatment of hæmoptysis—Lawrason Brown, M.D.

Manifestations of syphilis associated with pulmonary tuberculosis—John H. Pryor, M.D.

What may be accomplished with apparently hopeless cases of tuberculosis—Sherman G. Bonney, M.D.

A contribution to climatic phthisiotherapy—E. S. Bullock, M.D.

The hot morning bath for the tuberculous—Norman Bridge, M.D.

Tuberculous peritonitis—Richard Douglas, M.D.

The treatment of tuberculosis of the bones and joints—Joel E. Goldthwait, M.D.   ·

Tuberculous glands of the neck, based on five hundred cases—C. H. Mayo, M.D.

The portals of entry and sources of infection in tuberculosis in children—David Bovaird, Jr., M.D.

Treatment of tuberculosis in early life—J. P. Crozer Griffith, M.D.

The protection of infants and young children from tuberculous infection—John Lovett Morse, M.D.

The therapeutic value of sea air in non-pulmonary tuberculosis in children—John W. Brannan, M.D.

Report of the Committee on Clinical Nomenclature.

CHAPTER XIII
THIRD ANNUAL MEETING

THE third annual meeting of The National Association for the Study and Prevention of Tuberculosis was held at the New Willard Hotel, Washington, D. C., Monday, Tuesday, and Wednesday, May 6, 7, and 8, 1907.

The president of the Association, Dr. Hermann M. Biggs, occupied the chair at the general meeting. Over 300 members of the Association were present at the various sessions.

At the general meeting on the morning of May 6, following the addresses of President Biggs and Vice-President Flick, the following committee on resolutions was appointed: Dr. Victor C. Vaughan, Ann Arbor, chairman; Dr. Edward R. Baldwin, Saranac Lake; Dr. S. A. Knopf, New York; Dr. John H. Lowman, Cleveland; Dr. William S. Thayer, Baltimore.

The following committee to present nominations to fill vacancies on the board of directors was appointed: William H. Baldwin, Washington, Chairman; Dr. Frank Billings, Chicago; Dr. Lawrason Brown, Saranac Lake; Major George E. Bushnell, Fort Bayard; Dr. Charles R. Grandy, Norfolk; Dr. F. M. Pottenger, Los Angeles; Dr. Henry Sewall, Denver.

At the regular business meeting of the Association held on the evening of May 7 the following directors were unanimously elected for terms of five years: Dr. Hermann M. Biggs, New York; Dr. Frank Billings, Chicago; Dr. R. W. Corwin, Pueblo, Colo.; Edward T. Devine, New York; Dr. Lawrence F. Flick, Philadelphia; David R. Francis, St. Louis; Robert Garrett, Baltimore; Charles M. Lea, Philadelphia; Dr. C. F. McGahan, Aiken; W. C. Nones, Louisville; Dr. Mazÿck P. Ravenel, Philadelphia; Gen. George M. Sternberg, Washington.

The following resolution presented by the Advisory Council was adopted:

167

WHEREAS, In order to deal intelligently and effectively with the tuberculosis problem in any community a knowledge of the extent and location of the disease on the part of the health authorities is indispensable, therefore be it

Resolved, That The National Association for the Study and Prevention of Tuberculosis regards the compulsory notification and registration of tuberculosis as a necessary measure; and that where it does not already exist, legislation providing for such compulsory notification and registration of tuberculosis, with adequate provision for its enforcement, should be enacted.

At the meeting of the board of directors, held on the evening of Tuesday, May 7, the following officers were elected for the ensuing year: Dr. Frank Billings, president; Dr. Mazÿck P. Ravenel and Dr. John P. C. Foster, vice-presidents; Dr. Henry Barton Jacobs, secretary, Gen. George M. Sternberg, treasurer.

The following directors were elected to serve on the executive committee for the ensuing year: William H. Baldwin, Washington; Dr. Hermann M. Biggs, New York; Dr. Vincent Y. Bowditch, Boston; Dr. Lawrence F. Flick, Philadelphia; Dr. John P. C. Foster, New Haven; Dr. Edward G. Janeway, New York; Dr. Arnold C. Klebs, Chicago.

The board adopted unanimously the following resolutions on the death of Dr. S. E. Solly, a former member of the board:

WHEREAS, The Directors of The National Association for the Study and Prevention of Tuberculosis have learned with sincere sorrow of the death of their colleague, Dr. S. E. Solly, of Colorado Springs, and

WHEREAS, By his great medical ability and no less by his unusual personal charm he had both endeared himself to them and proven a wise counsellor in their deliberations, be it

Resolved, That in his death they have lost a member whose place cannot easily be filled; one whose distinguished professional attainments did honor to this body to which he belonged and whose remarkable gifts of heart equally with those of mind made him ever welcome in their midst; and further be it

Resolved, That the Secretary be directed to send a copy of these resolutions and assurances of our deep sympathy to his bereaved family; that a copy be spread on our minutes and that they be published in Colorado Medicine, the official organ of the Colorado State Medical Society, in the Journal of the American Medical Association, in the Medical Record, and in the Journal of the Outdoor Life, the official organ of The National Association for the Study and Prevention of Tuberculosis.

The summarized report of the treasurer, Gen. George M. Sternberg is as follows:

```
Balance on hand April 30, 1906............... $4,085.30
Receipts.................................... 10,812.13
Expenditures............................... 12,281.79
                                            ----------
Balance on hand April 30, 1907............... $2,615.64
```

At the meeting of 1906 there were reported to exist in the United States 32 tuberculosis associations, to which 22 were added during 1906–1907. To the 27 dispensaries 9 were added during the same period; and 12 sanatoria and special hospitals to the existing 106.

A list of officers and directors for 1906 to 1907 follows:

President, Dr. Hermann M. Biggs; honorary vice-presidents, Theodore Roosevelt, Grover Cleveland, and Dr. William Osler; vice-presidents; Dr. Lawrence F. Flick and Dr. Vincent Y. Bowditch; treasurer, Gen. George M. Sternberg; secretary, Dr. Henry Barton Jacobs; directors, Dr. Howard S. Anders, Philadelphia; William H. Baldwin, Washington; Ernest P. Bicknell, Chicago; Dr. Hermann M. Biggs, New York; Dr. Frank Billings, Chicago; Dr. John J. Black, New Castle, Del.; Dr. Sherman G. Bonney, Denver; Dr. Vincent Y. Bowditch, Boston; Dr. Henry M. Bracken, St. Paul; Dr. Norman Bridge, Los Angeles; Maj. George E. Bushnell, Fort Bayard; Dr. William S. Carter, Galveston; Otis H. Childs, Pittsburgh; Dr. T. D. Coleman, Augusta, Ga.; Edward T. Devine, New York; Charles W. Fairbanks, Washington; Dr. Lawrence F. Flick, Philadelphia; Dr. W. H. Flint, Santa Barbara, Cal.; Homer Folks, New York; Dr. John P. C. Foster, New Haven; David R. Francis, St. Louis; Dr. John S. Fulton, Baltimore; Robert Garrett, Baltimore; Samuel Gompers, Washington; Rowland G. Hazard, Peace Dale, R. I.; James J. Hill, St. Paul; Frederick L. Hoffman, Newark; Dr. John N. Hurty, Indianapolis; Dr. Henry Barton Jacobs, Baltimore; Dr. Walter B. James, New York; Dr. Edward G. Janeway, New York; Dr. Arnold C. Klebs, Chicago; Dr. S. A. Knopf, New York; Dr. George M. Kober, Washington; Charles M. Lea, Philadelphia; Dr. John H. Lowman, Cleveland; Dr. C. F. McGahan, Aiken, S. C.; Dr. Alfred Meyer, New York; Dr. Charles L. Minor, Asheville; Dr. Edward O. Otis, Boston; Dr. Leonard Pearson, Philadelphia; C. E. Perkins, Burlington, Iowa; Henry Phipps, New York; Dr. William Porter, St. Louis; Dr. Charles O. Probst, Columbus; Redfield Proctor, Jr., Proctor, Vt.; Dr. Mazÿck P. Ravenel, Philadelphia; W. T. Sedgwick, Boston; Dr. Henry Sewall, Denver; Dr. S. E. Solly, Colorado Springs; A. A. Sprague, 2d, Chicago; General Geo. M. Sternberg, Washington; Dr. Edward L. Trudeau, Saranac Lake; Dr. Victor C. Vaughan, Ann Arbor; Dr. Joseph Walsh, Philadelphia; John Seely Ward, Jr., New York; Dr. Wiliam H. Welch Baltimore; Benjamin I. Wheeler, Berkeley, Cal.; General Walter Wyman, Washington.

Executive secretary, Dr. Livingston Farrand.

The following is a list of papers read before the respective sections at the meeting of May 6–8, 1907:

Report on the International Congress on Tuberculosis—Lawrence F. Flick, M.D.

The campaign against tuberculosis in the United States—Livingston Farrand, M.D.

Address of the chairman of the Advisory Council—William H. Baldwin.

Compulsory notification and registration of tuberculosis—Hermann M. Biggs, M.D.

The class method of treating consumption in the homes of the poor—Joseph H. Pratt, M.D.

Country treatment of city cases—B. H. Waters, M.D.

A working program for a small city—Oscar H. Rogers, M.D.

Schools and tuberculosis—John H. Lowman, M.D.

The detection and treatment of cases of tuberculosis among factory employees in Providence—Frank T. Fulton, M.D.

Address of the chairman of the Clinical and Climatological Section—George Dock, M.D.

Some experience with tuberculin—L. Rosenberg, M.D.

Varieties of tuberculosis according to race and social condition—Woods Hutchinson, M.D.

Phagocytosis, etc., in sputum as a measure of resistance in tuberculosis—Albert H. Allen, M.D.

Bacteriological examination of the feces as a means of early diagnosis in tuberculosis—Myer Solis Cohen, M.D.

Split products of the tubercle bacillus and their effects upon animals—Victor C. Vaughan, M.D., and Sybil May Wheeler.

Further notes on the technique of the tuberculo-opsonic test—Hugh M. Kinghorn, M.D., David C. Twichell, M.D., and Norman M. Carter, M.D.

Homologous bacteria as a vaccine in tuberculosis—Albert H. Allen, M.D.

The pleural pressure after death from tuberculosis—W. B. Stanton,M .D.

Disseminated focal necroses due to tubercle bacilli—A. S. Warthin, M.D.

Localized tuberculosis of the liver—A. S. Warthin, M.D.

The leucocytes in various complications of pulmonary tuberculosis—Frank A. Craig, M.D.

Occult blood findings in tuberculous ulceration of the intestines—H. R. M. Landis, M.D.

The living pathology of tuberculosis of the bones in early life—Thomas Morgan Rotch, M.D., and Arial W. George, M.D.

Recent advances in the knowledge of tuberculosis in early life—Charles Hunter Dunn, M.D.

The present status of the transmissibility of bovine tuberculosis as illustrated by infants and young children—Henry L. K. Shaw, M.D.

Are tuberculous infants and children in the first five years of life liable to be
sources of infection?—Samuel S. Adams, M.D.

The treatment of surgical tuberculosis by hyperemia (Bier)—Dr. V. Schmieden.

Present status of the opsonic theory and the treatment by tuberculins—Rufus
I. Cole, M.D.

The advantages and limitations of the x-ray in the treatment of surgical tuberculosis—Henry K. Pancoast, M.D.

Report of the Committee on Clinical Nomenclature.

Report of the Committee on Medication in Tuberculosis.

Report of the Committee on Mixed Infection in Tuberculosis.

CHAPTER XIV

FOURTH ANNUAL MEETING

THE fourth annual meeting of The National Association for the Study and Prevention of Tuberculosis was held at the Auditorium Hotel, Chicago, Ill., on Friday and Saturday, June 5 and 6, 1908. The president of the Association, Dr. Frank Billings, occupied the chair at the general meeting.

At the general meeting on the afternoon of Friday, June 5, following the addresses of President Billings, Vice-President Flick, and the executive secretary, the following committee was appointed by the president to present nominations to fill vacancies on the board of directors: Dr. Norman Bridge, Los Angeles, chairman; Dr. Henry M. Bracken, St. Paul; Alexander M. Wilson, Chicago; Dr. John L. Dawson, Charleston, S. C.; Dr. Herbert Maxon King, Liberty, N. Y.

The following committee on resolutions was appointed: Dr. John H. Lowman, Cleveland, chairman; Dr. Henry B. Favill, Chicago; Dr. Gerald B. Webb, Colorado Springs; Dr. Thomas D. Coleman, Augusta; Dr. Hugh M. Kinghorn, Saranac Lake.

At the regular business meeting of the Association, held on Saturday, June 6, at 12.30 P. M., the following directors were unanimously elected for terms of five years: Dr. Edward R. Baldwin, Saranac Lake; C. B. Boothe, Los Angeles; A. B. Cummins, Des Moines; Samuel Gompers, Washington; James J. Hill, St. Paul; Frederick L. Hoffman, Newark; Dr. John N. Hurty, Indianapolis; Dr. S. A. Knopf, New York; Dr. Rudolf Matas, New Orleans; Dr. Charles L. Minor, Asheville; Redfield Proctor, Jr., Proctor, Vt.; Dr. Victor C. Vaughan, Ann Arbor. W. K. Bixby, St. Louis, was elected a director to fill the unexpired term of C. E. Perkins, deceased.

At a meeting of the board of directors, held at the Auditorium Hotel on Saturday afternoon, June 6, the following officers were elected for the ensuing year: Dr. Vincent Y. Bowditch, president; Homer Folks and Dr. Charles L. Minor, vice-presidents; Dr. Henry Barton Jacobs, secretary and Gen. George M. Sternberg, treasurer.

The following directors were elected to serve on the executive committee for the ensuing year: William H. Baldwin, Washington; Dr. Hermann M. Biggs, New York; Homer Folks, New York; Dr. John P. C. Foster, New Haven; Dr. Edward G. Janeway, New York; Dr. Edward O. Otis, Boston; Dr. Leonard Pearson, Philadelphia.

Following the joint meeting of the Advisory Council and the Sociological Section of the Association, Alexander M. Wilson, of Chicago, was elected chairman of the Advisory Council for the next annual meeting.

The summarized report of the treasurer, Gen. George M. Sternberg, is as follows:

Balance on hand April 30, 1907	$2,615.64
Receipts	21,720.39
Expenditures	18,236.32
Balance on hand April 30, 1908	$6,099.71

At the meeting of 1908 there were reported an addition of 50 associations to the already existing 54; 28 dispensaries were added during the year to the existing 36; and 30 special hospitals and sanatoria were added to the existing 118.

A list of officers and directors for 1907 to 1908 follows

President, Dr. Frank Billings; honorary vice-presidents, Theodore Roosevelt, Grover Cleveland, and Dr. William Osler; vice-presidents, Dr. Mazÿck P. Ravenel and Dr. John P. C. Foster; treasurer, Gen. George M. Sternberg; secretary, Dr. Henry Barton Jacobs; directors, Dr. Howard S. Anders, Philadelphia; William H. Baldwin, Washington; Ernest P. Bicknell, Chicago; Dr. Hermann M. Biggs, New York; Dr. Frank Billings, Chicago; Dr. John J. Black, New Castle, Del.; Dr. Sherman G. Bonney, Denver; Dr. Vincent Y. Bowditch, Boston; Dr. Henry M. Bracken, St. Paul; Dr. Norman Bridge, Los Angeles; Maj. Geo. E. Bushnell, Ft. Bayard; Dr. William S. Carter, Galveston; Otis H. Childs, Pittsburgh; Dr. T. D. Coleman, Augusta, Ga.; Dr. R. W. Corwin, Pueblo, Colo.; Edward T. Devine, New York; Charles W. Fairbanks, Washington; Dr. Lawrence F. Flick, Philadelphia; Dr. W. H. Flint, Santa Barbara, Cal.; Homer Folks, New York; Dr. John P. C. Foster, New Haven;

David R. Francis, St. Louis; Dr. John S. Fulton, Baltimore; Robert Garrett, Baltimore; Samuel Gompers, Washington; Rowland G. Hazard, Peace Dale, R. I.; James J. Hill, St. Paul; Frederick L. Hoffman, Newark; Dr. John N. Hurty, Indianapolis; Dr. Henry Barton Jacobs, Baltimore; Dr. Walter B. James, New York; Dr. Edward G. Janeway, New York; Dr. Arnold C. Klebs, Chicago; Dr. S. A. Knopf, New York; Dr. George M. Kober, Washington; Charles M. Lea, Philadelphia; Dr. John H. Lowman, Cleveland; Dr. C. F. McGahan, Aiken, S. C.; Dr. Alfred Meyer, New York; Dr. Charles L. Minor, Asheville; W. C. Nones, Louisville; Dr. Edward O. Otis, Boston; Dr. Leonard Pearson, Philadelphia; C. E. Perkins, Burlington, Iowa; Henry Phipps, New York; Dr. William Porter, St. Louis; Dr. Charles O. Probst, Columbus; Redfield Proctor, Jr., Proctor, Vt.; Dr. Mazÿck P. Ravenel, Madison, Wis.; W. T. Sedgwick, Boston; Dr. Henry Sewall, Denver; A. A. Sprague, 2d, Chicago; Gen. Geo. M. Sternberg, Washington; Dr. Edward L. Trudeau, Saranac Lake; Dr. Victor C. Vaughan, Ann Arbor; Dr. Joseph Walsh, Philadelphia; John Seely Ward, Jr., New York; Dr. William H. Welch, Baltimore; Benjamin I. Wheeler, Berkeley, Cal.; Gen. Walter Wyman, Washington.

Executive secretary, Dr. Livingston Farrand; assistant secretary, Philip P Jacobs, Ph.D.

The following is a list of papers read before the respective sections at the meeting of June 5-6, 1908:

Report on the International Congress on Tuberculosis—Lawrence F. Flick, M.D.
The campaign in the United States—Livingston Farrand, M.D.
With a state sanatorium secured, what next?—Symposium.
Tuberculosis in hospitals for the insane—H. A. Tomlinson, M.D.
Tuberculosis in prisons—H. C. Sharp, M.D.
The orphan asylum and its duties toward its wards—Ethan A. Gray, M.D.
Employment for arrested cases of tuberculosis—Charles J. Hatfield, M.D.
Tuberculin tests—Arnold C. Klebs, M.D.
Clinical study of the effect of tuberculin treatment on the serum agglutination of tubercle bacilli—Hugh M. Kinghorn, M.D., and David C. Twichell, M.D.
Immunity production by inoculation of increasing numbers of bacteria, beginning with one organism. Preliminary report—Gerald B. Webb, M.D., and William W. Williams, M.D.
The heart in pulmonary tuberculosis—Lawrason Brown, M.D.
The changes in the lungs in systemic blastomycosis as contrasted with those of tuberculosis—E. R. LeCount, M.D.
Acute pylephlebogenous miliary tuberculosis of the liver, with clinical picture of acute infectious jaundice; primary tuberculosis of mesenteric glands—Alfred Scott Warthin, M.D.
The clinical application of bacterial vaccines in cases of pulmonary tuberculosis—Sherman G. Bonney, M.D.

Explanation of seeming paradoxes in modern phthisio-therapy, with particular reference to sun, air, water, and food as remedial agents—S. Adolphus Knopf, M.D.

The municipal anti-tuberculosis work in Boston—Edwin A. Locke, M.D.

Hemoptysis in pulmonary tuberculosis—F. C. Smith, M.D.

The tuberculo-opsonic index, the von Pirquet tuberculin skin test, and the conjunctival tuberculin test in the diagnosis of tuberculosis—Mary C. Lincoln, M.D.

Tuberculous abscesses: their management—Edwin W. Ryerson, M.D.

Children of the tuberculous—Theodore B. Sachs, M.D.

Vertebral auscultation in the diagnosis of bronchial adenopathy, preliminary report—Ethan Allen Gray, M.D.

Report of the Committee on Clinical Nomenclature.

CHAPTER XV

FIFTH ANNUAL MEETING

THE fifth annual meeting of The National Association for the Study and Prevention of Tuberculosis was held at the New Willard Hotel, Washington, D. C., on May 13, 14, and 15, 1909. In the absence of the president, Dr. Vincent Y. Bowditch, the first vice-president, Mr. Homer Folks, occupied the chair at the general meetings.

On the afternoon of Friday, May 14, a public meeting was held in coöperation with the Washington Association for the Prevention of Tuberculosis and the Washington Academy of Sciences. Addresses were made on that occasion by Mr. Homer Folks, chairman, Right Honorable James Bryce, Hon. Joseph G. Cannon, Dr. William Osler, and Dr. William H. Welch.

At the opening meeting on Thursday, May 13, following the address of the vice-president and the report of the executive secretary, in accordance with the regular procedure of the Association a committee was appointed by the chair to present nominations to fill vacancies on the board of directors, as follows: Dr. Henry M. Bracken, St. Paul, chairman; Dr. William C. White, Pittsburgh; Dr. Charles R. Grandy, Norfolk; William H. Baldwin, Washington; Dr. Joseph H. Pratt, Boston.

The following committee on resolutions was also appointed by the chair: Dr. George M. Kober, Washington, chairman; Dr. John S. Fulton, Baltimore; Dr. S. A. Knopf, New York; Dr. Joseph Walsh, Philadelphia; Alexander M. Wilson, Boston.

At the regular business meeting of the Association, held on Friday, May 14, at 12.30 P. M., the following directors were unanimously elected for terms of five years: Dr. Robert H. Babcock, Chicago; Dr. W. F. Drewry, Petersburg, Va.; John M. Glenn, New York; Dr. Edward G. Janeway, New York; Dr. George M. Kober, Washington; Dr. John H. Lowman, Cleve-

land; R. B. Mellon, Pittsburgh; Dr. E. A. Pierce, Portland, Ore.;
Dr. Joseph Y. Porter, Key West, Fla.; Professor W. T. Sedgwick,
Boston; Dr. W. R. Steiner, Hartford, Conn.; Dr. Joseph Walsh,
Philadelphia.

The following resolutions were reported favorably by the committee and were unanimously adopted by the Association·

Resolved, That The National Association for the Study and Prevention of
Tuberculosis urges the centralization of the health activities of the United
States Government.

Resolved, That The National Association for the Study and Prevention of
Tuberculosis hails with gratification the efforts of the George Washington
Memorial Association to provide in the capital of the nation a permanent
home and meeting place for the national, patriotic, scientific, educational,
literary, and art activities, including a great hall and rooms for large congresses.

Resolved, That the need of such a building was emphasized during the International Congress on Tuberculosis, which was held in Washington during
September and October, 1908.

Resolved, That this Association indorses the project, and while pledging
cordial coöperation also recommends the undertaking as worthy of popular
support.

WHEREAS, Detailed knowledge of population, births, and deaths is a fundamental need of civilized governments; and

WHEREAS, The government of the United States, through its Census Bureau,
can furnish the necessary information concerning population only, the power
and the duty of recording births and deaths belonging to the States; and

WHEREAS, The government of the United States has assumed obligations to
furnish to foreign governments authoritative information concerning the
deaths of aliens in this country, the several States being party to these treaty
obligations the Government of the United States does not discharge, and cannot discharge except through the proper exercise by the States of their reserved
rights; and

WHEREAS, The government of the United States has more than once been
advised by foreign governments of its default in these obligations, and has
more than once called the attention of State governments to the existing
foreign obligations; and

WHEREAS, Only 16 of the States are able to furnish reliable accounts of
current mortality, while none can furnish reliable accounts of births; by these
defaults burdening their citizens, their courts, their boards of health, education,
charity, and labor with expensive and inferior substitutes for official and
authoritative records, and by the default in mortality registration, exposing the

12

government of the United States in the rôle of a defaulter in foreign relations: therefore, be it

Resolved, That The National Association for the Study and Prevention of Tuberculosis coöperate with other agencies in extending and strengthening the practice of registration of deaths and births in all parts of the United States.

At a meeting of the board of directors held on Friday afternoon, May 14, the following resolution was adopted by the board:

It having been demonstrated that typhoid fever, scarlet fever, tuberculosis, and certain other infectious diseases of man may be contracted by the use of impure (infected) milk, the board of directors of The National Association for the Study and Prevention of Tuberculosis desires to express its approval of all efforts to secure for the public generally, and especially for children, a pure milk supply.

The board of directors, at its meeting on May 14, elected the following officers for the ensuing year: Dr. Edward G. Janeway, New York, president; Mr. Edward T. Devine, New York, and Dr. Henry Sewall, Denver, vice-presidents; Dr. Henry Barton Jacobs, Baltimore, secretary; Gen. George M. Sternberg, Washington, treasurer.

The following directors were elected to serve on the executive committee for the ensuing year: William H. Baldwin, Washington; Dr. Hermann M. Biggs, New York; Edward T. Devine, New York; Homer Folks, New York; Dr. George M. Kober, Washington; Dr. John H. Lowman, Cleveland; Dr. Joseph Walsh, Philadelphia.

Following the meeting of the Advisory Council on the evening of May 13, Dr. Henry M. Bracken, of St. Paul, was unanimously elected chairman of the Advisory Council of the next annual meeting.

The summarized report of the Treasurer, Gen. George M. Sternberg, is as follows:

Balance on hand April 30, 1908............... $6,099.71
Receipts..................................... 24,256.62
Expenditures................................. 26,087.69
_____
Balance on hand April 30, 1909............... $4,268.64

At the meeting of the Association in 1909 there were reported an addition of 41 anti-tuberculosis associations to the already existing 104. To the 64 previously existing dispensaries were added 85 during the period 1908–1909; and 36 sanatoria and special hospitals were added to the previously reported 148.

A list of officers and directors for 1908 to 1909 follows:

President, Dr. Vincent Y. Bowditch; honorary vice-presidents, Theodore Roosevelt, and Dr. William Osler; vice-presidents, Mr. Homer Folks, and Dr. Charles L. Minor; treasurer, Gen. George M. Sternberg; secretary, Dr. Henry Barton Jacobs; directors, Dr. Howard S. Anders, Philadelphia; Dr. Edward R. Baldwin, Saranac Lake; William H. Baldwin, Washington; Ernest P. Bicknell, Chicago; Dr. Hermann M. Biggs, New York; D. Frank Billings, Chicago; W. K. Bixby, St. Louis; Dr. John J. Black, New Castle, Del.; Dr. Sherman G. Bonney, Denver; C. B. Boothe, Los Angeles; Dr. Vincent Y. Bowditch, Boston; Dr. Henry M. Bracken, St. Paul; Dr. Norman Bridge, Los Angeles; Maj. George E. Bushnell, Fort Bayard; Dr. William S. Carter, Galveston; Otis H. Childs, Pittsburgh; Dr. T. D. Coleman, Augusta, Ga.; Dr. R. W. Corwin, Pueblo, Colo.; Albert B. Cummins, Des Moines; Edward T. Devine, New York; Dr. Lawrence F. Flick, Philadelphia; Dr. W. H. Flint, Santa Barbara, Cal.; Homer Folks, New York; Dr. John P. C. Foster, New Haven; David R. Francis, St. Louis; Dr. John S. Fulton, Baltimore; Robert Garrett, Baltimore; Samuel Gompers, Washington; Rowland C. Hazard, Peace Dale, R.I.; James J. Hill, St. Paul; Frederick L. Hoffman, Newark, N. J.; Dr. John N. Hurty, Indianapolis; Dr. Henry Barton Jacobs, Baltimore; Dr. Edward G. Janeway, New York; Dr. Arnold C. Klebs, Chicago; Dr. S. A. Knopf, New York; Dr. George M. Kober, Washington; Charles M. Lea, Philadelphia, Dr. John H. Lowman, Cleveland; Dr. C. F. Mc Gahan, Aiken, S. C.; Dr. Rudolf Matas, New Orleans; Dr. Alfred Meyer, New York; Dr. Charles L. Minor, Asheville; W. C. Nones, Louisvile; Dr. Edward O. Otis, Boston; Dr. Leonard Pearson, Philadelphia; Henry Phipps, New York; Dr. Charles O. Probst, Columbus, O.; Redfield Proctor, Jr., Proctor, Vt.; Dr. Mazÿck P. Ravenel, Madison, Wis.; W. T. Sedgwick, Boston; Dr. Henry Sewall, Denver; A. A. Sprague, 2d, Chicago; Gen. Geo. M. Sternberg, Washington; Dr. Edward L. Trudeau, Saranac Lake; Dr. Victor C. Vaughan, Ann Arbor; Dr. Joseph Walsh, Philadelphia; John Seely Ward, Jr., New York; Dr. William H. Welch, Baltimore; Gen. Walter Wyman, Washington.

Executive secretary, Dr. Livingston Farrand; assistant secretary, Philip P. Jacobs, Ph.D.

The following is a list of papers read before the respective sections at the meeting of May 13–15, 1909:

Tuberculosis legislation—Victor C. Vaughan, M.D.
Relation of the public school to the anti-tuberculosis movement—A. B. Poland.

Boston's outdoor school—James J. Minot, M.D., and Miss Isabel F. Hyams.
The organization of local tuberculosis campaigns by a state association—John A. Kingsbury.
After-care of local committees—Homer Folks
Economic and efficient construction—Arnold C. Klebs, M.D.
Improved organization and management—A. H. Garvin, M.D.
On the construction of an efficient and economic diet in tuberculosis—Herbert Maxon King, M.D.
Work for patients as an economic factor—Lawrence F. Flick, M.D.
Work for patients as an immediate and ultimate therapeutic factor—Frederick I. Hills, M.D.
Clinical diagnosis of pulmonary tuberculosis—James Alexander Miller, M.D.
The laboratory methods of diagnosis in tuberculosis—Randle C. Rosenberger, M.D.
Diagnosis of intestinal tuberculosis—Joseph Walsh, M.D.
Studies of tuberculin reaction with a new index to dosage in tuberculin treatment—William Charles White, M.D., D. A. L. Graham, M.B., and K. H. Van Norman, M.D.
Some hematological studies in tuberculosis—G. B. Webb, M.D., and W. W. Williams, M.D.
The value of the tuberculo-opsonic test in the diagnosis of pulmonary tuberculosis—Hugh M. Kinghorn, M.D., David C. Twichell, M.D., and Norman Carter, M.D.
The tuberculo-opsonic index in its relation to the temperature curve in active tuberculosis and its value in diagnosis in suspected or arrested cases—Herbert Maxon King, M.D.
The heart in one hundred and ten cases dying of tuberculosis—William B. Stanton, M.D.
Primary location and development of tuberculosis in the lungs—Joseph Walsh, M.D.
The amount of lung involvement at the onset of pulmonary tuberculosis—Harry Lee Barnes, M.D.
Some results of the injection of Beck's bismuth paste in the treatment of tuberculous sinuses—William S. Baer, M.D.
Chloroform rather than ether anesthesia in tuberculosis—Joseph Walsh, M.D.
Address of the chairman of Section on Tuberculosis in Children—John H. Lowman, M.D.
The diagnosis of tuberculosis in young children—Henry L. K. Shaw, M.D., and Arthur T. Laird, M.D.
A study of the symptomatology of pulmonary tuberculosis among children—Henry I. Bowditch, M.D.
Treatment of surgical tuberculosis—John W. Brannan, M.D.

CHAPTER XVI

SIXTH ANNUAL MEETING

THE sixth annual meeting of The National Association for the Study and Prevention of Tuberculosis was held at the New Willard Hotel, Washington, D. C., on May 2 and 3, 1910. The president of the Association, Dr. Edward G. Janeway, occupied the chair at the general meeting held at noon on Monday, May 2. Following the address of the president and the report of the executive secretary, in accordance with the regular procedure of the Association, the following committee was appointed by the chair to present nominations to fill vacancies on the board of directors: Dr. Walter R. Steiner, Hartford, chairman; Dr. Henry M. Bracken, St. Paul; Dr. John S. Fulton, Baltimore; Dr. Charles O. Probst, Columbus, Ohio; Frank E. Wing, Chicago.

The following committee on resolutions was also appointed by the chair: Homer Folks, New York, chairman; Dr. Hermann M. Biggs, New York; Dr. G. Walter Holden, Denver; Dr. John H. Lowman, Cleveland; Gen. George M. Sternberg, Washington.

At the regular business meeting of the Association held on the evening of Monday, May 2, the following were unanimously elected directors of the Association for terms of five years: William H. Baldwin, Washington; William K. Bixby, St. Louis; Jeffrey R. Brackett, Boston; Dr. Thomas D. Coleman, Augusta, Ga.; Dr. George Dock, St. Louis; Dr. G. Walter Holden, Denver; Dr. Alfred Meyer, New York; Julius Rosenwald, Chicago; Dr. F. F. Wesbrook, Minneapolis; Alexander M. Wilson, Philadelphia; Gen. Walter Wyman, Washington.

Dr. John L. Dawson, Charleston, S. C., was elected a director to fill the unexpired term of the late Dr. Charles F. McGahan. Dr. Elmer E. Heg, Seattle, Wash., was elected a director to fill the unexpired term of the late Dr. John J. Black.

181

The following resolutions were reported favorably by the committee on resolutions and were unanimously adopted by the Association:

WHEREAS, Hundreds of thousands of human lives are lost annually from tuberculosis and other preventable diseases, and

WHEREAS, There is great need of some agency of national scope whose functions shall be the investigation of problems of public health, the dissemination of information relating thereto, and such other duties pertaining to public health as may properly fall within the field of Federal authority, and

WHEREAS, The work of this character which should be undertaken by a national agency is beyond the resources of private effort and should have not only the larger resources, but the dignity and prestige of Federal authority; and

WHEREAS, A bill has been introduced in Congress by Senator Owen and Representative Craeger establishing a Federal Department of Health in which are to be brought together all Federal agencies now dealing with these subjects and by which should be undertaken such new duties relative to public health as the national government might properly undertake, therefore,

Resolved, That we very heartily endorse the general principle of the Owen-Craeger bill and place on record our conviction that its enactment would be of great service in the prevention of tuberculosis, and of other infectious and preventable diseases.

1. *Resolved*, That a thorough, efficient, and continuous official supervision of dairies and herds and of the milk from the dairy to the consumer is of the first importance in securing a clean and pure milk supply, which is essential to public health.

2. *Resolved*, That the production and handling of milk under such satisfactory sanitary conditions as to insure its complete reliability (*i. e.*, the production of what is known as certified milk) at the present time unfortunately increases its cost to such an extent as to make the use of such milk for general consumption impracticable.

3. *Resolved*, That the efficient pasteurization of the general milk supply (excepting certified milk) when supplementing dairy inspection and applied to milk from inspected dairies and done under official supervision is desirable for the destruction of the ordinary micro-organisms of fermentation and putrefaction and as an additional protection against possible infection by typhoid fever, scarlet fever, diphtheria, tuberculosis, and possibly some other specific infectious diseases.

4. *Resolved*, That pasteurization of milk for sale should not be permitted except under official supervision and on conditions definitely prescribed by competent sanitary authorities; and should not be permitted as a method for the preservation of old or dirty milk.

5. *Resolved*, That milk intended for infant feeding should be considered

apart from that intended for general consumption; and should be certified milk when obtainable.

6. *Resolved*, That in the opinion of this Association it has been proven, apparently, that a small percentage of the cases of non-pulmonary human tuberculosis, especially tuberculosis of the lymph-nodes in children under five years of age, is due to infection by tubercle bacilli of bovine origin.

WHEREAS, The State of Nebraska has recently passed a law making it obligatory for hospitals and sanatoria receiving tuberculous patients supported by the public to use treatment of immunization (vaccine therapy); and

WHEREAS, In the opinion of the members of this Association the present state of knowledge of specific immunization and vaccine therapy in tuberculosis does not justify any state in enacting such legislation; therefore

Resolved, That The National Association for the Study and Prevention of Tuberculosis deplores the above named act of the State Legislature of Nebraska as most unwise, and wholly unjustifiable. Be it further

Resolved, That the Executive Secretary of the Association transmit a copy of these resolutions to the Governor of the State of Nebraska and the Speakers of the Senate and the House of Representatives of that State.

WHEREAS, The Board of Medical Examiners of the State of Oklahoma refuses to grant licenses to physicians afflicted with tuberculosis; and

WHEREAS, All applicants for such a license must subscribe and swear to a so-called tuberculosis affidavit in which they must not only declare that they are not suffering with tuberculosis in any form but also swear that they have not, within the last three years, lived in the house with or nursed any one suffering from said disease;

WHEREAS, In the opinion of the members of this Association such action of the State Board of Medical Examiners of Oklahoma is not based on sound scientific or economic considerations; and

WHEREAS, It is the conviction of the members of this Association that neither the careful tuberculous physician nor the well trained tuberculous patient pursuing his occupation should be considered a menace to society, be it therefore

Resolved, That this Association deplores the action of the State Board of Medical Examiners of Oklahoma as unjustifiable and prejudicial to the best interests of the community, and

Resolved, That the Executive Secretary transmit a copy of these resolutions to the President and Secretary of the Oklahoma State Board of Medical Examiners and to the Governor of that State.

Resolved, That this Association observes with great interest and satisfaction the marked progress throughout the United States and particularly in the District of Columbia during the past year, of the playground movement; and expresses the earnest hope that the National Congress will make adequate appropriations for continuing and extending in the District of Columbia these opportunities for healthful open-air exercise and play.

Resolved, That we urge upon municipalities a study of housing conditions with special reference to tenement and cheap lodging houses and urge a vigorous effort to improve congested districts, believing that such improvement will decrease the tuberculosis death-rate.

At a meeting of the board of directors held on Tuesday afternoon, May 3, the following officers were elected for the ensuing year: Dr. William H. Welch, Baltimore, president; Dr. George Dock, St. Louis, and Dr. Victor C. Vaughan, Ann Arbor, vice-presidents; Dr. Henry Barton Jacobs, Baltimore, secretary; General George M. Sternberg, Washington, treasurer.

The following directors were elected to serve on the executive committee for the ensuing year: William H. Baldwin, Washington; Dr. Hermann M. Biggs, New York; Homer Folks, New York; Dr. John N. Hurty, Indianapolis; Dr. Edward G. Janeway, New York; Dr. George M. Kober, Washington; Dr. Joseph Walsh, Philadelphia.

Following the meeting of the Advisory Council on the evening of May 2, Dr. William Charles White, of Pittsburgh, was unanimously elected chairman of the Advisory Council for the next annual meeting.

The summarized report of the Treasurer, Gen. George M. Sternberg, is as follows:

Balance on hand April 30, 1909	$4,268.64
Receipts	24,948.76
Disbursements	28,696.26
Balance on hand April 30, 1910	$521.14

At the meeting of the Association in 1910, there was reported a membership of 2,107. The number of anti-tuberculosis associations was 297; dispensaries 222; sanatoria and special hospitals 298, with a capacity of over 15,000 beds. This marvelous gain has to be ascribed to the interest which was aroused in the movement by the International Tuberculosis Congress which was held in Washington in 1908.

A list of officers and directors for 1909 to 1910 follows:

President, Dr. Edward G. Janeway; honorary vice-presidents, Theodore Roosevelt and Dr. William Osler; vice-presidents, Mr. Edward T. Devine and Dr. Henry Sewall; treasurer, General George M. Sternberg; secretary, Dr. Henry Barton Jacobs; directors, Dr. Robert H. Babcock, Chicago; Dr. Edward R. Baldwin, Saranac Lake; William H. Baldwin, Washington; Ernest P. Bicknell, Chicago; Dr. Hermann M. Biggs, New York; Dr. Frank Billings, Chicago; W. K. Bixby, St. Louis; Dr. John J. Black, New Castle, Del.; Dr. Sherman G. Bonney, Denver; C. B. Boothe, Los Angeles; Dr. Vincent Y. Bowditch, Boston; Dr. Henry M. Bracken, St. Paul; Dr. William S. Carter, Galveston; Otis H. Childs, Pittsburgh; Dr. T. D. Coleman, Augusta, Ga.; Dr. R. W. Corwin, Pueblo, Colo.; Albert B. Cummins, Des Moines; Edward T. Devine, New York; Dr. W. F. Drewry, Petersburg, Va.; Dr. Lawrence F. Flick, Philadelphia; Dr. W. H. Flint, Santa Barbara, Cal.; Homer Folks, New York; David R. Francis, St. Louis; Dr. John S. Fulton, Baltimore; Robert Garrett, Baltimore; John M. Glenn, New York; Samuel Gompers, Washington; Rowland G. Hazard, Peace Dale, R. I.; James J. Hill, St. Paul; Frederick L. Hoffman, Newark; Dr. John N. Hurty, Indianapolis; Dr. Henry Barton Jacobs, Baltimore; Dr. Edward G. Janeway, New York; Dr. Arnold C. Klebs, Chicago; Dr. S. A. Knopf, New York; Dr. George M. Kober, Washington; Charles M. Lea, Philadelphia; Dr. John H. Lowman, Cleveland; Dr. C. F. McGahan, Aiken, S. C.; Dr. Rudolf Matas, New Orleans; R. B. Mellon, Pittsburgh, Pa.; Dr. Alfred Meyer, New York; Dr. Charles L. Minor, Asheville; W. C. Nones, Louisville; Dr. Edward O. Otis, Boston; Henry Phipps, New York; Dr. E. A Pierce, Portland, Ore.; Dr. Joseph Y. Porter, Key West, Fla.; Dr. Charles O. Probst, Columbus, O.; Redfield Proctor, Jr., Proctor, Vt.; Dr. Mazÿck P. Ravenel, Madison, Wis.; W. T. Sedgwick, Boston; Dr. Henry Sewall, Denver; A. A. Sprague, 2d, Chicago; Gen. George M. Sternberg, Washington; Dr. Walter R. Steiner, Hartford, Conn.; Dr. Edward L. Trudeau, Saranac Lake; Dr. Victor C. Vaughan, Ann Arbor; Dr. Joseph Walsh, Philadelphia; Dr. William H. Welch, Baltimore.

Executive secretary, Dr. Livingston Farrand; assistant secretary, Philip P. Jacobs, Ph.D.

The following is a list of papers read before the respective sections at the meeting of May 2-3, 1910:

Insurance against tuberculosis—Lee K. Frankel.
Budget and program for a local anti-tuberculosis campaign—James Jenkins, Jr.
The question of employment—A. M. Forster, M.D.
The enforcement of anti-spitting laws—Robert J. Newton.
The school child and tuberculosis: a plea for preventoria—Henry Farnum Stoll, M.D.
Medical and board of health supervision of boarding houses and sanatoria for the treatment of tuberculosis—David P. Butler, M.D.

State phthisiophilia and state phthisiophobia, with a plea for justice to the consumptive—S. Adolphus Knopf, M.D.

The teaching of tuberculosis—A plea for its specialization in medical schools—A. P. Francine, M.D.

Prognosis of tuberculous lesions involving the whole of or more than one lobe—Joseph Walsh, M.D.

The responsibility for relapse of tuberculous patients after discharge—W. L. Dunn, M.D.

Early changes in the larynx in pulmonary tuberculosis—Charles L. Minor, M.D.

Gastric disturbances in pulmonary tuberculosis—H. R. M. Landis, M.D.

Some results of sanatorium treatment of pulmonary tuberculosis in children—Henry S. Goodall, M.D.

The diagnostic value of local tuberculin reactions—Theodore B. Sachs, M.D.

The relation of the cutaneous to the subcutaneous tuberculin test—Thomas DeWitt Gordon, M.D.

An individual quantitative basis for dosage in tuberculin treatment—William Charles White, M.D., and K. H. Van Norman, M.D.

Cutaneous and conjunctival tuberculin tests in pulmonary tuberculosis—a report of 1,000 cases—Louis Hamman, M.D., and Samuel Wolman, M.D.

The diagnosis of tuberculosis of the bronchial glands—Henry Farnum Stoll, M.D.

A contribution to the study of pulmonary tuberculosis in its relation to albuminuria—John Ritter, M.D.

Stereoscopic radiography as diagnostic aid in pulmonary tuberculosis—Emil G. Beck, M.D.

Artificial lymphocytosis in tuberculosis—Gerald B. Webb, M.D., William Whitbridge Williams, M.D., and A. F. Basinger, M.D.

A study of the leucocytes in pulmonary tuberculosis (a preliminary investigation)—Myer Solis-Cohen, M.D., and Albert Strickler, M.D.

The gross pathology in fatal cases of tuberculosis of the lungs—Joseph Walsh, M.D.

The relative importance of the bovine and human types of tubercle bacilli in different forms of human tuberculosis—William H. Park, M.D., and Charles Krumwiede, Jr., M.D.

The bovine type of tuberculosis associated with three cases of tuberculosis in man—Marshall Fabyan, M.D.

The reaction curve of the human and the bovine type of the tubercle bacillus in glycerin bouillon—Theobald Smith, M.D.

CHAPTER XVII

SEVENTH ANNUAL MEETING

THE Seventh Annual Meeting of The National Association for the Study and Prevention of Tuberculosis was held at the Brown Palace Hotel, Denver, Colorado, on June 20 and 21, 1911.

The Colorado members entertained the Association at luncheon on June 20, and also acted as hosts on the occasion of a mountain trip over the Moffat Road on the afternoon and evening of June 21. On Tuesday, June 22, many of the members visited Colorado Springs as guests of that city, and had an opportunity of inspecting the various sanatoria of the vicinity.

The president of the Association, Dr. William H. Welch, called the Association to order on the morning of June 20. Following the address of the president and the report of the executive secretary, in accordance with the regular procedure of the Association, the following committee was appointed by the chair to present nominations to fill vacancies on the board of directors: Dr. Henry M. Bracken, St. Paul, chairman; Dr. Dunning S. Wilson, Louisville; Dr. H. Wirt Steele, Baltimore; Dr. R. W. Corwin, Pueblo; Dr. Ethan A. Gray, Chicago.

The following committee on resolutions was also appointed by the chair: Dr. S. Adolphus Knopf, New York, chairman; Dr. Mazÿck P. Ravenel, Madison; Dr. Frank E. Wing, Chicago; J. Byron Deacon, Philadelphia; Dr. Will Howard Swan, Colorado Springs.

At the regular business meeting of the Association, held on the evening of Tuesday, June 20, the following members were unanimously elected directors of the Association for the term of five years: Dr. Joseph S. Ames, Baltimore; Miss Kate Barnard, Oklahoma City; Ernest P. Bicknell, Washington, D. C.; Dr. Vincent Y. Bowditch, Boston; Dr. John S. Fulton, Baltimore;

Dr. Charles Lyman Greene, St. Paul; Dr. Elmer E. Hegg, Seattle; Dr. Henry Barton Jacobs, Baltimore; Dr. Theodore B. Sachs, Chicago; Dr. Thomas D. Tuttle, Helena; Dr. Gerald B. Webb, Colorado Springs; Dr. William Charles White, Pittsburgh.

Dr. James Alexander Miller, New York, was elected a director to fill the unexpired term of the late Dr. Edward G. Janeway.

The following resolutions were recorded favorably by the com mittee on resolutions, and were unanimously adopted by the Association:

WHEREAS, It has pleased Divine Providence to remove from our midst our late President, Dr. Edward G. Janeway, and

WHEREAS, By his great diagnostic skill, and deep interest in all that appertains to the anti-tuberculosis movement in this country, he has been of invaluable service to our cause; be it

Resolved, That we the members of The National Association for the Study and Prevention of Tuberculosis deeply deplore the loss of our late President, who by his life and devotion to anti-tuberculosis work, should forever be an example for us to follow. Be it further

Resolved, That a copy of these resolutions be spread on the minutes of the Annual Meeting of The National Association for the Study and Prevention of Tuberculosis, that a copy of them be transmitted by the Executive Secretary to the family of the late Dr. Janeway, and also to the medical and lay press.

WHEREAS, It has been demonstrated experimentally by bacteriologists of high standing in this and other countries and by two governmental commissions, that the bovine tubercle bacillus causes serious and fatal tuberculosis in human beings; and

WHEREAS, Milk from tuberculous cattle appears to be the medium through which transmission of bovine tuberculosis to human beings most commonly takes place; be it ,l

Resolved, That The National Association for the Study and Prevention of Tuberculosis recognizes the danger to mankind from tuberculosis of cattle; and be it

Resolved, That this Association recommends that all cows furnishing milk for human consumption be subjected to the tuberculin tests, and that all animals which react to this test be excluded from dairy herds; and be it further

Resolved, That where these measures cannot be efficiently carried out, the Association recommends the efficient pasteurization of milk as a safeguard against the transmission of bovine tuberculosis to mankind.

WHEREAS, The care of advanced cases of tuberculosis has been found from experience to be particularly difficult in institutions located at a considerable distance from the homes of patients; and

WHEREAS, The municipality and the county have in most cases been found to be satisfactory units for the care of advanced cases; and

WHEREAS, The stamping out of tuberculosis depends so largely upon segregation of advanced cases; therefore be it

Resolved, That The National Association for the Study and Prevention of Tuberculosis approves a plan whereby municipalities and counties shall be encouraged to erect satisfactory institutions for treatment of advanced cases; and be it further

Resolved, That this Association approves a plan whereby municipalities and counties shall be encouraged to establish dispensaries for the discovery, treatment and prevention of cases of tuberculosis.

WHEREAS, The National Association for the Study and Prevention of Tuber-, culosis has enjoyed the bountiful hospitality of the Colorado members of the Association, be it

Resolved, That we hereby tender to the chairman and members of the various committees, to the Colorado medical profession and to the laity at large who have so liberally contributed to our entertainment, our most hearty thanks and appreciation.

At a meeting of the board of directors held on Wednesday, June 21, the following officers were elected for the ensuing year: Dr. Mazÿck P. Ravenel, president; John M. Glenn, New York, and Dr. G. Walter Holden, Denver, vice-presidents; Dr. Henry Barton Jacobs, Baltimore, secretary; Gen. George M. Sternberg, Washington, treasurer.

The following directors were elected to serve on the executive committee for the ensuing year: William H. Baldwin, Washington; Dr. Hermann M. Biggs, New York; Edward T. Devine, New York; Dr. S. A. Knopf, New York; Dr. George M. Kober, Washington; Dr. Walter R. Steiner, Hartford; Dr. William Charles White, Pittsburgh.

Following the meeting of the Advisory Council on the evening of June 20, Dr. Charles O. Probst, of Columbus, Ohio, was unanimously elected chairman of the Advisory Council for the next annual meeting.

The summarized report of the Treasurer, Gen. George M. Sternberg, is as follows:

Balance on hand April 30, 1910	$521.14
Receipts	33,080.59
Disbursements	31,058.60
Balance on hand April 30, 1911	$2,543.13

At the meeting of the Association in 1911 the Secretary reported a membership of 2,270; number of associations, 431; number of dispensaries, 286; and sanatoria and special hospitals, 393, with a capacity of 22,720 beds.

A list of officers and directors for 1910 to 1911 follows:

President, Dr. William H. Welch; honorary vice-presidents, Theodore Roosevelt and Dr. William Osler; vice-presidents, Dr. Victor C. Vaughan and Dr. George Dock; treasurer, Gen. George M. Sternberg; secretary, Dr. Henry Barton Jacobs; directors, Dr. Robert H. Babcock, Chicago; Dr. Edward R. Baldwin, Saranac Lake; William H. Baldwin, Washington; Dr. Hermann M. Biggs, New York; Dr. Frank Billings, Chicago; W. K. Bixby, St. Louis; C. B. Boothe, Los Angeles; Dr. Henry M. Bracken, St. Paul; Jeffrey R. Brackett, Boston; Dr. William S. Carter, Galveston; Otis H. Childs, Pittsburgh; Dr. T. D. Coleman, Augusta, Ga.; Dr. R. W. Corwin, Pueblo, Colo.; Albert B. Cummins, Des Moines; Dr. John L. Dawson, Charleston; Edward T. Devine, New York; Dr. George Dock, St. Louis; Dr. W. F. Drewry, Petersburg, Va.; Dr. Henry B. Favill, Chicago; Dr. Lawrence F. Flick, Philadelphia; Dr. W. H. Flint, Santa Barbara; Homer Folks, New York; David R. Francis, St. Louis; Robert Garrett, Baltimore; John M. Glenn, New York; Samuel Gompers, Washington; Rowland G. Hazard, Peace Dale, R. I.; Dr. Elmer E. Hegg, Seattle; James J. Hill, St. Paul; Frederick L. Hoffman, Newark; Dr. G. Walter Holden, Denver; Dr. John N. Hurty, Indianapolis; Dr. Henry Barton Jacobs, Baltimore; Dr. Edward G. Janeway, New York; Dr. S. A. Knopf, New York; Dr. George M. Kober, Washington; Charles M. Lea, Philadelphia; Dr. John H. Lowman, Cleveland; Dr. Rudolf Matas, New Orleans; R. B. Mellon, Pittsburgh, Pa.; Dr. Alfred Meyer, New York; Dr. Charles L. Minor, Asheville; W. C. Nones, Louisville; Dr. Edward O. Otis, Boston; Dr. E. A. Pierce, Portland, Ore.; Dr· Joseph Y. Porter, Key West, Fla.; Redfield Proctor, Jr., Proctor, Vt.; Dr. Mazÿck P. Ravenel, Madison, Wis.; Julius Rosenwald, Chicago; W. T. Sedgwick, Boston; Dr. Henry Sewall, Denver; Gen. George M. Sternberg, Washington; Dr. Walter R. Steiner, Hartford, Conn.; Dr. Edward L. Trudeau, Saranac Lake; Dr. Victor C. Vaughan, Ann Arbor; Dr. Joseph Walsh, Philadelphia; Dr. William H. Welch, Baltimore; Dr. F. F. Wesbrook, Minneapolis; Alexander M. Wilson, Philadelphia; Gen. Walter Wyman, Washington.

Executive secretary, Dr. Livingston Farrand; assistant secretary, Philip P. Jacobs, Ph.D.

The following is a list of papers read before the respective sections at the meeting of June 20–21, 1911:

Dr. Edward G. Janeway, late president of the National Association for the Study and Prevention of Tuberculosis; his contributions and activities— S. Adolphus Knopf, M.D.

The responsibility of the state in the tuberculosis problem—Homer Folks, LL.D.

The responsibility of the county in the tuberculosis problem—Hoyt E. Dearholt, M.D.

The responsibility of the city in the tuberculosis problem—Clyde E. Ford, M.D.

Open-air schools—Leonard P. Ayres, Ph.D.

Four months in the open air—a study of sixty children—O. W. McMichael, M.D.

Methods of school ventilation (by the Chicago Commission on Ventilation)— W. A. Evans, M.D.

Health of school children—Helen Marsh Wixson.

School health and hygiene exhibits—John B. Hawes, 2d, M.D.

The relief of families in which there is tuberculosis—H. Wirt Steele.

The past and future of the tuberculosis nurse—Edna L. Foley.

Tuberculosis as a factor in the increased cost of living—Edward F. McSweeney, Boston.

An economic study of 500 consumptives treated in the Boston Consumptives' Hospital—Edwin A. Locke, M.D., and Cleaveland Floyd, M.D.

A survey of Dunn county, Wisconsin—Hoyt E. Dearholt, M.D.

A county organized and equipped to control tuberculosis—George J. Nelbach.

The control of tuberculosis in the smaller towns—George R. Pogue, M.D.

A study of three small cities—J. Byron Deacon.

Report of traveling tuberculosis car of Missouri Association for the Relief and Control of Tuberculosis—Miss Winifred Doyle.

Boston's hospital school for tuberculous children—Edwin A. Locke, M.D., and Timothy J. Murphy, M.D.

The present attitude toward climate—Alexius M. Forster, M.D.

Experience with pulmonary tuberculosis during the past year—a clinical résumé—S. G. Bonney, M.D.

The albumin reaction in the sputum in pulmonary tuberculosis—Lawrason Brown, M.D., and W. H. Ross, M.D.

Sputum examinations with special reference to the antiformin method— Frederick Tice, M.D.

Bedside service in tuberculosis—William Porter, M.D.

The treatment of secondary anemia of tuberculosis by the hypodermic injection of iron—LeRoy S. Peters, M.D., and E. S. Bullock, M.D.

Hypotension and tachycardia in the tuberculous—John Ritter, M.D.

Studies on mixed infection in pulmonary tuberculosis. The isolation of the streptococcus and pneumococcus from the blood—Roswell T. Pettit, M.D.

Secondary infection in pulmonary tuberculosis (a study based on sputum examinations)—James L. Whitney, M.D.

The effect of tuberculin treatment upon the leucocytic picture—Myer Solis-Cohen, M.D., and Albert Strickler, M.D.

Prognosis in pulmonary tuberculosis—H. S. Mathewson, M.D.

Report of 34 cases of tuberculosis treated with tuberculins and 18 with mercury at the Marine Hospital Sanatorium, Fort Stanton, N. M.—L. D. Fricks, M.D., William Keiller, M.D., F. Simpson, M.D., and F. C. Smith, M.D.

Investigations into the nature of tuberculin sensitiveness—Edward R. Baldwin, M.D.

Control of bovine tuberculosis—Mazÿck P. Ravenel, M.D.

The specific tissue inoculation of vaccines—Gerald B. Webb, M.D., and G. Burton Gilbert, M.D.

A study of leukocytes in 100 cases of pulmonary tuberculosis—Henry D. Chadwick, M.D., and Roy Morgan, M.D.

Some remarks on the mode of infection and of dissemination of tuberculosis in man based on anatomical investigation—William Ophüls, M.D.

CHAPTER XVIII

EIGHTH ANNUAL MEETING

THE eighth annual meeting of The National Association for the Study and Prevention of Tuberculosis was held at the New Willard Hotel, Washington, D. C., on May 30 and 31, 1912. The president of the Association, Dr. Mazÿck P. Ravenel, called the Association to order at 11 o'clock on the morning of May 30. Following the address of the president and he report of the executive secretary, in accordance with the regular procedure of the Association, the following committee was appointed by the chair to present nominations to fill vacancies on the board of directors: Dr. William C. White, Pittsburgh, chairman; Dr. A. M. Forster, Colorado Springs; F. H. Mann, New York; W. S. Ufford, Washington; Dr. Gordon Wilson, Baltimore.

The following committee on resolutions was also appointed by the chair: Dr. H. R. M. Landis, Philadelphia, chairman; Dr. W. J. Barlow, Los Angeles; Dr. H. M. Kinghorn, Saranac Lake; Dr. T. B. Sachs, Chicago; J. R. Shillady, Buffalo

At the regular business meeting of the Association, held at noon on May 31, the following were unanimously elected directors of the Association for terms of five years: Dr. W. Jarvis Barlow, Los Angeles; Miss Mabel T. Boardman, Washington; Homer Folks, New York; Dr. Charles J. Hatfield, Philadelphia; John A. Kingsbury, New York; Col. J. L. Ludlow, Winston-Salem; Dr. Cabot Lull, Birmingham; Dr. C. O. Probst, Columbus, Ohio; Dr. E. C. Schroeder, Washington; Surgeon-General C. F. Stokes, Washington; Dr. E. L. Trudeau, Saranac Lake; Dr. W. H. Welch, Baltimore.

Dr. H. E. Dearholt, of Milwaukee, was elected a director to fill the unexpired term of the late Surgeon-General Walter Wyman.

The following resolutions were reported favorably by the committee on resolutions and were unanimously adopted by the Association:

Resolved, That the Executive Secretary be requested to correspond with the officers of the American Veterinary Medical Association, calling to their attention the following points:

1. The close relationship between the work of The National Association for the Study and Prevention of Tuberculosis and the work of the veterinary medical profession.

2. The small number of veterinarians who have joined The National Association for the Study and Prevention of Tuberculosis.

3. Inviting them individually to take membership in The National Association for the Study and Prevention of Tuberculosis.

4. Inviting the veterinarians to arrange a part of the program of the Pathological Section for the next annual meeting of the National Association.

Resolved, That The National Association for the Study and Prevention of Tuberculosis indorse the following terms of a resolution adopted by the Southwestern Conference on Tuberculosis, held at Waco, Texas, April 16, 1912:

"WHEREAS, Southwestern States have climatic and other natural advantages which have attracted people from other states for years past, and especially the sick—and as many of these people come into the Southwest with insufficient funds to maintain themselves until well, as a result of which they become public charges or suffer great privation, which counteracts all possible benefit of climate, and

"WHEREAS, The number of such indigent persons who are careless in their habits of living and spread their disease, not decreasing, it seems proper for us to issue a warning to the public, and especially to that portion of it afflicted with tuberculosis, and to all physicians, churches, lodges, labor unions, and charitable organizations; therefore be it

"*Resolved,* That the newspapers of the country be asked to give publicity to the following facts:

"(a) There are no free hospitals in the Southwest for other than citizens of Southwestern States.

"(b) No assistance can be given strangers by charitable associations because the public does not contribute funds for that purpose.

"(c) Owing to the large immigration of healthy people there is small chance for employment for sick persons. The number of factories is limited, cheap labor is performed by Mexicans and Negroes, ranch and farm work is strenuous, and invalids are not employed by land owners.

"(d) That invalids cannot hope to secure assistance from private individuals because the demands for aid from strangers have exhausted the patience of the people.

"(e) That invalids coming to the Southwest should have funds sufficient to carry them for one year, as they cannot hope for restoration to health and strength under that period of time.

"(*f*) That each community should provide proper hospitals, dispensaries, visiting nurses, etc., and care for its own people."

WHEREAS, Hospital care of advanced cases of tuberculosis is essential to the gradual reduction of the present incidence of this disease, and

WHEREAS, Experience has shown that patients will not enter or remain in institutions unless the surroundings are attractive and the care is of a higher standard than now prevails, be it

Resolved, That The National Association for the Study and Prevention of Tuberculosis, in its advocacy of sufficient institutional provision for the advanced consumptive, emphasize the importance of proper care of these unfortunate patients, including sufficient and efficient medical and nursing service, as well as a proper diet, and, further,

Resolved, That the Association indorses the efforts now being made by local communities for the proper care of advanced cases, and approves of the appointment by the Board of Directors of a Committee to investigate the present status of hospitals for advanced cases in this country and to formulate proper standards for their construction and management.

WHEREAS, Attention has been directed to the social and industrial causes of tuberculosis, the relation of dusty trades and other occupational factors to the morbidity and mortality from tuberculosis, and

WHEREAS, The prevalence of special tuberculosis clinics affords an opportunity for the recording of valuable information as to these important factors, therefore be it

Resolved, That the Board of Directors of The National Association for the Study and Prevention of Tuberculosis be requested to appoint a special committee to consider the possibility of securing the adoption of uniform dispensary records prepared with special reference to recording detailed data on industrial and social factors, past and present, in the patient's history.

WHEREAS, The double red cross has been used as the emblem of The National Association for the Study and Prevention of Tuberculosis for several years, having been adopted officially by said Association in 1906, and

WHEREAS, No fixed standards as to form or dimensions of the double red cross have ever been adopted by the Association, and

WHEREAS, There has been considerable variation in the forms and dimensions of the crosses used by the numerous anti-tuberculosis organizations in the United States and elsewhere, be it

Resolved, That the Board of Directors of The National Association for the Study and Prevention of Tuberculosis be requested to appoint a committee to consider the various questions involved in the history, artistic appearance, form, and proportions of the double red cross as the emblem of the anti-tuberculosis crusade in the United States, and that this Committee be directed to report to the Board of Directors for such action as the Board may deem advisable.

At the suggestion of the president it was voted unanimously that a telegram conveying the greetings and good wishes of the Association be sent to Dr. Edward L. Trudeau, the first president of the Association.

At a meeting of the board of directors, held on Friday afternoon, May 31, the following officers were unanimously elected for the ensuing year: Homer Folks, New York, president; Dr. Robert H. Babcock, Chicago, and Dr. Edward R. Baldwin, Saranac Lake, vice-presidents; Dr. Henry Barton Jacobs, Baltimore, secretary.

The following directors were elected to serve on the executive committee for the ensuing year: William H. Baldwin, Washington; Dr. Charles J. Hatfield, Philadelphia; Frederick L. Hoffman, Newark; Dr. S. A. Knopf, New York; Dr. George M. Kober, Washington; Dr. Walter R. Steiner, Hartford; Dr. William C. White, Pittsburgh.

General George M. Sternberg, having declined to accept re-election as treasurer of the Association, the responsibility of filling the office of treasurer was referred to the executive committee with power to act, and General Sternberg, upon request, consented to serve as acting treasurer until his successor should be elected.

The board of directors adopted the following resolution:

WHEREAS, General George M. Sternberg, who has been Treasurer of The National Association for the Study and Prevention of Tuberculosis since its organization in 1904, has found it necessary to ask to be relieved from further duty in that capacity, be it

Resolved, That the Board of Directors of the National Association, in reluctantly yielding to this request, desires to place on record its deep appreciation of the invaluable services of General Sternberg not only to the National Association, but to the entire anti-tuberculosis movement and the cause of public health in the United States.

Following the meeting of the Advisory Council on the evening of May 30, Dr. Charles J. Hatfield of Philadelphia was unanimously elected chairman of the Advisory Council for the next annual meeting.

The summarized report of the Treasurer, Gen. George M. Sternberg, is as follows:

Balance on hand April 30, 1911............... $2,543.13
Receipts................................... 36,230.15
Disbursements............................. 38,479.51

Balance on hand April 30, 1912.............. $293.77

At the meeting of the Association in 1912 there were reported by the secretary a membership of 2,223; 511 associations; 342 dispensaries, and 422 sanatoria and special hospitals with a capacity of 26,360 beds.

A list of officers and directors for 1911 to 1912 follows:

President, Dr. Mazÿck P. Ravenel; honorary vice-presidents, Theodore Roosevelt and Sir William Osler; vice-presidents, John M. Glenn and Dr. G. Walter Holden; treasurer, Gen. George M. Sternberg; secretary, Dr. Henry Barton Jacobs; directors, Joseph S. Ames, Baltimore; Dr. Robert H. Babcock, Chicago; Dr. Edward R. Baldwin, Saranac Lake; William H. Baldwin, Washington; Miss Kate Barnard, Oklahoma City; Ernest P. Bicknell, Washington; Dr. Hermann M. Biggs, New York; Dr. Frank Billings, Chicago; W. K. Bixby, St. Louis; C. B. Boothe, Los Angeles; Dr. Vincent Y. Bowditch, Boston; Jeffrey R. Brackett, Boston; Dr. T. D. Coleman, Augusta, Ga.; Dr. R. W. Corwin, Pueblo, Colo.; Albert B. Cummins, Des Moines; Dr. John L. Dawson, Charleston; Edward T. Devine, New York; Dr. George Dock, St. Louis; Dr. W. F. Drewry, Petersburg, Va.; Dr. Henry B. Favill, Chicago; Dr. Lawrence F. Flick, Philadelphia; David R. Francis, St. Louis; Dr. John S. Fulton, Baltimore; Robert Garrett, Baltimore; John M. Glenn, New York; Samuel Gompers, Washington; Dr. Charles Lyman Greene, St. Paul; Dr. Elmer E. Hegg, Seattle; James J. Hill, St. Paul; Frederick L. Hoffman, Newark; Dr. G. Walter Holden, Denver; Dr. John N. Hurty, Indianapolis; Dr. Henry Barton Jacobs, Baltimore; Dr. S. A. Knopf, New York; Dr. George M. Kober, Washington; Charles M. Lea, Philadelphia; Dr. John H. Lowman, Cleveland; Dr. Rudolf Matas, New Orleans; R. B. Mellon, Pittsburgh; Dr. Alfred Meyer, New York; Dr. James Alexander Miller, New York; Dr. Charles L. Minor, Asheville; W. C. Nones, Louisville; Dr. E. A. Pierce, Portland, Ore.; Dr. Joseph Y. Porter, Key West, Fla.; Redfield Proctor, Jr., Proctor, Vt.; Dr. Mazÿck P. Ravenel, Madison, Wis.; Julius Rosenwald, Chicago; Dr. Theodore B. Sachs, Chicago; W. T. Sedgwick, Boston; Gen. George M. Sternberg, Washington; Dr. Walter R. Steiner, Hartford, Conn.; Dr. Thomas D. Tuttle, Helena; Dr. Victor C. Vaughan, Ann Arbor; Dr. Joseph Walsh, Philadelphia; Dr. Gerald B. Webb, Colorado Springs; Dr. F. F. Wesbrook, Minneapolis; Dr. William Charles White, Pittsburgh; Alexander M. Wilson, Philadelphia.

Executive secretary, Dr. Livingston Farrand; assistant secretaries, Philip P. Jacobs, Ph.D., and Thomas Spees Carrington, M.D.

The following is a list of papers read before the respective sections at the meeting of May 30–31, 1912:

Should the prevention of tuberculosis be under exclusive official control?—C. O. Probst, M.D.

The relation of the health official to the anti-tuberculosis campaign—John H. Landis, M.D.

The relation of the physician to the anti-tuberculosis campaign—James Alexander Miller, M.D.

The relation of the layman to the anti-tuberculosis campaign—J. L. Ludlow, C.E.

A brief account of the treatment and care of tuberculous wage-earners in Germany—Frederick L. Hoffman, LL.D.

A preliminary study of the value of sanatorium treatment—Herbert Maxon King, M.D.

Employment of patients after leaving sanatoria—W. J. Vogeler, M.D.

A revised estimate of the economic cost of tuberculosis—Irving Fisher, Ph.D.

The unjustified prejudice of tuberculous patients against sanatoria and hospitals—S. Adolphus Knopf, M.D.

Examination of employees for tuberculosis—Theodore B. Sachs, M.D.

Misleading mortality statistics on tuberculosis—Philip P. Jacobs, Ph.D.

The visiting nurse and tuberculosis control—Miss Lillian Wald.

The New Jersey tuberculosis exhibit—Millard Knowlton, M.D.

Hygienic and economic features of the East River Homes Foundation—Henry L. Shively, M.D.

A home hospital for tuberculosis—John A. Kingsbury.

Adequate hospital control—Bertram H. Waters, M.D.

Adequate clinic control—F. Elisabeth Crowell.

An adequate educational campaign—Hoyt E. Dearholt, M.D.

The external use of water for enhancing resistance in tuberculosis—Simon Baruch, M.D.

The present status of the therapeutic use of tuberculin—Lawrason Brown, M.D.

The value of reactions in tuberculin therapy—William Charles White, M.D., and K. H. Van Norman, M.B.

The use of the tuberculin test (subcutaneous)—William L. Dunn, M.D.

The diagnostic use of tuberculin—Edward R. Baldwin, M.D.

Note on the death rate from tuberculosis in various large municipalities—Hermann M. Biggs, M.D.

Induced pneumothorax in the treatment of pulmonary disease—Louis Hamman, M.D., and Martin F. Sloan, M.D.

A report of 31 cases of pulmonary tuberculosis treated by compression of the lung—Mary E. Lapham, M.D.

Restoration of working efficiency after sanatorium treatment—Herbert Maxon King, M.D.

A study of the ultimate results in the dispensary treatment of tuberculosis—H. R. M. Landis, M.D.

Prevention of hemorrhage in pulmonary tuberculosis by the administration of autogenous vaccine—Roswell T. Pettit, M.D.

Advanced tuberculosis confined to one lung; a comparative analysis of 150 cases—F. C. Smith, M.D.

A further study of the prognostic value of Arneth's leukocytic blood-picture in pulmonary tuberculosis, based upon 729 counts in 475 patients—Paul H. Ringer, M.D.

The polynuclear neutrophile leukocytic count as a guide for the administration of tuberculin—Wallace J. Durel, M.D.

The effect of graduated work upon the leukocytes in pulmonary tuberculosis—Myer Solis-Cohen, M.D., and Albert Strickler, M.D.

Report of 150 cases of pulmonary tuberculosis treated with tuberculin—Harry Lee Barnes, M.D.

Acid agglutination of tubercle bacilli—Charles Krumwiede, Jr., M.D.

Some observations on tuberculous cattle—Charles F. Briscoe, A.M., and W. J. MacNeal, M.D.

Lime assimilation and tuberculosis—Ira Van Gieson, M.D.

The relation of animal fat to tubercle bacillus fat—William Charles White, M.D., and A. Marion Gammon.

The variation in the longevity of tubercle bacilli from different individuals—B. L. Arms, M.D., and E. Marion Wade, B.A.

The relation of the virulence of the tubercle bacillus to its persistence in the circulation—Alfred F. Hess, M.D.

The bacteriology of the blood in pulmonary tuberculosis: a preliminary report—Lawrason Brown, M.D., and S. A. Petroff.

Report of Committee on Nomenclature of the American Sanatorium Association—Lawrason Brown, M.D., chairman.

CHAPTER XIX

NINTH ANNUAL MEETING

THE ninth annual meeting of The National Association for the Study and Prevention of Tuberculosis was held at the New Willard Hotel, Washington, D. C., on Thursday and Friday, May 8 and 9, 1913.

The president of the Association, Mr. Homer Folks, called the Association to order at 11 o'clock on the morning of May 8. Following the address of the president and the report of the executive secretary, in accordance with the regular procedure of the Association, the following committee was appointed by the chair to present nominations to fill vacancies in the board of directors: Frederick L. Hoffman, New Jersey, chairman; Dr. J. W. Coon, Wisconsin; James Minnick, Illinois; Seymour H. Stone, Massachusetts; Dr. Linsly R. Williams, New York.

The following committee on resolutions was also appointed by the chair: Dr. Henry Barton Jacobs, Maryland, chairman; William H. Baldwin, District of Columbia; Dr. George H. Evans, California; Dr. John H. Lowman, Ohio; Dr. W. S. Rankin, North Carolina.

At the general meeting of the Association, held at noon on May 9, the regular order of business was varied to admit the presentation of a report on the status of the investigation of the Friedmann Treatment by the United States Public Health Service. The report was presented by Dr. John F. Anderson.

Following the report of the United States Public Health Service, the following resolutions were presented on behalf of the board of directors and after discussion were adopted:

WHEREAS, Wide-spread publicity has been given to the claims of an alleged cure for tuberculosis,

Resolved, That there is no information before The National Association for the Study and Prevention of Tuberculosis to justify the belief that any specific cure for tuberculosis has been discovered which deserves the confidence of the medical profession or of the people, and

Resolved, That it is the duty of the public to continue unabated all the present well-tried agencies for the treatment and prevention of tuberculosis.

At the business meeting of the Association the following were unanimously elected directors of the Association for terms of five years: Frederic Almy, Buffalo; Dr. Hermann M. Biggs, New York; Severance Burrage, Indianapolis; Dr. George H. Evans, San Francisco; Dr. Lawrence F. Flick, Philadelphia; Lee K. Frankel, New York; Dr. Herbert Maxon King, Liberty; Miss Julia Lathrop, Washington; Charles P. Neill, New York; Dr. W. S. Rankin, Raleigh; Dr. M. P. Ravenel, Madison, Wis.; Rt. Rev. F. S. Spalding, Salt Lake City.

The following resolution was reported favorably by the committee on resolutions and was unanimously adopted by the Association:

Resolved, That The National Association for the Study and Prevention of Tuberculosis recommend to the United States House of Representatives that it appoint from its body a Committee on Public Health.

The special committee on the form of the double-barred red cross through its chairman, Dr. Henry Barton Jacobs, presented a report. The recommendations of the committee were unanimously adopted.

At a meeting of the board of directors, held on Friday afternoon, May 9, the following officers were unanimously elected for the ensuing year: Dr. John H. Lowman, Cleveland, president; Miss Mabel T. Boardman, Washington, and Dr. Theodore B. Sachs, Chicago, vice-presidents; Dr. Henry Barton Jacobs, Baltimore, secretary; William H. Baldwin, Washington, treasurer.

The following directors were elected to serve on the executive committee for the ensuing year: William H. Baldwin, Washington; Dr. Hermann M. Biggs, New York; Homer Folks, New York; Dr. Charles J. Hatfield, Philadelphia; Dr. George M. Kober, Washington; Dr. Walter R. Steiner, Hartford; Dr. William Charles White, Pittsburgh.

In recognition of his long and eminent services Gen. George M. Sternberg was elected an honorary member of the Association.

The summarized report of the treasurer, Mr. William H. Baldwin, is as follows:

Balance on hand April 30, 1912................	$293.77
Receipts.......................................	37,191.91
Disbursements................................	34,951.31
Balance on hand April 30, 1913................	$2,534.37

At the meeting of the Association in 1913 the secretary reported a membership of 2,132; associations, 660; dispensaries, 373; sanatoria and special hospitals, 466; open-air schools, 95.

A list of officers and directors for 1912 to 1913 follows:

President, Homer Folks; honorary vice-presidents, Theodore Roosevelt and Sir William Osler; vice-presidents, Dr. Robert H. Babcock and Dr. Edward R. Baldwin; treasurer, William H. Baldwin; secretary, Dr. Henry Barton Jacobs; directors, Joseph S. Ames, Baltimore; Dr. Robert H. Babcock, Chicago; Dr. Edward R. Baldwin, Saranac Lake; William H. Baldwin, Washington; Dr. W. Jarvis Barlow, Los Angeles; Miss Kate Barnard, Oklahoma City; Ernest P. Bicknell, Washington; W. K. Bixby, St. Louis; Miss Mabel T. Boardman, Washington; C. B. Boothe, Los Angeles; Dr. Vincent Y. Bowditch, Boston; Jeffrey R. Brackett, Boston; Dr. T. D. Coleman, Augusta, Ga.; Albert B. Cummins, Des Moines; Dr. Hoyt E. Dearholt, Milwaukee; Dr. George Dock, St. Louis, Mo.; Dr. W. F. Drewry, Petersburg, Va.; Dr. Henry B. Favill, Chicago; Homer Folks, New York; Dr. John S. Fulton, Baltimore; John M. Glenn, New York; Samuel Gompers, Washington; Dr. Charles Lyman Greene, St. Paul; Dr. Charles J. Hatfield, Philadelphia; Dr. Elmer E. Hegg, Seattle; James J. Hill, St. Paul; Frederick L. Hoffman, Newark; Dr. G. Walter Holden, Denver; Dr. John N. Hurty, Indianapolis; Dr. Henry Barton Jacobs, Baltimore; John A. Kingsbury, New York; Dr. S. A. Knopf, New York; Dr. George M. Kober, Washington; Dr. John H. Lowman, Cleveland; Col. J. L. Ludlow, Winston-Salem; Dr. Cabot Lull, Birmingham, Ala.; Dr. Rudolf Matas, New Orleans; R. B. Mellon, Pittsburgh; Dr. Alfred Meyer, New York; Dr. James Alexander Miller, New York; Dr. Charles L. Minor, Asheville; Dr. E. A. Pierce, Portland, Ore.; Dr. Joseph Y. Porter, Key West, Fla.; Dr. Charles O. Probst, Columbus, O.; Redfield Proctor, Proctor, Vt.; Julius Rosenwald, Chicago; Dr. Theodore B. Sachs, Chicago; Dr. E. C. Schroeder, Washington; W. T. Sedgwick, Boston; Dr. Walter R. Steiner, Hartford, Conn.; Gen. C. F. Stokes, Washington; Dr. Edward L. Trudeau, Saranac Lake; Dr. Thomas D. Tuttle, Helena; Dr. Victor C. Vaughan, Ann Arbor; Dr. Joseph Walsh, Philadelphia; Dr. Gerald B. Webb, Colorado Springs; Dr. William H. Welch, Baltimore; Dr. F. F. Wesbrook, Minneapolis; Dr. William Charles White, Pittsburgh; Alexander M. Wilson, Philadelphia.

Executive secretary, Dr. Livingston Farrand; assistant secretaries, Philip P. Jacobs, Ph.D., and Thomas Spees Carrington, M.D.

The following is a list of papers read before the respective sections at the meeting of May 8–9, 1913:

The tuberculosis campaign—its influence on the methods of public health work generally—Hermann M. Biggs, M.D., and Charles F. Bolduan, M.D.

The tuberculosis problem from the sociological and medical points of view—John R. Commons.

The medical side of the tuberculosis problem—William Charles White, M.D.

Tuberculosis and public health—H. R. M. Landis, M.D.

The decline in the tuberculosis death-rate, 1871–1912—Frederick L. Hoffman, LL.D.

Is the economic problem of the sanatorium graduate being solved?—John H. Huddleston, M.D.

The relation of the industries to tuberculosis—B. S. Warren, M.D.

A method of finding early cases of pulmonary tuberculosis—Harry Lee Barnes, M.D.

One year's results at the Home Hospital—Edward C. Brenner, M.D.

The tuberculosis preventorium—Alfred F. Hess, M.D.

The tuberculosis problem of the country and small towns—Charles S. Prest, M.D.

The value of auto-inoculation in pulmonary tuberculosis—Harry Lee Barnes, M.D.

The occurrence and importance in treatment of secondary infection in pulmonary tuberculosis—Lawrason Brown, M.D., F. H. Heise, M.D., and S. A. Petroff.

The treatment of progressive cases of pulmonary tuberculosis—Mary E. Lapham, M.D.

Results on January 1, 1913, in Philadelphia patients discharged from Mont Alto in 1909—Albert P. Francine, M.D.

What became of one group of cases—E. S. Bullock, M.D., and L. S. Peters, M.D.

Clinical observations with the bacilli emulsion administered by the polynuclear neutrophile index method—Wallace J. Durel, M.D.

Report on a group of infants infected by a tuberculous attendant—Alfred F. Hess, M.D.

Further observations on vital stains in relation to tubercle—Paul A. Lewis, M.D.

The relation of the spleen in rats and mice to their resistance to experimental tuberculosis—Paul A. Lewis, M.D., and Arthur Georges Margot.

Observations on the products obtained from the tubercle bacillus by the method of Vaughan—Benjamin White, Ph.D.

Factors in immunity in tuberculosis—W. H. Manwaring, M.D., and J. Bronfen Brenner, Ph.D.

Chemo-therapeutic experiments with trypan-red compounds in experimental tuberculosis—Paul A. Lewis, M.D., and Robert B. Krauss.

The chemical composition of commercial tuberculins—William Charles White, M.D., and Lester Hollander, M.D.

Further observations on experimental tuberculosis of the cornea—Paul A. Lewis, M.D.

The comparative study of cultures from type cases of human pulmonary tuberculosis—Karl F. Meyer, M.D., and Paul A. Lewis, M.D.

The relative virulence of type cultures of B. tuberculosis for guinea-pigs Paul A. Lewis, M.D.

Some new biological relations between tubercle bacilli and other acid-fast forms—Allen K. Krause, M.D., and Edward R. Baldwin, M.D.

Variations of the tubercle bacillus when cultivated on potato media—S. A. Petroff.

The bacteriology of the blood in pulmonary tuberculosis—Lawrason Brown, M.D., Fred H. Heise, M.D., and S. A. Petroff.

Study of a case of generalized tuberculous lymphadenitis in an adult—Lever Stewart, M.D., and Arthur Georges Margot.

Further observations on tuberculous cervical adenitis—Paul A. Lewis, M.D., and Arthur Georges Margot.

Specimen showing cavitation of lung in an infant dying in the seventh month—B. M. Randolph, M.D.

Report of the Committee on Hospitals for Advanced Cases of Tuberculosis.

Report of the Committee on Clinical Nomenclature.

CHAPTER XX

TENTH ANNUAL MEETING

THE tenth annual meeting of The National Association for the Study and Prevention of Tuberculosis was held at the New Willard Hotel, Washington, D. C., on Thursday and Friday, May 7 and 8, 1914. The president of the Association, Dr. John H. Lowman, called the Association to order at eleven o'clock on the morning of May 7. Following the address of the president and the report of the executive office, in accordance with the regular procedure of the Association, the following committee was appointed by the chair to present nominations to fill vacancies in the board of directors: Dr. Walter R. Steiner, Connecticut, chairman; Dr. R. H. Bishop, Jr., Ohio; Dr. H. M. Bracken, Minnesota; Paul Kennaday, New York; Dr. William Charles White, Pennsylvania.

The following committee on resolutions was also appointed by the chair: Dr. George M. Kober, District of Columbia, chairman; William H. Baldwin, District of Columbia; Frederick L. Hoffman, New Jersey; Dr. Lawrence Litchfield, Pennsylvania; Dr. Theodore B. Sachs, Illinois.

At the regular business meeting of the Association, held at noon on May 8, the following were unanimously elected directors of the Association for terms of five years: Dr. Rupert Blue, Washington; Dr. Lawrason Brown, Saranac Lake; Dr. Livingston Farrand, Boulder, Colo.; Frederick L. Hoffman, Newark, N. J.; Dr. S. A. Knopf, New York; Dr. H. R. M. Landis, Philadelphia; Dr. David R. Lyman, Wallingford, Conn.; S. Livingston Mather, Cleveland; Dr. James Alexander Miller, New York; A. L. Mills, Portland, Ore.; Dr. Charles L. Minor, Asheville; John Mitchell, New York.

Upon motion made by Dr. Ravenel, and seconded by Mr. Baldwin, the following resolutions, passed by the board of directors at their meeting on March 7, 1914, were unanimously endorsed by the general meeting:

WHEREAS, Dr. Livingston Farrand, who has served as executive secretary of The National Association for the Study and Prevention of Tuberculosis since January 15, 1905, or practically during the entire existence of the organization, has resigned to accept the presidency of the University of the State of Colorado, and

WHEREAS, The executive secretary, Dr. Farrand, has been largely responsible both for suggesting the lines of policy and work of The National Association for the Study and Prevention of Tuberculosis and for carrying into effect the policies and lines of activity approved by the board of directors, and

WHEREAS, During the nine years of Dr. Farrand's incumbency of the position of executive secretary the number of organizations engaged in the prevention of tuberculosis has increased from a very few to over 1,200; the number of hospitals and sanatoria has increased to 550, with more than 35,000 beds; the number of dispensaries to 400; the number of visiting nurses to 3,000; the number of open-air schools and fresh-air schools to over 200; and advanced laws dealing with the treatment and prevention of tuberculosis have been enacted in 45 states, and

WHEREAS, These results are the most eloquent and conclusive justification possible of the policies suggested to the Association by Dr. Farrand during the early years of his incumbency of the position of executive secretary, therefore be it

Resolved, That The National Association for the Study and Prevention of Tuberculosis hereby places on record an expression of its recognition of the far-reaching benefit and value to the people of the country as a whole of the services which Dr. Farrand has rendered as executive secretary of The National Association for the Study and Prevention of Tuberculosis during the past nine years; of its appreciation of the admirable spirit he has shown in all his dealings with the officers and members of the Association; of his exceptional far-sightedness and sagacity in meeting the problems that have arisen from year to year; of his unqualified devotion to the success of the cause; of his sound judgment on the wide variety of medical, scientific, social, political, and practical questions arising in its work; and of the very great regard and affection felt for him by every member of the Association who has had the pleasure of working with him, and

Resolved, That we part from him as executive secretary with the greatest regret and extend to him our best wishes and confident assurance of his complete success in the new position to which he has been called, and urge him to continue, to the largest extent compatible with his new duties, his active interest in the cause of public health and in the work of this Association.

At a meeting of the Board of Directors, held on Friday afternoon, May 8, the following officers were elected for the ensuing year: Dr. George M. Kober, Washington, president; Lee K. Frankel, Ph.D., New York, and Dr. W. Jarvis Barlow, Los Angeles, vice-presidents; Dr. Henry Barton Jacobs, Baltimore, secretary; William H. Baldwin, Washington, treasurer.

The following directors were elected to serve on the executive committee for the ensuing year: William H. Baldwin, Washington; Dr. Hermann M. Biggs, New York; Homer Folks, New York; Dr. Charles J. Hatfield, Philadelphia; Dr. David R. Lyman, Wallingford; Dr. Theodore B. Sachs, Chicago; Dr. William Charles White, Pittsburgh.

The summarized report of the treasurer, Mr. William H. Baldwin, is as follows:

Balance on hand April 30, 1913	$2,534.37
Receipts	33,374.31
Disbursements	34,092.59
Balance on hand April 30, 1914	$1,816.09

At the meeting of the Association in 1914 the secretary reported a membership of 2,134; associations, 1,049; dispensaries, 400; sanatoria and special hospitals, 577; open-air schools, 169.

A list of officers and directors for 1913 to 1914 follows:

President, Dr. John H. Lowman; honorary vice-presidents, Theodore Roosevelt and Sir William Osler; vice-presidents, Miss Mabel T. Boardman and Dr. Theodore B. Sachs; treasurer, William H. Baldwin; secretary, Dr. Henry Barton Jacobs; directors, Frederic Almy, Buffalo; Joseph S. Ames, Baltimore; Dr. Robert H. Babcock, Chicago; William H. Baldwin, Washington; Dr. W. Jarvis Barlow, Los Angeles; Miss Kate Barnard, Oklahoma City; Ernest P. Bicknell, Washington; Dr. Hermann M. Biggs, New York; W. K. Bixby, St. Louis; Miss Mabel T. Boardman, Washington; Dr. Vincent Y. Bowditch, Boston; Jeffrey R. Brackett, Boston; Severance Burrage, Indianapolis; Dr. T. D. Coleman, Augusta, Ga.; Dr. Hoyt E. Dearholt, Milwaukee; Dr. George Dock, St. Louis; Dr. W. F. Drewry, Petersburg, Va.; Dr. George H. Evans, San Francisco; Dr. Henry B. Favill, Chicago; Dr. Lawrence F. Flick, Philadelphia; Homer Folks, New York; Lee K. Frankel, New York; Dr. John S. Fulton, Baltimore; John M. Glenn, New York; Dr. Charles Lyman Greene, St. Paul; Dr. Elmer E. Hegg, Seattle; Dr. G. Walter Holden, Denver; Dr. Henry Barton Jacobs, Baltimore; Dr. Herbert M. King, Loomis, N. Y.; John A. Kingsbury, New York; Dr. George M. Kober, Washington; Miss Julia C. Lathrop, Washington; Dr. John H. Lowman, Cleveland; Col. J. L. Ludlow, Winston-Salem; Dr. Cabot Lull, Birmingham, Ala.; R. B.

Mellon, Pittsburgh; Dr. Alfred Meyer, New York; Dr. James Alexander Miller, New York; Charles P. Neill, New York; Dr. E. A. Pierce, Portland. Ore.; Dr. Joseph Y. Porter, Key West, Fla.; Dr. Charles O. Probst, Columbus, O.; Dr. Watson S. Rankin, Raleigh, N. C.; Dr. Mazÿck P. Ravenel, Madison, Wis.; Julius Rosenwald, Chicago; Dr. Theodore B. Sachs, Chicago; Dr. E. C. Schroeder, Washington; W. T. Sedgwick, Boston; Rt. Rev. F. S. Spalding, Salt Lake City; Dr. Walter R. Steiner, Hartford, Conn.; Gen. C. F. Stokes, Washington; Dr. Edward L. Trudeau, Saranac Lake; Dr. Thomas D. Tuttle, Warm Springs, Mont.; Dr. Gerald B. Webb, Colorado Springs; Dr. William H. Welch, Baltimore; Dr. F. F. Wesbrook, Vancouver; Dr. William Charles White, Pittsburgh; Alexander M. Wilson, Philadelphia.

Executive secretary, Dr. Livingston Farrand; assistant secretaries, Philip P. Jacobs, Ph.D., and Thomas S. Carrington, M.D.; field secretary, Dixon Van Blarcom.

The following is a list of papers read before the respective sections at the meeting of May 7–8, 1914:

The campaign in Chicago for medical examinations of employes—Theodore B. Sachs, M.D.

An efficient system of medical examination of employes—Harry E. Mock, M.D.

The relation of medical examinations of employes to the hygiene of the working-place and the efficiency of the working force—James A. Britton, M.D.

Medical examination of employes as a part of industrial insurance—J. W. Schereschewsky, M.D.

Action of drugs on the pulmonary circulation—David I. Macht, M.D.

The treatment of advanced pulmonary tuberculosis—S. A. Knopf, M.D.

The occurrence of the Widal reaction in tuberculous people—Mazÿck P. Ravenel, M.D.

The prognosis of tuberculous infection among infants—Alfred F. Hess, M.D.

A scheme for promoting efficiency in state sanatoria—Walter C. Bailey, M.D. and Carl C. MacCorison, M.D.

Artificial pneumothorax, with report of gas analyses and experiments to determine the use of air or nitrogen—Gerald B. Webb, M.D., G. Burton Gilbert, M.D., T. L. James, M.D., and Leon C. Havens, M.A.

Exercise as a therapeutic measure in pulmonary tuberculosis—Charles W. Mills, M.D., and Herbert Maxon King, M.D.

Variation in tuberculin hypersensitiveness during the course of pulmonary tuberculosis—James B. Holmes, M.D.

The rôle of surgery in the treatment of pulmonary tuberculosis—a résumé— Edward Archibald, M.D.

Subsequent report of patients who received injections of Friedmann vaccine over a year ago—George Mannheimer, M.D.

A study of intravenous injections of stained organisms—John W. Churchman, M.D.

Tuberculocidal action of certain chemical disinfectants—Lydia M. DeWitt, M.D., and Hope Sherman.

Streptothrix infections and their differentiation from tuberculosis—Edith J. Claypole, M.D.

Blood platelets and tuberculosis—Gerald B. Webb, M.D., George Burton Gilbert, M.D., and Leon C. Havens, M.A.

Biological curves obtained during the onset and course of tuberculous infection—Alfred H. Cauldfeild, M.B., and F. S. Minns, M.B.

Tuberculin treatment based upon clinical and biological data—Alfred H. Cauldfeild, M.B., and F. S. Minns, M.B.

A study of tuberculous lesions in infants and young children, based on post-mortem examinations—Martha Wollstein, M.D., and Frederick H. Bartlett, M.D.

Some new features of interest about the pulmonary circulation and the fate therein of intravenously introduced fats—William Charles White, M.D., and A. Marion Gammon.

An attempt to immunize calves against tuberculosis by feeding the milk of vaccinated cows—W. L. Moss, M.D.

The work of the state livestock sanitary board of Pennsylvania upon the artificial immunization of animals against tuberculosis—S. H. Gilliland, V.M.D., M.D.

The effect of ligation of the pulmonary vein on the development of experimental tuberculosis—by G. L. Kite, M.D.

Studies on the morphology of living miliary tubercles—G. L. Kite, M.D.

The diagnosis of tuberculosis of biological methods—J. Bronfenbrenner, Ph.D.

The prognostic value of a study of the leukocytes—Henry D. Chadwick, M.D., and Roy Morgan, M.D.

The problem of infection in tuberculous families—John B. Hawes, 2d, M.D.

Prenatal and early childhood problems—William Charles White, M.D.

School child problems—Frank H. Mann.

The needs of patients discharged from tuberculosis sanatoria—Charles F. Bolduan, M.D.

Employment for post-sanatorium cases—Rabbi Sidney E. Goldstein.

The health aspect of the clothing industry—H. R. M. Landis, M.D., and Janice S. Reed.

The state health department and the tuberculosis problem—E. F. McCampbell, Ph.D., M.D.

The municipal health department and the tuberculosis problem—C. E. Ford, M.D.

Report of the Committee on Exhibits.

Report of Committee on Literature and Red Cross Seals.

CHAPTER XXI
ELEVENTH ANNUAL MEETING

THE eleventh annual meeting of The National Association for the Study and Prevention of Tuberculosis was held at Plymouth Congregational Church, Seattle, Washington, on Monday, Tuesday, and Wednesday, June 14, 15, and 16, 1915. The president of the Association, Dr. George M. Kober, called the meeting to order at nine o'clock on the morning of June 15. The address of the president was presented and filed for publication in the Transactions. The report of the executive office for the year ending April 30, 1915, was read and approved.

On motion from the floor, the following committee was appointed by the chair to present names to fill vacancies on the board of directors: Dr. Gerald B. Webb, Colorado, chairman; Dr. W. Jarvis Barlow, California; Dr. George T. Palmer, Illinois; Dr. Wilfred Manwaring, California; George J. Nelbach, New York.

The following committee on resolutions was also appointed by the chair: Dr. Edward O. Otis, Massachusetts, chairman; Dr. Christen Quevli, Washington; Dr. Alfred Meyer, New York; Dr. Theodore B. Sachs, Illinois; Dr. Thomas D. Tuttle, Washington.

At the business meeting of the Association, held on June 16, the following were elected directors of the Association for terms of five years: Dr. Edward R. Baldwin, New York; William H. Baldwin, District of Columbia; Dr. Hoyt E. Dearholt, Wisconsin; John M. Glenn, New York; Sherman C. Kingsley, Illinois; Dr. O. W. McMichael, Illinois; Dr. George T. Palmer, Illinois; Dr. LeRoy S. Peters, New Mexico; Dr. Christen Quevli, Washington; Seymour H. Stone, Massachusetts; Dr. E. R. Van der Slice, Nebraska; Miss Maude Van Syckle, Michigan.

Dr. Edward O. Otis, chairman of the committee on resolutions, presented the following resolutions with the endorsement of the committee. They were unanimously adopted by the general meeting:

Resolved, That The National Association for the Study and Prevention of Tuberculosis expresses its gratitude and appreciation of the courtesies extended to it by the Washington Association for the Prevention and Relief of Tuberculosis, the Seattle Red Cross Seal Committee, the Chamber of Commerce, the local Committee of Arrangements, the Tacoma and Pierce County Anti-Tuberculosis Association, the city and state officials, and to Mrs. Buchanan, Dr. and Mrs. Quevli, Mr. H. C. Henry, Mrs. W. E. Humphrey, and to all the good citizens of Seattle who have contributed so largely to the success of the meeting and entertainment and comfort of the attending members.

WHEREAS, State, city, and county tuberculosis hospitals and sanatoria are an important factor in the gradual attainment of control of tuberculosis in this country, and

WHEREAS, The efficiency of these institutions can be attained only through administration free from politics and by a personnel selected solely upon the consideration of their fitness, it is

Resolved by The National Association for the Study and Prevention of Tuberculosis that the boards of management of such institutions should always be chosen on the basis of their knowledge and experience in the different phases of the problem, and it is further

Resolved, That it is essential that all the administrative and medical officers of such institutions be selected by means of strict competitive civil service examinations.

Resolved, That The National Association for the Study and Prevention of Tuberculosis urge upon all local anti-tuberculosis associations the importance of co-operating with various official and voluntary associations having for their object the prevention of disease, and especially those associations dealing with the problems of housing; and

Resolved, That The National Association recommends that in communities where there are no housing associations the local tuberculosis association appoint an active committee to be known as the housing committee.

Resolved, That The National Association for the Study and Prevention of Tuberculosis approves of the plan for municipal regulation and supervision of the milk supply, such regulation and supervision supplementing state and federal control; and that such regulation include—(1) pasteurization of all milk for human consumption, if not of the grade of certified milk; (2) tuberculin tests for all dairy herds supplying milk for municipal consumption; and (3) the frequent inspection of dairy herds.

At a meeting of the board of directors, held on Wednesday,

June 16, the following officers were elected for the ensuing year: Dr. Theodore B. Sachs, Illinois, president; Dr. Edward R. Baldwin, New York, first vice-president; Dr. Christen Quevli, Washington, second vice-president; Dr. Henry Barton Jacobs, Baltimore, secretary; William H. Baldwin, Washington, treasurer.

The following directors were elected to serve on the executive committee for the ensuing year: William H. Baldwin, District of Columbia; Homer Folks, New York; John M. Glenn, New York; Dr. David R. Lyman, Connecticut; Dr. O. W. McMichael, Illinois; Seymour H. Stone, Massachusetts; Dr. William Charles White, Pennsylvania.

A resolution was adopted to the effect that it was the consensus of opinion that the next annual meeting shall be held in Cincinnati, but that the final decision shall be left to a later meeting of the executive committee or the board of directors.

The summarized report of the treasurer, Mr. William H. Baldwin, is as follows:

```
Balance on hand April 30, 1914..............  $1,816.09
Receipts....................................  36,226.92
Disbursements...............................  34,999.85
                                              ─────────
Balance on hand, April 30, 1915.............  $3,043.16
```

At the meeting of the Association in 1915 the secretary reported a membership of 2,419; number of associations, 1,210; dispensaries, 418; sanatoria and special hospitals, 468.

A list of officers and directors for 1914 to 1915 follows·

President, Dr. George M. Kober; honorary vice-presidents, Theodore Roosevelt and Sir William Osler; vice-presidents, Lee K. Frankel and Dr. W. Jarvis Barlow; treasurer, William H. Baldwin; secretary, Dr. Henry Barton Jacobs; directors, Frederic Almy, Buffalo; Joseph S. Ames, Baltimore; William H. Baldwin, Washington; Dr. W. Jarvis Barlow, Los Angeles; Miss Kate Barnard, Oklahoma City; Ernest P. Bicknell, Washington; Dr. Hermann M. Biggs, New York; W. K. Bixby, St. Louis, Mo.; Dr. Rupert Blue, Washington; Miss Mabel T. Boardman, Washington; Dr. Vincent Y. Bowditch, Boston; Dr. Lawrason Brown, Saranac Lake; Severance Burrage, Indianapolis; Dr. T. D. Coleman, Augusta, Ga.; Mrs. O. B. Colquitt, Dallas, Tex.; Dr. Hoyt E. Dearholt, Milwaukee; Dr. George Dock, St. Louis; Dr. George H. Evans, San Francisco; Dr. Livingston Farrand, Boulder, Colo.; Dr. Henry B. Favill, Chicago; Dr. Lawrence F. Flick, Philadelphia; Homer Folks, New York; Lee K. Frankel, New York; Dr. John S. Fulton, Baltimore;

Dr. Ethan A. Gray, Chicago; Dr. Charles Lyman Greene, St. Paul; Dr. Elmer E. Hegg, Seattle; Frederick L. Hoffman, New York; Dr. G. Walter Holden, Denver; Dr. Henry Barton Jacobs, Baltimore; Dr. Herbert M. King, Loomis, N. Y.; John A. Kingsbury, New York; Dr. S. A. Knopf, New York; Dr. H. R. M. Landis, Philadelphia; Miss Julia C. Lathrop, Washington; Col. J. L. Ludlow, Winston-Salem; Dr. Cabot Lull, Birmingham, Ala.; Dr. David R. Lyman, Wallingford, Conn.; S. Livingston Mather, Cleveland; Dr. Alfred Meyer, New York; Dr. James Alexander Miller, New York; A. L. Mills, Portland, Ore.; Dr. Charles L. Minor, Asheville; John Mitchell, New York; Charles P. Neill, New York; Dr. Charles O. Probst, Columbus, O.; Dr. Watson S. Rankin, Raleigh, N. C.; Dr. Mazÿck P. Ravenel, Madison, Wis.; Julius Rosenwald, Chicago; Dr. Theodore B. Sachs, Chicago; Dr. E. C. Schroeder, Washington; Gen. C. F. Stokes, Washington; Seymour H. Stone, Boston; Dr. Edward L. Trudeau, Saranac Lake; Dr. Thomas D. Tuttle, Warm Springs, Mont.; Dr. Gerald B. Webb, Colorado Springs; Dr. William H. Welch, Baltimore; Dr. F. F. Wesbrook, Vancouver; Dr. William Charles White, Pittsburgh; Alexander M. Wilson, Philadelphia.

Executive secretary, Charles J. Hatfield, M.D.; assistant secretary, Philip P. Jacobs, Ph.D.; field secretaries, Dixon Van Blarcom and Charles M. De Forest.

The following is a list of papers read before the respective sections at the meeting of June 14–16, 1915:

The child and the home—George M. Kober, M.D.

The child and the school—Sherman C. Kingsley.

The child and the community—Edward O. Otis, M.D.

Trachea position—Gerald B. Webb, M.D., Alexius M. Forster, M.D., and G. Burton Gilbert, M.D.

The cutaneous tuberculin vaccination method—John Ritter, M.D.

A study of Kroenig's isthmus in pulmonary tuberculosis—Walter C. Klotz, M.D.

The diagnosis of intra-thoracic tuberculosis in children—W. J. Dobbie, M.D.

A clinical study of 228 children in relation to tuberculosis exposure controlled by von Pirquet reaction—John B. Manning, M.D., and Howard James Knott, M.D.

Does the general practitioner utilize the means at his disposal for the diagnosis of early pulmonary tuberculosis?—James S. Ford, M.D.

The x-ray as an aid in the study of pulmonary tuberculosis—Ray W. Matson, M.D.

Prevention and care of laryngeal tuberculosis—Julius Dworetzky, M.D.

Pancreatic ferment determination in pulmonary tuberculosis—Ethan A. Gray, M.D., and Olga Pickman, M.D.

Essential points in the early determination of tubercle—Frederick Slyfield, M.D.

Non-tuberculous lesions of the lung—William Charles White, M.D.

The treatment of pulmonary hemorrhage by venesection—A. G. Shortle, M.D.

Artificial pneumothorax in the treatment of pulmonary tuberculosis—Theodore B. Sachs, M.D.

Artificial pneumothorax in the treatment of pulmonary tuberculosis—C. H. Vrooman, M.D.

A clinical report of sixty-nine cases treated by artificial pneumothorax—Henry Schwatt, M.D.

Clinical observations on artificial pneumothorax with report of 73 cases—Ralph C. Matson, M.D.

The influence of lung disease through artificial diaphragm paralysis ("phrenikotomie")—Ralph C. Matson, M.D., and Marr Bisaillon, M.D.

Exudates in artificial pneumothorax—LeRoy S. Peters, M.D.

A case of spontaneous pyopneumothorax complicated by hydro- or pyopneumopericardium—Alfred Meyer, M.D.

Sanatorium temperature records—David R. Lyman, M.D.

The serum diagnosis of tuberculosis in relation to immunization and prophylaxis—Enrico Castelli, M.D.

Immunity in tuberculosis—G. Burton Gilbert, M.D., and Gerald B. Webb, M.D.

The function of the spleen in the experimental infection of albino mice with bacillus tuberculosis—Paul A. Lewis, M.D., and Arthur Georges Margot.

Further observations on the presence of iodine in tuberculosis tissues—Paul A. Lewis, M.D., and Robert B. Krauss.

The bacteræmic nature of tuberculosis and leprosy—D. Rivas, M.D.

The value of copper in the treatment of tuberculosis—Lydia M. DeWitt, M.D.

On new methods of serum diagnosis of tuberculosis—J. Bronfenbrenner, Ph.D., and M. J. Schlesinger.

A study of the cultivation of the tubercle bacillus directly from the sputum—Robert A. Keilty, M.D.

The Widal reaction in tuberculous persons—A. J. Chesley, M.D., and E. M. Wade.

Some observations on streptothrix infections and their relation to tuberculosis—David John Davis, M.D.

Communicability of the avian tubercle bacterium to mammals—L. R. Himmelberger, M.D.

Tuberculosis of the ovary—C. E. Royce, M.D.

The official responsibility of the state in the tuberculosis problem—William Charles White, M.D.

The official responsibility of the city in the tuberculosis problem—Theodore B. Sachs, M.D.

The official responsibility of the county in the tuberculosis problem—George J. Nelbach.

The duties and opportunities of the state tuberculosis association—Miss E. L. M. Tate.

The duties and opportunities of the local tuberculosis association—James Minnick.

The relation state and local anti-tuberculosis associations should sustain to
each other—Charles J. Hatfield, M.D.
House infection: a potent source of tuberculosis—Isaac W. Brewer, M.D.
Relative prevalence of tuberculosis under good and bad housing conditions—
Charles J. Hastings, M.D.
Housing and tuberculosis—a legislative program—Lawrence Veiller.

CHAPTER XXII

TWELFTH ANNUAL MEETING

THE twelfth annual meeting of The National Association for the Study and Prevention of Tuberculosis was held at the New Willard Hotel, Washington, D. C., on Thursday and Friday, May 11 and 12, 1916. The president of the Association, Dr. Edward R. Baldwin, called the meeting to order at two o'clock on the afternoon of May 11. The address of the president was presented and filed for publication in the Transactions. The report of the executive office for the year ending April 30, 1916, was read and approved.

On motion from the floor, duly seconded and carried, the following committee was appointed by the chair to present names to fill vacancies on the board of directors: Dr. John H. Lowman, Ohio, chairman; Mrs. Bethesda Beals Buchanan, Washington; Dr. Alexius M. Forster, Colorado; Sherman C. Kingsley, Illinois; Dr. Walter R. Steiner, Connecticut.

Likewise on motion from the floor, seconded and carried, the following committee on resolutions was appointed by the chair: William H. Baldwin, District of Columbia, chairman; Dr. Robert H. Babcock, Illinois; Dr. Vincent Y. Bowditch, Massachusetts; Dr. Philip King Brown, California; Dr. Livingston Farrand, Colorado.

By unanimous vote of the members present the secretary was instructed to send a telegram to Mrs. Theodore B. Sachs, conveying the sympathy of the meeting and expressing appreciation of the great work accomplished by Dr. and Mrs. Sachs.

At the business meeting of the Association, held at noon on May 12, the following were elected directors of the Association for terms of five years: Dr. Robert H. Babcock, Illinois; Dr. H. M. Bracken, Minnesota; Dr. Philip King Brown, California; Dr. C. E. Edson, Colorado; Miss Edna L. Foley, Illinois; Dr. Louis

V. Hamman, Maryland; Dr. Henry Barton Jacobs, Maryland; H. McK. Jones, Missouri; Dr. George M. Kober, District of Columbia; R. B. Mellon, Pennsylvania; Dr. A. K. Stone, Massachusetts; Dr. Victor C. Vaughan, Michigan.

Mr. William H. Baldwin, chairman of the committee on resolutions, presented the following resolutions with the endorsement of the committee. They were unanimously adopted by the general meeting:

Resolved, That The National Association for the Study and Prevention of Tuberculosis express its hearty appreciation of the generous proposition of the Metropolitan Life Insurance Company to contribute $100,000 for conducting a community experiment in the control of tuberculosis.

In undertaking this trust the Association hopes that the results of the experiment may be commensurate with the desires which inspired the offer.

WHEREAS, The Prudential Insurance Company of America has recently issued an elaborate statistical treatise on the mortality from cancer throughout the world, in the furtherance of the cause of cancer control, under the auspices of the American Association for Cancer Research and the American Society for the Control of Cancer; and

WHEREAS, A corresponding treatise on the mortality from tuberculosis throughout the world, with a due consideration of the various medical and sociological aspects of the tuberculosis problem, would aid materially all those who throughout the country are engaged in the study and prevention of tuberculosis; and

WHEREAS, Heretofore no collective study of tuberculosis statistics of this world-wide problem in preventive medicine has been made, either under the direction of government or private enterprise; be it

Resolved, by The National Association for the Study and Prevention of Tuberculosis, in annual meeting assembled, that it be respectfully suggested to the president and board of directors of the Prudential Insurance Company of America that the said Company cause to be prepared, and make available for gratuitous distribution to those interested in the subject, a work on the mortality from tuberculosis throughout the world corresponding to the recently issued volume on the mortality from cancer; and be it further

Resolved, That the Association desires to place on record its appreciation of the active interest on the part of the Prudential in the campaign against tuberculosis.

WHEREAS, The death of Dr. Edward Livingston Trudeau, the physician, philanthropist, scientist, and first president of the Association, removes from us the leader in the sanatorium movement in America, one of the founders of this body, and an exponent of humanitarian principles of the highest order, and

WHEREAS, In the life history of this unique man, Providence has given to us in a gifted and lovable personality an example of rare usefulness in the face of adversity, an inspiration to those whom fate leads to tread the same road of invalidism, and a nobility of character developed as a result of suffering, a sympathy deepened and made invaluable to the world by personal experience of disease throughout a long life, and

WHEREAS, In the history of American medicine, there existed no finer example of the ideal physician, whose influence radiated far beyond his home in the forest, whose memory will be cherished by the strong and the weak, by the grief-stricken and disheartened in their struggle for life, whose comfort he was, whose presence brought faith and hope to the bedside, and who made an undying impression on the art and science of medicine in the field of tuberculosis, be it

Resolved, That this Association records these sentiments with a full consciousness of the debt we owe to his memory, and a deep appreciation of the glory shed upon his work as well as upon the history of American medicine, and be it further

Resolved, That a copy of these resolutions be sent to the family of the late Dr. Trudeau.

WHEREAS, In the death of Dr. Theodore B. Sachs, The National Association for the Study and Prevention of Tuberculosis has suffered the loss of its honored president, and the entire anti-tuberculosis movement a valued worker; and

WHEREAS, In a spirit of self-sacrifice and devotion to the cause of humanity he has given the best of his life to the anti-tuberculosis campaign; and

WHEREAS, His signal services in tuberculosis work, both as a clinician and an administrator, have proven of inestimable worth to the people of the United States and the rest of the world; be it

Resolved, That The National Association for the Study and Prevention of Tuberculosis deplores its own loss of a member, director and president, and expresses its deep and sincere appreciation of the valuable services Dr. Sachs has rendered; and be it further

Resolved, That a copy of these resolutions be read at and spread upon the minutes of the twelfth annual meeting of The National Association for the Study and Prevention of Tuberculosis, and that they be transmitted by the executive secretary to the family of Dr. Sachs.

WHEREAS, In the death of General George M. Sternberg this Association has lost one of its most highly valuable members, eminent for his service as an executive officer and for his attainments in medicine, as one of the leaders in the movement against tuberculosis and a co-worker with Dr. Robert Koch, and as one of the founders of this Association, be it

Resolved, That the secretary be requested to extend to his family the deep sympathy of the members of this Association, while expressing their appreciation of him, both as a man and a physician.

WHEREAS, The Senate Joint Resolution number 120, introduced into the United States Congress on April 11, 1916, makes it unlawful for any officer or employee of the Public Health Service of the Federal Government to be or become a member or officer of, or in any way connected with, any medical or private health association or organization of any kind, and

WHEREAS, In the opinion of The National Association for the Study and Prevention of Tuberculosis the spirit of said resolution is opposed to the aims and objects for which the Association was formed, and its passage would seriously interfere with the progress of the anti-tuberculosis movement in the United States, therefore be it

Resolved, That The National Association for the Study and Prevention of Tuberculosis records its absolute disapproval of said resolution and urges its members to take such steps as may be proper to prevent its adoption by the United States Congress.

WHEREAS, In the past the tendency of general hospitals has been to exclude cases of tuberculosis, and

WHEREAS, It has been demonstrated in a number of such institutions that this class of cases may be admitted into separate wards without detriment to other patients, and

WHEREAS, Both for humanitarian reasons and for purposes of instruction, there is need for a change of policy in this regard, therefore be it

Resolved, That The National Association for the Study and Prevention of Tuberculosis recommends to general hospitals, through both their medical and lay boards, that separate wards, one for each sex, be established for the care of such cases.

The report of the Committee on Nursing Education was received and accepted with thanks to the Committee for their labor upon it.

At a special meeting held on the afternoon of May 12 the report of the Committee on Standards of Diagnosis of Pulmonary Tuberculosis in Children was discussed and referred back to the committee for further consideration.

At a meeting of the board of directors, held on Friday, May 12, the following officers were elected for the ensuing year: Dr. Edward R. Baldwin, New York, president; Hon. Theodore Roosevelt, New York, and Sir William Osler, Oxford, honorary vice-presidents; Dr. Watson S. Rankin, North Carolina, and Dr. James Alexander Miller, New York, vice-presidents; Dr. Henry Barton Jacobs, Maryland, secretary; Mr. William H. Baldwin, District of Columbia, treasurer.

The following directors were elected to serve on the executive committee for the ensuing year: William H. Baldwin, District of Columbia; Dr. Hermann M. Biggs, New York; Homer Folks, New York; John M. Glenn, New York; Sherman C. Kingsley, Illinois; Dr. David R. Lyman, Connecticut; Dr. George T. Palmer, Illinois.

The summarized report of the treasurer, Mr. William H. Baldwin, is as follows:

Balance on hand April 30, 1915. . . . . $3,043.16
Receipts. 53,431.59
Disbursements. 45,546.27

Balance on hand April 30, 1916. . . . .$10,928.48

At the meeting of the Association in 1916 the secretary reported a membership of 2,505; number of associations, 1,334; dispensaries, 459; sanatoria and special hospitals, 491; open-air schools, 300.

A list of officers and directors for 1915 to 1916 follows:

President, Dr. Theodore B. Sachs; honorary vice-presidents, Theodore Roosevelt and Sir William Osler; vice-presidents, Dr. E. R. Baldwin and Dr. Christen Quevli; treasurer, William H. Baldwin; secretary, Dr. Henry Barton Jacobs; directors, Frederic Almy, Buffalo; Joseph S. Ames, Baltimore; Dr. Edward R. Baldwin, Saranac Lake; William H. Baldwin, Washington; Dr. W. Jarvis Barlow, Los Angeles; Miss Kate Barnard, Oklahoma City; Ernest P. Bicknell, Washington; Dr. Hermann M. Biggs, New York; Dr. Rupert Blue, Washington; Miss Mabel T. Boardman, Washington; Dr. Vincent Y. Bowditch, Boston; Dr. Lawrason Brown, Saranac Lake; Severance Burrage, Indianapolis; Dr. Hoyt E. Dearholt, Milwaukee; Dr. George H. Evans, San Francisco; Dr. Livingston Farrand, Boulder, Colo.; Dr. Lawrence F. Flick, Philadelphia; Homer Folks, New York; Lee K. Frankel, New York; Dr. John S. Fulton, Baltimore; John M. Glenn, New York; Dr. Charles Lyman Greene, St. Paul; Dr. Elmer E. Hegg, Seattle; Frederick L. Hoffman, Newark, N. J.; Dr. Henry Barton Jacobs, Baltimore; Dr. Herbert M. King, Loomis, N. Y.; John A. Kingsbury, New York; Sherman C. Kingsley, Chicago; Dr. S.ᵀA. Knopf, New York; Dr. H. R. M. Landis, Philadelphia; Miss Julia C. Lathrop, Washington; Col. J. L. Ludlow, Winston-Salem; Dr. Cabot Lull, Birmingham, Ala.; Dr. David R. Lyman, Wallingford, Conn.; Dr. O. W. McMichael, Chicago; S. Livingston Mather, Cleveland; Dr. James Alexander Miller, New York; A. L. Mills, Portland, Ore.; Dr. Charles L. Minor, Asheville; John Mitchell, New York; Charles P. Neill, Washington; Dr. George T. Palmer, Springfield, Ill.; Dr. LeRoy S. Peters, Albuquerque; Dr. Charles

O. Probst, Columbus, O.; Dr. Christen Quevli, Tacoma; Dr. Watson S. Rankin, Raleigh, N. C.; Dr. Mazÿck P. Ravenel, Columbus, Mo.; Dr. Theodore B. Sachs, Chicago; Dr. E. C. Schroeder, Washington; Gen. C. F. Stokes, Washington; Seymour H. Stone, Boston; Dr. Edward L. Trudeau, Saranac Lake; Dr. Thomas D. Tuttle, Seattle; Dr. E. R. Vander Slice, Kearney, Neb.; Miss Maude Van Syckle, Detroit; Dr. Gerald B. Webb, Colorado Springs; Dr. William H. Welch, Baltimore; Dr. William Charles White, Pittsburgh.

Executive secretary, Charles J. Hatfield, M.D.; assistant secretary, Philip P. Jacobs, Ph.D.; field secretaries, Charles M. DeForest and Frederick D. Hopkins.

The following is a list of papers read before the respective sections at the meeting of May 11–12, 1916:

Housing and tuberculosis—Lawrence Veiller.
The separation of tuberculosis from general medicine—Thomas McCrae, M.D.
The relation of the general hospital to tuberculosis—George Dock, M.D.
Observations on the teaching of tuberculosis—William S. Thayer, M.D.
Hemoptysis as a symptom—Frederick T. Lord, M.D.
Tuberculosis often of secondary importance to other pathological conditions—
    C. D. Parfitt, M.D.
Results obtained by the class method of home treatment in pulmonary tu-
    berculosis during a period of ten years—Joseph H. Pratt, M.D.
D'Espine's sign: its significance in pulmonary and glandular tuberculosis—
    H. S. Hatch, M.D.
The use of the x-ray in the diagnosis and study of pulmonary tuberculosis—
    Charles L. Minor, M.D.
The early diagnosis of pulmonary tuberculosis by x-rays: the Roentgeno-
    logical aspect—Frederick H. Baetjer, M.D.
The therapeutic value of the U. S. P. tincture of iodine in the treatment of
    tuberculosis and other infectious diseases when properly administered and
    given in progressively increasing doses—John Ritter, M.D.
Chronic non-tuberculous pulmonary infections—Louis Hamman, M.D., and
    S. Wolman, M.D.
The teeth in tuberculosis—David R. Lyman, M.D.
Rest of the individual lung by posture—Gerald B. Webb, M.D., Alexius M.
    Forster, M.D., and F. M. Houck, M.D.
Gastric function in pulmonary tuberculosis—Henry K. Mohler, M.D., and
    Elmer H. Funk, M.D.
The relation of tuberculosis of the bronchial glands to the diagnosis of tubercu-
    losis of the lungs—Mary E. Lapham, M.D.
Complement fixation in the diagnosis of tuberculosis—H. J. Corper, M.D.
A clinical and experimental study of complement fixation in tuberculosis—
    S. A. Petroff.
Complement fixation in pulmonary tuberculosis: some clinical observations—
    Alfred Meyer, M.D.

Diagnosis of tuberculosis by complement fixation test—J. Bronfenbrenner, Ph.D., and M. J. Schlesinger.

Attempts to alter the resistance of guinea-pigs to tuberculous infection and extension by anaphylactic shock—Allen K. Krause, M.D.

Experimental studies on cutaneous hyper-sensitiveness to tuberculo-protein—A. K. Krause, M.D.

Some unusual consequences of artificial pneumothorax—A. K. Krause, M.D.

Fatal hemorrhage in bone tuberculosis: case report and autopsy—Robert C. Paterson, M.D.

Cellular or tissue immunity to tuberculosis and its relation to the pathology of tuberculosis—A. K. Krause, M.D.

Demonstration of the lungs of rabbits immunized against tuberculous infection—Willard B. Soper, M.D.

Leucocytic counts in rabbits immunized against tuberculosis; a preliminary report—Robert C. Paterson, M.D., and E. N. Packard, Jr., M.D.

Some derivatives of methylene blue in tuberculosis chemo-therapy—Lydia M. DeWitt, M.D.

Influenza bacilli in the sputum of consumptives—Mary L. Hamblet, M.D., and H. L. Barnes, M.D.

Streptothricosis of the lungs with report of cases—William M. Stockwell, M.D.

Studies in tuberculin hypersensitiveness as determined by intracutaneous tests of different dosages—Myer Solis-Cohen, M.D.

The occurrence of living tubercle bacilli in river water contaminated by sewage from a health resort—Lawrason Brown, M.D., S. A. Petroff, M.D., and F. H. Heise, M.D.

The Diazo and urochromogen reactions in pulmonary tuberculosis—H. J. Corper, M.D., F. F. Callahan, M.D., and M. I. Marshak, M.D.

Interstate factors in the tuberculosis problem—Homer Folks, LL.D.

Interstate control of the tuberculosis problem—Hon. William Kent.

Interstate control of tuberculosis; Will the Kent Bill help?—Gertrude Vaile.

The solution of the interstate tuberculosis problem—Wilbur A. Sawyer, M.D.

Dispensary standards—F. Elisabeth Crowell.

Pay clinics for tuberculosis—Michael M. Davis, Jr., Ph.D.

Colored physicians and colored nurses for colored patients—H. R. M. Landis, M.D.

Health insurance—John B. Andrews, Ph.D.

Tuberculosis relief associations—Charles J. Hatfield, M.D.

Present status of medical examination of employees—Harry E. Mock, M.D.

Report of the Committee on Research.

Report of the Committee on Standards of Diagnosis of Pulmonary Tuberculosis in Children.

Report of Committee on Education for Student Nurses in Tuberculosis.

Eleventh midwinter meeting of the American Sanatorium Association.

Eleventh spring meeting of the American Sanatorium Association.

CHAPTER XXIII
THIRTEENTH ANNUAL MEETING

THE thirteenth annual meeting of The National Association for the Study and Prevention of Tuberculosis was held at the Hotel Sinton, Cincinnati, Ohio, on Wednesday, Thursday, and Friday, May 9, 10, and 11, 1917. The meeting of the Association was called to order by the president, Dr. Edward R. Baldwin, at 4.30 o'clock on Wednesday. The address of the president was presented and filed for publication in the Transactions. The report of the executive office for the year ending April 30, 1917, was read and approved.

On motion, duly seconded and carried, the following committee was appointed by the chair to nominate candidates for vacancies on the board of directors: William H. Baldwin, District of Columbia, chairman; Dr. Lawrason Brown, New York; Dr. David R. Lyman, Connecticut; Dr. Hoyt E. Dearholt, Wisconsin; Homer Folks, New York.

On motion, duly seconded and carried, the following committee on resolutions was appointed by the chair: Dr. John H. Lowman, Ohio, chairman; Dr. Vincent Y. Bowditch, Massachusetts; Dr. Robert H. Babcock, Illinois; Dr. H. M. Bracken, Minnesota; Dr. Philip King Brown, California.

The meeting was well attended, the registration being over 800, with a large representation from all parts of the United States. At the business meeting, held on Thursday afternoon, the following directors were elected for terms of five years each: Ernest P. Bicknell, District of Columbia; Dr. Vincent Y. Bowditch, Massachusetts; Dr. C. C. Browning, California; Dr. J. W. Coon, Wisconsin; Dr. H. K. Dunham, Ohio; Rev. George Eaves, Alabama; E. K. Gaylord, Oklahoma; Surgeon General W. C. Gorgas, District of Columbia; Dr. Allen K. Krause, Maryland; Dr. John

223

H. Lowman, Ohio; Dr. Gerald B. Webb, Colorado; Dr. William Charles White, Pennsylvania.

Dr. John H. Lowman, chairman of the committee on resolutions, presented the following resolutions with the endorsement of the committee. Each of the resolutions was unanimously adopted:

INASMUCH as Dr. Franklin Martin, of the Advisory Committee of the General Medical Board of the Council of National Defense, has written to the president of The National Association for the Study and Prevention of Tuberculosis, for recommendation to the Medical Board concerning tuberculosis, to be sent to the subcommittee of the Board, namely, Dr. Hermann M. Biggs, Chairman, Mr. Homer Folks, Dr. Lawrason Brown, Dr. George T. Palmer, and Dr. E. R. Baldwin, the following resolutions have been prepared:

WHEREAS, It has been the experience of the warring nations of Europe that cases of incipient and even moderately advanced tuberculosis are frequently unrecognized in the routine examination of recruits; and

WHEREAS, Inactive tuberculosisis frequently rendered active by the physical and mental strain and exposure of modern warfare; and

WHEREAS, The appalling prevalence of tuberculosis in the armies both in the field and in the concentration camps with the inevitable and widespread extension of the infection from these to the civilian population is the *greatest* of all health problems presented by the present war; and

WHEREAS, The extreme gravity of the situation demands that the services of all the most highly trained men available be utilized most effectively for protection against the occurrence of conditions now prevailing in France and other countries; and

WHEREAS, The continued presence in their several communities of men and women now engaged in tuberculosis and other health work is likewise necessary for the preservation of the health of our people, and to care for returning invalided soldiers; therefore be it

Resolved, That The National Association for the Study and Prevention of Tuberculosis in convention assembled pledges its loyal support to the Government; and further

Resolved, That The National Association for the Study and Prevention of Tuberculosis urges upon the Council of National Defense the following measures:

I. The registration and organization for the term of the war of the tuberculosis workers of our country, including clinicians, roentgenologists, laboratory workers, nurses, social workers, and administration officers, and their commission as reserve officers.

II. The division of the country into districts in which these new federal forces may be utilized without unduly interfering with the present vital work of conserving the health of their several localities.

III. The employment of these forces for the following specific purposes:

a. To make under the command of a ranking medical officer of the army corps, repeated routine examination and observation of recruits while in training and mobilization camps for the purpose of detecting any obscure tuberculous lesions;

b. To utilize and enlarge the existing sanatoria and hospitals of our country so that all cases of tuberculosis arising in our forces may be adequately cared for as near as possible to their own homes;

c. To work out in coöperation with existing health authorities a definite, comprehensive, and constructive program for adequate prevention and control of tuberculosis among the whole population.

WHEREAS, A large number of public health nurses have already enrolled or are being urged to enroll in the active service of the American Red Cross and other agencies for nursing work during the war; and

WHEREAS, The Red Cross and other bedside nursing can be done as well by the regular graduate and undergraduate nurses as by those who have had special training in public health work, while we have no substitutes available for the latter; and

WHEREAS, Our national efficiency, depending as it does upon our national health, demands of each of us that we give our services where they will be of the widest benefit rather than follow our personal inclinations therefore, be it

Resolved, That The National Association for the Study and Prevention of Tuberculosis urges upon all public health nurses, and particularly upon those who have had special training in tuberculosis work, that they can best serve our country in its present crisis by continuing, for the present at least, to employ their energies with the complicated health problems of our various communities.

WHEREAS, The National Association for the Study and Prevention of Tuberculosis has an organization extending throughout every State of the Union which is thoroughly conversant with health conditions and philanthropic activities, and

WHEREAS, The American Red Cross is confronted with the immense task of coördinating the health and philanthropic activities throughout the country; be it

Resolved, That The National Association for the Study and Prevention of Tuberculosis offers to the president of the American Red Cross the services of its organization for coöperation in promoting Red Cross work in any form that may be determined upon.

WHEREAS, Several of the European countries engaged in the great war have found it desirable to place themselves on a prohibition basis; and

WHEREAS, We wish to neglect nothing that will make for the general good of the service; and

WHEREAS, Our loyalty in such time of stress should lead us to ask nothing of those going to the front which those remaining are not willing to demand of themselves; therefore, be it

15

Resolved, That this Association place itself on record as favoring National Prohibition, both for soldiers and civilians during the war period and for one year thereafter.

WHEREAS, The National Association for the Study and Prevention of Tuberculosis is opposed to the vending of patent medicines and the self-administration of "cures" for various diseases; and

WHEREAS, The American Medical Association has also condemned the sale and use of self-administered "cures"; and

WHEREAS, The patent medicine interests of the United States have been seeking an outlet for their trade in foreign countries; and

WHEREAS, The United States Department of Commerce in its special Consular Report No. 76, issued in March, 1917, has advocated and urged upon the patent medicine interests of the United States that they exploit China and the Chinese people as a lucrative field for their business; be it

Resolved, That The National Association for the Study and Prevention of Tuberculosis condemns such action on the part of the United States Department of Commerce, and that the executive secretary be instructed to forward a copy of this resolution to the secretary of said department, urging that hereafter the influence of the United States Government should not be used in support of the patent medicine business.

WHEREAS, Since the year 1907, the Russell Sage Foundation has generously contributed to the work of The National Association for the Study and Prevention of Tuberculosis, making it possible for the Association to carry on such activities as publicity, the publication of the Directory and the development of work in the field, the financing of which would have been extremely difficult; and

WHEREAS, The trustees of the Russell Sage Foundation feel unable longer to continue their annual grant to the National Association; be it

Resolved, That The National Association for the Study and Prevention of Tuberculosis thus publicly expresses and records its appreciation and thanks for this service of the Russell Sage Foundation; and that the executive secretary be instructed to forward a copy of this resolution to the directors of the Russell Sage Foundation.

Resolved, That the thanks of The National Association for the Study and Prevention of Tuberculosis be extended to the Local Committee of Arrangements, to the Cincinnati Anti-Tuberculosis League, to the Cincinnati Chamber of Commerce, and to all of those who have helped to promote the attendance at this thirteenth annual meeting, and to make it a success.

The report of the Committee on the Expenditure of Red Cross Seal Funds was presented by the chairman, Homer Folks, and was adopted. The report is as follows:

REPORT OF SPECIAL COMMITTEE ON EXPENDITURE OF RED CROSS SEAL FUNDS, SHOWING AN EVALUATION OF THE PURPOSES TO WHICH THE PROCEEDS OF THE RED CROSS SEAL SALE MAY BE APPLIED

(Exact statements as to relative values are, of course, impossible, but the different purposes are stated in the order of their estimated value as preventive measures.)

1. *Aiding in the Development of a State Tuberculosis Association* which shall formulate a constructive program for the prevention of tuberculosis, and shall organize, coördinate, and unify measures adopted for the fulfilment of the program.

2. *Securing the Establishment, in State or Local Health Departments, of Divisions of Tuberculosis,* or of definitely organized tuberculosis activity, for the promotion of all forms of anti-tuberculosis work.

3. *Direct Educational Work* as to the nature, treatment, and prevention of tuberculosis, such educational work to be addressed, whenever practicable, to securing the adoption of certain definite community activities in the anti-tuberculosis campaign. This educational work should include the payment of the expenses of representatives of tuberculosis agencies in attending tuberculosis conferences.

4. *Propaganda Efforts,* for the establishment and operation by public authorities of survey, nursing, clinic, hospital, sanatorium, day or night camp, open-air school or class, or other kindred agencies.

5. Educational and other work for safeguarding infants and others from tuberculosis infection and for increasing their powers of resistance to such infection.

Note: In all communities having a population of more than, say, 30,000, the promotion of 1, 2, 3, 4, and 5 can most effectively be done by the employment of the anti-tuberculosis organization of a paid, full-time, trained executive secretary.

6. *Employment of Nurses for Tuberculosis Surveys* or temporarily (pending public provision) for assisting and nursing the tuberculous sick, securing admission to hospitals and sanatoria, etc.

7. *Organization and Temporary Operation of Clinics, Dispensaries, or Out-Patient Stations,* for the diagnosis and treatment of tuberculosis and for the expert medical examination of all persons who have been exposed to tuberculosis.

8. *Establishment and, if Need Be, Temporary Operation (Pending Public Provision) of Open-Air Schools* or Fresh Air Classes for Children who are pre-tubercular or have been exposed to tuberculosis.

9. *Establishment and, if Need be, Temporary Operation (Pending Public Provision) of Preventoria* for pre-tuberculous cases, or children's divisions of sanatoria or hospitals.

10. *Payment in Whole or Part for Maintenance of Patients in Hospitals or Sanatoria,* when efforts to secure funds therefor from relatives, employers, churches, lodges, or the public or other private relief agencies prove unavailing.

11. *After-Care: i. e.,* advice, employment, and, if need be, relief of patients leaving sanatoria as arrested or cured.

12. *Relief,* of whatever medical or material form may be needed (so far as efforts to procure it from other private or public sources, as set forth in No. 10 above, prove unavailing), for families in which there is a case of tuberculosis which cannot be placed in a hospital, provided that through definite medical nursing and social supervision conditions are maintained which will prevent further infections.

13. *Relief* (so far as it is not available from private or public sources, as set forth in No. 10 above) which may be needed to enable a patient who is a breadwinner or a caretaker of a family to accept hospital care.

We recommend:

1. That the report of the committee on a circular of advice as to policy in the use of Red Cross Seal funds, appointed in January last, be adopted.

2. That this Association recommend to the American Red Cross the adoption of the Committee's report as its definition of anti-tuberculosis work, in place of the existing definition.

3. That the National Association recommend to the State Associations and to local associations through State Associations, where such exist, the adoption of the program of work outlined in this Committee's report, with any modification called for by local conditions, in the expenditure of Red Cross Seal funds and any further available resources.

4. That the National Association secure annually from State Associations and from local associations through State Associations, where such exist, a financial statement, so far as practicable, for the year ending November 1, of the expenditure of their funds; subdivided so far as may be practicable on the lines indicated by the purposes enumerated in this report.

5. That a circular letter of explanation be framed to be addressed to the State Associations and local associations and through State Associations amplifying the Committee's report and dealing more fully with the relation between agencies and tuberculosis associations.

The Red Cross Seal banners awarded in the inter-city and interstate competition for 1916 were presented to the following states and cities: Wyoming, Minnesota, and New York; and Thornburg, Pa.; Hershey, Pa.; River Falls, Wis.; Sewickley, Pa.; Morristown, N. J.; Elmira, N. Y.; Troy, N. Y.; Rochester, N. Y.; Buffalo, N. Y.; and Brooklyn, N. Y.

At a meeting of the board of directors held on the afternoon of Thursday, May 10, the following officers were elected for the ensuing year: Dr. Charles L. Minor, North Carolina, president;

Theodore Roosevelt, New York, and Sir William Osler, England, honorary vice-presidents; Dr. David R. Lyman, Connecticut, and Frederick L. Hoffman, New Jersey, vice-presidents; Dr. Henry Barton Jacobs, Maryland, secretary; William H. Baldwin, District of Columbia, treasurer.

The following directors were elected to serve on the executive committee for the ensuing year: Dr. Edward R. Baldwin, New York; William H. Baldwin, District of Columbia; Dr. Hoyt E. Dearholt, Wisconsin; Dr. Lee K. Frankel, New York; John M. Glenn, New York; Dr. George Thomas Palmer, Illinois; Dr. William Charles White, Pennsylvania.

The vice-presidents were authorized by special resolution to serve as members of the executive committee for the ensuing year.

The summarized report of the treasurer, Mr. William H. Baldwin, is as follows:

Balance on hand April 30, 1916..............$10,928.48
Receipts................................... 66,061.48
Disbursements............................. 74,469.55

Balance on hand April 30, 1917.............. $2,520.79

At the meeting of the Association in 1917 the secretary reported a membership of 2,493; number of associations, 1,100; dispensaries, 437; sanatoria and special hospitals, 501.

A list of officers and directors for 1916 to 1917 follows:

President, Dr. Edward R. Baldwin; honorary vice-presidents, Theodore Roosevelt and Sir William Osler; vice-presidents, Dr. W. S. Rankin and Dr. James A. Miller; treasurer, William H. Baldwin; secretary, Dr. Henry Barton Jacobs; directors, Frederic Almy, Buffalo; Dr. Robert H. Babcock, Chicago; Dr. Edward R. Baldwin, Saranac Lake; William H. Baldwin, Washington; Dr. W. Jarvis Barlow, Los Angeles; Dr. Hermann M. Biggs, New York; Dr. Rupert Blue, Washington; Miss Mabel T. Boardman, Washington; Dr. H. M. Bracken, Minneapolis; Dr. Lawrason Brown, Saranac Lake; Dr. Philip King Brown, San Francisco; Severance Burrage, Indianapolis; Mrs. O. B. Colquitt, Dallas, Tex.; Dr. Hoyt E. Dearholt, Milwaukee; Dr. C. E. Edson, Denver; Dr. George H. Evans, San Francisco; Dr. Livingston Farrand, Boulder, Colo.; Dr. Lawrence F. Flick, Philadelphia; Miss Edna L. Foley, Chicago; Homer Folks, New York; Lee K. Frankel, New York; John M. Glenn, New York; Dr. Louis V. Hamman, Baltimore; Frederick L. Hoffman, Newark; Dr. Henry Barton Jacobs, Baltimore; H. McK. Jones, St. Louis; Dr. Herbert M. King, Loomis, N. Y.; John A. Kingsbury, New York; Sherman G. Kingsley, Chicago; Dr. S. A. Knopf, New York; Dr. George M.

Kober, Washington; Dr. H. R. M. Landis, Philadelphia; Miss Julia C. Lathrop, Washington; Dr. John H. Lowman, Cleveland; Col. J. L. Ludlow, Winston-Salem; Dr. Cabot Lull, Birmingham, Ala.; Dr. David R. Lyman, Wallingford; Dr. O. W. McMichael, Chicago; S. Livingston Mather, Cleveland; R. B. Mellon, Pittsburgh; Dr. James Alexander Miller, New York; A. L. Mills, Portland, Ore.; Dr. Charles L. Minor, Asheville; John Mitchell, New York; Charles P. Neill, Washington; Dr. George T. Palmer, Springfield, Ill.; Dr. LeRoy S. Peters, Albuquerque; Dr. Charles O. Probst, Columbus, O.; Dr. Christen Quevli, Tacoma; Dr. Watson S. Rankin, Raleigh, N. C.; Dr. Mazÿck P. Ravenel, Columbia, Mo.; Dr. F. C. Schroeder, Washington; Gen. F. C. Stokes, Washington; Dr. A. K. Stone, Boston; Seymour H. Stone, Boston; Dr. E. R. Vander Slice, Mason, Mich.; Miss Maude Van Syckle, Detroit; Dr. Victor C. Vaughan, Ann Arbor; Dr. William H. Welch, Baltimore; Dr. Dunning S. Wilson, Louisville.

Executive secretary, Charles J. Hatfield, M.D.; assistant secretaries, Philip P. Jacobs, Ph.D., and Donald B. Armstrong, M.D.; field secretaries, Charles M. DeForest and Frederick D. Hopkins.

The following is a list of papers read before the respective sections at the meeting of May 9–11, 1917:

Lessons from Canada's war experience with tuberculosis—Jabez M. Elliott, M.B.

The relation of the federal government to the anti-tuberculosis movement—F. C. Smith, M.D.

A war tuberculosis program for the nation—Hermann M. Biggs, M.D.

The nose in the tuberculous—G. W. Wagner, M.D.

Tuberculosis and pregnancy: A study of three hundred cases with a review of the literature—S. A. Douglass, M.D., and J. E. J. Harris, M.D.

The rôle of surgery in the treatment of intestinal tuberculosis—Edward Archibald, M.D.

A comparison between the skin tests, using various tuberculosis antigens and the complement fixation phenomenon—F. W. Wittich, M.D.

The Wassermann reaction and pulmonary tuberculosis—James S. Ford, M.D.

A tuberculosis preventorium for infants—Alfred F. Hess, M.D.

Medical aspects of the Michigan tuberculosis survey—Victor C. Vaughan, Jr., M.D.

Tuberculous abscess of the thoracic wall—Samuel Robinson, F.A.C.S.

The primary and secondary lobules of the lung—W. S. Miller, M.D.

Clinical observations derived from the examination of over three thousand chests checked by stereoroentgenograms—H. Kennon Dunham, M.D.

The interpretation of pathology visualized by the roentgen examination of the chest—Lewis G. Cole, M.D., and Joseph M. Steiner, M.D.

Diaphragmatic pleurisy in the tuberculous—Gerald B. Webb, M.D., Alexius M. Forster, M.D., and G. Burton Gilbert, M.D.

Are sanatoria worth while? A study of the present condition of 1,056 patients discharged from Massachusetts State Sanatoria from May, 1912, to May, 1914—Bernice W. Billings and John B. Hawes, 2d, M.D.

Prognosis in tuberculosis from the standpoint of the occurrence of hemoptysis and tubercle bacilli in the sputum—Fred H. Heise, M.D.

Deductions from four and one-half years' use of artificial pneumothorax in the treatment of pulmonary tuberculosis—Charles L. Minor, M.D.

Undergraduate instruction in tuberculosis—Allen K. Krause, M.D.

The seasonal variation of the weight-curve—Karl Schäffle, M.D.

Gold therapy of tuberculosis—Lydia M. DeWitt, M.D.

Experimental tuberculosis of the liver—W. B. Soper, M.D.

The correlation of certain sputum findings with the clinical symptoms in pulmonary tuberculosis—Joseph Elbert Pottenger, M.D.

The destruction of tubercle bacilli in the sewage of tuberculosis sanatoria—Arthur T. Laird, M.D.

The reaction of the local tubercle: a method for determining the value of indirect therapeutic agents in tuberculosis—H. J. Corper, M.D.

The pleural reaction to inoculation with tubercle bacilli in vaccinated and normal guinea-pigs—Robert C. Paterson, M.D.

The Wassermann and luetin reactions in tuberculosis—H. J. Corper, M.D., W. A. Gekler, M.D., and H. C. Sweany, M.D.

The cone and collateral lymphatic circulation in pulmonary tuberculosis—H. Kennon Dunham, M.D.

Bilateral spontaneous non-tuberculous pneumothorax, with autopsy—Alfred Meyer, M.D.

A state program for the promotion of tuberculosis nursing—Katherine M. Olmsted.

Three typical case problems in tuberculosis—Mrs. Henrietta E. Knorr.

A state bureau of tuberculosis hospital admissions and discharges—Amy L. Mercer.

A health center in a large city—Robert H. Bishop, Jr., M.D.

The social unit—Wilbur C. Phillips.

The Framingham health and tuberculosis demonstration—D. B. Armstrong, M.D., M.A., M.S.

Tuberculosis associations and relief agencies—Homer Folks, LL.D.

An adequate relief program for tuberculosis cases—Boris D. Bogen.

Rural nursing—Fannie F. Clement.

Medical examination of school children in the rural districts—J. N. Hurty, M.D.

Some problems of county tuberculosis hospitals—George J. Nelbach.

County tuberculosis hospital problems—Otto R. Eichel, M.D.

Budget and program—Arthur J. Strawson.

Publicity and education—why is a press agent?—E. A. Moree.

Report of Committee on Expenditure of Red Cross Seal Funds.

Twelfth mid-winter meeting of the American Sanatorium Association.

Twelfth spring meeting of the American Sanatorium Association.

CHAPTER XXIV

FOURTEENTH ANNUAL MEETING

THE fourteenth annual meeting of The National Tuberculosis Association was held at the Copley-Plaza Hotel, Boston, Mass., on Thursday, Friday, and Saturday, June 6, 7, and 8, 1918. The meeting of the Association was called to order by the president, Dr. Charles L. Minor, at 4.30 o'clock on Thursday. The address of the president was presented and filed for publication in the Transactions. The report of the executive office for the year ending April 30, 1918 was read and ordered filed.

On motion, duly carried, the following committee was appointed by the chair to nominate candidates for vacancies on the board of directors: Dr. Lee K. Frankel, New York, chairman; Dr. Vincent Y. Bowditch, Massachusetts; Dr. Hoyt E. Dearholt, Wisconsin; Dr. W. L. Dunn, North Carolina; Dr. Stephen J. Maher, Connecticut.

On motion, duly made and carried, the following committee on resolutions was appointed by the chair: William H. Baldwin, District of Columbia, chairman; Dr. Robert H. Babcock, Illinois; Frederick L. Hoffman, New Jersey; Dr. Edward O. Otis, Massachusetts; Dr. O. W. McMichael, Illinois.

The meeting was well attended, the registration totaling 548, representing every state in the union except nine. Three sessions of the Clinical Section, three of the Sociological Section, two of the Pathological Section, and one of the Advisory Council were held. In addition to these there was a mass meeting under the auspices of a local committee.

At the business meeting of the Association on Friday afternoon, the following directors were elected for the term of five years each: Mr. Isaac Adler, New York; Dr. W. Jarvis Barlow, California; Col. Frank Billings, Illinois; Col. George E. Bushnell,

District of Columbia; George F. Canfield, New York; Lieut.-Col. A. M. Forster, Colorado; Dr. Alfred Henry, Indiana; Mrs. F. G. Hodgson, Georgia; Dr. Thomas McCrae, Pennsylvania; Dr. Alfred Meyer, New York; W. Frank Persons, District of Columbia; Bolton Smith, Tennessee; Miss Agnes D. Randolph, Virginia (for unexpired term of Dr. Bracken).

On behalf of the committee on resolutions Mr. William H. Baldwin, chairman, presented the following resolutions with the endorsement of the committee. Each of the resolutions was unanimously adopted:

WHEREAS, The board of directors of the National Association at a meeting on March 16 last voted in accordance with Article VIII of the By-Laws of this Association to amend the name of this society from The National Association for the Study and Prevention of Tuberculosis to National Tuberculosis Association.

Resolved, That, in accordance with Article VIII of the By-Laws of the Association, the action of the board of directors is hereby approved and the name of this society shall be known hereafter as National Tuberculosis Association.

Resolved, That the Board of Directors of the National Tuberculosis Association be and they are hereby authorized, directed, and empowered to incorporate this Association under the laws of the state of Maine, or such other state as may be selected by them, and to transfer all the property and assets of every name and nature of this Association to such new corporation upon such terms and conditions as to them may seem desirable; and to do any and all other things in connection therewith.

Resolved, That the coöperation of the National Tuberculosis Association and its affiliated agencies be given to the fullest possible extent to the International Health Board of the Rockefeller Foundation in the study of the anti-tuberculosis movement being made by that organization.

Resolved, That the thanks of the National Tuberculosis Association be extended to the Bureau of Vocational Guidance of Harvard University for the work it is undertaking in a study of open-air schools in the United States, and

Resolved, Further, That the coöperation of the National Association and all its affiliated agencies be extended in the fullest possible measure to those who are making this investigation.

WHEREAS, It is vital to the progress of the medical profession that the valuable experience being gained at the present time in war medicine and surgery be gathered together and preserved for future generations; and

WHEREAS, The Army Medical Museum at Washington, D. C., is taking necessary steps to do this with the hope that it will eventually become, as it should be, a center for medical teaching and research; and

WHEREAS, Plans for a new building and new equipment and for the expansion of the Museum on a scale adequate to meet the growing needs brought about by the war have been made by those in charge,

Resolved, That the National Tuberculosis Association pledges its support to the directors of the Army Medical Museum in their efforts to secure appropriation from Congress, and in other ways.

WHEREAS, It has been found necessary by the American Red Cross and the National Tuberculosis Association to withdraw the rebates allowed from the ten per cent. of the gross sale of Red Cross Christmas Seals payable to the American Red Cross, and

WHEREAS, Certain agents have expressed themselves as unfavorable to this change in percentage because of the withdrawal of revenue from their treasuries,

Resolved, That in case any state or general agent appointed by the National Tuberculosis Association finds after the 1918 Seal Sale that his net return from the sale of Red Cross Seals has diminished below that of 1917 because of the withdrawal of rebates, the National Tuberculosis Association will recommend to the American Red Cross the adjustment of his returns to the extent of the deficit under the 1917 rate of rebate applied to the 1918 sale.

WHEREAS, The National Tuberculosis Association and its affiliated agencies fully appreciate the necessity for prompt increase in the number of beds available in tuberculosis hospitals and sanatoria throughout the United States; and

WHEREAS, The Federal Reserve Board of the United States Government, through its Capital Issues Committee, has taken the position in some cases brought before it that the issuance of bonds and other securities must be limited to construction of a temporary nature only; and

WHEREAS, The National Tuberculosis Association realizes that this action is in danger of decidedly hindering the construction of necessary tuberculosis hospital facilities throughout the country; and

WHEREAS, The National Tuberculosis Association and its affiliated agencies desire to work heartily and earnestly with the President and the Government in taking the course which will do the country the most good with the least harm,

Resolved, That the National Tuberculosis Association urges upon all communities of the United States the necessity of promptly increasing their hospital provisions, and of planning them in such a way as to minimize the difference between permanent and temporary construction; and

Resolved, Further, That the Capital Issues Committee be urged to allow permanent buildings to be constructed in all cases where the difference is not too great, in order that it may not be necessary to repeat the process a few years later, or to waste the money which it is so difficult to obtain for any kind of construction.

Resolved, That the National Tuberculosis Association would deplore the retirement of Surgeon General Gorgas from the office he now fills so admirably, and that we request that he be continued in active service in his present position, so that neither his work nor his plans may be interrupted.

Resolved, That the National Tuberculosis Association expresses its appreciation and thanks to the Massachusetts Anti-Tuberculosis League and the Boston Association for the Relief and Control of Tuberculosis for their assistance in arranging for this meeting; to the management of the Copley-Plaza Hotel for the use of its meeting rooms; to the organizations which have shown the interesting and instructive exhibits; and to the nurses and others who have given able assistance in making the conference a success.

Announcement of the winners of Red Cross Seal banners in the inter-state and inter-city competition for 1917 was made on behalf of the following states and cities: Wyoming, Minnesota, and Wisconsin; and Broadview, Mont.; Big Timber, Mont.; Kellogg, Idaho; Dillon, Mont.; Phoenix, Ariz.; Tulsa, Okla.; Oklahoma City, Okla.; Minneapolis, Minn.; Buffalo, N. Y.; and Brooklyn, N. Y.

At a meeting of the board of directors on Friday afternoon, June 7, the following officers were elected for the ensuing year: Dr. David R. Lyman, Connecticut, president; Hon. Theodore Roosevelt, New York, Sir William Osler, England, and Col. George E. Bushnell, District of Columbia, honorary vice-presidents; Dr. Lawrason Brown, New York, first vice-president; Lee K. Frankel, Ph.D., New York, second vice-president; Dr. Henry Barton Jacobs, Maryland, secretary; Mr. William H. Baldwin, District of Columbia, treasurer.

The following directors were elected to serve on the executive committee for the ensuing year: Dr. E. R. Baldwin, New York; Dr. Hoyt E. Dearholt, Wisconsin; Mr. Frederick L. Hoffman, New Jersey; Dr. O. W. McMichael, Illinois; Mr. William H. Baldwin, District of Columbia; Dr. George T. Palmer, Illinois; Mr. W. Frank Persons, District of Columbia.

The vice-presidents and honorary vice-presidents were authorized by special resolution to attend the meetings of the executive committee. The executive committee was authorized by the board of directors to consider itself a War Board and to take up actively all matters of concern in relation to tuberculosis and the war. It was also instructed to hold monthly meetings.

win, is as follows:

Balance on hand April 30, 1917	$2,520.79
Receipts	99,203.15
Disbursements	92,062.96
Balance on hand April 30, 1918	$9,660.98

At the meeting of the Association in 1918 the secretary reported a membership of 4,050; number of associations, 997; dispensaries, 457; sanatoria and special hospitals, 530.

A list of officers and directors for 1917 to 1918 follows:

President, Dr. Charles L. Minor; honorary vice-presidents, the Hon. Theodore Roosevelt and Sir William Osler; vice-presidents, Dr. David R. Lyman and Frederick L. Hoffman, Ph.D.; treasurer, William H. Baldwin; secretary, Dr. Henry Barton Jacobs; directors, Frederic Almy, Buffalo; Dr. Robert H. Babcock, Chicago; Dr. Edward R. Baldwin, Saranac Lake; Ernest P. Bicknell, Washington; William H. Baldwin, Washington; Dr. Hermann M. Biggs, New York; Dr. Rupert Blue, Washington; Dr. V. Y. Bowditch, Boston; Dr. H. M. Bracken, Minneapolis; Dr. Lawrason Brown, Saranac Lake; Dr. Philip King Brown, San Francisco; Dr. C. C. Browning, Los Angeles; Severance Burrage, Indianapolis; Mrs. O. B. Colquitt, Austin, Tex.; Dr. J. W. Coon, Stevens Point, Wis.; Dr. Hoyt E. Dearholt, Milwaukee; Dr. H. K. Dunham, Cincinnati; Rev. George Eaves, Birmingham, Ala.; Dr. C. E. Edson, Denver; Dr. Geo. H. Evans, San Francisco; Dr. Livingston Farrand, Boulder, Colo.; Dr. Lawrence F. Flick, Philadelphia; Miss Edna L. Foley, Chicago; Lee K. Frankel, New York; E. K. Gaylord, Oklahoma City; John M. Glenn, New York; Gen. W. C. Gorgas, Washington; Dr. Louis V. Hamman, Baltimore; Frederick L. Hoffman, Newark; Dr. Henry Barton Jacobs, Baltimore; H. McK. Jones, St. Louis; Dr. Herbert M. King, Loomis, N. Y.; Sherman C. Kingsley, Cleveland; Dr. S. A. Knopf, New York; Dr. George M. Kober; Washington; Dr. Allen K. Krause, Baltimore; Dr. H. R. M. Landis, Philadelphia; Miss Julia C. Lathrop, Washington; Dr. John H. Lowman, Cleveland; Dr. David R. Lyman, Wallingford, Conn.; Dr. O. W. McMichael, Chicago; S. Livingston Mather, Cleveland; R. B. Mellon, Pittsburgh; Dr. James Alexander Miller, New York; A. L. Mills, Portland, Ore.; Dr. Charles L. Minor, Asheville; John Mitchell, New York; Charles P. Neill, Washington; Dr. George T. Palmer, Springfield, Ill.; Dr. LeRoy S. Peters, Albuquerque; Dr. Christen Quevli, Tacoma, Wash.; Dr. Watson S. Rankin, Raleigh, N. C.; Dr. Mazÿck P. Ravenel, Columbia, Mo.; Dr. A. K. Stone, Boston; Seymour H. Stone, Boston; Dr. E. R. Vander Slice, Mason, Mich.; Miss Maude Van Syckle, Detroit; Dr. Victor C. Vaughan, Ann Arbor; Dr. Gerald B. Webb, Colorado Springs; Dr. William Charles White, Pittsburgh.

Managing director, Charles J. Hatfield, M.D.; assistant secretaries, Philip P. Jacobs, Ph.D. and Donald B. Armstrong, M.D.; field secretaries, Charles M. DeForest, Frederick D. Hopkins and H. A. Pattison, M.D.

The following is a list of papers read before the respective sections at the meeting of June 6–7, 1918:

The program of the Massachusetts state department of health against tuberculosis—Eugene R. Kelley, M.D.

Massachusetts and tuberculosis—the state sanatoria—Arthur K. Stone, M.D.

The municipal hospitals of Massachusetts—John F. O'Brien, M.D.

How America is helping France with her tuberculosis problem—James Alexander Miller, M.D.

How the United States is meeting the tuberculosis war problem—Col. George E. Bushnell, M.D.

How Canada is meeting the tuberculosis war problem—Lieut.-Col. Jabez H. Elliott, M.B.

The ultimate result in 1,654 cases of tuberculosis treated at the Modern Woodmen of America Sanatorium—J. A. Rutledge, M.D., and John B. Crouch, M.D.

An x-ray study of pulmonary tuberculosis with syphilis—Cleaveland Floyd, M.D., H. K. Boutwell, M.D., and R. L. Leonard, M.D.

The necessity for caring for the careless consumptive—John J. Lloyd, M.D.

A study of pulmonary and pleural annular radiographic shadows—H. L. Sampson, F. H. Heise, M.D., and Lawrason Brown, M.D.

Pain in the chest with special reference to pulmonary tuberculosis—John B. Hawes, 2d, M.D.

Pulmonary conditions simulating tuberculosis—Lieut.-Col. Jabez H. Elliott, M.B.

Methuselah and life in the open—Vincent Y. Bowditch, M.D.

The word tuberculosis—Allen K. Krause, M.D.

Rest and exercise in the treatment of pulmonary tuberculosis—Hugh M. Kinghorn, M.D.

A study of the effects of typhoid fever and anti-typhoid immunization on pulmonary tuberculosis: history of a typhoid fever epidemic at the Trudeau Sanatorium—Lawrason Brown, M.D., Fred H. Heise, M.D., S. A. Petroff, and George E. Wilson, M.D.

The clinical value of complement fixation in pulmonary tuberculosis based on a study of 540 cases—Lawrason Brown, M.D., and S. A. Petroff.

Diabetes complicated with tuberculosis, treated by means of the Allen Fasting Method—H. R. M. Landis, M.D., Elmer H. Funk, M.D., and C. M. Montgomery, M.D.

Artificial pneumothorax and pregnancy—S. A. Slater, A.B., M.D.

Institutional care of laryngo-pulmonary tuberculosis—Julius Dworetzky, M.D.

The treatment of laryngeal tuberculosis by reflected condensed sunlight—Charles W. Mills, M.D., and Lieut.-Col. Alexius M. Forster, M.D.

The recording of physical findings in chest examinations—D. MacDougall King, M.B.

Anti-tuberculosis organization in France for the period of the war—summarized by P. Armand-DeLille, M.D.

The struggle against infantile tuberculosis in France and the preservation of childhood against its ravages by the system of the Oeuvre Grancher—P. Armand-DeLille, M.D.

Tuberculosis as a war problem—Major Joseph H. Pratt, M.R.C., and Lawrason Brown, M.D.

Attempts to reduce the resistance of the guinea-pig to tuberculosis by means of various agents; Roentgen ray, benzene, thorium X, tuberculin, ether and chloroform—H. J. Corper, M.D.

Experiments on the effect of repeated protein injections on tuberculous infection—Allen K. Krause, M.D., and H. S. Willis, M.D.

Experimental arrested tuberculosis and subsequent infections—Edward R. Baldwin, M.D.

Notes on the experimental infection of guinea-pigs with virulent tubercle bacilli—Allen K. Krause, M.D., and Linda B. Lange, M.D.

Preliminary report on experiments performed to produce an immune serum for tuberculosis—H. J. Corper, M.D.

Mercury in the chemotherapy of experimental tuberculosis in guinea-pigs—Lydia M. DeWitt, M.D.

The urochromogen test as an aid in prognosis in far advanced pulmonary tuberculosis—Thomas H. A. Stites, M.D.

The complement fixation test for tuberculosis—Linda B. Lange, M.D.

A glycerine extract of tubercle bacilli as an antigen—S. A. Petroff.

X-ray chest manual—Kennon Dunham, M.D.

Tuberculosis of the lungs with especial reference to the importance of adenopathy—James A. Honeij, M.D.

New evidence on the cause of human tuberculosis—Burton R. Rogers, D.V.M.

Reclaiming the tuberculous soldier from the military and industrial army—Lieut.-Col. Harry E. Mock.

Problems in the vocational re-education of disabled men—C. A. Posser, Ph.D.

Ten years' experience with the Eudowood Farm Colony—Martin F. Sloan, M.D.

Eighteen years' experience with ergotherapy—Philip King Brown, M.D.

Occupations in relation to tuberculosis—Bayard T. Crane, M.D.

Occupation and industrial training of tuberculous soldiers in sanatoria—J. Roddick Byers, M.D.

Employment of post-tuberculous workers—George M. Price, M.D.

Three years' experience in the employment of the discharged tuberculous patients in factory work—Edward Hochhauser.

Promoting adult efficiency through child welfare—S. C. Kingsley.

The Framingham health program: first year results—D. B. Armstrong, M.D., M.A., M.S.

Consultation and medical examination work of the Framingham community health and tuberculosis demonstration—P. Challis Bartlett, M.D.

Framingham educational and organization activities—Mary A. Abel.

Thirteenth midwinter meeting of the American Sanatorium Association.

Thirteenth spring meeting of the American Sanatorium Association.

CHAPTER XXV

FIFTEENTH ANNUAL MEETING

THE fifteenth annual meeting of the National Tuberculosis Association was held at St. Paul's Methodist Episcopal Church, Atlantic City, N. J., on Saturday, Monday, and Tuesday, June 14, 16, and 17, 1919.

The meeting of the Association was called to order by the president, Dr. David R. Lyman, at 4.30 o'clock on Saturday. The address of the president was presented and filed for publication in the Transactions. The report of the executive office for the year ending May 31, 1919, was read and ordered filed.

The report of the committee previously appointed, Dr. James Alexander Miller, chairman, to nominate candidates for vacancies on the board of directors, was presented, and it was moved and carried that the report of the committee be accepted and that the names be forwarded for formal election to Portland, Me., where the corporate meeting was held on Monday, June 16, at 10 A. M., and the following directors were duly and legally elected for terms of five years each unless otherwise indicated: Dr. John S. Billings, New York, N. Y.; Dr. Charles V. Chapin, Providence, R. I.; Dr. Gordon K. Dickinson, Jersey City, N. J.; Dr. W. L. Dunn, Asheville, N. C.; Lee K. Frankel, New York, N. Y.; Dr. Paul A. Lewis, Philadelphia, Pa.; Dr. Harry T. Marshall, University, Va.; Dr. John H. Peck, Des Moines, Ia.; James H. Pershing, Denver, Colo.; Fred M. Stein, New York, N. Y.; Dr. Walter R. Steiner, Hartford, Conn.; Dr. Josephine Milligan, Jackson, Ill. (four years, in place of Mr. Isaac Adler); Henry B. Platt, New York, N. Y. (one year, in place of Dr. O. W. McMichael); Dr. Z. T. Scott, Austin, Tex. (three years, in place of Dr. John H. Lowman).

On motion duly made and carried, the following committee on resolutions was appointed by the chairman: Dr. Vincent Y.

Bowditch, Boston, chairman; Dr. Christen Quevli, Tacoma; Dr. G. W. Holden, Denver; Dr. Horace J. Howk, Mt. McGregor, N. Y.; Seymour H. Stone, Boston.

The meeting was well attended, the registration totaling 608, with representatives from every state in the Union and from Canada and England and other foreign countries. Three sessions of the Clinical Section were held, three of the Pathological, three of the Sociological, one of the Nursing Section, and one of the Advisory Council.

The announcement was made by the chair that Mr. Henry B. Platt, of New York, one of the newly elected directors, had consented to serve as treasurer of the Association, succeeding Mr. William H. Baldwin, who resigned after seven years of service.

On behalf of the committee on resolutions, Dr. Vincent Y. Bowditch, chairman, presented the following resolutions with the endorsement of the committee. Each of the resolutions was adopted unanimously:

WHEREAS, The National Tuberculosis Association has always advocated a maximum amount of sunlight and fresh air as a means of prevention and cure of tuberculosis, and

WHEREAS, The said Association considers the present daylight-saving law an aid in preserving the general health of the country, and in particular, a help in the prevention of tuberculosis, be it

Resolved, That the National Tuberculosis Association views with concern the present effort to abrogate the daylight-saving law, and hereby protests against any effort that shall tend to stop the operation of that law.

Be it Resolved, That the National Tuberculosis Association through its executive officers take immediate steps to secure the coöperation of all other great health organizations, especially the American Medical Association and state and territorial health officers in placing before the American people a united demand for the adoption of universal military service as a public health measure.

WHEREAS, The introduction of physical education into the schools, including instruction in health principles, direction in physical activities, and periodic physical examinations, is of vital importance in the prevention and combating of tuberculosis, and

WHEREAS, The National Physical Education Service has been established for the purpose of unifying the efforts of all interested organizations for the promotion of a physical education in the elementary and secondary schools, therefore, be it

Resolved, That the National Tuberculosis Association will coöperate in every practicable way with the National Physical Education Service in the promotion of physical education in the schools.

WHEREAS, It has become increasingly apparent that a Division of Tuberculosis of the United States Public Health Service is necessary and that the creation of such a division will be the greatest step forward in the struggle against this disease which it is possible to take at the present time, be it

Resolved, That the National Tuberculosis Association earnestly urges Congress to pass as promptly as possible the Ransdell-Esch bill (S. 1660, H. R. 3855) to provide such a Division of Tuberculosis in, and Advisory Council for, the United States Public Health Service.

Resolved, That a vote of thanks be given to the members of the St. Paul's Methodist Episcopal Church and to their pastor, Rev. A. A. Lucas; to the Local Committee of Arrangements, and the Committee on Registration for their splendid coöperation and assistance during this conference; and to Mr. Boyer, the Superintendent of Schools, for the use of the High School Auditorium.

On behalf of the Committee on Indigent Migratory Consumptives, Mr. James H. Pershing, chairman, presented the following report, which was ordered accepted and placed on file:

REPORT OF THE COMMITTEE ON INDIGENT MIGRATORY CONSUMPTIVES

In certain portions of the country, particularly the Southwest, the people are greatly concerned with the problem of the indigent migratory consumptives. This region is relatively sparsely populated and undeveloped. Therefore, the burden of indigence is sustained with difficulty. Besides, there has existed the feeling that with life in the arid regions tuberculosis is not a concomitant, but is the product of less salubrious climates, which is being shifted upon a people who are not responsible for its existence. The results are manifest. Not only is the migratory consumptive neglected, but the people of the arid regions fail to promote their own proper well-being by reason of the fear that by so doing they will be unduly burdened with responsibilities which belong to others.

Recognizing this situation, the National Tuberculosis Association, in December last, appointed a committee "to make a study of the problem of the indigent migratory consumptive in all of its various aspects and to outline and prepare a plan for dealing with the problem."

The present members of the committee are the following: Mr. James H. Pershing, Chairman, Denver, Colo.; Mr. William H. Baldwin, Washington, D. C.; Dr. Philip King Brown, San Francisco, Cal.; Dr. S. J. Crumbine, Topeka, Kas.; Mr. E. K. Gaylord, Oklahoma City, Okla.; Mr. John M. Glenn,

16

New York City; Dr. B. J. Lloyd, Hygienic Laboratory, U. S. Public Health
Service, Washington, D. C.; Dr. Z. T. Scott, Austin, Tex.; Mr. E. C. Shaw,
Akron, Ohio; Dr. A. G. Shortle, Albuquerque, N. Mex.; Mrs. E. L. M. Tate-
Thompson, Los Angeles, Cal.; Miss Gertrude Vaile, Denver, Colo.; Dr. Allen
Hamilton Williams, Phoenix, Ariz.

Dr. Severance Burrage, who in 1918 served as special public health investigator in Serbia with the Red Cross, and more recently on the staff of the United
States Public Health Service, was appointed by the National Association as the
executive secretary for the committee, with an office at 519 Chamber of Commerce Building, Denver, Colorado.

The committee met for organization at Santa Fé, New Mexico, on March
1, 1919. It appeared to the committee that the subject before it naturally
resolved itself into three branches:

1. The prevention of migration;

2. The measures to be taken for the relief of communities into which indigent consumptives most generally migrate; and

3. The relief of migrating indigent consumptives.

The matter of prevention resolves itself largely into a question of education
along three lines:

(a) Early diagnosis by the attending physician;

(b) Knowledge on the part of physician and patient that successful home
treatment is possible; and

(c) General diffusion of knowledge with respect to (a) and (b).

The Committee has suggested to the National Association the adoption of
an education program involving the following:

(a) The securing for the control of tuberculosis emphasis and publicity by
the Federal Government similar to that given to the control of venereal diseases.

(b) Assistance from the Federal Government directed to the medical profession by supplying information in aid of early diagnosis and home treatment.

(c) The exertion of influence which may lead to the adequate financing of the
Public Health Service through the appropriate Federal Department and by
means of appeals to such large private endowments as the Rockefeller Foundation.

The Committee also urges the creation of a special department of tuberculosis in the Federal Public Health Service.

Since March 1st, Dr. Burrage, the committee's secretary, has been making an
intensive study of the problem throughout the Southwest and on the Pacific
Coast. Dr. Burrage has not as yet completed his investigation, but in due
course will report his findings to the committee which will, in turn, report to
the National Association.

In view of the unfinished condition of the committee's investigations, it is
impossible at this time to state conclusions. The data at hand, however,
indicate, first, that the number of indigent consumptives who seek relief by
change of climate is not as great as the committee had been led to believe; and

second, that the number has been decreasing, at least during the period of the war. The problem has been complicated somewhat by the tuberculous soldier, a condition which may be expected to improve as the relief agencies provided by the Federal Government become better established.

In general it may be said that throughout the Southwest there is great want of public health legislation and no adequate enforcement of such laws as do exist. Aside from the fear of the burden of indigence, public opinion does not seem to be awake to the fact that there is a tuberculosis problem—California is the only resort state which is making community provision for the care of its resident patients. The Colorado legislature, recently adjourned, refused to adopt a measure before it for the reorganization of its State Board of Health; but in this connection it should be said that the New Mexico Legislature created a Board of Health. Denver, at the municipal election of May 20, defeated a proposed bond issue to provide a municipal sanatorium for the tuberculous. Undoubtedly the fear that such an institution would increase the influx of indigent consumptives was an influence against its establishment. The committee hopes to complete its work by September 1.

At a meeting of the board of directors the following officers were elected for the ensuing year: Dr. Victor C. Vaughan, Michigan, president; Sir William Osler, England, and Col. G. E. Bushnell, District of Columbia, honorary vice-presidents; Dr. Gerald B. Webb, Colorado, and Mr. John M. Glenn, New York, vice-presidents; Dr. Henry Barton Jacobs, Maryland, secretary; Mr. Henry B. Platt, New York, treasurer.

The following directors were elected to serve on the executive committee for the ensuing year: Dr. E. R. Baldwin, New York; Dr. George T. Palmer, Illinois; Dr. William Charles White, Pennsylvania; Dr. Vincent Y. Bowditch, Massachusetts; Dr. George M. Kober, District of Columbia; Dr. Hoyt E. Dearholt, Wisconsin; Mr. William H. Baldwin, District of Columbia.

The summarized report of the treasurer is as follows:

Balance, May 1, 1918	$9,660.98
Receipts	76,685.51
	$86,346.49
Disbursements	83,294.43
Balance, December 31, 1918	$3,052.06

Note: This report covers a period of eight months instead of one year, the fiscal year of the Association having been changed to correspond to the calendar year.

At the meeting of the Association in 1919 the secretary reported a membership of 4,066; number of associations, 1,024; dispensaries, 478; sanatoria and special hospitals, 572.

A list of officers and directors for 1918 to 1919 follows:

President, Dr. David R. Lyman; honorary vice-presidents, the Hon. Theodore Roosevelt, Sir William Osler, and Col. George E. Bushnell; vice-presidents, Dr. Lawrason Brown and Dr. Alfred Meyer; treasurer, William H. Baldwin; secretary, Dr. Henry Barton Jacobs; directors, Isaac Adler, Rochester, N. Y.; Dr. Robert H. Babcock, Chicago; Dr. Edward R. Baldwin, Saranac Lake; William H. Baldwin, Washington; Dr. W. Jarvis Barlow, Los Angeles; Ernest P. Bicknell, Washington; Col. Frank Billings, Chicago; Surg. Gen. Rupert Blue, Washington; Dr. Vincent Y. Bowditch, Boston; Dr. Lawrason Brown, Saranac Lake; Dr. Philip King Brown, San Francisco; Dr. C. C. Browning, Los Angeles; Col. Geo. E. Bushnell, Washington; George F. Canfield, New York; Dr. J. W. Coon, Stevens Point, Wis.; Dr. Hoyt E. Dearholt, Milwaukee; Dr. H. K. Dunham, Cincinnati; Rev. George Eaves, Birmingham, Ala.; Dr. C. E. Edson, Denver; Dr. Livingston Farrand, Boulder, Colo.; Miss Edna L. Foley, Chicago; Lieut. Col. A. M. Forster, New Haven; E. K. Gaylord, Oklahoma City; John M. Glenn, New York; Gen. W. C. Gorgas, Washington; Dr. Louis V. Hamman, Baltimore; Dr. Alfred Henry, Indianapolis; Mrs. F. G. Hodgson, Atlanta; Frederick L. Hoffman, Newark; Dr. Henry Barton Jacobs, Baltimore; H. McK. Jones, St. Louis; Sherman C. Kingsley, Cleveland; Dr. S. A. Knopf, New York; Dr. George M. Kober, Washington; Dr. Allen K. Krause, Baltimore; Dr. H. R. M. Landis, Philadelphia; Dr. John H. Lowman, Cleveland; Dr. David R. Lyman, Wallingford; Dr. Thomas McCrae, Philadelphia; Dr. O. W. McMichael, Chicago; S. Livingston Mather, Cleveland; Dr. Ralph C. Matson, Portland, Ore.; R. B. Mellon, Pittsburgh; Dr. Alfred Meyer, New York; Dr. James A. Miller, New York; A. L. Mills, Portland, Ore.; Dr. Charles L. Minor, Asheville; John Mitchell, New York; Dr. George T. Palmer, Springfield, Ill.; Dr. LeRoy S. Peters, Albuquerque; Dr. Christen Quevli, Tacoma, Wash.; Miss Agnes D. Randolph, Richmond; Bolton Smith, Memphis; Dr. A. K. Stone, Boston; Seymour H. Stone, Boston; Dr. E. R. Vander Slice, Ann Arbor; Miss Maude Van Syckle, Detroit; Dr. V. C. Vaughan, Ann Arbor; Maj. Gerald B. Webb, Colorado Springs; Dr. William Charles White, Pittsburgh.

Managing director, Charles J. Hatfield, M.D.; assistant secretaries, Philip P. Jacobs, Ph.D., Donald B. Armstrong, M.D.; medical field secretary, H. A. Pattison, M.D.; regional secretaries, Murray A. Auerbach, Atlanta; Leet B. Myers, New York; George Everson, Spokane; Severance Burrage, Ph.D., Denver; Modern Health Crusader executive, Charles M. DeForest; field secretary, Frederick D. Hopkins; publicity secretary, B. G. Eaves.

The following is a list of papers read before the respective sections at the meeting of June 14-17, 1919:

The national welfare—Victor C. Vaughan, M.D.

Experience abroad, showing relationship between tuberculosis and a general health program—Homer Folks, LL.D.

X-ray study of advanced tuberculosis of the lungs with autopsies—Joseph Walsh, M.D., James W. Wood, M.D., and Capt. James C. Thompson, M.C.

A preliminary study of clinical activity—Lawrason Brown, M.D., Fred H. Heise, M.D., S. A. Petroff, and Homer L. Sampson.

A study of thirty cases of pneumothorax found in the first 2,000 consecutive cases received at U. S. A. General Hospital No. 19—Major Kennon Dunham, M.C.

Spontaneous pneumothorax—Capt. Everett Morris, M.C.

Odds and ends in artificial pneumothorax—LeRoy S. Peters, M.D.

Physical reconstruction applied in the treatment of pulmonary tuberculosis—Col. Frank Billings, M.C.

The epidemiology of tuberculosis in the military service—Col. G. E. Bushnell.

Medical, hospital, and special aspects of reconstruction for the tuberculous—Lieut.-Col. Estes Nichols, M.C.

Tuberculosis among European nations at war—James Alexander Miller, M.D.

Clinical follow-up of influenza cases—P. Challis Bartlett, M.D.

The temperature of tuberculosis in its diagnostic and prognostic significance—Charles L. Minor, M.D.

Community machinery for the discovery of tuberculosis—D. B. Armstrong, M.D.

Employment of rest and exercise after tuberculous patients have returned to Work—Hugh M. Kinghorn, M.D.

Treatment in tuberculosis—Capt. C. B. Sylvester, M.C.

The classification of laryngeal tuberculosis—Julius Dworetzky, M.D.

Lung abscess following operation on the upper respiratory tract—Frederick Slyfield, M.D.

Etiological studies in tuberculosis—Lawrason Brown, M.D., S. A. Petroff, and Gilberto Pesquera, M.D.

The origin and relationship of the bronchial artery in the guinea-pig—H. S. Willis, M.D.

The circulatory relationships of experimental tubercle in the rabbit's lung—William Snow Miller, M.D.

An investigation on the acid fastness of tubercle bacilli—B. Suyenaga, M.D.

The mode and growth of the tubercle bacillus on fluid mediums—Paul A. Lewis, M.D.

Further observations on the inhibition of growth of the tubercle bacillus by chemical compounds—Paul A. Lewis, M.D.

Some observations which may lead to the classification of tubercle bacilli—S. A. Petroff and Gilberto Pesquera, M.D.

Tuberculosis and evolution—Lieut. John Paul Givler, S.C.

Continuous injection method in treatment of experimental tuberculosis—Julian H. Lewis, M.D., and Lydia M. DeWitt, M.D.

The influence of anæsthesia on experimental tuberculosis in guinea-pigs—Lawrason Brown, M.D., and S. A. Petroff.

The microörganisms, especially pneumococci and streptococci, in the sputum and blood of cases of pulmonary tuberculosis—Major H. J. Corper, M.C., Lieut. W. G. Donald, M.C., and Lieut. J. J. Enright, M.C

Streptococcus hæmolyticus in tuberculous lungs—Lieut. John N. Hayes, M.C.

A comparison of certain antigens used in complement fixation tests in pulmonary tuberculosis—Lieut. H. C. Young, S.C., and Lieut. J. P. Givler, S.C.

Some problems in complement fixation in tuberculosis—S. A. Petroff.

The types of tuberculous lesions found at autopsy in a military hospital—Lieut. E. D. Downing, M. C.

An interesting case of foreign body in the bronchus recovered at postmortem—James B. Dinnan, M.D.

Comparisons of stereoroentgenograms of the chest with autopsy findings at U. S. A. General Hospital No. 19, Oteen, N. C.—Major Kennon Dunham, M.C., and Lieut. J. N. Hayes, M.C.

Centralized control of tuberculosis through the United States Public Health Service—J. B. Lloyd, M.D.

Centralized control of tuberculosis by state commissions or divisions of tuberculosis—Eugene R. Kelley, M.D.

Centralized control of tuberculosis by divisions of tuberculosis in county or city boards of health—Gordon K. Dickinson, M.D.

Present status of soldiers and draft rejects with tuberculosis—William H. Baldwin, M.D.

Occupational therapy and prevocational training for soldiers about to be discharged—Capt. Samuel M. North, S. C.

The program of the Federal Board for Vocational Éducation—H. A. Pattison, M.D.

Relief in the home, by state, by municipalities, by private agencies—Walter S. Ufford.

Social insurance as a means of relieving poverty—John A. Lapp.

An intensive educational program—Mary A. Meyers, R.N.

A tuberculosis survey—Arthur K. Stone, M.D.

Preparation of the public health nurse for tuberculosis nursing—Mary Van Zile, R.N.

Report of the Committee on Indigent Migratory Consumptives.

Fourteenth midwinter meeting of the American Sanatorium Association.

Fourteenth spring meeting of the American Sanatorium Association.

CHAPTER XXVI

SIXTEENTH ANNUAL MEETING

THE sixteenth annual meeting of the National Tuberculosis Association was held at the Hotel Statler, St. Louis, Mo., April 21 to 24, 1920.

The meeting was called to order at 2 o'clock on Thursday afternoon by the president, Dr. Victor C. Vaughan. Following a few brief remarks of welcome by Archbishop Glennon, of St. Louis, the address of the president was presented and filed for publication in the Transactions. The report of the executive office for the year ending April 20, 1920, was read and ordered filed and published.

The report of the nominating committee, which had been appointed in March, was presented by the chairman, Dr. Vincent Y. Bowditch. The committee placed in nomination 12 directors to fill five-year terms, and two directors to fill vacancies caused by resignation. The report of the nominating committee was approved and the names were forwarded for formal election to Portland, Me., where the corporate meeting of the members of the National Tuberculosis Association was held on Friday, April 23, at 10 A. M. The following directors were duly and legally elected for terms of five years each, unless otherwise indicated: Dr. William N. Anderson, Omaha, Neb.; Dr. A. C. Bachmeyer, Cincinnati, O.; H. R. Cunningham, Helena, Mont.; Dr. George Dock, St. Louis, Mo.; Dr. Livingston Farrand, Washington, D. C.; Homer Folks, New York; Dr. David R. Lyman, Wallingford, Conn.; Dr. James A. Miller, New York; Henry B. Platt, New York; J. V. A. Smith, Seattle, Wash.; Prof. Reed Smith, Columbia, S. C.; Dr. Allen H. Williams, Phoenix, Ariz.; Miss Mary Beard, Boston, Mass. (three years in place of Mrs. F. G. Hodgson); Dr. Walter J. Marcley, Minneapolis, Minn. (one year in place of Dr. Henry Barton Jacobs).

On motion duly made and carried, the following committee on resolutions was appointed by the president: Dr. Gerald B. Webb, Colorado Springs, chairman; Dr. S. Adolphus Knopf, New York; Dr. Philip King Brown, San Francisco; Dr. W. L. Dunn, Asheville; Dr. Josephine Milligan, Jacksonville, Ill.

Over 800 persons were registered at the meeting, and it is estimated that there was a considerable number who were not registered.

The Clinical Section held two meetings and the Pathological Section one meeting. Two combined sessions of the Clinical and Pathological Sections were also held. The Advisory Council held one session, the Sociological Section three sessions, and the Nursing Section one session. On Friday evening, under the auspices of the local committee of arrangements and the Missouri Tuberculosis Association, a reception and Modern Health Crusader program was given.

On behalf of the committee on resolutions, Dr. Gerald B. Webb, chairman, presented the following resolutions with the endorsement of the committee. Each of the resolutions was adopted unanimously:

WHEREAS, In the death of Sir William Osler, Bart., the National Tuberculosis Association has suffered the loss of its first Honorary Vice-President and the three English-speaking countries, Canada, America, and England, a most distinguished physician, medical teacher, and anti-tuberculosis worker; and

WHEREAS, This Association is indebted to the late Sir William Osler for having been one of the prime movers in its formation and in no small measure responsible for its success from the beginning until now; and

WHEREAS, His interest in our Association was unabated even throughout the years of his sojourn as Regius Professor in Oxford; and

WHEREAS, By his wisdom, devotion, high ideal, and love for humanity he not only labored among physicians for a better understanding of the medical problems of tuberculosis but also labored untiringly for the improvements of the social conditions responsible for the spread of tuberculosis, and always took a special interest in the care of the consumptive poor, and during the World War in the medical and sanitary care of the British and Allied armies; and

WHEREAS, Sir William Osler, by his lovable personality, his genial spirit, veneration for his teachers, friendship for his colleagues, love for his pupils, great diagnostic skill, and devotion to his patients, endeared himself to thousands of American physicians and patients; be it

Resolved, That this Association record these attributes with the full consciousness of the profound debt it owes to the memory of Sir William Osler and a deep appreciation of the glory he has shed upon his work as well as upon the history of the anti-tuberculosis movement in the three English-speaking countries in which he lived and labored; and

Resolved, further, That these resolutions be spread on the minutes of this meeting of the Association and that they be engrossed and sent to Lady Osler with the expression of profound sympathy in the great sorrow which has befallen her in the passing away of her distinguished husband and her brave and only son, who made the supreme sacrifice on the field of battle in the recent world war.

WHEREAS, During the fifteen years of its existence the National Tuberculosis Association has encouraged the elaboration of new methods of handling tuberculosis, has co-ordinated existing methods, and has given its influence to the building up of a complete program for the treatment as well as the prevention of the disease; and

WHEREAS, There appears to be a sentiment on the part of most of our workers that the care of arrested cases demands further elaboration and machinery, and for some years past the farm colony and industrial community have been recommended for handling this side of the question, but have not had an adequate trial; and

WHEREAS, It is recognized that the trend from rural to urban life is a serious factor in complicating the prevention of tuberculosis, and that it is recognized that the very cases unsuited for the complications of urban life are particularly liable to break down from tuberculosis; and

WHEREAS, Various public and governmental agencies are asking for advice in regard to this phase of the problem, therefore be it

Resolved, That the National Tuberculosis Association recognizes the present necessity for a carefully planned trial of this measure and that the President is empowered to appoint a committee to investigate and to study the situation and to recommend a proper course for the organization of such colonies and communities.

WHEREAS, The campaign against tuberculosis is founded directly on medical research and animal experimentation and

WHEREAS, It is necessary in the development of new discoveries that laboratory experiments be made upon animals, and

WHEREAS, Existing laws for the prevention of cruelty to animals are adequate to prevent improper practices; be it

Resolved, That the National Tuberculosis Association approves of animal experimentation conducted under proper supervision and urges the further development of research in tuberculosis to the end that a greater knowledge of the means of prevention and treatment of the disease may be obtained; and

Resolved, That the National Tuberculosis Association considers unwise special legislative restriction of experimentation on animals.

WHEREAS, The National Tuberculosis Association, is fully aware of the widespread lack of suitable provision for the care, supervision and control of tuberculous patients in the country, either public or private, and

WHEREAS, The Federal Government has provided liberal pensions and skilled treatment for disabled soldiers, sailors and others entitled to care by reason of injuries and other diseases acquired in our country's service during the World War, but has not thus far done so for those afflicted with tuberculosis, be it

Resolved, That this Association urgently recommends immediate legislation to deal with this large problem. Furthermore and by reason of the investigation of a special committee appointed to advise with the U. S. Public Health Service, which is duly charged with responsibility for the care of these disabled soldiers, sailors, etc., after their discharge from the military and naval service, we specifically urge the following:

First, Immediate authorization for increased salaries for the personnel of the U.S. Public Health Service, without which it has been found and is clearly impossible to secure or train competent medical officers.

Second, Immediate appropriations for the construction of a sufficient number of sanatoria near the large centers of population and in salubrious surroundings, together with the ample provision for hospital cases in existing U. S. P. H. S. hospitals, or by establishing new units for this purpose.

Furthermore, We urge that provision be made for the training and employment of arrested tuberculous beneficiaries in such occupations as may be found suitable and under such conditions as will conduce to their continued health.

WHEREAS, In connection with the Open Air School movement—open window rooms—and classes for anemic and other children have demonstrated the value of these classes in ordinary school buildings;

WHEREAS, The school authorities in a number of the large cities of the United States have already adopted plans to provide open window rooms in all new school structures, be it

Resolved, That the National Tuberculosis Association recommends the adoption of plans by school authorities for the provision of a sufficient number of open window rooms in every new school building hereafter erected in the United States and further resolved that copies of this resolution be circulated among the Federal, State and Local School authorities throughout the United States.

WHEREAS, Tuberculosis among the Negro race is very prevalent and on the increase and due partly to bad housing, bad sanitation in general and lack of institutions for tuberculous cases in all stages of the disease of the Negro race; be it

Resolved, That this Association recommends the passage of better housing laws for the United States as a whole; more institutions for the treatment of tuberculous Negroes and the admission of colored physicians to post graduate courses in the study of tuberculosis.

Resolved, That the National Tuberculosis Association expresses its appreciation and thanks to the Local Committee on Arrangements, the St. Louis Society, and the Missouri Tuberculosis Association for their generous hospitality and their assistance in arranging for this meeting; to the Management of the Hotel Statler for the use of its meeting rooms and to all those who have helped to make the conference a success.

On behalf of the Committee on Indigent Migratory Consumptives, Mr. James H. Pershing, Chairman, presented a report. On motion duly made and carried, it was ordered that the report be accepted and the Committee be continued and enlarged. The report of the Committee follows:

FINAL REPORT OF COMMITTEE ON INDIGENT MIGRATORY CONSUMPTIVES

Your Committee, through its Secretary, has collected a large amount of data concerning the indigent migratory consumptive, largely from the southwestern states, but including a number of communities in other parts of the country as well. Unfortunately the records available have been so incomplete that authentic figures in regard to a number of the points investigated could not be obtained. We have however been able to learn certain definite facts.

First: That there is a large indigent migratory problem. The region most seriously affected is the Southwest,—Arizona, California, Colorado, New Mexico and Texas receiving by far the greater majority of migrants. Colorado and California have the largest number, but in proportion to the population Arizona, New Mexico and certain small communities in Texas are more seriously affected.

Certain communities in Kansas, Wyoming, Utah, eastern Texas and several cities in the Middle West may be looked upon as gateways, which receive cases stopping off en route to the so-called health resort states.

Second: That the problem also prevails more or less extensively in other health resort communities, particularly in Asheville, certain portions of Florida, and Saranac Lake. Also, there is a definite movement of tuberculous indigents toward and from the large industrial centers of the East and Middle West.

Third: That the ex-soldier is no longer to be regarded as a factor in the indigent migratory consumptive problem, because of Government care.

Fourth: That among these cases there is an unusually high death rate within the first year after migration. For example, in Arizona, out of 1,132 deaths from tuberculosis reported in 1918, 440 or 39 ⅔ per cent. had resided in the state less than twelve months.

Fifth: That, of the indigent tuberculous persons, a varying but large percentage are non-residents.

Sixth: That the principal causes of the migration of the indigent tuberculous are:

1. The advice of physicians.

Out of 1,786 cases reported from the southwestern States in the last six months 738 were advised to go there by their physicians.

2. By the advice of others.

250 of the 1,786 cases upon such advice.

3. The passing on of indigent cases by charity organizations of local officials. This cause is diminishing, apparently through better coöperation between social agencies.

4. The lack of knowledge and lack of facilities for treatment in home states. This applies not only to the lack of sanatoria, but more especially to the ignorance on the part of the public concerning the proper treatment of tuberculosis, and to the faulty diagnosis, as well as the indifference and ignorance in regard to the treatment on the part of many physicians. Thus, no other remedy being known to the patient, he is practically forced to seek a change of climate.

5. The alluring advertisements put out by some health resort communities. For example, an illustrated booklet from the chamber of commerce of a southwestern city states, "While the climate alone is almost a specific for incipient tuberculosis . . . there is ample provision for sufferers who need hospital treatment."

In view of these ascertained facts, your Committee has come to the following conclusions:

A. That the problem is a serious one demanding immediate attention, because

1. It is a menace to the public health. The indigent migratory consumptive is ignorant and careless, and is a danger to those about him both during his migration and after he arrives in a community not prepared to look after him.

2. It is a heavy financial drain on the communities to which the migration goes.

3. It is the cause of much needless suffering and loss of life.

Inadequate care, worry, homesickness, lack of proper food and often actual starvation, are the conditions frequently met. A certain number of these cases that die undoubtedly might have recovered had they stayed at home.

B. That the remedy for this whole situation lies in the education of the doctors and the public, and in increased facilities for the treatment of patients in their home states.

Your Committee therefore makes these general recommendations:

A. That an extensive campaign of education of physicians and the public be instituted by the following agencies:

1. The United States Public Health Service, through a division of tuberculosis.

2. The American Medical Association and its Journal, and the component state medical associations and their journals.

3. State Boards of Health and their publications.

4. The National, state, and local tuberculosis associations.

5. Agricultural and labor publications.

6. Chambers of commerce of health resort communities.

B. That persistent efforts be made to increase facilities for the early diagnosis and treatment of patients in their home states.

1. By the establishment of schools for the intensive study of tuberculosis similar to those at Trudeau and Colorado Springs.

2. By the construction of additional sanatoria and the establishment of more tuberculosis clinics.

C. That health resort communities be urged to make and enforce such rules and regulations as are necessary to protect themselves from the dangers caused by the presence of persons afflicted with tuberculosis. Such regulation and supervision are necessary in all states but especially so in those to which sufferers go from other states. Better control along these lines might become an important factor in actually reducing migration.

To assist in the practical and early fulfillment of these general recommendations your Committee makes the following specific suggestions:

First: That our Association urge the establishment of a division of tuberculosis in the United States Public Health Service, provided with adequate funds and personnel.

Second: That this Indigent Migratory Consumptive Committee be continued, with power to enlarge, for the purpose of further study, and particularly for the purpose of inaugurating the proposed educational and publicity work.

On behalf of the Committee on History of the National Association, Dr. S. Adolphus Knopf read a progress report and summary of the history as it was compiled to date. In connection with it he read short tributes to the departed leaders of the Association, *i. e.*, Grover Cleveland, honorary vice-president from 1905 to 1908; Theodore Roosevelt, honorary vice-president from 1906 to 1919; Edward Livingston Trudeau, the first president; Edward G. Janeway, president 1909–1910; Theodore B. Sachs, president 1915–1916; John Henry Lowman, president 1913–1914; Surgeon General George M. Sternberg, treasurer from 1904 to 1912; and lastly, Sir William Osler, honorary vice-president from 1905 to 1919. After the reading of the report, Dr. Knopf made the motion that the president request the audience to rise and remain standing in silence for a few moments in honor of the departed leaders of the Association.

At a meeting of the board of directors the following officers were elected for the ensuing year: Dr. Gerald B. Webb, Colorado, president; General William C. Gorgas, District of Columbia, honorary vice-president; Colonel George E. Bushnell, Massachusetts, honorary vice-president; Dr. Philip King Brown, California, and Dr. James Alexander Miller, New York, vice-presidents; Dr. George M. Kober, District of Columbia, secretary; Mr. Henry B. Platt, New York, treasurer; Mr. Wadleigh B. Drummond, Maine, clerk.

The following directors were elected to serve on the executive committee for the ensuing year: Dr. H. Kennon Dunham, Ohio; Dr. W. L. Dunn, North Carolina; Miss Edna L. Foley, Illinois; Dr. Alfred Henry, Indiana; Dr. Walter R. Steiner, Connecticut; Dr. Victor C. Vaughan, Michigan; Dr. William Charles White, Pennsylvania.

The summarized report of the treasurer, Mr. Henry B. Platt, is as follows:

Balance, December 31, 1918..............	$3,052.06
Receipts...............................	2,743,819.31
	$2,746,871.37
Disbursements.........................	2,728,159.35
Balance, December 31, 1919..............	$18,712.02

A list of officers and directors for 1919 to 1920 follows:

President, Dr. Victor C. Vaughan; honorary vice-presidents, Sir William Osler and Col. George E. Bushnell; vice-presidents, Dr. Gerald B. Webb and John M. Glenn; treasurer, Henry B. Platt; secretary, Dr. Henry Barton Jacobs; clerk, W. B. Drummond; directors, Dr. Robert H. Babcock, Chicago; Dr. Edward H. Baldwin, Saranac Lake; William H. Baldwin, Washington; Dr. W. Jarvis Barlow, Los Angeles; Ernest P. Bicknell, Washington; Col. Frank Billings, Chicago; Dr. John S. Billings, New York; Dr. Vincent Y. Bowditch, Boston; Dr. Philip King Brown, San Francisco; Dr. C. C. Browning, Los Angeles; Col. George E. Bushnell, Washington; George F. Canfield, New York; Dr. Charles V. Chapin, Providence; Dr. J. W. Coon, Stevens Point, Wis.; Dr. Hoyt E. Dearholt, Milwaukee; Dr. G. K. Dickinson, Jersey City; Maj. H. K. Dunham, Cincinnati; Dr. W. L. Dunn, Asheville; Rev. Geo. Eaves, Birmingham, Ala.; Dr. C. E. Edson, Denver; Miss Edna L. Foley, Chicago; Dr. A. M. Forster, Colorado Springs; Lee K. Frankel, New York; E. K. Gaylord, Oklahoma City; John M. Glenn, New York; Surg. Gen. W. C. Gorgas, Washington; Dr. Louis V. Hammon, Baltimore; Dr. Alfred Henry, Indianapolis; Dr. H. W. Hoagland, Colorado Springs; Mrs. F. G. Hodgson, Atlanta; Dr. Henry Barton Jacobs, Baltimore; H. McK. Jones, St. Louis; Sherman G. Kingsley, Cleveland; Dr. George M. Kober, Washington; Dr. Allen K. Krause, Baltimore; Dr. Paul A. Lewis, Philadelphia; Dr. Thomas McCrae, Philadelphia; Dr. Harry T. Marshall, University, Va.; Dr. Ralph C. Matson, Portland, Ore.; R. B. Mellon, Pittsburgh; Dr. Alfred Meyer, New

York; Dr. Josephine Milligan, Jacksonville, Ill.; Dr. George T. Palmer, Springfield, Ill.; Dr. John H. Peck, Des Moines; James H. Pershing, Denver; Dr. LeRoy S. Peters, Albuquerque; Henry B. Platt, New York; Dr. Christen Quevli, Tacoma, Wash.; Miss Agnes D. Randolph, Richmond; Dr. Z. T. Scott, Austin, Texas; Bolton Smith, Memphis, Tenn.; Fred M. Stein, New York; Dr. Walter R. Steiner, Hartford; Dr. A. K. Stone, Boston; Seymour H. Stone, Boston; Dr. E. R. Vander Slice, Ann Arbor; Miss Maude Van Syckle, Detroit; Dr. Victor C. Vaughan, Ann Arbor; Dr. Gerald B. Webb, Colorado Springs; Dr. William Charles White, Pittsburgh.

Executive Staff: Administrative Service, Charles J. Hatfield, M.D., managing director; Philip P. Jacobs, Ph.D., assistant secretary; A. J. Leverton, office secretary; Grace Douglass, assistant office secretary; L. B. Whitcomb, purchasing agent; F. W. Coriell, auditor.

Medical Service, H. A. Pattison, M.D., medical field secretary; T. B. Kidner, institutional secretary; Benjamin K. Hays, M.D., educational secretary; Mary E. Marshall, R.N., secretary for nursing.

Modern Health Crusade Service, Charles M. DeForest, crusader executive; Mildred Terry, assistant crusader executive.

Framingham Demonstration, Donald B. Armstrong, M.D., executive officer; P. Challis Bartlett, M.D., chief medical examiner.

Field Service, Frederick D. Hopkins, supervisor of field service.

Regional Secretaries, Murray A. Auerbach, Atlanta; Paul L. Benjamin, Philadelphia; George Everson, Portland, Ore.; Leet B. Myers, New York; Arthur J. Strawson, Indianapolis; John Tombs, Albuquerque, N. M.

Research Service, Jessamine S. Whitney, research secretary; Eleanor B. Conklin, research secretary; Josephine McK. Stults, librarian.

Publicity Service, Basil G. Eaves, publicity secretary; Helena V. Williams, assistant publicity secretary.

National Committee on Indigent Migratory Consumptives, Severance Burrage, D.P.H., secretary, Denver.

The following is a list of the papers read before the respective sections of the meeting of April 21–24, 1920:

The administrative problem of public health nursing—A. W. Freeman, M.D.
The Red Cross program for coöperation in public health nursing—Elizabeth G. Fox.
Coöperation in public health nursing between the state society and the state health organization—Robert G. Paterson, Ph.D.
The need of a unified nursing service—Katherine M. Olmsted.
Intrapleural hypertension for evacuating pus through bronchi in spontaneous pyopneumothorax—Alfred Meyer, M.D., and B. Stivelman, M.D.
The classification of pulmonary tuberculosis, based upon symptoms, physical and x-ray findings—Lawrason Brown, M.D., Fred H. Heise, M.D., and H. L. Sampson.

Physical diagnosis vs. the x-ray in disease of the lungs—George William Norris, M.D.

First infection with tuberculosis—Eugene L. Opie, M.D.

The relation of sound and light to the interpretation of x-ray examinations of the chest—J. J. Singer, M.D.

The classification of pulmonary tuberculosis as modified by stereoscopic Roentgenographs—Bertram H. Waters, M.D., and J. Burns Amberson, Jr., M.D.

The concurrence of intestinal tuberculosis in patients with pulmonary tuberculosis at the Trudeau Sanatorium—Lawrason Brown, M.D., Homer L. Sampson, and F. H. Heise, M.D.

Studies on pneumothorax and tuberculosis—H. J. Corper, M.D., Saling Simon, M.D., and O. B. Rensch, M.D.

How may the tuberculous patient secure an arrestment of his disease without becoming an invalid?—F. M. Pottenger, M.D.

Relationship of influenza to clinical pulmonary tuberculosis; deductions from the epidemic of 1918–1919—Martin F. Sloan, M.D.

Twenty years' experience with the subcutaneous tuberculin test—Lawrason Brown, M.D., and Fred H. Heise, M.D.

Serological studies in tuberculosis, third contribution, concerning precipitins and complement-fixing antibodies—Yoshio Nishida, M.D., and S. A. Petroff.

Masked juvenile tuberculosis—J. V. Cooke, M.D., and T. C. Hempelmann, M.D.

Studies on the inhibitory action of sodium cinnamate in tuberculosis—H. J. Corper, M.D., H. Gauss, M.D., and W. A. Gekler, M.D.

The influence of creosote, guaiacol, and related substances on the tubercle bacillus and on experimental tuberculosis—Lydia M. DeWitt, M.D., Binzi Suyenaga, M.D., and H. Gideon Wells, M.D.

Tb.—the proper abbreviation for the words "tuberculous" or "tuberculosis"— L. B. McBrayer, M.D., F.A.C.P.

Some problems in the differential diagnosis of pulmonary tuberculosis—James Alexander Miller, M.D.

Pulmonary findings in circulatory changes—J. S. Pritchard, M.D., and M. A. Mortensen, M.D.

Influenza as a factor in the activation of latent tuberculosis—Louis C. Boisliniere, M.D.

Tuberculosis among the Negroes—H. G. Carter, M.D.

The influence of smallpox and vaccination on pulmonary tuberculosis— Horace John Howk, M.D., and William E. Lawson, M.D.

A study of the effect of pulmonary tuberculosis on vital capacity, first report— F. W. Wittich, M.D., J. A. Myers, Ph.D., and F. L. Jennings, M.D.

Elimination of tuberculosis from the army—Ralph C. Matson, M.D.

Climate—LeRoy S. Peters, M.D.

Pregnancy and pneumothorax—Ethan A. Gray, M.D.

The importance of physical signs in the prognosis of pulmonary tuberculosis—Francis B. Trudeau, M.D.

Artificial heliotherapy in pulmonary tuberculosis—Selig Simon, M.D.

Silence in the treatment of pulmonary tuberculosis—S. W. Schaefer, M.D.

Extrapleural thoracoplasty and a modification of the operation of apicolysis, utilizing muscle flaps for compression of the lung—Edward Archibald, M.D.

Pulmonary hemorrhage in Banti's disease—Herbert M. Rich, M.D.

A report of the results by heliotherapy in surgical tuberculosis after six and one-half years' use at the J. N. Adam Memorial Hospital—Clarence L. Hyde, M.D., and Horace LoGrasso, M.D.

An investigation on the acid fastness of tubercle bacilli, II—Binzi Suyenaga, M.D.

The utilization of amino acids by tubercle bacilli and other acid fast organisms—Esmond R. Long, Ph.D.

Hypernephrectomy and experimental tuberculosis—Gerald B. Webb, M.D., G. B. Gilbert, M.D., J. B. Hartwell, M.D., and C. T. Ryder, M.D.

Possibilities of producing local lung lesions in smaller animals—William Charles White, M.D.

Weight curves of tuberculous guinea-pigs—Lydia M. DeWitt, M.D.

Studies on the relation of dust to tuberculosis—a preliminary report on the effect of inhaled granite dust on pulmonary tuberculosis—LeRoy U. Gardner, M.D.

Experimental arrested tuberculosis and subsequent infections—Edward R. Baldwin, M.D.

The effect of heat on experimental tuberculosis—H. J. Corper, M.D., and H. Gauss, M.D.

The effect of bleeding upon tuberculosis in the guinea-pig—H. J. Corper, M.D.

Experimental studies on the leucocytes with particular reference to tubercle bacillus infections—J. B. Rogers, M.D.

Possible modifications in tuberculosis programs on the basis of recent Framingham experience—D. B. Armstrong, M.D.

Some findings in regard to the economic costs of tuberculosis—Jessamine S. Whitney.

Sociology and public health—H. W. Hill, M.D.

The industrial colony in the campaign against tuberculosis—Alexius M. Forster, M.D.

Let the public know—B. L. Taliaferro, M.D.

Rehabilitation of discharged tuberculous service men—John W. Turner, M.D.

Control of tuberculosis in industrial organizations—John S. Billings, M.D.

The program of the American Red Cross with reference to tuberculosis and other diseases—Ervin A. Peterson, M.D.

A broader attack on tuberculosis—Joseph Herzstein.

Tuberculosis in the Philippines—Carmelo Penaflor, M.D.

Nutrition classes for undernourished children—Mrs. Ira Couch Wood.

The relations of feeble-mindedness and tuberculosis—K. A. Menninger, M.D.

17

The crusade in the school and the community—M. Grace Osborne.

University leadership in public health—John Sundwall, Ph.D., M.D.

Some considerations on tuberculosis—Sir Arthur Newsholme, M.D., K.C.B.

Occupational therapy and tuberculous patients—Bertha Thompson.

The value of occupational therapy in tuberculosis sanatoria from a medical administrative standpoint—Glenford L. Bellis, M.D.

Missouri Association for Occupational Therapy—Idelle Kidder.

Final Report of Committee on Indigent Migratory Consumptives.

Report of Committee on History.

Final Report of the Committee on Standardization of Sanatoria of the American Sanatorium Association.

Fifteenth midwinter meeting of the American Sanatorium Association.

Fifteenth spring meeting of the American Sanatorium Association.

CHAPTER XXVII

SEVENTEENTH ANNUAL MEETING

THE seventeenth annual meeting of the National Tuberculosis Association was held at the Waldorf Astoria Hotel, New York City, on June 14, 15, 16, and 17, 1921.

The meeting was called to order at 2 o'clock on Tuesday afternoon by the president, Dr. Gerald B. Webb.

Following the address of welcome by Dr. Hermann M. Biggs, chairman of the honorary committee of arrangements, the address of the president was presented and filed for publication in the Transactions. The report of the executive office for the year ending June 1, 1921, was read and ordered filed.

The report of the nominating committee, which had been appointed in March, was presented by the chairman, Dr. Lee K. Frankel.

In view of the fact that a new constitution and by-laws were ratified by the board of directors at its meeting on March 11, 1921, following the recommendation of the committee on reorganization, it became necessary for the nominating committee to nominate a new board of directors under the new by-laws. The board is to consist of representative directors, nominated by "represented affiliated" associations and, in addition, 50 directors at large. The report of the nominating committee is as follows:

DIRECTORS TO SERVE ONE YEAR TERM

Representative Directors: Dr. William N. Anderson, Omaha, Neb.; Mr. George F. Canfield, New York City, N. Y.; Mr. H. M. Cass, Huron, S. D.; Dr. J. W. Coon, Stevens Point, Wis.; Dr. O. C. Gebhart, St. Joseph, Mo.; Dr. Charles R. Grandy, Norfolk, Va.; Major R. J. Guinn, Atlanta, Ga.; Dr. Alfred Henry, Indianapolis, Ind.; Dr. G. Walter Holden, Denver, Colo.; Dr. A. T. Laird, Nopeming, Minn.; Dr. Charles H. Lerrigo, Topeka, Kan.; Dr. Thomas McCrae, Philadelphia, Pa.; Dr. E. D. Merrill, Foxcroft, Me.; Dr. Edward O. Otis, Boston, Mass.; Mr. J. F. Owens, Oklahoma City, Okla.; Mrs. H. E. Pearce, Birmingham, Ala.; Dr. J. W. Pettit, Ottawa, Ill.; Dr. D.

L. Richardson, Providence, R. I.; Dr. Thomas J. Riley, Brooklyn, N. Y.; Dr. E. O. Schroeder, Bethesda, Md.; Dr. Z. T. Scott, Austin, Texas; Mr. J. V. A. Smith, Seattle, Wash.; Col. Kenneth P. Williams, Little Rock, Ark.; Mr. R. B. Wilson, Raleigh, N. C.; Dr. John M. Wise, Glencliff, N. H. *Directors at large:* Dr. Edward R. Baldwin, Saranac Lake, N. Y.; Mr. William H. Baldwin, Washington, D. C.; Dr. Hermann M. Biggs, New York City, N. Y.; Dr. Vincent Y. Bowditch, Boston, Mass.; Dr. C. C. Browning, Los Angeles, Cal.; Col. George E. Bushnell, Bedford, Mass.; Dr. S. J. Crumbine, Topeka, Kansas; Dr. H. K. Dunham, Cincinnati, Ohio; Dr. W. L. Dunn, Asheville, N. C.; Dr. Livingston Farrand, Washington, D. C.; Dr. Lee K. Frankel, New York City, N. Y.; Mr. E. K. Gaylord, Oklahoma City, Okla.; Mrs. John M. Glenn, New York City, N. Y.; Father Charles Hannigan, Baltimore, Md.; Mr. A. W. Jones, Jr., St. Louis, Mo.; Mr. John A. Kingsbury, New York City, N. Y.; Mrs. R. C. McCredie, Sunnyside, Washington; Dr. O. W. McMichael, Chicago, Ill.; Dr. Josephine Milligan, Jacksonville, Ill.; Dr. Charles L. Minor, Asheville, N. C.; Dr. B. S. Pollak, Secaucus, N. J.; Dr. Theobald Smith, Princeton, N. J.; Dr. Gerald B. Webb, Colorado Springs, Colo.; Dr. William H. Welch, Baltimore, Md.; Dr. William Charles White, Pittsburgh, Pa.

DIRECTORS TO SERVE TWO YEAR TERM

Representative Directors: Dr. G. H. Barksdale, Charleston, W. Va.; Dr. Robert H. Bishop, Jr., Cleveland, Ohio; Dr. Henry Boswell, Sanatorium, Miss.; Dr. T. Z. Cason, Jacksonville, Fla.; Mr. H. R. Cunningham, Helena, Mont.; Dr. S. B. English, Glen Gardner, N. J.; Dr. A. F. Fischer, Hancock, Mich.; Dr. John W. Flinn, Prescott, Ariz.; Mrs. John M. Fulton, Reno, Nev.; Dr. J. Grassick, Grand Forks, N. D.; Dr. Ethan A. Gray, Chicago, Ill.; Dr. A. T. McCormack, Louisville, Ky.; Dr. Stephen J. Maher, New Haven, Conn.; Dr. Ralph C. Matson, Portland, Ore.; Dr. James Alexander Miller, New York City, N. Y.; Dr. Charles R. Mowery, Wallace, Idaho; Dr. John H. Peck; Des Moines, Iowa; Dr. Robert A. Peers, Colfax, Cal.; Dr. Edward J. Rogers, Pittsford, Vt.; Dr. J. D. Shingle, Cheyenne, Wyo.; Dr. Martin F. Sloan, Baltimore, Md.; Mr. Henry Teitlebaum, Nashville, Tenn.; Mr. John P. Thomas, Jr., Columbia, S. C.; Mr. James H. Wallis, Salt Lake City, Utah; Mr. Edward A. Woods, Pittsburgh, Pa. *Directors at large:* Dr. Wallace S. Allis, Norwich, Conn.; Dr. A. C. Bachmeyer, Cincinnati, Ohio; Dr. W. Jarvis Barlow, Los Angeles, Cal.; Dr. Max Biesenthal, Chicago, Ill.; Dr. Frank Billings, Chicago, Ill.; Dr. James A. Britton, Chicago, Ill.; Dr. Lawrason Brown, Saranac Lake, N. Y.; Dr. Hoyt E. Dearholt, Milwaukee, Wis.; Dr. William DeKleine, Flint, Mich.; Mr. Henry S. Dennison, Framingham, Mass.; Dr. Oscar Dowling, New Orleans, La.; Mr. Homer Folks, New York City, N. Y.; Dr. A. M. Forster, Colorado Springs, Col.; Mr. Hugh Frayne, New York City, N. Y.; Mr. Morton D. Hull, Chicago, Ill.; Mr. Sherman C. Kingsley, Philadelphia, Pa.; Dr. Roger I. Lee, Cambridge, Mass.; Dr. Paul A. Lewis, Philadelphia, Pa.; Dr. David R. Lyman, Wallingford, Conn.; Dr. Alfred Meyer, New York City, N. Y.; Dr. George M. Price, New York City,

N. Y.; Mr. Julius Rosenwald, Chicago, Ill.; Mr. Fred M. Stein, New York City, N. Y.; Dr. Charles Stover, Amsterdam, N. Y.; Mrs. F. E. Whitley, Webster City, Iowa.

The report of the nominating committee was approved and the names were forwarded for formal election to Portland, Me., where the corporate meeting of the members of the National Tuberculosis Association was held on Wednesday, June 15, at 12 o'clock noon, and the directors were duly and legally elected.

Over 1,000 persons were registered at the meeting and a considerable number who attended were not registered.

The Clinical Section held three meetings and the Pathological Section two meetings. A combined session of the Clinical and Pathological Sections was also held. The Advisory Council held one session, the Sociological Section three sessions, the Nursing Section two sessions. There was also a combined session of the Sociological and Nursing Sections. Under the direction of the local committee on arrangements several unique features were provided, among which were an exhibit, a demonstration by the health clown, "Humpty Dumpty," and a pageant, "The Spirit of the Double-Barred Cross."

The following committee on resolutions was appointed by the president: Dr. George M. Kober, Washington, D. C., chairman; Dr. Philip King Brown, San Francisco; Dr. Vincent Y. Bowditch, Boston; Dr. E. R. Baldwin, Saranac Lake; Dr. J. W. Pettit, Ottawa, Ill.

On behalf of the committee on resolutions, Dr. George M. Kober, chairman, presented the following resolutions with the endorsement of the committee. Each of the resolutions was adopted unanimously.

WHEREAS, The National Tuberculosis Association has always been deeply concerned with the subject of medical education in tuberculosis, and

WHEREAS, The movement for the inauguration of special departments of tuberculosis has as yet been taken up by very few of our medical schools, and

WHEREAS, We regard the spread of this movement as of vital importance to the future development of all tuberculosis work, be it therefore

Resolved, First, that the medical schools of our country be urged to take special account in the development of their curricula of the necessity for the establishment of such departments.

Second, that in the question of the location of new sanatoria due consideration be given to placing them, whenever possible, where their facilities will be available for the development of such special tuberculosis departments in our medical schools.

WHEREAS, The rehabilitation of our tuberculous ex-service men and women is at once our most imperative duty and the biggest problem in public health before our people, and

WHEREAS, The National Tuberculosis Association through the coöperation with the government services, both of the executive staff and of its individual members, has acquired a close familiarity with the work of these various services and especially that of the tuberculosis hospitals, and

WHEREAS, The best results in these hospitals can only be attained by the maintenance of a close coöperation of physicians and patients under strict disciplinary regulations, and

WHEREAS, Such conditions do not at present generally exist in government tuberculosis hospitals in spite of the continuous and conscientious effort of government departments, and

WHEREAS, The chief causes of this fatal defect are: first, the demoralizing influence upon many of the men of the present compensation act and its administration; second, the failure of the public, of the Congress, of the local posts of the American Legion and of other organizations interested in the welfare of ex-service men, to familiarize themselves with the facts of the tuberculosis situation and to bring to the aid of the government departments that intelligent coöperation which they sorely need and without which they cannot do their best work; be it therefore

Resolved, That it be urged upon Congress both by the executive office of the National Tuberculosis Association and by each affiliated state association through the members of its state delegation, that the government departments be given the assistance necessary to establish the discipline so essential to the maintenance of this needed morale by:

First, such changes in the compensation act as will result in the immediate and material reduction in compensation for those cases who refuse to make proper use of the facilities provided for their benefit, and

Second, by making the welfare of the men and of the country at large, and *not* the desires of the individual constitutents, the basis of action both as regards appointments of those *charged* with the care of these men, and as regards the individual cases of the men themselves.

Resolved, That the National Tuberculosis Association hereby expresses its appreciation and commendation of the efforts thus far of the national officials of the American Legion to have corrected the defects in legislation pertaining to rehabilitation of ex-service men, and its administration, and urges the Legion to continue these efforts and to see that its local posts throughout the country give their full coöperation to the government departments in their efforts to prevent an uncontrolled minority of the ex-service men from seriously interfering, as they now do, with the chance of the recovery of their fellow patients.

Resolved, That the local tuberculosis associations throughout the country be urged to inaugurate immediately a campaign of publicity, which will give the people of their respective localities the true facts of the situation, and will develop in all parts of the country that educated public opinion, the lack of which has been largely responsible for the present unfortunate situation.

Resolved, That the National Tuberculosis Association approves the principles involved in sheltered training and employment for the tuberculous, and the necessity for providing various forms of sheltered employment as a necessary and important factor in the management of the tuberculosis problem.

In view of the various existing means for providing such sheltered employment and the extension of these ideas into the consideration of various plans for industrial and agricultural settlements by governmental and non-governmental agencies, the National Tuberculosis Association invites the attention of these agencies to the large amount of data gathered by its Committee on Farm Colonies and Industrial Communities for the Tuberculous, which the executive office is directed to place at the disposal of all of those interested in the problem.

It is the sense of the National Association that the many difficulties, objections and criticisms of proposals for agricultural and industrial settlements demand a most careful and continued study of all the medical, economic and political factors involved, and it desires to express its interest in the elaboration of these proposals; and therefore directs the continuation of this Committee, to prepare and present at the next annual meeting a complete digest of the information that it gathers.

WHEREAS, The admission of immigrants with tuberculosis has provided our state and municipal institutions with a large number of cases of pulmonary tuberculosis because of the absence of a physical examination on entrance into this country, and

WHEREAS, These immigrants with tuberculosis create a social and economic problem which is likely to be greater and more important during the present period of depression in Europe, therefore be it

Resolved, That the National Tuberculosis Association in conference assembled ask that the United States Public Health Service detail medical examiners especially trained in tuberculosis work to be stationed at ports of debarkation and further that steamship companies be encouraged to protect themselves from the burden of returning such cases by some type of examination or health certificate at port of embarkation.

WHEREAS, The National Tuberculosis Association has lost by death Major General William Crawford Gorgas, U. S. A., Honorary Vice-President, therefore be it

Resolved, First, that this Association commemorates the great services of General Gorgas as a sanitarian whose worldwide activities have resulted in the practical elimination of one of the worst scourges of mankind, yellow fever, and in the successful combating of other communicable diseases.

Second, That it deplores the loss of this great man, this good friend and modest and kindly gentleman, whose memory will always be cherished not only on account of his unparalleled services to humanity but also for his qualities of mind and heart.

Third, That the National Tuberculosis Association extends the sympathy of its members to the wife and family of its deceased member.

Fourth, That a copy of these resolutions be forwarded to Mrs. Gorgas.

WHEREAS, There exist between this country and the Republic of Mexico many common health problems the chief of which is tuberculosis, and

WHEREAS, The President of Mexico through the Department of Public Health has extended an invitation to the National Association to hold its meeting in 1922 in Mexico City, be it

Resolved, That this Association express to the President of Mexico its appreciation of the invitation and its desire to further the intimate consideration of that special part of our common medical problem for which this Association was organized, and

That the Association regrets its inability to accept the invitation for 1922 on account of the triennial meeting of all the national medical societies in Washington that year; and be it

Further Resolved, That this Association invite the Department of Public Health and the interested members of the profession in Mexico to meet with it on the occasion of the next annual meeting in Washington, D. C.

WHEREAS, The National Tuberculosis Association has always advocated that advanced cases of tuberculosis be cared for in separate wards in the general hospitals of their own towns, and

WHEREAS, There is an unfortunate tendency in some quarters to interpret this to mean that the incipient or favorable case can also be treated efficiently in such local hospitals, be it therefore

Resolved, That the National Tuberculosis Association, while strongly reaffirming its previous stand on the local hospitalization of advanced cases, does not approve of the suggestion of caring for the incipient or favorable case in like manner, and for the following reasons:

(1) It has been well proven that the favorable case can have his best chances only in institutions situated outside of the cities and with a régime centered on the education of the patient for his after life, along with his physical rehabilitation, and

(2) It is disadvantageous to arrange for the treatment of the curable case in connection with the advanced cases, because of the depressing mental effect which prevents the incipient case coming for treatment at the only time when it can be prevented from developing into an open case and an active focus for the spread of the disease.

The following resolution was presented in connection with the Summary Report of the Committee on Dusty Trades to the Executive Committee and approved, with the understanding that the resolution be published with the resolutions adopted at the Annual Meeting.

The Directors of the National Tuberculosis Association having completed an investigation of the mortality from tuberculosis in the granite industry under the auspices of a special committee, after which an x-ray and physical examination was made of more than 400 men in the city of Barre, Vermont, hereby make the following resolutions:

WHEREAS, It has been demonstrated by the death certificates of men employed for varying periods, ranging from ten to forty years in the trade of granite stone cutting, that an unusually high and increasing death rate from pulmonary tuberculosis prevails,

(2) That this occurs in men of good physique and previous good health who usually undergo heavy work with ease.

(3) That the repeated inhalation of fine dust resulting from the cutting of granite, especially since the introduction of pneumatic tools, induces in the large majority of men so employed a condition known as silicosis, due to deposits of this dust in the lungs which predisposes them to tuberculosis and aggravates any existing disease of the lungs.

(4) That by means of an x-ray and physical examination of the chest these diseases can be recognized in an early stage, be it

Resolved, That this Association urges:

(1) The adoption of more efficient methods of removing the fine dust, the isolation of the most dusty operations so far as may be practicable and of general sanitary measures to prevent infection in the sheds.

(2) The introduction of a system of periodic physical examinations by trained physicians selected for this duty; also that obligatory x-ray examinations by skilled technicians shall be required at the same time for all men entering the trade and while engaged therein.

At a meeting of the board of directors on Wednesday, June 15, the following officers were elected for the ensuing year: Dr. James Alexander Miller, New York, president; Hon. Warren G. Harding, District of Columbia, honorary vice-president; Col. George E. Bushnell, Massachusetts, honorary vice-president; Dr. Lawrason Brown, New York, vice-president; Dr. Ralph Matson, Oregon, vice-president; Dr. George M. Kober, District of Columbia, secretary; Mr. Henry B. Platt, New York, treasurer.

The following directors, in addition to the president, the vice-president, the secretary, and the treasurer, ex-officio, were elected to serve on the executive committee for the ensuing year: Dr. William Charles White, Pennsylvania; Dr. Kennon Dunham, Ohio; Dr. Alfred Henry, Indiana; Dr. W. L. Dunn, North Carolina; Homer Folks, New York; Dr. David R. Lyman, Connecticut, Sherman C. Kingsley, Pennsylvania.

The summarized report of the treasurer, Mr. Henry B. Platt, is as follows:

Balance, December 31, 1919	$18,712.02
Receipts	227,841.49
	$246,553.51
Disbursements	174,749.82
Balance, December 31, 1920	$71,803.69*

A list of officers and directors for 1920 to 1921 follows:

President, Dr. Gerald B. Webb; honorary vice-presidents, Gen. W. C. Gorgas, Col. George E. Bushnell; vice-presidents, Dr. James Alexander Miller, Dr. Philip King Brown; treasurer, Henry B. Platt; secretary, Dr. George M. Kober; clerk, W. B. Drummond. Directors, Dr. William N. Anderson, Omaha; Dr. Robert H. Babcock, Chicago; Dr. A. C. Bachmeyer, Cincinnati; Dr. W. Jarvis Barlow, Los Angeles; Miss Mary Beard, Boston; Ernest P. Bicknell, Washington; Dr. Frank Billings, Chicago; Dr. John S. Billings, New York; Dr. Vincent Y. Bowditch, Boston; Dr. Philip King Brown, San Francisco; Dr. C. C. Browning, Los Angeles, Cal.; Col. George E. Bushnell, Concord, Mass.; George F. Canfield, New York; Dr. Charles V. Chapin, Providence; Dr. J. W. Coon, Stevens Point, Wis.; H. R. Cunningham, Helena, Mont.; Dr. Gordon K. Dickinson, Jersey City; Dr. George Dock, St. Louis; Dr. H. K. Dunham, Cincinnati; Dr. W. L. Dunn, Asheville; Rev. George Eaves, Birmingham, Ala.; Dr. C. E. Edson, Denver; Dr. Livingston Farrand, Washington; Miss Edna L. Foley, Chicago; Homer Folks, New York; Dr. A. M. Forster, Colorado Springs; Lee K. Frankel, New York; E. K. Gaylord, Oklahoma City; Gen. W. C. Gorgas, Washington; Dr. Louis V. Hamman, Baltimore; Dr. Alfred Henry, Indianapolis; Dr. Henry W. Hoagland, Colorado Springs; H. McK. Jones, St. Louis; Dr. George M. Kober, Washington; Dr. Allen K. Krause, Baltimore; Dr. Paul A. Lewis, Philadelphia; Dr. David R. Lyman, Wallingford; Dr. Thomas McCrae, Philadelphia; Dr. Walter J. Marcley, Minneapolis; Dr. Harry T. Marshall, University, Va.; Dr. Ralph C. Matson, Portland, Ore.; R. B. Mellon, Pittsburgh; Dr. Alfred Meyer, New York; Dr. James Alexander Miller, New York; Dr. Josephine Milligan, Jacksonville; Dr. John H. Peck, Des Moines; James H. Pershing, Denver; Henry B. Platt, New York; Miss Agnes D. Randolph, Bisbee, Ariz.; Dr. Z. T. Scott, Austin, Tex.; Bolton Smith, Memphis, Tenn.; J. V. A. Smith, Seattle; Reed Smith, Columbia, S. C.; Fred. M. Stein, New York; Dr. Walter R. Steiner, Hartford; Dr. A. K. Stone, Boston; Dr. V. C. Vaughan, Ann Arbor, Mich.; Dr. Gerald B. Webb, Colorado Springs; Dr. William Charles White, Pittsburgh; Dr. Allen H. Williams, Phoenix, Ariz.

Executive staff,† Dr. Charles J. Hatfield, managing director; Frederick D.

* Not including expenditures on Campaign.
† As of January 1, 1922.

Hopkins, administrative secretary; Amelia T. Dutcher, administrative assistant; S. M. Sharpe, business manager; L. B. Whitcomb, purchasing agent; Grace Douglass, office secretary; Dr. Donald B. Armstrong, assistant secretary and executive officer of the Community Health and Tuberculosis Demonstration at Framingham; Dr. H. A. Pattison, supervisor medical service; Dr. Edgar Thomson Shields, medical field secretary; T. B. Kidner, institutional secretary: Mary E. Marshall, R.N., secretary for nursing; Walter I. Hamilton, industrial research secretary; George T. Eddy, industrial research librarian; Philip P. Jacobs, Ph.D., publicity director; Basil G. Eaves, campaign secretary; Helena V. Williams, assistant publicity secretary; Elizabeth Cole, assistant publicity secretary; Eleanor B. Conklin, editorial assistant; Arthur J. Strawson, supervisor field service; Jessamine S. Whitney, statistician; Charles M. DeForest, Modern Health Crusader executive; M. Grace Osborne and Louise Strachan, assistant Crusader executives.

The following is a list of papers read before the respective sections at the Seventeenth Annual Meeting of the National Tuberculosis Association, June 14th to 17th, 1921:

How compensation is provided for ex-service beneficiaries by the Bureau of War Risk insurance—Haven Emerson, M.D.

Provision for hospital and dispensary care of tuberculous ex-service patients by the Public Health Service—F. C. Smith, M.D.

Vocational training for arrested tuberculous patients by the Federal Board for Vocational Education—Hon. Uel W. Lamkin.

The limitations and possibilities in the federal care of tuberculous ex-service patients—David R. Lyman, M.D.

Di-chloramine T in tuberculous abscesses—Edward J. Murray, M.D.

The management of pleural effusions in the course of therapeutic pneumothorax—Barnett P. Stivelman, M.D., and Joseph Rosenblatt, M.D.

Theoretical explanation of the formation of Roentgenographic pleural annular shadows—J. Burns Amberson, M.D.

Theoretical considerations on the application of ultraviolet radiation to tuberculous laryngitis—Edgar Mayer, M.D.

Results in one hundred cases of pulmonary and intestinal tuberculosis with the use of the ultraviolet ray—Sidney F. Blanchet, M.D.

A comparison of vital capacity readings and x-ray findings in pulmonary tuberculosis—J. A. Myers, M.D.

The curative value of pneumothorax in non-tuberculous lesions of the lung—disappearance of osteo-arthropathy—William Charles White, M.D.

Certain manifestations of hypertrophic osteo-arthropathy in pulmonary tuberculosis: a survey of a sanatorium group of patients—H. J. Corper, M.D., and Philip Cosman, M.D., in collaboration with William H. Gilmore, M.D., and Louisa T. Black, M.D.

Lymphatism and tuberculosis—Maurice Fishberg, M.D.

A workshop for the rehabilitation of the tuberculous—Grant Thorburn, M.D., and John S. Billings, M.D.

Clinical and therapeutic aspects of the Framingham work—P. Challis Bartlett, M.D.

Undergraduate instruction in tuberculosis—Walter C. Klotz, M.D.

Post-graduate education in tuberculosis—Edward R. Baldwin, M.D.

Some problems of medical education in tuberculosis—Allen K. Krause, M.D.

Interim report on cases of extra-pleural thoracoplasty—Edward Archibald, M.D.

Dettweiler and his methods—Hugh M. Kinghorn, M.D.

Small pneumothorax in tuberculosis—abstract of a monograph—Nathan Barlow, M.D., and James C. Thompson, M.D.

Physical and clinical variations in a study of seven hundred tuberculous young women—Philip King Brown, M.D.

The taking of temperature in the diagnosis and treatment of tuberculosis—George Thomas Palmer, M.D.

The safe removal of tonsils by the desiccation method with the high frequency current in poor surgical risks, with especial reference to the tuberculous—P. P. McCain, M.D.

Further observations on heredity as influencing natural resistance to tuberculosis—Paul A. Lewis, M.D., and Sewall Wright, Ph.D.

Fundamental features of the complement deviation reaction as applied to tuberculosis—Paul A. Lewis, M.D., and Joseph D. Aaronson, M.D.

The destruction of tubercle bacilli in sewage by chlorine—John M. Conroy, M.D., Bernice Brasted Conroy, and Arthur T. Laird, M.D.

The survival and virulence of tubercle bacilli in excised animal lymph nodes—G. B. Webb, M.D., C. T. Ryder, M.D., and G. B. Gilbert, M.D.

The Griffith method for direct isolation of the tubercle bacillus—Harold W. Lyall, Ph.D.

Tuberculosis of the heart—with the report of two cases—Edward Weiss, M.D.

The course of pulmonary tuberculosis in guinea-pigs produced by the inhalation of a low-virulent strain—Leroy U. Gardner, M.D.

Studies of the influence of carbon dioxide on the resistance to tuberculosis: the effect of carbon dioxide upon the tubercle bacillus—H. J. Corper, M.D., H. Gauss, M.D., and O. B. Rensch, M.D.

Studies with morphine in experimental tuberculosis—H. J. Corper, M.D., H. Gauss, M.D., and O. B. Rensch, M.D.

The significance of allergy in tuberculosis—Allen K. Krause, M.D.

Chemical problems in the bacteriology of the tubercle bacillus—Esmond R. Long, Ph.D.

Arrangement of the musculature of the bronchioli and its relation to certain pathological conditions in the lung—William Snow Miller, M.D.

Finer divisions of the air spaces in man and some of the laboratory animals—William Snow Miller, M.D.

Normal radiographic appearance of the chests of children—a symposium—(a) Kennon Dunham, M.D., and Kenneth D. Blackfan, M.D.; (b) H. K.

Pancoast, M.D., and H. R. M. Landis, M.D.; (c) Charles R. Austrian, M.D., and F. H. Baetjer, M.D.

Progress report on the investigation of the chemotherapeutics of chaulmoogric acids in tuberculosis—Ernest Linwood Walker.

The effect of artificial pneumothorax on the collateral lung—Saling Simon, M.D.

A clinical study of granite dust inhalation—D. C. Jarvis, M.D.

The results of an experimental study of the dietary requirements in tuberculosis —William S. McCann, M.D.

The clinic for Negroes at the Henry Phipps Institute—H. R. M. Landis, M.D.

Comprehensive coöperation in the tuberculosis program—W. McN. Miller, M.D.

An experiment in organization of rural tuberculosis work in Albemarle County, Virginia—Walter C. Klotz, M.D.

Framingham yardsticks—Donald B. Armstrong, M.D.

Post-sanatorium care of Canadian ex-soldiers—Lieut.-Col. W. M. Hart.

The sanatorium care of tuberculous soldiers by the federal government— George Thomas Palmer, M.D., and Henry W. Hoagland, M.D.

The care of tuberculous ex-service men: a correlation of local and Public Health Service work—C. Howard Marcy, M.D.

When is an exhibit?—E. G. Routzahn.

Health education through the school—Willard S. Small, Ph.D.

Tuberculosis, marriage and maternity—Maurice Fishberg, M.D.

The evidence of intensive anti-tuberculosis effort upon the death rate—Lee K. Frankel, Ph.D.

Report of a study of the indigent migratory tuberculous in certain cities of the Southwest—Jessamine S. Whitney.

Industrial nursing as a means of fighting tuberculosis—Lee K. Frankel, Ph.D.

Tuberculosis nursing by specialized staff—Mary E. Edgecomb, R.N.

Tuberculosis nursing by a generalized staff—Anne Sutherland, R.N.

Detection and control of contact and arrested tuberculous cases—Edith M. Blades, R.N.

Malnutrition and tuberculosis—W. R. P. Emerson, M.D.

Practical applications for the tuberculosis program—Lucinda N. Stringer, R.N.

Recommendations of the Committee on Indigent Migratory Consumptives.

Sixteenth midwinter meeting of the American Sanatorium Association.

Sixteenth spring meeting of the American Sanatorium Association.

PART III

BIOGRAPHIES OF THE OFFICERS
OF THE ASSOCIATION

INTRODUCTORY NOTE

THE biographies of the honorary vice-presidents are given first, and are followed in turn by those of the presidents, treasurers, secretaries, vice-presidents, and some of the executives on the staff. A bibliography of the principal contributions to tuberculosis literature is appended to each biographical sketch.

In the preparation of these biographies no effort has been made to give an exhaustive personal history of each official, but rather to stress particularly those events that have to do with tuberculosis history.

CHAPTER XXVIII

GROVER CLEVELAND

HONORARY VICE-PRESIDENT OF THE NATIONAL TUBERCULOSIS ASSOCIATION
FROM 1905 TO 1908

THE first layman on whom was conferred by unanimous election the title of honorary vice-president of the National Tuberculosis Association was Grover Cleveland, ex-president of the United States, and at the time of his election member of the board of trustees of and professor of jurisprudence at Princeton University. Our society honored itself by making Grover Cleveland its honorary vice-president, in 1906.

Grover Cleveland was born in Caldwell, N. J., March 18, 1837. His father was the Rev. Richard Falley Cleveland, and his mother, Anne Neal Cleveland. His interest in medicine and in the unfortunate sick and disabled dates back to 1853, when he became a teacher in the Institute for the Blind, located at Ninth Avenue and 34th Street, in the city of New York. He was drawn to the study of law, however, and admitted to the bar in 1859. He became assistant district attorney in January, 1863, was elected sheriff of Erie County, New York, in 1870, mayor of Buffalo in 1881, and governor of the State of New York by a majority of 192,000 on November 1, 1882. Two years later, on November 4, 1884, he was elected to the presidency of the United States and he was elected for the second time November 8, 1892.

Mr. Cleveland on repeated occasions showed deep interest in medicine and disease prevention. His address on the occasion of the fiftieth anniversary of the New York Academy of Medicine on January 29, 1897, may be seen in its autographed form on the walls of the Academy by all who care to read it. It shows that he was well informed on the advances in medicine and sanitation, yet at the same time in touching words he paid his tribute to the village doctor of fifty years ago. After saying that those not born yesterday were living monuments to the faithful care of the village doctor, he continued as follows:

"He, too, alleviated suffering and saved human life. We know that it was not given to him to see the bright lights that now mark the path of medicine and surgery, but you cannot convince us that he groped entirely in the dark. We remember with abhorrence his ever ready lancet, and the scars of his blood-letting found in every household. We endure with complacency the recollection of his awful medicine case, containing bottles, powders, and pills, which, whatever might be thought of them now, seemed then to be sufficient for all emergencies, to say nothing of the tooth-pulling tools and other shiver-breeding instruments sometimes exposed to view. If he was ignorant of many of the remedies and appliances now in use, he in a large measure supplied the deficiency by hard-headed judgment, well-observed experience, and careful nursing. Besides, it was in his favor that he did not have to bother his head with many of the newly invented and refined diseases that afflict mankind to-day. He had no allotted hours for his patients, but was always on duty, and we knew the sound of his gig as he rattled past in the night.

"Your ways are better than his; but we desire you to regard this admission as all the more valuable because it is carved out of our loyalty to our old village doctor, who brought us through the diseases of childhood without relapse, who saved from death our parents and our brothers and our sisters in many a hard combat with illness, and who, when vanquished and forced to surrender, was present in the last scene to close the eyes of his dying patient and sympathize with those who wept."

The concluding words of this remarkable address, warning us against neglect of civic duties, are as applicable to conditions of to-day as they were twenty-three years ago:

"We cannot accuse you of utter neglect of your duty to the country; and yet we cannot keep out of mind the suspicion that if your professional work in exposing evils was more thoroughly supplemented by labor in the field of citizenship, these evils would be more speedily corrected. If laws are needed to abolish abuses which your professional investigations have unearthed, your fraternity should not be strangers to the agencies which make the laws. If enactments already in force are neglected or badly executed, you should not forget that it is your privilege and duty to insist upon their vigorous and honest enforcement. Let me also remind you of the application to your case of the truth embodied in the homely injunction, 'If you want a job well done, do it yourself.' If members of your profession were oftener found in our national and State legislative assemblies, ready to advocate the reformatory measure you have demonstrated to be necessary, and to defend your brotherhood against flippant and sneering charges of impracticability, the prospect of your bestowal upon your fellow-men of the ripened results of your professional labor would be brighter and nearer."

GROVER CLEVELAND

Perhaps the solution of our tuberculosis problem would be nearer if Grover Cleveland's advice had been followed two decades ago.

The address delivered by Mr. Cleveland on the occasion of the one hundredth annual meeting of the Medical Society of the State of New York, held at Albany on February 6, 1906, was a veritable gem of oratory, marked by a keen sense of humor, and at the same time a deep penetration into all that is faulty and also all that is true and noble in our profession. Here follows a portion of this memorable oration:

"For the purpose of argument, let us divide humanity in two sections—one composed of a few doctors, and the other embracing the many millions of their actual prospective patients. I appeal for myself and those millions, and I claim at the outset that, notwithstanding our large majority, the medical section of 'mankind has, in one way or another, curtailed the opportunity of freedom of thought and considerate hearing, to which we are entitled by 'the laws of Nature and of Nature's God.' We acknowledge that the world owes this minority a living. With a generous delicacy which reaches sublimity we are on their account not over-obedient to the laws of health; and we sometimes pay their bills. When sick, we submit with more or less humility to their orders. If we recover, it is only to take our place on the waiting list, still subject to further service. If we do not recover, it is left to us to do the dying.

"In view of these facts, I think I do not mistake the temper of my clients when I represent that there is growing up among them a feeling that there ought to be less mystery and high and mighty aloofness on the part of their medical advisers. We have long been wont to treat with a kind of amused toleration the names in pigeon Latin or Greek given by the doctors to very common things, and to diseases which already had names both simple and significant. But all this seems to have much increased with the discovery of new remedies, and the chase after new diseases; and this increase has apparently been accompanied by additional mystery and additional inclination on the part of our doctors to remind us of their stately superiority.

"We fully appreciate the tremendous advance that has been made in medical knowledge and practice within the memory of those not yet old. There are but few left who bear the scars of blood-letting which depleted the veins of a former generation. In these days the fever-stricken wretch who begs for a drop of water to cool his tongue is heard with more favor than was the rich man who cried out to Father Abraham from the flaming torments of the bottomless pit. We are now told that germs and microbes, more or less deadly, countless in number, of every conceivable size and shape, and given to habits and tastes adjusted to every emergency of their existence, not only inhabit the earth beneath us and the atmosphere about us, but lurk in every corner and cranny of our bodies with murderous intent. Another marked and startling indication of progress in medical knowledge is found in the sentence of removal and destruction lately passed by medical science upon a certain annex or attachment of the human body, which has for centuries substantially escaped more serious accusation than that of inactive uselessness. Its detection in conspiracy against life and health has stimulated our doctors in such hot pursuit that the man who carries his appendix about with other personal belongings is probably just as comfortable if he has never heard the story of the way the devil lost his tail.

"In all seriousness, therefore, I desire to concede, without the least reservation, on behalf of the great army of patients, that they owe to the medical profession a debt of gratitude which they can never repay, on account of hard, self-sacrificing work done for their benefit, and for beneficent results accomplished in their interest. But at the same time we are inclined to insist that, while our doctors have wonderfully advanced in all that increases the usefulness and nobility of their profession, this thing has not happened without some corresponding advance in the intelligent thought and ready information of their patients along the same lines. We have come to think of ourselves as worthy of confidence in the treatment of our ailments; and we believe if this were accorded to us in greater measure it would be better for the treatment and better for us."

This extract from President Cleveland's address was selected because it applies so markedly to tuberculosis workers. We have perhaps in a measure endeavored to follow this advice. The conscientious physician treating a tuberculous patient usually takes him into his confidence, realizing that, in this disease at least, the coöperation of the patient and his full knowledge of the character of his affliction are essential to the cure, but we cannot say that this practice is universal. A repetition of Grover Cleveland's wise counsel is not untimely.

Of his personal interest in tuberculosis it was the biographer's privilege to learn from a letter he received a few years before President Cleveland's death. Expressing his satisfaction at having become acquainted with some of the author's writings, which had aroused his interest in the tuberculosis problem some years ago, he closed his letter by saying: "Hoping that the movement on foot for the study and prevention of this direful disease may be upon such lines as will make it practical and effective, I am, etc."

Grover Cleveland passed away on June 24, 1908, at his home in Princeton, universally regretted, forever to be remembered as one of the ablest and most conscientious of statesmen, and a most efficient chief executive of our country.

CHAPTER XXIX

THEODORE ROOSEVELT

HONORARY VICE-PRESIDENT OF THE NATIONAL TUBERCULOSIS ASSOCIATION
FROM 1905 TO 1919

THE second layman to receive a unanimous election as honorary vice-president of the National Tuberculosis Association was Colonel Theodore Roosevelt. He honored the Association by his acceptance of the office in 1906, during his first term as President of the United States. Of all the statesmen of this and foreign countries, there has perhaps never been a man whose name has been more familiar to the masses than that of Theodore Roosevelt, nor any man of whom there have been written more eulogies and more biographies. The high and the low, the rich and the poor, men and women in all walks of life, have felt a deep admiration for this wonderful man. No public character in American history has ever combined such boundless energy and exuberant enthusiasm with such versatility of achievements. In the present sketch we shall consider mostly what Theodore Roosevelt has meant to public sanitation and medicine in general and to the tuberculosis problem in the United States in particular.

Theodore Roosevelt, the son of Theodore and Martha Bulloch Roosevelt, was born October 27, 1858. He received his early education partially from private tutors and by attending the Cutler preparatory school. He entered Harvard, graduating in 1880. Then began a career so varied, so interesting, and so full of achievement that each of the various positions he occupied and the distinction he received therein might be a subject for an essay in itself. He was a member of the New York legislature from 1882 to 1884. He then became a rancher, a cowboy, civil service commissioner, New York police commissioner, assistant secretary of the navy, soldier, governor, vice-president, and president. He entered upon his presidential duties October 14, 1901, on the

277

death of William McKinley. In November, 1904, he was elected president for the term 1905 to 1909. After his retirement from the presidency he became traveler, explorer, naturalist, big game hunter, editor, and author.

It has been said that Roosevelt himself as a child must have been tuberculous, but this has not been confirmed, although the possibility exists that there had been a tuberculous diathesis. That he suffered from asthma and was very delicate as a child is well known. If he had a tuberculous diathesis or a pronounced predisposition to tuberculosis, he certainly knew how to master it by choosing the life of a rancher and devoting a number of years to building himself up to strong and vigorous manhood. The occasional asthmatic attacks seem to have remained with him. According to Dr. Alexander Lambert, for many years his private physician, whenever Roosevelt was attacked with bronchitis he would have "tremendous asthmatic spasms of his lungs." Asthma seems to be antagonistic to the development of tuberculosis, and so we may perhaps be grateful that only asthma was his chief malady in youth.

Roosevelt as a police commissioner became intensely interested in public sanitation, clean streets, better housing, etc. His friend, Jacob A. Riis, who was at the time engaged in the "battle with the slums," had shown him the iniquity of allowing the existence of overcrowded, unclean, and unsanitary tenements, factories, and sweatshops in the city of New York, with their invariable train of tuberculosis and other diseases.

Throughout his official life, and even after his retirement from public office, Roosevelt always had a deep interest in the welfare of the laboring class, in their proper housing, and in factory and workshop sanitation. In an address delivered in Chicago on August 6, 1912, he referred to these vital problems of the nation's welfare in the following words:

"In the last twenty years an increasing percentage of our people have come to depend on industry for their livelihood, so that to-day the wage workers in industry rank in importance side by side with the tiller of the soil. As a people we cannot afford to let any group of citizens, or individual citizens, live or labor under conditions which are injurious to the common welfare. We must protect the crushable elements at the base of our present industrial structure."

THEODORE ROOSEVELT

As governor of the state of New York he looked with favor on the then rising tide of anti-tuberculosis propaganda, and as President of the United States he was, of course, interested in the larger problem of public health of the nation.

Dr. Lambert had been asked whether by reason of his intimate relation as family physician to Roosevelt he could not write something worth reproducing in this biography, showing Roosevelt's interest in state hygiene, in public health in general, and in tuberculosis in particular. With Dr. Lambert's permission part of his letter to the author is here reproduced:

"You can say that it was through Roosevelt's knowledge and appreciation of the problems of sanitation and public health, as shown in the problems involved in the Panama Canal, that he raised Gorgas from a petty, hampered, bureau chief to a Commissioner with equal powers to the others, in order that Gorgas might make the place safe and livable for the workmen to build the Canal. . . . The President was greatly interested in the Tuberculosis Congress of 1908, and talked to me a good deal about it when I was in Washington just after it had occurred."

Roosevelt's great interest in the International Congress on Tuberculosis referred to by Dr. Lambert was manifest by his acceptance of the presidency of that great scientific gathering, to which all the civilized nations of the world sent their representatives. In his letter of acceptance of the presidency of the Tuberculosis Congress he said: "The modern crusade against tuberculosis brings hope and bright prospects of recovery to hundreds and thousands of victims of the disease who, under old teachings, were abandoned to despair." The letter of acceptance speaks volumes for the Colonel's comprehension of the tuberculosis problem and will be found printed in full in the chapter on the Congress (p. 143). The Congress was held in Washington September 21 to October 12, 1908. At the closing session the President made a short but very brilliant address, which shows perhaps more than anything else, how well versed he was in public sanitation and how appreciative of what medical science had done to prolong the average of life and add to the happiness of the human race. Mr. Roosevelt said:

"I could not deny myself the privilege of saying a word of greeting to this noteworthy gathering. It is difficult for us to realize the extraordinary changes, the extraordinary progress, in certain lines of social endeavor during the last two or three generations; and in no other manifestation of human activity have the changes been quite so far reaching as in the ability to grapple with disease. It is not so very long, measuring time by history, since the attitude of man toward a disease such as that of consumption was one of helpless acquiescence in what he considered to be the mandates of a supernatural power. It is but a short time since even the most gifted members of the medical profession knew as little as any layman of the real causes of a disease like this, and therefore necessarily of the remedies to be invoked to overcome them. It is an affair of decades,—I am almost tempted to say an affair of years,—when we go back to cover the period in which the real progress has been made. Take, for instance, the work the United States government is now doing in Panama. When the first railroad was built across Panama, it was said, with some foundation of truth, with but slight exaggeration, that 'every sleeper laid cost the life of a man.' Now the work on the canal, in that identical place, is being prosecuted, on an infinitely larger scale of course, than the mere building of a railroad, under conditions which make the locality stand above the ordinary locality in the United States in point of health. The Isthmus of Panama, which was a byword for fatal disease, has become well-nigh a sanatorium; and it has become so because of the investigations of certain medical men which enabled them to find out the real causes of certain diseases, especially yellow fever and malarial fever, and to take measures to overcome them. The older doctors here, when they were medical students, would have treated the suggestion of regarding mosquitos as the prime source of disease like that as a subject for mirth. Is not that literally true? These utterly unexpected results have followed patient, laborious, dangerous, and extraordinarily skilful work that has enabled the cause of the disease to be found and the diseases themselves to be combated with extraordinary success. I said dangerous work. That success had its martyrs; doctors laid down their lives to secure the results of which I have spoken, showing exactly as much heroism as ever was shown by the soldier on the field of battle.

"At this moment, in the middle of the great continent of Africa, there is a peculiarly fatal and terrible disease—the sleeping sickness; a disease which, if it had been known to our ancestors in the middle ages, would have been spoken of as the black death was spoken of in the middle ages—as a scourge sent of God, possibly as something connected with a comet, or some similar explanation would have been advanced. We know now that it is due to the carrying of a small and deadly blood parasite by a species of biting fly, there being this very curious genus of biting flies in Africa, one form of which, although harmless to wild animals and men, conveys by its bite a fatal infection to all domestic animals, and even to the closest allies of the wild animals, to which its bite is fatal; while the other form, which does not seem to be fatal to domestic or wild animals, is responsible for the spread of this terrible disease, the sleeping sickness, which in one region killed two hundred thousand out of three hundred thousand inhabitants—a rate of slaughter, of course, infinitely surpassing that of any modern war. And the chance to control that disease lies in the work of just such men as and, indeed, of some of the men who are assembled here. You who have come here, however, have come to combat not a scourge confined to the tropics, but what is, on the whole, the most terrible scourge of the people throughout the world. But a few years ago hardly an intelligent effort was made or could be made to war against this peculiarly deadly enemy of the human race. The chance successfully to conduct that war arose when the greatest experts in the medical world turned their trained intelligence to the task. It remains for them to find out just what can be done. The task then will be for the representatives of the governments to give all possible effect to this conclusion of the scientific men.

"The change in the status of the man of science during the last century has been immeasurable. A hundred years ago he was treated as an interesting virtuoso, a man who was capable of giving amusement, but with whom no practical man dealt with any idea of standing on a footing of equality. Now more and more the wisest men of affairs realize that the great chance for the advancement of the human race in material things lies in the close inter-relationship of the man of practical affairs and the man of science, so that the man of practical affairs can give all possible effect to the discoveries of the most unforeseen and unexpected character now made by the man of science.

"I feel that no gathering could take place fraught with greater hope for the welfare of the people at large than this. I thank you all, men and women of this country, and you, our guests, for what you have done and are doing. On behalf of the nation I greet you, and hope you will understand how much we have appreciated your coming here."

The interest this great man took not only in the political, economic, and social, but also in the sanitary, welfare of the nation was so varied that he did not even recall in detail the many things he had done for the betterment of the physical condition of the masses during his official life. The author of this sketch had occasion to correspond with Mr. Roosevelt a few years after he had gone out of office concerning certain episodes in the tuberculosis movement of the past. In reply he wrote: "I cannot at the moment recall the details of my action as Governor and as President, but I have always taken a very real and great interest in the anti-tuberculosis cause—I should not regard myself a good citizen if I had failed to do so."

His life-long friend, Major-General Wood, wrote the author that Roosevelt always manifested the greatest interest in preventive medicine and tuberculosis. The same assurance of his interest in tuberculosis was given by Mrs. Douglas Robinson, the sister of Mr. Roosevelt. Mrs. Robinson says that in many conversations with her brother he had shown his deep interest in the tuberculosis campaign.   In a personal letter to the author she writes: "His whole life was an endorsement of preventive measures along the line of medicine and sanitation."

It is interesting to note that, at the instance of the National Tuberculosis Association, Mr. Roosevelt, as President of the United States, issued an executive order prohibiting promiscuous spitting and providing for individual drinking cups and other sanitary arrangements in all Federal offices.

While believing that the consumptive should be conscientious in the disposal of his sputum and favoring rigid rules concerning this vital point in the prevention of tuberculosis, Roosevelt's heart was with the consumptive sufferer.   A case in point is that of an Irishman who had lived many years in America and raised a family, but who, by some oversight or carelessness, had failed to become an American citizen, although he had taken out his first papers years before.   He returned to visit his native country and while there tuberculosis, which had probably been latent for many years, suddenly became active.   He hastened to return to his family in the United States, but because of the evident symptoms which the man showed and the new law prohibiting those who are not American citizens from entering the United States when tuberculous, he was detained at Ellis Island.   The invalid sought legal aid, and the author was called in as expert to testify that as long as the man was instructed and careful concerning the disposal of his sputum and had sufficient means to enter a private sanatorium at once he would be neither a burden to the community nor a danger to his fellow-men.   The lawyer's eloquent plea before the court, as well as this testimony, was in vain.   Our last resort was to appeal to the magnanimity and generous heart of President Roosevelt.   This did not fail, and the man was permitted to reënter the United States.

Theodore Roosevelt was indeed an ideal citizen.   This necessarily inadequate biographical sketch has sought to record mainly events of interest to the medical profession, and particularly to tuberculosis workers.   Of his character and patriotism his successor in the presidential chair, the Hon. William H. Taft, has said:

"Over and above everything Theodore Roosevelt was a deeply patriotic American. He had intensified his passionate love of his country that was natural in him by acquiring an intimate knowledge and a profound appreciation of the great sacrificial struggle needed to make her great. He left no doubt of his willingness himself to render the ultimate sacrifice in her behalf. His spirit of patriotic devotion was web and woof of his character. He sent his four boys forth to war with the pride of a Roman Tribune. Through his father's tears for Quentin's death there shone the stern joy that a son of his had been given to die the death he would himself have sought on the field of battle in his country's cause. Theodore Roosevelt's example of real sacrifice was of inestimable value to our country in this war. The nation has lost the most commanding, the most original, the most interesting, and the most brilliant personality in American public life since Lincoln."

Roosevelt passed away peacefully, on the night of January 5, 1919, mourned by untold numbers in this and other countries. His grave on the hillside in the beautiful little cemetery near his home at Sagamore Hill is the object of pilgrimage for thousands, old and young, high and low, rich and poor, all eager to do homage to the man they had admired and loved as the third of that great trinity of American Presidents, Washington, Lincoln, Roosevelt.

For the loan of the excellent photograph of Theodore Roosevelt from which the accompanying photogravure is made the author is indebted to his friend, Dr. Ralph Waldron, of Newark. This is the last photograph of Roosevelt taken before his last illness. Whether or not he felt the approaching end intuitively, the picture shows Theodore Roosevelt in serious mood. Perhaps he thought of the world war and all that it meant to the world at large, to the American nation, and to himself. On his lapel we notice the insignia showing how very close the war had come to his own family. There we see the four stars representing Theodore Roosevelt, Jr., Kermit Roosevelt, Archibald Bullock Roosevelt, and Dr. Richard Derby, who all served in the war, but fortunately returned. In the midst of these stars we notice a golden one, the star of the heroic Quentin Roosevelt, who did not return, having made the supreme sacrifice, and whose body rests in the soil of France surrounded by those of his comrades.

Well may we reiterate here the words of Warren G. Harding, President of the United States, expressed on October 27, 1921, the sixty-third anniversary of Roosevelt's birth, "He was the greatest American of his time."

CHAPTER XXX

SIR WILLIAM OSLER, Bart., M.D., LL.D

HONORARY VICE-PRESIDENT OF THE NATIONAL TUBERCULOSIS ASSOCIATION
FROM 1905 TO 1919*

THE first physician to receive the distinction of a unanimous election as honorary vice-president of the National Tuberculosis Association was the late Sir William Osler, who, when at Baltimore, as has already been stated in the preceding pages, was one of the prime movers in its formation. His interest in the tuberculosis problem, in its social as well as its medical aspects, was always uppermost.

He was closely identified with the anti-tuberculosis movement in America as well as in England, and his counsel was sought as an expert in all that appertains to this most wide-spread of diseases. The accompanying bibliography comprises some 50 of his most important contributions on the subject of tuberculosis. To Dr. Osler is due the formation of the Laennec Society for the Study of Tuberculosis, which is allied with Johns Hopkins Medical School. In 1900 he established the first social service division in connection with the tuberculosis work at the Johns Hopkins Hospital.

This universally beloved physician is justly claimed by three countries—Canada, the United States, and England. He was born in Bond Head, Ontario, on July 12, 1849. He came from a family of culture. His father was the Rev. F. L., and his mother, Ellen Frere Pickton Osler. He started out in life with high ambitions and noble aims, graduating from Trinity College, Toronto, in 1868, and taking his medical degree at McGill University, Montreal, in 1872. He went abroad for a post-graduate course, study-

* The accompanying picture is a reproduction of a photograph Sir William kindly had taken shortly before his last illness to enable the author to illustrate the biographical sketch for this history. It is generally conceded to be the best portrait of him in existence. The picture was sent from England by Lady Osler shortly after the death of Sir William.

SIR WILLIAM OSLER

ing at London, Berlin, and Vienna. On his return in 1874 he was made professor of the Institute of Medicine of McGill University, where he remained until 1884, and then accepted a call as professor of clinical medicine at the University of Pennsylvania. With the foundation of the medical department of Johns Hopkins University in 1889 Dr. Osler became professor of theory and practice of medicine at that institution, and at the same time physician-in-chief of Johns Hopkins Hospital. He remained in these positions until the spring of 1905.

In the fall of 1904 he had received and accepted a call from Oxford, to become Regius Professor of Medicine of that world-renowned university. In reply to the author's congratulation, he wrote:

"Naturally, I am very loath to leave America, where I have been so well treated and where I have so many warm friends, but it really is an act of self-preservation. I could not possibly stand for very long the high pressure of my present life. The position is almost purely academic, and I still have an abundance of time for my literary work."

When Osler left America, a dinner was given to him, the memory of which will be forever cherished by those who were present. He was eulogized as a teacher, clinician, consultant, and author by such men as Tyson, Shepard, Wilson, Welch, Jacobi, and Mitchell. Osler's reply was full of expressions of gratitude and appreciation. Among other things he said:

"Why so much happiness has come to me I know not. But this I know, that I have not deserved more than others, and yet a very rich abundance of it has been vouchsafed to me. I have been singularly happy in my friends, and for that I say, 'God be praised!' I have had exceptional happiness in the profession of my choice, and I owe all of this to you.   I have been happy, too, in the public among whom I worked—happy in my own land in Canada, happy here among you in the country of my adoption."

His mother and his wife were seated in one of the boxes, and turning a grateful glance upward, he said:

"Of the greatest of all happiness I cannot speak—of my home. Many of you know it, and that is enough. . . . I have had three personal ideals. One, to do the day's work well and not to bother about to-morrow. The second ideal has been to act the Golden Rule, as far as in me lay, toward my professional brethren and toward the patients committed to my care. The third has been to cultivate such a measure of equanimity as would enable me to bear success with humility, the affection of my friends without pride, and to be ready when the day of sorrow and grief came to meet it with the courage befitting a man."

The honors bestowed upon Osler are almost too numerous to recount. He received the honorary degree of LL.D. from McGill University in 1895, from the universities of Aberdeen and Edinburgh in 1898, from the University of Toronto in 1899, from Yale University in 1901, from Harvard University in 1904, and from Johns Hopkins in 1905. The degree of Doctor of Civil Law was conferred by Trinity University, Toronto, in 1902, and the University of Durham in 1913; the degree of Doctor of Science from Oxford University in 1904, Liverpool University in 1910, and the University of Dublin in 1912. He was made a fellow of the Royal College of Physicians in 1883, and a fellow of the Royal Society in 1898. In 1911 Osler was created a Baronet of the United Kingdoms by King George V. In 1918 Sir William was made president of the British Classical Association, a rare honor to be bestowed upon one whose training had been that of a physician purely and simply.

Osler's interest in America, in its medical institutions, and in his countless friends and pupils was genuine and lasting until the end. His work in Oxford equaled his achievements in Montreal, Philadelphia, and Baltimore. In answer to an inquiry prior to the publication of an article on "The Tuberculosis Situation After the World War," Sir William wrote the author under date of May 26, 1919, "All goes well here and I hope we will get the tuberculosis problem settled ere long on national lines." During the war he worked for the health of the English and Allied armies. The death of his only son in the world war was a terrible blow to this great and good man, but he bore up under it bravely. In reply to a letter of condolence from the author, after expressing his thanks with his usual warmheartedness, Sir William merely added: "It has, of course, been a pretty hard business." Then, forgetful of his own sorrow, he went on to speak of our duties as physicians in the world war. He kept on working for the soldiers and with the soldiers. He talked to them on subjects of hygiene, how to preserve their health and to prevent tuberculosis. The July, 1919, number of the *Johns Hopkins Hospital Bulletin* was entirely devoted to tributes to Osler. Thomas, Barker, Councilman, MacCallum, Thayer, Brown, McCrae, Hamman, Futcher, Jacobs, Brush, Woods, Chatard, Noyes, Hurd, Kelly, and Boggs, all of whom had been either Osler's co-workers or pupils, related their personal experiences, showing the wide spheres of his activities as a teacher, sanitarian, physician, citizen, scholar, and lover of books. The articles which are of particular interest to us as students of tuberculosis were those of Louis V. Hamman, who wrote on "Osler and the Tuberculosis Work of the Hospital," and of Henry Barton Jacobs, on "Osler as a Citizen and His Relation to the Tuberculosis Crusade in Maryland."

In November, 1919, Osler contracted pneumonia, but he himself hoped for an early recovery, and on Christmas day he sent a typically cheerful cablegram to Johns Hopkins Hospital, announcing that he was making a good fight. Four days later he died. Perhaps he only sent that message to give Christmas cheer to his many friends on this side of the Atlantic. He must have analyzed the seriousness of his condition, for after his death the following note, dated December 23, 1919, was found among his effects: "Dear friends, the harbor is nearly reached, after a splendid voyage with such companions all the way; and my boy waiting for me." How the soul of this great man is revealed in these simple words!

Cheerfulness and unbounded capacity for work, a devotion to the highest ideals of medicine and humanity, a marvelous scholarship, loyalty to his friends, and kindliness to the humblest of the humble, were the outstanding characteristics of Sir William Osler. His life-long friend, Professor William H. Welch, of Baltimore, well said of him: "To Osler nothing human was foreign. His home, both in Baltimore and Oxford, was a center of hospitality." Those who had the rare privilege of walking with Professor Osler through the medical wards or who had the good fortune of being present at some of his receptions to students will never forget the human side of his character.

Osler's loyalty to his friends was indeed genuine, particularly when they were in need or in distress, as the author has reason to remember with deepest gratitude. Osler was still smarting under the ignominious slander manufactured by a sensational news-seeking press which had taken seriously a jocular remark he had made on the subject of euthanasia when, as a result of a statement the author had occasion to make at a meeting of the National Tuberculosis Association, he had to suffer a similar experience.   During a discussion on the use of morphin in tuberculosis the author ventured to say that in his opinion it was an almost indispensable remedy to assuage pain in the hopelessly ill consumptive.   The statement was apparently approved by all present, for it is well known that by the judicious administration of morphin we not only make the patient more comfortable, but in reality prolong life.   Yet, to the amazement of nearly everybody who heard it, among whom were the leading authorities on tuberculosis in this country, the author was denounced the following morning in a Philadelphia paper as having openly favored the administration of enough morphin to hopelessly ill tuberculous patients to end their lives.   As is usual with such sensational so-called news items, this statement quickly made the rounds of the American and European press.   On learning of this calumnious attack leveled against a younger colleague, Osler's indignation had no bounds.   His own sufferings from a similar experience he had borne with that equanimity of resignation characteristic of his great soul, but when it befell somebody else it was different.   He urged the author to start legal proceedings against that newspaper at once, offered his private purse to defray expenses, and assured him the support of the American profession at large.   He stood by him to the end of a very hard but finally victorious battle, defending him publicly and comforting him in private by letters of sympathy and friendship, which helped him to bear up under a most trying and painful experience.

Osler was devoted to his pupils, but he was also devoted to his teachers, and the veneration and enthusiasm he expressed when he spoke of his own masters and the masters of us all was an inspiration that not only stimulated the interest in historic medicine, but aroused gratitude for the inheritance which the teachers of past generations have left us.   On October 5, 1905, he took the American delegation, which had attended the Fifth International Tuberculosis Congress in Paris, to the cemetery of

AMERICAN DELEGATION AT THE TOMB OF LOUIS IN 905

Rea   from le t to ri ht Klebs Ka   R   Whitman McCarth   Norton Os er

Mont Parnasse to deposit a wreath on the tomb of Louis, the French physician, at whose feet so many American physicians of the past generation had sat. It was a touching tribute and gave the younger men a lesson in gratitude to our teachers. The accompanying picture of that occasion shows Osler in a thoughtful attitude after having made a short and impressive address to the American delegation by whom he is surrounded. The delegation included Drs. Whitman, Norton, Leonard Pearson, George H. Evans, Arnold C. Klebs, D. J. McCarthy, A. J. Magnin, Henry Barton Jacobs, John W. Brannan, A. Kayserling, Henry Beyer, John H. Lowman, F. M. Pottenger, and S. Adolphus Knopf.

Such a biographical sketch as this must necessarily be incomplete. Osler was one of the greatest physicians of the Anglo-Saxon race of the present day, but we are considering mainly his activities as a tuberculosis worker. As such he instructed thousands of students by word of mouth and by his writings on early diagnosis, practical prophylaxis, and rational treatment. In a lecture he delivered soon after his arrival in England he said:

"Probably 90 per cent. of mankind has latent tuberculosis, and if I had an instrument here with which I could look into the chest and abdomen of each of you I would probably find somewhere a small area of the disease. So widespread is the germ that practically all humans, by the time they become adults, harbor the bacillus of the disease. But we do not die, because we are not guinea-pigs and rabbits. We have attained a certain immunity. But the germ is in us, though negative, and with all of us there is the possibility of slipping into the dangerous state. But when workers have living wages, when the house becomes the home, and the nation spends on food what it now spends on drink, then there will be millions instead of thousands with practically continuous immunity. For the enemy has been tracked to its stronghold, which is defended by three allies—poverty, bad housing, and drink."

Characteristic of William Osler and his labors are the words which grace the photograph he presented to those who bade him farewell on May 2, 1905, when he was about to leave for Oxford. They were the immortal words of Abou Ben Adhem, "Write me as one that loves his fellow-men."

The tributes paid to Osler by some of his pupils, colleagues and friends are most touching. Harvey Cushing, one of his favorite pupils, closes his remarks in the *Annals of Medical History* with,

19

the following words: "In 1910 'Man's Redemption of Man' was delivered at a service for the students at the University of Edinburgh.   Osler unconsciously chose as his text from Isaiah what he himself has been to those who knew him: 'And a man shall be as an hiding-place from the wind, and a covert from the tempest; as rivers of water in a dry place; as the shadow of a great rock in a weary land.'"

Howard S. Anders, one of Osler's Philadelphia pupils, recalls in his tribute the master's saying that "there is no higher mission in this life than nursing God's poor."   And Henry Sewall, the first pupil to matriculate and to graduate from Johns Hopkins, wrote: "If I tried to characterize Osler, three words would suffice, *sweetness and light.*"

Dr. Field H. Garrison, of Washington, D. C., describes Osler's lovable personality in his tribute in "Science" of January, 1920, in the following words:

"Osler's warm glance and utter friendliness of manner told how naturally fond he was of people.   He had the gift of making almost anyone feel for the moment as if he were set apart as a valued particular friend, and so became, in effect, a kind of universal friend to patients, pupils and colleagues alike."

Prof. Charles L. Dana, Osler's New York friend, characterized the great physician's personality in the following terms:

"Sir William Osler was altogether the best known and best loved physician that this or any other country has produced.   His influence and achievements are not to be measured by the books he wrote, the students he taught, or the scientific observations he made.   Through the influence of his ideas, his personality and the mellowing activities of his career, he enriched the medical profession and greatly helped to raise its art to a point which now compels for it the esteem of society in general."

Another beautiful side of Osler was expressed in the tribute paid to him by Prof. F. J. Shepherd in the *Journal of the Canadian Medical Association*, wherein he said:

"As a clinical teacher, Osler was at his best; not only was he an acute diagnostician and a clear expositor, but he treated his hospital patients most kindly, as human beings and not as mere cases.   His example was one which made a great impression on his students and the Osler tradition of gentleness and sympathy with patients was handed on."

Osler was a sanitarian to the end. As a demonstration of his firm belief that cremation is the most rational, sanitary, and economic disposal of the dead, he had expressed the wish that his body should be thus disposed of. His life-long friend and colleague, Professor J. George Adami, of McGill University, Montreal, in the Memorial Number of the *Journal of the Canadian Medical Association*, describes the funeral service of Sir William, and among other things says:

"From one end of the Dominion to the other there will be those deeply attached to Osler—'Our Osler'—who hunger to possess a fuller and more personal knowledge of the illness that took him from among us, and of the solemnly beautiful last service at Oxford on New Year's Day. Most touching at Christ Church was the Psalm 'Lord Thou hast been our refuge.' Clear and yet subdued, the balanced voices of the choir led the congregation that filled the narrow Norman nave, transepts, and chancel of the Cathedral and poured over into the side aisles.   After a most impressive service the congregation was dismissed, and with the benediction dispersed, leaving all that was mortal of the great physician at rest for the night in the Lady Chapel, by the grave of his old friend, Burton, of 'the Anatomy of Melancholy.' The next morning his remains were conveyed to London to the crematorium, where Lady Osler and her sister, Mrs. Chapin, Mr. Frank Osler, Dr. W. Francis, and Dr. Molloch were alone present at the Committal Service.

"Doubtless by the time this reaches Canada it will be known that, in accordance with the expressed desire and as a last gift, Sir William's ashes are to be conveyed to Montreal, there to be deposited in the midst of his books in the Medical College of his student days, in which he held his first Chair, and which, to the end, retained his deep affection. With loving care those books were brought together, the first and the finest editions of the masterpieces of medical literature. How he loved to expatiate over their virtues! With what enjoyment he hunted for and acquired each rare volume! In that collection is concentrated the whole history of medical progress. There is nowhere so choice and well-selected a corpus of medical literature. Noble in itself, the gift is doubly ennobled by having associated with it all that is mortal of the great physician whose remains, after all his wanderings, are to come thus to rest in the country of his birth. McGill is to become his shrine, and for generations to come those who love medicine and its history will find their inspiration in that room where, surrounded by the books he loved so well, repose the ashes of Sir William Osler. Could there be nobler gifts or greater service to Canadian medicine?"

This gift will be deeply appreciated in the land of his birth, but the scientific work done by Osler, the influence he exerted as a medical teacher, the friendships he formed wherever he went, belong to us all. On one occasion, when making a farewell address, he said:

"I have loved no darkness, sophisticated no truth,
Nursed no delusion, allowed no fear."

To those wonderful words, expressing his ideals, we who remain behind may add as our farewell: "You made countless friends among the rich and poor, the humble and the great. Your life was an inspiration to old and young. You gave your heart and devoted the powers of your great intellect to the lessening of suffering that the world should be made better. You put into practice the maxim that service to man is the highest service to God."

The bibliography of Sir William Osler follows:

On the pathology of miner's lung. Can. Med. and Surg. Jour., 1876, p. 145–168.

Phthisical cavities in left lung: gangrene of pulmonary tissue about one of them. Can. Med. and Surg. Jour., 1877–78, p. 114.

Pleura. Small fibroid thickenings on visceral layer. Can. Med. and Surg. Jour., 1877–78, p. 115–116.

Diabetes, phthisical cavity in right lung surrounded by hepatized tissue. Montreal Gen. Hosp. Path. Rep., 1878, p. 34–35.

Chronic phthisis; almost entire destruction of both lungs. Healthy portion involved in a pneumonia. Montreal Gen. Hosp. Path. Rep., 1878, p. 35.

Chronic phthisis; perforation of lungs; pneumothorax; dermoid cyst of right ovary. Montreal Gen. Hosp. Path. Rep., 1878, p. 39–40.

Acute tubercular inflammation of the peritoneum. Small caseous mass in left lung. Right-sided pleurisy. General hyperplasia of the bone marrow. Montreal Gen. Hosp. Path. Rep., 1878, p. 52–56.

Tuberculous disease in right kidney, pelvis, ureter, and bladder. Tubercles in left kidney and lungs. Perforation of tuberculous ulcer in bladder. Peritonitis. Montreal Gen. Hosp. Path. Rep., 1878, p. 72–73.

Old scrofulous disease of right kidney, which is converted into cyst. Recent affection of the left. Mont. Gen. Hosp. Path. Rep., 1878, p. 73–74.

Old disease of the right kidney, which is converted into five or six cysts, filled with a putty-like material. Extensive tuberculous disease of the organ. Miliary tubercles in lungs. Albuminoid spleen. Montreal Gen. Hosp. Path. Rep., 1878, p. 74–75.

Miner's phthisis. Can. Med. and Surg. Jour., 1878–79, p. 452–54.

Chronic pleurisy; flattening of sides of chest. Can. Med. and Surg. Jour., 1879–80, viii, 109–111.

Perforation of pulmonary artery by ulcer of left bronchus; sudden death from hæmoptysis; chronic bronchitis, emphysema, phthisis. Montreal Gen. Hosp. Path. Rep., 1880, i, 282–283.

Pneumonia phthisis. Montreal Gen. Hosp. Rep., 1880, i, 295–297.

Clinical lecture on a case of fibroid phthisis. Can. Med. and Surg. Jour., 1880–81, ix, 641–650.

Cestode tuberculosis. A successful experiment in producing it in a calf. Am. Vet. Rev., 1882–83, vi, 6–10.

Pulsating pleurisy. Tr. Assn. Am. Phys., 1888, iii, 330–338.

The anatomical tubercle. Montreal Med. Jour., 1888–89, xvii, 418.

Note on endocarditis in phthisis. Johns Hopkins Hosp. Rep., 1890, ii, 62–64.

Tubercular peritonitis; general considerations; tubercular abdominal tumors; curability. Johns Hopkins Hosp. Rep., 1890, ii, 67–113.

Diagnosis of tuberculous broncho-pneumonia in children. Arch. Pediat., 1891, viii, 825–829.

Acute phthisis; erosion of a large branch of the pulmonary artery; sudden fatal hæmoptysis. Tr. Path. Soc., Phila., 1891, xiv, 169.

Report on the Koch Treatment in Tuberculosis. Bull. Johns Hopkins Hosp., 1891, ii, 7–14.

The healing of tuberculosis. Climatologist, Phila., 1892, ii, 149–153.

Tuberculous pericarditis. Am. Jour. Med. Sc., Phila., 1893, 20–27.

Cases of sub-phrenic abscess. Tr. Assn. Am. Phys., Phila., 1893, 257–267.

Profound toxemia with slight tuberculous lesions. Medical News, Phila., 1893, lxiii, 632.

Notes on tuberculosis in children. Arch. Pediat., N. Y., 1893, x, 979–986.

Toxæmia in tuberculosis. Practitioner, London, 1894, iii, 26–30.

The registration of pulmonary tuberculosis. Phila. Polyclin., 1894, p. 65.

Pleuro-peritoneal tuberculosis. Bull. Johns Hopkins Hosp., 1896, p. 79.

Ephemerides, 1895: xi. Is the coin sound distinctive of pneumothorax? Montreal Med. Jour., 1895–96, xxiv, 518 to 969.

The preventive and remedial treatment of tuberculosis (Discussion). Brit. Med. Jour., 1899, ii, 1155.

The home treatment of consumption. Maryland Med. Jour., 1900, p. 8–12.

On the study of tuberculosis. Phila. Med. Jour., 1900, vi, 1029–30.

The home in its relation to the tuberculosis problem. Med. News, N. Y., 1903, p. 1105–10; also in Sanitarian, N. Y., 1904, p. 322–336; Canada Lancet, Toronto, 1904–05, p. 600–612; Revue Internat. de la Tuberculose, Paris, 1905, vii, 403–413.

The "phthisiologia" of Richard Morton, M.D. Med. Libr. & Hist. Jour., Brooklyn, 1904, ii, 1–7.

Address of the vice-president. Tr. Nat. Tuberc. Assn., i, 20, 1905.

Acute tuberculous pneumonia. Brooklyn Med. Jour., 1905, xix, 57–61.

Address before National Tuberculosis Association, Fifth Annual Meeting. Tr. Nat. Tuberc. Assn., v, 31, 1909.

Edward L. Trudeau—An appreciation. Jour. Outdoor Life, 1910, vii, 162.

Men and books: VII, Letters of Laennec. Can. Med. Assn. Jour., 1912, ii, 247–248.

Men and books: XI, George Bodington. Can. Med. Assn. Jour., 1912, p. 526–27.

Bacilli and bullets: an address to the officers and men in the camps at Churn. Brit. Med. Jour., 1914, ii, 569–70.

A tribute to Dr. Edward L. Trudeau: a medical pioneer. Am. Med., 1915, n.s. x, p. 20.

An address on the tuberculous soldier. Lancet, 1916, 220–221.

Graduated exercise in prognosis. Lancet, 1918, i, 231.

Tuberculosis. In Amer. Textbook Dis. Child. (Starr), Phila., 1894, p. 94 126. Also in his collected reprints, 1892–97, iii, no. 134.

Tuberculosis. In Syst. pract. med. (Loomis), N. Y. & Phila., 1897, i, 731–848.

Tuberculosis. In Amer. text book dis. child. (Starr), 2d edition, Phila., 1898, p. 270–302.

The principles and practice of medicine; designed for the use of practitioners and students of medicine, a textbook of which eight editions have appeared, containing valuable chapters on tuberculosis. Appleton, N. Y., 1917. This book has been translated into French, German, and Chinese.

CHAPTER XXXI

COLONEL GEORGE E. BUSHNELL, M.C., U.S.A.

HONORARY VICE-PRESIDENT OF THE NATIONAL TUBERCULOSIS ASSOCIATION
FROM 1918

DR. GEORGE E. BUSHNELL, Colonel of the United States Army, Retired, was unanimously chosen honorary vice-president of the National Tuberculosis Association at the annual meeting in 1918, in special recognition of the great service he had rendered in the prevention of tuberculosis in the army during the world war.

George Ensign Bushnell was born in Worcester, Mass., September 10, 1853, his parents being George and Mary Elizabeth Bushnell. He graduated with the degree of A.B. from Yale in 1876, and obtained the degree of M.D. at the same school in 1880. He passed the examination for assistant surgeon in the United States Army, and was appointed in February, 1881. He passed through the various grades, finally reaching that of colonel, and was retired as such on account of age limit September 10, 1917.

Since 1903 Colonel Bushnell has paid particular attention to the study of tuberculosis. At that time he had been assigned to duty at the army sanatorium for the tuberculous at Fort Bayard, New Mexico. In 1904 he was in command of the hospital, where he remained until June 2, 1917, when he was assigned to duty in the office of the Surgeon General and placed in charge of all matters appertaining to tuberculosis in the army. Although officially retired on September 10, 1917, so experienced a physician could not be spared at such a time, and the Colonel remained on active duty throughout the war. His services at the head of the tuberculosis section of the Army Medical Corps have been invaluable.

One of the most effective circulars brought out during the war was S.G.O. Circular No. 20, which was issued upon his recommendation from the Surgeon General's office. This circular was highly approved by Major General Gorgas, then Surgeon General, and later by his successor, Major General Ireland. Prior to being issued it had been submitted for revision to two of our most eminent internists, Professor William P. Thayer and the late Professor Theodore C. Janeway, both of Johns Hopkins University, but these authorities found only some slight changes to recommend and returned it to the Surgeon General's office with their absolute approval. Its purpose was to standardize the methods of examination in order to secure uniformity in the rejection or acceptance of doubtful cases of tuberculosis. Bushnell well said:

"Military examinations must differ from those in civil life in three respects: (1) The statements of the men examined could not be taken at their face value; the examinations must, therefore, be based on objective facts. (2) Besides the interests of the individual, only considered usually in civil practice, there must be borne in mind the interests of the Government. It was important, above all things, to obtain soldiers; men must, therefore, not be rejected on doubtful indications—the diagnosis upon which rejection was based must be based upon positive, distinctly marked signs and symptoms. (3) The examinations must be rapidly performed in order to clear the army of the unfit at an early date for the army's sake, and examinations must be early to prevent claims that the disabilities found had been incurred in line of duty— this for the sake of the taxpayer."

Because of the scientific, practical, economic, historical, and above all patriotic value of this circular, it will be well worth while to reproduce here the essential parts of it. The circular was issued on June 13, 1917, for the information of the medical officers to be used in connection with examinations for pulmonary tuberculosis in military service:

"The duties of the examiner are:
"1. To exclude cases of manifest tuberculosis from the army.
"2. To hold to service men who allege tuberculosis as a ground for exemption or discharge on the basis of insufficient or incorrectly interpreted signs and symptoms.
"3. To determine in the case of soldiers accepted for the military service the existence of pulmonary tuberculosis, and to decide whether or not the disease has been incurred in the line of duty."
"The following signs will not be regarded as evidence of pulmonary disease in the absence of other signs in the same portion of the lungs:
"1. Slightly harsh breathing, slightly prolonged expiration over the right

GEORGE E. BUSHNELL

apex above the clavicle anteriorly and to the third dorsal vertebra posteriorly. The same signs at the extreme apex left side.

"2· Same signs second interspace right anteriorly near sternum (proximity of right main bronchus or trachea).

"3· Increased vocal resonance, slightly harsh breathing immediately below center of left clavicle.

"4· Fine crepitations over sternum heard when stethoscope touches the edge of that bone.

"5. Clicks heard during strong respiration or after cough in the vicinity of the sternocostal articulations.

"6· The so-called atelectatic râles heard at the apex during the first inspiration which follows a deeper breath than usual or cough.

"7· Sounds resembling râles at base of lung (marginal sounds), especially marked in right axilla, limited to inspiration.

"8· Similar sounds heard at apex of heart on cough (lingula)

"9· Slightly prolonged expiration at left base posteriorly.

" 10. Very slight harshness of respiratory sounds with prolonged expiration in the lower paravertebral regions of both lungs posteriorly, most marked at about angle of scapula, disappearing a short distance above that point, equal on both sides, or slightly more marked at the angle of one side, more frequently the left."

"Incipient tuberculosis of the apex is often erroneously diagnosticated:

" 1. On account of misinterpretation of normal signs.

"2· Because the importance of minor differences between the two sides is exaggerated.

"3· Because signs of a healed lesion are considered to indicate an incipient lesion."

"The only trustworthy sign of activity of apical tuberculosis is the presence of persistent moist râles."

Concerning the diagnosis of acute lesions, the following are striking sentences:

"If small, this lesion is manifested by râles, with or without changes in breath sounds, percussion note, and voice transmission. The more acute the lesion the greater the probability that its presence will be indicated only by râles. . . . Large acute lesions are rarely found in candidates for enlistment and the small acute lesion is also comparatively rare. Tuberculosis as it presents itself to the Army examiner is usually of a chronic type."

"An arrested chronic lesion is characterized by harshness of breath sounds and prolongation of expiration, by increased vocal fremitus and resonance and by more or less pronounced dullness on percussion."

"An active chronic localized lesion is denoted by the presence of râles, together with the other signs described under the arrested lesion. Râles do not necessarily show that the lesion is extending nor that the activity is of much clinical importance, but in military practice the presence of râles accompanied by breath changes and other signs should be an indication for rejection. The more active and recent the chronic lesion the less marked the breath changes and the more conspicuous the râles."

"True miliary tuberculosis is not likely to come to the attention of the military examiner. The peribronchial type is common and frequently not recognized. In the adolescent the peribronchial tuberculosis may be extending from the deep lung without as yet developing a superficial focus. It may be manifested only by the presence of distant râles with or without slight changes in the breath sounds which are of a slightly bronchovesicular quality. If the case is well marked there will be impairment of expansibility of the affected side and increased vocal resonance. Less pronounced cases are distinguished from chronic bronchitis only by the character of the râles (coarser in bronchitis) and by their typical distribution."

"A definitely demonstrated tuberculous lesion of more than insignificant size below the apex is cause for rejection whether such lesion be active or inactive. . . . No examination for tuberculosis is complete without auscultation following a cough."

"The Method of 'Expiration and Cough.'—It is best executed as follows: Starting from the state of rest of the lung the subject forcibly expels the air from the lungs, reserving the last portion of the expiration for a short cough, after which inspiration immediately follows, but only enough air is inhaled to return the lung to the state of rest. The idea is to diminish the size of the bronchi as much as may be by expiration, then to cough to stir up forcibly such fluid as may be present in them. The moisture is more likely to be moved by the current of air and so produce râles when the tubes are of their least caliber. This procedure should invariably be employed in examinations in order to determine the activity of lesions found by other signs and also to detect the existence of fresh disseminated tuberculosis."

"The presence of tubercle bacilli in the sputum is cause for rejection."

"Tuberculin.—It is well recognized that a positive reaction to tuberculin, especially in the young adult, is not a proof of the presence of active clinically important tuberculosis. Tuberculin only demonstrates activity of the tuberculous process in the clinical sense when it can be shown to produce a focal reaction. Such reaction is not without danger. Since, therefore, tuberculin rarely leads to a correct diagnosis and may do injury, its general use in the diagnosis of tuberculosis in examinations for enlistment is prohibited."

"Résumé of Indications from X-ray Negatives.—The X-ray shows: 1. Tuberculous disease confined to region of hilus in deep lung. 2. Extension upward toward apex or downward and outward toward base, confined to deep lung. 3. A fine line or two extending to apex with or without small focus or foci there—condition not determinable by physical signs. 4. Clouding of apex without marked lines from hilus, probably largely pleuritic. 5. Well-marked lines extending to superficies of apex, usually, but not necessarily, with foci there—lesion accessible to physical examination. 6. Lines extending toward shoulder as well as apex. (a) If confined to deep lung may mean early and now obsolete exacerbation. (b) If extending to superficies denote larger lesion and less immunity than 5. 7. More or less widely diffused spots, lines, and streaks through a considerable portion of the lower lobe approaching periphery of lung, with few or no auscultatory signs—deep peribronchial tuberculosis. 8. More extensive streaked opacities involving greater part of one or both lungs and extending to periphery with few or many physical signs—fibrocaseous tuberculosis, fibrosis preponderating in proportion to scantiness of more or less rounded spots or dots.

"Conditions as shown by 1, 2, 3, 4, and 6(a) are not causes for rejection. Cases under 5 are to be determined by physical examination. Cases under 6(b), 7, and 8 are to be rejected."

Concerning the reception of this circular by the examiners of the army, Colonel Bushnell said in an address, delivered before the National Tuberculosis Association on March 6, 1918:

"These were novel ideas for our examiners, but they grasped them soon and carried them out loyally. The attempt to standardize indications was per-haps a bold one. Naturally, the ideas advanced in Circular No. 20, though before its publication it had received the approval of some of the leading internists in the country, did not fail to arouse some opposition, which cannot be said to be overcome even now. Almost any statement concerning a disease with regard to which such divergent views are held, as is the case with tuberculosis, will meet with some dissenters. Still I think it may be said that, though imperfect, a standard is better than no standard, under the conditions of this examination."

It was the writer's privilege to see the methods of examination indicated in Circular No. 20 put into practice at Camp Plattsburg, and it was indeed astonishing to see how much could be accomplished and how reasonably sure one could be of not having made a serious mistake by following the directions given by order of the Surgeon General through Colonel Bushnell. The following figures certainly will give food for thought: During the mobilization period of the war in 1917–1918 the draft boards rejected 62,000 men because of tuberculosis. The examinations, as a rule, were made by civilian practitioners. All men sent to camps and cantonments as fit for military service and free from tuberculosis were again examined by military surgeons according to the indications in Circular No. 20, and as a result 25,000 more were rejected on account of tuberculosis, which had escaped the examiners at the draft boards.

Colonel Bushnell's activity while at the head of the tuberculosis section of the Army Medical Corps was, of course, not confined to inaugurating effective diagnostic work. It was under his direction that ample provision was made in eight newly erected government hospitals for those in our army who had contracted or developed tuberculosis during service here or abroad.

Below will be found the valuable bibliography of Colonel Bushnell's literary activity on behalf of the prevention and cure of tuberculosis in the army.   Colonel Bushnell has now retired, enjoying a well-deserved rest.   He can amply afford to do this with the consciousness of having done his duty and having given not only the best of his years, but even the years of later life, which he had a right to enjoy in peace and quiet, to the service of his country.

The Colonel, however, does not seem to believe that retirement from active service should be followed by complete inactivity, and so he surprised and delighted his friends and admirers recently by the publication of a remarkable book, entitled "A Study of the Epidemiology of Tuberculosis; With Especial Reference to Tuberculosis of the Tropics and of the Negro Race."   This should be considered one of the most authoritative books that have appeared on the subject, showing, as it does, the wide reading of the author and his vast experience as an army surgeon in various parts of the country and under diverse climatic conditions.

The bibliography of Col. George E. Bushnell follows:

Marginal sounds in the diagnosis of pulmonary tuberculosis.   Med. Rec., Dec. 21, 1912.
Immunity through tuberculous infection.   Mil. Surgeon, Jan., 1913.
The diagnosis of tuberculosis in the military service.   Mil. Surgeon, June, 1917; also in Med. Rec. and Am. Rev. Tuberc., i, 325–352, 1917.
Tuberculosis in the army.   Address before South. Med. Assn., Memphis, Tenn., Nov. 13, 1917.   South. Med. Jour., Dec., 1917.
Tuberculosis and war.   Address before Am. Sanatorium Assn., Dec. 14, 1917. Med. Rec., Jan. 5, 1918.
Complement fixation in tuberculosis with the "partial antigens" of Deycke and Much (With A. Woods and C. Maddux).   Jour. Immunol., April, 1917.
Extension of tuberculosis of the lungs as shown by the x-ray.   Southwestern Med., May, 1917.
Manifest pulmonary tuberculosis.   Mil. Surgeon, April, 1918; also in Med. Rec. and Am. Rev. Tuberc.

The treatment of tuberculosis. Mil. Surgeon, June, 1918; also in Med. Rec. and Amer. Rev. Tuberc.

Sanatorium treatment in the appropriate climate, Tr. Nat. Tuberc. Assn., i, 362, 1905.

Lessons from the war as to tuberculosis. Address before Nat. Jewish Hosp. for Cons., Jan. 13, 1918. Jour. Am. Med. Assn., March 9, 1918.

The army in relation to the tuberculosis problem. The Jerome Cochran Lecture read before the Alabama State Med. Assn., April 17, 1918. Jour. Am. Med. Assn., June 15, 1918.

How the United States is meeting the tuberculosis war problem. Am. Rev Tuberc., Sept., 1918; also in Tr. Nat. Tuberc. Assn., xiv, 93, 1918.

Experimental evidence as to immunity from tuberculous infection. Med. Rec., Jan. 18, 1919.

The epidemiology of tuberculosis in the military service, Tr. Nat. Tuberc. Assn., xiv, 155, 1919.

A study of the epidemiology of tuberculosis; with especial reference to tuberculosis of the tropics and of the Negro race. William Wood & Co., New York, 1920.

CHAPTER XXXII

MAJOR GENERAL WILLIAM C. GORGAS, M.C., U.S.A.

HONORARY VICE-PRESIDENT OF THE NATIONAL TUBERCULOSIS ASSOCIATION IN 1920

A T ITS meeting in April, 1920, in St. Louis, the National Tuberculosis Association honored itself by the unanimous election of General William C. Gorgas to the honorary vice-presidency. General Gorgas had belonged to the Association officially as a director since 1917, but as an honorary vice-president he was ours only a few months, for he died on July 4, 1920. Of the many obituaries which appeared at the time of the great General's death, in all of which high tributes were paid to his achievements, one of the most touching was that by his successor, Merritt W. Ireland, Surgeon General of the United States Army.

William Crawford Gorgas, the son of General Josiah and Amelia Gayle Gorgas, was born in Mobile, Ala., October 3, 1854. General Ireland writes of the parents and their son William as follows:

"General Josiah Gorgas was Chief of Ordnance of the Confederate Army during the Civil War, and later president of the University of the South at Sewanee, Tenn. His mother was Amelia Gayle, a famous beauty, daughter of the War Governor of Alabama. In lineage and personality the late Surgeon General was a typical southerner. He had what might be called the Alabama temperament, a pleasant, suave, affable manner, and an attractive disposition, which, wherever he went, made him many friends."

William C. Gorgas received his preliminary and classical education at the University of the South from which he was graduated in 1875. He then entered Bellevue Hospital Medical College, receiving his degree in 1879. He subsequently served there as intern for two years. Entering the army in 1880, he received a commission as first lieutenant. His first post was Fort Brown, Texas. It was here that we may say he was fortunate enough to

302

WILLIAM C. GORGAS

contract yellow fever, which rendered him immune for the great work he was to do later on. He was promoted to captain in 1885. During the Spanish-American War he served as major and brigadier surgeon of volunteers. On July 6, 1898, he received his commission as major in the regular army. At the close of the Spanish-American War Major Gorgas was made Chief Sanitary Officer of Havana, in which capacity he served from 1898 to 1902.

General Gorgas' achievements in combating yellow fever in Cuba and in the Panama Canal Zone are so well known and have been referred to so often in his obituaries and biographies that we shall merely quote here the following statements from General Ireland's tribute:

"When de Lesseps started his ill-fated venture at canal building in 1880, the French occupants found the Isthmus a death-trap and during the nine years of occupancy they lost 22,819 laborers from the disease. At this time Panama was called 'the White Man's Grave.' When the United States took charge of the Canal in 1904, the death rate was as high as ever and a yellow fever epidemic was actually going on. In less than a year's time, the disease was completely wiped out and there was not a single case since May, 1906."

For his work in Cuba Gorgas was made a Colonel and Assistant Surgeon General by special act of Congress in March, 1903. In 1907 he was made a member of the Isthmus Canal Commission, and as such he remained in charge of the sanitation of the Isthmus until the winter of 1913.

In 1913, at the request of the British government, Gorgas went to South Africa to investigate conditions in the Rand mines, where the natives were dying in large numbers from pneumonia, miners' consumption, malarial fever, and tuberculosis. It was here that for the first time the General's interest was centered publicly upon tuberculosis, although it is known that he had always felt a profound interest in the combat of this disease, and he had been a member of our Association for a number of years. General Gorgas had a deep insight into the primary causes of tuberculosis, such as bad housing, underfeeding, overwork, and he did not hesitate to state publicly that our present taxation evils, grants, and immunities represent an unjust social order that is largely responsible for insufficient and unsanitary housing, poverty, and want in general. He was an ardent disciple of Henry George and firmly believed in the single tax system.

Gorgas was an idealist, but an intensely practical one. In one of his most remarkable addresses, entitled "Economic Causes of Disease," delivered in Cincinnati, September 29, 1914, he said:

"While dwelling upon thoughts such as these (better housing, better food, and better clothing for the laborers in order to combat disease) I came across 'Progress and Poverty.' I was greatly impressed by the theory and was soon convinced that the single tax would be the means of bringing about the sanitary conditions I so much desired, and was striving for. It was impressed upon me in a concrete form everywhere, in the United States, in the tropics and particularly in Panama; the great benefit that some such scheme of taxation would confer upon sanitation."

The entire address which to the men engaged in tuberculosis work has a deep significance, was published by Dr. Walter Mendelson, of New York, and endorsed by many of our leading sanitarians, medical teachers, sociologists, and economists throughout the country.

In South Africa, where General Gorgas had complete command of the situation, he at once inaugurated a campaign for the combat of pneumonia, tuberculosis, miners' consumption, etc., based on the principles of rational hygiene and general human welfare, such as we apply in the prevention of tuberculosis—more air space for sleeping and living quarters, a pure water supply, a sewer system, the destruction of flies and mosquitoes, and a better food supply.

On January 16, 1914, Gorgas was appointed Surgeon General of the United States Army with the rank of Brigadier General and in 1915 he was made Major General. During the summer and fall of 1916 he spent several months in South America making a preliminary survey for the Rockefeller Foundation, of localities still infested with yellow fever.

With the entrance of the United States into the World War in 1917, General Gorgas fulfilled the duties of his high office in a remarkably efficient way. The subject of tuberculosis was, of course, of particular interest, because so much work had to be done in order to safeguard our troops from contracting the disease. General Gorgas selected for this work the best talent among the military and civilian population. In the general history of our Association and in Colonel Bushnell's biography the work done by the division of tuberculosis in the Surgeon General's Office has already been referred to in detail.

General Gorgas showed his wisdom and interest in the tuberculosis problem of the army by appointing Colonel Bushnell to the task of looking after that disease and in seeing to it that no interference was placed in his way. It is characteristic of General Gorgas that, having selected the men that he needed, he left them alone in the confidence that they would do the right thing and without the wish to add to his own renown by taking credit for what was accomplished.

In recognition of General Gorgas' service to medical science and to humanity at large, many honors were conferred upon him. He was awarded the Distinguished Service Medal of the United States and was made Commander of the Legion of Honor of France; he was knighted by King George of England and decorated by King Albert of Belgium, as well as by rulers of other foreign countries. Honorary degrees were conferred on him by the University of Pennsylvania, the University of the South, the University of Alabama, and by Harvard, Brown, Tulane, Johns Hopkins, Oxford, Lima, and other universities. His alma mater, now the New York University and Bellevue Hospital Medical College, conferred on him the degree of LL.D. in June, 1918, in the midst of the great war. A brilliant assembly gathered in the amphitheater of the college to pay homage to their distinguished fellow alumnus. The gathering was largely composed of physicians training for or already active in war work. At the conclusion of the ceremonies which conferred the degree of LL.D. upon William Crawford Gorgas, the General responded in felicitous terms thanking the faculty for the honor conferred upon him. He then took occasion to express his appreciation of the willingness of the American medical profession to do its duty in the great war. He congratulated those present on having the privilege of serving their country in an hour of greatest need, bidding them an affectionate God speed. He concluded by saying that he hoped soon to meet many of their number in France, for which country he was about to sail with Secretary of War Baker. In addition to the just mentioned honors conferred on General Gorgas, he was awarded the Mary Kingsley medal from Liverpool School of

20

Tropical Medicine (1907), a gold medal of the American Museum of Safety (1914), and a special medal from the American Medical Association, 1914. Besides being president of the American Medical Association in 1909–1910, he was a member of the American Society of Tropical Medicine, American Public Health Association, and Association of Military Surgeons; honorary fellow of the New York Academy of Medicine and of the College of Physicians of Philadelphia, and associate member of the Société de pathologie exotique de Paris.

After his retirement from active duty in the army during the year 1919, General Gorgas was occupied with yellow fever investigations at Guayaquil and other South American foci. In 1920 the question of exploring the African foci came up. General Gorgas reached London on his way to West Africa on May 19, apparently in the best of health, and after a short period of travel on the continent, during which time he was decorated by King Albert of Belgium, he returned to London on May 29. On the following day he had a stroke of apoplexy from which he never recovered. The funeral ceremonies in London and in Washington were conducted with the military and civil honors becoming his rank and his distinction as an officer and scientist.

To characterize the man Gorgas, we may be permitted to quote again from General Ireland's tribute:

"Reticent and shy in public address, kindly, modest, and unselfish in authority, patient and open-minded, General Gorgas stands as one of the great figures in the application of science to the conquest of disease."

To have known him intimately was indeed a privilege, and his kindly face will never be forgotten by those who served with him or under him, or came into personal contact with him socially. We are indebted to Mrs. Gorgas for the picture of the General, which she considers the best ever taken of him. It was taken just before his retirement from the army.

With the death of General Gorgas the world lost one of the greatest medical authorities, a true benefactor of mankind, an ideal soldier, and a most lovable man. His achievements in preventive medicine have placed his name among the immortals of the age.

The remains of General Gorgas were interred at Arlington Cemetery at Washington with impressive military and civilian ceremonies. A special memorial service in honor of the late Major General was held in Washington on Sunday evening, January 16, 1921. Besides the diplomats, officers of the army and navy, members of Congress and other officials, there was present a large gathering of the many friends and admirers of General Gorgas. The exercises were under the auspices of the Southern Society of Washington, of which he was the former president. Major General Peter C. Harris, the Adjutant General of the United States Army, who presided, paid a glowing tribute to the life and career of General Gorgas. The other speakers who followed in the same vein were: Dr. Clarence J. Owens, Past President of the Southern Society; His Excellency Mr. J. J. Jusserand, Ambassador of the French Republic; His Excellency Señor Don Frederico Alfonzo Pezet, Ambassador of Peru; The Hon. Dr. Carlos Manuel de Cespedes, Minister of Cuba; Hon. Scñor Dr. Don Rafael H. Elizalde, Minister of Equador; Hon. Newton D. Baker, Secretary of War; Hon. Josephus Daniels, Secretary of the Navy; Hon. Señor Don J. E. Lefevre, Charge d'Affaires ad interim of Panama; Major General H. K. Bethell, Military Attache to the British Embassy; Dr. L. S. Rowe, Director General, Pan-American Union. Cablegrams of tribute to General Gorgas were read from the residents of Uruguay and Costa Rica and from the government of Columbia.

Since Major General Gorgas' death a number of movements have been started to honor his memory. A Senate joint resolution by Senator Heflin, of Alabama, is before Congress, which would authorize the expenditure of $50,000 in the erection of a monument in the city of Washington. Another movement purposes to raise a fund of $2,000,000 to establish a medical school as a memorial to Major General William C. Gorgas. The present plan is to have the entire nation contribute to the fund and to locate the school at Tuscaloosa, Ala., where General Gorgas lived as a boy. Dr. Seale Harris, of Birmingham, Ala., is chairman of the National Committee. Lastly, a Gorgas memorial institute has already been established in Washington, D. C. The purpose of the executive committee is to further a movement to introduce the sanitary methods devised by the late Surgeon General Gorgas into all the civilized countries of the world.

CHAPTER XXXIII

WARREN G. HARDING

Honorary Vice-President of the National Tuberculosis Association, 1921

TO HAVE the President of the United States as an honorary vice-president of any association is indeed a great distinction, and to be permitted to incorporate a biographical sketch of the first citizen of the United States in the history of the anti-tuberculosis movement in this country, because he has honored us by accepting the honorary vice-presidency, is a privilege which every member of the Association deeply appreciates.

Warren G. Harding is the son of a physician, the venerable Dr. George Tryon Harding of Marion, Ohio. Dr. Harding, although he has been nearly fifty years in practice, is still hale and hearty and following his profession. Such an ancestry speaks well for the President. The Hardings are of good, old Colonial stock. They settled first in Connecticut, removing later to the Wyoming Valley, Pennsylvania, where some of them were massacred and others fought in the Revolutionary War. The mother of the President, Phoebe Elizabeth Dickerson, was descended from an old-time Holland Dutch family, the Van Kirks; so that in Warren G. Harding is found the blending of the blood of the hardy Holland Dutch and the fearless, alert, and liberty-loving Scotch. His interest in medical science, preventive medicine, and, what concerns us particularly, the tuberculosis problem, he has evidently acquired directly from his father.

Warren G. Harding was born in Blooming Grove, Morrow County, Ohio, November 2, 1865. Of his boyhood an unknown biographer says: "He was just a natural, healthy, robust boy, endowed with the supremest gifts of nature—good, hard common sense, a rugged constitution, a sunny disposition, and a heart full of the milk of human kindness." He attended the village school until fourteen years of age, when he entered the Ohio Central

308

WARREN G. HARDING

College of Iberia from which he was graduated, standing high in scholarship; and it was there, as editor of the college paper, that he first displayed a talent for journalism. Like most aspiring young men in those days, he was obliged to stop for a time now and then to earn the money with which to pursue his college course. At one time we find him cutting corn; at another painting his neighbor's barns; at still another driving a team and helping to grade the roadbed of the T. & O. C. Railroad, which was then being built through that community. At the age of seventeen we find him teaching a district school, and "tooting a horn" in the "brass band" of the village. When young Harding was nineteen, having completed his college course, his father, Dr. Harding, removed to Marion, Ohio, the county seat of the adjoining county, where he still resides.

Warren G. Harding engaged in the newspaper business at Marion, and in 1884 became president of the Harding Publishing Company which published the Daily Star. In 1900 he was elected to the Ohio Senate and served as State Senator until 1904 when he became Lieutenant-Governor, remaining in that position until 1906. He became United States Senator from Ohio in 1915 and remained a member of the Senate until 1921, having been elected President of the United States on November 2, 1920, by an overwhelming majority.

An admirer of the President said of him prior to his election: "Were Warren G. Harding elected President of the United States, the country would have a good listener, a man capable of selecting a strong cabinet of good advisers, a wholesome man of good physical proportion, a man loving peace but unyielding in the demand for protection of the American ideals of right living."

When Mr. Charles M. DeForest wrote to the President that the children of the District of Columbia had won the Silver cup offered in the intercity contest of the Modern Health Crusade, President Harding in a charming way consented to present the cup and afterwards wrote the following letter:

"The White House, Washington.
"My dear Mr. DeForest: September 27, 1921.
   "I was very much interested to-day in presenting, on behalf of the National Tuberculosis Association, the silver cup won by the school children of the Dis-

trict of Columbia because of their larger enlistment, relatively, in the Modern Health Crusade, particularly in their enlistment to make effective warfare against tuberculosis. I may quite sincerely express the hope that in every American city and country district a like large proportion of boys and girls will make themselves knights by faithful attention to their own habits and their care and concern for the health of the nation.

"Very truly yours,
(Signed) "Warren G. Harding."

Mr. Charles M. DeForest,
    National Tuberculosis Association,
        New York City, N. Y.

President Harding was indeed a good listener, on this occasion listening even to little children. His letter to Mr. DeForest shows not only his love for little children but also his deep interest in the physical well-being and the health of the nation at large.

His special interest in the tuberculosis problem is shown by a splendid letter written to Dr. Charles J. Hatfield, the Managing Director of the National Tuberculosis Association, in answer to a letter referring to the Christmas Seal Campaign. It reads as follows:

"The White House, Washington.
"My dear Dr. Hatfield: November 10, 1921.
    "I am glad to note the splendid success of the campaign against tuberculosis, as shown by the decline of the death rate in 1920, to the remarkably low level of 114 per 100,000. The enormous saving of life reflected by these figures clearly indicates the success of the work of the National Tuberculosis Association and its affiliated organizations.

    "As Honorary Vice-President of the Association, I will be glad to have you convey to all who are interested in the prevention of tuberculosis my earnest hope that the coming Fourteenth Annual Christmas Seal Sale may be completely successful, in order that your splendid work may be further developed. I trust that there may be a generous response to your appeal.

"Yours sincerely,
(Signed) "Warren G. Harding."

Dr. Charles J. Hatfield,
    Managing Director,
    National Tuberculosis Association,
        370 Seventh Avenue, New York City.

President Harding's attitude toward the anti-tuberculosis work is further shown by the following letter which accompanied the excellent autographed photograph of the President reproduced in this History, and which the author will always cherish among his most valuable documents:

"The White House, Washington.
"My dear Dr. Knopf: March 1, 1922.
    "I am glad to receive your communication, with enclosures, and to learn that the National Tuberculosis Association has undertaken the publication of "A History of the Anti-Tuberculosis Movement in the United States.
    "My attention has recently been directed to the beneficent results achieved by the intensive anti-tuberculosis effort, as evidenced by Dr. Frankel's paper at the Annual Meeting of the National Association last June.   It is certainly gratifying to know that sixty thousand fewer deaths occurred in the United States Registration Area from pulmonary tuberculosis in 1919, than would have occurred if the 1900 death rate had prevailed.   The knowledge of such impressive facts cannot fail to be an inspiration to all engaged in preventive medicine and in the mitigation of human suffering and distress.
    "With all good wishes for the continuing success of your efforts, I remain
                                "Yours sincerely,
                                (Signed) "Warren G. Harding."

Dr. S. Adolphus Knopf,
    16 West 95th St.,
    New York City.

The interest in the tuberculosis problem taken by the Harding family is not confined to the President alone.   In the Bulletin of the National Tuberculosis Association of December, and reproduced in this volume in chapter VI, entitled "The Tuberculosis Christmas Seal," a charming picture is shown of Mrs. Harding purchasing her first sheet of Christmas Seals from a small Modern Health Crusader.

In his letter to Dr. Hatfield and in the one addressed to the author, President Harding referred to the remarkably low level of the tuberculosis death rate in 1919 and in 1920.   With the President's deep interest in the problem, with his ever present anxiety for the care of the tuberculous ex-soldiers and the war veterans afflicted with other diseases or still suffering from wounds received in battle, and with his ardent advocacy of all measures tending to improve the health of the nation, may we not be certain that during the years while he is President the morbidity and mortality not only of tuberculosis but also of other preventable and curable diseases will continue to decrease?

The great French scientist, Louis Pasteur, the father of modern bacteriology, to whom preventive medicine is perhaps more indebted than to any other man, set before his pupils and disciples an ideal to strive for when he pronounced the immortal phrase which has now become classic: "Il est dans le pouvoir de l'homme de faire disparaitre toutes les maladies parasitaires du monde."*

May our country be privileged under the presidency of Warren G. Harding to show to the rest of mankind that we are in earnest in our efforts to realize this goal, as far as it is humanly possible, by combating all infectious and contagious diseases and their accompanying or causative abnormal social and economic conditions. Thus, we shall make our country a beacon of light in the onward march of civilization, by ourselves becoming spiritually, morally, and physically a strong and happy nation.

*It is in the power of man to cause all parasitic (germ) diseases to disappear from the world.

CHAPTER XXXIV

EDWARD LIVINGSTON TRUDEAU, M.D.

PRESIDENT, NATIONAL TUBERCULOSIS ASSOCIATION, FROM 1904 TO 1905

EDWARD LIVINGSTON TRUDEAU was the first president of the National Tuberculosis Association. He was unanimously elected on June 6, 1904, and on retiring a year later from the office he was made the first honorary member. The outstanding qualities of this great man as a pioneer in sanatorium treatment in the United States, his many contributions to tuberculosis science, and his philanthropic work on behalf of the tuberculous poor and those of moderate means, give him a unique position in the history of the tuberculosis movement in this country. Many biographies have been written of Trudeau, the best perhaps being that of Stephen Chalmers, entitled, "The Beloved Physician—Edward Livingston Trudeau." Of greatest interest and value, however, is his autobiography. We shall content ourselves here with a relatively short sketch of the life of this pioneer in the American tuberculosis movement.

Dr. Edward Livingston Trudeau, son of a prominent practitioner in New York, was born in that city October 5, 1848. The father, being of French descent, decided to give his son a thorough knowledge of that language, and sent him to Paris to get his preliminary education. There he attended the celebrated Lycée Bonaparte.

After the completion of his studies in the French capital young Trudeau came back to the United States in 1867, undecided what career to choose. He finally secured an appointment as midshipman in the Naval Academy, but remained there a very short time. His brother had become ill, and the disease proved to be tuberculosis. Trudeau's career as a tuberculosis fighter began by his nursing the hopelessly ill brother with that self-sacrifice and devotion characteristic of all the things he did throughout his long, eventful life. He cared for his brother until the latter's death, hardly ever leaving his bedside. Precautions to avoid infection were then unknown, and open windows and fresh air were considered contraindications.

There is no doubt that Edward contracted tuberculosis from his brother, yet one cannot help feeling that a Divine Providence ordained it to be thus, for his brother's illness led young Trudeau to choose medicine as a career, and his own illness made him a pioneer in the life-saving open-air treatment. A brilliant student of tuberculotherapeutics, a beloved physician, a savior of countless lives, and last, but not least, the teacher of a great many men who are now carrying on the work in all parts of the United States.

After graduating from the College of Physicians and Surgeons in 1871, Trudeau started in general practice, becoming an associate of Dr. Fessenden Otis. He worked hard to gain a foothold in practice, but the disease he had contracted from his brother became seriously active and he was obliged to give up. He consulted Professors Loomis and Janeway, who advised a climatic change. He went South, but returned to New York with very little, if any, improvement.

Recalling the delightful times he had had during vacations when hunting and fishing in the Adirondacks, and having always been an ardent lover of nature, he decided to spend his last days in the midst of what was to him the most congenial of environments. He had given up all thought of practising medicine. The Adirondack climate and the outdoor life, coupled with his good, sound judgment, which led him not to overdo, with plenty of complete rest whenever possible, restored the young physician to almost perfect health within a few years, to the surprise of himself as well as his friends. The cold season, which was feared by all other invalids who came to the Adirondack Mountains, did even more for him than the summer, and to the astonishment of the inhabitants of Paul Smith's, where the doctor had made his home, he remained with them through the most rigorous winters. Trudeau proved that tuberculosis is curable in pure air independent of the seasons of the year, by means of a careful, regulated outdoor life.

EDWARD LIVINGSTON TRUDEAU

A mind like that of Trudeau's could not be idle, and a heart like his could not see a suffering patient without offering help; but he had his own notions of how to prescribe for the poor. It is told of him that once, in the early days, Fitz Hallock, his guide, friend, and neighbor, came in to tell the doctor that a poor family who lived back in the woods were in trouble and had sent him to get them medicine. The doctor took a prescription pad and wrote on it "A sack of flour and a strip of bacon," and said: "Here is some money; get that prescription filled at the store and take it to them."

The writings of Hermann Brehmer, of Germany, on the open-air, hygienic and dietetic treatment of tuberculosis in closed institutions (sanatoria) and the discovery of the tubercle bacillus by Koch awoke in Trudeau an ardent desire to devote his entire life to the study and cure of tuberculosis. The story of how he established his first laboratory to confirm Koch's experiments of isolating the tubercle bacillus in sputum, and of his later original experiments in the hope of producing artificial immunity, is full of romance. He selected a little room in his own house which he called a laboratory, and made his own thermostat, which was heated by a kerosene lamp. The laboratory was heated by a wood stove, which on many a cold night the doctor had to get up to replenish. Yet in spite of all these difficulties he succeeded in isolating the tubercle bacillus. In 1893, while Trudeau was on a visit to New York, word reached him that the lamp which was connected with the thermostat had exploded and his home and laboratory had burned to the ground. When Osler heard of the misfortune, he wrote the following characteristic lines: "Dear Trudeau: Sorry to hear of your misfortune, but take my word for it there is nothing like a fire to make a man do the Phoenix trick." In reality it was not very long before a magnificent building of stone and tile was erected at Saranac Lake which compares well with any of the best equipped laboratories of the country, and which has been a Mecca for students from all over the world.

There has, perhaps, never been a physician who had so many kind-hearted and wealthy friends and grateful patients as Trudeau. Mr. George C. Cooper built the laboratory, Mr. A. A. Anderson endowed it, and Mr. Horatio W. Garrett, of Baltimore, presented the institution with a splendid library.   From the laboratory many valuable contributions have gone out into the world and have done honor to American tuberculosis research.   In 1908, on the occasion of Trudeau's sixtieth birthday, his former pupils and assistants presented to him a *Festschrift* containing the results of work done in the laboratory.   Trudeau's own careful studies on the use of tuberculin as a therapeutic agent have done much to show that its indiscriminate use in the hands of inexperienced practitioners is dangerous.   His conservatism and painstaking care in all his investigations made him the ideal phthisiotherapist.

But if the history of the laboratory, of which Trudeau remained director until his death, is interesting and far-reaching, the story of the sanatorium itself is of as great if not greater importance. It was in 1884 that the guides and residents of Saranac Lake donated money enough to buy five acres of land near the village in a spot selected by Trudeau because, as he used to say, he could always light his pipe there, showing that it was sheltered from the strong winds by the conformation of the hills and woods.   Two little shacks were erected.   They constituted the nucleus of what is to-day one of the greatest and most splendidly equipped institutions for the treatment of the tuberculous poor and those in moderate circumstances in the United States, if not in the world, the Trudeau Sanatorium.

Although a great admirer of the teachings of Brehmer as to outdoor life, and of Dettweiler's theory of the rest cure, Trudeau never favored the one-house system characteristic of the German sanatorium.   It is to him that we are indebted for what is known as the cottage plan sanatorium for the treatment of tuberculous patients.   Over 40 cottages accommodating from four to six patients each, an administration building, a library, a nurses' home, and a church, called "St. Luke the Beloved Physician," besides the laboratory already mentioned, to-day comprise the institution.   It has served as a model for many of the existing sanatoria now in operation in the United States.   The patients who, passing through the institution, have gained their health and been restored to their earning capacity, thanks to the genius of Trudeau, can be numbered by the thousands.   How Trudeau, with virtually no means of his own, was nevertheless able to build this vast institution and maintain its workings has been a wonder to the world. The explanation is to be found in his optimism and in the generosity of his countless wealthy friends who were always willing to give when he asked for money for the building of a cottage or for this or for that.

Those who came into close contact with Trudeau will recall his personal charm. Tall, slender but wiry, with a wonderful head and pleasing smile, he was the ideal physician and friend. His humor never left him no matter how trying the hour. A few years ago, when he had had one of his unpleasant relapses, the author of this sketch had occasion to write him and closed the letter wishing him a speedy recovery, to which Dr. Trudeau replied as follows: "I am still on my chair on my porch, to which I am glued like the fly on the fly-paper, and still have a nurse. I am afraid I don't 'enjoy' poor health as some people seem to, and it is much preferable to play the part of doctor to that of patient."

Few men of the medical profession were so greatly beloved and honored as he. His alma mater, the College of Physicians and Surgeons, now the medical department of Columbia University, conferred on him the honorary degree of M.Sc. in 1899, and McGill University of Montreal gave him the degree of LL.D. in 1905. In 1910 he was tendered the presidency of the Congress of American Physicians and Surgeons, one of the highest honors within the gift of the medical profession. In May, 1913, he received the degree of LL.D. from the University of Pennsylvania. Custom requires the presence of those about to receive the degree, but in this case, owing to his illness at the time, precedent was waived and the degree conferred "in absentia," an added honor.

We have already referred to the enthusiastic reception (see p. 31) which was given him in Atlantic City at June, 1904, when he was elected president of the National Tuberculosis Association, and have quoted the remarks he made in his address of acceptance. The scene which preceded his acceptance, however, is of sufficient historical interest to be related here. Trudeau's name was proposed as president and his election was proclaimed by a unanimous vote, but Dr. Trudeau declined. Dr. Osler and Dr.

Henry Barton Jacobs then took hold of his arms and marched him up to the platform. The audience stood and would not listen to his declination, but on the contrary a loud and continued "No" arose from the vast assembly. At the International Congress on Tuberculosis in September, 1908, in Washington, Trudeau received an ovation whenever he appeared on the platform, and what he said as greeting to the delegates illustrates the man's labors and great modesty. Speaking of the achievements in tuberculosis work from the time when he started his professional career up to that date, he said:

"For thirty-five years I have lived in the midst of a perpetual epidemic, struggling with tuberculosis both within and without the walls, and no one can appreciate better than I do the great meaning of such a meeting. I have lived through many of the long and dark years of ignorance, hopelessness, and apathy, when tuberculosis levied its pitiless toll on human life unheeded and unhindered; when, as Jaccoud has tersely put it, 'The treatment of tuberculosis was but a meditation on death.' But I have lived also to see the dawn of the new knowledge, to see the fall of the death-rate of tuberculosis, to see hundreds who have been rescued, to see whole communities growing up of men and women whose lives have been saved, and who are engaged in saving the lives of others. I have lived to see the spread of the new light from nation to nation until it has encircled the globe and finds expression to-day in the gathering of the International Congress of Tuberculosis, with all that it means to science, philanthropy, and the brotherhood of men."

During the last years of his life Trudeau suffered a great deal from his old tuberculous lesion. When artificial pneumothorax came into vogue a few years ago, he submitted himself to this treatment, and for a time it gave very gratifying results. Later he gave it up, feeling that it did not help him. Though illness and the loss of two beloved grown-up children—a son and a daughter —had left an impress of sadness on Trudeau, he kept up admirably, was optimistic and cheerful most of the time, and until the very last took the keenest interest in the institutional and laboratory work of the sanatorium.

We are indebted to him for a most remarkable address on "The Value of Optimism in Medicine," which should be read and reread by every physician. This wonderful address was delivered before the Congress of American Physicians and Surgeons in 1910. To give the full weight and meaning to the address on optimism we will quote Mr. Alfred L. Donaldson's description of the circumstances under which it was written.

"He had been suffering from one of his most serious relapses—high fever, acute coughing spells, and broken sleep. He woke in the small hours of each morning, and lay tossing uncomfortably on his bed. Then it occurred to him that instead of lying there idly between coughs, thinking of himself and his troubles, he might better concentrate his mind on some preparation for the great meeting over which he had been asked to preside. So he turned on the light near his bed, reached for pad and pencil, and began the rough draft of this notable address on optimism. Not long after he was able to leave his bed and deliver it in person. What it means to turn out optimistic literature under such conditions only those who have tasted them can realize; but the unusual feat is essentially typical of Dr. Trudeau's whole career."

The same all-pervading optimism, faith in God, and faith in his friends and colleagues, faith in the present and the future, permeated the life of this beloved physician from the beginning to the end of his earthly career. He died November 15, 1915, at the age of sixty-seven. By his own life, with its sufferings and trials, he showed us how to forget self, and taught us that by consecrating our lives to high ideals and true service to our fellow-men we are rendering the highest service to God.

A few weeks before his death there occurred an event that must have tended to make the last hours of the great Trudeau supremely happy. An ardent admirer of his, Mr. Samuel Mather, of Cleveland, made it possible, through a magnificent gift, for a post-graduate medical institution, to be known as the Trudeau School for Instruction in Tuberculosis Science, to be established at Saranac Lake. Thus Trudeau's noble wish to spread the best scientific knowledge of the prevention and cure of tuberculosis became realized. Several societies whose object is the scientific study of tuberculosis have also been named in his honor.

On August 10, 1918, a distinguished company of physicians, friends, and former patients of Dr. Edward L. Trudeau gathered in the grounds of the Sanatorium at Saranac Lake, N. Y., to witness the unveiling of a memorial statue of the noted physician. In this life-size bronze the sculptor, Gutzon Borglum, has succeeded in reproducing in a marvelous manner the spiritual expression so characteristic of the great teacher. The statue is the gift of 1,200 of Doctor Trudeau's former patients, and the formal presentation to the institution was made by one of these patients, Miss Louise E. Bonney, now a high-school teacher in New York.

The statue is mounted on a marble pedestal and placed on the terrace in front of the main building, in which are located the administration offices. From this point one has a wonderful view of the mountains in all their grandeur. The front of the pedestal bears the following inscription

EDWARD L. TRUDEAU

THOSE WHO HAVE BEEN HEALED IN THIS
PLACE
HAVE PUT THIS MONUMENT HERE
A TOKEN OF THEIR GRATITUDE
AUGUST 10, 1918.

On the reverse of the pedestal, in the original French, are the words:

GUERIR QUELQUEFOIS
SOULAGER SOUVENT,
CONSOLER TOUJOURS.

(To cure sometimes, to relieve often, to comfort always.)

Some day, when the Great White Plague shall be no more, the name of Edward Livingston Trudeau will be gratefully remembered as one who taught us how to fight and conquer this great enemy of mankind.

The bibliography of Dr. Edward Livingston Trudeau follows:

Infectiousness of non-bacillary phthisis. Am. Jour. Med. Sc., Oct., 1885.

Environment experiment in relation to bacterial invasion. Am. Jour. Med. Sc., July, 1887; also in Tr. Am. Clim. and Clin. Assn., iv, 131, 1887.

Sulphuretted hydrogen vs. the tubercle bacillus. Med. News, li, 570, 1887.

Environment experiments repeated. Tr. Am. Clim. and Clin. Assn., v, 91, 1888.

Hydrofluoric acid as a destructive agent to tubercle bacilli. Med. News, lii, 486, May 5, 1888.

Hot-air inhalations in pulmonary tuberculosis. Med. News, Sept. 28, 1889; also in Tr. Assn. of Am. Physicians, iv, 287, 1889.

Some cultures of the tubercle bacillus illustrating variations, growth and pathogenic properties. Tr. Assn. Am. Physicians, v, 183, 1890.

Limitation of prevalence of tuberculosis. (Discussion.) Tr. Assn. Am. Physicians, v, p. 207, 1890.

MONUMENT TO EDWARD LIVINGSTON TRUDEAU

Study of preventive inoculations in tuberculosis. Med. Rec., Nov. 22, 1890.

Treatment by Koch's tuberculin, Hunter's modification and other products of the tubercle bacillus. Med. News, Sept. 3, 1892; also in Tr. Assn. Am. Physicians, 1892, p. 87.

Results of employment of tuberculin and modifications at the Adirondack Cottage Sanitarium. Med. News, Sept. 10, 1892; also in Tr. Am. Clim. and Clin. Assn., ix, 18, 1892.

Eye-tuberculosis and anti-tubercular inoculization in the rabbit. N. Y. Med. Jour., July 22, 1893; also in Tr. Assn. Am. Physicians, 1893, p. 108.

Creosote in pulmonary tuberculosis. (Discussion.) Tr. Assn. Am. Physicians, viii, 194, 1893.

Sarcoma of the lung, Diagnosis of. (Discussion.) Tr. Assn. Am. Physicians, viii, 194, 1893.

Ultimate results of eye-tuberculosis and anti-tuberculosis inoculation in the rabbit. Med. News, Sept., 1894; also in Tr. Assn. Am. Physicians, 1894, p. 168.

Letter on Klebs' "Anti-Phthisin." Feb. 8, 1896.

Sanitaria for the treatment of incipient tuberculosis. N. Y. Med. Jour., Feb. 27, 1897.

The tuberculin test in incipient and suspended tuberculosis. Med. News, May 29, 1897.

The need of improved technique in the manufacture of "T. R." Med. News, Aug. 28, 1897.

Remarks on artificial immunity in tuberculosis. Brit. Med. Jour., Dec. 25, 1897.

Résumé of experimental studies on the preparation and effects of antitoxins for tuberculosis. Tr. Assn. Am. Physicians, xiii, 1898.

The Adirondack Cottage Sanitarium for the Treatment of Tuberculosis. Practitioner, Feb., 1899.

The present aspect of some vexed questions in tuberculosis. Bull. Johns Hopkins Hosp., July, 1899.

The sanitarium treatment of tuberculosis and its results. Med. News, June 2, 1900.

The first people's sanitarium in America for the treatment of tuberculosis. Zeitschr. f. Tuberk. u. Heilstwn., i, no. 3, 1900.

Recent research work on the chemistry of the tubercle bacillus. Tr. Assn. Am. Physicians, 1900.

The importance of the recognition of the significance of early tuberculosis in relation to its treatment. Tr. Assn. Am. Physicians, 1901.

The history of the work of the Saranac Laboratory for the Study of Tuberculosis. Bull. Johns Hopkins Hosp., Sept., 1901.

Artificial immunity in experimental tuberculosis. N. Y. Med. Jour., July 18, 1903; also in Tr. Assn. Am. Physicians, 1903.

Bovine, avian and human tuberculosis. (Discussion.) Tr. Assn. Am. Physicians, 1903.

The history of the tuberculosis work at Saranac Lake.   Med. News, Oct. 24, 1903.

Address of the president.   Tr. Nat. Tuberc. Assn., i, 13, 1905.

Two experiments in artificial immunity against tuberculosis.   Tr. Nat. Tuberc. Assn., i, 157, 1905; also in Med. News, Sept. 30, 1905.

The therapeutic use of tuberculin combined with sanitarium treatment of tuberculosis.   Tr. Nat. Tuberc. Assn., ii, 297, 1906; also in Am. Jour. Med. Sc., August, 1906.

Tuberculin immunization in the treatment of pulmonary tuberculosis.   Am. Jour. Med. Sc., June, 1907.

Antibacterial and antitoxic immunization in tuberculin treatment.   Jour. Am. Med. Assn., Jan. 23, 1909.

Animal experimentation and tuberculosis.   Pamphlet II, Defense of Research, Am. Med. Assn., 1909.

The value of optimism in medicine.   President's address to the Congress of American Physicians and Surgeons, 1910.   Am. Jour. Med. Sc., cxl, 1, 1910.

Letter in answer to E. G. Bullock.   Brit. Jour. Tuberc., Aug. 25, 1915.

Relative immunity in tuberculosis and the use of tuberculin.   Brit. Jour. Tuberc., January, 1916.

An autobiography.   Lea & Febiger, Philadelphia, 1915.

CHAPTER XXXV

HERMANN M. BIGGS, M.D., Sc.D., LL.D.

PRESIDENT OF THE NATIONAL TUBERCULOSIS ASSOCIATION FROM 1905 TO 1907

DR. HERMANN M. BIGGS was president of the National Tuberculosis Association for two years—from 1905 to 1907.

The son of Melissa T. Pratt and Joseph Hunt Biggs, he was born in Trumansburg, N. Y., September 29, 1859. He attended Cornell University and was graduated in 1882. He received his degree of M.D. from Bellevue Hospital Medical College, New York, in 1883. He served as intern in Bellevue Hospital from 1883 to 1884. With the formation of the Bellevue Hospital Alumni Association he became its first president. In 1910 New York University conferred the degree of LL.D. upon Dr. Biggs, and in 1917 he received the same degree from the University of Rochester. In 1920 Harvard University conferred upon him the degree of Doctor of Sciences.

From the time of his graduation from Bellevue Hospital Dr. Biggs has served as pathologist and visiting or consulting physician to many of our leading New York hospitals and tuberculosis sanatoria. Dr. Biggs was also professor of pathological anatomy at Bellevue Hospital Medical College from 1885 to 1894, professor of therapeutics and clinical medicine from 1897 to 1907, associate professor of medicine from 1907 to 1914. He now occupies the position of professor of medicine of the University and Bellevue Hospital Medical College. He is a member of the International Health Board of the Rockefeller Foundation, and has been a member of the Board of Scientific Donation of the Rockefeller Institute for Medical Research since its foundation. Dr. Biggs is an honorary fellow of the Royal College of Physicians of Edinburgh and of the Royal Sanitary Institute of Great Britain. He is now president of the Association of American Physicians and of the

American Social Hygiene Association.   Dr. Biggs was decorated by the King of Spain for the valuable services he has rendered the world as a hygienist and sanitarian.

Besides having made many valuable contributions to nearly all the clinical, pathological, and bacteriological branches of internal medicine, Dr. Biggs has rendered the most conspicuous services to sanitary science, and particularly in the prevention of tuberculosis.   He occupied the position of General Medical Officer of the Department of Health of the city of New York from 1901 to 1914.   Since that date he has been the Health Commissioner of the State of New York.   As General Medical Officer of New York city, Dr. Biggs was responsible more than any other medical man in this or any other country for obtaining the official recognition of tuberculosis as a communicable and reportable disease in order to combat it successfully.   As already mentioned in our general history, it was due to the efforts of Dr. Biggs and his co-workers, Dr. T. Mitchell Prudden and Dr. Joseph D. Bryant, that a voluntary notification of private cases of tuberculosis and a compulsory notification of all cases treated in institutions was inaugurated by the New York Health Department in 1893, and that in 1897 the Department adopted regulations requiring the notification of all cases.

But Dr. Biggs was not satisfied with a mere statistical control of tuberculosis.   He inaugurated at the same time a system whereby an early and definite diagnosis of all cases of tuberculosis could be obtained.   This consisted in the gratuitous examination of any specimen of sputum sent to the Health Department's laboratory for that purpose.   To this Dr. Biggs added educational measures.   Circulars teaching the simple rules of the prevention of tuberculosis, designed to reach the different classes of the community, were widely distributed.   For the foreign population these were translated into their respective languages.

In 1902, when the author presented an appeal for the formation of a committee or society for the prevention of tuberculosis in New York, Dr. Biggs was the first to sign, and from the day of its first meeting he has been a most active member of the Committee for the Prevention of Tuberculosis of the Charity Organization Society, now the New York Tuberculosis Association.

HERMANN M. BIGGS

Under the inspiration of Dr. Biggs this committee worked hand in hand with the Health Department in the educational propaganda.

Again it was through the initiative of Dr. Biggs that the first municipal dispensary (clinic) for the treatment of the consumptive poor was established in the city of New York. In the course of years these dispensaries have been multiplied so that to-day there are no less than twenty dispensaries distributed throughout the city under the Health Department's direction. Following the example of the Health Department, 10 tuberculosis clinics connected with the larger hospitals have been established in a comparatively short time. To coördinate their activities, the Association of Tuberculosis Clinics of the city of New York was founded, and under Dr. Biggs' direction and with the coöperation of Dr. James Alexander Miller, the Health Department issued a pamphlet outlining the purposes of the association, which are in brief as follows:

First.—To organize dispensary control of pulmonary tuberculosis in New York city.
Second.—To develop a uniform system of operation of such dispensaries as are organized for this purpose.
Third.—To retain patients under observation until they are satisfactorily disposed of, and to prevent them from drifting from one dispensary to another.
Fourth.—To establish and maintain a district system of dispensary treatment.
Fifth.—To facilitate the attendance of patients at the dispensary most convenient to their homes.
Sixth.—To facilitate the work of visiting nurses in the homes of patients.
Seventh.—To provide for each patient requiring it assistance by special funds or benevolent organizations, and proper hospital or sanatorium care.
Eighth.—To coöperate with, and assist as far as possible, the Department of Health in the supervision of pulmonary tuberculosis.

In 1904 Dr. Biggs established the Riverside Hospital-Sanatorium for advanced cases on North Brother Island as one of the Health Department's activities, particularly designed to remove cases of tuberculosis constituting centers of infection in their homes.

When the first New York municipal sanatorium was opened at Otisville, N. Y., in 1906, Dr. Biggs was made the medical director and physician-in-chief. He occupied the position until 1914, and from its inception took the keenest interest in this institution. To-day it is one of the largest sanatoria of its kind, having three units (males, females, children) with 600 beds. To Dr. Biggs' initiative is due the employment of that invaluable adjuvant in the modern treatment of pulmonary tuberculosis known as work therapy, which is successfully employed at the Otisville Sanatorium. Dr. Biggs has also the distinction of having been president of the first tuberculosis preventorium for children, which was founded some years ago in Farmingdale, N. J., largely through the munificence of Mr. Nathan Straus.

The tuberculosis work, inaugurated by Dr. Biggs and being carried on by the Health Department of the city of New York, has served as a model to many cities in this and other countries. It may be summarized as follows:

(1) Notification and registration of all cases of tuberculosis.

(2) Free bacteriological examination of sputum, to aid notification and to facilitate the early and definite diagnosis.

(3) Educational measures of various kinds—circulars, lectures, exhibits, newspaper articles.

(4) Visitation of consumptives in their homes. Continuous supervision of cases in tenement houses by corps of trained nurses.

(5) Free disinfection by the Department of Health, and issuance of orders for the renovation of rooms vacated by consumptives.

(6) Referring needy cases to the proper charitable organizations.

(7) Three classes of institutions are provided:

    (a) Free clinics (dispensaries) for ambulant cases unable to go to sanatoria.

    (b) Free sanatoria for incipient and early cases.

    (c) Free hospitals for advanced cases.

(8) Forcing certain classes of patients into a hospital and retaining them there.

(9) Enforcing regulations concerning spitting in public places.

(10) Research studies concerning the mode of infection, the rôle of bovine tuberculosis, characteristics of the tubercle bacillus, etc.

What was the result of all these activities inaugurated under the leadership of Dr. Biggs? In 1887 he was one of the consulting pathologists of the Department of Health of the city of New York. He had felt for several years the primary importance and necessity for administrative action in relation to tuberculosis, and he urged upon the Board of Health of New York city the immediate enactment of suitable regulations for the sanitary surveillance of this disease. The year previous—in 1886—the mortality from pulmonary tuberculosis was 355 per 100,000 population; in 1910 the mortality was 185. This means virtually a reduction of the mortality from tuberculosis by one-half during a quarter of a century's labors and tuberculosis activities, such as were directed by Dr. Biggs. In 1920 the death-rate in New York city for pulmonary tuberculosis had been reduced to 110.7 per 100,000 population.

Since Dr. Biggs has been at the helm of the New York State Department of Health he has transferred his enthusiasm and interest in the tuberculosis problem to the state at large. He inaugurated a special tuberculosis division of the State Department of Health for educational propaganda, and a few years ago was instrumental in working out a plan for traveling clinics. These clinics are of invaluable help in the discovery of early cases of tuberculosis, in the supervision of former sanatorium cases, and in education in the prevention of tuberculosis through visiting nurses. The local physicians are invited to coöperate and to visit these clinics.

Dr. Biggs came to the New York State Health Department immediately upon its reorganization in 1914. His administrative skill and far-seeing vision are best shown in the decline of the death-rate from tuberculosis. In 1914 for "upstate" New York, the pulmonary tuberculosis rate was 118.8 per 100,000 population. In 1920 it had dropped to 98.0 per 100,000 a decline of 17.5 per cent.

Dr. Biggs' activities in anti-tuberculosis work and his vast knowledge and experience were, of course, utilized during the recent World War. He became a member of the Council of National Defence, of the Advisory Committee of the United States Food Administration, and of the American Red Cross. The Rockefeller Foundation sent him to France to investigate the unfortunate tuberculosis situation which was reported to exist throughout that country, particularly in the war zone. Dr. Biggs' report on his return from France resulted in the appointment of a tuberculosis commission under the leadership of Dr.

Livingston Farrand, which has done incalculable good not only in taking care of the immediate needs, but in stimulating an active anti-tuberculosis propaganda and in establishing clinics and sanatoria throughout France. In the fall of 1920 Dr. Biggs took over temporarily the direction of the General Medical Department of the League of Red Cross Societies, with headquarters at Geneva, Switzerland.

Well may it be said of Dr. Biggs that his lifelong enthusiasm and devotion to the tuberculosis cause and to preventive medicine in general have had the widest and most beneficent influence, not only throughout the United States, but throughout the entire civilized world.

The bibliography of Dr. Hermann M. Biggs follows·

The accidents incidental to the use of the exploring needle for diagnosis. 1888.
The sanitary supervision of tuberculosis as practiced by the New York City Board of Health. (With John H. Huddleston, M.D.) Jour. Am. Med. Assn., Jan., 1895.
The health of the city of New York. Wesley M. Carpenter Lecture, Nov. 7, 1895.
The conduct of an isolation period for communicable disease in a home.
Provision for the care of advanced cases of tuberculosis.
Preventive medicine in the city of New York. 1897.
Sanitary science, the medical profession and the public. 1897.
The registration of tuberculosis. 1900.
An ideal health department. (With C. F. H. Winslow, M.D.) Minneapolis.
Tuberculosis—its causation and prevention. New York, 1901.
Brief history of the campaign against tuberculosis in New York. (With Charles F. Bolduan, M.D.)
Preventive medicine, its achievements, scope, and possibilities. 1904.
The reduction in the tubercular death rate in children in New York City. 1904.
Address of the vice-president. Tr. Nat. Tuberc. Assn., i, 23, 1905.
Address of the president. Tr. Nat. Tuberc. Assn., iii, 16, 1907.
Compulsory notification and registration of tuberculosis. Tr. Nat. Tuberc. Assn., iii, 39, 1907.
The health of the city. 1868–1910.
Administrative control of tuberculosis. 1912.
Comments on some plans of hospital construction. (Monograph) 1912.
The municipal sanatorium at Otisville. (Reprint) 1913.
Note on the death rate from tuberculosis in various large municipalities. Tr. Nat. Tuberc. Assn., viii, 357, 1912.
Facts every emigrant should know. How to enjoy health and how to avoid sickness. 1913.

The tuberculosis campaign, its influence on the methods of public health work
   generally. (With C. F. Bolduan.) Tr. Nat. Tuberc. Assn., ix, 39, 1913.

The infectiousness of tuberculosis. 1915.

What has been learned about tuberculosis since the International Congress of
   1908? 1916.

Tuberculosis in France. Am. Jour. Pub. Health, July, 1917.

A war tuberculosis program for the nation. Tr. Nat. Tuberc. Assn., xiii,
   73, 1917; also in Am. Rev. Tuberc., July, 1917.

CHAPTER XXXVI

FRANK BILLINGS, M.D., Sc.D.

PRESIDENT OF THE NATIONAL TUBERCULOSIS ASSOCIATION FROM 1907 TO 1908

D R. FRANK BILLINGS succeeded Dr. Hermann M. Biggs as the third president of the National Tuberculosis Association (1907–1908).

He was born April 2, 1854, at Highland, Iowa County, Wisconsin, the son of Henry M. and Anne Bray Billings. He graduated from the medical department of the Northwestern University in 1881, and obtained the degree of M.S. in 1890. He served as intern in the Cook County Hospital from 1881 to 1882, and studied in Vienna, London, and Paris from 1885 to 1886. Dr. Billings obtained the title of Doctor of Science from Harvard in 1915.

Beginning as a humble demonstrator of anatomy, by his untiring energy, intense application, and hard study, Dr. Billings rose in a relatively short time to be professor of medicine and dean of Rush Medical College in Chicago. He served as attending and consulting physician to many of the most important hospitals of that city. He was Shattuck lecturer in Boston in 1902, and Lane medical lecturer at the Leland Stanford University in 1915. Although a general medical consultant, his interest in tuberculosis, in its social as well as its medical aspects, has always been intense.

From 1906 to 1912 Dr. Billings was president of the Illinois State Board of Charities. He is a member of the medical societies of his State and city, and was president of the Chicago Medical Society in 1891. The American medical profession at large made him president of the Association of American Physicians and of the American Medical Association. In coöperation with Drs. Henry B. Favill, Arnold C. Klebs, Theodore B. Sachs, and others, he was instrumental in calling into life the Chicago Tuberculosis Institute. As one of the most active members of the National

FRANK BILLINGS

Tuberculosis Association, his discussions in the clinical, pathological, and sociological sections have always been inspiring and helpful. His presidential address at the meeting of the Association in 1908 was full of sound advice and prophetic vision.

It goes without saying that a personality such as Dr. Billings, with his vast medical experience and his splendid executive ability, had to be called upon by our War Department during the recent war. Thus he was made chairman of the American Red Cross Mission to Russia, where he rendered valuable service. On his return he entered active service, and attained the rank of colonel on April 30, 1918, being attached to the Surgeon General's office in Washington and devoting his vast knowledge and energy to the rehabilitation of wounded, sick, and disabled soldiers. For his admirable work at the head of the Rehabilitation Department of the Surgeon General's office he was awarded the Distinguished Service Medal. He published a number of lectures on rehabilitation of the disabled which, because of their clearness and precision, attracted a great deal of attention.

Although Dr. Billings modestly claims not to have done or written anything of note on tuberculosis, those who have had the privilege of working with him know what an invaluable factor he has been in the combat of tuberculosis in general among the civilian population, and of his recent work on behalf of the tuberculous soldiers.

Colonel Billings is an enthusiast regarding the value of curative work in wards, schools, shops, garden, and field for the recovery of tuberculous soldiers, and justly considers it of the greatest psychological and material value in the treatment of pulmonary tuberculosis generally.

The bibliography of Dr. Frank Billings follows:

Address of the president. Tr. Nat. Tuberc. Assn., iv, 15, 1908.

The standards of physical examinations and the selective service. Jour. Am. Med. Assn., July 6, 1918.

Rehabilitation of the disabled. Jour. Am. Med. Assn., May 24, 1919.

The physical and mental rehabilitation of disabled soldiers of the United States Army. Congress Amer. Phys. and Surg., June 16, 1919.

Physical reconstruction applied in the treatment of pulmonary tuberculosis. Jour. Am. Med. Assn., Oct. 4, 1919; also in Tr. Nat. Tuberc. Assn., xv, 146, 1919.

CHAPTER XXXVII

VINCENT Y. BOWDITCH, M.D.

OUR fourth president, unanimously elected to serve for the year 1908–1909, was Dr. Vincent Y. Bowditch. He had already served the Association as vice-president from 1906 to 1908.

The son of Dr. Henry I. and Olivia Yardley Bowditch, he was born July 7, 1852, at Weston, Mass. He was graduated from Harvard in 1875, and received his M.D. in 1879 from the Harvard Medical School. He was house officer in the Massachusetts Gen eral Hospital from 1878 to 1879, instructor in clinical medicine at Harvard Medical School from 1892 to 1899, and attending physician to the Carney and Boston City Hospitals.

His father, the elder Bowditch, as has been mentioned on p. 4, was a great physician, and particularly interested in diseases of the lungs. To him we are indebted for the introduction of the operation known as paracentesis thoracis (tapping of the chest to remove accumulations of fluid). One of the most inspiring and instructive works it has ever been the author's privilege to read, not only on medicine, but also on philosophy, religion, and politics, are the two volumes entitled "Life and Correspondence of Henry Ingersoll Bowditch," by his son, Vincent Y. Bowditch, who dedicated this wonderful biography to the memory of his mother, the thought of whom was his constant inspiration while writing the book.[1]

The mantle of the older Bowditch could not have fallen upon worthier shoulders than those of young Vincent. With the example of so much wisdom, patriotism, gentleness, and devotion to high ideals, it is no wonder that Dr. Vincent Y. Bowditch has become one of the most beloved and distinguished physicians of New England and one of the most ardent tuberculosis workers.

---

[1] Houghton, Mifflin & Co., Boston and New York, 1902.

VINCENT Y. BOWDITCH

We have referred to the Sharon Sanatorium in Massachusetts as the first to be established near a large center of population and independent of any climatic advantages. (See p. 10.) This unique institution owes its inception to Dr. Bowditch's enthusiasm and devotion. It was opened in March, 1891, and has demonstrated that more could be done for the tuberculous at low altitude, near the sea, in an inclement climate, than had been thought possible before. The object of the Sharon Sanatorium was to supply a suitable institution for the treatment of incipient pulmonary disease arising in women who are unable, for pecuniary and other reasons, to seek distant health resorts. The institution has now been in existence for almost thirty years, and its constant growth and the splendid results obtained show the wisdom of the enterprise. Dr. Bowditch's demonstration of the possibility of treating the tuberculous of the state of Massachusetts in their home climates, resulted in the establishment of the Rutland State Sanatorium, the first institution of its kind. It is but natural that Dr. Bowditch should be one of its visiting physicians, a position which he held for many years. The universal esteem in which Dr. Bowditch has been held by sanatorium workers resulted in his election as the first president of the American Sanatorium Association in 1905. When the Massachusetts Tuberculosis League was formed in 1914 he was also chosen president of that organization.

As the accompanying bibliography shows, Dr. Bowditch's publications on the subject of tuberculosis have been numerous and his labors on behalf of the consumptive poor worthy of the distinguished name he bears. Because of the historic and classic interest of the elder Bowditch's introduction of paracentesis into the treatment of pleuritic effusions, we may note with special interest the fact that one of the first papers Dr. Vincent Y. Bowditch published was in regard to 96 cases of pleuritic effusion occurring in the private practice of his father, covering a period of thirty years, in which he followed up the cases and gave the after-results as evidence of the possibility of active pulmonary disease showing itself in later life after an attack of pleurisy. The result showed a more favorable aspect than that which had been given previously by Dr. Landouzy, of Paris.

Unfortunately, owing to serious illness, Dr. Bowditch was prevented from delivering the usual presidential address, and the vice-president, Mr. Homer Folks, had to take his place on that occasion. We rejoice in Dr. Bowditch's complete recovery, which has enabled him since to accomplish so much good work on behalf of the tuberculosis cause.

The bibliography of Dr. Vincent Y. Bowditch follows:

A case of traumatic linear atrophy.   Boston Med. and Surg. Jour., June 25, 1885.

The treatment of pulmonary disease by means of "pneumatic differentiation." Boston Med. and Surg. Jour., July 16, 1885.

A case of phthisis with numerous bacilli.   Complete arrest of the disease. Boston Med. and Surg. Jour., Dec. 10, 1885.

The use of strophanthus hispidus in heart disease.   Boston Med. and Surg. Jour., March 17, 1887.

Homœopathy as viewed by a member of the Massachusetts Medical Society. Address before the Hahnemann Society of the Boston University School of Medicine.   Boston Med. and Surg. Jour., June 24 and 30, 1886.

Comparative importance of different climatic attributes in the treatment of pulmonary consumption.   Med. News, Oct. 13, 1888.

Two cases of phthisis treated by intra-pulmonary injections.   Read before Mass. Med. Socy., March 13, 1889.

Comparative results in ninety cases of phthisis pulmonalis.   Delivered before Am. Clim. and Clin. Assn., June, 1889.

The establishment of sanatoria for pulmonary diseases in the vicinity of our great cities.   Boston Med. and Surg. Jour., Feb. 25, 1892.

The effect of change of posture upon heart murmurs.   Internat. Med. Magazine, Nov., 1892.

Three years' experience with sanitarium treatment of pulmonary diseases near Boston.   Tr. Am. Clim. and Clin. Assn., 1894.

Suggestions: The result of recent experiences with phthisical patients.   Tr. Am. Clim. and Clin. Assn., 1898.

State sanatoria for tuberculosis.   Read at meeting of the Providence Med. Assn., December 3, 1900.

The home (sanitarium) treatment versus the climatic treatment of consumption.   Boston Med. and Surg. Jour., Sept. 19, 1901.

The care of consumptives in state and private sanatoria in Massachusetts. Address before Maryland Public Health Assn., Jan. 28, 1902.

Subsequent histories of seventy-nine arrested cases treated at the Sharon Sanatorium, 1891–1902.   Tr. Am. Clim. and Clin. Assn., 1903.

Origin and growth of sanatoria for tuberculosis in Massachusetts.   Jour. Tuberc., April, 1903.

Arrested tuberculosis; subsequent histories of cases treated at the Sharon Sanatorium.   Boston Med. and Surg. Jour., March 17, 1904.

Pulmonary tuberculosis and sanatorium treatment.   Boston Med. and Surg. Jour., Dec. 1, 1904.

Six years' experience at the Massachusetts State Sanatorium for Tuberculosis. (With H. B. Dunham.)   Tr. Nat. Tuberc. Assn., i, 349, 1905;   also in Jour. Am. Med. Assn., June 24, 1905.

The scope and aim of state sanatoria for tuberculosis.   Tr. Nat. Tuberc. Assn., ii, 287, 1906.

Subsequent histories of one hundred and sixty "arrested cases" of pulmonary tuberculosis treated at the Sharon Sanatorium.   Tr. Am. Clim. and Clin. Assn., 1907.

The English sanatorium.   Jour. Outdoor life, iii, 461, 1907.

Tuberculosis in Massachusetts.   Prepared by Mass. State Committee for Tuberc. Congress, 1908.   Edited by Edwin A. Locke, M.D.

The movement for the control and eradication of tuberculosis in Massachusetts. In "Festschrift" in honor of R. W. Philip, M.D., Edinburgh, 1911.

A retrospect.   A few thoughts and suggestions based upon twenty-five years' experience with tuberculosis.   Boston Med. and Surg. Jour., July 20, 1911.

Memorabilia.   Extracts from notes made by the late Henry Ingersoll Bowditch, M.D., of Boston.   Tr. Am. Clim. and Clin. Assn., 1912;   also in Boston Med. and Surg. Jour., Oct. 31, 1912.

After results in tuberculous patients treated during the years 1891–1911 at the Sharon Sanatorium.   (With Dr. W. A. Griffin.)   Jour. Am. Med. Assn., Dec. 14, 1912.

The origin and aims of the Massachusetts Anti-Tuberculosis League.   Boston Med. and Surg. Jour., Aug. 12, 1915.

What the general practitioner should know about incipient pulmonary tuberculosis.   Boston Med. and Surg. Jour., Nov. 25, 1915.

The history of the growth of the anti-tuberculosis movement in Massachusetts, and the lesson to be learned therefrom.   Address delivered at the Trudeau School of Tuberc., Saranac Lake.   Boston Med. and Surg. Jour., Dec. 14, 1916.

Methuselah and life in the open.   Tr. Nat. Tuberc. Assn., xiv, 197, 1918;   also Am. Rev. Tuberc., July, 1918.

Medical reminiscences: I. Visits to Brehmer's and Dettweiler's sanatoria. Jour. Outdoor Life, March, 1919.   II. Memorial service to Florence Nightingale.   April, 1919.   III. Personal reminiscences of episodes in the medical career of Henry Ingersoll Bowditch, M.D., June, 1919.

Life and correspondence of Henry Ingersoll Bowditch, 2 volumes.   Houghton, Mifflin & Co., 1902.

CHAPTER XXXVIII

EDWARD G. JANEWAY, M.D., LL.D.

PRESIDENT OF THE NATIONAL TUBERCULOSIS ASSOCIATION FROM 1909 TO 1910

D R. EDWARD G. JANEWAY, the fifth president of the National Tuberculosis Association, served in that capacity from 1909 to 1910.

He was born in Middlesex County, New Jersey, August 31, 1841, received his preliminary education at Rutgers College, and was graduated with the degree of A.B. in 1860. He took his medical course at the College of Physicians of Columbia University, from which he was graduated with the degree of M.D. in 1864. The honorary degree of LL.D. was conferred upon him by the Princeton University in 1904.

Dr. Janeway's medical career began as intern in Bellevue Hospital. From 1868 to 1873 he was curator and instructor of pathological anatomy in the Bellevue Hospital Medical College; from 1873 to 1886 professor of pathological anatomy and clinical medicine; in 1886 he succeeded the late Dr. Austin Flint to the chair of principle and practice of medicine and clinical medicine, and later on, with the amalgamation of the University and Bellevue Medical Colleges, he became dean of that institution.

Dr. Janeway's interest in public sanitation, and particularly in tuberculosis, was characteristic throughout his medical career. Although perhaps the greatest fame he attained was because of his unusual diagnostic skill as a general consultant, his activity in the tuberculosis field was greater than the seeming scarcity of his publications on tuberculosis would indicate. Serving as health commissioner of the city of New York from 1875 to 1882, he showed a deep interest in the housing conditions predisposing to tuberculosis, and maintained the then unpopular theory that tuberculosis was a transmissible disease.

Among his first publications on the subject there are some of a

EDWARD G. JANEWAY

very remarkable character, as, for example, one on the contagiousness of tuberculosis, published as far back as 1882, prior to Koch's discovery of the tubercle bacillus as the factor of contagion; and a second article, entitled "Danger of Errors in Diagnosis between ,Chronic Syphilitic Fever and Tuberculosis."

Dr. Janeway was among the first American teachers who, after Koch's discovery, taught the value of the bacteriological examina tion of sputum as an important diagnostic means. The inval uable help he gave to the New York Health Department, particularly to Dr. Biggs, in the latter's early struggles for municipal control of tuberculosis, is a matter of record, and cannot be better illustrated than by quoting what Dr. Biggs said in a letter to the author of this biographical sketch in reference to it:

"Dr. Janeway was always one of our strongest and most unswerving supporters. Dr. Janeway and Dr. Prudden and Dr. Frank Foster were almost the only men prominent in medicine twenty-five years ago in New York city who actively supported the measures proposed and later adopted by the Department of Health for the restriction and prevention of tuberculosis. The first assurance of this effect came, I think, in 1887, when Dr. Bryant sent a letter to a number of prominent physicians in New York asking for advice as to the adoption of the recommendations which had been made to the board by Dr. Prudden, Dr. Loomis, and myself. From that date onward Dr. Janeway's attitude never changed, and it was to him that I went more frequently, in the early days of my connection with the Department of Health, for advice and assistance, than to any other man in New York. Dr. Janeway, Dr. Bryant, and Dr. Prudden were the three men who have never been found wanting in support of any measures to improve the public health in New York city."

Dr. Janeway was an examining physician of the Adirondack Cottage Sanatorium from 1895 to the time of his death, and he had likewise been connected with the Loomis Sanatorium since 1900 as a member of the medical board. He was on the consulting staff of the Sea Breeze Sanatorium for tuberculous joint diseases (now the Neponsit Beach Hospital for Children) from the very foundation of the institution, and he was also a member of the advisory board of the Stony Wold Sanatorium for tuberculous working girls and children.

In 1901 Dr. Janeway was honorary vice-president of the British Congress on Tuberculosis, and one of the official delegates for the

22

United States. In an interesting paper read before the Academy of Medicine on December 19 of that year he gave a very complete review of the work of that congress, and made some valuable suggestions concerning prophylactic measures. At the International Tuberculosis Congress in Washington in 1908 he was a vice-president of the clinical section.

In 1902 Dr. Janeway was one of the first to sign a call for the formation of a local tuberculosis committee, which developed into the permanent Committee on the Prevention of Tuberculosis of the Charity Organization Society of New York city, on which he served as one of the most faithful and active members during the remainder of his life. He was one of the first to join The National Association for the Study and Prevention of Tuberculosis, of which he became a director and member of the executive committee in 1906 and president in 1909. He was also a member of the Committee on the Prevention of Tuberculosis of the State Charities Aid Association from the time of its formation in 1907.

Dr. Janeway always had the greatest sympathy for the consumptive sufferer, and expressed on many occasions his belief in the unwisdom of individual, state, or governmental phthisiophobia. On one occasion, when he had heard that a refined and cultured tuberculous invalid of English nationality, who had come to visit the United States on some important family affair, was held at Ellis Island because of the new regulation not permitting tuberculous immigrants to land, he called the author's attention to the injustice being done and asked his coöperation to obtain the gentleman's admittance to the United States. He added his humble efforts to Dr. Janeway's strong appeal to the authorities in Washington, and the Englishman was finally permitted to enter this country.

Dr. Janeway was opposed to the unfortunate Goodsell-Bedell law, which made the establishment of sanatoria in the state of New York virtually impossible for a number of years, and, as a member of the various tuberculosis committees, helped in its ultimate repeal. He combated phthisiophobia, whether it originated in the minds of statesmen, laymen, or physicians. He strongly opposed the action of the State Board of Medical Examiners of Oklahoma, whereby tuberculous but otherwise well-qualified practitioners were to be excluded from practising in that state, and physicians were forced to sign a sworn statement that they had not in the last three years lived in the house with or nursed any one suffering from said disease (tuberculosis). The following is what Dr. Janeway wrote on this subject:

"I think that it is a very oppressive measure, and one not either humane or just. As regards the affidavit, I think that is an additional oppression, especially the part which requires the practitioner to say 'he has not lived in the house with a consumptive or nursed any one suffering from the disease.' These measures, it seems to me, are ill calculated to advance the best interests of the struggle against tuberculosis."

This was one of the last messages on tuberculosis he gave to the world.

In his presidential address of 1910, reviewing the medical and sanitary progress which had been made during the previous decade, this far-seeing physician, teacher, and lover of his kind again warned us not to slacken our efforts on behalf of the betterment of the social and living conditions of the poor, and he wisely said, in the conclusion of his address: "The contest will not be considered carried to the highest point unless at the same time measures are taken to secure the avoidance of overcrowding by the obtaining of suitable dwelling places for the masses."

Dr. Janeway's tact, diagnostic skill, and wisdom in dealing with the consumptive individual, the many physicians who were, or thought themselves to be, afflicted with tuberculosis who went to him for an opinion, and the great number of general practitioners who sought his counsel, will never be forgotten by those who were fortunate enough to come in contact with him. Edward G. Janeway never claimed to be a tuberculosis specialist, but there is hardly any one who may aspire to this title who has done more for the tuberculosis cause in general and for the individual patient or pupil, as a teacher, physician, or friend.

Evidence of the deep interest Dr. Janeway showed throughout his life in the tuberculosis problem is shown by a letter the author received from Mrs. Janeway after the death of her husband in acknowledgement of a tribute to him as teacher and physician. After warmly expressing her thanks, she added: "My husband gave a great deal of his time and his wisdom to the prevention and cure of tuberculosis, long before it became such a world-wide question, and it is especially gratifying to me and my children that you have recognized the fact in your tribute. He certainly had the respect and confidence of the best men in his profession and that was the thing he cared the most about."

The bibliography of Dr. Edward G. Janeway follows:

Possible contagion of phthisis.   Arch. of Medicine, viii, 219, 1882.
Danger in error in diagnosis between chronic syphilis and tuberculosis. Tr. Am. Physicians, 1898.
Some notes on the British Congress on Tuberculosis.   Med. News, Feb. 22, 1902.
Address of the president.   Nat. Tuberc. Assn., vi, 19, 1910.

CHAPTER XXXIX

WILLIAM H. WELCH, M.D., LL.D.

PRESIDENT OF THE NATIONAL TUBERCULOSIS ASSOCIATION FROM 1910 TO 1911

WILLIAM H. WELCH, who was president of the National Tuberculosis Association from 1910 to 1911, was born in Norfolk, Conn., April 8, 1850. His father was Dr. William Wickham Welch, his mother Emeline Collins Welch. He graduated from Yale with the degree of A.B. at the age of twenty, and five years later, in 1875, took his degree of M.D. at Columbia University. He served as intern in Bellevue Hospital until 1876, when he went abroad to take post-graduate courses at the universities of Strassburg, Leipzig, Breslau, and Vienna, from 1876 to 1878. On his return he was made professor of pathological anatomy and general pathology at the Bellevue Hospital Medical College, where he established a pathological laboratory and remained until 1884. He then went abroad again to study a year at the universities of Berlin, Munich, and Göttingen, working with Koch and Flügge in bacteriology. With the formation of a nucleus for medical treaching in Johns Hopkins University Dr. Welch became Baxley Professor of Pathology of that institution and pathologist to the Johns Hopkins Hospital, which position he occupied from 1884 to 1916. From 1893 to 1898 he was dean of the medical faculty of Johns Hopkins Medical School. On the creation of the new School of Hygiene and Public Health of the same university in 1916 he was made its director.

The story of how Dr. Welch was called to Baltimore is one which cannot fail to awaken a thrill of pride and patriotism in every American. When Dr. Gilman, who had been placed at the head of Johns Hopkins University, began to look for the right kind of man to fill the chair of pathology he communicated with leading German pathologists, among others with Professor Cohnheim, then at Breslau, and later at Leipzig. "Why do you

341

come to us Germans?" asked Professor Cohnheim. "There is a young American perfectly competent to take that professorship. He is going to be one of the world's greatest authorities in the science of pathology. Why don't you ask him to become the professor at Johns Hopkins?" "Who is he? What is his name?" asked Dr. Gilman's emissary. "His name is William H. Welch, and the world is going to hear of him." President Gilman began negotiations which resulted in securing the services of Dr.Welch for Johns Hopkins, where he has ever since remained.

Professor Welch's brilliant careeɪ may well be illustrated by the honors which have been conferred upon him in this and other countries. He received the honorary degree of M.D. from the University of Pennsylvania; of LL.D. from the Western Reserve University, from Yale, from Harvard, from Toronto, from Columbia, from Jefferson Medical College, from Princeton, from Washington University, and from the University of Chicago. He has been president of the Maryland State Board of Health since 1898; president of the Board of Directors of the Rockefeller Institute for Medical Research since 1901; and trustee of the Carnegie Institution of Washington since 1906. He was Huxley lecturer at the Charing Cross Hospital Medical School in London in 1902, president of the Medical and Chirurgical Faculty of Maryland from 1891 to 1892, president of the Congress of American Physicians and Surgeons in 1897, president of the Association of American Physicians in 1901, of the American Association for the Advancement of Science from 1906 to 1907, of the American Medical Association from 1910 to 1911, of the National Academy of Science from 1913 to 1916, and of the American Social Hygiene Association in 1916. Dr. Welch is a fellow of the Academy of Arts and Sciences and of the College of Physicians of Philadelphia, an Honorary Fellow of the Royal Society of Medicine, and of the Royal Sanitary Institute, London, and honorary member of the Pathological Society of Great Britain and Ireland, foreign associate of the Academy of Medicine, Paris, and of the Royal Academy of Medicine of Belgium, and an honorary member of the medical societies of Berlin and Vienna. He was chairman of the Section on Pathology and Bacteriology of the Sixth International Congress on Tuberculosis. He has been decorated by

WILLIAM H. WELCH

the Emperor of Japan with the Order of the Rising Sun, and was awarded the gold medal of the National Institute of Social Sciences.

Dr. Welch's renown as a hygienist is as great as his fame as a pathologist. He was one of the prime movers in the creation of the National Tuberculosis Association. As already stated in the historical section, he presided over the first meeting, which resulted in the establishment of The National Association for the Study and Prevention of Tuberculosis. It was he, in coöperation with Drs. Osler, Fulton, and others, who was responsible for the first tuberculosis exhibit in this country. Those of us who were privileged to visit that remarkable exposition will recall the inspiring and instructive talks that were given on that occasion by Professor Welch. His interest in the tuberculosis problem has been unabated. He has served not only as president, but has been active as a director and member of the executive committee of the National Tuberculosis Association. His advice is frequently sought by the officers of the Association, whether he happens to be on the board of directors or not.

It is Dr. Welch's unique and marvelous ability to judge the merit of educational enterprises and his keen appreciation of worthy scientific endeavors which have caused his counsel to be sought by philanthropic men and philanthropic organizations prior to making donations to an institution of learning or societies or individuals engaged in scientific research.

.Professor Welch has always taken the greatest interest in all that appertains to public health and public welfare. On more than one occasion his powerful pen has combated the nefarious efforts of well-meaning but ill-advised men and women to curb vivisection for purposes of medical research. He has appeared before legislative bodies and by cogent reasoning has shown that, thanks to the results obtained by scientific vivisection, we have obtained the mastery over some of the most fatal and prevalent infectious diseases. Dr. Welch is an ideal teacher whom those who have been privileged to listen to his lectures on pathology will be able best to appreciate, and is possessed of a charming personality. It is, therefore, no wonder that he is so universally beloved by his colleagues and pupils.

On April 2, 1910, 500 men of reputation in the world of science, literature, and finance, gathered in Baltimore at a banquet in honor of Dr. Welch's twenty-fifth anniversary as professor of pathology at Johns Hopkins. On this most interesting occasion appropriate addresses were made by distinguished men. A gold medallion was presented to Professor Welch as an enduring memorial of the event. On one side is Dr. Welch's portrait in relief, with the words, "William H. Welch," and on the reverse side is a sprig of laurel, intertwined with a spray of roses, emblematic of success and friendship, with the inscription, "From his friends."

Dr. Welch is also well known as a public speaker. Seldom does any great event occur in the medical world of the United States without his voice being heard and eagerly listened to. His interest in medical education, medical research, sanitation, hygiene, and tuberculosis, besides his vast knowledge of pathological science, is shown by his writings, which have been collected and reprinted in three large volumes under the editorship of Dr. Walter C. Burket, who has recently compiled a bibliography dating from 1875 to 1917, comprising no less than 335 contributions. Of these, 32 deal with the subject of tuberculosis.

In the great war a man like Dr. Welch, with vast experience and sound judgment in all things medical, sanitary, and educational, was sure to be called upon to serve his country. He became a member of the Medical Advisory Committee of the American Red Cross, entered the Medical Reserve Corps as Major in 1917, was transferred to active service with the rank of lieutenant colonel, and served as such to the end of the war. He is now commissioned Brigadier General in the Officers' Reserve Corps. When the great prevalence of tuberculosis among the French civilian and military population was made known by Dr. Hermann M. Biggs on his return from France, the author of this sketch wrote a little pamphlet, entitled "What the American Soldier Now Fighting in France Should Know About Tuberculosis," which was translated into French and widely circulated in this country, in Canada, and in France. For this pamphlet Professor Welch contributed a preface, from which the following is quoted:

"Particularly interesting is the suggestion that our soldiers possessed of such knowledge as the pamphlet imparts and trained in habits of cleanly, healthy living may be missionaries of health as well as comrades in arms to their French colleagues.

"Everything possible must be done to protect our soldiers from the risks of tuberculosis, and I believe that the public may be assured that this will be done. Undoubtedly the education of the individual soldier is an important part of these efforts. There is every reason to anticipate that our army will be spared the pitiful experience of the French in this matter of tuberculosis."

Professor Welch's activities as a colonel in the United States Medical Corps, and the fact that a number of our best medical men were joined with him as advisers to the Surgeon General, are doubtless in part responsible for the relatively small morbidity and mortality from general diseases, including tuberculosis, in our own army as compared with those of our allies and the armies of the Central Powers.

The bibliography of Dr. William H. Welch follows:

Zur pathologie des lungenödems. Arch. f. path. Anat., Berlin, lxxii, 375–412, 1878.

Annual address—Modes of infection. Tr. Med. and Chir. Fac., Maryland, 1887, pp. 67–87.

How far may a cow be tuberculous before her milk becomes dangerous as an article of food? Tr. Assn. Am. Phys., iv, 285–286, 1889.

Tuberculosis of the lip. (Discussion.) Bull. Johns Hopkins Hosp., i, 114, 1889–90.

The frequency of the localization of phthisis pulmonalis in the upper lobes. (Discussion.) Tr. Assn. Am. Phys., vi, 52, 1891.

Sanitation in relation to the poor. Address before Charity Organization Society of Baltimore, Nov. 14, 1892.

The treatment of experimental tuberculosis by Koch's tuberculin, Hunter's modifications, and other products of the tubercle bacillus. (Discussion.) Tr. Assn. Am. Phys., vii, 101, 1892.

Eye tuberculosis and anti-tubercular inoculation in the rabbit. (Discussion.) Tr. Assn. Am. Phys., viii, 113–114, 1893.

Pseudo-tuberculosis in animals. Johns Hopkins Hosp. Med. Society, Feb. 4, 1895.

Relations of laboratories to public health. Address before Am. Public Health Assn., Minneapolis, Oct. 31, 1899. Am. Pub. Health Assn. Rep., xxv, 460–465, 1899.

The present system of sanitary reporting with some suggestions for its simplification and improvement. Jour. San. Inst., Lond., p. 722–30, 1902–03.

Theory of pulmonary edema.   In Edema, a Consideration of the Physiologic and Pathologic Factors Concerned in its Formation (Meltzer).   Am. Med., Philad., viii, 195–196, 1904.

Acute miliary tuberculosis, historical note.   Address before meeting of the Laennec Society, Feb. 24, 1904.

The healing of pulmonary tuberculosis, anatomical condition.   Address before meeting of the Laennec Society, Nov. 18, 1904.

Tuberculosis of the kidney.   Pathology.   Address before meeting of the Laennec Society, Dec. 15, 1904.

Report of a commission on certain features of the federal meat-inspection regulations (William H. Welch, chairman).   Rep. Bureau Animal Indust., 1907; Washington, 1909, 361–373.

Address at the fifth annual meeting of the National Association for the Study and Prevention of Tuberculosis, Washington, D. C., May 13, 1909.   Tr. Nat. Tuberc. Assn., v, 34–36, 1909.

Introductory remarks, the Laennec Society, its history and its aims.   Address before meeting of the Laennec Society, Jan. 21, 1909.

The influence of the ingestion of dead tubercle bacilli upon infection.   (Discussion.)   Tr. Assn. Am. Phys., xxiv, 144, 1909.

Tuberculosis of the liver.   (Discussion.)   Bull. Johns Hopkins Hosp., xx, 294, 1909.

Marmorek's serum in the treatment of pulmonary tuberculosis.   (Discussion.)   Bull. Johns Hopkins Hosp., xx, 295, 1909.

The significance of the great frequency of tuberculous infection in early life for prevention of the disease.   Address of the president at the Seventh Annual Meeting of the National Association for the Study and Prevention of Tuberculosis, June 20–21, 1911.   Tr. Nat. Tuberc. Assn., vii, 17–28, 1911.

The influence of Koch and his students.   Address before meeting of the Laennec Society, commemorative of Robert Koch, March 27, 1911.

The duties of a hospital to the public health.   Proc. Nat. Conf. Char., 1915, p. 209–218.

The School of Hygiene and Public Health at the Johns Hopkins University.   Science, New York and Lancaster, Pa., 1916, xliv, 302.

Medical problems of the war.   (Abstr.)   Proc. Johns Hopkins Hosp. Med. Society, Nov. 20, 1916.   Med. Bull. Johns Hopk. Hosp., 1917,154–157.

A treatise on the principles and practice of medicine; designed for the use of practitioners and students of medicine.   (The pathological sections.)   Sixth ed. revised and largely rewritten by the author, assisted by A. Flint and A. Flint, Jr., Lea Bros. & Co., Philadelphia, 1886.

CHAPTER XL

MAZŸCK P. RAVENEL, M.D.

PRESIDENT OF THE NATIONAL TUBERCULOSIS ASSOCIATION FROM 1911 TO 1912

MAZŸCK P. RAVENEL, son of Henry Edmund and Salina E. R. Ravenel, was our seventh president, officiating from 1911 to 1912. He had already served the Asso ciation as vice-president from 1907 to 1908.

Dr. Ravenel was born at Pendleton, S. C. His classical education was obtained at the University of South Carolina, from which he was graduated in 1881. He obtained his medical degree from the Medical College of the state of South Carolina in 1884, and then went to the University of Pennsylvania for post-graduate work, obtaining the Scott fellowship in 1903. He became lecturer on diseases of children to the Charleston Medical School, and later assistant bacteriologist at the University of Pennsylvania. Dr. Ravenel went abroad for further post-graduate work, devoting special attention to the study of bacteriology at the Pasteur Institute of Paris and at the Institute of Hygiene at Halle on the Saale. On his return he became director of the Laboratory of Hygiene at Princeton, and bacteriologist of the Live Stock Sanitary Board of Pennsylvania, which position he held from 1897 to 1907. From 1898 to 1903 he was also lecturer on bacteriology of the Veterinary Department of Pennsylvania. With the founding of the Phipps Institute in 1903 he became assistant medical director and chief of its laboratory. In 1907 Dr. Ravenel was called to the chair of bacteriology of the University of Wisconsin, and a year later became director of the State Hygienic Laboratory. In 1914 he accepted the chair of preventive medicine and of medical bacteriology at the University of Missouri, and was also made director of the Public Health Laboratories.

Dr. Ravenel has enriched our knowledge of bacteriological

science in no small degree. The accompanying bibliography gives evidence of his untiring energy and enthusiasm in his chosen specialty. To him belongs the credit of having first called attention to the importance of tuberculous infection of the digestive tract. He was one of the first to demonstrate beyond any doubt the infection of human beings with the bovine type of the tubercle bacillus. His experiments concerning this important bacteriological discovery were published in 1902 in the Transactions of the Annual Meeting of the Philadelphia Pathological Society.

Many honors were conferred upon Dr. Ravenel by the United States Government, which appointed him as delegate to the various international congresses, such as the one on hygiene, which convened in Berlin in 1908; the International Congress on Alimentary Hygiene in Brussels in 1910; and the International American Congress at Buenos Aires in 1910. Not only the government, but also many scientific societies, honored Dr. Ravenel. Honorary membership was conferred upon him by the Cleveland Academy of Medicine, the Philadelphia Pathological Society, the College of Physicians of Philadelphia, and the Philadelphia Pediatric Society. Besides being a fellow of these associations, Dr. Ravenel was made President of the American Public Health Association in 1920. He is also a member of the American School Hygiene Association, the American Philosophic Society, and the Wisconsin Anti-Tuberculosis Association, of which he is also an ex-president.

It is only natural that a man of Dr. Ravenel's attainments should have offered his services to his country during the world war. Having joined the Medical Reserve Corps in 1910 as a First Lieutenant, he was commissioned Major July 19, 1917, and ordered for training to Fort Riley, where he remained until November, 1917, doing sanitary and some epidemiological work at Camp Funston, assisting the Division Sanitary Inspector of the Eighty-ninth Division. In November, 1917, he was ordered to Roumania, and sailed from San Francisco on December 5. The transport, however, was called back by wireless owing to the Bolshevists' riots and the impossibility of getting through Russia. In June, 1918, he was ordered to Camp Kearney, Cal.,

MAZŸCK P. RAVENEL

where he served as Epidemiologist, Division Sanitary Inspector of the Fortieth Division, and finally as Camp Surgeon, which position he held when the armistice was signed. He was discharged after nineteen months' of service on June 25, 1919, with the rank of Lieutenant Colonel.

The bibliography of Dr. Mazÿck P. Ravenel follows:

Tuberculosis and milk supply. 1897.

Three cases of tuberculosis of the skin following accidental inoculation with bovine tubercle bacillus. 1900.

Dissemination of tubercle bacilli by cows in coughing a source of contagion. 1900.

Case of pneumonomycosis due to aspergillus fumigatus. 1900.

Comparative virulence of tubercle bacilli from human and bovine sources. 1901.

A case of tuberculosis of skin from accidental inoculation with bovine tubercle bacilli. 1902.

Intercommunicability of human and bovine tuberculosis. 1902.

The warfare against tuberculosis. 1903.

The passage of tubercle bacilli through normal intestinal wall. 1903.

Occurrence of tubercle bacilli of exalted virulence in man. 1903.

The influence of bovine tuberculosis on human health. 1904.

The animal tuberculoses and their relation to human health. 1904.

Report on bacillus of tuberculosis in man and in animals. 1905.

Tabes mesenterica due to bovine tuberculosis. 1905.

Studies on agglutination. (With H. R. M. Landis.) Tr. Nat. Tuberc. Assn., i, 140, 1905.

Report on comparative study of various forms of tuberculosis. 1905.

Studies on mixed infection in tuberculosis. (With J. W. Irvin.) Tr. Nat. Tuberc. Assn., i, 231, 1905.

The etiology of tuberculosis. 1907.

Maragliano's method of preparing serum for tuberculosis—also Marmorek's serum. 1907.

Transmission of tuberculosis through milk. 1908.

Aetiologie der tuberkulose. 1908.

Tuberculous infection through the alimentary canal. 1908.

Routes of infection in tuberculosis. 1908.

Mixed infection in tuberculosis. 1908.

Modes and sources of infection in tuberculosis. 1909.

Detection of tubercle bacilli in blood by Rosenberger's method. 1909.

Presence of tubercle bacilli in circulating blood. 1909.

Prevention of tuberculosis in children by guarding milk supply. 1910.

Passage of tubercle bacilli through intestinal wall. 1911.

Control of bovine tuberculosis. Tr. Nat. Tuberc. Assn., vii, 358, 1911.

Address of the president. Tr. Nat. Tuberc. Assn., viii, 19, 1912.

Occurrence of the Widal reaction in tuberculous people.   Tr. Nat. Tuberc.
   Assn., x, 89, 1914.
Control of bovine tuberculosis.   1911.
Bovine tuberculosis.   1914.
Present views in respect to modes and periods of infection in tuberculosis.
   1916.
Modes and periods of infection in tuberculosis.   1917.

CHAPTER XLI

HON. HOMER FOLKS, LL.D.

PRESIDENT OF THE NATIONAL TUBERCULOSIS ASSOCIATION FROM 1912 TO 1913

TRUE to its intention not to be exclusively a medical society, the National Tuberculosis Association, at the meeting in 1912, elected for its eighth president a layman, Mr. Homer Folks, and the choice was indeed a happy one. He had already served the Association as vice-president from 1908 to 1909.

Among the lay members of the society perhaps no one has done more constructive work in the tuberculosis campaign in the United States than Mr. Homer Folks. He was born February 18, 1867, in Hanover, Mich., graduated with the degree of A.B. from Albion College in 1889, and from Harvard with the same degree in 1890. The degree of LL.D. was conferred upon him by Albion College and also by Ohio Wesleyan University in 1911.

Mr. Folks was one of the first of what is now a large group of university men who have chosen the field of social work as a career. In August of 1890 he became General Superintendent of the Children's Aid Society of Pennsylvania, with headquarters in Philadelphia. In February, 1893, he accepted the secretaryship of the New York State Charities Aid Association, an unofficial organization working for the improvement of public charities and public health in New York State. This position he has since held, except during his term of office as Commissioner of Public Charities of New York city, and during his service abroad with the American Red Cross.

As secretary and chief executive officer of this Association, Mr. Folks has taken an active part in organized movements for the improvement of public institutions and the promotion of public health in the city and state of New York since 1893. Among these were the establishment of the Craig Colony for Epileptics,

351

the securing of a constitutional amendment reorganizing the State Board of Charities and giving it power to control the granting of public aid to private charities, the division of the Department of Charities and Correction of New York city into two separate departments, the establishment of a State Hospital for consumptives, the revision of the Charities Chapter of the Greater New York Charter in 1897, the creation of a Children's Court in New York city in 1901, and the reorganization of the State Department of Health in 1914.

He was elected in 1897 a member of the first Municipal Assembly of Greater New York from the twenty-ninth assembly district, on the Citizen's Union ticket, for a term of two years. In the winter of 1899–1900 he was a special agent of the United States Commission to the Paris Exposition, and assisted in securing a comprehensive exhibit on the subject of American Charities.

In April, 1900, at the request of General Leonard Wood, Military Governor of Cuba, Mr. Folks spent six weeks in Cuba studying the public relief of that island. He prepared a Charities Law which was enacted in July, 1900, creating a Cuban Department of Charities, establishing State institutions for destitute and delinquent children and the insane, and a Bureau for Placing Children in Families.

As Commissioner of Public Charities in New York city during the years 1902–1903, in the administration of Major Low, Mr. Folks was in control of hospitals, almshouses, and other institutions containing an average of over 9,000 inmates, having more than 2,000 employees and with an annual expenditure of $2,000,-000. Early in 1902 he organized the first municipal hospital for consumptives in the United States, which developed within two years to a hospital with nearly 500 patients. During these two years the Department was practically reorganized, and was carried on in such a manner as to receive the unanimous commendation of the press and of the public generally.

The State Charities Aid Association, through a special committee, in 1907 began a systematic movement for the prevention of tuberculosis in the state of New York outside of New York city. As Secretary of the Association, Mr. Folks had direct charge and control of what rapidly became the most compre-

HOMER FOLKS

hensive and successful of the state campaigns for the prevention of tuberculosis, resulting in the enactment of a number of important statutes and the establishment, throughout the state, of a series of tuberculosis hospitals and tuberculosis dispensaries, and the employment of a large number of tuberculosis visiting nurses.

Mr. Folks was president of the National Conference of Charities and Correction at the time it met in Boston, in 1911, and was president of the American Association for the Study and Prevention of Infant Mortality in 1915.

One of the by-products of the tuberculosis campaign in the state of New York was the establishment of a special Public Health Commission in 1913, to recommend an entire revision of the public health law. Mr. Folks was secretary of this commission which secured the enactment by the legislature of an entirely new public health law for the state, which has since been copied in substance by a number of other states, including Massachusetts. One of the provisions of the law was for the establishment of a State Public Health Council, with power to enact sanitary regulations having the force of law throughout the state. Mr. Folks was appointed a member of this Council, and has served as such since its establishment.

In July, 1917, Mr. Folks went to France for the American Red Cross and organized and directed its Department of Civil Affairs. In this department were developed bureaus dealing with tuberculosis, child welfare, cripples, relief in the war zone, and relief of refugees through France. Large numbers of physicians, nurses, and trained social workers were secured from America. In less than a year the department had a well-organized staff of 1,400 workers and its expenditures for the relief of French war victims amounted to $4,000,000 per month. At the end of the war Mr. Folks, then a Lieutenant Colonel of the American Red Cross, was asked to make a survey of the condition and needs of the civilian populations of Italy, Greece, Serbia, and Belgium, as well as of France, for the use of the American Red Cross in outlining its further plans for war relief in Europe. He acquitted himself of this difficult task in his usual thorough manner

The tuberculosis and, in fact, the entire public health movement in New York state has had no more valiant and worthy

23

champion than Homer Folks. His creative imagination, his
diplomatic perseverance, and his unswerving integrity make him
one of the foremost leaders in all affairs—civic, social, and political—in the Empire State.

The bibliography of Mr. Homer Folks follows:

Health as an investment.   Tr. Nat. Tuberc. Assn., i, 37, 1905.

With a state sanatorium secured, what next?   Tr. Nat. Tuberc. Assn., iv, 45,
    1908.

A state aroused: Effective control of tuberculosis in small cities and rural com-
    munities.   Proc. Internat. Cong. on Tuberc., Washington, D. C., Sept.
    21 to Oct. 12, 1908.

Conditions in Albany and vicinity in relation to tuberculosis.   Proc. of the
    public meeting on prevention of tuberculosis, Albany, N. Y., January 27,
    1908.

Hope.   A tract on tuberculosis (consumption).   Its nature, cure, and prevention.
    (With John A. Kingsbury.)   Published by State Charities Aid Assn., 1909.

After care of local committees.   A discussion of the functions and problems
    of local committees on the prevention of tuberculosis.   Tr. Nat. Tuberc.
    Assn., v, 100, 1904; also Jour. Outdoor Life, July, 1909.

County hospitals for tuberculosis.   State Charities Aid Assn., 1909.

Address of the vice-president.   Tr. Nat. Tuberc. Assn., v, 21, 1909.

A conference with a purpose and the forecast and prophecy.   Addresses at
    conference of local committees on the prevention of tuberculosis of the
    State Charities Aid Assn., Albany, March 18–19, 1910.

Responsibility of the state in the tuberculosis problem.   Tr. Nat. Tuberc.
    Assn., vii., 44, 1911.

Points of contact between the health officer and the social worker.   Am.
    Jour. Pub. Health, ii, 776–781, 1912.

The present status of the movement for the prevention of tuberculosis in New
    York State.   Jour. Outdoor Life, Sept., 1912.

Some adverse factors of the present year.   Tr. Nat. Tuberc. Assn., ix, 17, 1913.

Address of the president.   Tr. Nat. Tuberc. Assn., ix, 17, 1913.

A seven years' campaign.   Review of measures and statement of results of
    the tuberculosis movement in New York State outside of New York City.
    Address delivered at opening session, State Conference of Tuberculosis
    Workers, Syracuse, N. Y., Nov. 11, 1914.

The next eight years.   Address before N. Y. State Tuberc. Conference and
    North Atlantic States Tuberc. Conference, Albany, N. Y., Nov. 4, 1915.

Interstate factors in the tuberculosis problem.   Tr. Nat. Tuberc. Assn., xii,
    305, 1916.

Tuberculosis associations and relief agencies.   Tr. Nat. Tuberc. Assn., xiii,
    414, 1917.

Experience abroad, showing relationship between tuberculosis and a general
    health program.   Tr. Nat. Tuberc. Assn., xv, 6, 1919.

CHAPTER XLII

JOHN H. LOWMAN, M.D

PRESIDENT OF THE NATIONAL TUBERCULOSIS ASSOCIATION FROM 1913 TO 1914

THE ninth president of the National Tuberculosis Association, who was unanimously chosen at the meeting of 1913, was Dr. John H. Lowman, of Cleveland, O.

John Henry Lowman was born in Cleveland on October 6, 1849, where his ancestors had lived for two generations. His preliminary education was obtained in the public schools of his native city. In 1871 he took the degree of A.B. at Wesleyan University, and in 1874 his Alma Mater conferred upon him the degree of A.M. In 1873 he graduated in medicine at Wooster. The year following Dr. Lowman served as intern in the Cleveland Charity Hospital. In 1875 he obtained the post of house surgeon to the New York Hospital on Blackwell's Island. In 1876 he received a degree of M.D. at Columbia. While there he was instrumental in starting the first nose and throat dispensary in New York. In 1877 he became Professor of Materia Medica and Therapeutics at Western Reserve University, and in 1889 Professor of Medicine, being, during this time, the head of the department. In 1919 he relinquished the professorship of medicine in favor of a full-time professor, and from then until his death he occupied the chair of clinical medicine at the Western Reserve University. Thus Dr. Lowman was a professor at the Medical School of Western Reserve University for forty-two years.

Until 1902 Dr. Lowman's labors were largely confined to the institutional side of medical education, and to the care of his own enormous private practice. In that year he visited the most prominent tuberculosis sanatoria and institutions in Germany and France, and in 1905 attended the International Congress on Tuberculosis held in Paris. Upon his return he conceived the idea of and founded the Anti-tuberculosis League of Cleveland, an association that later became responsible for the development of the municipal department of tuberculosis and the Warrensville Sanatorium. He was most active in the International Tuberculosis Congress held in Washington in 1908.

In "an appreciation" of Dr. Lowman, Dr. Henry J. Gerstenberger writes:

"In the building of the Cleveland Anti-tuberculosis League he again showed his clear conception of the problem and his good judgment of the methods for the solution by drawing together, as members of its board of trustees, representatives of the various groups of society who were already working through well-equipped organizations for the improvement of Cleveland's educational and social conditions, thus accomplishing the very important work of establishing an enduring relationship between these representatives themselves, and of making the local tuberculosis movement from the start a powerful coöperative alliance. The Anti-tuberculosis League of Ohio counted him as one of its founders and he became its first president. . . Owing to his gracious modesty very few people realized how quick he was to seize an opportunity to improve any work in which he was interested and to secure its benefits for his community, nor how willing he was to give liberally of his valuable time and counsel."

The following incident well illustrates what Dr. Gerstenberger says: Toward the end of 1905, on a certain Tuesday, Dr. Lowman learned of the development in Germany of prophylactic tuberculosis clinics for the members of the families, especially for children, of all patients attending the regular tuberculosis clinics. On the following Saturday he caused the first prophylactic family clinic in this country to be opened. It was the same with the further enlargement of the infant welfare activities in Cleveland.

In the narrow margin of time left to him after the performance of his regular professional duties Dr. Lowman lectured before labor unions, schools, church societies, settlements, and wherever he could stir up or create a sound public opinion concerning the combat against tuberculosis.

Dr. Gerstenberger recounts that Italy was for Dr. Lowman always a land of enchantment and delight. It was mainly during a stay in that country as a young man that his inborn interest and appreciation of the esthetic values in life blossomed out in pure adoration and enjoyment of things beautiful and great.

JOHN H. LOWMAN

In 1893 he was destined to be in Rome again as one of the vice-presidents of the International Congress of Medicine there assembled. He went to Italy in September, 1918, to act as Medical Director of the American Red Cross Tuberculosis Unit, and to establish not only a cordial relationship with the Italian physicians, but also an understanding of the purpose of the Commission which would make secure and unhampered the coöperation that is so essential to success in such undertakings. His physical condition, however, undermined by the vicissitudes of the ocean voyage and war-time continental travel, and seriously affected by an attack of influenza contracted soon after reaching Rome, largely prevented him from carrying out his mission. He died in New York city on January 23, 1919.

To quote again from the "Appreciation":

"Dr. Lowman was a man of rare ability and in every sense a gentleman. He was a generous friend, a kindly and sound advisor, and a source of comfort and support to countless others besides the members of his immediate family. When his Samaritan efforts bore fruits he was pleased and grateful, and when they did not, his philosophical mind saw and understood the reasons and his big heart forgave and forgot.

"His modesty hid from view many of his accomplishments. Some 70 sonnets were written by him in work and play. As an essayist he had no equal in the medical profession of Cleveland. His memorial addresses on Gustav C. E. Weber, Edward Fitch Cushing, Dudley P. Allen, and Henry Swift Upson are classics. He was the cultured physician of Cleveland, beloved by many in all walks of life, both rich and poor. The variety of his interests and accomplishments served but to make him more completely and entirely the physician and to develop in him that broader view and deeper understanding of life which made of him so wise a counselor and so sound a diagnostician. In every sense he was a physician of the highest type."

Dr. Lowman was a speaker of no small ability. By the clear way in which he set forth the essentials in popular tuberculosis work, he knew how to hold his audience spell-bound and to show them their duties in the fight against the Great White Plague.

In Cleveland he was probably best known among the general lay public as an expert on tuberculosis. He realized that he had done more than all the rest of the profession in that city to stimulate interest in the fight against this disease, but at the same time he knew that his other activities and the duties of a heavy practice did not give him time for the minute and intensive research work upon this subject which men who are devoting their whole lives exclusively to the study and prevention of tuberculosis are able to do.

The accompanying relatively short list of contributions to the tuberculosis literature does not by any means represent all he has written on the subject nor does it include the many lectures he had carefully prepared and delivered on behalf of the cause. Characteristic of the man's modesty is what Mrs. Lowman wrote when the author asked her kind assistance to complete the biography: "Dr. Lowman did not feel that he had written anything in the real sense of the word, and he always looked forward with the keenest anticipation to the time when he could withdraw from his overbusy life and spend a few years in contemplation and study." In sending this short list of contributions and apologizing for the delay, Mrs. Lowman added:

"However, I do think also that half unconsciously I have been influenced by a feeling that Dr. Lowman would not have called these fragmentary bits of work writing, in any real sense, nor a true indication of his feeling in the matter. About seventeen or eighteen years ago, when he was trying to stir up a more effective and general interest in Ohio in the combat against tuberculosis, he gave a great many talks and lectures before colleges, schools, church societies, settlements, labor unions, and factory operatives. I have some of these addresses in type-written form. He put a vast amount of energy and earnestness into informing the general public concerning their duties and responsibilities in regard to this common enemy, and he succeeded in arousing the kind of interest which caused people to go to work at the problem and to persist in their endeavors."

All the charming qualities and fine traits of mind and heart, so well described by Dr. Gerstenberger, will long be remembered by all his co-workers of the National Tuberculosis Association who had the privilege of knowing Dr. Lowman intimately, and his memory will be cherished by all his friends and countless patients. Dr. Livingston Farrand, who was the executive secretary of the National Tuberculosis Association for nine years, and who is now president of Cornell University, speaks of Dr. Lowman as "one of the best and finest men that the medical profession of America has known," and goes on to say of him, "Of all the many physicians with whom I have been associated in the last fifteen years, I know of no one toward whom I felt the same sense of personal attachment, as well as of high admiration."

Dr. Lowman's death was typical of his life. He made the supreme sacrifice as surely as any American soldier on the battle-fields of Flanders or in France. When he was called to direct the anti-tuberculosis work in Italy under the auspices of the American Red Cross, he knew the risk he was taking, but he answered the call. He returned in broken health and lived but a short time thereafter.

Former Secretary of War, the Hon. Newton D. Baker, speaks of Dr. Lowman's passing away in the following impressive words: "When the world's great test came, he could not help sacrificing himself to minister to the stricken and suffering. Surely he died a soldier's death after living, in the best sense of the words, a physician's life."

The bibliography of Dr. John H. Lowman follows:

Account of the general sanitary condition of Cleveland, Ohio. Nat. Board Health Bull., 1879–80, i, 258.

A study of fever. Ohio Med. Jour., 1881–2, i, 159–166.

The conflict with tuberculosis. Cleveland Med. Jour., 1902, 485–96.

The anti-tuberculosis dispensary. Cleveland Med. Jour., 1903, 404–14.

Tuberculosis and the sanatorium. Columbus Med. Jour., 1903, 145–167.

An ideal sanatorium with notes on the black forest. Cleveland Med. Jour., 1903, ii, 18–27.

The opening of the tuberculosis dispensary in Cleveland. Cleveland Med. Jour., 1904, iii, 488–93.

The anti-tuberculosis movement in Cleveland. Cleveland Med. Jour., 1905 iv, 205–212.

Schools and tuberculosis. Tr. Nat. Tuberc. Assn., iii, 107, 1907.

The care of healthy children in tuberculous families. Tr. Int. Cong. on Tuberc., 1905, ii, 200.

The Paris Congress of Tuberculosis, 1905. Cleveland Med. Jour., 1906, v, 1–20.

Tuberculosis and the Schools, Charities, New York, 1907, 657–662.

Address of the President. Tr. Nat. Tuberc. Assn., x, 17, 1914.

CHAPTER XLIII

GEORGE M. KOBER, M.D., LL.D

PRESIDENT OF THE NATIONAL TUBERCULOSIS ASSOCIATION FROM 1914 TO 1915

D R. GEORGE M. KOBER served as president of the National Tuberculosis Association during the year 1914–1915 and presided over the very interesting meeting of that year in Seattle.

George Martin Kober, son of Jacob and Dorothea Behr Kober, was born at Alsfeld, Hessen-Darmstadt, Germany, March 28, 1850. He was educated at the public and grand-ducal "Realschule" of his native town. His father was a revolutionist in 1848, and had made a vow that none of his sons should serve under a German king or any prince or potentate. His oldest son emigrated in 1854 and served in the United States Cavalry on the frontiers of Kansas, New Mexico, and Utah, and subsequently throughout the Civil War. In April, 1867, the younger brother George came to the United States, securing an assignment to the Hospital Corps at Carlisle Barracks, Pa., and commencing his medical studies under Surgeon Joseph J. B. Wright, of the United States Army. In January, 1870, he was appointed hospital steward and was ordered to Frankford arsenal near Philadelphia, where he continued his studies under Dr. Robert B. Burns until October, 1871, when he was ordered to duty in the Surgeon General's office, Washington, D. C. He entered the medical department of Georgetown University the same year, following up his studies in addition to the regular courses under the instruction of his preceptors, Drs. Johnson Eliot and Robert Reyburn, and was graduated in March, 1873. In the following winter he was the first graduate of a post-graduate course inaugurated by Drs. Thompson, Busey, Ashford, and others, at the Columbia Hospital, Washington, D. C.

In July, 1874, Dr. Kober was appointed acting assistant sur-

GEORGE M. KOBER

geon, United States Army, and was post surgeon at Alcatraz Island, Cal., from July to November, 1874; post surgeon at Fort McDermit, Nev., from November, 1874, to July, 1877. In the fall of 1875 he served with the First United States Cavalry in the Southeastern Nevada expedition against hostile Indians, and in 1877 he served in the Nez-Perces War, and was in charge of the field hospital at Kamiah on the Clearwater, Idaho, from July to October, 1877. He was post surgeon at a camp near Spokane Falls, Wash., and at Fort Coeur d'Alene, Idaho, to November, 1879; Fort Klamath, Oregon, to June, 1880; and post surgeon at Fort Bidwell, Cal., to November, 1886. While in this station he was engaged in a large practice among the civilians, and continued there, after severing his connection with the army until June, 1887, when he traveled extensively in America and Europe, returning to Fort Bidwell the following year.

In the fall of 1888 Dr. Kober returned to Washington, D. C., with a view to devoting his time to college, hospital, and literary work. In 1889 he was appointed professor of hygiene and state medicine in Georgetown Medical School. During the winter of 1889–90 he directed attention to the sewage pollution of the Potomac River water, as an important factor in the undue prevalence of typhoid fever in Washington. In August, 1890, he was a member of the Tenth International Medical Congress, held in Berlin, and there read a paper on the Etiology of Typhoid Fever, with special reference to water-borne epidemics, and was appointed honorary secretary of the section of medical geography, history, etc. In December, 1890, his California investments necessitated his return to Bidwell, where he engaged in the practice of his profession, and for a year or more was again attending surgeon at the post.

In the fall of 1893 Dr. Kober returned to Washington, resumed his professional work at the Georgetown Medical School, and became deeply engaged in the health and housing problems of the city and its social and industrial betterment. In 1895, at the request of the Health Officer, he investigated the causes of typhoid fever in Washington, and in his report pointed out for the first time the agency of flies in the transmission of the disease. His public addresses on the relation of water-supply and sewers to the health of the city, as well as his researches into the relative merits of slow sand and mechanical filtration, aided materially toward securing the necessary sanitary legislation and requisite appropriations by Congress.

Dr. Kober is an honorary member of the Association of Military Surgeons of the United States and of the Association of American Physicians.   He is a fellow of the American Medical Association, the American Public Health Association, and the Anthropological Society; also a member of the board of directors of the Associated Charities of Washington, D. C., and of the local tuberculosis society.   He designed the Tuberculösis Hospital of the District of Columbia in Washington, which was formally opened in June, 1908.   Dr. Kober's affiliations with scientific and philanthropic societies are too numerous to mention here, as are also his achievements in experimental medicine, industrial and general hygiene, medical education, and anthropological investigations.   He is the author of no less than 110 monographs, chapters, and text-books, journal articles and reviews on medical, surgical, and sociological subjects.   Dr. Kober's tabulation of 330 milk-borne epidemics, his monograph on "Milk in Relation to Public Health," and his first book on "Industrial Hygiene," published as Senate Documents, are regarded as pioneer contributions to American medical literature. In 1916, in collaboration with Dr. Hansen, he published a volume of nearly 1,000 pages, entitled, "Diseases of Occupation and Vocational Hygiene," which is recognized as one of the foremost works on this subject.

At the annual meeting of the National Tuberculosis Association at St. Louis in 1920, a new honor was conferred upon Dr. Kober by his unanimous election to the office of secretary of the Association, succeeding Dr. Henry Barton Jacobs, who had served the Association in this capacity since its formation in 1904.

On March 28, 1920, Dr. Kober attained his seventieth birthday.   This was made the occasion of a complimentary dinner to him by his countless friends all over the United States.   The dinner was held under the auspices of the Medical Society of the District of Columbia and allied scientific and civic organizations. It was the privilege of the author of this sketch to present for that occasion the following tribute, which sets forth in a concise way the great achievements of Dr. Kober:

To GEORGE M. KOBER, M.D., LL.D.,

Soldier, Scientist, Physician, and Philanthropist,

On His Seventieth Birthday, March 28, 1920.

Your cradle stood on foreign soil,
But love of liberty was your inheritance;
Your father was of those who suffered long
From persecution and from tyranny.
He vowed that you should never be
The simple minion of a lord of war,
Bowing to king and potentate;
But if a soldier you should wish to be,
You then should serve in freedom's holy cause.
So you came here and cordial greeting found,
For men like you Columbia gladly welcomes;
And you repaid her well.
You served her first as humble helper
To sick and wounded heroes of the war.
A faithful student of our noble art you next became,
And soon attained a magister's degree.
As soldier and physician you combined
True bravery with sympathy of heart, and thus
Became the friend of many a suffering soul;
And when to former comrades in the field you bade adieu,
All said, "Well done, God speed you on your way."
A life of great devotion then began,
To civic welfare, art, and science given;
Your earnest studies fitted you to teach
To show the younger men what hygiene means,
And prove prevention of disease surpasses cure.
By your endeavors, plagues and water-borne disease
Were banished from within your city fair;
You found the reason why so many died
Of that disease of all diseases;
And better housing of the poor became your passion.
Now sanitary homes for black and white
Arose where once was wilderness.
Next to housing of the laboring men
You studied how to make his occupation safe
And thus prevent disease among the workers.
So manifold your triumphs were
In battling with disease and death,

In this small space I cannot count them all,
And in your modesty you will not tell
What greater things you did for God and man.
Throughout your long and earnest life
Your greatest joy has been to work,
But never for yourself.   To serve,
To help wherever there was greatest need
Was your ideal, the motive of your life.
So then be thanked on this your honor day,
For inspiration and example you have given
To pupils and to friends,
For countless deeds of mercy and of good
You gave to others.
Now may reward of peace and happiness
Be yours for many years to come,
And may no cloud of sorrow cast a shadow
On the evening of your life.

The bibliography of Dr. George M. Kober follows:

The etiology and prevention of tuberculosis.   Report of Board of Health of Calif., xi, Sacramento, 1890.

A plea for the prevention of tuberculosis.   Proc. State Sanitary Convention, Sacramento, 1894.

Morbific and infectious milk.   Pub. Health Rep., Feb. 14, 1896.

Milk in relation to health and disease.   Biannual Health Report of California, Sacramento, 1896.

Milk in relation to public health.   Senate Document No. 441, 59th Congress, Govt. Printing Office, 1902.

The transmission of bovine tuberculosis by milk.   Tr. Assn. of Am. Phys., 1903.

The prevention and treatment of tuberculosis by state methods.   Pan-Am. Med. Congress, Panama, 1906, ii, 249–258.

The tuberculosis hospital in Washington, D. C., designed by George M. Kober, 8 plates.   Published by Board of Charities, D. C., 1908.

Unterbringung von schwerkranken Schwindsüchtigen und der luftkur bedürftigen leichtkranken Tuberkulosen in einem und demselben Krankenhaus. XIV. Intern. Kongr. f. Hygiene u. Demographie, Berlin, 1907, bd. iv, 432.

The fight against tuberculosis in various countries.   Opening discussion, 6th Internat. Congr. on Tuberc., Washington, D. C., 1908, vol. iv, part I, p. 105–110.

Tuberculosis;   report of committee on social betterment of the President's Homes Commission.   Senate Document No. 644.   60th Congress, 2nd Session, Jan. 8, 1909.

The influence of sewers and general sanitation upon the prevalence of tuberculosis.   Bull. Johns Hopkins Hosp., vol. xx, March, 1909.

The general movement of typhoid fever and tuberculosis in the last thirty years. Jour. Med. Sciences, Nov., 1909.

Discussion of dispensary tuberculosis work. Washington Med. Annals. p. 370–371, Jan., 1910.

Tuberculosis as a disease of the masses. Lecture before the School of Health Officers. Bull. Vermont State Board of Health, 1912, no. 1.

Tuberculosis with special reference to its prevention. Address of the president. Tr. Nat. Tuberc. Assn., xi, 17–26, 1915.

The child and the home. Nat. Tuberc. Assn., xi, 41–45, 1915.

Tuberculosis with special reference to its epidemiology, transmissibility and prevention. Pub. Health Rep., Oct. 29, 1915.

Avoid house dust. Washington Health Rules, 1915.

Occupation in relation to tuberculosis. Tr. College of Phys., Philadelphia, 1919; Pub. Health Rep., March 26, 1920.

Diseases of occupation and vocational hygiene (Kober and Hanson), 918 pp. Blakiston's Son & Co. 1916.

CHAPTER XLIV

THEODORE B. SACHS, M.D.

PRESIDENT OF THE NATIONAL TUBERCULOSIS ASSOCIATION FROM 1915 TO APRIL, 1916

THEODORE B. SACHS was elected president of the National Tuberculosis Association at the Eleventh Annual Meeting held in Seattle, Washington, in June, 1915. But his tragic death on April 2, 1916 prevented his serving his full term. He had already served the Association as vice-president from 1913 to 1914.

Born in Dinaberg, Russia, May 2, 1868, the son of Bernard and Sophie Sachs, he was graduated from the Kherson high school and later, in 1891, received his degree in law from the Imperial New Russian University of Odessa. While at the University, he reported for military duty and was placed on the reserve list in 1887. His removal to America in 1891 was doubtless prompted by a winter's exile, imposed upon him and several fellow-students because of their participation in a debate which did not meet with the approval of the local authorities.

After his arrival in this country Dr. Sachs determined to study medicine, and gave up his legal career to enter the Medical Department of the University of Illinois, from which he graduated in 1895. After two years of work as an intern in the Michael Reese Hospital, he entered general practice, devoting himself particularly to diseases of the lungs. In 1901 Dr. Sachs was appointed instructor in internal medicine at his alma mater, and in 1903 he was appointed attending physician to Cook County Hospital. Even in the earlier days of his medical career, as a struggling young practitioner endeavoring to gain a foothold, he saw how conditions were with reference to tuberculosis in Chicago at that time, and he could not refrain from doing something to help. At no little sacrifice and expense, he personally made an

366

THEODORE B. SACHS

investigation of the prevalence of tuberculosis in some of the crowded quarters of the city, particularly in the districts where the Jewish population was in evidence. These studies, among the first of their kind, gave Dr. Sachs considerable prominence at the International Congress on Tuberculosis in 1908, and won for him special honorable mention from the jury of awards.

Dr. Sachs was greatly interested in the Chicago Tuberculosis Institute, which he helped to call into life, and of which he remained one of the most active and representative workers. He served as president of the Institute from January, 1913, until his death. He was one of the most ardent advocates of the routine examinations of employees of large establishments. His advice and example in this respect have since been followed by many corporations and large business concerns throughout the country. It was largely due to Dr. Sachs' influence that Mrs. Keith Spalding donated the funds for the Edward Sanatorium at Naperville, of which institution he became the director and physician in chief. Besides his activities in the Edward Sanatorium he was attached to the Chicago Winfield Sanatorium, the West Side Dispensary, and the Chicago Municipal Sanitarium. Concerning his interest in the latter, Dr. Philip P. Jacobs says:

"Of all the many activities in which he engaged, however, none claimed so large a share of Dr. Sachs' personality and skill as the Chicago Municipal Tuberculosis Sanitarium. In a very real sense the Sanitarium was and is Dr. Sachs. It breathes his personality and his genius from almost every ward and brick. Into it he put his very body and soul. He was active in the passage of the Glackin Law, which made the sanatorium possible. He was a prime mover in the monstrous referendum campaign when hundreds of thousands of people voted 'yes' for the municipal sanatorium. He was the chairman of the Building Committee which secured the site and conceived the sanatorium long before a brick or a stone had been laid, putting into this effort thousands of dollars' worth of time and sacrifice, and countless miles of travel to visit the best institutions that the world provided. Later he became president of the board and its chief administrative director. While the sanatorium was in construction he spent hours daily at no little sacrifice to his practice, and gave of himself unstintedly to see that the people of Chicago should have an institution which would be both of service for the purpose for which it was constructed and which would not squander one dollar of the people's money."

In the spring of 1915 a new administration came into office in the city of Chicago, which, it was universally admitted at the time, was responsible for Dr. Sachs' untimely death. He had made the Chicago Municipal Sanitarium an ideal institution, but the Thompson administration refused to reappoint him until practically forced to do so by the people of Chicago. Politics finally gained the upper hand, however, and Dr. Sachs was forced to resign; but even after his resignation nefarious politics made life a burden for this brave pioneer who had unselfishly devoted the best years of his life to the welfare of the consumptive poor of the great city of Chicago.

In an article entitled "The Civic Martyrdom of Dr. Sachs," Dr. Graham Taylor, the distinguished social worker, says:

"No altar of civic patriotism ever held a more loyal offering than that on which Dr. Theodore B. Sachs sacrificed himself in life and death to save Chicago's Municipal Tuberculosis Sanitarium from ruthless partisan spoilsmen. In truth, many altars and offerings seemed to unite in that one costly sacrifice. Such supreme devotion to a cause as the Jewish religious spirit can beget, such self-sacrifice as the Russian oppression of the Jew incites, such idealism as only the Orient inspires, such sensitivity as the heritage of suffering weaves into the very texture of the soul, such humanitarian achievements as are possible only in America—all combined to make the achieving life and the tragic death of Dr. Sachs profoundly impressive."

As the accompanying bibliography of Dr. Sachs indicates, his achievements as a clinician and specialist in tuberculosis are equal to his attainments as a propagandist and administrator. He founded the Robert Koch Society for the Study of Tuberculosis, and read before that body a number of interesting and valuable papers on the various phases of tuberculosis science. A few months before his death (February, 1916) he was elected a fellow of the Institute of Medicine in Chicago. His devotion to high ideals, his passionate love for humanity, his integrity and faithfulness to all things which he undertook, are best shown in a passage from his letter of resignation from the Municipal Sanitarium Board, wherein he said:

"My service to the Sanitarium during the last six years has been prompted by the earnest desire to give the best in me to this community in which I have resided during the last twenty-seven years. .   I have refused to betray the community that has given me confidence. I have great faith in the city

MONUMENT TO THEODORE B. SACHS

of Chicago and its citizens. I have passed through ten months of continuous nightmare in trying to avert the politicalization of a great institution. But I find it impossible to continue. Single-handed at present I cannot fight a big political machine."

In this connection the following copy of a letter which Dr. Sachs received from his patients at the Edward Sanatorium a few months before his death is significant:

"We the undersigned patients of the Edward Sanatorium wish to take this privilege of expressing our admiration for the stand you have taken in regard to politics in connection with the Municipal Sanitarium of Chicago—your untiring and unselfish interest in humanity. None of the grossly unjust criticisms of you by anyone who does not know you or your methods will have the slightest influence on us who have implicit confidence in your ability as a practitioner and as a man. The past records of a man who possesses your international reputation cannot be easily tossed aside."

The end came at the sanatorium of the Chicago Tuberculosis Institute in the quiet little town of Naperville. There, after his day's work in town, he sought rest all alone in the quiet of the library. And there they found him the next morning, at peace in his last sleep, which he had himself induced.

The National Tuberculosis Association, at its meeting in May, 1916, at which Dr. Sachs should have presided, passed appropriate resolutions which are incorporated in the minutes of the meeting of 1916. (See p. 218.)

The body of Dr. Sachs was interred on the grounds of the Naperville Sanatorium, and on the memorial tablet indicating the site, of which we give herewith an illustration, we read the following impressive words by the great blind physician, Dr. Robert H. Babcock, who had never seen Theodore B. Sachs, but whose spiritual insight must have been more keen than many a seeing physical eye:

"In Memory of DR. THEODORE B. SACHS, whose life was spent in disinterested efforts to relieve the condition of the unfortunate, never indifferent to the distress of others, he labored unselfishly and untiringly in their behalf, and this Sanatorium in which ground he sleeps is a monument to his unusual greatness of heart and singleness of purpose. He loved his neighbor as himself and was in truth a good Samaritan."

24

Over the portals of that other monument to Sachs' genius, the Municipal Sanitarium, which had become a part of his very life, are to be placed the following words: "Conceived in boundless love of humanity and made possible by years of toil."

The bibliography of Dr. Theodore B. Sachs follows:

Tuberculosis in the Jewish district of Chicago.   Jour. Am. Med. Assn., Aug. 6, 1904.
A plea for the poor consumptives.   Reform Advocate, Oct. 29, 1904.
The mission of local sanatoria in the crusade against tuberculosis.   Jewish Exponent, May 25, 1906.
Local sanatoriums and tuberculosis.   Charities and the Commons, May 26, 1906.
The tuberculosis nurse.   Am. Jour. Nursing, May, 1908.
Some observations on the ophthalmo-tuberculin reaction.   Med. Rec., May 30, 1908.
Children of the tuberculous.   Tr. Nat. Tuberc. Assn., iv, 283, 1908; also in Jour. Am. Med. Assn., Oct. 24, 1908.
A ten year fight against tuberculosis in the Jewish districts of Chicago.   Reform Advocate, Jan. 30, 1909.
The diagnostic value of local tuberculin reactions.   Tr. Nat. Tuberc. Assn., vi, 203, 1910; also Jour. Am. Med. Assn., Jan. 21, 1911.
Care of advanced consumptives.   Survey, June 17, 1911.
Examination of employees for tuberculosis.   Survey, Oct. 21, 1911.
When is a case of tuberculosis curable?   Time required for cure and subsequent precautions to be observed.   Illinois Med. Jour., Dec., 1911.
Examination of employes for tuberculosis.   Tr. Nat. Tuberc. Assn., viii, 157, 1912.
Superintending health of employes.   The Survey, Oct. 11, 1913.
Campaign in Chicago for medical examination of employes.   Tr. Nat. Tuberc. Assn., x, 35, 1914.
Official responsibility of the city in the tuberculosis problem.   Tr. Nat. Tuberc. Assn., xi, 278, 1915.
Artificial pneumothorax in the treatment of pulmonary tuberculosis.   Tr. Nat. Tuberc. Assn., xi, 150, 1915; also Jour. Am. Med. Assn., Nov. 27, 1915.

CHAPTER XLV

EDWARD R. BALDWIN, M.D.

PRESIDENT OF THE NATIONAL TUBERCULOSIS ASSOCIATION FROM 1916 TO 1917

AFTER the sudden death of Theodore B. Sachs, Edward R. Baldwin, the vice-president for the year 1915–1916, assumed the function of president until the next election, which was held at the regular meeting at Washington, D. C., May 11 and 12, 1916, at which time he was elected president of the National Tuberculosis Association for the ensuing year. He had already served the Association as vice-president from 1912 to 1913 and 1915 to 1916.

Dr. Baldwin comes from an old New England stock, being the son of the Rev. Elijah C. and Frances M. Hutchinson Baldwin. He was born in Bethel, Conn., September 8, 1864, and attended the New Haven high school from 1878 to 1882. His parents destined their son for the clerical profession, wishing him to be some day a congregational minister like his father. Edward, however, did not take kindly to the career of a clergyman. In spite of his father's illness and early breakdown, and consequently impaired finances, young Baldwin started out early in life to work his way through Yale Medical school, from which he graduated in 1890. This struggle and hard work had, however, impaired the young man's constitution, which was at best not any too strong. While serving in the Hartford City Hospital as intern he developed symptoms of tuberculosis, which were not fully recognized. After leaving the hospital he entered general practice in the office of his maternal grandfather, who had been deceased for some years, but who had been a well-known physician in the Connecticut Valley. Dr. Edward R. Baldwin remained one year in the town of Cromwell in general practice, which was a very valuable experience and an excellent preparation for the future specialist. But after six months of practice symptoms of tuberculosis again made their appearance, and at the completion of a year Dr. Baldwin decided to go to Saranac Lake and place himself under the care of Dr. Trudeau, where he became his assistant and his close associate.

The entrance of Dr. Baldwin into the Trudeau Sanatorium meant so much both to Dr. Trudeau and Dr. Baldwin, to medical science and the tuberculosis movement in this country and throughout the civilized world, that it is of historic interest to quote here what Edward L. Trudeau has to say in his autobiography concerning this episode:

"In December, 1892, a slender and pale young man rang my door-bell one morning and told me he was a doctor, had contracted tuberculosis, and wanted to go to the Sanitarium. Little did I know then how much the coming of this strange young man would mean to me personally, to my work, to Saranac Lake, and to the world at large! He told me his name was Edward R. Baldwin, that he was from New Haven; and when I asked what made him think he had tuberculosis, he quite floored me by his answer: that he had used his microscope and knew he had it. Truly Koch's teaching was beginning to bring practical results. I admitted him to the Sanitarium.

"Through many long years of friendly fellowship, through many long years of work side by side, through many long years of physical misery and suffering, my debt to Dr. Baldwin has steadily grown, until it has become a debt which I can never hope to·repay but by affection and gratitude; a coin in which many debts, I find, are paid to him, because it is a coin he cannot possibly refuse to accept. Riches, fame, and praise he scorns, but he cannot escape the heritage of affection and gratitude he so unconsciously and abundantly calls forth."

Dr. Baldwin took a deep interest in the laboratory work and Dr. Trudeau affectionately writes of this:

"Dr. Baldwin in those days, of course, knew even less than I did about the new science of bacteriology, and I gladly taught him all I knew; and as gladly does he teach me now the latest advances in a branch of medical science in which he is an expert and an acknowledged authority. Many happy hours did we spend working in the laboratory together; and now that I cannot work with him any more, he brings to my bedside the latest literature, and tells me of the work he and the others are doing. . Until Dr. Baldwin's arrival in Saranac Lake I had had no one to discuss my work with, and I had no help of any kind but the manual assistance of a poor Irish patient of mine."

With Dr. Trudeau's illness and ultimate death Dr. Baldwin proved himself a worthy successor to the great physician. Al-

EDWARD R. BALDWIN

though apparently a laboratory man, as the many invaluable contributions in the accompanying bibliography would indicate, as a patient in the sanatorium and as assistant physician under Dr. Irving H. Hance, and also as examining physician in the sanatorium, he had acquired the knowledge of an expert clinician, and his fame as such rose rapidly. He is now vice-president of the Trudeau Sanatorium, and director of the Edward L. Trudeau Foundation and Trudeau School of Tuberculosis. The Saranac Lake Reception Hospital, which was established through the efforts of Dr. Trudeau, has been under the management and the direction of Dr. Baldwin from its beginning. The Vermont State Sanatorium, which was built by the Proctor family, as well as the Gaylord Farm Sanatorium at Wallingford, Conn., are both indebted to Dr. Baldwin for his great interest in helping to call these institutions into life. The General Hospital in Saranac Lake was also promoted largely through Dr. Baldwin's efforts.

Dr. Baldwin has an enviable war record. On May 5, 1917, he was appointed a member of the subcommittee on tuberculosis of the General Medical Board of the Council of National Defense. He was Chairman of the Medical Advisory Board No. 32 of his district during the selective service examination, and served as a Four-Minute Man in the speech-making campaigns for all the different purposes for which this form of publicity was used. During the month of January, 1918, he served as contract surgeon on the tuberculosis examining board, as referee at Camp Devens, and as a member of the executive committee of the National Tuberculosis Association he was most active in the work of that organization. In 1919 he was invited to join the Inter-Allied Red Cross Medical Conference at Cannes.

The two presidential addresses of Dr. Baldwin are to be found on page 19 of the Association's Transactions of 1916, and on page 23 of the Transactions for 1917.

The bibliography of Dr. Edward R. Baldwin follows:

The effects of peppermint inhalation on experimental tuberculosis. N. Y. Med. Jour., lxi, 623, 1895.

A chemical and experimental research on "antiphthisin" (Klebs), (with E. L. Trudeau). Med. Rec., xlviii, 871, 1895.

The need of an improved technique in the manufacture of Koch's T. R. (with E. L. Trudeau). Med. News, lxxi, 257, 1897.

Infection from the hands in pulmonary phthisis. Phila. Med. Jour., Dec. 3, 1898.

Experimental studies on the preparation and effects of antitoxins for tuberculosis (with E. L. Trudeau). Am. Jour. Med. Sc., Dec., 1898, and Jan., 1899.

A case of lymphatic leucæmia combined with pulmonary tuberculosis (with J. A. Wilder). Am. Jour. Med. Sc., June, 1899.

The conditions of tuberculosis infection and their control. Yale Med. Jour., March, 1900.

Some results of the climatic and sanatorium treatment of tuberculosis in the Adirondacks. Albany Med. Ann., xxi, 213, 1900.

Recent work on tuberculosis. Proc. 28th Annual Meeting Am. Pub. Health Assn., Oct. 22–26, 1900.

Bacteriology in health and disease. Bacterio-therapeutics with especial reference to tuberculosis. Tr. Cong. Am. Phys. and Surg., v, 1900.

The action of proteolytic enzymes on bacterial toxines (with P. A. Levene). Jour. Med. Research, vi, 120, 1901.

The selection of favorable cases of pulmonary tuberculosis for sanatorium treatment. Internat. Clin., iii, 11th series, 1901.

The tuberculous patient—when and to what extent shall his liberty be limited? Med. Rev. of Rev., Jan., 1903.

The rational application and value of specific treatment for tuberculosis. Jour. Am. Med. Assn., Nov. 26, 1904.

Studies on the tuberculin reaction (with E. L. Trudeau and H. M. Kinghorn). Studies from the Saranac Laboratory, 1900–1904.

On the anti-hemolytic action of some cell and tissue constituents (with P. A. Levene). Studies from the Saranac Laboratory, 1900–1904.

Studies on tuberculosis serum and bacteriolysis of bacillus tuberculosis. Studies from the Saranac Laboratory, 1900–1904.

Anti-tuberculin or tuberculin precipitin serums. Studies from the Saranac Laboratory, 1900–1904.

Differences in precipitins produced by tubercle bacilli. Studies from the Saranac Laboratory, 1900–1904.

Studies on immunity in tuberculosis: the properties of the serum of immunized rabbits (with H. M. Kinghorn and A. H. Allen). Tr. Nat. Tuberc. Assn., i, 143, 1905; also Med. News, Sept. 30, 1905.

Studies on immunity in tuberculosis, III: Experiments with leucocytes, lymph glands and bone marrow extracts of immunized animals (with J. Woods Price). Tr. Nat. Tuberc. Assn., ii, 281, 1906.

Die "Aggressine" der Tuberkelbazillen (with J. Woods Price). Centralbl. f Bak., Parasit. u. Infekt. Krankhtn., I. Anteil, 1906, Nr. 24–25.

The mechanism of resistance to tuberculosis. Proc. Pathol. Soc., Phila., 1907. new series, ix, 7.

Opsonins in tuberculosis. Tr. Assn. Am. Phys., 1907.

Review of theoretical considerations and experimental works relative to opsonins with observations at the Saranac Laboratory. N. Y. Med. Jour., June 27, 1908.

Conclusions from 1097 conjunctival tuberculin tests by a uniform method. Tr. Internat. Cong. on Tuberc., 1908.

The problem of immunity in tuberculosis. Tr. Internat. Cong. on Tuberc., 1908.

Hypersusceptibility to tuberculin in tuberculosis; its physiological and clinical importance. 1908.

General principles of tuberculin diagnosis and treatment. 1908.

Ophthalmo-tuberculin diagnostic test. Jour. Am. Med. Assn., xlix, 1969, 1909.

Progress and changes in the treatment of tuberculosis during the past twenty years.

Investigations into the nature of tuberculin sensitiveness. Tr. Nat. Tuberc. Assn., vii, 351, 1911.

Diagnostic use of tuberculin. Tr. Nat. Tuberc. Assn., viii, 345, 1912.

Allergy and reinfection in tuberculosis. Bull. Johns Hopkins Hosp., July, 1913.

Tuberculin treatment, address before N. Y. State Med. Soc., Rochester, 1913.

Some new biological relations between tubercle bacilli and other acid-fast forms (with Allen K. Krause). Tr. Nat. Tuberc. Assn., ix, 334, 1913

Experimental studies on the blood-serum of cows immunized against tuberculosis: "sensitization" of living tubercle bacilli. Arch. Int. Med., May, 1914.

Immunity in tuberculosis: with special reference to racial and clinical manifestations. Harvey Lecture. Am. Jour. Med. Sc., June, 1915.

An address: delivered on the occasion of the second commencement of the D. Ogden Mills Training School for Nurses, Trudeau, N. Y. 1915.

The consumptive and his neighbor. Survey, July 22, 1916.

Address of the president. Tr. Nat. Tuberc. Assn., xii, 19, 1916.

The advantages of special training in tuberculosis in sanatorium surroundings. Tr. Am. Clim. and Clin. Assn., 1916.

Therapy as related to the immunology of tuberculosis. N. Y. Med. Jour., March 18, 1916.

Address of the president. Tr. Nat. Tuberc. Assn., xii, 19, 1916.

Address of the president. Tr. Nat. Tuberc. Assn., xiii, 25, 1917.

Latent tuberculosis: its importance in military preparation. Cleveland Med. Jour., June, 1917.

Address of the president. Tr. Nat. Tuberc. Assn., xiii, 25, 1917.

Research problems in tuberculosis. Boston Med. and Surg. Jour., Jan., 1918.

Tuberculin in 1917. Therap. Gaz., March 15, 1918.

Experimental arrested tuberculosis and subsequent infections (abstract). Tr. Nat. Tuberc. Assn., xiv, 364, 1918.

Experimental arrested tuberculosis and subsequent infections. Second report. Tr. Nat. Tuberc. Assn., xvi, 350, 1920.

CHAPTER XLVI

CHARLES L. MINOR, M.D.

CHARLES L. MINOR, our thirteenth president, was elected for the term 1917–1918. He had already served the Association as vice-president from 1908 to 1909.

He was born in Brooklyn, N. Y., on May 10, 1865, the son of James Monroe and Ellen Josephine Pierpont Minor. He received his early education in private schools in Europe and in the United States. He graduated from the University of Virginia School of Medicine in 1888. Dr. Minor served as intern in the St. Luke's Hospital, New York, from 1888 to 1890, then went abroad for post-graduate study, chiefly in Vienna, but also in Munich, Berlin, London, and Dublin. In 1892 he settled in Washington. His interest in tuberculosis arose from being personally slightly afflicted with the disease. In 1884 he moved to Asheville, N. C. He soon recovered his health and became an enthusiastic phthisio-therapeutist, and one of the leading physicians of his city and state, where he is widely known. His medical skill, his high ideals, and his attractive personality have endeared Dr. Minor to his countless patients and friends in the profession. His practice is confined exclusively to the treatment of tuberculous diseases.

Dr. Minor is a member of the Delta Psi Fraternity, of the Phi Beta Kappa honorary fraternity, of the American Medical Association, of the North Carolina Medical Society, of the Buncombe County Medical Society, a member and one of the founders of the National Tuberculosis Association, a member of the American Climatological and Clinical Association and its president in 1916, a member of the Southern Medical Association, and a member of the staff of the Asheville Mission Hospital.

As the accompanying bibliography shows, Dr. Minor has been a prolific writer on the subject of tuberculosis. His most im-

CHARLES L. MINOR

portant contribution is perhaps the one on "Symptomatology of Pulmonary Tuberculosis" in Klebs' "Treatise of Tuberculosis by American Authors." Dr. Minor's elaborate article on the subject, covering 240 pages of Klebs' system, is recognized as one of the best expositions of the subject and is as up to date to-day as it was ten years ago when it was written. His presidential address is to be found on page 23 of the Transactions of the Fourteenth Annual Meeting, 1918, of the National Tuberculosis Association. Among the most widely used and quoted of Dr. Minor's writings is his little pamphlet, entitled "Hints and Help for Tuberculous Patients."

The bibliography of Dr. Charles L. Minor follows:

On the feasibility and management of a hygienic cure of pulmonary tuberculosis outside of closed sanatoria. N. Y. Med. Jour., Dec. and Jan., 1902.

Hygiene vs. drugs in the treatment of pulmonary tuberculosis. N. Y. Med. Jour., Jan., 1899.

On the use and abuse of pulmonary gymnastics in the treatment of pulmonary tuberculosis. Tr. Nat. Tuberc. Assn., ii, 368, 1906; also in Therap. Gaz., Oct., 1906.

Notes on some common errors in the technique of sputum staining for tubercle bacilli (with Paul Ringer). Tr. Nat. Tuberc. Assn., ii, 246, 1906.

Treatment of tuberculous patients in their homes and in places other than sanatoria. Jour. Am. Med. Assn., March, 1909.

Hints and helps for tuberculous patients. Printed several times in Jour. Outdoor Life.

What you should know about tuberculosis (with David R. Lyman). Prepared for Nat. Tuberc. Assn. Pamphlet 106.

Use of the x-ray in the diagnosis of pulmonary tuberculosis. N. Y. Med. Jour., March, 1910.

Early changes in the larynx in pulmonary tuberculosis. Tr. Nat. Tuberc. Assn., vi, 186, 1910.

The psychological handling of the tuberculosis patient. Internat. Clin., ii, series 28.

Problem of rest or exercise in the treatment of pulmonary tuberculosis. Med. Rec., Oct. 7, 1916.

The rôle of the x-ray in the physical examination of the lungs. Tr. Am. Clim. and Clin. Assn., 33, 1917.

Importance of the control of childhood infection in the crusade for the eradication of tuberculosis. South. Med. Jour., Feb., 1917.

Address at thirteenth annual meeting. Tr. Nat. Tuberc. Assn., xiii, 41, 1917.

Deductions from four and one-half years' use of artificial pneumothorax in the treatment of pulmonary tuberculosis. Tr. Nat. Tuberc. Assn., xiii, 218, 1917; also Am. Rev. Tuberc., Nov., 1917.

Artificial pneumothorax.   Its application to the arrest or cure of pulmonary tuberculosis.   North Amer. Clinics, 1918.

War in its effects upon the development of tuberculosis.   South. Med. Jour., Jan., 1918.

On the present tendency to nihilism in drug therapeutics.   Therap. Gaz., May 15, 1918.

Temperature of tuberculosis in its diagnostic and prognostic significance.   Tr. Nat. Tuberc. Assn., xv, 207, 1919.

Pulmonary tuberculosis.   Internat. Clin., iii, series 26.

Symptomatology of pulmonary tuberculosis.   Article in Klebs' Treatise of Tuberculosis by American Authors, pp. 149 to 296, 1909.

Physical examination, ibid., 197–324.

Diagnosis, ibid., 325–387.

CHAPTER XLVII

DAVID R. LYMAN, M.D.

PRESIDENT OF THE NATIONAL TUBERCULOSIS ASSOCIATION FROM 1918 TO 1919

DAVID RUSSELL LYMAN was born in Buffalo, N. Y., March 8, 1876, the son of Henry Leslie and Jane Ellen Newman Lyman. He was the youngest man who ever served as president of the National Tuberculosis Association. He was elected to this honor in 1918, on his return from France, where he had served with distinction as associate director of the Rockefeller Tuberculosis Commission. He had already served the Association as vice-president from 1917 to 1918.

Dr. Lyman received his collegiate and medical education at the University of Virginia, with the degree of M.D. in 1899. He became instructor in histology and in anatomy at his alma mater, and after serving in this capacity for one year he became assistant resident physician at Johns Hopkins Hospital. In 1901 a slight tuberculous trouble caused him to seek the Adirondack Cottage Sanitarium, where he soon became assistant resident physician and pupil of Trudeau. When the Gaylord Farm Sanatorium was established and the directors looked longingly to Saranac Lake for a competent physician-in-chief for their institution, they found such a person in David R. Lyman, who took charge of the institution at Wallingford, Conn. It is the privilege of the author of this biographical sketch to have been associated in the capacity of honorary director of the Gaylord Farm Sanatorium from its very beginning, and thus he has been able to watch the progress of this wonderful institution under the able directorship of Dr. Lyman.

This is not the place to trace the development of any individual institution, but since the success of the Gaylord Farm Sanatorium as an institution for the treatment of tuberculosis has been almost exclusively due to Dr. Lyman's genius as a physician, organizer, and executive officer, it may be permissible to repeat here something from an address delivered by the author at the fifteenth anniversary of Gaylord Farm Sanatorium on September 13, 1919:

"Up to the tenth anniversary of the Gaylord Farm Sanatorium, at which it was also my privilege to be present, this institution had expended $800,000. Now, what have the patients given back to the state in return for these expenditures which made them breadwinners again and supporters of their families? Dr. Lyman, who has kept a careful record of the earning capacity of those who have left the sanatorium as cured or practically cured, finds that they have added something like $2,000,000 to the wealth of the country since they left the institution. That pays surely even if the elimination of a certain number of state liabilities and the decrease of the total sum of unhappiness are not taken into account. Ninety per cent. of the graduates who went to Gaylord Farm in the early stages of tuberculosis are in good health after ten years of work. That percentage cannot be exceeded outside of sanatorium ranks. If the first thousand men passing a given corner were caught and earmarked to-day, it is not likely that 900 of them would be alive and vigorous ten years later. In the moderately advanced cases 60 per cent. of the patients were restored to health at the sanatorium, and 10 per cent. even of the apparently hopeless cases were turned out well men."

Dr. Lyman's invaluable services to the commonwealth of the state of Connecticut have been recognized by the state authorities. He was elected a member of the Connecticut State Tuberculosis Commission, and served in this capacity for four years. In the year 1908 the medical faculty of Yale University appointed Dr. Lyman a clinical lecturer on tuberculosis, and Yale University conferred upon him the honorary degree of Master of Arts in 1916. Besides being a member of the National Tuberculosis Association, Dr. Lyman is also a member of the American Climatological and Clinical Association, the American Public Health Association, the New Haven County Medical, Connecticut State Medical, and American Medical Associations. In 1919 he had the honor of being president of the New Haven County Medical Association.

Dr. Lyman's service on behalf of the tuberculosis movement has been universally recognized. He was most active in organizing tuberculosis dispensaries in France, particularly in the Department of Eure et Loir. As already stated, on his return he was unanimously elected as the fourteenth president of the National

DAVID R. LYMAN

Tuberculosis Association. In the fall of 1919 he was again chosen to represent the National Tuberculosis Association at the British Tuberculosis Conference in London. His value to the National Association was again recognized when he was made chairman of a committee of seven appointed to recommend changes in the organization of the Association. The report of this committee was presented to the board of directors at its meeting on December 8, 1920, and resulted in the adoption of the new by-laws of the Association.

The bibliography of Dr. David R. Lyman follows:

The cutaneous reaction of Lautier and some studies in controls. Tr. Am. Clim. and Clin. Assn., 1909.

The employment of arrested cases. Jour. Outdoor Life, Jan., 1911.

Diet in tuberculosis. Jour. Outdoor Life, Oct., 1911.

The use of artificial pneumothorax in the treatment of pulmonary tuberculosis. Tr. Conn. State Med. Soc., 1913.

After the sanatorium—what? (Symposium). Jour. Outdoor Life, xi, Sept., 1914.

The problem of the discharged sanatorium patient. St. Paul Med. Jour., xvii, p. 270–80, April 1, 1915.

The tuberculosis work in Connecticut, its development in the last decade, and its future needs. Boston Med. and Surg. Jour., clxxii, 657–60, May 6, 1915.

The work of the State Tuberculosis Commission, its development and present outlook. Proc. Conn. State Med. Socy., 1915.

Visiting nurses in the fight against tuberculosis. Virginia Med. Semi-Month., xx, 376–80, Nov. 12, 1915.

Sanatorium temperature records. Tr. Nat. Tuberc. Assn., xi, 205–208, 1919.

Some of the present needs of the tuberculosis work in Connecticut. Address before the Litchfield County Pub. Health Assn., May 25, 1916. Printed in pamphlet form.

The development of the tuberculosis crusade and its needs. Lancet-Clinic, cxvi, 193–199, Aug., 26, 1916.

The teeth in tuberculosis. Tr. Nat. Tuberc. Assn., xii, 178, 1916.

A case of unsuspected spontaneous pneumothorax. Tr. Amer. Climat. and Clin. Assn., 1916.

When is the diagnosis of tuberculosis without positive sputum justified? Boston Med. and Surg. Jour., clxxvii, no. 5, Aug. 2, 1917.

The control of the careless consumptive. Am. Rev. Tuberc., ii, no. 1, 36–42, March, 1918.

Following up the discharged sanatorium patient. Am. Rev. Tuberc., ii, no. 10, Dec., 1918.

Address of the president. Tr. Nat. Tuberc. Assn., xv, 17, 1919.

CHAPTER XLVIII

VICTOR C. VAUGHAN, M.D

PRESIDENT OF THE NATIONAL TUBERCULOSIS ASSOCIATION FROM 1919 TO 1920

VICTOR C. VAUGHAN occupied the presidential chair of our Association from 1919 to 1920. He had already served the Association as vice-president from 1910 to 1911.

Dr. Vaughan was born October 27, 1851, at Mount Airy, Randolph County, Mo., the son of John and Adelina Demeron Vaughan. Concerning his early boyhood, he has given us some very interesting information which explains in no small degree his practical sense, his thoroughness in his studies, his patriotism, and his later great achievements as a physician, educator, and military surgeon.

On his father's farm in Missouri everything he wore except his Sunday clothes was made from fibers grown on the farm—wool, flax, hemp, and, during the Civil War, cotton. These fibers were carried through every process necessary to convert them into clothing on the farm. The hides of cattle were tanned and made into shoes. Even the buttons were made on the farm. Spinning-wheels and looms were busy the year around. The cradles in which the children were rocked and the coffins in which the aged were buried were made on the farm. Concerning these early experiences he writes:

"I have visited and studied in divers universities in this country and in Europe, but the biggest university I ever went to was my father's farm. There I learned more than I could have learned at any university or polytechnic school in the world. I lived in Missouri during the Civil War. My father had both legs broken before the Civil War and did not serve in either army. My uncle, Moses Vaughan, commanded a Mississippi brigade in the Confederate Army. We were known as southern sympathizers, and the family received rather rude treatment from Missouri and Iowa home guards, organizations of which occupied Missouri during the Civil War. In February, 1865, with my mother, younger brother, and sister, I fled by night from Mis-

382

VICTOR C. VAUGHAN

souri to southern Illinois, where at that time there were many southern sympathizers. We remained in Illinois until the close of the war, when we returned to our farm in Missouri. Before and during the first part of the war my father and some of his neighbors maintained a private school. The school building was a single-roomed house a short distance from my father's home in the woodland pasture. My most impressive teacher at this time was a Scotchman who taught me to speak Latin, although I never really knew anything of Latin grammar until I went to college."

In 1867 young Vaughan went to Central College, Fayette, Missouri, where he remained one year. From there he went to Mt. Pleasant College, Huntsville, Mo., and completed his undergraduate course, tutoring and giving instruction in Latin in order to pay his way. In fact, when he graduated he was professor of Latin in this college. He spent one semester teaching Latin in Hardin College, Mexico, Mo., a college for girls, and in 1874 came to the University of Michigan, taking an M.S. degree in 1875, a Ph.D. degree in 1876, and an M.D. degree in 1878. Dr. Vaughan has received the following honorary degrees: Sc.D. , University of Pittsburgh; M.D., University of Illinois; LL.D., University of Michigan, Central College, Jefferson Medical School. In 1888 he took a course in bacteriology in the University of Berlin in Koch's laboratory. At that time Karl Frankel gave the laboratory course and Professor Koch gave the lectures.

Dr. Vaughan's professional career has indeed been a remarkable one, full of attainments in the field of physical and medical chemistry, therapeutics, hygiene, and medico-military science. He occupied the position of assistant in the chemical laboratory of the Michigan University from 1875 to 1883; he was lecturer on medical chemistry from 1879 to 1880; assistant professor in medical chemistry from 1880 to 1883; professor of physiological and pathological chemistry and associate professor in therapeutics and materia medica from 1883 to 1887; professor of hygiene and physiological chemistry and director of the hygienic laboratory from 1887 to 1909. Besides these many teaching positions, Professor Vaughan has been dean of the department of medicine and surgery of the University of Michigan since 1890; member of the Michigan State Board of Health from 1883 to 1895, and since 1901 president of the Board.

Dr. Vaughan is a member of many learned societies, such as the American Philosophical Society, the American National Association of Sciences, the French and Hungarian Societies of Hygiene. In 1909 he was the president of the Association of American Physicians, and in 1915 the president of the American Medical Association.

Dr. Vaughan served in the Santiago campaign in 1898 as Major and surgeon of the Thirty-third Michigan Volunteer Infantry. He was soon appointed a Division Surgeon and gradually rose to the rank of Surgeon General.   Because of his distinction as a hygienist and as one of our greatest authorities on physiological chemistry, Dr. Vaughan has been made a member of many national and foreign societies, and during the recent World War he served with distinction as Colonel and as Assistant Surgeon General.   He is a member of the American Advisory Board of the Red Cross.

All of Dr. Vaughan's five sons served in the World War and distinguished themselves by bravery and devotion.   Unfortunately, the oldest son, Major Victor C. Vaughan, Jr., was accidentally drowned in France.

Dr. Vaughan's text-book on Physiological and Pathological Chemistry is perhaps the most important work existing on the subject.   Among some two hundred papers on medical and scientific subjects published by him in this country and in Europe, there are a number of highly interesting contributions relating to the subject of tuberculosis, of which a partial list is attached to this sketch.

In the tuberculosis movement of his own state, Dr. Vaughan has been most active and is largely responsible for the formation of the state tuberculosis association and the foundation of the admirable Michigan State Sanatorium for the tuberculous.   The appended bibliography does not by any means comprise all of the numerous and instructive addresses on behalf of the tuberculosis cause which Dr. Vaughan delivered during his long and interesting career.   He has been a faithful attendant at nearly all the meetings of the National Tuberculosis Association, and his addresses and discussions have always been most enlightening and instructive.   We will make especial mention only of the wonderful address on "The National Welfare," which appears in the Transactions of the meeting at Atlantic City in the year 1919.

The bibliography of Dr. Victor C. Vaughan follows:

Healthy homes and healthy foods for the working classes. The Lomb prize essays. First published in 1886.

The infection of meat and milk. Tr. 7th Internat. Congr. on Hygiene and Demography, London, iii, 118–129, 1891.

The treatment of tuberculosis with yeast nuclein. Med. News, lxv, 157–175, 1894.

The restriction of tuberculosis. Med. News, lxviii, 255, 1896.

The crusade against tuberculosis. Mich. Publ. Health Jour., iii, 49–54, 1908.

The problem of tuberculosis. Wisc. Med. Jour., iv, 59–71.

The split products of the tubercle bacillus and their effects on animals (with Sybil May Wheeler). Tr. Nat. Tuberc. Assn., iii, 237–243, 1907.

The fight against tuberculosis. Jour. Lab. and Clin. Med., ii, 134.

Tuberculosis Legislation. Tr. Nat. Tuberc. Assn., 239, 1909.

National Welfare. Tr. Nat. Tuberc. Assn., xv, 55, 1919.

Address of the president. Tr. Nat. Tuberc. Assn., xvi, 24, 1920.

The service of medicine to civilization. Jour. Am. Med. Assn., lxii, 2003–2012, 1914.

Die Phänomene der Infektion. Berlin, 1914, J. Springer.

Infection and immunity. In Commemoration volume. Am. Med. Assn., 1915.

CHAPTER XLIX

GERALD B. WEBB, M.D.

PRESIDENT OF THE NATIONAL TUBERCULOSIS ASSOCIATION FROM 1920 TO 1921

GERALD BERTRAM WEBB was one of the youngest men to serve as president of the Association. Born in England in 1871, he received his preliminary education at Dean Close Memorial School, Cheltenham. As a child he had the privilege of playing in the home of the celebrated Jenner at Berkeley. He began his medical studies at Guy's Hospital, London, in 1891, and remained there until 1895. He came to the United States and was graduated from the University of Denver in 1896. He went to Europe in 1905 and pursued special studies on immunity and tuberculosis with Sir A. E. Wright, and did clinical work, particularly in tuberculosis, with Lorenz, Covacs, Ghon, and others at the Allgemeine Krankenhaus in Vienna, and also at some of the other European tuberculosis sanatoria. On his return to America in 1906 he established himself at Colorado Springs, paying particular attention to tuberculosis practice. In 1910 he took over the Cragmor Sanatorium, which was founded by Dr. S. E. Solly in 1905. He has completely rebuilt this sanatorium and enlarged its capacity from 20 to 100 beds.

In 1912 Dr. Webb represented the National Tuberculosis Association at the International Congress on Tuberculosis in Rome.

During the World War Dr. Webb served as Lieutenant Colonel of the Medical Corps of the United States Army. He had active charge of the tuberculosis work of the American Expeditionary Force in France. After his honorable discharge he resumed his work in Colorado Springs and founded the Colorado School of Tuberculosis, of which he became the president. He is now consulting physician to the Cragmor and Sunny Rest sanatoria at Colorado Springs. He is a member of the American Medical Association, the American Association of Physicians, the Amer-

GERALD B. WEBB

ican Climatological and Clinical Association, and the American Association of Immunologists.

Dr. Webb was unanimously elected President of the National Tuberculosis Association in 1920.

In the same year he was chosen to represent the United States at the International Union against Tuberculosis in Paris, and in 1921 he again represented our country before the same body in London.

Dr. Webb has been from the very beginning of his medical career an ardent student of experimental and clinical tuberculosis, and in later years has done valuable and original research work in immunization.

The bibliography of Dr. Gerald Bertram Webb follows:

Experimental

Immunity production by inoculation of increasing numbers of bacteria, beginning with one organism (with Williams). Preliminary report, Tr. Nat. Tuberc. Assn., iv, 113, 1908; Tr. 6th Internat. Congress on Tub., 1908.

Immunity production by inoculation of increasing numbers of bacteria, beginning with one living organism (with Williams and Barber). Jour. Med. Res., Jan., 1909.

The integumental tuberculin reactions, with report of 155 more inunction reactions (with Williams). Colo. Medicine, Jan., 1909.

Some immunity problems in tuberculosis (with Williams). Colo. Medicine, April, 1909.

Some hematological studies in tuberculosis (with Williams). Tr. Nat. Tuberc. Assn., v, 231, 1909.

Artificial lymphocytosis as a possible aid in the treatment of tuberculosis; preliminary report (with Williams and Basinger). Colo. Medicine, Jan., 1910.

Artificial lymphocytosis in tuberculosis (with Williams and Basinger). Tr. Nat. Tuberc. Assn., vi, 279, 1910. (These papers include first observations on lymphocyte increase in high altitudes.)

Immunity in tuberculosis; a further report on its production by the inoculation of increasing numbers of bacilli (with Williams). Jour. Med. Res., Jan., 1911.

Immunity in tuberculosis; its production in monkeys and children (with Williams). Jour. Am. Med. Assn., Oct. 28, 1911.

Immunity in tuberculosis by inoculation of living tubercle bacilli. New Mexico Med. Jour., Dec., 1911.

Immunity in tuberculosis (with Gilbert). Tr. Nat. Tuberc. Assn., xi, 227, 1915.

Studies in tuberculosis.   Bull. Johns Hopkins Hosp., Aug., 1912.

Blood platelets—some studies in connection with altitude and tuberculosis; preliminary report (with Gilbert and Havens).   Colo. Medicine, Jan., 1914.

Immunity in tuberculosis; further experiments (with Gilbert).   Jour. Am Med. Assn., Sept. 26, 1914.

Blood platelets and tuberculosis (with Gilbert and Havens).   Tr. Nat. Tuberc. Assn., x, 180, 1914; also Arch. Int. Med., Nov., 1914

Immunity in tuberculosis; inoculation with tubercle bacilli mixed with lymphocytes (with Gilbert).   Tr. Nat. Tuberc. Assn., xi, 227, 1915.

Immunity in tuberculosis.   Jour. Lab. and Clin. Med., March, 1916.

An attempt to produce immunity by transplanting tuberculous lymph nodes into normal animals (with Ryder and Gilbert).   Am. Rev. Tuberc., Feb., 1918.

Transplantation of tuberculous lymph nodes (with Ryder and Gilbert).   Tr. Assn. Amer. Phys., 1918.

Hypernephrectomy and experimental tuberculosis (with Gilbert, Hartwell, and Ryder).   Tr. Nat. Tuberc. Assn., xvi, 336, 1920; also Am. Rev. Tuberc., Oct., 1920.

The survival of virulence of tubercle bacilli in excised animal lymph nodes; further studies (with Ryder and Gilbert).   Am. Rev. Tuberc., July, 1921. Tr. Nat. Tuberc. Assn., 1921.

The adrenals and thyroid in experimental tuberculosis (with Gilbert and Ryder).   Am. Rev. Tuberc., May, 1921.

Address of the president.   Tuberculosis: the rationale of research.   Tr. Nat. Tuberc. Assn., xvii, 26, 1921; also Am. Rev. Tuberc., June, 1921.

Clinical

Some opsonic and bacterial vaccine experiences.   Colo. Medicine, March, 1908.

Vaccine therapy—theories regarding certain failures; preliminary report (with Gilbert).   Colo. Medicine, Feb., 1911.   Second Note, Colo. Medicine, April, 1911.

The specific tissue inoculation of vaccines (with Gilbert).   Tr. Nat. Tuberc· Assn., vii, 375, 1911.

Tuberculosis carriers.   Jour. Outdoor Life, Oct., 1912.

Artificial pneumothorax; with report of gas analyses and experiments to determine the use of air or nitrogen (with Gilbert, James, and Havens). Tr. Nat. Tuberc. Assn., x, 101, 1914; also Arch. Int. Med., Dec., 1914.

Recent progress in the diagnosis and treatment of pulmonary tuberculosis; Pan-American Surg. and Med. Jour., June, 1915.

Sunlight treatment of tuberculosis.   Jour. Outdoor Life, Sept., 1915.

Trachea position (with Forster and Gilbert).   Tr. Nat. Tuberc. Assn., xi, 69, 1915; also Jour. Am. Med. Assn., Sept. 18, 1915.

Rest of the individual lung by posture (with Forster and Houck). Preliminary report. Colo. Medicine, May, 1916; also Tr. Nat. Tuberc. Assn., xii, 182, 1916; Jour. Am. Med. Assn., Nov. 11, 1916.

Diaphragmatic pleurisy in the tuberculous (with Forster and Gilbert). Tr. Nat. Tuberc. Assn., xiii, 193, 1917.

The effect of inhalation of cigarette smoke on the lungs. Am. Review Tuberc., March, 1918.

Bronchiectasis and bronchitis associated with accessory sinus disease (with Gilbert). Jour. Am. Med. Assn., March 12, 1921.

Postural rest for pulmonary tuberculosis (with Forster and Gilbert). Jour. Am. Med. Assn., March 26, 1921.

CHAPTER L

JAMES ALEXANDER MILLER, M.D.

JAMES ALEXANDER MILLER, who has already served the Association as vice-president from 1916–1917 and from 1920–1921, was born in Roselle, N. J., March 27, 1874, being the son of Charles Dexter and Julia Hope Miller. Young Miller became a Bachelor of Arts of Princeton in 1893, an A.M. of the same university in 1894, and an M.D. of Columbia University, 1899. He served as intern in the Presbyterian Hospital, New York, from 1899 to 1901. Dr. Miller's interest in tuberculosis was aroused by no less a teacher and pioneer in tuberculosis science than the famous Trudeau. The summer after leaving the Presbyterian Hospital Dr. Miller went up to Paul Smith's to assist Dr. Trudeau who then did general practice during the summer months at that resort. It was but natural that the young physician, being inspired by Dr. Trudeau's personality, enthusiasm, and achievements in tuberculosis, should himself become so deeply interested as to make tuberculosis his life's work. On his return to New York and to the Vanderbilt Dispensary, to which he was attached, he urged the establishment of special tuberculosis classes. He was supported in this work by his teacher and friend, Dr. Walter B. James, then professor of medicine at the College of Physicians and Surgeons, the medical department of Columbia University. Dr. Miller is now himself professor of clinical medicine in that school. From the time he inaugurated the tuberculosis classes connected with the Vanderbilt Hospital he has been an untiring worker in his chosen specialty, so that to-day he occupies the enviable position of leader in the anti-tuberculosis work in New York city. He is visiting physician at Bellevue Hospital; physician in charge of the tuberculosis division of Bellevue Hospital; special consultant

JAMES ALEXANDER MILLER

in tuberculosis at the Presbyterian Hospital, New York. He is consulting physician to the Sea View Hospital, Staten Island, Sprain Ridge Sanatorium, Yonkers, and the Trudeau Sanatorium, Saranac Lake. He is also secretary of the Board of Trustees of the Trudeau Sanatorium.

But Dr. Miller is not contented with clinical work in tuberculosis. From the very beginning of his career as a tuberculosis worker he has realized the importance of the social aspect of this disease and was instrumental in reorganizing the former Tuberculosis Committee of the New York City Charity Organization Society into the flourishing New York City Tuberculosis Association, of which he is now the president. To Dr. Miller we are also indebted for the formation of the Association of Tuberculosis Clinics, which is doing such admirable work under his presidency. As secretary of the Public Health Committee of the Academy of Medicine, member of the Advisory Council of the Phipps Institute, Philadelphia, of the Central Council of the Charity Organization Society, of the Board of Directors of the Association for Improving the Condition of the Poor, of the Board of Directors of the State Charities Aid Association, and as chairman of the Health Service Committee of the New York County Chapter, American Red Cross, he has been instrumental in furthering the anti-tuberculosis cause perhaps more than any other individual tuberculosis worker. Not the least among the many important positions he occupies at the head of the various anti-tuberculosis movements, is that of editor-in-chief of the *Journal of the Outdoor Life*. During the world war Dr. Miller did admirable service in France from 1917 to 1918, as associate director of the Rockefeller Commission for the Prevention of Tuberculosis in France and as Major in the American Red Cross in France. The French Government honored Dr. Miller by the bestowal of the decoration of Chevalier de Légion d'honneur.

Dr. Miller is a fellow of the Association of American Physicians, of the New York County and State Medical Societies and of the American Medical Association. He served from 1915 to 1916 as president of the American Climatological and Clinical Society.

At its meeting in June, 1921, the National Tuberculosis Association honored itself by electing Dr. Miller president in recognition of the valuable clinical and social work which he has carried on in the field of tuberculosis.

The bibliography of Dr. James Alexander Miller follows:

A clinical study of the children of tuberculous parents (with I. Ogden Wood-ruff, M.D.).   Jour. Am. Med. Assn., lii, 1016, 1909.

Clinical diagnosis of pulmonary tuberculosis.   Tr. Nat. Tuberc. Assn., v, 195, 1909.

Relation of the physician to the anti-tuberculosis campaign.   Tr. Nat. Tuberc. Assn., viii, 52, 1912.

Studies of the leukocytes in pulmonary tuberculosis and pneumonia (with Margaret A. Reed).   Arch. Int. Med., ix, 609, 1912.

Hospital ventilation from the point of view of the clinician.   Jour. Am. Med. Assn., lxiii, 1623, 1914.

The effect of changes in atmospheric conditions upon the upper respiratory tract (with Gerhard H. Cocks, M.D.).   Tr. Am. Clim. and Clin. Assn., xxxi, 31, 1915.

The effects of exposure to cold upon experimental infection of the respiratory tract (with Willis C. Noble).   Jour. Exper. Med., xxiv, 223, 1916.

Some physiological effects of various atmospheric conditions.   Am. Jour. Med. Sci., cliii, 412, 1917.

Some problems of differential diagnosis in chronic pulmonary disease.   New York Med. Jour., April 28, 1917.

Subacute and chronic non-tuberculous pulmonary infections.   Tr. Nat. Tuberc. Assn., xiv, 78, 1918; also Am. Jour. Med. Sci., xliv, 805, 1917.

How America is helping France with her tuberculosis problem.   Am. Rev. Tuberc., ii, 409, 1918.

Tuberculosis among European nations at war.   Am. Rev. Tuberc., iii, 337, 1919.

Some problems in the differential diagnosis of pulmonary tuberculosis.   Tr. Nat. Tuberc. Assn., xvi, 197, 1920; also Am. Rev. Tuberc., iv, 502, 1920.

Pulmonary tuberculosis.   In Nelson's Loose Leaf System of Medicine, 1921.

CHAPTER LI

GENERAL GEORGE M. STERNBERG, M.C., U.S.A.

TREASURER OF THE NATIONAL TUBERCULOSIS ASSOCIATION FROM 1904 TO 1912

SURGEON GENERAL GEORGE M. STERNBERG served the National Tuberculosis Association as its faithful treasurer from the time of the formation of the society in 1904 to the year 1912.

He was born June 8, 1838, in the city of New York and was the son of the Rev. Levi and Margaret Levering Miller Sternberg. He received his preliminary education at the Hartwick Seminary of Otsego County, N. Y., and graduated in medicine from the College of Physicians and Surgeons, New York, in 1860.

General Sternberg was an honorary fellow of Johns Hopkins University from 1880 to 1881 and from 1885 to 1887; he was president of the American Public Health Association in 1887, of the Washington Biological Society in 1896, the American Medical Association in 1897, the Washington Philosophical Society in 1897, and the Association of Military Surgeons in 1899. He was also a member of the American Bacteriological Society, the Association of American Physicians and of the American Association for the Advancement of Science.

General Sternberg's career as a scientist, physician, medical officer in the United States Army, and worker for the civic welfare of Washington was indeed a brilliant one. Entering as an assistant surgeon in 1861, he was made a captain and then major in the United States Army "for faithful and meritorious services" during the Civil War, and a lieutenant colonel "for gallant service in performance of his professional duty under fire in action against the Indians at Clearwater, Idaho, July 12, 1877." General Sternberg participated in many engagements, including the first battle of Bull Run, on which occasion he was wounded and taken prisoner.   He escaped from Fairfax Court House shortly afterward, and at once rejoined his regiment.   He was under heavy fire while caring for the wounded at the battles of Gaines Mill and Malvern Hill, and afterward suffered a severe attack of typhoid fever.   He was executive officer of the United States general hospital at Portsmouth Grove, R. I.; was with General Banks' expedition to the Gulf of Mexico, and, at the close of the war, was serving as officer in charge of the United States general hospital at Cleveland, Ohio.

Dr. Sternberg was in the field in various Indian campaigns from 1868 to 1870.   Among his many details was one at Fort Columbus, in New York harbor, during the yellow fever epidemic in 1871, and in Florida during similar epidemics in 1873 and 1875.   He participated in the expedition against the Nez Perce Indians in 1877, and was a member of the Havana yellow fever commission in 1879.   He was a delegate from the United States to the international sanitary conference held in Rome, Italy, in 1885, and in 1887 was detailed to make investigations in Brazil, Mexico, and in Cuba relating to the etiology and prevention of yellow fever.

On May 28, 1893, Colonel Sternberg was made Surgeon General on account of his scientific work and his gallantry and bravery on various battlefields.   Within a month after his appointment he recommended the establishment of the Army Medical School.   This institution marks an epoch in American medicine, and it would seem but just and fitting that it should be made a lasting monument to the great soldier physician.   He also recommended the establishment of the sanatorium at Fort Bayard in New Mexico for the treatment of pulmonary tuberculosis, with Dr. George E. Bushnell in charge.   This institution has accomplished great good not merely by restoring many men to active duty again, but also by the humane care extended to the hopeless cases and the protection afforded to the families of the afflicted and thus to the community at large.   Since the time of its establishment in 1899 to March 31, 1920, it has cared for 12,984 patients.

As Surgeon General of the Army, Sternberg's work in the establishment and improvement of army hospitals and laboratories is acknowledged to be of the greatest importance.   During the

GEORGE M. STERNBERG

Spanish-American War he established general hospitals at Key West, Savannah, Fort Thomas, Ky., Fort McPherson, Ga., Fort Monroe, Va., Fort Myer, Washington Barracks, and San Francisco, and upon his recommendation two hospital ships were purchased and equipped. All volunteer surgeons and contract surgeons were appointed on his recommendation. He organized the female nurse corps and the corps of dental surgeons in compliance with acts of Congress passed on his recommendations At the outbreak of the conflict he issued a circular calling attention to the danger of typhoid in camps and organized the "typhoid fever board," with Major Walter Reed as chairman. He organized the yellow fever commission of 1900, with the now famous Major Reed and Drs. Carroll, Lazear, and Aramonte as members. In 1901 he recommended that the medical department be increased to correspond with the increase in the army made at that time.

Surgeon General Sternberg was retired from the army on account of age in 1902. Up to his passing away he devoted his energy, knowledge, and experience to the betterment of health in the capital of our country. He died on November 3, 1915, at the age of seventy-eight, and was buried with military honors becoming his rank. On November 5, 1919, a simple but imposing monument in granite was unveiled at the Arlington National Cemetery, to mark the place where Surgeon General Sternberg had been laid at rest. Tributes were paid on this occasion by Major General Merritt W. Ireland, Surgeon General of the United States Army, Brigadier General Walter D. McCaw, Colonel Edward L. Monson, and Colonel Frederick R. Russell. Dr. George M. Kober, his life-long friend, pronounced the following eulogy on his life's work:

"Dr. Sternberg was not only a great scientist, he was also a philanthropist in the fullest and most beautiful meaning of the word. A review of his scientific work shows that he always sought the application of science to the amelioration of human ills. His first important work in bacteriology was on disinfectants and disinfection as a means of preventing the so-called germ diseases; a work of incalculable value to mankind. He never lost an opportunity to impress on the profession and the public that the eradication of preventable diseases is the highest aim of scientific medicine.

"It was not possible for a man of Dr. Sternberg's humanitarian attributes to rest content with the scientific knowledge that polluted water and infected milk are potent factors in the spread of typhoid fever, bovine tuberculosis, etc., and that unsanitary houses and low standards of living are largely responsible for the prevalence of tuberculosis, but he must make practical application of this knowledge.   We therefore found him in the front rank and as a leader in the campaign for pure water and milk, removal of slums, and the creation of sanitary houses in the National Capital.   As a result of his efforts the Washington Sanitary Housing Companies were organized, which have erected healthful houses at reasonable rentals for over 800 families.

"Having been the first in America to demonstrate the tubercle bacillus discovered by Koch in 1881, and familiar with the cause and prevention of tuberculosis, it was natural that he should labor long and faithfully in the campaign against this disease.   He was a charter member of the National Association and took a deep interest and participated in many discussions at the annual meetings, and at the International Congress on Tuberculosis.   As president of the local Association from its organization until his death in 1915, he was the leader of a great educational campaign.   He established several dispensaries, urged the erection of the municipal hospital for indigent tuberculous patients, and also established a sanatorium for the middle class victims of this disease.   He was instrumental in securing the enactment of a law providing for the condemnation of houses unfit for human habitation and the compulsory registration of tuberculous patients."

Thus was the monument dedicated as General Ireland said: "To the memory of a remarkable man, whose name is writ large in the military and scientific annals of this country."

Professor William H. Welch and his associates on the committee had selected the following sentences to be inscribed on the stone as expressive of the achievements of this remarkable man:

"Pioneer American Bacteriologist.   Distinguished by his studies of the causation and prevention of infectious diseases, by his discovery of the microorganism causing pneumonia, and scientific investigation of yellow fever, which paved the way for the experimental demonstration of the mode of transmission of this pestilence."

"Veteran of three wars.   Brevetted for bravery in action in the Civil War and Nez Perces War.   Served as Surgeon General of the U. S. Army for the period of nine years, including the Spanish-American War.   Founder of the Army Medical School.   Scientist, author, and philanthropist.   M.D., LL.D."

Surgeon General Sternberg's biography, written by Mrs. Sternberg and published by the American Medical Association,* contains a complete bibliography of the General's writings on

* George M. Sternberg, a biography, by his wife.   American Medical Association, Chicago, 1920.

yellow fever, malarial fever, tuberculosis, and other infectious diseases.

The bibliography of Gen. George M. Sternberg follows:

Report of microscopical examination of suspended particles found in the atmosphere. Nat. Bd. Health Report 2, p. 387–396, 1880.

A fatal form of septicæmia in the rabbit, produced by the subcutaneous injection of human saliva. (The discovery of the organism causing croupous pneumonia.) Nat. Bd. Health Bull., 2, p. 781–783, 1881; also 3, p. 87–92, 1881.

Experiments with disinfectants. Nat. Bd. Health Bull., 3, p. 21, 68, 181.

Bacteria and the germ theory of disease. Tr. Med. Society, California, 12, p. 193–198, 1882.

Bacterial organisms. Western Lancet 11, p. 198–203, 1882.

Is tuberculosis a parasitic disease? Medical News, 1892, p. 730.

Sanatorium treatment for the tuberculous. Washington Med. Annals, 1905.

First fifty cases of tuberculosis treated at Star Mount Sanatorium. Washington Med. Annals, 1907

Building of model homes. Report of the President's Home Commission, 1908.

Housing the working classes a factor in the prevention of tuberculosis. Jour. Outdoor Life, 1910.

Results of treatment at the Star Mount Tuberculosis Sanatorium. Washington Medical Annals, 1911. .

Small homes within the city limits for unskilled wage earners. 2nd edition, Nat. Housing Assn. Public no. 27, 1915.

Manual of bacteriology. 1893.

Textbook on bacteriology. 1901.

CHAPTER LII

WILLIAM HENRY BALDWIN

TREASURER OF THE NATIONAL TUBERCULOSIS ASSOCIATION FROM 1912 TO 1919

WILLIAM HENRY BALDWIN, who served our National Tuberculosis Association so faithfully as treasurer from 1912 to 1919, was born in Youngstown, Ohio, July 16, 1851. He was the son of Timothy D. and Lucretia K. Manning Baldwin. He obtained his degree of A.B. from the Western Reserve University in 1871. He became cashier of the First National Bank of Youngstown in 1877, its vice-president in 1889; manager of the Arms-Bell Company in 1887, secretary of the Youngstown Iron and Steel Company in 1890, and of the Union Iron and Steel Company in 1892; secretary and treasurer of the Ohio Steel Company in 1894, and of the National Steel Company in 1899.

In 1901 Mr. Baldwin retired and devoted himself to social work. We owe it to Dr. Charles O. Probst, of Columbus, Ohio, one of the pioneers and an enthusiastic worker for the tuberculosis cause in this country and particularly in the state of Ohio, that Mr. Baldwin, a layman, entered with heart and soul into the tuberculosis movement and brought with him a keen sense of the responsibility which all good citizens have in the social and hygienic welfare of the nation.

Mr. Baldwin's business training fitted him eminently for the many positions of trust which he has occupied since he settled in Washington, D. C. Aside from being treasurer of the National Tuberculosis Association he has served as a director and member of its executive committee for many years. He was a member of the President's Home Commission; official delegate of the National Tuberculosis Association to the International Conference on Tuberculosis in Brussels in 1910, and an official delegate of the United States to the International Congress on Tuberculosis

WILLIAM H. BALDWIN

in Rome in 1912; a member of the Conference of Commissioners on Uniform State Laws from the District of Columbia; Vice-Chairman of the American Association of Societies for Organizing Charity; and member of the Advisory Council of the Henry Phipps Institute. With the entrance of the United States into the World War it was, of course, evident that Mr. Baldwin would. do his share, and in 1917 he became chairman of the District Council of Defense for the District of Columbia.

We append here only a very short list of valuable papers Mr. Baldwin has written on the social aspect of tuberculosis. Coming from a layman so intimately associated with the tuberculosis movement in the United States, they are of incalculable value and will serve as classical treatises for many years to come.

Mr. Baldwin's social activities, however, were not confined specifically to tuberculosis subjects. Poverty, want, and social unhappiness, all of which contribute toward the propagation of tuberculosis, received his attention and devotion. Mr. Baldwin's book on "Family Desertion and Non-Support Laws," published in 1904, and various papers and reprints on the same subject, are monuments to his philanthropy and eagerness to serve. In connection with the Associated Charities in Washington since 1909 he has been chairman of the Citizen's Committee on the Loan Shark Law, which has stopped the payment of more than $500,000 illegal interest in our capital each year.

Although he has retired as our treasurer, we still rejoice in having Mr. Baldwin as a member of our Association, feeling sure that he will never fail to help us with his valued advice in all matters appertaining to the social and economic side of the tuberculosis problem.

The bibliography of Mr. William H. Baldwin follows:

The progress of the sanatorium movement in America. Tr. Nat. Tuberc. Assn., i, 70, 1905; also Am. Med., ix, no. 24, 995–1000, June 17, 1905.

Influence of a tuberculosis sanatorium on the value of surrounding property. Tr. Nat. Tuberc. Assn., ii, 51, 1906; also in Jour. Am. Med. Assn., Dec. 22, 1906, 2054–58.

Reports and registration of cases of tuberculosis. Printed for the Committee on the prevention of consumption, Washington, Nov. 14, 1906.

Compulsory reports and registration of tuberculosis in the United States. New York Med. Jour., Dec. 8, 1906.

The movement against tuberculosis in Washington, D. C.   Jour. Outdoor
   Life, Sept., 1907.
The army and tuberculosis.   Printed in the Washington Star, March 30, 1919,
   under the title Tuberculosis war is army problem.
Present status of soldiers and draft rejects with tuberculosis.   Tr. Nat. Tuberc.
   Assn., xv, 366, 1919; also in Am. Rev. Tuberc., iii, no. 6, Aug., 1919.

HENRY B. PLATT

CHAPTER LIII

HENRY BARSTON PLATT

TREASURER OF THE NATIONAL TUBERCULOSIS ASSOCIATION, FROM 1919

MR. PLATT, the present treasurer of the National Tuberculosis Association, is modesty personified. It was with great difficulty that a few data were obtained to enable the author to make this short biographical sketch.

Henry Barston Platt was born in New York City, February 2, 1860. He is the son of the late Senator Thomas C. and Ellen Barston Platt. After his preliminary education in the public schools, young Platt went to Yale, where he finished his classical education in 1882. After graduating from college he went into the manufacturing business for about three years and became superintendent of coal properties in Pennsylvania. Later on he was made general superintendent of the United States Express Company. He is now vice-president of the Fidelity and Deposit Company of Maryland. During the world war Mr. Platt naturally wished to do his duty, and in the year 1918 served as director of the Bureau of Personnel of the Atlantic Division of the American Red Cross. The National Tuberculosis Association is to be congratulated on Mr. Platt's acceptance of this most important position in our Association.

CHAPTER LIV

HENRY BARTON JACOBS, M.D.

AT THAT historic meeting in Baltimore on January 28, 1904, when the National Tuberculosis Association was suggested, the choice of a secretary fell tentatively upon Dr. Henry Barton Jacobs. With the establishment of the society this office was definitely conferred upon him and this position he filled until his resignation in 1920. While the duties of secretary were largely performed by the executive secretary, yet Dr. Jacobs' interest in the tuberculosis cause has never flagged, and his voice in the development of the organization has always been raised with enthusiasm for all that marked progress and efficiency in the work of the Association.

Dr. Jacobs was born in South Scituate, Plymouth County, Mass., June 2, 1858. His parents were Barton Richmond and Frances Almira Ford Jacobs. We are informed of the remarkable fact that through these parents he is a direct descendant of seven of the passengers on the "Mayflower," which arrived in Plymouth December 29, 1620. Dr. Jacobs received his preliminary education at the High School in Hingham, Mass., and at the Phillips Exeter Academy, Exeter, N. H. He took his bachelor's degree at Harvard in 1883, and was graduated with the degree of M.D. from the Harvard Medical School in 1887. He then became a medical intern for one and a half years in the Massachusetts General Hospital on the East Side Service under Dr. Reginald H. Fitz and his colleagues. Dr. Jacobs left the hospital in the spring of 1888 and was appointed physician to the Boston Dispensary, opening an office for general practice at 8 Hancock Street, Boston. In August, 1888, he became the private physician of Robert Garrett, president of the Baltimore and Ohio Railroad, and after spending the winter of 1888–89 in Ringwood, N. J., moved to

HENRY BARTON JACOBS

Baltimore, where he has since resided. He was present at the opening of the Johns Hopkins Hospital in May, 1889, and soon became attached to the dispensary service of that hospital under Dr. William Osler, the physician-in-chief. In 1896 he was made associate in medicine in the Johns Hopkins University, and was engaged in teaching the early classes in the medical school in physical diagnosis and in therapeutics.

With the departure of Professor Osler to Oxford in 1905, Dr. Jacobs resigned his position in the medical school and soon afterward was made a trustee of the Johns Hopkins Hospital. Since then he has devoted his time largely to public health and educational matters. He is a trustee of the Peabody Institute, of the Maryland Institute, of the Church Home and Infirmary, and of the Hospital School for Children; president of The Hospital for Consumptives of Maryland, and president of the Maryland Tuberculosis Association. He was one of the original directors of the Maryland State Tuberculosis Sanatorium, and with Dr. H. Warren Buckler chose the site and matured the plans of this institution. Dr. Jacobs is also a director of the Baltimore Museum of Art, a member of the executive committee of the Baltimore Society of the Friends of Art, and of the Newport Art Society. He has collected extensively prints illustrating medical portraiture, and also medals illustrating the same subject. Books too have interested him and he serves on the library committee of the Peabody Institute, and Medical and Chirurgical Faculty, and the Redwood Library, Newport. Since he gave up his teaching at the Johns Hopkins Medical School Dr. Jacobs has not engaged in practice, but he has retained his membership in various medical societies, and together with the crusade for the suppression of tuberculosis, medical history has held his special attention. For a number of years he was president of the Johns Hopkins Medical Historical Society, as well as the Laennec Society, also the Book and Journal Club of the State Medical Society, which was a medical historical club. He is still a member of the Medical Historical Society of Paris, and one of the associate editors of the Annals of Medical History.

Dr. Jacobs until his resignation was a faithful attendant at the executive committee and board meetings. He rarely failed to attend the national meetings, and at the various international tuberculosis congresses and conferences abroad he has always ably represented the Association. At the final session of the Paris Congress in 1905, when Dr. Flick moved to invite the international gathering to be the guest of the American nation in 1908, Dr. Jacobs seconded the motion and arranged, by means of the cable, through the assistance of Dr. Welch, to have President Roosevelt confirm the invitation which then was accepted.

Aside from Dr. Jacobs' valuable service as secretary of the Association for the first sixteen years of its existence, he has contributed a number of notable papers on the treatment, prevention, and history of tuberculosis. His most important article is perhaps the one entitled "A Farm Colony Experiment," which he presented at the Sixth International Tuberculosis Congress. Since then a number of institutions have imitated with gratifying success this farm colony system. The plan was first inaugurated at the Eudowood Sanatorium near Baltimore during the superintendency of Dr. Alexius M. Forster, who originated the idea, and who with the coöperation of Dr. Jacobs, the president, made every effort to demonstrate its usefulness in caring for convalescent and arrested cases.

On November 19, 1901, before the semi-annual meeting of the Maryland State Medical Society, Dr. Jacobs read a paper on "The Treatment of Consumption in Local Sanatoria," in which he demonstrated from the results in Massachusetts that consumption could be as successfully treated in eastern local sanatoria as in western mountain resorts, and he made an earnest plea to the members of the society to urge upon the Legislature of Maryland the necessity of establishing a state sanatorium on the slopes of the Blue Mountain chain. In this paper in 1901 Dr. Jacobs was the first to advocate the Maryland State Sanatorium. He followed up the plea at the annual meeting of the State Medical Society April, 1903, by a paper "Maryland's Need of a Mountain Sanatorium for Indigent Consumptives." Thus it was that the voice of Dr. Jacobs was the first to be raised in Maryland for the State Sanatorium, in the building of which later on he took so much interest. He was influential in choosing its site and in determining its type of buildings and its policy. Perhaps the article of Dr. Jacobs which has attracted most notice is his essay on "Some Distinguished American Students of Tuberculosis," in which he was the first to bring together data in regard to the eminent early students of the disease in this country. The paper was published in the Johns Hopkins Hospital Bulletin.* In later years Dr. Jacobs has been making efforts to compile the early history of vaccination with special reference to Dr. Jenner himself. His collection of autograph letters of Jenner is probably by far the largest and most important in this country.

The bibliography of Dr. Henry Barton Jacobs follows:

The treatment of consumptives in local sanatoria. Maryland Med. Jour., Dec., 1901.

International medical congress in Paris. Boston Med. and Surg. Jour., Jan., 1901.

Some distinguished American students of tuberculosis. Bull. Johns Hopkins Hosp., xiii, 199–208, Aug.–Sept., 1902.

Maryland's need of a mountain sanatorium for indigent consumptives. Maryland Med. Jour., Oct., 1903.

Remarks upon the International Congress on Tuberculosis, Paris, 1905. Bull. Johns Hopkins Hosp., Nov., 1906.

The onward march in Maryland. Jour. Outdoor Life, April, 1907.

The tuberculosis situation in Maryland. Proc. Maryland Tuberc. Assn., April, 1907.

The prevention of tuberculosis among school children. Maryland Med. Jour., March, 1908.

Hygienic instruction in schools. Proc. Sixth Internat. Congr. on Tuberc., Washington, 1908.

A farm colony experiment. Proc. Sixth Internat. Congr. on Tuberc., Washington, 1908.

The sanatorium school. Proc. 5th Cong. Amer. School Hygiene Assn., New York, Feb., 1911.

Osler as a citizen and his relation to the tuberculosis crusade in Maryland. Bull. Johns Hopkins Hosp., July, 1919.

President's reports on the work of the Hospital for Consumptives of Maryland (The Eudowood Sanatorium). In the annual reports of the Hospital for Consumptives of Maryland, 1906–1919.

* Johns Hopkins Hosp. Bull., xiii, 199–208, Aug.-Sept., 1902.

CHAPTER LV

LIVINGSTON FARRAND, M.D.

D R. LIVINGSTON FARRAND, who was the first executive secretary of the National Tuberculosis Association, was born in Newark, N. J., June 14, 1867. His father was Samuel A. and his mother Louise Wilson Farrand. Dr. Farrand obtained his degree of A.B. at Princeton University in 1888, and in the year 1891 he received simultaneously the degree of A.M. from Princeton and of M.D. from the College of Physicians and Surgeons of New York city. He studied in Cambridge, England, and in Berlin, devoting a great deal of time to psychology and anthropology. He was instructor in psychology at Columbia University from 1893 to 1901, adjunct professor from 1901 to 1903, and professor of anthropology from 1903 to 1914.

Dr. Farrand served as executive secretary of the National Tuberculosis Association from 1905 to 1914. He left the National Association, much to the regret of the board of directors and his associates, to accept the presidency of the University of Colorado, over which institution he presided until the year 1917. His work as college president was marked by the same great executive ability and tact which characterized his invaluable work as executive secretary of the Association. The University of Colorado conferred upon him the degree of LL.D. during the first year of his presidency. Besides being intensely interested in his specialties of anthropology and tuberculosis, Dr. Farrand was also most active in the American Psychological Association and the American Public Health Association, and served the latter association as treasurer and as editor of the American Journal of Public Health from 1912 to 1914.

The growth of the National Tuberculosis Association during

LIVINGSTON FARRAND

the nine years from 1905 to 1914, during which time Dr. Farrand devoted his best energies to the tuberculosis movement in the United States, bears eloquent testimony to his devotion to our cause. When Dr. Farrand began his activities as executive secretary of the Association the latter had a membership of less than 500. In 1905 there were in the United States 32 tuberculosis associations, societies, and committees, 24 tuberculosis dispensaries, and 96 sanatoria and special hospitals. In the year 1914 the membership of the Association had grown to 2,256; there were 1,200 associations, 400 dispensaries, 550 sanatoria and special hospitals, and 250 open-air schools.

Such executive ability and such knowledge of the methods of combating tuberculosis as Dr. Farrand possessed could not have remained unutilized during the great World War, and it was but natural that when the Rockefeller Foundation decided to help tuberculosis-stricken France, Dr. Farrand should be chosen to head the Commission sent to that country to help in an effective anti-tuberculosis campaign. Dr. Farrand speaks in a modest way about the work in a letter to the author, saying:

"The most definitely constructive piece of work I have ever been engaged in, aside from the development of the general tuberculosis work in this country, was the campaign in France in 1917–18–19. The essential point in that campaign was that we were able to gather the results of the work done in different places in America during the last fifteen or twenty years and apply them in concentrated form in a country aroused by the war to a realization of its peril from the point of view of tuberculosis. In other words, we were able to start model equipments in certain selected places in France which were in many ways more completely worked out than anything we have in operation in this country. It is too soon yet to predict results, but I believe the campaign was soundly laid and that the ultimate results will be not only great but obvious."

The French medical profession and the French government appreciated fully Dr. Farrand's invaluable work and the French government bestowed upon him the decoration of an officer of the Legion of Honor. Another great honor was in store for him on his return to this country when he was made chairman of the Central Committee of the American Red Cross. Dr. Farrand had a very high and patriotic conception of the organization over whose destinies he was called to preside. In the Red Cross

Magazine of March, 1920, he expressed himself concerning the destinies of the American Red Cross as follows:

"I don't want to see our Red Cross stand for anything but organized Americanism. It represents us all. Because of that fact it can be made America's most powerful agent in community effort. It represents no single class or creed. It stands for the great essential in any community—service. In its every activity it is building up a sound citizenship through community effort."

Through his position as chief executive of the American Red Cross he was able to exert a powerful influence in the formation of the National Health Council, of which he was made the first president. Thus was realized a goal in public health coördination for which he had striven for many years.

What Dr. Farrand hoped to do in the responsible position of chairman of the Central Committee of the Red Cross, how keenly he felt the immensity of the task before him, he expressed to the author in the following words:

"I feel that there is a tremendous opportunity in working out a program which will place the energy of this great organization behind the general movement in this country and the world for the improvement of the public health and for building up the vitality of Europe which has been shattered by the war. Certainly it is a task big enough and inspiring enough to challenge the interest of any one, and I am giving whatever I have to that work."

He succeeded well in his task for which he was so eminently fitted; but a greater honor was still in store for him. Several months ago, when the position of president of Cornell University became vacant by the resignation of Dr. Jacob Gould Schurman, the choice of the board of trustees fell upon Dr. Farrand. A better choice could hardly have been made in view of his vast experience as an educator and an executive officer. On Thursday, October 20, 1921, with most impressive ceremonies, Dr. Farrand was duly installed at Ithaca, N. Y., as president of Cornell University.

He has the very best wishes of his former associates of the National Tuberculosis Association for a brilliant career in his new field.

The bibliography of Dr. Livingston W. Farrand follows:

First annual meeting of the National Association for the Study and Prevention of Tuberculosis. Charities, xiv, 801–6, June 3, 1905.

Tuberculosis nomenclature. Am. Med., x, 893, 1905.

War against disease. In Proc. New York State Conference of Charities and Correction. 1906, 271–76.

Year's fight against tuberculosis. Charities, xvii, 9–11, Oct. 6, 1906.

Looking ahead in the tuberculosis campaign. Charities, xix, 875–6, Oct. 12, 1907.

The campaign against tuberculosis in the United States. Tr. Nat. Tuberc. Assn., iii, 28–34, 1907.

The campaign in the United States. Ibid., iv, 24–26, 1908.

Educational methods in the campaign against tuberculosis. Jour. Am. Med. Assn., xlix, 815–18, 1907.

A comprehensive program for the prevention of tuberculosis. Tr. Sixth Internat. Cong. on Tuberc., iii, 236–44, 1908.

The National Association. Jour. Outdoor Life, v, 140, 180, 218, 263, May–Aug., 1908; vi, 20, 47, 78, 111, 142, 178, 211, 242, 275, 306, 337, 368, Jan.–Dec., 1909. Department edited by Dr. Farrand.

Advantages of institutional care. In New York State Charities Aid Association publication No. 116, 95–99, 1910.

The National Association for the Study and Prevention of Tuberculosis. Am. Pub. Health Assn., i, 334–37, 1911.

Report of the executive secretary. Tr. Nat. Tuberc. Assn., v, 17–20, 1909; vi, 27–32, 1910; vii, 29–33, 1911; viii, 30–37, 1912; ix, 23–28, 1913.

Strategy in tuberculosis. Survey, xxvi, 693–4, Aug. 12, 1911.

The development of the educational efforts in public and personal hygiene in America. Fifteenth Internat. Congr. on Hygiene and Demography. Tr. Wash. (1912), iv, 17–28, 1913.

Introductory remarks to Advisory Council. Tr. Nat. Tuberc. Assn., xii, 59–60, 1916.

Medical education and public health. Colo. Medicine, xiv, 15–17, Jan., 1917.

Future coöperation between the American Red Cross and the public health agencies. Am. Jour. Pub. Health, ix, 583–85, Aug., 1919.

CHAPTER LVI

CHARLES J. HATFIELD, M.D.

EXECUTIVE SECRETARY AND MANAGING DIRECTOR OF THE NATIONAL TUBERCU-
LOSIS ASSOCIATION FROM 1914

CHARLES JAMES HATFIELD, son of Daniel Keyser and Margaret Alexander Hatfield, was born January 23, 1867, in Philadelphia. He received his preliminary education at the Hill School at Pottstown, Pa. He was graduated with the degree of A.B. from Princeton in 1888, with the degree of A.M. from the same university in 1891, and took the degree of Doctor of Medicine at the University of Pennsylvania in 1900. He took post-graduate courses in medicine at the universities of Göttingen in 1901 and of Vienna in 1902.

On his return to the United States in 1903 he established himself in general practice in Philadelphia. Intensely interested in tuberculosis work, and identified with the tuberculosis movement in his own state and city, he became a member of the medical staff and later (in 1912) was chosen executive director of the Henry Phipps Institute for the Study and Prevention of Tuberculosis. He is a visiting physician to the White Haven Sanatorium for the tuberculous, a Fellow of the College of Physicians of Philadelphia, member of the American Medical Association and of the Clinical and Climatological Society, and a director of the American Public Health Association. During the organization of the Sixth International Congress Dr. Hatfield had the difficult position of chairman of the Committee of Awards. The work of this committee extended over several years and was completed to the general satisfaction of the exhibitors.

Dr. Hatfield has been a member of the board and of the executive committee of the National Tuberculosis Association for many years, and with the retirement of Dr. Farrand as executive secretary he was unanimously elected to this office. His title as execu-

CHARLES J. HATFIELD

tive secretary was changed December 5, 1918, to that of managing director. Dr. Hatfield has indeed most ably succeeded Dr. Farrand. Under his directorship the Association has been growing rapidly and its activities have extended, particularly during the World War when so much and such useful work was done by the officers of the Association. Dr. Hatfield devoted himself energetically to the development of the field policy, with the result that the National Association's field service has been one of the most distinctive forces in contributing to the development of tuberculosis work in this country. In his efforts toward coöperation and coördination of our work with that of various public health agencies and with local and state agencies affiliated directly with the National Association, Dr. Hatfield has shown consummate skill. In these fields, requiring careful and diplomatic handling, he has always upheld the traditions of the National Tuberculosis Association, but at the same time has never hesitated to sacrifice tradition to take a new step forward.

Dr. Hatfield ably represented our Association at the recent Conference on Tuberculosis in London and on that occasion visited and conferred with the French tuberculosis authorities as to the best means of furthering the international relations in anti-tuberculosis work. He was instrumental in helping to promote a French National Tuberculosis Committee modeled after our Association.

One of the most important features of the many increased activities since Dr. Hatfield has been at the helm of the executive office, is his work in coördinating the fight against tuberculosis with the other public health activities, especially the American Red Cross and the American Public Health Association through the National Health Council.

The creation and rapid development of the Modern Health Crusade movement during Dr. Hatfield's administration reflects not only his judgment in the guidance of this new movement, but also his encouragement of those who have directly contributed to making it a success.

Dr. Hatfield is chairman of the S. E. Pennsylvania (Philadelphia) Chapter of the American Red Cross, president of the Whittier Center Housing Company for Negroes, and a member of

the executive committee of the Philadelphia Health Council and
Tuberculosis Committee and of the Pennsylvania Tuberculosis
Society.   He is the author of numerous papers on various phases
of tuberculosis and Red Cross work.

The gradual development of the Red Cross Seal Sale, the appropriation of $2,500,000 for the budget in 1919, and the subse-
quent development of the Christmas Seal independently of the
Red Cross reflect the diplomacy and tact of Dr. Hatfield in dealing
with situations that at various times threatened to disrupt the
entire tuberculosis movement.   The wise guidance of the Christmas seal campaign under his leadership has no doubt been the
most significant factor in placing the tuberculosis movement
where it is to-day.

The bibliography of Dr. Charles J. Hatfield follows:

History-taking in cases of pulmonary tuberculosis.   Med. News, Sept. 17,
   1904.
Modes of infection in tuberculosis.   Sanitation, i, 253–55, 1904–1905.
Tuberculosis exhibit at the Louisiana Purchase Exposition.   Second annual
   report Henry Phipps Institute, 1904–05, 405–409.
Report on serum treatment.   Third annual report Henry Phipps Institute,
   1905–1906, 90, 94.
Report of the Henry Phipps Institute Training School for Nurses.   Third
   annual report Henry Phipps Institute, 1905–1906; 388; Fifth annual
   report, 1907–1908, 444.
Training for professional nursing in institutions for tuberculous patients.   Tr.
   Sixth Internat. Congr. on Tuberc., iii, 407, 1908.
Employment for arrested cases of tuberculosis.   Tr. Nat. Tuberc. Assn., iv,
   82, 1908.
The relation state and local anti-tuberculosis associations should sustain to
   each other.   Tr. Nat. Tuberc. Assn., xi, 321, 1911.
Introductory remarks to Advisory council.   Tr. Nat. Tuberc. Assn., ix, 37,
   1913.
Tuberculosis relief associations.   Tr. Nat. Tuberc. Assn., xii, 406, 1916.
War and tuberculosis.   Boston Med. and Surg. Jour., clxxviii, 863, 1918.
Economic aspect of tuberculosis.   Proc. Nat. Conference of Social Work,
   1919.
Henry Phipps Institute.   Special report and prospectus, 1919.   (Type-
   written.)
Report of the executive secretary.   Tr. Nat. Tuberc. Assn., x, 23–29, 1914;
   xi, 27–36, 1915; xii, 24–36, 1916; xiii, 29–40, 1917; xiv, 32–46, 1918; xv,
   26–42, 1919; xvi, 33–48, 1920; xvii, 32–53, 1921.

CHAPTER LVII

PHILIP P. JACOBS, Ph.D.

PUBLICITY DIRECTOR OF THE NATIONAL TUBERCULOSIS ASSOCIATION

PHILIP PETER JACOBS, for many years our able assistant secretary and now publicity director of the Association, was born in Syracuse, N. Y., March 28, 1879, the son of Theodore B. and Dorothy Jacobs. He received his preliminary education at the Binghamton High School. From Syracuse University he graduated with the degree of A.B. in 1903, from the Drew Theological Seminary with the degree of B.D. in 1908, and from Columbia University with the degree of Ph.D. in 1910.

Dr. Jacobs entered the service of the National Tuberculosis Association on March 1, 1908. His first work was the preparation of the tuberculosis directory, entitled, "The Campaign Against Tuberculosis in the United States," published as a special volume for the International Congress under the auspices of the Russell Sage Foundation. Subsequent directories of a similar character were published by the National Tuberculosis Association in 1911 and 1916, and a new edition in three parts appeared in 1919.

From the fall of 1908 until the resignation of Dr. Farrand in the spring of 1915 Dr. Jacobs served as assistant secretary, giving special attention to publicity and organization. Since the resignation of Dr. Farrand he has still served under the title of assistant secretary, but has been more directly in charge of the executive work of the office, under the direction of Dr. Charles J. Hatfield. He has conducted eight institutes for the training of tuberculosis workers in coöperation with the New York School of Social Work.

To Dr. Jacobs' genius and executive ability we are greatly indebted for the solution of the problems connected with the organization of state and local societies and the general progress of the tuberculosis work. Besides some 30 odd publications under his name, Dr. Jacobs has written many valuable editorials in the

Journal of the Outdoor Life, of which periodical he is the treasurer and managing editor. The growth of this journal in importance and circulation has been already referred to in the general history, but the fact that under the guidance of the managing editor the circulation has been increased from about 2,000 in 1910 to nearlv 6,500 in 1921, deserves special mention here.

Both Dr. Farrand and Dr. Hatfield have frankly stated on many occasions their belief that Dr. Jacobs, by his long association with the work of the National Tuberculosis Association, has accumulated a greater store of knowledge of the details of tuberculosis work in the United States than has any other single individual in this country.

It would indeed be ungrateful did the author of this biographical sketch fail to embrace this opportunity to express again to Dr. Jacobs his profound gratitude for the invaluable help he has given in the preparation of the History of the National Tuberculosis Association.

The bibliography of Philip P. Jacobs follows:

Ambulance service in Greater New York.   Published by N. Y. State Charities
    Aid Assn., 1907.
New hospitals needed in Greater New York.   Published by N. Y. State Chari-
    ties Aid Assn., 1908.
Tuberculosis directory.   Published by Nat. Tuberc. Assn., 1908, 1911, 1916
    and 1919.
German sociology.   Columbia doctor's thesis.   Published privately 1909.
Tuberculosis.   Charities, xxi, 686–90, Jan. 16, 1909.
Eight million dollars to prevent tuberculosis.   Survey, xxii, 821–822, Sept. 18,
    1909.
National Tuberculosis Association.   Survey, xxii, 327–329, May 29, 1909.
Trend of anti-tuberculosis crusade.   Survey, xxii, 710–713, Aug. 21, 1909.
Bird's-eye view of the anti-tuberculosis campaign.   Survey, xxiii, 579–82,
    Jan. 29, 1910.
National Tuberculosis Association meeting.   Survey, xxiv, 290–293, May 14,
    1910.
New York Tuberculosis Conference.   Survey, xxiv, 49–51, April, 1910.
Campaign of 1910.   Jour. Outdoor Life, viii, 17, 1911.
Welfare work of the Metropolitan Life Insurance Company.   Survey, xxiv,
    705–707, Aug. 13, 1910.
Christmas seals.   Survey, xxix, 307–308, Dec. 7, 1912.
Tuberculosis prevention costs in 1911.   Survey, xxvii, 1612–13, Jan. 20, 1912.

PHILIP P. JACOBS

Year's trend in the prevention of tuberculosis. Survey, xxviii, 443–444, June 15, 1912.

Expenditures in 1911. A review of what tuberculosis prevention costs. Jour. Outdoor Life, ix, 35, 1912.

The part of the Red Cross Seal in the anti-tuberculosis campaign. Jour. Outdoor Life, ix, 181, 1912.

Tuberculosis in motion pictures. Jour. Outdoor Life, ix, 302, 1912.

Tuberculosis in the state legislatures. Jour. Outdoor Life, x, 138, 1913.

Theodore B. Sachs. An appreciation. Jour. Outdoor Life, xiii, 129, 1916.

Our equipment for success against tuberculosis. Survey, xxx, 288–289, May 24, 1913.

Misleading mortality statistics on tuberculosis. Am. Jour. Public Health, iii, 431–447, 1913.

Fake consumption "cures." Metropolitan Life Insurance Company publication, 1913.

What a western woman did with Red Cross Seals. Ladies' Home Journal, xxxi, 56, Dec., 1914.

Red Cross Seals and the anti-tuberculosis campaign. Jour. Outdoor Life, xii, 17, 1915.

The consumptive. Survey, xxxvii, 359, Dec. 30, 1916.

Tuberculosis. A bibliography. Bull. Russell Sage Foundation Library, Aug., 1916.

Survey nurse and nurse's survey for a small community. National Tuberc. Assn. publication, 1917.

Trend of the tuberculosis campaign. Jour. Outdoor Life, xvi, 213, July, 1919.

Programs and policies for 1920. Bull. Nat. Tuberc. Assn., Dec., 1919.

On to St. Louis. Bull. Nat. Tuberc. Assn., April, 1920.

CHAPTER LVIII

DONALD B. ARMSTRONG, M.D.

SECOND ASSISTANT SECRETARY OF THE NATIONAL TUBERCULOSIS ASSOCIATION
SINCE 1916

D R. DONALD B. ARMSTRONG, our second assistant
secretary, was born on December 19, 1886, at Bangor,
Pa., and is the son of Elmer R. and Sadie Budd Armstrong. He received his preliminary education at the public school
of Easton, Pa., and Lerch's preparatory school of the same place,
and graduated from Lafayette College as Ph.B. in 1908. Four
years later he graduated from Columbia University as A.M. and
M.D., and in 1913 as M.S. from the Massachusetts Institute of
Technology.

The positions which Dr. Armstrong has occupied since he left
the Massachusetts Institute of Technology show a wide range of
activity. He was superintendent of the Bureau of Public Health
and Hygiene of the New York Association for Improving the
Condition of the Poor from 1913 to 1914; director of the Depart-
ment of Social Welfare of the New York A.I.C.P. from 1914 to
1916; chairman of the Advisory Council, Department of Street
Cleaning, New York City, from 1913 to 1916; chairman of the
Committee on Sanitation, Advisory Council, Department of
Health, New York City, from 1913 to 1916; chairman of the
Committee on Food Supply, Borough President's Office, New
York City, from 1914 to 1915; lecturer at Teachers College, New
York, from 1915 to 1916; at the New York University Medical
School from 1914 to 1916, and at the College of the city of New
York from 1914 to 1915. At the meeting of the American Public
Health Association in 1916 Dr. Armstrong was chairman of the
Sociological Section.

In 1916 he became assistant secretary of the National Tuberculosis Association and executive officer of the Framingham

DONALD B. ARMSTRONG

Community Health and Tuberculosis Demonstration. (See p. 70.) To Dr. Armstrong's activities and achievements in this capacity we have already referred in the general history when recording the results of this unique experiment. Since the creation of the National Health Council, Dr. Armstrong has served as acting executive officer of that organization. He has recently resigned as executive officer of the Framingham Community Health and Tuberculosis Demonstration and is now executive officer of the National Health Council. We are indebted to Dr. Armstrong for a number of valuable publications which show his ability as a physician and administrator, eminently fitted for that important task to which he has been assigned.

The bibliography of Dr. Donald B. Armstrong follows:

LIST OF FRAMINGHAM PUBLICATIONS AND REPORTS ISSUED IN CONNECTION WITH THE COMMUNITY HEALTH AND TUBERCULOSIS DEMONSTRATION

Monographs and General Publications

Framingham Monographs: No. 1—General series, i, The program.
" " No. 2—Medical series, i, The sickness census.
" " No. 3—Sanitary series, i, Vital statistics.
" No. 4—Medical series, ii, Medical examination campaigns.
" No. 5—Medical series, iii, Tuberculosis findings.
" No. 6—Sanitary series, ii, Schools and factories.
" No. 7—General series, ii, The children's summer camp.
" " No. 8—General series, iii, Health letters.
Diagnostic standards (4 editions).
Report of the Committee on Appraisal.
Framingham—keep fit.
Healthy homes make happiness.
Advice to persons having consumption.
What has the health demonstration done thus far for Framingham?
Framingham's opportunity.
Your annual medical examination.
Framingham Yardsticks. Four Years of the Demonstration.

Reprints

The Framingham Health and Tuberculosis Demonstration. Tr. Nat. Tuberc. Assn., xiii, 398, 1917; also in Am. Jour. Pub. Health, vii, no. 3, March, 1917.

27

Health administration in cities of less than 20,000 population. Jour. Am. Med. Assn., Nov. 2, 1918.

Civilian tuberculosis control following war conditions.   Am. Jour. Pub. Health, viii, 12, Dec., 1918.

The Framingham health program: the first year results.   Tr. Nat. Tuberc. Assn., xiv, 478, 1918.

Community machinery for the discovery of tuberculosis.   Tr. Nat. Tuberc. Assn., xv, 214, 1919; also Boston Med. and Surg. Jour., Aug. 28, 1919.

The consultation service in tuberculosis work.   Mod. Med., Nov., 1919.

The sanitarian's definition of a living wage.   Mod. Med., Feb., 1920.

The state, the municipality, and the private tuberculosis associations in the control of tuberculosis.   Jour. Outdoor Life, xvii, 9, Jan., 1920.

Possible modifications in tuberculosis programs on the basis of recent Framingham experience.   Tr. Nat. Tuberc. Assn., xvi, 381, 1920.

CHAPTER LIX

JOHN S. FULTON, M.D.*

SECRETARY GENERAL OF THE SIXTH INTERNATIONAL CONGRESS ON TUBERCU-
LOSIS

MARYLAND has been fortunate in the development of its public health and tuberculosis work, both because of the fact that it has had an institution of such international importance as the Johns Hopkins Medical School and also because of the fact that it has had, for over twenty years, state health officers of strong and vigorous personalities. Such a man has been Dr. John Samuel Fulton. Without Dr. Fulton much of the progressive leadership that Maryland has enjoyed in the tuberculosis movement might have been retarded or indefinitely postponed.

Dr. Fulton was born in a rectory at Freemont, Ohio, in 1859, his parents being Rev. William Fulton, D.D., a native of Glasgow, Scotland, and Nancy Organ Fulton, of Cable, Ohio. In 1861 the family moved to Snow Hill, Maryland. Dr. Fulton's education, therefore, began in the rectory of All Hallows Parish, on the eastern shore of Maryland, with his parents for teachers. The lot of a clergyman in the South during the Civil War was hard enough. There were not fewer than five Scottish born clergymen on the eastern shore in those days, two of them Fultons, and all of them had to teach for a living. Any boy in a rectory or a manse had, therefore, quite superior educational advantages.

Dr. Fulton received his A.B. degree from St. John's College, Annapolis, in 1876, and began the study of medicine immediately thereafter as student assistant to Dr. Stephen Purnell Dennis, of Salisbury. He taught two years in the public schools, and graduated in medicine at the University of Maryland in 1881. In 1897 Dr. Fulton became secretary of the State Board of Health,

* As Secretary-General of the International Congress Dr. Fulton was a recognized officer of the National Tuberculosis Association.

expecting to continue in private practice, as did the health officers in most of the states at that time. After he had forgotten a few important appointments in private practice he concluded that state medicine had his real affection, and should become his sole pursuit.

In 1898 Dr. Fulton sought and secured the appointment of Dr. William H. Welch as a member of the State Board of Health. Dr. Welch became president of the Board of Health, and still retains that office. It is, therefore, not surprising that the Maryland State Board of Health should have led a campaign for the enactment of the first registration law requiring reporting of living cases of tuberculosis, a law which has been a model for practically every state in the Union; or that with such backing Dr. Fulton, and his assistant, Dr. Marshall L. Price, should have planned and realized the first tuberculosis exposition, held in Baltimore in February, 1904, where the first action in regard to the formation of the National Tuberculosis Association was taken.

When it was definitely decided to hold the Sixth International Congress on Tuberculosis in this country, the general committee having the arrangements for the Congress in charge in casting about for a man who could serve as secretary-general, selected Dr. Fulton. This arduous task he held from 1906 until about a year after the close of the Congress in 1909. The success of the Congress itself, mention of which is made in other pages of the volume, is sufficient testimony to the ability of Dr. Fulton. The reputation that he gained in this connection brought him into such world-wide prominence that he was selected as secretary-general of the Fifteenth International Congress on Hygiene and Demography held in Washington in 1913.

During the war Dr. Fulton served in the Medical Reserve Corps with a commission of Lieutenant Colonel. At the present time he is again serving as secretary of the State Department of Health of Maryland.

JOHN S. FULTON

CHAPTER LX
LAWRENCE F. FLICK, M.D.*

VICE-PRESIDENT OF THE NATIONAL TUBERCULOSIS ASSOCIATION FROM 1905 TO 1908

TO THE pioneer in any field of human endeavor there must always come many hours of discouragement. If, however, he has the perseverance to continue, he will sooner or later be heartened by the continuing development of the movement that he has started. Dr. Lawrence F. Flick was a pioneer in every sense of the word. He had the vision, the conviction, and the perseverance of the true pioneer. The nation-wide campaign against tuberculosis, to which he as an individual contributed so much, must today bring him great encouragement in contrast with the numerous discouragements to which he was subjected in the earlier days of his work.

Dr. Flick was born at Carrolltown, Cambria County, Pa., on August 10, 1856. He was the son of an Alsatian farmer and one of a numerous family of children. As a boy he attended the township schools, and when thirteen entered the Benedictine School, Latrobe, Pa. During his first year in college his health broke down and he returned home with a mild attack of tuberculosis. He made a fair recovery by living largely out-of-doors at home, but he did not become very strong and robust. The result was that after a few months of teaching in Newark, N. J., he again broke down, and after a second recovery, taught school for two winters in the mountains near his home.

Because of the unsatisfactory condition of his health he decided to study medicine, hoping thus to find the way to his own cure. After a year's preliminary work in a country doctor's office, he matriculated in 1877 at the Jefferson Medical College in Philadelphia and graduated from that school in 1879. After a

* Written by Philip P. Jacobs.

year of internship he took up the general practice of medicine. At the same time he began the study of law to gratify an old ambition, registering as a student in the office of Benjamin Harris Brewster, of Philadelphia. The strain of practising medicine and studying law, however, was too much for him, and he again broke down. Hoping to improve his health by life at sea, he applied for assignment in the United States Navy, but was rejected on physical grounds. The naval physicians advised him to go west. With a few dollars in his pocket he started for Colorado, and after countless hardships and calling upon several of his friends for assistance he reached Los Angeles by way of Texas and Arizona in December, 1881, with $25 in borrowed money as his total assets. He was thrown from a horse while looking for work the day after he reached Los Angeles, and was taken back to his boarding-house in a grocery wagon. For somewhat over six months he struggled for existence, all the time, however, improving his health. He says that his poverty was the principal reason for his cure because he was compelled to live largely on milk, drinking as much as six quarts a day. From this personal experience he gathered many interesting suggestions in regard to diet in tuberculosis that he put into practice in later life.

In September, 1882, he resumed his practice in Philadelphia and rapidly began to develop a reputation as a specialist in tuberculosis. From that time on he did not suffer seriously on account of tuberculosis. He married and reared a family of seven children, all of whom are living at this time.

Dr. Flick's early contributions to tuberculosis excited a considerable amount of opposition, not only because of the fact that his general views regarding the communicability and curability of the disease were counter to the notions of most of his professional brothers, but also because he had developed from his own personal experience very positive convictions regarding the climatic treatment of tuberculosis.

As early as 1888 he developed and presented a paper on the con tagiousness of phthisis, and began to advocate the registering and reporting of living cases of tuberculosis in Philadelphia.

His daily practice in one of the most congested districts of Philadelphia convinced him of the necessity of free treatment and

LAWRENCE F. FLICK

diagnosis. He saw all about him the evidences of tuberculosis and the inability of the average tenement-house dweller to secure adequate diagnosis or proper treatment. He was perplexed as to the cause of tuberculosis, and for years struggled singlehanded in research on tuberculosis.

The Rush Hospital for Consumption and Allied Diseases, incorporated in September, 1890, realized only in part his ambitions and ideals. It was not until the White Haven Sanatorium, for which he had worked for several years, became an actual fact in 1900 that Dr. Flick began to see the consummation of his dream. Here was an institution where the poor could receive treatment free of charge or at reasonable rates.

In 1901, through the influence of a member of the State Board of Charities, Dr. Flick met Mr. Henry Phipps, and out of the meeting grew and developed a friendship which bore fruit in a great many different ways. Commenting on Mr. Phipps' first visit to the White Haven Sanatorium in 1901, Dr. Flick says:

"It was a rainy day and the grounds were muddy. Overhead everything was gloomy. Mr. Phipps found the patients lodged in an old barn, their beds ranged on the threshing floor and in the hay-mows. The administration building was a small and dilapidated farm-house. There were about forty patients in the institution. As Mr. Phipps left me on Saturday afternoon at Bethlehem he said, 'You may hear from me again,' but I was very much downcast and feared that the sanatorium had made a bad showing indeed. Imagine my surprise when at four o'clock the next morning I was routed out of bed by a special delivery letter from Mr. Phipps which read, 'It really surprises me how much good you are doing with so little money at your command. It is very creditable to your management. If you had been a business man in any line you would have been a serious competitor, but you wisely selected a better line than that of business, that of conferring benefits on your fellow-men. Please accept my check enclosed for $2,500, which please use in any way you may prefer for the benefit of the Free Hospital for Poor Consumptives.'"

In October, 1901, Dr. Flick had occasion to tell Mr. Phipps about his ideas regarding a dispensary in one of the congested districts of Philadelphia. Imagine his surprise when Mr. Phipps, on learning of the plan, offered to buy a whole block and equip a hospital for him. Out of this conversation grew the Henry Phipps Institute for the Study and Prevention of Tuberculosis, and later the Phipps Tuberculosis Dispensary in Baltimore and the Phipps

Model Tenement Houses in New York. In 1903 the Phipps Institute was opened with 52 beds and with laboratories, dispensaries, and full facilities for research and clinical observation. For several years Dr. Flick remained Director of the Institute until, in 1910, it was turned over to the University of Pennsylvania.

Shortly after the formation of the Henry Phipps Institute the discussion regarding a national association in the United States began to grow intense. As early as 1898 Dr. Flick, in correspondence with Dr. Otis, Dr. Bowditch, Dr. Knopf, and others, had discussed with them the possibilities of a national association in this country. In 1892 he had formed the Pennsylvania Society for the Prevention of Tuberculosis; the first organized society of its type in the world. In coöperation with Dr. Edward L. Trudeau, Dr. William Osler, Dr. William H. Welch, General Sternberg, Dr. Henry Barton Jacobs, Dr. Charles L. Minor, Dr. M. P. Ravenel, Dr. Hermann M. Biggs, Dr. S. A. Knopf, and others, he helped to organize The National Association for the Study and Prevention of Tuberculosis which was formed in 1904.

In 1905 he took a leading part in arranging for bringing to this country the International Congress on Tuberculosis and was made the chairman of the Central Committee of the Congress. He devised the plan for financing the Congress and was most active in raising the funds which made the gathering possible. The success of this gathering in 1908 is due largely to his hard and painstaking endeavor, as well as to his far-seeing vision, a fact which has been suitably acknowledged by the members of the Central Committee and the Board of Directors of the National Association.

In his own community and state Dr. Flick has been the originator of almost every line of work against tuberculosis that is now in operation; in the national organization he has been a leader and potent factor; internationally he is recognized as one of the pioneers in the world-wide anti-tuberculosis campaign.

Dr. Flick published a popular book on tuberculosis in the summer of 1903. It was called "Consumption, a Curable and Preventable Disease—What the Layman Should Know About It." An abbreviated edition of this book was also published later. Both have had a very wide and continuous sale since that date.

During the many years of his active life Dr. Flick has contributed numerous articles on various phases of tuberculosis treatment and prevention to the leading medical journals of the United States and foreign countries.

After the International Congress on Tuberculosis Dr. Flick retired from active participation in the national campaign against tuberculosis. He is now devoting himself to the preparation of a magnum opus, a comprehensive treatise on the subject of tuberculosis, to which he has devoted his life. It is sincerely hoped that he will be spared to complete this work.

The bibliography of Dr. Lawrence F. Flick follows:

The hygiene of phthisis. Tr. Phila. Co. Med. Soc., 1888.

The contagiousness of phthisis. Tr. Med. Soc. State of Pennsylvania, 1888.

How to take care of the lungs. Tr. Alumni Association of the Phila. College of Pharmacy, 1889.

A review of the cases of tuberculosis which terminated in death in the fifth ward of the city of Philadelphia during the year 1888. Tr. of the Phila. Co. Med. Soc., 1889.

The mode of entrance of the tubercle bacillus into the system. Times and Register, Oct. 19, 1889.

Special hospitals for the treatment of tuberculosis. Tr. of the College of Physicians of Phila., 1890; also Times and Register, March, 1890.

The treatment of tuberculosis. Med. News, Nov. 15, 1890.

The prevention of tuberculosis. Tr. Am. Pub. Health Assn., 1890; also Sanitarian, 1891.

Some points in the treatment of tuberculosis. Tr. Phila. Co. Med. Soc., 1891.

A further report on the treatment of tuberculosis by iodoform inunctions. Med. News, March, 1892.

The influence of the doctrine of contagion upon the death rate from tuberculosis in the city of Philadelphia. Med. News, May, 1892.

The early recognition of tuberculosis. Penn. University Med. Magazine, Nov., 1893.

Practical measures for the prevention of tuberculosis. Med. News, Oct. 21, 1893.

The registration of tuberculosis. Phila. Polyclinic, Feb. 17, 1894.

Prophylaxis in the treatment of tuberculosis. Penn. University Med. Magazine, Oct., 1894.

The control of tuberculosis. Twelfth annual report of the State Board of Health of Pennsylvania.

Contagiousness of tuberculosis. Annual report of the Woman's Health Protective Assn. of the U. S., 1897.

Immunity as against heredity in tuberculosis. Jour. of Tuberc., Oct., 1899.

Consumption: its nature, history, curability, and prevention.   Annual report, Phila. Col. of Pharmacy, 1897.

Nitroglycerine as a hemostatic in hemoptysis.   Phila. Med. Jour., Feb., 1898.

Immunity the fundamental principle underlying all treatment of tuberculosis. Jour. Am. Med. Assn., Oct., 1898.

Contagion: its meaning and limitations.   Phila. Med. Jour., Jan., 1899.

The treatment of tuberculosis.   Med. News, Sept., 1899.

The therapeutics of tuberculosis.   Therap. Gaz., Jan., 1900.

The registration of tuberculosis.   Phila. Med. Jour., June, 1900.

The treatment of tuberculosis.   Hare's System of Therapeutics, 1901.

Home treatment of tuberculosis.   Proc. Phila. Co. Med. Soc., Feb., 1901.

Primary abdominal tuberculosis.   Courier of Med., Dec., 1901.

The implantation of tuberculosis.   Courier of Med., July, 1902.

Are meat and milk a source of seed supply for human tuberculosis?   Jour. of Tuberc., Oct., 1902.

A year's work at the White Haven Sanatorium of the Free Hospital for Poor Consumptives.   Phila. Med. Jour., Nov., 1902.

Differential diagnosis between tuberculosis of the lungs and diseases which resemble it.   Internat. Clin., iv, 12th series.

The Henry Phipps Institute for the Study, Treatment, and Prevention of Tuberculosis.   Phila. Med. Jour., Jan., 1903.

House infection of tuberculosis.   Am. Med. Jour., Feb., 1904; also in Med. News, Feb., 1904.

Communities without health departments in the crusade against tuberculosis. Tr. of the Scranton Society for Prevention and Cure of Tuberc.; also in New York Med. Jour. and Phila. Med. Jour., 1904.

Municipalities in the crusade against tuberculosis.   Med., April, 1904.

The treatment and control of the tuberculous patient in his home.   Am. Med., July, 1904.

Report of the committee on tuberculosis.   Am. Pub. Health Assn., Havana, Jan., 1905.   Published in Transactions.

The hospital and the dispensary in the warfare against tuberculosis.   Am. Med., May, 1905.

The pneumococcus as a factor in hemoptysis (with Ravenel and Irwin).   From the Laboratory of the Henry Phipps Institute.   Med. News, Sept., 1905.

Prognosis in tuberculosis.   Am. Med., Jan., 1906.

Vicarious action of the bowels for the kidneys in tuberculosis (with Joseph Walsh).   From the Laboratory of the Henry Phipps Institute.   Tr. Nat. Tuberc. Assn., i, 198, 1905; also in Am. Med., July, 1905.

America and the International Congress on Tuberculosis.   One hundred thousand dollar fund proposed for the great Washington gathering of 1908.   Charities, Dec., 1905; also in Jour. Outdoor Life, March, 1907.

The relative value of home treatment of tuberculosis.   Tr. Nat. Tuberc. Assn., ii, 442, 1906.

Address of the vice-president. The duties, responsibilities and opportunities of the National Association for the Study and Prevention of Tuberculosis. Tr. Nat. Tuberc. Assn., ii, 14, 1906.

The way of infection in tuberculosis. Med., Dec., 1906.

The essentials in the crusade against tuberculosis. N. Y. Med. Jour., March, 1907.

The crusade against tuberculosis. Bull. Johns Hopkins Hosp., Aug., 1907.

Report on the International Congress on Tuberculosis. Tr. Nat. Tuberc. Assn., iii, 20, 1907; also Tr. Nat. Tuberc. Assn., iv, 18, 1908.

The hospital for advanced cases of tuberculosis. Internat. Clin., i, 19th series.

The influence of the International Congress on Tuberculosis in Washington, 1908. Read at the opening of the International Tuberculosis Exhibit of New York, Dec., 1908.

Our consumptive brethren. Sunday School Times, Dec., 1908.

The crusade against tuberculosis in Pennsylvania. Annual report of the Free Hospital for Poor Consumptives, 1908.

Work for patients as an economic factor. Tr. Nat. Tuberc. Assn., v, 181, 1909.

State appropriations to hospitals not under state control. Objections to the Pennsylvania method. Penn. Med. Jour., Jan., 1910.

Present status of the tuberculosis campaign and the essentials for thorough and prompt success. New York Med. Jour., Feb. 5, 1910.

The tuberculosis situation in Pennsylvania in the year 1909. Privately printed 1910.

The medical profession in relationship to preventive medicine. Interstate Med. Jour., xvii, no. 6, 1910.

Skin inunction as a therapeutic measure. Monthly Cyclopedia and Med. Bull., Aug., 1910.

The crux of the tuberculosis problem. Med. Rec., May, 1910.

Tuberculosis among the poor. Tr. Conference of Catholic Charities, Washington, D. C., 1910.

Advantages of local care and treatment of tuberculosis. Interstate Med. Jour., xvii, no. 12, 1910.

The progress in the tuberculosis campaign in Pennsylvania up to 1911. Tr. College of Physicians of Phila., 1911; also Interstate Clinics, ii, 21st series.

Tuberculosis as it concerns the physician. Interstate Med. Jour., xviii, no. 2, 1911.

Crusade against tuberculosis. Consumption a curable and preventable disease. P. Reilly, Phila., 1903. Several editions.

CHAPTER LXI

JOHN P. C. FOSTER, M.D.

VICE-PRESIDENT OF THE NATIONAL TUBERCULOSIS ASSOCIATION FROM 1907 TO 1908

D R. JOHN PIERPONT CODDINGTON FOSTER, who was one of our early vice-presidents, is no longer with us, but to convey an idea of the life of this fine and interesting man, scholar, and physician, we cannot do better than to quote from the admirable tribute paid to Dr. Foster by his pupil and friend, Dr. David R. Lyman, which appeared in the Transactions of the American Climatological and Clinical Association of 1910.

"Dr. Foster was born in New Haven, Connecticut, on March 2, 1847. He prepared for college at Russell's Collegiate Institute in New Haven. He graduated from Yale Medical School in 1875, and settled in New Haven, where his family had borne a prominent part in the town's history since its foundation. In 1878 he was appointed instructor in anatomy in the Yale Art School, which position he held up to his death. He was for many years port surgeon of the United States Marine Hospital Service and consulting physician to the Yale Infirmary. Deeply enthusiastic, untiring, and unselfish in his devotion to his profession, he has left behind him a lasting impression of his life work such as is equaled by few men.

"He was best known to the general public through his work in tuberculosis, in recognition of which Yale conferred upon him the honorary degree of M.A. in June, 1909. He knew from personal experience what it meant to fight through life handicapped by the disease. He combined a deep insight into the mental unrest of those first facing the fight against it with an ever-ready sympathy for them and a thorough knowledge of their needs. He spared himself nothing if he could lighten the burden of a tuberculous patient. This unselfishness, which characterized his private practice, he carried into his public work, and to his untiring devotion Connecticut is indebted to-day for four of its existing sanatoria.

"To Dr. Foster belongs the distinction of having been the first physician in America to apply Koch's tuberculin for therapeutic purposes.

"He was on the original board of directors of The National Association for the Study and Prevention of Tuberculosis, and was vice-president of the Association in 1908. He was one of the incorporators of the New Haven County Anti-Tuberculosis Association, and as chairman of its executive committee was more than any one man personally responsible for the character

JOHN P. C. FOSTER

and success of the Gaylord Farm Sanatorium. When Governor Woodruff appointed a commission to study the tuberculosis problem in Connecticut he chose Dr. Foster as its chairman. His report to the Governor is one of the most exhaustive and practical of the many that have been submitted by like commissions. Recognizing the fact that the greatest need in the work was a proper provision for the care of the advanced cases, he insisted that the state's duty was primarily to these, leaving the sanatoria for curable cases to the care of private philanthropy. When his report was brought before the legislature it was largely through his energy that a bill was passed carrying two all-important provisions—the compulsory notification of tuberculosis and the establishment of county homes under the control of the State Commission, where all classes of cases could be received. He was appointed chairman of the permanent commission and given an appropriation of $175,000 to open three such institutions of 100 beds each. Few believed that the appropriation could be made to accomplish so much. These institutions are now in operation and accommodate 330 patients.

"But the accomplishment cost the state dear, as the great labor entailed was largely responsible for Dr. Foster's death. He had hoped to hold out until their completion before taking a sorely needed rest. While on a business trip to one of them he contracted pneumonia, and died six days later. Realizing that his end was near, he concentrated his energies for these six days in planning the completion of his work with the least possible disorganization after his death.

"He was best known in Yale through his work among the students. Many a young man has had cause to be thankful for having come under his influence. As Professor Phelps said in introducing him for his degree: 'But perhaps greater than all his honors is the daily quiet work that Dr. Foster has done for many years among the undergraduates of Yale. Trusted by the faculty and students, he has been of material assistance to both, and many a man to-day owes his health and character largely to the kindly counsel he received at the critical period of adolescence.'

"By those of us privileged to be counted among his friends, he was, as President Hadley says, 'If possible, loved even more than he was respected,' and has left to us an inspiring memory of one who lived and died 'a gentleman unafraid.'"

There is little to be added to this fine and well-deserved eulogy. The author had the privilege of knowing Dr. Foster intimately and will never forget a lengthy and interesting visit he had with him a few weeks prior to his passing away. Dr. Foster maintained to the end his enthusiasm and desire to be helpful in all that concerned the solution of the tuberculosis problem. His name will be cherished by all workers in tuberculosis and all patients who had the privilege of coming in contact with him.

CHAPTER LXII

EDWARD THOMAS DEVINE, Ph.D., LL.D.

EDWARD THOMAS DEVINE was born in Union, Hardin County, Iowa, May 6, 1867, the son of John and Laura Hall Devine. He obtained his degree of A.B. from Cornell College, Iowa, in 1887, of A.M. in 1890, and of Ph.D. from the University of Pennsylvania in 1893. The degree of LL.D. was conferred upon him by Cornell College in 1904. He studied also at the University of Halle, Germany, and was a fellow of the University of Pennsylvania from 1891 to 1895.

Dr. Devine was principal of the schools at Albion, Marshalltown, and Mt. Vernon in Iowa from 1886 to 1890. From 1891 to 1896 he was staff lecturer on economics and the secretary of the American Society for the Extension of University Teaching. In 1896 he became general secretary of the New York Charity Organization Society, which position he occupied until 1917. He was professor of social economy at Columbia from 1905 to 1919, director of the School of Philanthropy from 1904 to 1907, and from 1912 to 1917. Dr. Devine was editor of the Survey from 1897 to 1912, and has been serving in the capacity of associate editor ever since. He was chief of the Bureau of Refugees and Home Relief under the American Red Cross Commission to France from 1917 to 1918. Prior to these important positions Dr. Devine had been active as special representative of the American Red Cross in charge of relief work in San Francisco in 1906 after the earthquake and fire, and he served again as special representative for the American Red Cross in charge of Storm and Flood Relief in Dayton, Ohio, in 1913, and as special agent to the American Embassy in Petrograd in 1916. Because of this great executive ability Dr. Devine was chosen president of the

EDWARD T. DEVINE

National Conference of Charities and Correction in 1906, chairman of the Section of Hygienic, Social, Industrial, and Economic Aspects of Tuberculosis of the International Congress on Tuberculosis in Washington in 1908. In 1909 he was elected vice-president of the National Tuberculosis Association. He has served on many commissions for the improvement of prison conditions, industrial relations, etc., and has been especially interested in the social aspect of the tuberculosis problem.

The author of this history is greatly indebted to him for the help extended in 1902 in the formation of a local tuberculosis committee. When the appeal for such a committee was shown him bearing the signatures of eleven leading physicians, Dr. Devine at once offered his services and became its first lay member and secretary. The valuable work which that committee did is referred to in the historical part of this book. Dr. Devine was equally helpful in the formation of the National Tuberculosis Association in 1904. He was a member of the Association's first executive committee and was largely responsible for raising the initial funds that made possible the selection of Dr. Livingston Farrand as executive secretary in January, 1905.

As secretary of the New York Committee on the Prevention of Tuberculosis, and as editor of the Survey, Dr. Devine has written many interesting articles and circulars, which, unfortunately, never bore his signature, and for this reason we are deprived of a tuberculosis bibliography of this distinguished leader in the anti-tuberculosis crusade.

Dr. Devine has become world famous as a leader and organizer in social relief work. The National Tuberculosis Association may congratulate itself that he has been and still is one of its most enthusiastic workers in the combat of the social causes of tuberculosis.

Among his published works which bear on the tuberculosis problem we must not fail to mention here his valuable contributions, entitled "Misery and Its Causes," 1909; "The Family and Social Work," 1912; "Disabled Soldiers and Sailors," 1919.

CHAPTER LXIII

HENRY SEWALL, M.D., Ph.D., Sc.D.

VICE-PRESIDENT OF THE NATIONAL TUBERCULOSIS ASSOCIATION FROM 1909 TO 1910

H ENRY SEWALL, the son of Thomas and Elizabeth Waters Sewall, was born at Winchester, Va., May 25, 1855. He received the degree of B.S. from the Wesleyan University of Connecticut in 1876, of Ph.D. from Johns Hopkins University in 1879, Hon. M.D. from the University of Michigan in 1888, M.D. from the University of Denver in 1889, and Sc.D. from the University of Michigan in 1912. Dr. Sewall was assistant fellow and associate in biology at Johns Hopkins University from 1876 to 1881, professor of physiology at the University of Michigan from 1882 to 1889, professor of physiology at the Denver and Gross College of Medicine from 1890 to 1908, professor of medicine at the same school from 1911 to 1917, and lecturer in medicine at the University of Colorado from 1917 to 1919.

Dr. Sewall was a member of the National Board of Medical Examiners until 1919 and secretary of the Colorado State Board of Health from 1893 to 1899. He is a member of the American Physiological Society and of the Association of Physicians, whose president he was from 1915 to 1916. He is also a member of the American Climatological Association and was its president from 1914 to 1915. He is a member of the Colorado State Medi cal Society and of the American Medical Association. The numerous degrees, medical and purely scientific, which Dr. Sewall is entitled to add to his name are evidence of the great achievements in scientific medicine for which we are indebted to him. The bibliography of Dr. Sewall, shows how much we owe him for the many valuable contributions on the subject of tuberculosis. In Colorado he is justly considered as one of the State's pioneers in tuberculosis work.

HENRY SEWALL

The bibliography of Dr. Henry Sewall follows:

On the relations of diaphragmatic and costal respiration (with M. E. Pollard). Jour. Physiol., xi, 159, 1890.

On tuberculosis contracted in Colorado.   Tr. Colo. State Med. Soc., 1895, 385.

Clinical uses of stethoscopic pressure.   N. Y. Med. Jour., lxvi, 758, 1897.

Comparison of physical signs and x-ray pictures of the chest in early stages of tuberculosis (with S. B. Childs).   Arch. Int. Med., 1912, x, 45.

Bimanual palpatory percussion.   Arch. of Diagnosis, v, 13, 1912.

On what do the hygienic and therapeutic properties of the open air depend? Jour. Am. Med. Assn., lviii, 174, 1912.

Rôle of the stethoscope in physical diagnosis.   Am. Jour. Med. Sc., cxlv, 234, 1913.

The auscultatory determination of early pathologic changes in the lungs.   Jour. Am. Med. Assn., lx, 2027, 1913.

Another view on ventilation.   Interstate Med. Jour., xxiii, 23, 1916.

Experimental tuberculosis in guinea pigs following preliminary treatment with tuberculin by the nose (with C. F. Hegner and C. Powell).   Am. Rev. Tuberc., i, 220, 1917.

Experimental asthma in guinea pigs.   Jour. Lab. and Clin. Med., ii, 874, 1917.

Diagnosis of tuberculosis.   Colo. Med., xiv, 286, 1917.

On occult tuberculosis.   Am. Rev. Tuberc., iii, 665, 1920.

Importance of subliminal symptoms and period of alternation of rest and exercise in the treatment of tuberculosis.   Am. Rev. Tuberc., v, 236, 1921.

The effects of limiting the respiratory excursions of the upper thorax in refractory cases of pulmonary tuberculosis (with S. Swezey).   Am. Rev. Tuberc., v, 547, 1921.

CHAPTER LXIV

GEORGE DOCK, M.D., Sc.D.

VICE-PRESIDENT OF THE NATIONAL TUBERCULOSIS ASSOCIATION FROM 1910 TO 1911

GEORGE DOCK was born at Hopewell, Pa., April 1, 1860. He was the son of Gilliard and Lavinia Lloyd Bombaugh Dock. He received his preliminary education at the common school of Lancaster, Pa., and at the Harrisburg, Pa., Academy. He was graduated in 1884 with the degree of M.D. from the University of Pennsylvania; in 1895 he received the honorary degree of A.M. from Harvard, and in 1904 the degree of Sc.D. from the University of Pennsylvania. Dr. Dock was assistant to the chair of Clinical Pathology at the University of Pennsylvania from 1887 to 1888, professor of pathology of the Texas Medical College and Hospital from 1888 to 1891, professor of theory and practice of medicine and clinical medicine at the University of Michigan from 1891 to 1908, and professor of theory and practice of medicine at Tulane University from 1908 to 1910. He now occupies the chair of professor of medicine at the Washington University Medical School, St. Louis, where he has been since 1910, and also the position of physician-in-chief of the Barnes Hospital, connected with the school of medicine.

Dr. Dock is a member of the Association of American Physicians (president, 1916–1917), also of the American Medical Association, and of numerous other medical bodies. His contributions on various subjects in medicine and his practical clinics have given him an enviable reputation. He has always been deeply interested in the tuberculosis problem and was most helpful in the work of the local tuberculosis associations as well as the National. Some of his most important contributions on the subject of tuberculosis may be found in the following bibliography.

GEORGE DOCK

The bibliography of Dr. George Dock follows:

Sputum examination for the diagnosis of tuberculosis. Texas Cour.-Rec. Med., Dallas, March, 1890.

An etiologic study of tuberculosis in country people (with T. L. Chadbourne). Phila. Med. Jour., Nov. 5, 1898.

Tuberculosis. Physician and Surg., Sept., 1900.

Tuberculosis hospital at Ann Arbor. Physician and Surg., May, 1902.

Address of the chairman of clinical section. Tr. Nat. Tuberc. Assn., iii, 341, 1907.

Clinical and pathological possibility of spontaneous healing in renal tuberculosis without destruction of kidney. Tr. Am. Urolog. Assn., 1916.

The relation of the general hospital to tuberculosis. Tr. Nat. Tuberc. Assn., xii, 89, 1916.

CHAPTER LV

JOHN M. GLENN, A.M., LL.D.

VICE-PRESIDENT OF THE NATIONAL TUBERCULOSIS ASSOCIATION FROM 1911–1912
AND 1919–1920

JOHN MARK GLENN, the son of William Wilkins and Ellen Mark Smith Glenn, was born in Baltimore, Md., October 28, 1858. He received the degree of A.M. at the Washington and Lee University in 1879, took up special studies at Johns Hopkins University from 1879 to 1880, became LL.B. of the University of Maryland in 1882, and an honorary A.M. of Johns Hopkins Hospital in 1902. He was admitted to the bar in 1882. Washington and Lee University conferred upon him the degree of LL.D. in 1897.

Mr. Glenn's activities have been preëminently philanthropic, and in the interest of social work and public welfare. He was one of the supervisors of the City Charities of Baltimore from 1898 to 1907, and from 1904 to 1907 was president of the board. In 1907 he was selected director of the Russell Sage Foundation, a fund of $10,000,000 set aside by the late Mrs. Russell Sage for the betterment of the social and living conditions. It was fortunate, indeed, that Mr. Glenn was chosen to administer that fund. Being deeply interested in the tuberculosis problem, he has been not only sympathetic, but most helpful to the work which the National Tuberculosis Association is doing. Through his interest grants of considerable sums were made to the National Tuberculosis Association beginning with 1907, and extending over a period of several years. These funds did much to start the struggling National Association on its career of usefulness. Mr. Glenn was chosen president of the National Conference of Charities and Correction in 1901. He is a member of the Administration Commission of the Federal Council of Churches, of the Joint Commission of Social Service of the Protestant Episcopal Church, and of the Central Commission of the American Red Cross, and a trustee of the Johns Hopkins Hospital.

JOHN M. GLENN

G. WALTER HOLDEN, M.D.

VICE-PRESIDENT OF THE NATIONAL TUBERCULOSIS ASSOCIATION FROM 1911 TO 1912

DR. G. WALTER HOLDEN was born at Barre, Mass., September 17, 1866. His parents were James E. and Harriet A. Wheelock Holden. He received his preliminary education at the Mount Hermon Academy, Northfield, Mass., and graduated as Doctor of Medicine of the University of Vermont in 1895. Dr. Holden was in general practice in North Brookfield, Mass., from 1896 to 1898, and at Denver, Colo., from 1898 to 1904, when he became director of the Agnes Memorial Sanatorium. As such he has been identified nationally and internationally with anti-tuberculosis work since 1907, when he was elected a member of the International Tuberculosis Conference. In April, 1908, he formed the Colorado State Organization of the International Congress on Tuberculosis, which was held from September 21 to October 12 of that year in Washington, D. C. Among the exhibits sent by the Colorado State Organization to this International Congress was one submitted by Dr. Holden of new architectural plans for a sanatorium for the treatment of curable cases of tuberculosis among the working classes. This exhibit was awarded a silver medal.

The Colorado State Organization became a permanent organization in 1908, with Dr. Holden as its first president. On retiring from this office in 1912 he was made an honorary life member and is still the only member of the Colorado Association to hold this title. He has continued his interest and constant assistance in the anti-tuberculosis work in Colorado, as a member of the executive committee both of the Colorado Tuberculosis Association and of the Denver Anti-Tuberculosis Society, which latter was organized in October, 1917.

Dr. Holden has also been closely connected with the work of the

National Tuberculosis Association. He was a director from 1910 to 1915, holding the office of vice-president from 1911 to 1912. In 1912 he also represented the National Association at the Fifteenth International Congress on Hygiene and Demography, held at Washington, D. C., in September. In this same year he was appointed United States official delegate to the Seventh International Congress on Tuberculosis held at Rome in April, 1912. He was again elected a director of the National Tuberculosis Association in June of 1921 to represent the State of Colorado.

During the war Dr. Holden was a member both of the executive committee and the ways and means committee of the Denver Chapter of the Red Cross and has served constantly on these committees ever since. He gave much time in 1918 to the organization of first aid and home nursing classes. For several months of this same year he served as chairman of the Medical Advisory Board, examining chests of drafted men several mornings a week. During the World War he was appointed a captain of the Medical Corps, United States Army, and stationed at General Hospital 21, near Denver.

Notwithstanding these many services so generously given, Dr. Holden still supervised the work at the Agnes Memorial Sanatorium, an institution of 150 beds, and held it unswervingly to the same high standards which he has always maintained. He has been superintendent and medical director of this institution since it was planned. In preparation for the building of the Agnes Memorial, Dr. Holden visited all the important tuberculosis sanatoria of Europe and, on his return in 1903, superintended the building and equipping of this now justly famous sanatorium.

From the very beginning of his work as a sanatorium director, Dr. Holden doubted the wisdom of excessive feeding of patients which was in vogue in the early days in many European and also in some American sanatoria. Six meals a day was the accepted custom. While he continued this method of "stuffing" with half of his patients he allowed the other half only three meals a day. At the end of three months the latter group had made better gains in weight, had better appetites, and slept better. Dr. Holden was also one of the early advocates of rest before and after each meal.

G. WALTER HOLDEN

Dr. Holden is a member of the International Anti-tuberculosis Association, the American Climatological Association, the American Public Health Association, and the National Association of Hospital Superintendents, of which he is a vice-president.

The bibliography of Dr. G. W. Holden follows:

The advantages of sanatorium over home treatment of pulmonary tuberculosis. Denver Med. Times, xxv, 707–17, June, 1906.

Agnes Memorial Sanatorium. The Hospital, 1906.

A case of pulmonary and glandular aspergilosis. Am. Clim. and Clin. Assn., xxxi, 97–105, 1 pl., 1915. Digested in New York Med. Jour., cii, 479, Aug. 28, 1915.

Does Colorado climate influence tuberculosis? Read before Colorado Springs Society.

Duties of municipality and state in control of tuberculosis. Jour. Am. Med. Assn., ccvii, 10, 1907.

The mother's responsibility in the prevention of tuberculosis. Read before Mothers' Congress, Denver, 1910.

Open-air pavilions for the tuberculous. Brochure, Internat. Congr. on Tuberc., 1908.

Prevention of tuberculosis. Lecture at Cesa Virinda, Pueblo, 1908.

Report of committee on model health ordinances for a city which is a resort of consumptives. [American Medical Association. Section on preventive medicine.] Chicago, 1911. 10 p. Reprint Jour. Am. Med. Assn., Dec. 9, 1911.

Sanatorium treatment of tuberculosis in Colorado. Ill. Med. Jour., ix, 14–24, 1906; also Medical Age, Detroit, xxiv, 41–84, 1906.

Suggestions to physicians in the care of the consumptive. Tr. Med. Assn. of Alabama, 404–15, 1906.

CHAPTER LXVII

ROBERT H. BABCOCK, M.D., LL.D.

VICE-PRESIDENT OF THE NATIONAL TUBERCULOSIS ASSOCIATION FROM 1912 TO 1913

ROBERT HALL BABCOCK was born at Watertown, N. Y., July 26, 1851. He was the son of Robert Stanton and Emily M. Hall Babcock. His father was of old New England stock, having been born at Stonington, Conn., but he was for many years a merchant and banker in Kalamazoo, Mich., where he died in 1885. Dr. Babcock's mother was also of old New England stock. She died in her eighty-sixth year at Washington, D. C.

When one considers that Dr. Babcock lost his eyesight at the age of thirteen, one cannot help being moved to admiration at his achievements. Educated in the Institute for the Blind from 1864 to 1867, he entered the preparatory department of Olivet College of Michigan in 1867. After remaining there for two years he went to the Western Reserve College (1869 to 1873), from which he was graduated with the degree of A.B. He entered the literary department of the University of Michigan in 1873, and remained there for one year. Dr. Babcock began his illustrious medical career by entering the medical department of the same university in 1874 and received the degree of M.D. in 1876. He studied at the Chicago Medical College in 1878, the College of Physicians and Surgeons in New York in 1879, and continued his medical studies in Berlin, Munich, and Würzburg up to 1883, when he established himself in practice in Chicago. His alma mater, the University of Michigan, conferred upon him the degree of A.M. in 1897, and the degree of LL.D. in 1910.

In spite of his blindness, his indomitable energy and his fine training have made him one of the most distinguished citizens of Chicago. He was chosen professor of clinical medicine and physi-

ROBERT H. BABCOCK

cal diagnosis of the Chicago Post-Graduate Medical School, and remained there from 1887 to 1892. He was professor of clinical medicine and diseases of the chest at the College of Physicians and Surgeons of Chicago from 1901 to 1905, and attending physician to the Cook County Hospital from 1891 to 1897, when he became one of its consultants. He is a consulting physician to a number of other Chicago institutions, a member of the Association of American Physicians, the Climatological Association, and many other medical associations, among them the Medico Chirurgical Society of Edinburgh and the International Anti tuberculosis Association. From the day of the untimely death of the late Theodore B. Sachs until January first of the year 1921 Dr. Babcock served faithfully as director of the Chicago Tuberculosis Institute.

Dr. Babcock's interest in the tuberculosis problem has been unusual. When asked to send a list of his contributions on the subject of tuberculosis, he modestly wrote: "I have contributed a few articles to current medical literature on subjects pertaining to pulmonary tuberculosis, but cannot now give their titles or dates." This is much to be regretted because he has written much more than his bibliography would indicate. His outstanding work is his book, entitled, "Diseases of the Lungs," which, although published more than a decade ago, is still considered and will for a long time to come be considered as a classic.

The author now desires to digress from the usual order of these biographies to relate the circumstances of his first meeting with this great blind master of medicine. During the author's student days in the late eighties at the Bellevue Hospital Medical College, Dr. Babcock, while attending one of the clinics held at the old amphitheater, was introduced to the class. All were deeply moved and impressed when Professor Edward G. Janeway introduced the blind physician from Chicago. A patient was brought in, and Dr. Janeway courteously asked whether our honored guest would care to examine the case. He consented. Gently palpating over the posterior and anterior portions of the chest, he turned to the class and said: "This is an aneurism of the aorta." He made the diagnosis even without placing the ear or stethoscope to the chest. Dr. Janeway then examined the case, confirming the diagnosis, and an ovation was given to Dr. Bab cock such as is seldom seen in a medical amphitheater.   It was a scene which will never be forgotten by those who were privileged to be present.

The bibliography of Dr. Robert H. Babcock follows:

The treatment of consumption, 1895.

The open air treatment of consumptives who cannot seek change of climate. Jour. Am. Med. Assn., April 6, 1895.

The treatment of hemoptysis.   Medicine, Sept., 1896.

Antitoxin or serum therapy.   North Am. Practitioner, Oct., 1896.

The diagnosis of pulmonary tuberculosis.   Jour. Am. Med. Assn., Oct. 20, 1900.

The home treatment of pulmonary tuberculosis.   N. Y. Med. Jour., July 13, 1901.

Cases of pleurisy with more or less permanent pneumonic induration—are they tuberculosis?   Internat. Clin., i, series 12.

Pulmonary tuberculosis and syphilis, with reports of three cases.   Lancet-Clinic, April 15, 1911.

The early diagnosis of pulmonary tuberculosis.   Ill. Med. Jour., June, 1915.

Diseases of the lungs—a practical presentation of the subject for the use of students and practitioners of medicine.   D. Appleton & Co., 1907.   809 pages.

CHAPTER LXVIII

MABEL T. BOARDMAN, A.M., LL.D.

VICE-PRESIDENT OF THE NATIONAL TUBERCULOSIS ASSOCIATION FROM 1913 TO 1914

MABEL THORPE BOARDMAN was born in Cleveland, Ohio, and was the daughter of William Jarvis and Florence Sheffield Boardman. Miss Boardman received her preliminary education in private schools in Cleveland and New York and also studied in Europe. She received the honorary degree of A.M. from Yale University in 1911, and of LL.D. from Western Reserve University, Smith College, and the Georgetown University. She also holds the degree of D.H.L. from Converse College.

Miss Boardman is a member of the Central Committee of the American Red Cross, and was delegated to the Eighth and Ninth International Red Cross Conferences in London in 1907, and in Washington in 1912. She is now the secretary and a member of the executive committee of the American Red Cross. The remarkable preparedness of the American Red Cross in the recent world war was largely due to the broad vision and leadership of Miss Boardman, who was instrumental in stimulating the organization of Red Cross medical units long before our country entered the war. For her activities she has been decorated by the King of Sweden and the Emperor of Japan.

Miss Boardman served as Commissioner of the District of Columbia, 1920 to 1921, for which position she was so eminently qualified because of her executive and business ability. It was a source of great disappointment to the citizens of the national capital that she was not reappointed, so that she might have continned her splendid efforts for the welfare of 165,455 women and 132,316 children out of a total population of 437,571.

Miss Boardman is the author of a valuable work entitled

"Under the Red Cross Flag." Because of her Red Cross work she has, as a matter of course, always been intensely interested in the tuberculosis problem and has rendered important financial aid by promoting the Red Cross Christmas Seal Sale and numerous other health activities. It was due largely to Miss Boardman that the Red Cross Seal became a part of the program of the American Red Cross in 1908.

MABEL T. BOARDMAN

CHAPTER LXIX

LEE K. FRANKEL, Ph.D.

VICE-PRESIDENT OF THE NATIONAL TUBERCULOSIS ASSOCIATION FROM 1914 TO 1915

LEE KAUFMAN FRANKEL, the son of Louis and Aurelia Lobenburg Frankel, was born in Philadelphia August 13, 1867. He received the degree of B.S. from the University of Pennsylvania in 1887, and of Ph.D. in 1891. He was an instructor in chemistry at the University of Pennsylvania from 1888 to 1893, practised as consulting chemist in Philadelphia from 1893 to 1899, served as Manager of the United Hebrew Charities of New York from 1899 to 1908, and subsequently for one year was a special investigator for the Russell Sage Foundation. In 1909 Dr. Frankel entered the Metropolitan Life Insurance Company as head of the welfare work for its many employees. It was this position which caused him to become intensely interested in the social problem of tuberculosis. He not only inaugurated an educational campaign among the policy-holders of the company, but was also largely instrumental in the establishment of the Mount McGregor Sanatorium for tuberculous employees of the Metropolitan Life Insurance Company. This institution may well be considered as one of the finest in this country, and is doing incalculable good by furthering the health and physical welfare of the Company's numerous employees. To Dr. Frankel we are also indebted for the conception of the Framingham Health and Tuberculosis Demonstration, which has been one of the most important features of the anti-tuberculosis campaign of our country. He has served as a member of the National Committee of the Framingham Demonstration from its very beginning, and besides, has shown his deep interest in the tuberculosis problem as a member of the executive committees of our national, state, and local tuberculosis associations.

445

Dr. Frankel, however, has not limited his activities to the prevention of tuberculosis alone. He is an honorary member of the American Social Hygiene Association, a member of the General Committee of the Child Health Organization, and a director of the American Public Health Association, which body has honored him with the position of treasurer and president. He is the delegate from the American Public Health Association to the National Health Council, of which he is chairman, and in 1917 he was president of the New York Conference of Charities and Correction. He is also intensely interested in public health nursing, and originated and organized the visiting nurse service of the Metropolitan Life Insurance Company.

Dr. Frankel's reputation as a welfare worker is indeed national, if not international, and the United States Government has recognized his experience and authority. In spite of his multiple duties as the head of the Welfare Department of the Metropolitan Life Insurance Company, of which he is now the third vice-president, he accepted without pay the big contract of organizing a welfare department of the United States Post-Office. His official title is Welfare Director of the United States Post-Office Department, and the Government and former Postmaster General Hays may well be congratulated on having secured the services of so able a man.

The bibliography of Lee K. Frankel follows:

Tuberculosis as affecting charity organization. Address before National Conference of Jewish Charities, June 12, 1900.

Coöperation and health insurance for consumptives. Proc. N. Y. State Conference of Charities and Correction, Nov., 1901, 253–274.

Insurance against tuberculosis. Tr. Nat. Tuberc. Assn., vi, 35, 1910.

Statement showing that German sickness insurance will eventually reduce percentage of tuberculosis. Tr. Nat. Tuberc. Assn., viii, 175–76, 1912.

Influence of private life insurance companies on tuberculosis. Internat. Tuberc. Conference, Berlin, 1913.

Discussion on the needs of patients discharged from tuberculosis sanatoria. Tr. Nat. Tuberc. Assn., x, 306–308, 1914.

Fighting the white plague. Nat. Safety Council, round table discussion, Oct. 15, 1914, 216–218.

Plea for a Federal commission on tuberculosis. Address before Mississippi Valley Conference on Tuberculosis, Sept. 30, 1915.

LEE K. FRANKEL

Tuberculosis from the industrial point of view. Boston Assn. for the Relief and Control of Tuberculosis. Report, 1916, 25–27.

Study of mortality statistics of southern communities from typhoid fever malaria, pellagra, tuberculosis, and all causes. Address before Southern Sociological Congress, New Orleans, April 12, 1916.

Framingham Health and Tuberculosis Demonstration. Tr. Nat. Tuberc. Assn., xiii, 407–409, 1917.

Community Health and Tuberculosis Conference Demonstration. Safety Engineering, July, 1917, 380–381.

The evidence of intensive anti-tuberculosis effort upon the death rate. Tr. Nat. Tuberc. Assn., xvii, 505–514, 1921.

Industrial nursing as a means of fighting tuberculosis. Tr. Nat. Tuberc. Assn., xvii, 525–531, 1921.

CHAPTER LXX

W. JARVIS BARLOW, M.D.

VICE-PRESIDENT OF THE NATIONAL TUBERCULOSIS ASSOCIATION FROM 1914 TO 1915

WALTER JARVIS BARLOW was born in Ossining, N. Y., January 22, 1868. He was the son of William Henry and Catherine Lent Barlow, and received his preliminary education at the Mount Pleasant Military Academy at Ossining, N. Y., and his classical education at the Columbia University School of Arts, from which he was graduated with the degree of A.B. in 1889. He entered the medical department of Columbia University, and was graduated with the degree of M.D. in 1892. The same university conferred upon him the honorary degree of A.M. in 1919 for his valuable professional work on the Pacific Coast.

Dr. Barlow served for two and a half years as intern in the Mount Sinai Hospital, also one year in the Sloan Maternity Hospital. Breaking down in health, he was sent by his teacher and friend, Dr. Janeway, to Los Angeles, where he completely recovered and established himself in practice in 1897. He soon became one of the prominent practitioners of that city, and was honored by the presidency of the Los Angeles County Medical Association. Subsequently he was made professor of medicine and dean of the Los Angeles Medical Department of the University of California.

From the very beginning of his career in Los Angeles Dr. Barlow took the deepest interest in the tuberculosis problem. He became president of the California Tuberculosis Association, and on his retirement from the presidency became secretary-treasurer of the Association, which position he still holds. Besides being a member of the Los Angeles County Medical Society, he is a member of the American Medical Association and the American Climatological and Clinical Association.

W. JARVIS BARLOW

As one of the greatest achievements in Dr. Barlow's life work we must mention the Barlow Sanatorium, which was founded in 1903 and which is one of the most flourishing philanthropic institutions of its kind in the West. It is located in the Chavez Ravine, within the city of Los Angeles. Dr. Barlow was its founder and is its physician in chief. A further evidence of Dr. Barlow's scientific and philanthropic interest is the Barlow Medical Library which he has established and which is one of the most important medical libraries on the Pacific Coast.

The bibliography of Dr. W. Jarvis Barlow follows:

Climatic therapeutics. Article in Klebs' Tuberculosis. A Treatise by American Authors, Appleton, 1909.
Practical climatic therapy. Article in Hare's Therapeutics.
Sanatorium treatment. Tr. Los Angeles County Med. Assn., 1909.
Medical organization—conservation of public health. Tr. Los Angeles County Med. Assn., 1911.
Chronic nephritis. Am. Med. Assn., lxv, 1915.

CHRISTEN QUEVLI, M.D

VICE-PRESIDENT OF THE NATIONAL TUBERCULOSIS ASSOCIATION FROM 1915 TO 1916

CHRISTEN QUEVLI was born in Norway, June 26, 1864, and was the son of Anders and Gorrina Quevli. He came to the United States at the age of five, when his father settled at Windom, Minnesota, and engaged in mercantile business. Young Quevli attended the public schools, and later on the St. Olaf's College at Northfield, Minn. He graduated in medicine from the Minnesota College Hospital in 1886, and after that he went to Christiania, Norway, where he took a post-graduate course. In 1888 he returned to the United States and established himself in practice at Tacoma, Washington, where he remained until 1892, when he again began to do post-graduate work, visiting New York, Berlin, and the medical centers of Norway, Denmark, England, and France.

Returning to Tacoma he became health officer of the city, in which capacity he served for two years. In 1901 he went abroad again, studying mainly at the University of Vienna. On his return to Tacoma he took deep interest in tuberculosis work, and in 1911 was made president of the Washington Tuberculosis Association, which flourished remarkably under his administration. When he entered upon this office there was no tuberculosis legislation in the state of Washington, there were no leagues, no visiting nurses, no sanatoria, and the treasury of the association was empty. To-day there are 4 county sanatoria, 25 visiting nurses, 30 leagues, and a number of clinics in operation, and the treasury is far from being empty. All these achievements are due to Dr. Quevli's indomitable energy and enthusiasm.

CHRISTEN QUEVLI

CHAPTER LXXII

WATSON S. RANKIN, M.D.

VICE-PRESIDENT OF THE NATIONAL TUBERCULOSIS ASSOCIATION FROM 1916 TO
1917

WATSON S. RANKIN was born in Mooresville, N. C., on January 18, 1879. He was the son of John Alexander and Minnie Isabella McCorkle Rankin. His preliminary education was received in the high schools of Mooresville and Statesville, N. C., and he began his medical studies at the North Carolina Medical College, continuing at Davidson Medical College. He was graduated from the University of Maryland with the degree of M.D. in 1901. Dr. Rankin served as intern in the University of Maryland Hospital for eighteen months, and did postgraduate work in Johns Hopkins Medical School for one year. He was also a resident in the obstetrical department of the University of Maryland for six months, and resident pathologist at the University of Maryland Hospital for thirteen months. Dr. Rankin was called to the chair of pathology of the Medical Department of Wake Forest College, which position he occupied until 1905. He then became dean of the School of Medicine; this position he occupied until 1909. From that date on he has served the state of North Carolina as one of its most efficient state health officers. Between 1904 and 1905 he distinguished himself by making important investigations regarding the frequency of hookworm disease in North Carolina. At the present time he is a trustee of the Wake Forest College and of the North Carolina Sanatorium for the Treatment of Tuberculosis, a member of the American Medical Association, and of the American Public Health Association, having been president of the latter from 1919 to 1920, and a member of the executive committee. He also was secretary and later president of the Conference of State and Provincial Health Authorities, a vice-president of the

451

National Association for the Prevention of Infant Mortality, and a member of the National Health Council. In nearly all his contributions on public health and sanitation, of which there are many, Dr. Rankin has never failed to advocate the prophylaxis of tuberculosis and also sanatorium provision. Unfortunately, no separate works on the subject of tuberculosis have been written by him, and so the author is unable to attach any distinct tuberculosis bibliography of this distinguished vice-president.

W. S. RANKIN

CHAPTER LXXIII

FREDERICK L. HOFFMAN, LL.D.

FREDERICK L. HOFFMAN, the son of Augustus F. and Antoinette von Laar Hoffman, was born May 2, 1865, at Varel, Germany. He received his education in private and public schools, equivalent to what might be considered here a grammar school grade. This brilliant statistician very frankly admitted to the author that he never graduated from any school, and was almost always the last in his class and a grade or two behind. He came to the United States in 1884, and, after a varied commercial career, entered the business of life insurance with the Metropolitan Company at Somerville and Waltham, Mass., in 1888. He remained with that company for some years, then changed to the Life Insurance Company of Virginia, and in 1895 accepted a position with the Prudential Insurance Company.

In 1900 Mr. Hoffman had charge of the Prudential's Exhibit in Paris and in 1904 received the Grand Prix on life insurance methods and results contributed to the Louisiana Purchase Exposition. In 1906 he represented the United States Government at the International Actuarial Congress held in Vienna and the International Statistical Institute held in Paris that year. Ever since Mr. Hoffman has been active in various international statistical and also tuberculosis congresses. He is a member of the American Association for the Advancement of Science, a fellow of the Royal Anthropological Institute, the Society of Arts, the Royal Sanitary Institute, etc. He is an honorary member of the Swiss Actuarial Society and an associate fellow of the American Medical Association. In 1911 Tulane University conferred upon Mr. Hoffman together with the late Major General Gorgas the honorary degree of LL.D. in recognition of the services rendered to the cause of southern sanitation and mortality research.

453

Dr. Hoffman's contributions to statistical science are numerous. His first article was on the Vital Statistics of the Negro, published in the *Arena* of Boston, and his first book was "The Race Traits and Tendencies of the American Negro." Dr. Hoffman is an ardent American patriot, and during the recent world war was one of the most active members of the American Friends of German Democracy, a fact which was recorded in Mr. Creel's book, prefaced by Mr. Baker, Secretary of War. In his busy life Dr. Hoffman has found time and opportunity to devote much of his energy to the anti-tuberculosis cause in the United States. Twenty-four most important contributions on the various phases of tuberculosis are the product of his fertile pen.

The bibliography of Frederick L. Hoffman follows:

Industrial insurance and prevention of tuberculosis. Address before British Congress on Tuberc., July 23, 1901.

Coöperation and health insurance for consumptives. Second N. Y. State Conference of Charities and Corrections, Albany, Nov. 19, 1901.

The statistical laws of tuberculosis. Maryland Tuberc. Conference, 1904.

The detection and prevention of tuberculosis in factories. Tr. Nat. Tuberc. Assn., May 6, 1907.

Logical position of the government and insurance companies in the crusade against tuberculosis. Address before Am. Assn. of Med. Examiners, June 3, 1907.

The relation of occupation to tuberculosis. Address before Assn. of Med. Examiners, Atlantic City, June 3, 1907.

Tuberculosis as an industrial disease. Internat. Congress on Tuberc., Washington, Sept. 21, 1908.

Mortality from consumption in dusty trades. U. S. Bureau of Labor, Bulletin 79, 1908.

Relation of life insurance institutions to the problem of tuberculosis prevention. Internat. Tuberc. Exhibition, Philadelphia, March 10, 1909.

Mortality from consumption in certain occupations—exposing to municipal and general organic dust. Bureau of Labor Stat., Bull. 82, May, 1909.

Insurance against tuberculosis. Discussion of paper by Dr. Lee K. Frankel. Tr. Nat. Tuberc. Assn., vi, 50–56, 1910.

Pulmonary disease among miners. Engineer. and Mining Journal, March 11, 1911.

A brief account of the treatment and care of tuberculous wage-earners in Germany. Tr. Nat. Tuberc. Assn., viii, 75, 1912; Bull. 101, U. S. Bureau of Labor, July, 1912.

The decline in the tuberculosis death-rate, 1871–1912. Tr. Nat. Tuberc. Assn., ix, 101, 1913.

FREDERICK L. HOFFMAN

Letter on the tuberculosis death rate. N. Y. Evening Sun, Nov. 18, 1914.

Tuberculosis as an occupational disease. Address before Second North Atlantic Conference and Second N. Y. State Conference of Tuberc. Workers, Albany, Nov. 4, 1915.

Mortality from tuberculosis in dusty trades. In Kober & Hanson's Diseases of Occupation and Vocational Hygiene, Nov., 1915.

The tuberculosis death rate for 1917. Spectator, N. Y. City, June 6, 1918.

Mortality from respiratory diseases in dusty trades (inorganic dusts). U. S. Bureau of Labor Bulletin 231, June, 1918.

Mortality from tuberculosis in dusty trades. First preliminary report, Dec. 5, 1918; second report, Sept., 1919.

The tuberculosis problem. Spectator, N. Y. City, June 19, 1919.

Mortality from tuberculosis, 1900–1919. Spectator, N. Y. City, Sept. 23 and 30, 1920.

Sanatorium benefit under British national health insurance. Address before Mississippi Valley Conference on Tuberc., Duluth, Minn., Sept., 1920.

The mortality from dust phthisis in the granite stone industry of Vermont (in press).

CHAPTER LXXIV

LAWRASON BROWN, M.D.

VICE-PRESIDENT OF THE NATIONAL TUBERCULOSIS ASSOCIATION FROM 1918 TO 1919

LAWRASON BROWN, the son of William Judson and Mary Louise Lawrason Brown, was born in Baltimore, Maryland, September 29, 1871. He was educated in the private and public schools of Baltimore and received his degree of A.B. from Johns Hopkins University in 1895, and of M.D. from Johns Hopkins Medical School in 1900. Dr. Brown went to the Adirondacks for his health first in 1898. In 1900 and 1901 he was assistant resident physician at the Adirondack Cottage Sanitarium, now the Trudeau Sanatorium; resident physician 1901–1912; visiting physician 1912–1914, and since 1914, chairman of the medical board, consulting physician and trustee. He served on the village board of Saranac Lake Village; was the first president of the Stevenson Society of America. He started the *Journal of the Outdoor Life* in 1904 and conducted it until 1909, when it was turned over to the committee at present in charge of it. He was the first president of the Adirondack Good Roads Association which helped to bring about the system of good roads now in existence throughout the mountains. He is a Trustee of the Ray Brook State Sanatorium for Incipient Tuberculosis. During the war he was a member of the Medical Advisory Board of Saranac Lake; member of the Tuberculosis Committee of the Medical Section of the National Council of Defence; served as contract surgeon at Camp Devens for a short time, and was a "four minute man."

Dr. Brown's contribution to tuberculosis literature is an extensive one. He is the author of "Rules for Recovery from Tuberculosis," a handbook for patients which has gone through several editions, of "Diagnostic Theses," later enlarged to "Theses, Diagnostic, Prognostic, and Therapeutic," which has

456

LAWRASON BROWN

been reprinted for distribution by several societies. He is a lover of books, member of the Grolier Club of New York, possesses an extensive library on tuberculosis, including some rare first editions, which he intends to donate to the Trudeau Sanatorium as soon as the library building is completed. Dr. Brown has been president of the American Clinical and Climatological Association. He is a member of the Association of American Physicians, American Medical Association, American Public Health Association, American Association for Thoracic Surgery, Ecological Society, Association for the Advancement of Science, Medical Library Association. He has made a number of contributions to medical literature.

We are indebted to Dr. Lawrason Brown, perhaps more than to any one else, for the formation of the American Sanatorium Association, which has done and is doing so much toward improving our knowledge of sanatorium construction, sanatorium management, sanatorium treatment, and classification of cases according to the extent of invasion and symptoms. He is now president of this important organization. Besides being a fertile writer, Dr. Brown is one of the principal teachers at the celebrated Trudeau School, to which he has been attached from its very beginning.

The bibliography of Dr. Lawrason Brown follows:

Sputum examination in pulmonary tuberculosis and its prognostic value. Montreal Med. Jour., Oct., 1901.

The prognostic value of tubercle bacilli in sputum. Jour. Am. Med. Assn., Feb. 21, 1903.

A study of weights in pulmonary tuberculosis. Am. Med., April 25, 1903.

Zomotherapy in tuberculosis. Am. Jour. Med. Sci., June., 1903, cxxv, 1071 1078.

An analysis of fifteen hundred cases of tuberculosis. Jour. Am. Med. Assn., Nov. 21, 1903.

Some weather observations in the Adirondacks. Med. News, Aug. 20, 1904.

The shape of the chest in health and in tuberculosis (E. G. Pope). Am. Jour. Med. Sci., Oct., 1904, 619–636.

Treatment of the digestive disturbances occurring in pulmonary tuberculosis. Internat. Clin., iii, 14th series, 1904, 124–139.

The early physical signs of pulmonary tuberculosis. Med. News, Oct. 15, 1904.

The post-discharge mortality among the patients of the Adirondack Cottage Sanitarium (E. G. Pope). Am. Med., Nov. 19, 1904, 879–882.

A study of the cases of pulmonary tuberculosis treated with tuberculin at the Adirondack Cottage Sanitarium. Zeitschr. f. Tuberk. u. Heilstättenw., Band vi, Heft 4, 235–254, 1904.

Some points in the diagnosis and treatment of tuberculosis. Albany Med. Annals, April, 1906.

Suggestion in the treatment of hæmoptysis. Tr. Nat. Tuberc. Assn., ii, 459, 1906.

The prevention of tuberculosis. Brehmer Rest, Third Annual Report, 1907.

A brief study of a diphtheria epidemic at the Adirondack Cottage Sanitarium (A. H. Allen and E. J. S. Lupton). Am. Jour. Med. Sci., Feb., 1907.

The ultimate test of sanatorium treatment of pulmonary tuberculosis and its application to the results obtained in the Adirondack Cottage Sanitarium (E. G. Pope). Zeitschr. f. Tuberk., bd. xii, ht. 3, 1908, 206–15.

The sanatorium. Internat. Clin., i, 18th series, 1–21.

The early diagnosis of pulmonary tuberculosis. Albany Med. Annals, April, 1908. New York State Jour. of Med., May, 1908.

Dissecting aneurism of the aorta and pulmonary artery following rupture of the arch of the aorta. N. Y. Med. Jour., July 4, 1908.

The diagnostic and therapeutic use of tuberculin. Boston Med. and Surg. Jour., July 23, 1908, 97–106.

The hygienic requirements for the construction and equipment of sanatoriums. Internat. Tuberc. Conference, Phila., Sept., 24–26, 1908.

The ultimate results of sanatorium treatment. Tr. Sixth Internat. Congr. on Tuberc., i, part 2, 927–949, 1908.

The heart in pulmonary tuberculosis. Tr. Nat. Tuberc. Assn., iv, 116, 1908; also Am. Jour. Med. Sci., Dec., 1908, and Feb., 1909.

The clasification of pulmonary tuberculosis and statistical reports of sanatoria. Jour. Am. Med. Assn., Jan. 30, 1909, 341–348.

An outline for a co-ordinated attack upon tuberculosis. N. Y. Med. Jour. Nov. 20, 1909.

Some studies with the cutaneous tuberculin test. A preliminary report. Tr. Assn. Am. Phys., 1909, 104–144.

The cultivation of tubercle bacilli directly from sputum by the use of antiformin (Daniel Smith). Jour. Med. Research, June, 1910.

Properly regulated rest and exercise in pulmonary tuberculosis. Jour. Outdoor Life, June, 1911, 149–152.

The specificity, danger and accuracy of the tuberculin test. Am. Jour. Med. Sci., Oct., 1911, 469–475.

The causes of death in pulmonary tuberculosis. Tr. Am. Clim. and Clin. Assn., 1911, 65–86; also Zeitschr. f. Tuberk., bd. xviii, h. 1, 1911, 43–52.

The albumin reaction in the sputum in pulmonary tuberculosis (with W. H. Ross). Tr. Nat. Tuberc. Assn., vii, 260–289, 1911.

The present status of the tuberculin test. Tr. Assn. Am. Phys., 1911, 22–32.

A study of the blood of patients with pulmonary tuberculosis undergoing sanatorium and tuberculin treatment (A. F. Miller and E. J. S. Lupton). Am. Jour. Med. Sci., May, 1912, 683–693.

Tuberculin, its history, preparation and value (A. F. Miller). Jour. Outdoor Life, Jan., 1912, 12–13.

Routine medical work in a sanatorium (H. L. Barnes and V. F. Cullen). Boston Med. and Surg. Jour., Oct. 31, 1912, 613–614.

Recent advances in the treatment of pulmonary tuberculosis by air, food and rest. Jour. Am. Med. Assn., June 1, 1912, 1678–1681.

The therapeutic use of tuberculin, a working hypothesis and some personal observations. Tr. Nat. Tuberc. Assn., viii, 23, 1912; also Am. Jour. Med. Sci., Oct., 1912, 524–535.

The bacteriology of the blood in pulmonary tuberculosis, a preliminary report (S. A. Petroff). Tr. Nat. Tuberc. Assn., viii, 505–511, 1912.

Preliminary talk to patients undergoing treatment for pulmonary tuberculosis. Jour. Outdoor Life, Dec., 1912, 289–292.

The bacteriology of the blood in pulmonary tuberculosis (F. H. Heise and S. A. Petroff). Tr. Nat. Tuberc. Assn., ix, 344–361, 1913.

The occurrence and importance in treatment of secondary infection in pulmonary tuberculosis (F. H. Heise and S. A. Petroff). Tr. Tuberc. Assn., ix, 254–269, 1913.

The uncertainties of the treatment of pulmonary tuberculosis by artificial pneumothorax (A. K. Krause). Tr. Assn. Am. Phys., 1913, 441–448.

When is a tuberculous patient cured? Tr. Clim. and Clin. Assn., 1914, 315–321.

How and when do we contract tuberculosis? Jour. Outdoor Life, April, 1914.

Some errors in the diagnosis and treatment of pulmonary tuberculosis. Bull. Johns Hopkins Hosp., April, 1914, 117–127.

Tuberculin therapy (E. N. Packard). Medical Annual, 1914.

An attempt to immunize guinea pigs against tuberculosis by the use of graduated, repeated doses of living tubercle bacilli (F. H. Heise and S. A. Petroff). Jour. Med. Research, July, 1914, 475–485.

Honesty, sympathy and humbleness in nursing. Address at the first commencement of the Adirondack Cottage Sanitarium Training School for Nurses, Oct. 1, 1914.

The significance of tubercle bacilli in the urine. Jour. Am. Med. Assn., March 13, 1915, 886–890.

Diagnostic theses in pulmonary tuberculosis. Jour. Am. Med. Assn., June 12, 1915, 1977–1978.

Ueber das vorkommen von tuberkel-bazillen im blute von patienten mit lungentuberkulose (F. H. Heise and S. A. Petroff). Zeitschr. f. Tuberk., band 24, heft 2, 1915.

Sanatoria in the fight against tuberculosis. Virginia Med. Semi-Monthly, Nov. 12, 1915, 369–372.

The occurrence of living tubercle bacilli in river water contaminated by sewage from a health resort (F. H. Heise and S. A. Petroff). Tr. Nat. Tuberc. Assn., xii, 287, 1916, Am. Jour. Pub. Health, Nov., 1916, 1148–1152.

Tuberculosis theses: diagnostic, prognostic, therapeutic. Am. Rev. Tuberc., June, 1917, 193–205.

A preliminary study of the clinical value of complement fixation in tuberculosis (S. A. Petroff). Tr. Nat. Tuberc. Assn., xiii, 528–534, 1917.

Herbert Maxon King: 1864–1917 (Tribute). Am. Rev. Tuberc., Aug., 1917, 321–324.

Value of Roentgen ray in diagnosis of pulmonary tuberculosis in war time. Jour. Am. Med. Assn., Feb. 23, 1918, 516–519.

Tuberculosis as an army problem.   Tr. Nat. Tuberc. Assn., xiv, 318, 1918; also Am. Rev. Tuberc., Aug., 1918, 335.

The clinical value of complement fixation in pulmonary tuberculosis based on a study of 540 cases (S. A. Petroff).   Tr. Nat. Tuberc. Assn., xiv, 250, 1918; also Am. Rev. Tuberc., Nov., 1918.

A study of pulmonary and pleural annular radiographic shadows.   Tr. Nat. Tuberc. Assn., xiv, 171, 1918; also Am. Rev. Tuberc., Jan., 1919.

A study of the effects of typhoid fever and antityphoid immunization on pulmonary tuberculosis.   (History of a typhoid fever epidemic at the Trudeau Sanatorium) (Heise, Petroff and Wilson).   Tr. Nat. Tuberc. Assn., xiv, 230, 1918; also Am. Rev. Tuberc., Feb., 1919.

The early Roentgen diagnosis of ulcerative tuberculous colitis (H. L. Sampson). Jour. Am. Med. Assn., July 12, 1919, 77–85.

Etiological studies in tuberculosis (Petroff and Pesquera).   Tr. Nat. Tuberc. Assn., xv, 259, 1919; also Jour. Am. Med. Assn., Nov. 22, 1919, 1576–1578.

A preliminary study of clinical activity (Heise, Petroff and Sampson).   Tr. Nat. Tuberc. Assn., xv, 87, 1919.

The influence of anesthesia on experimental tuberculosis in guinea pigs (S. A. Petroff).   Tr. Nat. Tuberc. Assn., xv, 292, 1919.

The place of the sanatorium in the study of tuberculosis.   Am. Rev. Tuberc. May, 1920.

Twenty years' experience with the subcutaneous tuberculin test (F. H. Heise). Tr. Nat. Tuberc. Assn., xvi, 147, 1920; also Am. Rev. Tuberc., June, 1920.

The classification of pulmonary tuberculosis based upon symptoms and physical and x-ray findings (Heise and Sampson).   Tr. Nat. Tuberc. Assn., xvi, 79, 1920; also Am. Rev. Tuberc., Aug., 1920.

Adrenalin hypersensitiveness in definite and unproved pulmonary tuberculosis (Heise and Brown).   Am. Rev. Tuberc., iv, no. 8, 1920.

The occurrence of intestinal tuberculosis in patients with pulmonary tuberculosis, at the Trudeau Sanatorium (Heise and Sampson).   Tr. Nat. Tuberc. Assn., xvi, 114, 1920; also Am. Rev. Tuberc., Aug., 1920.

Certain points in the diagnosis and treatment of pulmonary tuberculosis; also Am. Jour. Med. Sci., Sept., 1920, 324.

On personal experience and the value of a medical society to its members. Am. Rev. Tuberc., Sept., 1920.

Rules for recovery from tuberculosis.   Lea and Febiger, Philadelphia, 1916.

Specific treatment.   In Tuberculosis, by Arnold C. Klebs, published by D. Appleton and Co., New York, 1909, p. 508–588.

The symptoms, etc., of tuberculosis.   In Modern Medicine, by William Osler, published by Lea and Febiger, Philadelphia, 1907.   p. 248–435.

The anti-tuberculosis movement in the United States: control and eradication of tuberculosis, by many authors.   Published by William Green and Son, Edinburgh and London, 1911, 256–277.

CHAPTER LXXV

ALFRED MEYER, M.D.

VICE-PRESIDENT OF THE NATIONAL TUBERCULOSIS ASSOCIATION FROM 1918 TO 1919

ALFRED MEYER was born in New York city June 18, 1854, a son of Isaac and Mathilda Langenbach Meyer. He received a liberal classical education in Columbia University, graduating in 1874 with the degree of Bachelor of Arts. He was graduated from the College of Physicians and Surgeons in 1877, and entered at once upon post-graduate work as an intern in the Mount Sinai Hospital, N. Y. Completing his internship, he spent over two years in clinical and laboratory work, mainly in Leipzig and Vienna, with visits to the hospitals of London, Paris, Frankfort, Rome, and Amsterdam.

In 1881 Dr. Meyer engaged in general private practice in New York, and for the past twenty-five years has limited himself to consultation work. Besides being clinical professor of medicine at the New York University and Bellevue Hospital Medical College, he is consulting physician to the Mount Sinai Hospital, the Montefiore Hospital for Chronic Diseases, and the Bedford Sanatorium for Consumptives.

Dr. Meyer has long been identified with the anti-tuberculosis movement in New York city and state, and with the national movement throughout the country. For many years he has been a member of the board of directors of the New York City Tuberculosis Association. He served on the original small committee that prepared for the International Congress on Tuberculosis in Washington, 1908, going abroad in 1906 to stimulate interest in the Congress, and visiting many countries. In the Parliament Building at The Hague Dr. Meyer delivered an address on the plan and scope of the Congress, receiving a silver medal for his exhibit of a dairy illustrating the sanitary production of milk.

461

After the Congress he was largely instrumental in bringing to New York the great international exhibit which was visited by 750,000 people, and to which undoubtedly may be traced a greatly heightened interest in the social significance of the disease.

Dr. Meyer is a member of the following medical organizations: The American Medical Association, New York Academy of Medicine, Medical Society of the State of New York, the Harvey Society, New York County Medical Society, the Alumni of Mount Sinai Hospital.

The bibliography of Dr. Alfred Meyer follows:

The city and its consumptive poor: a plea for a municipal sanatorium outside of the corporate limits.

State care of consumptive poor, with an account of the first state sanatorium. Med. Rec., Oct. 28, 1899.

State care of the consumptive poor. Med. Rec., Jan. 13, 1900.

Relationship of fistula in ano to pulmonary tuberculosis. Mount Sinai Hospital Rep., no. 2, 1901.

Municipal sanatoria. Med. Rec., Dec. 14, 1901.

Tuberculosis in the tenements. N. Y. Med. Jour., July 4, 1903.

History and work of the Bedford Sanitarium. Tr. Nat. Tuberc. Assn., i, 438, 1905; Med. Rec., July 8, 1905.

Complement fixation in pulmonary tuberculosis. Tr. Nat. Tuberc. Assn., xii, 219, 1916; also Med. Rec., Aug. 5, 1910.

After-care of discharged cases. Med. Rec., Aug. 10, 1912.

A case of spontaneous pyopneumothorax complicated by hydro- or pyopneumopericardium. Tr. Nat. Tuberc. Assn., xi, 193, 1915; also Med. Rec., Dec. 11, 1915.

A case of bilateral spontaneous non-tuberculous pneumothorax. Tr. Nat. Tuberc. Assn., xiii, 330, 1917; also N. Y. Med. Jour., June 30, 1917.

Influenza in a tuberculosis sanatorium. Med. Rec., April 12, 1919.

Intrapleural hypertension for evacuating pus through bronchi in spontaneous pyopneumothorax. Tr. Nat. Tuberc. Assn., xvi, 75, 1920; also Jour. Am. Med. Assn., July 24, 1920.

ALFRED MEYER

CHAPTER LXXVI

PHILIP KING BROWN, M.D.

VICE-PRESIDENT OF THE NATIONAL TUBERCULOSIS ASSOCIATION FROM 1920 TO 1921

PHILIP KING BROWN, the son of Henry Adams and Charlotte Amanda Blake Brown, was born in Napa, Cal., June 24, 1869. He received his preliminary education in San Francisco public schools and in Belmont School, California, and took his academic degrees at Harvard University in 1890 and Harvard Medical School in 1893. Dr. Brown was an attending physician to the San Francisco Hospital from 1896 to 1918, being in charge of the medical and tuberculosis wards. He is now a consulting physician to the Mount Zion Hospital and the Southern Pacific Railroad Hospital. Dr. Brown has accomplished perhaps his greatest and most important work as founder and medical director of Arequipa Sanatorium for early tuberculosis in wage-earning women, where he instituted a successful sociological experiment in the treatment of tuberculous working girls. He has done other important pioneer work in ergo-therapy in tuberculosis and in the blood studies in patients at the San Francisco Leprasorium. Dr. Brown has twice been president of the California Academy of Medicine, and is now president of the California Tuberculosis Association. He is a member of the Association of American Physicians and of the Climatological and Clinical Association. During the war Dr. Brown served as Deputy Commissioner for the Red Cross in France, and as Assistant Medical Director of the Department of Medical Research and Intelligence.

The bibliography of Dr. Philip King Brown follows:

A study of the blood in 73 cases of bone tuberculosis in children, with reference to prognosis and treatment. Occidental Med. Times, San Francisco, xi, 462, 1897; also Tr. M. Soc. Cal., S. F., 1897, 169–176.

Individual factors in hygiene (with R. C. Cabot). Boston Med. and Surg. Jour., 1905, 689; also Detroit Med. Jour., 1905–06, v, 73.

Primary infection with tubercle bacilli, with special reference to thoracic glands. Calif. State Jour. of Med., 1913, 346.

Early lesions of tuberculosis in the lungs. Tr. Am. Clim. and Clin. Assn., xxix, 34, 1913.

Primary infection with tubercle bacilli, with special reference to thoracic glands. Tr. Assn. Am. Phys., 1913, 408–421.

Arequipa Sanatorium, a sociological and economic experiment in cases of tuberculous wage-earning girls. Cal. State Jour. of Med., 1914, 327.

Sociologic experiment in treatment of tuberculosis working women. Jour. Sociolog. Med., Easton, Pa., 1915, 209.

Potteries of Arequipa Sanatorium. Mod. Hosp., viii, 394, 1917.

Tuberculosis in army. Boston Med. and Surg. Jour., 1917, 134.

Clinical manifestations of various joint affections and their bearing on diagnosis. Internat. Clin., i, 93, 1918.

Training of nurses and social workers in present emergency. Calif. State Jour. of Med., xvi, 281, June, 1918.

Army and tuberculosis. Med. and Surg., St. Louis, April, 1918.

Subsequent history of cases discharged apparently cured from Arequipa Sanatorium for wage-earning women during six years. Am. Rev. Tuberc., Feb., 1919.

Eighteen years' experience with ergo-therapy. Tr. Nat. Tuberc. Assn., xiv, 434, 1918.

Teamwork in fight against tuberculosis. Jour. Outdoor Life, 1919, 174.

PHILIP KING BROWN

APPENDICES

30

ANTI-TUBERCULOSIS WORK DONE DURING AND AFTER THE WORLD WAR BY THE SURGEON GENERAL'S OFFICES OF THE UNITED STATES ARMY, THE UNITED STATES NAVY, AND THE UNITED STATES PUBLIC HEALTH SERVICE

UNITED STATES ARMY

IN April, 1917, the United States entered the world war. The orders issued from the Surgeon General's office of the army concerning the general, careful, and thoroughly scientific measures taken to exclude the tuberculous from Army and Navy, have already been referred to in the biographies of Major General Gorgas and Col. George E. Bushnell. It seems desirable, however, to outline briefly here, as an important historical item in the anti-tuberculosis crusade in the United States, the admirable work done under the direction of the Surgeon General's office by the draft and camp surgeons. We are indebted to Major General Ireland, the present Surgeon General, for the following valuable statistics showing the rejection of selective service men by local and camp examining boards:

Among the 3,764,101 men examined, there were 58,916 found actually suffering from pulmonary tuberculosis, 17,055 with suspected tuberculosis, and 9,410 afflicted with tuberculosis of other organs than the lungs. Seven thousand, three hundred and sixty (7,360) were rejected because of defective physical development, 2,299 for deficient chest measurement, 70,608 because of underweight, and 769 for malnutrition. These four latter conditions are well known to be predisposing to tuberculosis. This would mean that 166,417 men were either actually tuberculous, suspected of tuberculosis or, by reason of their physical defects, predisposed to the disease. If we add to this figure 9,674 afflicted with syphilis and its sequelæ, which also predisposes to tuberculosis, we have a total of 176,091 individuals either already tuberculous or strongly predisposed to developing or contracting the disease, who were prevented from entering the Army.

REJECTIONS, SELECTIVE SERVICE MEN, LOCAL AND CAMP EXAMINING BOARDS

	Local Boards	Camp Boards
Total...................................	549,099	206,622
Pulmonary tuberculosis..................	44,305	14,611
Suspected tuberculosis..................	16,899	156
Tuberculosis of other organs.............	8,731	679
Mental deficiency......................	33,636	7,963
Defective physical development...........	5,604	1,756
Deficient chest measurement.............	2,105	194
Underweight...........................	59,022	11,586
Underheight...........................	6,556	2,060
Malnutrition...........................	676	93
Bones and organs of locomotion..........	113,287	58,533
Arthritis..............................	3,934	2,539
Syphilis...............................	4,541	4,261
Tabes.................................	425	153
Paresis................................	159	135

The actual number of selective service men, first and second registration, examined by the local boards was 3,764,101.

The actual number of selective service men, first and second registration, examined by the camp boards was 2,745,073.

The statistics for 1,961,692 selective service men as published in "Defects Found in Drafted Men" have been raised proportionately to cover the complete number 2,745,073.

Thus, the dissemination of tuberculous diseases in the army was guarded against by the exclusion of the tuberculous, and the development of the disease was prevented in the strongly predisposed. The majority of the latter would probably have fallen victims to tuberculosis as a result of the stress and strain inevitably connected with camp life and warfare. In this way a truly great life-saving work was done by the Surgeon General and his staff, not only during the war by the surgeons in the field, but also at home through the work of the physicians on the draft and camp boards. The National Tuberculosis Association, with the aid of the Surgeon General's records, took it upon itself to trace as many as possible of the cases definitely declared tuberculous, so that they could be placed under medical care and in suitable institutions (see page 41).

In comparison with the armies of our allies, the number of soldiers who developed or contracted tuberculosis during the war and had to be returned at once, was exceedingly small. Because of a too hasty examination or incorrect interpretation of Roentgen pictures, some men were returned, who upon subsequent examination here, were found simply to be suffering from chronic bronchitis or residual fraction of pneumonia. To avoid as far as possible a repetition of such errors, Dr. Gerald B. Webb was appointed Colonel and chief consultant in tuberculosis in the American Expeditionary Forces and sent to France in March, 1918. On his arrival Colonel Webb established centers for the correct sifting out of all chest cases, one at Savenay with the New York Post-Graduate Unit, under Colonel Samuel Lloyd; one at Vauclaire with the Mount Sinai Unit, under Colonel Lilienthal; and another center at Guyon with the Pennsylvania Unit. Colonel Webb visited almost every hospital of the American Expeditionary Force, hoping that through his instruction and standardization of diagnostic methods, mistakes might be reduced to a minimum and only positive sputum and hemorrhage cases sent home.

In spite of the admirable work of Dr. Webb, the errors in diagnosis increased because of unforeseen complications which arose in handling the problem of the tuberculous, those afflicted with other chest diseases, and the suspected tuberculous cases. One must draw this conclusion from an article in the Annual Report of 1920 by Colonel Brooke in which he says:

"The seemingly large number of cases in the above category was unexpected and was apparently brought about by two conditions not anticipated at the beginning of the war. First, the acute respiratory infections in 1918, largely influenza and pneumonia, resulted in a residual chronic pulmonary infection usually caused by the hemolytic streptococcus that clinically, even to the physical signs, simulated pulmonary tuberculosis; second, shortly after the signing of the armistice the tuberculosis-hospital centers in France were broken up and a large number of cases were sent home with a tentative diagnosis of tuberculosis that otherwise would have been sifted out overseas."

With a foresight that cannot be too highly commended, the

Surgeon General of the Army, upon the declaration of war, began to plan for the care and treatment of a large number of tuberculous patients who he thought might escape detection upon examination or develop tuberculosis while in the service. At the time war was declared, only the U. S. General Hospital at Fort Bayard, New Mexico, with 500 beds, was available. It was early apparent that it would be necessary to have a series of hospitals located in the east and as near the port of debarkation as possible, thus reducing discomfort and fatigue incident to railroad travel to a minimum. Following this policy, hospitalization for tuberculous patients was planned and executed as follows:

	Capacity
United States General Hospital, Fort Bayard, New Mexico	1,850
United States General Hospital, No. 8, Otisville, N. Y.	1,000
United States General Hospital, No. 16, New Haven, Conn.	500
United States General Hospital, No. 17, Markleton, Pa.	200
United States General Hospital, No. 18, Waynesville, N. C.	600
United States General Hospital, No. 19, Oteen, N. C.	1,300
United States General Hospital, No. 20, Whipple Barracks, Ariz.	500
United States General Hospital, No. 21, Denver, Colo. (Fitzsimmons).	1,500
United States General Hospital, No. 42, Spartanburg, S. C.	1,000
	8,450

No other nation has ever in such a short time constructed, equipped with all necessities and refinements, and placed in operation such an efficient chain of tuberculosis hospitals for military personnel. The number of beds which General Gorgas estimated would be necessary to care for the tuberculous sick was fully justified by subsequent admissions. Even though there was some slight delay incident to the Public Health Service taking over these patients, at no time was there any permanent congestion in any of these tuberculosis institutions. When the Public Health hospitals were ready to receive them, the majority was gradually absorbed, but many of these patients remained in Army hospitals as beneficiaries of the Bureau of War Risk Insurance (now U. S. Veterans' Bureau). As time elapsed it became possible to close or turn over to the Public Health Service all of the hospitals above named except the Fitzsimmons General Hospital at Denver, Colo. The bed capacity of this hospital has been increased from 1,000 to 1,740, and on this date it is caring for 782 beneficiaries of the Veterans' Bureau.

UNITED STATES NAVY

With our entrance into the world war the Bureau of Medicine and Surgery of the Department of the U. S. Navy early recognized the fact that there would be an increased number of tuberculous patients and took steps to enlarge its tuberculosis hospital at Fort Lyon, Colo., equipping it with the most modern type of x-ray apparatus, heliotherapy facilities, etc.

On October 3, 1921, this hospital was transferred by executive order to the Veterans' Bureau, which was obligated to care for the discharged personnel of the Government Services, the Navy having decided, as a result of its experience, that it was not economical to continue men in the service after they had developed tuberculosis. Before the War Risk Act of 1917, the Navy was under obligations to care for those who developed tuberculosis, and this was the more imperative because private and state sanatoria were disinclined to care for cases which had been discharged from the Navy.

Confronted with a large increase in personnel during the world war, the Navy Department fully realized the importance of eliminating at the recruiting office those men who were suffering with tuberculosis. Every endeavor was made to eliminate by physical examination at training stations cases that had escaped detection at the earlier examination. At the training stations latent cases also were detected as well as those which lighted up after strenuous training. Inasmuch as such men had already been enlisted, the navy accepted the obligation of caring for them and transferred them to the Naval Hospital at Fort Lyon.

Briefly, the following is the scheme which has been adopted by the Navy Department for the prevention and treatment of tuberculosis:

1. Elimination of the infected or predisposed individual at the recruiting office.
2. The holding of all recruits for a definite period, usually six months, for medical observation during training period before being sent to sea.
3. Physical examination of all men before being transferred and upon re-enlistment.

4. Special attention to carefully balanced ration, ventilation, physical exercise, and general personal hygiene of all men in the navy and Marine Corps.
5. A definite policy of early detection and segregation of all men suffering with tuberculosis.
6. Hospitalization. Formerly at Fort Lyon, now through Veterans' Bureau facilities.
7. At the present time all enlisted men suffering with tuberculosis are discharged from the service as soon as a definite diagnosis of tuberculosis can be made, and in many cases are held as supernumeraries until they can be taken care of by the Veterans' Bureau. In the case of enlisted men who have entered the navy since February 9, 1922, and those who are not eligible for benefit under the Veterans' Bureau, hospitalization is still afforded from naval sources.
8. The Bureau could not discharge officers except by retirement and, therefore, arrangements have been made with the Surgeon General, U. S. Army, to take care of officer patients until they are ordered before a retiring board. The army hospital utilized in this connection is the Fitzsimmons General Hospital, near Denver, Colo. This hospital also receives enlisted men of the navy suffering with tuberculosis.

PUBLIC HEALTH SERVICE

With the gradual return of all the sick and wounded there was naturally a considerable increase in the number of soldiers and sailors who had either contracted or developed tuberculosis in service as a result of war work or as sequelæ of influenza or pneumonia, and in 1919 the U. S. Public Health Service was required to make physical examinations and to furnish medical care for the disabled veterans applying for compensation.

To meet the serious emergency which then arose, the medical corps was quickly increased to more than 5,000 physicians, of whom 2,700 were full-time medical officers. Hospitals were rapidly organized and the field force made contact with applicants in every county in the United States. One-third of the patients admitted to hospitals were tuberculous.

A program for necessary hospital construction was prepared in conjunction with the War Risk Insurance Bureau, proposing 51 new hospitals at a total estimated cost of $85,000,000. Of these, 19 with an aggregate of 9,330 beds, were designed for the tuberculous. While this program, which was published December 5, 1919, Public Document No. 481, of the Sixty-sixth Congress, was considered by the Congress as too pretentious, subsequent events indicate that the forecast was approximately correct.

By order of Surgeon General Cumming, authorized by the Secretary of the Treasury, a Section of Tuberculosis was organized in the U. S. Public Health Service at Washington under the direction of Surgeon F. C. Smith, not as a substitute for the Division of Tuberculosis, which has several times been recommended by the National Tuberculosis Association, but only to meet urgent relief problems related to the care and examination of disabled veterans. Tuberculosis Sections were established as a part of each of the fourteen district offices, the chiefs of which undertook the task of securing from their field medical officers adequate chest examinations and accurate diagnoses. During the first two years approximately 1,000,000 physical examinations of all kinds were made.

To train medical officers in diagnosis and treatment, to open new hospitals, many of which were of temporary and unsatisfactory construction and unfavorably situated, to facilitate admissions, provide a proper standard of treatment, facilitate discharge when treatment was completed and prevent unnecessary transfers from hospital to hospital, were large problems. By December, 1920, more than 15,000 tuberculosis patients had been discharged from hospitals and nearly 10,000 tuberculous were under treatment, of which 5,300 were in Public Health Service hospitals, 219 in Army and Navy hospitals, about 500 in those belonging to the National Homes for Disabled Volunteer Soldiers, and the remainder scattered in contract hospitals. The task grew rapidly. One hundred and ninety dentists and about 2,000 trained nurses, reconstruction aides and dietitians were added to the corps. Dispensaries were established and follow-up care of tuberculous patients living at home was undertaken, thousands of standard packages of sputum cups and paper handkerchiefs being distributed.

Practically every large service tuberculosis hospital has become a continuous training school for physicians. The one at Oteen, N. C., has conducted a special summer school for nurses as well as medical officers. Several hundred physicians not stationed in hospitals have been given the short course in diagnosis at various points in the field. A report of the schools of instruction conducted in the Eighth District, which includes the States of Wisconsin, Illinois and Michigan, was published in Public Health

Reports December 2, 1921. Chief among the scientific articles offered for publication by Service officers is a report of two years' research carried out at Hospital No. 41, New Haven, Conn. This monograph, "Small Pneumothorax in Tuberculosis," by Surgeons (Reserve) Nathan Barlow and James C. Thompson, is being published as a bulletin of the Hygienic Laboratory.

Valuable coöperation has been constantly received from the National Tuberculosis Association, whose Advisory Committee outlined measures which were immediately included in the objectives. An expert in construction, Mr. T. B. Kidner, collaborated in the preparation of standard hospital plans, a report of which appeared in Public Health Reports June 17, 1921. A number of specialists consented to inspect the tuberculosis hospitals and the Supervisor of Medical Service, National Tuberculosis Association, also makes inspections from time to time at the request of the Surgeon General. The recommendations made by these highly trained men have been of very great assistance in providing proper standards of sanatorium treatment. A large number of well-known members of the Association assisted in conducting training courses in the field. It is regretted that the space here available is insufficient to give the desired credit to the individual members.

VETERANS' HOSPITALS FOR TUBERCULOSIS OPERATED BY THE
U. S. PUBLIC HEALTH SERVICE

	Bed Capacity
No. 24, Palo Alto, California	639
No. 26, Greenville, South Carolina	650
No. 27, Alexandria, Louisiana	554
No. 41, New Haven, Connecticut	500
No. 50, Prescott, Arizona	765*
No. 51, Tucson, Arizona	290
No. 55, Fort Bayard, New Mexico	1,120†
No. 59, Tacoma, Washington	278
No. 60, Oteen, North Carolina	1,100‡
No. 64, Camp Kearney, California	550
No. 79, Dawson Springs, Ky. (not yet open)	500
No. 80, Fort Lyon, Colorado	750
Excelsior Springs, Mo. (not open yet)	200
Walla Walla, Wash. (not yet open)	240
Rutland, Mass. (not yet open)	300

* New construction is under way to increase the capacity 422 beds.
† New construction is under way to increase the capacity 250 beds.
‡ New construction is under way to increase the capacity 200 beds.

In addition to the above named Veterans' hospitals with an aggregate of approximately 8,000 beds, three of the original Marine hospitals are devoted to tuberculous patients, the largest one, that at Fort Stanton, New Mexico, having 225 beds. All hospitals operated by the Public Health Service have tuberculosis wards, some of which, among them the large hospitals in Boston, New York, Baltimore and Chicago, contain several hundred beds. The general hospitals serve as observation points to clear up obscure diagnoses, and the tuberculosis wards are clearing stations from which patients are transferred to sanatoria proper. A considerable number of the tuberculous patients under treatment in them, however, are those unsuitable for transfer or who are unwilling to be removed to hospitals outside the city.

APPENDIX II

PUBLICATIONS OF THE NATIONAL TUBER CULOSIS ASSOCIATION

I T WOULD be impossible to give a complete list of all of the publications of the National Tuberculosis Association since its beginning. Much of the printed matter issued by the Association is of ephemeral value and is designed merely for occasional use. A list of the more stable and permanent publications of the Association, however, is of value in this record. Such a list follows:

Transactions of the annual meetings of the National Tuberculosis Association, beginning with Vol. I, 1905, to and including Vol. XVII, 1921. These annual volumes contain all of the papers read at the annual meetings, lists of members, a record of the meeting, resolutions adopted, reports of the treasurer, managing director, and other reports. Volumes range in size from about 350 pages to nearly 700 pages. A cumulative index of the Transactions has been published, covering the years 1905–1920.

Journal of the Outdoor Life, the official organ of the National Tuberculosis Association published monthly since 1904. The Journal of the Outdoor Life is not owned by the National Tuberculosis Association, but since 1910 has been published in close relation with the Association. It is the lay publication of the Association, designed to carry articles of information and inspiration for tuberculosis patients, tuberculosis workers and tuberculosis specialists. Each volume consists of twelve numbers.

Monthly Bulletin of the National Tuberculosis Association, published monthly since 1914. Prior to that date a mimeographed confidential bulletin was published at occasional intervals. The Bulletin is recognized in popular parlance as the "house organ" of the National Tuberculosis Association. It deals primarily with technique of tuberculosis work, that is, with methods and programs and with the news of the National Association.

American Review of Tuberculosis, published monthly since March 1917. The Review is the medical organ of the Association. Each volume begins with the March number and consists of twelve issues, separately paged for original articles and abstracts of tuberculosis articles.

Pamphlet No. 101, "Sleeping and Sitting in the Open Air," 24 pp., 1917. A pamphlet entitled "Directions for Living and Sleeping in the Open Air," was originally published by the National Tuberculosis Association in 1913. The present pamphlet 101 is an adaptation of the original one.

Pamphlet No. 102, "The Effect of Tuberculosis Institutions on the Value and Desirability of Surrounding Property," 64 pp., 1914.

Pamphlet No. 103, "Selling Red Cross Seals," a symposium presented before the North Atlantic Tuberculosis Conference, 1914, 16 pp., out of print.

Pamphlet No. 104, "Tuberculosis Legislation in the United States," 64 pp., 1915, out of print.

Pamphlet No. 105, "Working Men's Organizations in Local Anti-Tuberculosis Campaigns," 64 pp., 1916.

Pamphlet No. 106, "What You Should Know About Tuberculosis," a standard pamphlet prepared by a special committee of the National Tuberculosis Association, 32 pp., 1916.

Pamphlet No. 107, "Dispensary Method and Procedure," by F. Elisabeth Crowell, 120 pp., 1916. This pamphlet is now being revised.

Pamphlet No. 108, "Red Cross Seal Percentages," out of print.

Pamphlet No. 109, "What Tuberculosis Workers Should Know About Discharged Soldiers and Rejected Men," 16 pp., 1919, out of print.

Pamphlet No. 110, "A Directory of Tuberculosis Associations in the United States," 112 pp., 1919.

Pamphlet No. 111, "A Directory of Sanatoria, Hospitals and Day Camps for the Treatment of Tuberculosis in the United States," 100 pp., 1919.

Pamphlet No. 112, "A Directory of Dispensaries, Clinics, and Classes for the Special Treatment of Tuberculosis in the United States," 56 pp., 1919.

Pamphlet No. 113, "An Outline of Lectures on Tuberculosis," for nurses, occupational aides and social workers, 15 pp., 1921.

Modern Health Crusade Manual, 35 pp., 1921. The first Manual of the Modern Health Crusade was published in 1917. In addition to the Manual, the Crusade issues the chore record charts in three editions— standard, primary and senior. It also publishes other material for the Modern Health Crusade.

"Hints and Helps for Tuberculosis Patients," by Dr. Charles L. Minor, 16 pp., 1921, reprinted from the Journal of the Outdoor Life.

"Becoming Acquainted with the Enemy Tuberculosis," a four-page circular published in 1921, in 17 foreign languages and in English.

"Sanatorium Administration Standards," prepared by the Committee of the American Sanatorium Association, reprinted from the Transactions, 1920, 16 pp.

"Diagnostic Standards of the National Tuberculosis Association," prepared by a committee of the Framingham Community Health and Tuberculosis Demonstration, 1920, 16 pp.

Health Plays, a series of 15 playlets entitled "Miss Fresh Air, Visiting Nurse," "Judith and Ariel," "A Pageant of Average Town," "Health and His Enemies," "The Friends of Health," "The Imps and the Children," "Don't Care," "The New Child," "Good News from Babyland," "Playing Visit," "The Passing of the Littlest Pageant," "The Theft of Thistledown," "The Narrow Door," "David and the Good Health Elves," and "Wee Davie." Some of these plays are out of print, but a new edition of these and others is being prepared.

"To the Children of America," originally published by the American Commission for the Prevention of Tuberculosis of the Rockefeller Foundation and the Bureau of Tuberculosis of the American Red Cross in France, 20 pp., 1919.

The Framingham Monographs as follows:

No. 1—The Program.

No. 2—The Sickness Census.

No. 3—Vital Statistics.

No. 4—Medical Examination Campaigns.

No. 5—Tuberculosis Findings.

No. 6—Schools and Factories.

No. 7—The Children's Summer Camp.

No. 8—Health Letters.

The Framingham Community Health and Tuberculosis Demonstration has also published circulars as follows:

"What Has the Health Demonstration done for Framingham?"

"Report of the Committee on Appraisal."

"Framingham Yardsticks."

"Tuberculosis Hospital and Sanatorium Construction," by Thomas Spees Carrington, 182 pp., 1914, out of print.

The Christmas Seal, issued annually since 1908. With the Christmas Seal has been brought out each year a large and increasing volume of posters, circulars, and other literature.

APPENDIX III

BIBLIOGRAPHY OF THE AUTHOR
S. ADOLPHUS KNOPF, M.D.

Koch's lymph in Paris. South. California Praet., Feb., 1891.

Les sanatoria, traitement et prophylaxie de la phtisie pulmonaire. Thése pour le Doctorat. Paris, June, 1895.

Sanatoria for consumptives. South. California Praet., Oct., 1895.

Sanatoria for the treatment and prophylaxis of pulmonary phthisis. N. Y. Med. Jour., Oct. 5 and 12, 1895.

Les sanatoria des phtisiques sont-ils un danger pour le voisinage? Revue de la Tuberculose, Dec., 1895.

Should we treat pulmonary tuberculosis as a contagious or as a communicable disease? South. California Pract., May, 1896.

Are sanatoria for consumptives a danger to the neighborhood? N. Y. Med. Jour., Oct. 3, 1896.

La phtisiotherapie et les sanatoria. Presse méd., Oct. 14, 1896.

The hygienic, educational, and symptomatic treatment of pulmonary tuberculosis with a plea for sanatoria. Med. Rec., Feb. 13, 1897.

Tuberculosis and the board of health. N. Y. Med. Jour., April 3, 1897.

The communicability of tuberculosis and special hospitals for pulmonary consumption. Med. Rec., April 3, 1897.

Aerotherapeutics and hydrotherapeutics in the treatment and prevention of pulmonary tuberculosis. N. Y. Med. Jour., July 24, 1897.

Anti-streptococcic serum in the mixed infection of tuberculosis. Jour. Am. Med. Assn., Sept. 25, 1897.

The present status of preventive means against the spread of tuberculosis in the various states of the Union critically reviewed. Jour. Am. Med. Assn., Oct. 30, 1897.

The urgent need of sanatoria for the consumptive poor of our large cities. Med. Rec., Nov. 27, 1897.

A new binaural stethoscope with armamentarium for complete physical examination. Jour. Am. Med. Assn., Jan. 1, 1898.

Ueber Volksheilstätten für Lungenkranke in Amerika. Heilstätten Korrespondenz., Jan. 1, 1898.

Ein neues binaurales Stethoskop mit Armamentarium für vollständige Auskultation und Perkussion. Zeitschr. f. Krankenpflege, March, 1898.

State and municipal care of consumptives. Med. Rec., Sept. 24, 1898.

The tuberculosis problem in the United States. North Am. Rev., Feb., 1899; also Lancet, London, May 6, 1899.

Organized charities and tuberculosis. Charities, March 4, 1899.

Pulmonary tuberculosis: its modern prophylaxis and the treatment in special institutions and at home. 343 pages. Alvarenga Prize Essay, May, 1899. P. Blakiston's Son & Co., Philadelphia.

Die Tuberkulose als Volkskrankheit und deren Bekämpfung. Prize essay of Internat. Tuberc. Congr., Berlin, July, 1899.

The compulsory reporting of tuberculosis. N. Y. Med. Jour., Sept. 23, 1899.

Early recognition of pulmonary tuberculosis. Jour. Am. Med. Assn., Dec. 9, 1899.

Les sanatoria, traitement et prophylaxie de la phtisie pulmonaire. Second edition, 495 pages, Paris, Jan., 1900.

The California quarantine against consumption. The Forum, Jan., 1900.

Sanatorium treatment at home for patients suffering from pulmonary tuberculosis. Med. Rec., Jan. 27, 1900.

The sanatorium movement. Charities, Feb. 10, 1900.

Tenements and tuberculosis. New York Daily News, Feb. 21, 1900; also Jour. Am. Med. Assn., May 12, 1900; The Sanitarian, and Charities, Sept., 1900.

L'infection des livres par le bacille de la tuberculose. Presse méd., Feb. 24, 1900.

Tuberculosis—diagnosis, prognosis, prophylaxis, and treatment. In Twentieth Century Practice of Medicine, xx, 1900. Wm. Wood & Co., New York.

Die Früherkennung der Tuberkulose. Zeitschrift für Tuberk. u. Heilstättenw., April and July, 1900.

The anti-tuberculosis crusade in France. N. Y. Med. Jour., June 9, 1900.

On the reporting of tuberculous cases to the health authorities. Med. Press, July 19, 1900.

Dispensaries for the poor versus a hospital for consumptives. Charities, Oct. 6, 1900.

Some thoughts on overcrowding and tuberculosis. Jour. Am. Med. Assn., Oct. 10, 1900.

The ætiology of pulmonary tuberculosis, its course and termination. N. Y. Med. Jour., Oct. 13, 1900.

Tuberculosis in prisons and reformatories. Med. Rec., March 2, 1901.

Our duties toward the consumptive poor. Med. News, March 9, 1901.

Tuberculosis literature for the general practitioner and his work against the great white plague. South. California Praet., April, 1901.

The anti-tuberculosis crusade in the United States and the sanatorium movement during the year 1900. Zeitschr. f. Tuberk. u. Heilstättenw., April, 1901.

Municipal care of the consumptive poor. Boston Med. and Surg. Jour., May 2, 1901.

Tuberculosis as a disease of the masses and how to combat it. American edition, March, 1901. This international prize essay has been translated into the following languages: Arabic, Bohemian, Brazilian, Bulgarian, Chinese (2), Dutch, English, Finnish, French, Hebrew, Hindu (2), Hungarian, Icelandic, Italian (2), Japanese, Mexican (Spanish), Norwegian, Polish, Russian (2), Serbian, Spanish, Swedish, Turkish, and French-Canadian.

Relation of the medical profession in the twentieth century to the tuberculosis problem. Jour. Am. Med. Assn., June 15, 1901.

The value of local sanatoria in the combat of pulmonary tuberculosis. Med. Record, July 6, 1901.

The woman of the tenement and her three great enemies— ignorance, alcoholism, and tuberculosis. Jour. Med. and Science, Aug., 1901.

A plea for the alien consumptive. Jour. Med. and Science, Aug., 1901.

Prevention of tuberculous disease in infancy and childhood. Maryland Med. Jour., Aug., 1901; also Bull. Johns Hopkins Hosp., Sept., 1901.

Respiratory exercises in the prevention and treatment of pulmonary diseases. Bull. Johns Hopkins Hosp., Sept., 1901.

Ein Aufruf zur Gründung einer deutschen Lungenheilstätte in gross-New York als zweig der New Yorker and Brooklyner deutschen Hospitäler. Zeitschr. für Tuberk. u. Heilstättenw., Oct., 1901.

State and individual prophylaxis of tuberculosis during childhood and the need of children's sanatoria. N. Y. Med. Jour., Nov. 30, 1901; also Zeitschr. f. Tuberk. u. Heilstättenw., Jan., 1902.

Sanatorium versus hospital for incipients. Med. Rec., Dec. 21, 1901.

A McKinley memorial—A seaside sanatorium with a pavilion for every state for the treatment of American children suffering from tuberculous and scrofulous diseases, or predisposed to consumption. Charities, Oct. 12, 1901; Jour. of Med. and Science, Nov. 1901.

The deportation of consumptive immigrants. Charities, Dec. 14, 1901.

Allure generale de la lutte contre la tuberculose aux Etats Unis. La Lutte Antituberculose, Aug. 31, 1901.

Die Massnahmen der stadt New York zur Bekämpfung der Tuberkulose. Hyg. Volksblatt, Jan., 1902.

Official and private phthisiophobia. Med. Rec., Jan. 11, 1902.

Some unsolved problems in tenement house life. The Sanitarian, Feb., 1902; also Charities, Feb. 22, 1902.

The tuberculosis problem in the United States. North American Rev., March, 1902.

The mission of societies for the prevention of consumption in the anti-tuberculosis crusade. Tr. Can. Med. Assn., April, 1902; also Montreal Med. Jour., April, 1902; N. Y. Med. Jour., April 26, 1902.

A few thoughts on the medical and social aspects of tuberculosis at the beginning of the twentieth century. v. Leyden's Festschr., May, 1902.

Another chapter on phthisiophobia. Med. News, May 3, 1902.

The need of a Masonic sanatorium. Trs., Masonic Standard, May 17, 1902.

What shall we do with the consumptive poor? Nat. Hosp. Rec., June, 1902; also Med. Rec., July 5, 1902.

The anti-tuberculosis movement in the United States. Tuberculosis, Berlin, i, no. 8, Aug., 1902.

The exclusion of non-pauper tuberculous immigrants and alien tuberculous visitors from American shores. Zeitschr. f. Tuberk. u. Heilstättenw., Oct., 1902.

Prevention of tuberculosis and what every one should know about it; address before New Jersey Sanitarian Assn., Oct. 24, 1902.

The Burke Foundation and a plea for proper homes for the convalescent poor. N. Y. Med. Jour., Nov. 1, 1902.

The present aspect of the tuberculosis problem in the United States. Jour. Am. Med. Assn., Nov. 22, 1902.

Report on the care of the sick poor of the state of New York. With suggestions for the establishment of convalescent homes, psychopathic hospitals as reception stations for the insane and special pavilions for the treatment of the tuberculous insane and epileptics; also sanatoria, special hospitals, tuberculosis dispensaries and agricultural colonies for consumptives dependent on public charity. Med. News, Dec. 13, 1902.

Tuberculosis. Supplement to Twentieth Century Practice of Medicine. William Wood & Co., Jan., 1902.

The treatment and care of consumptives at their homes and the value of local sanatoria. Med. Rec., Feb. 21, 1903.

A practical talk to nurses of tuberculous patients. Am. Jour. of Nurses, March, 1903.

The duties of the individual and the government in the combat of tuberculosis as a disease of the masses. Charities, March 7, 1903.

The special dispensary as a factor in the combat of tuberculosis as a disease of the masses. N. Y. Med. Jour., March 28, 1903.

The duties of the school teacher in the combat of tuberculosis as a disease of the masses. Am. Med., July 11, 1903.

What shall we do with the consumptive who cannot leave the city during the hot season? N. Y. Med. Jour., July 18, 1903.

The mental status of phthisis. Letter to Jour. Am. Med. Assn., Oct. 3, 1903.

The treatment and management of post-operative tuberculous patients and a plea for the establishment of seaside sanatoria and convalescent homes. N. Y. Med. Jour., Nov. 28, 1903; Annals of Gynecol. and Pediatry, Dec., 1903.

American and international congresses on tuberculosis and tuberculosis exhibits, 1904–1905. Am. Med.; also Med. News, Dec. 5, 1903.

A multiplicity of tuberculosis congresses. N. Y. Med. Jour., Dec. 12, 1903.

A plea for justice to the consumptive—a reply to recent attempts to discriminate against the consumptive, not only on account of his physical infirmity but also on account of his alleged mental and moral defects. Med. Rec., Jan. 2, 1904.

What labor unions might do to stop the spread of tuberculosis among their members. Weekly Bull. of the Clothing Trades, Jan. 27, 1904.

The psychical relation of tuberculosis. Med. Rec., Feb. 13, 1904, and April 30, 1904.

Peter Dettweiler—obituary. N. Y. Med. Jour., Feb. 20, 1904.

Pulmonary consumption and the possibility of its eradication through the combined efforts of a wide government, well-trained physicians and an intelligent people. Maryland Med. Jour., March, 1904.

The first tuberculosis exposition in the United States, held in Baltimore, from Jan. 25 to Feb. 1, 1904. Tuberculosis, Berlin, April, 1904.

A few thoughts on the solution of the tuberculosis problem. Critic and Guide, May, 1904.

The tuberculosis epidemic among the street sweepers of the City of New York. N. Y. Med. Jour., May 14, 1904.

The patient's duty. Jour. Outdoor Life, July, 1904.

The place of the sanatorium in the prevention and treatment of tuberculosis. Bull. Vermont State Board of Health, Dec., 1903.

The National Association for the Study and Prevention of Tuberculosis. Med. Rec. and N. Y. Med. Jour., July 2, 1904; also Am. Med., July 16, 1904; Zeitschr. f. Tuberk. u Heilstättenw., Bd. vi, no. 3, 1904.

Hermann Brehmer and the semi-centennial celebration of Brehmer's sanatorium for the treatment of consumptives, the first institution of its kind. N. Y. Med. Jour., July 2, 1904.

The modern tuberculosis dispensary. Med. Rec., July 23, 1904.

How may the public school be helpful in the prevention of tuberculosis? N. Y. Med. Jour., Sept. 3, 1904.

Every man's duty regarding tuberculosis. World's Work, Oct., 1904.

The family physician as a factor in the solution of the tuberculosis problem. Jour. Am. Med. Assn., Oct. 22, 1904.

Woman's duty toward the health of the nation. N. Y. Med. Jour., Nov. 5, 1904.

The problem of ventilation of our new subway. N. Y. Med. Jour., Nov. 12, 1904.

A visit to the American tuberculosis exposition at Baltimore, with short reports of the lectures of Hoffman, Flick, Ravenel, Knopf, Adami, Welch, Huber and Osler. Zeitschr. f. Tuberk., April, 1904.

Consumptive heroes. Colo. Med. Jour., Sept., 1904.

Sanatoria for consumptives. Letter to N. Y. State Jour. Med., Jan., 1905.

The tuberculosis problem and Mr. Henry Phipps' philanthropy. Editorial, N. Y. Med. Jour., Jan. 21, 1905.

Geheimrath Dr. Dettweiler. Eulogy pronounced on the occasion of the first anniversary of his death. Med. Rec., Jan. 28, 1905.

Present status of anti-tuberculosis work in the United States. Suggestions for a more effectual coöperation of authorities, philanthropists, physieiaus and laymen. Jour. Am. Med. Assn., Feb. 11, 1905.

Die antituberkulose Bewegung in den Vereinigten Staaten im Anfang des Jahres, 1905. Zeitschr. f. Tuberk. u. Heilstättenw., vii, no. 1, 1905.

The open air treatment at home for tuberculous patients, with a description of a window-tent and a half tent. N. Y. Med. Jour., March 4, 1905.

The possible victory over the great white plague. St. Louis Courier of Med., March, 1905.

Elevated railways in the congested districts of the poor and its bearing on tuberculosis. Editorial N. Y. Med. Jour., March 18, 1905.

The tuberculosis situation in prisons, with especial reference to the state prison at Sing Sing and the state prison at Columbus, Ohio. Med. Rec., May 13, 1905.

Subway ventilation and its bearing on tuberculosis. Editorial, N. Y. Med. Jour., June 17, 1905.

Respiratory exercises in the prevention and treatment of pulmonary tuberculosis. Jour. Outdoor Life, July, 1905.

Jewish immunity from consumption. Letter to New Era Illustrated Magazine, Aug., 1905.

The sanatorium for tuberculous patients and its medical and social mission. N. Y. Med. Jour., Oct. 21, 1905.

The treatment and care of advanced cases of pulmonary tuberculosis. Tr. Nat. Tuberc. Assn., i, 371, 1905; also Med. Rec., Nov. 18, 1905.

Early clinical diagnosis of pulmonary tuberculosis. Jour. Med. Soc. of New Jersey, Nov., 1905.

The first annual meeting of the National Association for the Study and Prevention of Tuberculosis of the United States held at Washington, D. C., May 18 and 19, 1905. Zeitschr. f. Tuberk., Band viii, no. 1, 1905.

The marriage of the tuberculous and the size of the family in their bearing on the tuberculosis problem. Am. Med., Jan. 6, 1906.

Heilstätten für tuberkulose Patienten und deren medizinische und soziale Aufgabe. Tuberculosis, Berlin, v, no. 1; and N. Y. Med. Monatsschr, Jan., 1906.

The teacher's part in the tuberculosis problem. Med. Rec., Feb. 17, 1906.

Le sanatorium pour tuberculeux, sa mission medicale et sociale. Zeitschr. f. Tuberk., Band iii, no. 4, 1906.

Medicine and law in relation to the alcohol, venereal disease, and tuberculosis problem. Med. Rec., June 2, 1906.

How can the physician and layman accomplish more in the fight against tuberculosis. Brooklyn Med. Jour., June, 1906.

Maxims for the selection of climate in pulmonary, laryngeal, and bone tuberculosis. N. Y. Med. Jour., July 28, 1906.

The early diagnosis and the prognosis of pulmonary tuberculosis. South. California Pract., Aug. 19; also Med. Examiner and Pract., Sept., 1906.

Tuberculosis, a social disease. Jour. Am. Med. Assn., June 16, 1906; also Bull. Johns Hopkins Hosp., Dec., 1906.

The home treatment of tuberculosis. Proc. 6th Annual Confer. of Sanit. Officers of the State of New York, Oct. 24, 1906; and North Am. Jour. of Homoeopathy, Sept., 1907.

The tuberculosis problem in prisons and reformatories. N. Y. Med. Jour., Nov. 17, 1906.

Quacks and quackeries—their blighting influence on the lives of the tuberculous. Some fake remedies and the harm they do—chloroform and prussic acid combined in one "cure"—bad whiskey the basis of many nostrums.

Proc. 32d Annual Meeting of the New Jersey San. Assn., Nov. 16 and 17, 1906; also Jour. Outdoor Life, Jan., 1907.

A plea for cremation in tuberculosis and similarly infectious diseases. Jour. Am. Med. Assn., Jan. 26, 1907.

Professor Joseph J. Grancher of Paris; the life story of a distinguished physician. Zeitschr. f. Tuberk., Bd. ix, Heft 6, 1907.

In memoriam of Professor J. J. Grancher of Paris, France, 1843–1907. N. Y. Med. Jour., Sept. 28, 1907.

Aerotherapy in cold weather. N. Y. Med. Jour., May 25, 1907.

The mission of the municipal and state sanatorium for the tuberculous, and the urgent need of more institutions of this kind. Texas State Jour. of Med., Dec., 1907.

A war upon consumption—the duty of the citizen in the fight against tuberculosis. Lecture before Kentucky Anti-tuberc. Assn., Louisville, Ky., Dec. 11, 1907.

Some thoughts on the etiology, prophylaxis and therapeutics of laryngeal tuberculosis. Med. Rec., Feb. 22, 1908.

Sun, air, and water; their use in the preservation of health and the cure of disease. Life and Health, Feb. and June, 1908.

The social aspect of tuberculosis. Mobile Med. and Surg. Jour., June, 1908.

A plea for more sanatoria for the consumptive poor in all stages of the disease. N. Y. Med. Jour., July 11; also Post-Graduate, July, 1908.

How to adapt sanatorium methods to treatment of consumptives at their homes. N. Y. Post-Graduate, Aug., 1907; and Zeitschr. f. Tuberk., Bd. 13, H. 4, 1908.

Early diagnosis of tuberculosis. St. Louis Med. Rev., Sept., 1908.

The relation of the medical profession to the housing problem. Med. Rec., Sept. 12, 1908.

Le sanatorium, le dispensaire et l'hopital special pour le traitement des tuberculeux. L'Union Medicale du Canada, Aug., 1908; also Tuberculosis, Berlin, no. 9, Sept., 1908.

Sunlight and tuberculous disease. N. Y. Med. Jour., Sept. 26, 1908.

Explanation of seeming paradoxes in modern phthisiotherapy. Tr. Nat. Tuberc. Assn., iv, 189, 1908; also N. Y. Med. Jour., Sept. 26, 1908.

The popular lecture in the crusade against tuberculosis. N. Y. Med. Jour., Oct. 31, 1908.

The Red Cross in the anti-tuberculosis war—a plea for contribution through a Christmas stamp. N. Y. Med. Jour., Nov. 28, 1908.

L'adaption a domicile du traitement des tuberculeux tel qu'on le preconise dans les sanatoria. L'Union Médicale du Canada, Dec., 1908.

Sunlight and solartherapy in its relation to tuberculosis. Am. Med., Aug., 1908.

Overcoming the predisposition to tuberculosis and the danger from infection during childhood. Med. Rec., Dec. 5, and Pediatrics, Dec., 1908.

Der Internationale Tuberkulosekongress in Washington vom 21. September bis 12. Oktober, 1908. Zeitschr. f. Tuberk., Bd. 13, H. 5, 1908.

Die moderne Tuberkulosebekämpfung vom sozialmedizinischen Standpunkte betrachtet. N. Y. Med. Monatsschr., Dec., 1908; also Tuberculosis, Berlin, no. 6, 1909.

The responsibility of the family physician toward tuberculosis. N. Y. Med. Jour., Jan. 2, 1909.

The popular lecture in the crusade against tuberculosis. Tuberculosis, Berlin, no. 1, 1909.

Einiges aus dem internationalen Tuberkulosekongress in Washington. N. Y. Med. Monatsschr., Feb., 1909.

Moyens de defense contre la predisposition a la tuberculose et contre l'infection pendant l'enfance. Bull. méd. de Québec, Feb., 1909.

A window-tent for the prevention and treatment of tuberculosis. Med. Era, May, 1909.

The starnook and the window-tent—two devices for the rest cure in the open air and for outdoor sleeping. N. Y. Med. Jour., April 22, 1911.

Tuberculosis, a preventable and curable disease, modern methods for the solution of the tuberculosis problem. 394 pages, Moffat, Yard & Co., June, 1909; second edition, 1911.

Public measures in the prophylaxis of tuberculosis. Article in Klebs' American Treatise on General Tuberculosis. 130 pages; D. Appleton & Co., July, 1909.

The hopeful outlook of the tuberculosis problem in the United States; Interstate Med. Jour.; also Jour. Outdoor Life, Aug., 1909.

Life insurance in its relation to the prevention of tuberculosis. Med. Rec., Aug. 21; also Med. Examiner and Genl. Practitioner, Aug., 1909.

Tuberculosis and congestion. Pediatrics, Aug., 1909; also N. Y. Med. Jour., Sept. 4, 1909.

A new type of phthisophobia. Jour. Am. Med. Assn., Sept. 25, 1909.

Robert Koch—an appreciation. Jour. of Tuberc., London, Oct., 1909.

The anti-tuberculosis war and the Red Cross Christmas stamp—an appeal. N. Y. Med. Jour., Dec. 11, 1909.

What may be done to improve the hygiene of the city dweller. Med. Rec., Jan. 8, 1910.

The subjective fremitus as diagnostic means and a new adjuvant in determining the localization and magnitude of the objective fremitus in chest examinations. N. Y. Med. Jour., Jan. 22, 1910.

Der subjektive Fremitus in der Frühdiagnose der Tuberkulose und die Beschreibung eines neuen Hilfsmittels zur besseren Erkennung und genaueren Lokalisierung des objektiven Fremitus. Zeitschr. f. Tuberk., Bd. xv, H. 5, 1910.

La tuberculose; French address before the League Anti-tuberculose de Quebec. L'Union Médicale du Canada, May, 1910; and Le Soleil, Quebec, May 10, 1910.

Dr. Edward Livingston Trudeau, zum 25-jährigen Jubiläum des Adirondack Cottage Sanitarium. Zeitschr. f. Tuberk., xv, no. 6, 1910.

The local hospital-sanatorium as one of the most important phases in the anti-tuberculosis crusade. Med. Rec., May 21, 1910.

Robert Koch—in memoriam. Med. Rec., June 4; also N. Y. med. Monats- schr., June; Zeitschr. f. Tuberk., xvi, no. 2, 1910.

Robert Koch—the passing of a pioneer. Estimates by Trudeau, Park and Knopf. Jour. Outdoor Life, July, 1910.

State phthisiophilia and state phthisiophobia, with a plea for justice to the consumptive. Tr. Nat. Tuberc. Assn., vi, 139, 1910; also N. Y. Med. Jour., July 9, 1910.

Edward Livingston Trudeau—an appreciation. British Jour. of Tuberc., July, 1910.

The relation of modern dentistry to the tuberculosis problem. Jour. Am. Med. Assn., Aug. 13, 1910.

A tuberculosis sermon. Jour. Outdoor Life, Aug.; also The Messiah Pulpit, Sept., 1910.

Le fremissement subjectif comme moyen de diagnostic, comme procede nouveau permettant de localiser et de determiner l'amplitude du fremisse- ment objectif dans les examens du pumon. L'Union Méd. du Canada, Dec., 1910.

Licht- und schattenseiten antituberkulöser Bestrebungen in den vereinigten Staaten. Med. Monatsschr., Nov., 1910; and Zeitschr. f. Tuberk., xvii, heft 1, 1911.

Memorial address on Dr. Robert Koch, by John A. Wyeth, M.D., LL.D., and S. A. Knopf, M.D. Med. Rec., Jan. 21, 1911.

The hygiene of public conveyances. Med. Rec., March 18, 1911.

The starnook—a new device for the rest-cure in the open air and for outdoor sleeping. Bull. Johns Hopkins Hosp., Aug., 1911.

Halving the tax rate on buildings; the relation of congestion to the tubercu- losis problem. A plea for more sanatoria and tuberculosis hospitals and better tenements. Survey, Sept. 23, 1911.

Robert Koch—the father of the modern science of tuberculosis. Bull. Johns Hopkins Hosp., Dec., 1911.

Primary sources of tuberculous infection; their relation to eugenics, and the cost of tuberculosis. N. Y. Med. Jour., June 29, 1912.

The immigration of the tuberculous into the United States. A problem for every nation. Med. Rec., July 13, 1912; Bull. Am. Acad. Med., June, 1913; also Zeitschr. f. Tuberk., xix, no. 2.

The relation of atmospheric air to tuberculosis. The 6th International Tu- berculosis Congress held in Washington in 1908, awarded in 1912 to this essay half of the Smithsonian Institution prize of $1500; the other half being awarded to Dr. Guy Hinsdale, of Hot Springs, Va. A revised edition of this essay is in preparation.

The unjustified prejudice of tuberculous patients against sanatoria and hos- pitals. Tr. Nat. Tuberc. Assn., viii, 140, 1912; also Med. Rec., Sept. 28, 1912.

Some modern medico-sociologic conceptions of the alcohol, venereal diseases, and tuberculosis problems.   Illinois Med. Jour., Oct., 1912; also Am. Practitioner, Feb., March and April, 1913.

Tuberculosis and other diseases in schools and colleges.   Open air schools and open air instruction with breathing exercises as preventive measures. N. Y. Med. Jour., Jan. 25, 1913.

Some newer problems and some newer phases of the anti-tuberculosis warfare in the United States.   Med. Rec., Feb. 1, 1913.

Artificial pneumothorax—indications and contraindications.   N. Y. Med. Jour., March 22, 1913.

Euthanasia in tuberculosis.   Med. Rev. of Rev., March, 1913.

Discarded battleships to be used as sanatoria and open-air schools.   N. Y. Med. Jour., Sept. 13, 1913.

Resolutions offered to the Fourth International Congress on School Hygiene, at Buffalo, Aug. 25–30, 1913, on sanatoria for children.   Med. Rev., Nov., 1913; also Zeitschr. f. Tuberk. band xxi, H. Jan. 2; Tuberculosis, Berlin, No. 9, 1913, in English, German and French.

Rest and exercise for the tuberculous and the predisposed child at school; with practical demonstrations of breathing exercises and a device combining open air study and the window tent.   Med. Rec., Nov. 15, 1913.

The occupations of afebrile tuberculous patients.   Med. Rec., Jan. 24, 1914.

Some suggestions for a more rational solution of the tuberculosis problem in the United States.   Paper read at the National Conference of Race Betterment held at Battle Creek, Mich., Jan. 8–12, 1914; Med. Rev., January, 1914; South. California Pract., Feb., 1914; also Med. Rev. of Rev., June, 1914.

A practical apparatus for the production of therapeutic pneumothorax; with some notes on the modus operandi, indications, and contra-indications. Am. Jour. Med. Sc., March, 1914.

The Friedmann serum and the Society of German Sanatorium Physicians. Med. Rec. and N. Y. Med. Jour., April 16, 1914; also Jour. Outdoor Life, May, 1914.

The treatment of advanced pulmonarv tuberculosis.   Tr. Nat. Tuberc. Assn., x, 74, 1914; also Med. Rec., Oct. 31, 1914; Tuberculosis, Berlin, no. 5, 1914.

The tuberculosis nurse and the tuberculosis problem.   The Nurse, July, 1914.

Methodes modernes de combattre la tuberculose, maladie des masses. L'Union Medicle du Canada, Aug., 1914.

The modern warfare against tuberculosis as a disease of the masses.   Fourteenth annual report of the Canad. Assn. for the Prev. of Tuberc.; also N. Y. Med. Jour., Oct. 3, 1914.

The health officer and the tuberculosis problem in rural communities.   Med. Rec., Oct. 10, 1914.

Is the modern anti-tuberculosis crusade really a failure?   A reply to Dr. Thomas J. Mays' communications.   N. Y. Med. Jour., Nov. 7, 1914.

Tuberculosis as a cause and result of poverty.   Jour. Am. Med. Assn., Nov. 14, 1914.

Phthisiophobia. A caution against exaggerated fear of the tuberculous. N. Y. Times, Dec. 29, 1914; also Pacific Med. Jour., Jan., 1915.

Sunlight in the treatment of tuberculosis. Am. Med., Dec., 1914.

The tuberculosis problem in rural communities—its modern aspect and the duty of health officers. Pub. Health Rep., Dec. 18, 1914.

Ueber die Behandlung der vorgeschrittenen Lungentuberkulose. Zeitschr. f. Tuberk., Band 23, Heft 4, 1915.

Tuberculosis as a social disease. Long Island Med. Jour., June, 1915.

The tuberculosis problem and section 1142 of the penal code of the State of New York. N. Y. Med. Jour., June 12, 1915.

Birth control and tuberculosis. Survey, July 10, 1915. Woman's Med. Jour., Sept., 1915.

Water in the prevention and cure of tuberculosis—with a plea for public baths for old and young and swimming pools particularly in connection with public schools. Med. Rec., July 31, 1915.

Dr. John Henry Huddleston—in memoriam. Med. Rec., Nov. 13, 1915.

Tuberculosis infection. Woman's Med. Jour., Jan., 1916.

The period of life at which infection from tuberculosis occurs most frequently. How may we diminish the frequency of those infections and prevent them from becoming tuberculous diseases? Med. Rec., Jan. 8, 1916; also Jour. of Pub. Health, Sept., 1916.

Edward Livingston Trudeau—in memoriam. Jour. Am. Med. Assn., Jan. 22, 1916; also Zeitschr. f. Tuberk., Jan.; British Jour. of Tuberc., April, 1916.

Tuberculosis of the lungs—pathology. Article in Reference Handbook of the Medical Sciences. Wm. Wood & Co., 1916.

Woman's duty in the anti-tuberculosis crusade. Med. Rec., July 8, 1916.

Woman's duty in the combat of tuberculosis. Jour. Outdoor Life, Nov., 1916.

Birth control, its medical, social, economic, and moral aspects. N. Y. Med. Jour., Nov. 18; Survey, Nov. 18, 1916; Am. Jour. of Pub. Health, Feb., 1917. 2d Edition, 1919, N. Y. Woman's Publ. Co., New York.

The story of the window tent. Jour. Outdoor Life, Jan., 1917.

Is there any relation between tuberculosis, mental disease, and mental deficiency? A plea for justice to the sane and compassion and pity for the insane consumptive. Med. Rec., Jan. 6, 1917.

Constructive suggestions toward the control of tuberculosis in times of peace and in times of war. N. Y. Med. Jour., June 23, 1917.

Herbert Maxon King—in memoriam. Med. Rec., July 14, 1917; also Jour. Outdoor Life, Aug., 1917.

The effects of civilization on the morbidity and mortality of tuberculosis. Med. Rec., July, 1917; also Jour. Sociol. Med., Feb., 1919.

What the American soldier now fighting in France should know about tuberculosis. Med. Rec., Nov. 3, 1917; also Interstate Med. Jour., Nov., 1917; West. Med. Times, Dec., 1917; Jour. Outdoor Life, Jan., 1918; Canad. Jour. of Med. and Surgery, Feb., 1918; Trained Nurse and Hosp. Rev., Feb., 1918.

The Same; pocket edition, 1918; also revised edition, 1918.

Ce que le soldat americain, qui combat actuallement en France, devrait savoir sur la tuberculose. L'Union Médicale du Canada, Nov., 1917.

How our army in France can avoid the menace of tuberculosis. Nation, Jan. 10, 1918.

Pneumonia among soldiers in camps, cantonments and at the front. Causes, prevention, treatment and after care to prevent tuberculosis. N. Y. Med. Jour., Jan. 26, 1918.

The statue of Edward Livingston Trudeau. N. Y. Med. Jour., Aug. 24, 1918.

La pneumonie parmi les soldats dans les camps, les cantonnements et au front—causes, prévention, traitement—précautions á prendre aprés la guérison. L'Union Méd. du Canada, Oct., 1918.

Prevention of relapses in cases of arrested tuberculosis among soldiers and sailors. Jour. Am. Med. Assn., Feb. 22, 1919; also South. California Pract., July, 1919.

Some additional notes on the prevention of relapses in cases of arrested tuberculosis. June, 1919.

Official provision for the tuberculous soldier and what he should know about his disease. N. Y. Med. Jour., March 15, 1919.

La prévention des rechutes parmi les soldats et marins gueris de la tuberculose. L'Union Méd. du Canada, June, 1919.

The tuberculosis problem after the world war. Med. Rec., July 26; also Jour. Outdoor Life, Sept., 1919.

Drug addicts and the tuberculous in one institution. Med. Rec., Aug. 16, 1919.

Le probléme de la tuberculose aprés la guerre mondiale. L'Union Méd. du Canada, Sept., 1919.

Ideals in the treatment of tuberculosis—the ideal sanatorium, the ideal physician, the ideal nurse, and the ideal patient. N. Y. Med. Jour., Oct. 18, 1919; also Jour. Outdoor Life, Feb., 1920; Am. Rev. Tuberc., April, 1920.

Réné Theophile Hyacinthe Laennec and the hundredth anniversary of his book on mediate auscultation. Med. Rec., Dec. 27, 1919.

Sir William Osler, Bart.—in memoriam. Am. Rev. of Tuberc., May, 1920.

Tuberculosis and the life and work of Sir William Osler—a tribute. Brit. Jour. Tuberc., July, 1920.

The anti-tuberculosis movement in the United States prior to and since the formation of the National Tuberculosis Association. With brief tributes to its departed leaders. Med. Rec., June 26, 1920.

International Association of pneumothorax artificialis. Med. Rec., Sept. 11, 1920.

Major General William C. Gorgas, M.C., U. S. A.,—in memoriam. Am. Rev. Tuberc., Dec., 1920.

The soul of the consumptive—a plea for justice. N. Y. Med. Jour., Jan. 1, 1921; also Jour. Outdoor Life, March, 1920.

The tuberculosis problem of the present day. Editorial, N. Y. Med. Jour., Jan. 1, 1921.

In memoriam—Sir William Osler, Bart. On the first anniversary of his
death. Am. Med., Jan., 1921.

To the sixtieth birthday of the honorary secretary of the International Anti-
tuberculosis Association, Prof. Gotthold Pannwitz, M.D. Tuberculosis,
International Anti-tuberculosis Association correspondence, July, 1921.

A plea for the sale of Christmas seals on behalf of the anti-tuberculosis campaign. Med. Rec., Dec. 3, 1921; also in N. Y. Med. Jour., Dec. 21, 1921.

Eugenics and euthenics in their relations to the tuberculosis problem. Med.
Rec., Dec. 21, 1921.

The present-day tuberculosis problem in Europe and in the United States.
Med. Rec., April 22, 1922.

The patient's part in the solution of the tuberculosis problem. Jour. Outdoor
Life, April, 1922.

A physiological adjuvant in the rest cure of pulmonary tuberculosis. Am.
Rev. Tuberc., vi, 5, 1922.

INDEX

No effort has been made to make an exhaustive index. The references are chiefly to persons, places, and institutions. For those who are interested in the detailed proceedings of the Association there is available in pamphlet form a cumulative index of the Transactions covering the years 1905–1920 inclusive.

INDEX

Adami, J. G., 28.
Addams, Jane, 19.
Adirondack Cottage Sanitarium, 10.
  See also *Trudeau Sanatorium.*
Advanced cases, hospitals for, 9–10.
Agnes Memorial Sanatorium, 438.
Aiken Cottage Sanatorium, 10–11, 129.
Alabama, associations and work in, 77–78.
Alaska, 78.
Allen, Charles L., 19.
Altro Manufacturing Company, 20.
American Congress for the Prevention of Consumption, 22–27
American Congress on Tuberculosis, 22–27.
American Red Cross, 35–36, 56–62.
American Review of Tuberculosis, 15–16.
American Sanatorium Association, 12.
Anders, H. S., 30.
Anderson, A. A., 315.
Andrews, Glenn, 77.
Angney, W. M., 28.
Animal tuberculosis, 21.
Annual meetings, 157–269; *1st*, 157–161, *2nd*, 162–166, *3d*, 167–171, *4th*, 172–175, *5th*, 176–180, *6th*, 181–186, *7th*, 187–192, *8th*, 193–199, *9th*, 200–204, *10th*, 205–209, *11th*, 210–215, *12th*, 216–222, *13th*, 223–231, *14th*, 232–238, *15th*, 239–246, *16th*, 247–258, *17th*, 259–269.
Arequipa Sanatorium, 463.
Arizona, associations and work in, 78–80.
Arkansas, associations and work in, 80–81.
Armstrong, Donald B., 49, 70, 73; biography, 416–418.
Associated Tuberculosis Auxiliaries, 118.

Association of Tuberculosis Clinics, 391.
Associations, 34, 35, 37, 39; first, 18, 124; local, 20, 34–35; number of, 53, 407; state, 37, 44, 76–140; contracts in regard to Christmas seal, 64. See also *Congresses and under name of state.*
Athey, Catherine R., 90.
Atlantic City meeting, 1904, 31.
Auerbach, Murray A., 94.
Auxiliaries to clinics, 13.

Babcock, Robert H., 19, 28, 30, 369; biography, 440–442.
Baker, W. W., 135.
Baldwin, E. R., iv, 16, 68, 69, 216, 223; biography, 371–375.
Baldwin, William Henry, 18; biography, 398–400.
Baltimore Congress, 1904, 27–28.
Bang, Bernard, 146, 147.
Barlow, W. Jarvis, biography, 448–494.
Barlow Sanatorium, 449.
Barre granite workers' survey, 134, 264–265.
Barrel, Finley, 53.
Barrick, E. J., 23.
Barrier, Dr., 31.
Bartlett, P. Challis, 49.
Beatty, T. B., 132.
Becker, Joseph W., 91.
Bell, Clark, 23, 24, 29, 141.
Bell Congress, 24, 26, 27.
Bend, Beatrice, 13.
Bengoechea, Ramon, 146.
Bermingham, Edward J., 12.
Beyer, H. G., 34, 141, 145.
Bicknell, Ernest P., 56, 58, 59, 90.
Bigelow, Enos H., 70.
Biggs, Hermann M., 6, 8, 9, 12, 13, 17, 18, 28, 29, 30, 31, 141, 162, 167, 337, 344, 424; biography, 323–329.
Billings, Frank, 19, 26, 162, 172; biography, 330–331.

495

CPSIA information can be obtained
at www.ICGtesting.com
Printed in the USA
LVOW13s0042110517
534008LV00034B/1754/P